MACROECONOMICS

Theory and Policy

VANITA AGARWAL

Associate Professor of Economics,
Department of Commerce
Lakshmibai College,
University of Delhi

Pearson

Assistant Acquisitions Editor: Anshul Yadav
Associate Production Editor: Ruchi Sachdev
Composition: Pen2Print Media Solutions
Printer

Published by Dorling Kindersley (India) Pvt. Ltd., licensees of Pearson Education in South Asia.

ISBN: 978-81-317-3149-9

10 9 8 7 6 5 4 3 2 1

Published by Pearson India Education Services Pvt. Ltd, CIN: U72200TN2005PTC057128.

Head Office: 15th Floor, Tower-B, World Trade Tower, Plot No. 1, Block-C, Sector 16,
Noida 201 301, Uttar Pradesh, India.

Registered Office: 7th Floor, SDB2, ODC 7, 8 & 9, Survey No.01 ELCOT IT/ ITES SEZ,
Sholinganallur, Chennai – 600119, Tamil Nadu, India.
Phone: 044-66540100
Website: in.pearson.com, Email: companysecretary.india@pearson.com

Digitally printed in India by Manipal Technologies Limited. in the year of 2022

TO
MY PARENTS

Contents

UNIT VI INFLATION AND UNEMPLOYMENT

UNIT VII THE OPEN ECONOMY MACROECONOMICS AND THE FRAMEWORK OF MACROECONOMIC POLICIES

Figures

Preface

Macroeconomics: Theory and Policy examines and analyses the performance of the economy as a whole. Various macroeconomic issues appear in the news and the press on a routine basis—these relate to topics such as economic growth, inflation, employment, the comparison of a country's trade performance with other countries (i.e., the balance of payments), the extent of success or failure of government economic policies and the decisions made by the country's central bank. Without even realizing, we all become experts of the subject called macroeconomics.

A conscious attempt has been made to make this book different from the others, it is not only simple to understand but it also brings the classroom directly to the student with its lucid language. This book covers most of the topics that are relevant and essential at an undergraduate level and also designed for use in courses on macroeconomics at the undergraduate level of most Indian universities.

SALIENT FEATURES

The purpose of this book is to make the study of macroeconomics simple for students and enable them to apply it to everyday situations. The various tools used in this book are as follows:

- **Topics Chosen for Discussion:** The topics chosen for discussion cover various aspects of macroeconomics, which are relevant to undergraduate students.
- **Learning Objectives:** At the beginning of each chapter, learning objectives are mentioned to help students focus on the main aspects of the subject.
- **Boxes:** In every chapter, there are some FYI boxes, which contain interesting features and supplementary material relevant to the chapter for additional information.
- **Definitions of Important Concepts:** In every chapter, the definitions are given in margin boxes making it simpler for the student to review and learn these important concepts.
- **RECAP at the End of Every Section:** At the end of each section, a recap has been given to assist the student in recapitulating and reviewing the text discussed in every section.
- **Chapter Summary:** Each chapter has a brief summary, which is especially useful during examinations for a quick recollection of the chapter.
- **Review Questions:** At the end of every chapter, there are review questions, categorized under true and false, very short, short and long answer questions, which aim at checking the understanding of students.
- **Numerical Illustrations:** Some of the chapters, wherever required, contain numerical illustrations which improve the student's understanding of the text.
- **Diagrams:** The chapters are illustrated with diagrams to assist in clarifying the concepts.
- **Solved Numericals:** Some chapters contain solved numericals, which are related to the chapter and which will provide hands-on practice with the theory.
- **Unsolved Numericals:** By attempting to find a solution to the unsolved numericals, the student can check his/her understanding of the mathematical problems.
- **Relevance to the Indian Economy:** References to the Indian economy are given in the chapters wherever considered relevant for better insight.
- **Appendixes:** Appendixes are given at the end of the book.
- **Glossary:** Key terms have been included and defined in the glossary.

I sincerely hope that this book will prove handy and helpful to both students and teachers alike. I would, at all times, welcome any observations and suggestions for further improvement.

ACKNOWLEDGEMENTS

A textbook is not a solitary venture of its author but a collaborative project of a team of dedicated and competent people. I extend special thanks to the team of editors, Praveen Tiwari, Anshul Yadav and Ruchi Sachdev, for their superb work, efforts, care and expertise.

I am also grateful for the contributions and inputs of the reviewers and colleagues who offered very useful comments during the various stages of preparation of the drafts of the book. Specifically, I would like to acknowledge the encouraging comments and invaluable suggestions from Professor B. P. Singh, ex-Head, Department of Commerce, Delhi School of Economics, University of Delhi; Dr Karuna Kaushik, Principal, Lakshmibai College, University of Delhi; and Dr A. K. Singh, Department of Commerce, Delhi School of Economics.

I would also like to thank my husband Pradeep and children, Tanay and Prakriti, for their continuous encouragement, patience and support.

Vanita Agarwal

An Introduction to Macroeconomics

1

After studying this topic, you should be able to understand

- *Economics studies as to how the society can allocate its limited resources most efficiently.*
- *The field of economics has been divided into distinct areas of study: microeconomics and macroeconomics.*
- *With the advent of Keynes' book, The General Theory of Employment, Interest and Money in the year 1936 began the Keynesian era. It was followed by the development of the supply side economics.*
- *Whether it is an individual, consumer, firm, or government, macroeconomics is important for all.*
- *The variables in any economic model can be a stock or a flow.*
- *A static relationship exists when all variables relate to the same time period and a dynamic relationship exists when all the variables relate to different time periods.*
- *A given set of relationships between the variables may lead to an equilibrium or a disequilibrium solution.*

MACROECONOMICS AND MICROECONOMICS

The word *economy* is believed to have been derived from a certain Greek word which means a person who manages a *household*. A household has to make many decisions. Similar to a household, a society is also involved in making many decisions. A society also faces the same problem of limited resources (which include capital, labour force, natural resources, entrepreneurship, and technology) and unlimited wants like a household.

Since all our resources are limited in comparison to our wants and needs, both individuals and nations will have to make decisions as to the goods and services they can purchase and the ones they have to forgo.

So due to the problem of scarcity, individuals and economies have to make decisions in the allocation of their resources. Economics seeks to study as to why we make these decisions and how we can allocate our resources most efficiently.

The field of economics has been divided into two distinct areas of study: microeconomics and macroeconomics. *Microeconomics is that branch of economics which analyses the market behaviour and decision-making process of the individual consumers and firms and also the interactions between individual buyers and sellers.* Microeconomics focuses on the demand, supply, and equilibrium, and the price and output determination in individual markets.

> *Microeconomics is that branch of economics which analyses the market behaviour and decision-making process of the individual consumers and firms.*

Macroeconomics, on the other hand, is the study of how the national economy as a whole grows and the changes that occur over time. Thus, it analyses the big or the macro picture. Hence, the basic concerns of macroeconomics are to measure as to how well an economy performs, works, and then try to improve the performance of the economy. Macroeconomics is very complicated and influenced by many factors. These factors can be analysed through various economic indicators that tell us about the overall health of an economy. Thus, macroeconomics deals with big issues like price stability or inflation and full employment or unemployment.

BOX 1.1

On 23 October 1929, the Wall Street (which is the New York Stock Exchange) crashed. This was no ordinary crash. This financial catastrophe crippled not only the US economy but also affected the rest of the world. Successful people became paupers overnight leading to an increase in the suicide rates. For the world, the years ahead seemed to be the most financially difficult years possible. Before the crash, unemployment was about 3 per cent in US, while by 1933 it had increased to a quarter of the US labour force who found themselves unemployed. The high level of unemployment resulted in a fall in demand since the public did not have any money to spend. This lowered the prices of the goods. The agriculture, basic consumer goods industries, and others were affected badly. This heralded what is termed as the Great Depression, only Germany appeared to be sailing on safe water, which emerged as one of the most powerful nations economically. This was remarkable because it had been completely destroyed by the World War I. Germans had achieved this success through sheer hard work, which helped them to restore its industries. This led to an increase in the total production leading to a low level of unemployment and more spending, which in turn led to an increased production.

Micro- and macroeconomics are both intertwined. By improving their knowledge of certain phenomena, economists can help individuals and nations in making more efficient decisions in allocating the resources. It is important to note that what microeconomics considers as given, the total output, total employment, and total expenditure on the goods and services, macroeconomics takes it as one of its most important variables. On the other hand what macroeconomics takes as given, the distribution of the total output, total employment, and total expenditure among the goods and services of the different firms and the different industries, microeconomics takes it as a variable to be determined.

Although a distinction has often been made between microeconomics and macroeconomics, strictly speaking there is only one 'economics'. While the foundation of microeconomics lies in macroeconomics, the foundation of macroeconomics lies in microeconomics. Thus, an analysis of an economy cannot be conducted in two separate watertight compartments of macroeconomics and microeconomics.

RECAP

- Microeconomics analyses the market behaviour and decision-making process of the individual consumers and firms.
- Macroeconomics is the study of how the national economy as a whole grows and changes, which occur over time.

BACKGROUND OF MACROECONOMICS

The founder of the field of microeconomics is thought to be Adam Smith. As already discussed, it is that branch of economics, which is concerned with the behaviour of individual entities like firms, households and markets. These are the issues that Adam Smith has addressed in his book *The Wealth of Nations*.

Macroeconomics, the other major branch of economics, is of relatively recent origin as compared to microeconomics. However, it did exist earlier also but not with the same popularity that it gained with Keynes. One can trace the origin of macroeconomics by dividing it into three stages:

(1) **Classical School of Thought:** Karl Marx was responsible for the origin of the term 'classical'. He used this term to include the theories of David Ricardo, James Mill, and the other economists who preceded him. Later on, Keynes extended the term classical to include the followers of Ricardo including Marshall, J. S. Mill, Pigou and Edgeworth.

(2) **The Keynesian Economics:** In the 1930s, the most dramatic developments took place. The US economy, even with a quarter of its resources lying idle (a less than full employment situation), plunged into a depression. The classical school failed to provide any explanation to this turn of events.

The answer to the problems that the US economy faced came in the form of Keynes' book, *The General Theory of Employment, Interest and Money* in the year 1936. The book provided a theory to explain the events, which plagued the US economy at that particular time. The book with its embedded theories was well received and began the Keynesian era.

The response of the classical school to the situation was the argument that full employment was the normal situation in any economy. However, departures in the form of less than full employment could temporarily occur. But the automatic forces present in a competitive market would push the economy back to the full employment equilibrium. The experiences of the US economy with the relatively few but temporary depressions in the early twentieth century lend credence to these views. Their basic tenet was that it was not possible for aggregate demand for goods and services to fall short of aggregate supply except for a temporary period.

Keynes' general theory was an alternative theory that explained the determination of employment and output, and also the explanation as to why the market forces in an economy would not automatically generate a level of aggregate demand which was required for full employment. Keynes' theory addressed the issues pertaining to the economic disaster in the form of the Great Depression and provided an explanation for this disaster. In this new theory, Keynes had developed an analysis as to what causes unemployment and the downturns, how the consumption and investment levels are determined, how a central bank manages the money and the interest rates in an economy, and most important of all as to why some nations prosper while others stagnate.

Keynes' theory was followed by refinements, termed as *Keynesian economics*, which were later applied to tackle the analysis of inflation during and after World War II. With its growing success in providing a solution to the major macroeconomic issues, the Keynesian theory held sway into the 1960s.

The success faced by the US economy was, however, short lived. The various restrictive policy measures, recommended by the Keynesian theory, were not successful in checking the inflation and, in fact, responsible for pushing the US economy towards a recession in 1970, which was later followed by double digit rate of inflation that gripped the US economy. In such a situation, Keynesian economics, where the tools were designed for the specific purpose of controlling aggregate demand, could not provide a solution to the problem of controlling inflation and a recession, simultaneously. What were required were tools to manage the long neglected supply side. This was followed by the development of what is called the *supply side economics*.

(3) **The Post-Keynesian Economics:** Notwithstanding the tremendous success which Keynes and his book received, it could not in any way prevent the further developments that occurred on the classical front to appear under the heading of neo-classical, especially during the 1950s.

Starting in the 1950s and continuing till today is the development of another extension of the classical theory, which assigns a very critical role to money as a major factor in determining whatever happens in an economy. The theory is known as the *monetarism*. In fact in the 1960s and the 1970s, the theory gained so much importance that it was thought to be a counter-revolution. Monetarists like Milton Friedman were responsible for making the theory popular worldwide.

In the 1970s, the classical theory took a new turn with the introduction of the concept of *rational expectations*. This was the latest theoretical development on the classical front whose roots were firmly embedded in the classical theory. The emphasis here was on the role played by the individual's rational expectations regarding future economic events. Later on, there appeared the supply side economists with their emphasis on the factors operating on the supply side.

BOX 1.2

It was the Keynesian macroeconomics and the implementation of the proper plans and in the right directions which were responsible, to some extent, in building up the US economy in the aftermath of the Great Depression. Today, most of the economies in Africa and even in parts of South America are facing struggle, which is worse than what the US faced at the time of the Great Depression. Faced with the problems of poverty, issues of health and education, these economies are in a dire need of economic policies, which can help them in coming out of such doldrums. However, these policies can be determined only after a thorough study of the macroeconomic issues, which affect these economies.

RECAP

- The answer to the problems in the US economy came in the form of Keynes' book.
- In the 1960s and 1970s, the theory that gained popularity is known as monetarism.

NEED TO STUDY MACROECONOMICS

From the viewpoint of an individual: Macroeconomics may exercise a strong influence on the individual investor. For understanding and analysing the long-term trends and also the aggregate market behaviour, the principles of macroeconomics play a very important role. Thus for an individual who is managing his own asset portfolio, it may be of considerable importance to be aware of the current fiscal policy and also as to what will be its repercussions on the value of the government bond holdings. Depending on the objectives of the fiscal policy, the government may buy back the bonds or it may issue more bonds.

From the viewpoint of the consumers, firms and governments: The macroeconomists try to anticipate the economic conditions to be able to help the consumers, the firms and the governments in making their decisions.

(1) The consumers' interest lies in knowing how easy or difficult it will be for them to be able to find work. They are also concerned about the price of the goods and service and also as to how much may be the cost of borrowing.

(2) The interest of the business lies in knowing whether or not to expand production. They are also concerned about whether the consumer will have sufficient purchasing power to buy the product.

(3) The government is concerned with the macroeconomy when planning its budget and taxes, deciding on the interest rates and making its other policy decisions in national interest.

From the viewpoint of an economy's performance: An economy's performance is of considerable importance to all of us. We evaluate the performance of the macroeconomy by essentially looking at the national output, the rate of unemployment, the inflation rate and the trade performance. Even though it is the consumers who play the most important role in determining the direction that an economy traverses, the government also plays its role through the fiscal and monetary policy. A study of macroeconomics helps us to evaluate the success or failure of the economic policies of the government and the Central Bank of the country.

From the viewpoint of an economy's stability and growth: Although macroeconomics involves a wide field of study, there are two areas which are typical of the discipline:

(1) *The business cycle:* Macroeconomists are involved in trying to analyse the short-run fluctuations in the national income that lead to the business cycles.

(2) *Increase in the national income:* The *determinants* of long-run economic growth are of great interest to the macroeconomists, which are responsible for the increase in the national income.

(3) Both the government and the corporations utilize the macroeconomic models and their forecasts to foster the process of development, and also in the evaluation of economic policies and the business strategies. This would help in maintaining stability and attaining growth.

In the present scenario with the world in the grips of recession, macroeconomists are busy in trying to diagnose the cause of the recession and to find the policies or the mix of policies that will help the different economies of the world to pull out of the recession.

RECAP

- Macroeconomics helps to evaluate the performance of the economy, in terms of the national output, the rate of unemployment, the inflation rate and the trade performance.

CONCEPTS IN MACROECONOMICS

The variables in any economic model can be a stock and/or a flow. A relationship is postulated among these variables in the model. If all the variables in the model relate to the same time period, then it is a static relationship, while if the variables relate to different time periods it is a dynamic relationship. A given set of relationships between the variables may lead to an equilibrium or a disequilibrium solution. An equilibrium solution can be analysed through a static methodology, whereas a disequilibrium solution can be analysed through a dynamic methodology. If the model pertains to a situation where one equilibrium position is succeeded by another equilibrium position, then it can be analysed through comparative statics.

Stocks and Flows

Stock is a quantity, which is measured at a point in time.

Both stocks and flows are variables. Both are quantities that may increase or decrease over time. However, there is a difference between them, *stock is a quantity measured at a point in time wheeras flow is a quantity measured over a period of time.*

Some macro stock variables are the money supply, the total number of people employed in an economy, the total stock of capital, the total labour force, etc. Some macro flow variables are the savings, investment, change in inventories, change in the money supply, etc.

Flow is a quantity measured over a period of time.

It is important to note that often stock and flow are related. This is because a flow is actually the change in the stock. For example, while the total number of people employed in an economy is a stock variable, the numbers of people who take up new jobs or leave jobs are flow variables. While money is a stock variable, the expenditures in money or the spending of money is a flow variable. While inventories is a stock variable, the change in inventories is a flow variable.

It is not necessary that there should be a flow counterpart to every stock variable. Imports and exports, taxes, wages and salaries, and dividends are flows. There is no direct stock counterpart to them. However, though they do not have a stock counterpart, it is important to note that they do influence the other stock variables. For example, imports may affect the size of the stock of capital and also the stock of inventories, while wages and salaries may have an effect on the stock of housing.

For the flow variables where a direct stock counterpart exists, any change in the amount of the stock between two specific points of time will depend on the changes in the flow variables between those specific points of time. For example, the change in an economy's capital stock between two specific points in time depends on additions to the stock of capital and the consumption of capital goods.

While a change in stock occurs due to a change in the flow, a change in flow may also be influenced by a change in the stock. For example, a change in inventories is brought about by many factors including a change in the stock of capital. An excessive stock of capital may necessitate a decrease in the flow of investment and may thus be responsible for a business going downhill. However, it is important to note that stock can influence flows only in long run.

Equilibrium and Disequilibrium

In the simplest terms, *equilibrium is a state of balance or a state where there is no change.* The forces acting in the system may bring about a change in the economy. However, the net effect of the change is that the equilibrium position does not, in any way, get disturbed. On the other hand, *disequilibrium is a state of imbalance.*

Equilibrium is a state of balance or a state where there is no change.

The macroeconomic model, which can be considered here, is related to aggregate demand and aggregate supply as shown in Figure 1.1.

Here,

x-axis = aggregate quantities of all the commodities in the economy
y-axis = the price level
AD = aggregate demand
AS = aggregate supply
E = equilibrium

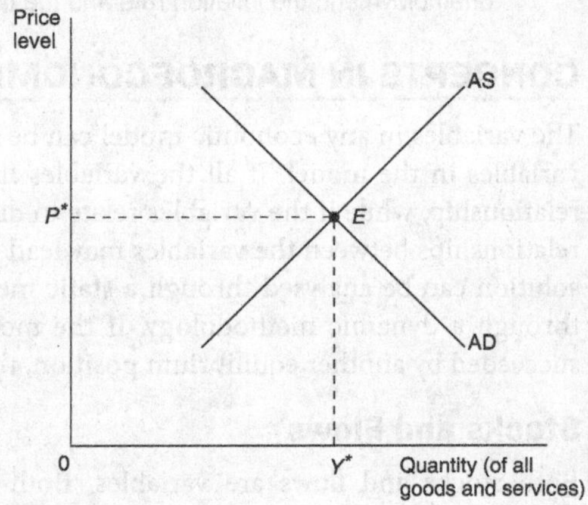

Figure 1.1 Aggregate Demand and Aggregate Supply

The aggregate demand, AD, curve relates to the aggregate quantity of all the goods and services demanded or in the other words it is the summation of the spending by the individuals, businesses, government and the net exports at each price level. The aggregate supply, AS, is the amount produced and supplied by the business at each price level. An equilibrium is determined at the intersection of the aggregate demand and aggregate supply curves at point E with the equilibrium output at Y^* and the equilibrium price at P^*. Thus at P^*, the aggregate quantity of the goods and services demanded and supplied is equal.

Disequilibrium will exist at any price higher or lower than P^*. At a price higher than P^*, the aggregate quantity of the goods and services demanded will be less than the aggregate quantity supplied and, therefore, the price level will fall until equilibrium is achieved. At a price lower than P^*, the aggregate quantity of the goods and services demanded will be more than the aggregate quantity supplied and, therefore, the price level will rise until equilibrium is achieved.

Flow equilibrium can be taken as the short-run equilibrium, while a stock equilibrium can be taken as the long-run equilibrium. It is necessary to remember that a stock equilibrium cannot exist without flow equilibrium because long-run equilibrium cannot exist without short-run equilibrium.

The concept of equilibrium is of utmost importance, it identifies that position where the variables are in a balanced state. Disequilibrium is again of importance, as it is more close to economic reality than equilibrium. The Keynesian model is, in fact, built upon the disequilibrium analysis.

Statics, Dynamics and Comparative Statics

We have already focused on the stock and flow variables found in the economic models. Equilibrium and disequilibrium are the two positions that these models are in at any point in time. Two methods employed in the construction of these economic models are statics and dynamics.

In *static models*, the relations between different variables relate to the same period in time. There is no need to be concerned about the problem of dating. Thus, static models are not able to trace the changes in the values of different variables over time. Hence, these models are unable to explain the process of change. They apply to models which are in a state of equilibrium.

Static models are those where the relationship between the different variables relates to the same period in time.

A special case of a static model is what is called a *stationary equilibrium*. Here, there are no changes and the same equilibrium position is repeated from one period to another.

Dynamic models trace the changes that occur in the values of the different variables over time. They apply to models that are in a state of disequilibrium. Disequilibrium is a state where there are changes in the values of the variables over time. To analyse a model that is in a state of disequilibrium, dynamics is used. Hence, dynamics traces the changes in the values of the variables as they move through the different disequilibria to arrive at the position of equilibrium.

Dynamic models are the models that trace the changes that occur in the values of the different variables over time.

Comparative Statics: While static models relate to a study of the equilibrium at a particular point of time, comparative statics compares two or more such equilibrium states. Comparative statics can be used to analyse, for example, the changes in an equilibrium price and quantity brought about by the shifts in the demand and/or supply curves. However, it is important to note that the process or the path through which one equilibrium position moves to another equilibrium position is not analysed under the domain of comparative statics, which is discussed under dynamics. Comparative statics performs the task of bridging the gap between the two equilibrium positions, but is unable to explain the path which has been traversed.

Comparative statics is of relevance only when an old equilibrium is succeeded by a new equilibrium position. When the old equilibrium is succeeded by a new disequilibrium position, comparative statics is not relevant.

Partial Equilibrium and General Equilibrium

Economists often distinguish between partial and general equilibrium analyses.

In a partial equilibrium analysis, which is the basis of study in microeconomics, more factors are assumed to be held constant as compared to a general equilibrium analysis. Hence, only a small number of variables are allowed to change while all the other variables are assumed to be constant.

Partial equilibrium approach involves the determination of the equilibrium price and output in each market, ceteris paribus.

A partial equilibrium analysis is based on the assumption of *ceteris paribus*, that is, we assume everything other than the market we are analysing, to be constant. For example, in an analysis of the maximization of the utility of the consumer we assume that his income is constant. In analysing the demand for say commodity X, we assume all factors, other than the price of commodity X including income, tastes and price of other commodities to be constant. In the product market, the interaction of the buyers and sellers determines the equilibrium price and output, *ceteris paribus* or in other words ignoring the relationship with the other markets. Thus, *a partial equilibrium approach involves the determination of the equilibrium price and output in each market, ceteris paribus.*

The main problem with a partial equilibrium approach is that it ignores the interdependence and the linkages between the different markets. For example, in analysing the demand for say commodity X, we assume all factors other than the price of commodity X including income, tastes, and price of other commodities to be constant. However in reality, the demand for commodity X depends not only on the price of commodity X but also on the individual's income, his tastes and the price of the other commodities, which may be substitutes or complements to the commodity.

General equilibrium analysis involves a state where all the markets and the decision-making units in the economy are in a simultaneous equilibrium. Hence, it studies the simultaneous equilibria in a group of interrelated markets emphasizing the interdependence between the different economic units in the economy.

General equilibrium approach involves a state where all the markets and the decision-making units in the economy are in a simultaneous equilibrium.

A general equilibrium approach analyses an economy in its totality taking into consideration the linkages between the different sectors in the economy. It does not consider the restrictive assumptions used in the partial equilibrium analysis. As compared to a partial equilibrium analysis, it allows many more variables to change.

While Marshall's name is associated with partial equilibrium analysis, general equilibrium analysis is associated with the French economist Leon Walras. He analysed an economic system where the firms were perfectly competitive and the consumers were utility maximizers. The model showed that under such conditions, a unique stable equilibrium can exist. However, economists have raised doubts about the stability and the uniqueness of such equilibrium.

In the modern world economics, while Marshall's partial equilibrium analysis is said to be relevant for the learners as well as the non-interventionist arts academicians, real economists are more interested in Walras's general equilibrium analysis.

RECAP

- A stock is measured at a point in time, while flow is measured over a period of time.
- Equilibrium is a state of balance where there is no change.
- In static models, the relations between different variables relate to the same period in time.
- General equilibrium is a state where all the markets and the decision-making units in the economy are in a simultaneous equilibrium.

SUMMARY

MACROECONOMICS AND MICROECONOMICS

1. Like a household, a society also faces the problem of limited resources and unlimited wants.
2. Due to the problem of scarcity, individuals and economies have to make decisions for the allocation of their resources.
3. The field of economics has been divided into two distinct areas of study: microeconomics and macroeconomics, which are both intertwined.
4. Microeconomics is that branch of economics, which analyses the market behaviour and decision-making process of the individual consumers and firms.
5. Macroeconomics, on the other hand, is the study of how the national economy as a whole grows and the changes that occur over time.

BACKGROUND OF MACROECONOMICS

1. The founder of the field of microeconomics is thought to be Adam Smith.
2. Macroeconomics, the other major branch of economics, is of relatively recent origin as compared to microeconomics. One can trace the origin of macroeconomics by dividing it into three stages.
   (a) The classical school of thought includes the theories of David Ricardo, James Mill, Marshall, J. S. Mill, Pigou and Edgeworth.
   (b) The Keynesian economics provided an alternative theory to explain the determination of employment and output.
   (c) The post-Keynesian economics, the monetarism, assigns a critical role to money.
3. In the 1970s, the classical theory took a new turn with the introduction of the concept of rational expectations.

NEED TO STUDY MACROECONOMICS

1. From the viewpoint of an individual, macroeconomics may exercise a strong influence on the individual investor. For an individual who is managing his own asset portfolio, it may be of considerable importance to be aware of the current fiscal policy.

2. From the viewpoint of the consumers, firms, and governments, macroeconomics is again important. The consumer's interest lies in knowing how easy or difficult it will be for them to be able to find work, about the price of the goods and service and also as to how much may be the cost of borrowing. The interest of the business lies in knowing whether or not to expand the production. The government turns to macroeconomics when planning its budget and taxes, deciding on the interest rates and making its other policy decisions.
3. From the viewpoint of an economy, its performance is evaluated by the national output, the rate of unemployment, the inflation rate, and the trade performance.
4. From the viewpoint of an economy's stability and growth, macroeconomists are involved in trying to analyse the short-run fluctuations in the national income, which lead to the business cycles.

CONCEPTS IN MACROECONOMICS

1. Stock is a quantity which is measured at a point in time, whereas flow is a quantity measured over a period of time.
2. A change in stock occurs due to a change in the flow, whereas a change in flow may also be influenced by a change in stock.
3. Equilibrium is a state of balance or a state where there is no change. On the other hand, disequilibrium is a state of imbalance.
4. Flow equilibrium can be taken as short-run equilibrium, whereas a stock equilibrium can be taken as long-run equilibrium.
5. Two methods employed in the construction of these economic models are statics and dynamics.
6. In static models, the relations between the different variables relate to the same period in time. Hence, these models are unable to explain the process of change.
7. A special case of a static model is what is called a stationary equilibrium where there are no changes and the same equilibrium position is repeated from one period to another.
8. Dynamic models trace the changes that occur in the values of the different variables over time.

PARTIAL EQUILIBRIUM AND GENERAL EQUILIBRIUM

1. Economists often distinguish between partial and general equilibrium analysis.
2. A partial equilibrium analysis is based on the assumption of *ceteris paribus*, that is, we assume everything other than the market we are analysing to be constant.
3. General equilibrium analysis involves a state where all the markets and the decision-making units in the economy are in a simultaneous equilibrium.
4. Marshall's name is associated with partial equilibrium analysis. On the other hand, general equilibrium analysis is associated with the French economist Leon Walras.
5. In the modern world of the twentieth century economics, Marshall's partial equilibrium analysis is said to be relevant for the learners as well as the non-interventionist arts professors, real economists are more interested in Walras's general equilibrium analysis.

REVIEW QUESTIONS

TRUE OR FALSE QUESTIONS

1. Macroeconomics is that branch of economics, which analyses the market behaviour and decision-making process of the individual consumers and firms.
2. Flow is a quantity which is measured at a point in time, whereas stock is a quantity measured over a period of time.
3. Static models are those models that trace the changes that occur in the values of the different variables over time.
4. General equilibrium approach involves a state where all the markets and the decision-making units in the economy are in a simultaneous equilibrium.
5. Marshall's name is associated with general equilibrium analysis. On the other hand, partial equilibrium analysis is associated with the French economist Leon Walras.

VERY SHORT-ANSWER QUESTIONS

1. What is microeconomics?
2. What is macroeconomics?
3. Write a short note on the classical school of thought?
4. How important is macroeconomics from the viewpoint of an economy's performance?
5. Differentiate between a stock and a flow.

SHORT-ANSWER QUESTIONS

1. Differentiate between microeconomics and macroeconomics.
2. Discuss the need for macroeconomics from the viewpoint of the consumers, firms, and governments.
3. Distinguish between static and dynamic models.
4. What is comparative statics? How is it different from statics?
5. Differentiate between a partial equilibrium approach and a general equilibrium approach.

LONG-ANSWER QUESTIONS

1. Trace the origin of macroeconomics through its three stages.
2. Write a short note on the Keynesian economics.
3. What is the relationship between a stock and a flow? Explain with examples.
4. Write a short note on equilibrium and disequilibrium.
5. Write a short note on statics, dynamics and comparative statics.

ANSWERS

TRUE OR FALSE QUESTIONS

1. **False.** Microeconomics is that branch of economics which analyses the market behaviour and decision-making process of the individual consumers and firms.
2. **False.** Stock is a quantity which is measured at a point in time, while flow is a quantity measured over a period of time.
3. **False.** Dynamic models are those models that trace the changes that occur in the values of the different variables over time.
4. **True.** General equilibrium approach, as compared to a partial equilibrium approach, is a state where all the markets and the decision-making units in the economy are in a simultaneous equilibrium.
5. **False.** While Marshall's name is associated with partial equilibrium analysis, general equilibrium analysis is associated with the French economist Leon Walras.

The Circular Flow of Income and Expenditure

2

After studying this topic, you should be able to understand

- ✓ *In a two sector economy, the sum total of the factor incomes earned by the households is equal to the total of the expenditures by the households on the goods and services.*
- ✓ *There exist withdrawals and injections, which prevent the circular flow of income and money from remaining constant.*
- ✓ *The main source of revenue for the government is through taxes.*
- ✓ *The government may follow a balanced, deficit or a surplus budget.*
- ✓ *A flow of income may exist between the government sector and the capital market.*
- ✓ *The import and export of goods and services influence the circular flow of income.*
- ✓ *In general, the exports of a country are rarely equal to the imports.*

INTRODUCTION

A modern economy produces a variety of goods. Firms use the various factors of production–namely, land, labour, capital and entrepreneurship—to produce the goods that are then sold in the market. This chapter analyses the flow of the factors of production, goods and services, and money in two sector, three sector and four sector economies. It also includes a discussion on the various withdrawals and injections, which form a part of these economies. In any economy, there are following two kinds of flows:

Real flows include the flows of the factors of production and the goods and services between different sectors.

(1) **Real flows**, which include the flows of the factors of production and the goods and services between the different sectors.

(2) **Money flows**, which include the monetary flows between the different sectors.

Money flows include the monetary flows between different sectors.

Our discussion on the circular flow includes both the real flows and the money flows.

THE CIRCULAR FLOW OF INCOME IN A TWO SECTOR ECONOMY

In a two sector economy, there are only two sectors, households and firms. There is no government sector and no foreign sector. There exists a flow of services from the households to the firms and a corresponding flow of factor incomes from the firms to the households who own all the factors of production.

By definition, the national income is equal to the national expenditure. Thus, the sum total of the factor incomes earned by the households is equal to the total of the expenditures by the households on the goods and services. In any economy, for every transaction, there exists a seller and a buyer. Hence, every rupee of expenditure by a buyer must be accompanied by a rupee of income by the seller. Hence in a two sector economy, the total income earned by the households must be equal to the total expenditure in the economy.

BOX 2.1

The circular flow of income involves a process through which money and goods move between the different sectors in the economy. The concept of the circular flow was developed by Francois Quesnay, a French economist, in the eighteenth century. The model is used for analysing the macroeconomic relationships. It is used as the basis for studying macroeconomic relationships. The national income accounts also have the concept of the circular flow as their basis.

The firms are engaged in the task of production by combining the different factors of production; namely, land, labour, capital and entrepreneurship. The owners of these factors are the households, which receive wages for labour, rent on land, interest on the capital and profit on the entrepreneurship. The goods produced by the firms are bought by the households and the payments made by them for these goods and services are utilized by the firms to make the factor payments.

Assumptions

(1) Households spend all their income on the purchase of goods and services produced by the firms. In other words, there are no savings by the household sector.

(2) Firms produce the goods and services demanded by the households. However, the production by the firms is just enough to satisfy the demand by the households. In other words, there are no inventories.

(3) The firm distributes all that it earns from the sale of goods as wages, salaries, rent interest and profits. Thus, there are no retained earnings by the firms.

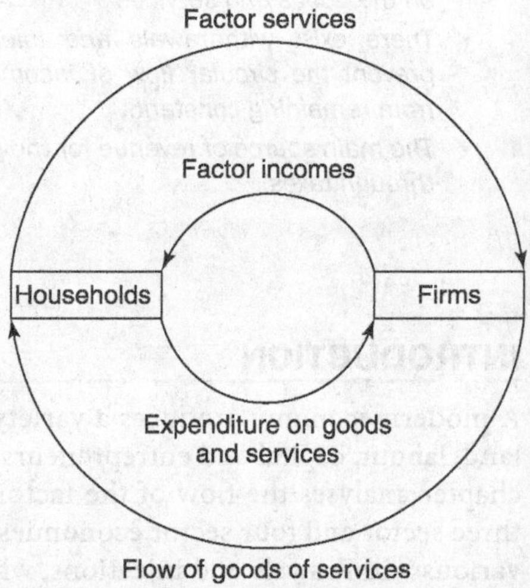

Figure 2.1 The Circular Flow of Income in a Two Sector Economy

Figure 2 .1 depicts the circular flow of income in a two sector economy. It shows the economic transactions between the households and the firms. There are two loops: inner loop and outer loop.

Inner Loop: This represents the money flows. It consists of following two parts:

(1) The flow of factor incomes, namely, wages, rent, interest and profits from the firms to the households.

(2) The flow of expenditures on the goods and services from the households to the firms.

Outer Loop: This represents the real flows. It consists of following two parts:

(1) The flow of factor services including land, labour, capital and entrepreneurship from the households to the firms.

(2) The flow of goods and services from the firms to the households.

Figure 2.1 also depicts two ways of calculating the national income:

(1) as the total income from the production of the goods and services which equals the sum of wages, rent, interest and profits. In Figure 2.1, this is represented by the top half of the circular flow of money or, in other words, by the top half of the inner loop.

(2) as the total expenditure on the goods and services. In Figure 2.1, this is represented by the bottom half of the circular flow of money or, in other words, by the bottom half of the inner loop.

BOX 2.2

A more realistic model is the five sector model of the circular flow of income. It relaxes all the assumptions made in the two sector model. The five sectors in the model include the households, firms, government, the foreign sector and the financial sector. In such a model also, the equilibrium occurs when the total leakages equal the total injections in the economy.

These two alternative ways of calculating the national income have to be equal as the expenditure on the goods and services (according to the accounting rules) is income for the sellers of the goods and services.

Withdrawals and Injections in an Economy

Before we embark on a discussion of the three and four sector economies, it is necessary to throw light on the concept of withdrawals and injections.

Withdrawal is income, which is generated in the production of the national output and which does not become a part of the circular flow of income.

The circular flow of income and money would remain constant as long as what is spent on the goods and services by the households is all distributed by the firms as factor payments. However, reality presents a different picture where there exist withdrawals and injections of income, which prevent the circular flow of income and money from remaining constant.

Withdrawal (or leakage) is income, which is generated in the production of the national output and which does not become a part of the circular flow of income. There are three types of withdrawals: saving, taxes and imports.

We had assumed that households spend all their income on the purchase of goods and services produced by the firms. This implies that there are no savings by the household sector. However, in reality every individual in an economy saves. Thus,

$$S = Y - C$$

where, S = saving
Y = income
C = consumption

As saving represents income not consumed, the very act of saving implies a reduction in the consumption expenditures. Thus, saving is a withdrawal of income and leads to a decrease in the income level. The savings by the firms also represent a withdrawal and lead to a decrease in the income level. Similarly, taxes and imports represent withdrawals and hence lead to a decrease in the circular flow of income.

Injection is an amount of money, which is spent by the different sectors in the economy and which is in addition to their incomes generated in the circular flow of income. There are following three types of injections, which are as follows:

Injection is an amount of money, which is spent by different sectors in the economy and which is in addition to their incomes generated in the circular flow of income.

(1) Investment
(2) Government expenditure
(3) Exports

Investment includes expenditure on plant and equipment, machinery and inventories. Investment expenditures are incurred by the firms to facilitate the process of production. It is financed from retained earnings, borrowings from the capital market, banks and others. These activities result in an addition to the circular flow of income.

Similarly, government expenditure and exports represent injections and hence lead to an increase in the circular flow of income.

The circle of money flowing through the economy is as follows: total income is spent (with the exception of 'leakages' such as consumer savings), while that expenditure allows the sale of goods and services, which in turn allows the payment of income (such as wages and salaries). Expenditure based on borrowings and existing wealth—i.e., 'injections' such as fixed investment—can add to total spending.

In equilibrium, the leakages are equal to the injections and the size of the circular flow remains the same. If injections are greater than the leakages, the circular flow will grow and there is prosperity in the economy. If on the other hand injections are less than leakages, the circular flow will become smaller in size and there is recession in the economy.

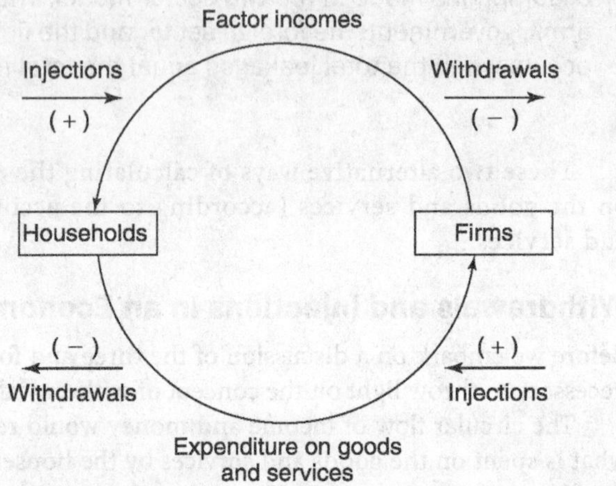

Figure 2.2 Withdrawals and Injections in an Economy

Figure 2.2 depicts withdrawals as deductions and injections as additions to the circular flow of income. As far as the household sector is concerned, withdrawals take the form of saving, personal income tax, sales tax, and imports whereas injections include government expenditures. As far as the firms are concerned, withdrawals take the form of corporation tax, business taxes and business savings whereas injections include government expenditures, investment expenditures and exports of goods and services.

RECAP

- In an economy, by definition, the national income is equal to the national expenditure.
- In a two sector economy, the inner loop represents the money flows whereas the outer loop represents the real flows.
- Withdrawal is the income, which is generated in the production of the national output and which is not part of the circular flow of income.
- Injection is an amount of money, which is spent by the different sectors in the economy and which is in addition to their incomes generated in the circular flow of income.

THE CIRCULAR FLOW IN A THREE SECTOR ECONOMY

Till now, we have discussed a two sector economy. We now introduce a third sector, the government sector. The inclusion of the government sector makes the model more realistic as the government plays an important role in the economy.

Just like any other sector in the economy, the government is involved in many activities.

(1) It raises its revenue from many sources. However, its main source of revenue is taxes. For the sake of keeping our analysis simple, we assume that taxes form the only source of revenue for the government. These taxes include:

(a) Taxes levied on the household sector: These can be direct taxes like the income tax or indirect taxes like the sales tax and excise duties on the consumer goods.

(b) Taxes levied on the firms: These can be direct taxes like the corporate income tax or indirect taxes like the sales tax and excise duties.

Thus, we have

$$T = T_H + T_F$$

where, T = total taxes

T_H = taxes levied on the households sector

T_F = taxes levied on the firms

(2) It has to incur expenditure on many heads. They include government expenditure on administration, justice, defense, development, social welfare activities, subsidies and so on. We can divide the government expenditures under four heads:

(a) Payments made to the household sector for the services rendered by them; for example, for those working in the armed forces, civil services and others.

(b) Payments made to the firms for the goods and services bought from them.

(c) Subsidies given to the firms to encourage production in certain areas and in certain sectors in the economy.

(d) Payments made for social security and welfare; these include pensions, unemployment compensations and other transfer payments.

Thus, we have

$$G = G_H + G_F + G_S + G_T$$

where, G = total government expenditure.

G_H = payments made to the household sector for the services rendered by them.

G_F = payments made to the firms for the goods and services bought from them.

G_S = government subsidies to the firms.

G_T = government payments for social security and welfare.

Like an individual, the government may follow a balanced, deficit or a surplus budget. The classical economists are in favour of a balanced budget where the government expenditure is always equal to the government revenue or where $G = T$. Hence, the amount of income withdrawn from the circular flow as taxes *re-enters* the flow as government expenditure.

In today's world, the government often follows a deficit budget. Often, the government expenditure is much greater than their revenue or $G > T$. The difference is financed from loans from the capital market. Such a budget implies net injections and thus an expansion in the circular flow of income.

In a surplus budget, the government expenditure is less than their revenue or $G < T$. Such a budget implies net withdrawals and thus a contraction in the circular flow of income.

Figure 2.3 depicts the circular flow of income in a three sector economy. It shows the economic transactions between the households, firms and the government sector. There are the same two loops of a two sector economy. It is important to note that:

(1) a part of the flows between the households and the firms now gets diverted to the government sector;

(2) a part of the household income goes to the government sector in the form of taxes;

(3) a part of the firms' earnings go to the government sector in the form of taxes;

(4) a part of the tax revenue is spent by the government as government expenditure on services and transfer payments to the household sector; and

(5) a part of the tax revenue is spent by the government as government expenditure on goods and subsidies to the firms.

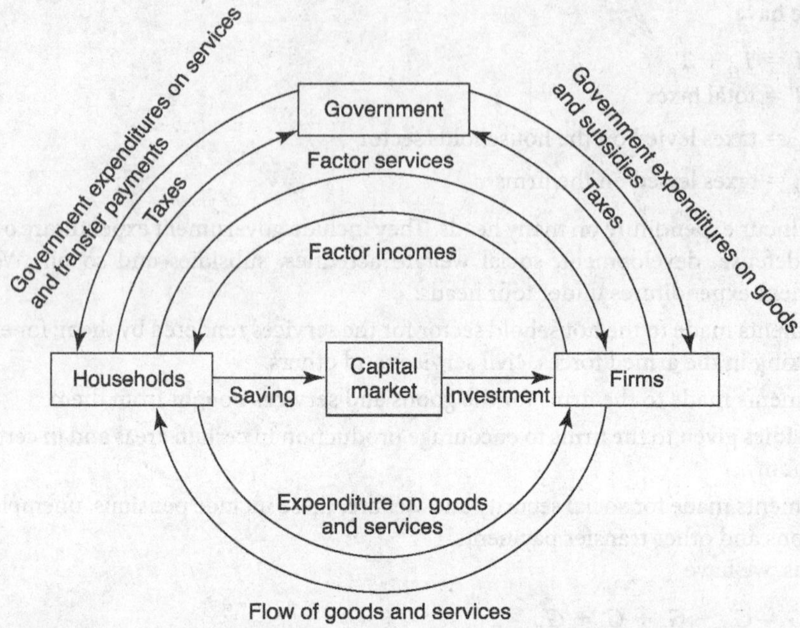

Figure 2.3 The Circular Flow of Income in a Three Sector Economy

In addition, a flow of income between the government sector and the capital market may also exist.

(1) In case the government follows a deficit budget and the government expenditure is greater than the revenue or $G > T$, the difference is financed from loans from the capital market. Hence, money will flow from the capital market to the government sector.

(2) In case the government follows a surplus budget and the government expenditure is less than the revenue or $G < T$, money will flow to the capital market from the government sector. However, in today's world this seems to be a rare occurrence.

RECAP

- Taxes levied by the government include those on the households sector and those on the firms.
- In today's world, the government often follows a deficit budget, which implies net injections into the economy and thus an expansion in the circular flow of income.
- For a deficit budget, money flows from the capital market to the government sector.

THE CIRCULAR FLOW OF INCOME IN A FOUR SECTOR ECONOMY

No economy in the world functions in isolation. It is linked with the other economies through trade. This brings us to an analysis of a four sector economy where besides the household, firms and the government, the fourth sector is the foreign sector.

Although the foreign sector is engaged in many activities, we will here concentrate only on the import and export of goods and services.

(1) When a country imports goods and services, the expenditure incurred by the residents of the domestic country leads to an increase in the income of the factors of production of the country which is exporting the goods and services (and not the domestic country). Hence, imports lead to an outflow of income and thus to a decrease in the circular flow of income.

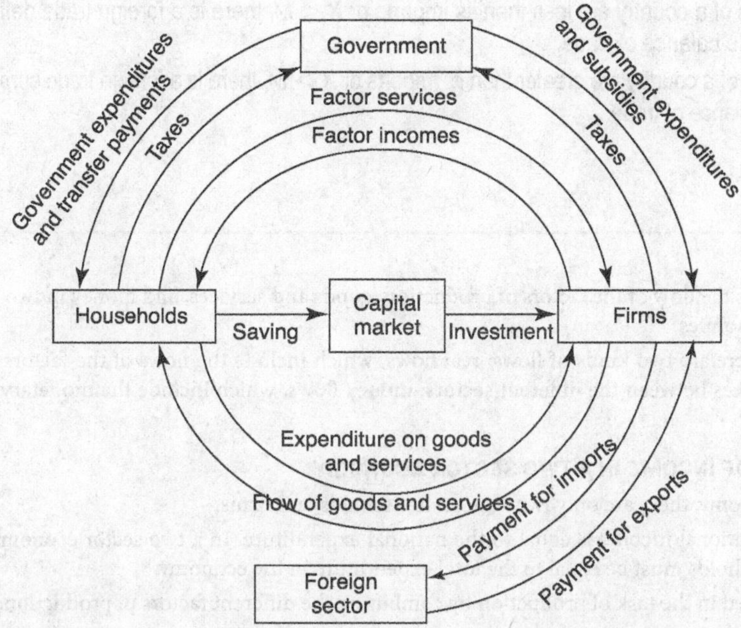

Figure 2.4 The Circular Flow of Income in a Four Sector Economy

(2) When a country exports goods and services, the expenditure incurred by the residents of the foreign country leads to an increase in the income of the factors of production in the domestic country which is exporting the goods and services. Hence, exports lead to an inflow of income and thus to an increase in the circular flow of income.

Rarely does a situation occur where the exports of a country equal the imports. In general, two situations are possible:

(a) The exports of a country are less than its imports or $X < M$: Hence, there is a foreign trade deficit equal to $(M - X)$ or an unfavourable balance of trade. As imports are greater than imports, or in other words, withdrawals are greater than injections there will be a decrease in the circular flow of income.

(b) The exports of a country are greater than its imports or $X > M$: Hence, there is a foreign trade surplus equal to $(X - M)$ or a favourable balance of trade. As exports are greater than imports, or in other words, injections are greater than withdrawals there will be an increase in the circular flow of income.

Figure 2.4 depicts the circular flow of income in a four sector economy. It shows the economic transactions between the households, firms, government and the foreign sector. The figure is an extension of figure 2.3 where the bottom part of the figure depicts the foreign sector. Though the exports of goods and services add to the circular flow of income, imports of goods and services reduce the circular flow of income. (In a four sector economy, we have discussed only a simple model which does not include the other aspects of foreign trade as this will complicate the analysis.)

RECAP

- Imports lead to an outflow of income and hence to a decrease in the circular flow of income.
- Exports lead to an inflow of income and hence to an increase in the circular flow of income.

- When the exports of a country are less than its imports or $X < M$, there is a foreign trade deficit equal to $M - X$ or an unfavourable balance of trade.
- When the exports of a country are greater than its imports or $X > M$, there is a foreign trade surplus equal to $X - M$ or a favourable balance of trade.

SUMMARY

INTRODUCTION

1. The chapter analyses the flow of the factors of production, goods and services, and money in two sector, three sector and four sector economies.
2. In any economy, there are two kinds of flows: real flows, which include the flows of the factors of production and the goods and services between the different sectors; money flows, which include the monetary flows between the different sectors.

THE CIRCULAR FLOW OF INCOME IN A TWO SECTOR ECONOMY

1. In a two sector economy, there are only two sectors: households and firms.
2. By definition, the national income is equal to the national expenditure. In a two sector economy, the total income earned by the households must be equal to the total expenditure in the economy.
3. The firms are engaged in the task of production by combining the different factors of production.
4. The owners of these factors are the households.
5. The goods produced by the firms are bought by the households and the payments made by them for these goods and services are utilized by the firms to make the factor payments.
6. Assumptions: There are no savings by the household sector; there are no inventories; there are no retained earnings by the firm.
7. The circular flow of income in a two sector economy can be depicted in a diagram showing the inner and the outer loops.

WITHDRAWALS AND INJECTIONS IN AN ECONOMY

1. Withdrawal (or leakage) is income, which is generated in the production of the national output and which does not become a part of the circular flow of income.
2. There are three types of withdrawals in an economy: saving, taxes and imports. Withdrawals lead to a decrease in the circular flow of income.
3. Injection is an amount of money, which is spent by the different sectors in the economy and which is in addition to their incomes generated in the circular flow of income.
4. There are three types of injections in an economy: investment, government expenditure and exports.

THE CIRCULAR FLOW IN A THREE SECTOR ECONOMY

1. We now introduce a third sector, the government sector.
2. It is assumed that taxes form the only source of revenue for the government. These taxes include those levied on the households sector and those levied on the firms.
3. We can divide the government expenditures under four heads: payments made to the household sector, payments made to the firms for the goods and services bought from them, subsidies given to the firms and payments made to social security and welfare.
4. The government may follow a balanced, deficit or a surplus budget. In today's world, the government often follows a deficit budget. Such a budget implies net injections and thus an expansion in the circular flow of income.
5. It is important to note that a part of the flows between the households and the firms now gets diverted to the government sector. In addition, a flow of income between the government sector and the capital market may also exist.

THE CIRCULAR FLOW IN A FOUR SECTOR ECONOMY

1. In a four sector economy besides the household, firms and the government, the fourth sector is the foreign sector.
2. Imports lead to an outflow of income and thus to a decrease in the circular flow of income.
3. Exports lead to an inflow of income and thus to an increase in the circular flow of income.
4. When the exports of a country are less than its imports or $X < M$, there is a foreign trade deficit equal to $M - X$ or an unfavourable balance of trade.
5. When the exports of a country are greater than its imports or $X > M$, there is a foreign trade surplus equal to $X - M$ or a favourable balance of trade.

REVIEW QUESTIONS

TRUE OR FALSE QUESTIONS

1. Real flows include the flows of money between the different sectors.
2. In a two sector economy, the national income is equal to the national expenditure.
3. Withdrawal is income, which is generated in the production of the national output and which does not become a part of the circular flow of income.
4. Injection is an amount of money, which is spent by the different sectors in the economy and which is generated in the circular flow of income.
5. A surplus budget implies net injections and thus an expansion in the circular flow of income.

VERY SHORT-ANSWER QUESTIONS

1. Which are the two kinds of flows in an economy?
2. Name the different types of withdrawals in an economy.
3. Name the different types of injections in an economy.
4. Name some of the taxes levied on the household sector and the firms.
5. 'Rarely does a situation occur where the exports of a country equal the imports.' Comment.

SHORT-ANSWER QUESTIONS

1. 'By definition, the national income is equal to the national expenditure.' Explain for a two sector economy.
2. What are the assumptions necessary for an analysis of a two sector economy?
3. Depict the circular flow of income in a two sector economy explaining the inner and outer loops?
4. With the help of a diagram, explain the two ways of calculating the national income.
5. What are the implications of a balanced, deficit or a surplus government budget on the circular flow of income? Discuss.

LONG-ANSWER QUESTIONS

1. Describe the circular flow of income in a two sector economy.
2. What is a withdrawal? What are the different types of withdrawals in an economy? Discuss.
3. What is an injection? What are the different types of injections in an economy? Discuss.
4. In a three sector economy, 'like any other sector in the economy, the government is involved in many activities.' Comment.
5. Describe the circular flow of income in a four sector economy.

ANSWERS

TRUE OR FALSE QUESTIONS

1. **False.** Real flows include the flows of the factors of production and the goods and services between the different sectors.
2. **True.** The sum total of the factor incomes earned by the households is equal to the total of the expenditures by the households on the goods and services. Hence in a two sector economy, the total income earned by the households must be equal to the total expenditure in the economy.

3. **True.** Withdrawal or leakage is income, which is generated in the production of the national output and which does not become a part of the circular flow of income. There are three types of withdrawals: saving, taxes, and imports. They all lead to a decrease in the circular flow of income.
4. **False.** Injection is an amount of money, which is spent by the different sectors in the economy and which is in addition to their incomes generated in the circular flow of income. There are three types of injections: investment, government expenditure and exports. They all lead to an increase in the circular flow of income.
5. **False.** In a deficit budget, the government expenditure is much greater than their revenue or $G > T$. The difference is financed from loans from the capital market. Such a budget implies net injections and thus an expansion in the circular flow of income.

National Income

3

After studying this topic, you should be able to understand

- ✓ *GNP is a measure of the value of goods and services that the nationals or residents of the country produce regardless of where they are located.*
- ✓ *GDP is the total value of all the final goods and services produced by all the enterprises within the domestic territory of a country in a particular year.*
- ✓ *Personal income is the income received by the households and the non-corporate businesses.*
- ✓ *Disposable personal income is the amount, which is actually available to the households and to the non-corporate businesses after they have fulfilled their tax obligations to the government.*
- ✓ *GDP is one of the most important macroeconomic variables and one of the best measures to judge an economy's performance.*
- ✓ *Three approaches to calculating the GDP are the output approach, the income approach and the expenditure approach.*

INTRODUCTION

In macroeconomics, we deal with economic aggregates like saving, consumption, investment, employment, national income and national product. Though all these aggregates play an important role, this chapter focuses on an analysis of the national income, national product and related aggregates like personal income and disposable personal income. It is not only important to have an understanding of the different concepts but also equally important to understand as to how these aggregates are measured.

NATIONAL INCOME AGGREGATES

Here we focus on the different concepts of the national income and the related aggregates.

Gross National Product

Gross national product (GNP) is a measure of the value of goods and services that the nationals or residents of the country produce regardless of where they are located.

Gross national product (GNP) is defined as the total value of all the final goods and services produced in a country in a particular year, plus the income which is earned by its citizens who are located abroad minus the income of non-residents located within that country. GNP is a measure of the value of goods and services that the nationals or residents of the country produce regardless of where they are located. It is, thus, the total income of a nation as earned by the citizens of a nation.

BOX 3.1

The need for accurate measures of aggregate economic activity was felt somewhere around the Great Depression. Thus, the initial efforts to develop such measures date back to the late 1920s and 1930s. Colin Clark and Simon Kuznets initiated the process followed by Richard Stone. In the US, the first formal national accounts were available by 1947. The United Nations System of National Accounts defines the international rules relating to national accounting.

Gross Domestic Product

Gross domestic product (GDP) is the total value of all the final goods and services produced by all the enterprises within the domestic territory of a country in a particular year.

Gross domestic product (GDP) is defined as the total value of all the final goods and services produced by all the enterprises (both resident and non-resident) within the domestic territory of a country in a particular year.

The GDP, one of the most essential macroeconomic variables, can be said to measure both a nation' total income and its total output of goods and services. It is believed to be one of the best indicators of judging an economy' performance.

In calculating the GDP,

(1) only market prices are used as they reveal the willingness of the public to pay for a good or a service;

(2) only the value of currently produced goods and services are included.

Treatment of Inventories in the GDP

In general when a firm adds to its inventories of goods, it involves expenditure by the firms. Hence like production for the final sale of the product, the accumulation of inventories also increases the GDP.

Treatment of Intermediate Goods in the GDP

Production involves many stages: raw materials, intermediate goods and then the finished goods. It is important to note that only the values of the final goods are included in the GDP. The values of the intermediate goods are already a part of the market price of the final goods in the production of which they are used. This avoids duplication.

Imputations in the GDP

Nominal GDP is the total of the value of the goods and services calculated at current prices.

Imputed values have to be used in the GDP calculations for goods, which are not sold in the market. For example, for people living on their own for durable goods which are owned by households, meals which are cooked at home, etc.

Nominal GDP and Real GDP

Real GDP is the total of the value of the goods and services calculated at constant prices.

Nominal GDP is the total of the value of the goods and services calculated at current prices. Real GDP is the total of the value of the goods and services calculated at constant prices.

Overall GDP Growth in India

Table 3.1 shows the overall growth of GDP in India. The rate of growth of GDP in India (at factor cost at constant 1999–2000 prices) in 2008–09, as per revised estimates released by the Central Statistical Organization

Table 3.1 Overall growth of GDP in India (2003–2004 to 2008–2009)

Year	Rate of growth of total GDP at factor cost in India (in per cent)
2003–2004	8.5
2004–2005	7.5
2005–2006	9.5
2006–2007	9.7
2007–2008	9.0
2008–2009	6.7

BOX 3.2

The GDP deflator or the implicit deflator is the ratio of the nominal GDP to the real GDP. GDP Deflator = nominal GDP/real GDP. This deflator deflates (or in other words takes out inflation from) the nominal GDP to give the real GDP. Hence, it reflects as to what is really happening to the general price level in an economy.

(CSO) (29 May 2009) was 6.7 per cent. The growth of GDP represents a deceleration from high growth of 9.0 per cent and 9.7 per cent in 2007–08 and 2006–07, respectively.

GDP and Economic Activity

It is important to note that, often, the value of many goods and services do not get included in the GDP. Also, the imputations involved in the calculations of the GDP may not be accurate. Hence, the GDP is an imperfect measure of economic activity.

To some extent it can be pointed out that real GDP, as compared to nominal GDP, is a better measure of economic well being because it is not affected by a change in the prices.

Measurement of Real GDP

Real GDP can be calculated in following two ways:

(1) by using base year prices;
(2) by using chain weighted measures.

In general, and most often, the two methods are interlinked and used to measure variations in the production of goods and services in the economy.

GDP and the Other Measures of Income

From the GDP, we can arrive at the other measures of income in the national income accounts.

Gross National Product (GNP)

$$\text{GNP} = \text{GDP} + \text{factor payments from abroad} - \text{factor payments to abroad}$$

Net National Product (NNP)

$$\text{NNP} = \text{GNP} - \text{depreciation}$$

National Income (NI)

NI = NNP − Indirect business taxes

where, depreciation = quantity of the economy' stock of plants and equipment that wears out during the period of a year.

indirect business taxes = like sales tax and value added taxes account for the difference between the price received by the firms and the price paid by the consumers for a good.

Personal income is the income received by the households and the non-corporate businesses. It includes income from all sources.

Personal Income = National Income (NI) − (Corporate Profits + Social Security Contributions + Net Interest) + (Dividends + Transfers from Government to individuals + Personal Interest Income)

We can arrive at the personal income from the national income by making some adjustments in the following sectors:

(1) Corporate sector:
   (a) Deduction to be made from the national income of undistributed corporate profits (or retained earnings) and the corporate taxes paid to the state.
   (b) Addition to be made to the national income of dividends.

(2) Government sector:
   (a) Deduction of the contributions to social insurance.
   (b) Addition to be made of the net amount the government pays as transfer payments to the individuals.

(3) Household sector:
   (a) Deduction of net interest.
   (b) Addition to be made of the personal interest income.

Disposable personal income is the amount, which is actually available to the households and to the non-corporate businesses after they have fulfilled their tax obligations to the government.

Disposable Personal Income

Personal income is the income received by the households and the non-corporate businesses.

Disposable personal income or personal disposable income is the amount, which is actually available to the households and to the non-corporate businesses after they have fulfilled their tax obligations to the government. It is the income available to the households for saving and consumption.

Disposable Personal Income = Personal Income − Personal Tax and Non-tax Payments

RECAP

- Real GDP, as compared to nominal GDP, is a better measure of economic well being because it is not affected by a change in the prices.
- Real GDP can be calculated in two ways: by using base year prices and chain-weighted measures.

TABLE 3.2 Selected Indicators of the Indian Economy (*Source*: Economic Survey 2008–09)

	0.1 Selected Indicators										
	1950–51	1960–61	1970–71	1980–81	1990–91	2000–01	2004–05	2005–06	2006–07	2007–08	2008–09
1	2	3	4	5	6	7	8	9	10	11	12
Eonomic Indicators											
GDP at factor cost: at current prices Rs. Cr.	9719	16512	42981	132520	515032	1925017	2877701	3282385	3779384	4320892^{Q}	4933183^{R}
GDP at factor cost: at constant prices Rs. Cr.	224786	329825	474131	641921	1083572	1864300	2388768	2616101	2871120	3129717^{Q}	3339374^{R}
Per capita Net National Product: at constant prices Rs.	5708	7121	8091	8594	11535	16172	19331	20868	22580	24295^{Q}	25494^{R}
Gross Domestic Capital Formation as percentage to GDP: at current market prices	8.4	14.0	15.1	19.9	26.0	24.3	32.1	35.5	36.9	39.1^{Q}	NA
Gross domestic savings as percentage to GDP: at current market prices	8.6	11.2	14.2	18.5	22.8	23.7	31.7	34.2	35.7	37.7^{Q}	NA
Index of agricultural production (Base: triennium ending 1981–82)	46.2	68.8	85.9	102.1	148.4	165.7	177.3	191.9	200.7	207.1	188.7
Index of industrial production[a] (Base: 1993–94 = 100)	7.9[b]	15.6	28.1	43.1	91.6	162.6	204.8	221.5	247.1	268.0	274.3
Wholesale Price Index average (Base: 1993–94 = 100)	6.8	7.9	14.3	36.8	73.7	155.7	187.3	195.8	206.2	215.8	234.0

(Continued)

TABLE 3.2 (continued)

	1950–51	1960–61	1970–71	1980–81	1990–91	2000–01	2004–05	2005–06	2006–07	2007–08	2008–09
1	**2**	**3**	**4**	**5**	**6**	**7**	**8**	**9**	**10**	**11**	**12**
Consumer Price Index for industrial Workers[e] average (Base 1982 = 100)	17.0	21.0	38.0	81.0	193.0	444.0	520.0	542.0	125	133	145
Output (a) Foodgrains (million tonnes)	50.8	82.0	108.4	129.6	176.4	196.8	198.4	208.6	217.3	230.8	229.9[d]
(b) Finished Steel[e] (million tonnes)	1.0	2.4	4.6	6.8	13.5	31.2	41.3	44.4	50.2	53.3	53.5
(c) Cement (million tonnes)	2.7	8.0	14.3	18.6	48.8	99.2	125.3	140.5	154.7	167.8	181.4
(d) Coal and lignite[f] (million tonnes)	32.3	55.2	76.3	119.0	225.5	332.6	413.0	437.1	462.1	491.1	NA
(e) Crude oil (million tonnes)	0.3	0.5	6.8	10.5	32.2	32.4	34.0	32.2	34.0	34.1	33.5
(f) Electricity generated (utilities only) (Billion KWH)	5	17	56	111	264	499	587	617	663	704	724
Plan outlay (Rs. Crore)	260[g]	1117	2524	15023	58369	185737	193114	247178	244230	292338	375486
Foreign Trade											
(i) Exports											
Rs. Crore	606	642	1535	6711	32553	203571	375340	456418	571779	655864	766935
US $ million	1269	1346	2031	8486	18143	44560	83535	103092	126361	162904	168704

TABLE 3.2 (continued)

	1950–51	1960–61	1970–71	1980–81	1990–91	2000–01	2004–05	2005–06	2006–07	2007–08	2008–09
1	2	3	4	5	6	7	8	9	10	11	12
(ii) Exports											
Rs. Crore	608	1122	1634	12549	43198	230873	501065	660409	840506	1012312	1305503
US $ million	1273	2353	2162	15869	24075	50536	111516	149167	185749	251439	287759
Foreign exchange reserves[h] (excluding gold. SDRs and Reserve Tranche Position at IMF):											
Rs. crore	911	186	438	4822	4388	184482	593121	647327	836597	1196023	1230066
US $ million	1914	390	584	5850	2236	39554	135571	145108	191924	299230	241426

[R] Revised estimates.
[Q] Quick estimates.
NA: Not available.
[a] The index of industrial Production has been revised since 1993–94.
[b] Relates to the calender year 1950.
[c] Data until 2005–06 is at base 1982 = 100, since january, 2006 new series of CPI (IW) has been introduced with base 2001 = 100. The conversion factor for deriving the data at base 1982 = 100 is 4.63.
[d] 3rd Advance Estimates.
[e] Including secondary producers.
[f] Coal output includes Meghalaya Coal from 2001–02 onwards.
[g] Relates to 1951–52.
[h] As on end March.

MEASUREMENT OF NATIONAL INCOME

Many measures are used to estimate the aggregate economic activity in a country, mainly GDP, GNP and NNP. Among these, GDP is perhaps one of the most important macroeconomic variables and one of the best measures to judge an economy' performance. Three approaches to calculating the GDP are the output approach, the income approach and the expenditure approach. Theoretically, the three approaches must yield the same result because the total expenditures on goods and services (GNE) must be equal to the total income paid out to the producers (GNI), and that in turn must also be equal to the total value of the output of goods and services (GNP).

We now attempt an analysis of the three approaches:

(1) **The output approach:** It is also called the product method or the value added method. To estimate the GDP by this approach, the total value of all the final goods and services produced in an economy during a given time period are estimated.

The stages involved are:

(a) Estimation of gross value of the domestic product: Firstly, this involves a classification of the production enterprises according to their activities. The three sectors here are the primary sector that relates to agriculture and allied activities, secondary sector (manufacturing sector) that includes all units engaged in producing material goods and tertiary sector (services sector) that includes all the units engaged in producing services like banking and transport.

Secondly, the gross value or the value of the output is estimated from all the sectors in two ways:

(i) By multiplying the output of each sector with the respective price and then summing them up.

(ii) By adding up the sales and change in stocks.

(b) Estimation of the intermediate cost of production and depreciation: While intermediate costs are estimated by including expenditure on non-factor inputs like raw materials, electricity and fuel used in the production process, depreciation may be estimated as a percentage of output or as a percentage of capital.

(c) Deduction of the intermediate cost of production and depreciation from the gross value to arrive at the net value of the domestic product.

(2) **The income approach:** It is also called the factor income method or factor share method. To estimate the GDP by this approach, the total sum of the factor payments received during a given period is estimated. Depending on the way the income is earned, it can be classified into five components:

(a) **Employee' compensation,** which includes the wages, salaries, and the fringe benefits received by the workers.

(b) **Proprietor' income,** which includes the incomes of non-corporate businesses including small firms.

(c) **Rental income,** which includes all the rental income earned by the owners of properties including the imputed rent on the houses which are self owned.

(d) **Corporate profits,** which include the incomes of corporations after having made payments to the workers, creditors and others.

(e) **Net interest,** which includes the interest paid by the domestic business after deducting the interest received and also interest earned from abroad.

All the different categories of income are added together to obtain the GDP from the income method.

(3) **The expenditure approach:** The GDP can be classified into following four components of expenditure:

(a) **Private Consumption Expenditure:** It includes goods and services, which are purchased by households. These can be further grouped into three categories:

(i) Non-durable goods are goods, which last only for a short period like food and clothing.

(ii) Durable goods are goods, which last for a long period like cars and electronic goods.

(iii) Services include the work performed or services provided by firms, individuals and others for the benefit of the consumers like banking, accounting and auditing services.

(b) **Investment Expenditure:** It consists of goods and services bought for use in the future. It can be further grouped into three categories:

(i) Business fixed investment is the purchase of new plant and equipment by firms.

(ii) Residential investment is the purchase of new housing by households and others.

(iii) Inventory investment is the change in the inventory of goods of the firm. This change can be positive or negative depending on whether the inventories increase or decrease.

(c) **Government Purchases:** They include the goods and services bought by the different governments like defense equipment. It is to be noted that transfer payments to the individuals like social security payments are not included in the GDP as they are not the payments for any goods and services.

(d) **Net Exports:** They are the values of goods and services exported to other countries minus the value of goods and services imported into the country.

A sum of all these different expenditures will give the GDP by the expenditure method.

Net Income from Abroad

It is important to understand that all the three methods discussed above yield the GDP at market price or the GDP for a closed economy. To arrive at the GDP for an open economy, we need to add to it the net factor incomes earned from abroad. Hence we will now obtain what is called the Gross National Income, GNI.

As already mentioned, theoretically, the three approaches must yield the same result. However, in practice there exist minor differences in results obtained from the various methods for several reasons; some of them are:

(1) Changes in inventory levels and errors in the statistics. This occurs because the goods, which are in inventory have been produced (and are therefore included in GNP), but they are not yet sold (and are therefore not yet included in GNE).

(2) Issues relating to timing can cause a slight difference between the value of goods produced (GNP) and the payments to the factors involved in the production of the goods. This is particularly so if the inputs are bought on credit, and also because the wages are often collected after the production period.

RECAP

- To estimate the GDP by the output approach, the total value of all the final goods and services produced in an economy during a given time period is estimated.
- To estimate the GDP by the income approach, the total sum of factor payments received during a given period is estimated.

SUMMARY

INTRODUCTION

The present chapter focuses on an analysis of the national income, national product and related aggregates like personal income and disposable personal income.

NATIONAL INCOME AGGREGATES

1. GNP is the total value of all the final goods and services produced in a country in a particular year, plus the income which is earned by its citizens who are located abroad minus the income of non-residents located within that country.
2. GDP is the total value of all the final goods and services produced by all the enterprises (both resident and non-resident) within the domestic territory of a country in a particular year. It is taken to be one of the best indicators of judging an economy' performance.
3. In calculating the GDP, only market prices are used and only the value of currently produced goods and services are included.
4. As far as inventories are concerned, accumulation of inventories also increases the GDP.
5. As far as intermediate goods are concerned, in the GDP only the value of the final goods (and not the intermediate goods) is included. This avoids duplication.
6. Imputed values have to be used in the GDP calculations for the goods that are not sold in the market.
7. Nominal GDP is the total of the value of the goods and services calculated at current prices whereas real GDP is the total of the value of goods and services calculated at constant prices.
8. GDP is an imperfect measure of economic activity because, often, the value of many goods and services do not get included in the GDP and the imputations involved in the calculations of the GDP may not be accurate. Real GDP is a better measure of economic well being because it is not affected by a change in the prices.
9. Real GDP can be calculated either by using base year prices or by using chain weighted measures.
10. GNP = GDP + Factor payments from abroad − Factor payments to abroad
11. NNP = GNP − Depreciation
12. NI = NNP − Indirect business taxes

PERSONAL INCOME

1. Personal Income is the income received by the households and the non-corporate businesses from all sources.
2. Personal Income = National Income (NI) − (Corporate Profits + Social Security Contributions + Net Interest) + (Dividends + Transfers from Government to individuals + Personal Interest Income).

DISPOSABLE PERSONAL INCOME

1. Disposable personal income or personal disposable is the amount, which is actually available to the households and to the non-corporate businesses after they have fulfilled their tax obligations to the government.
2. Disposable Personal Income = Personal Income − Personal Tax and Non-tax payments.

MEASUREMENT OF NATIONAL INCOME

1. GDP is one of the most important macroeconomic variables and one of the best measures to judge an economy's performance.
2. Three ways of calculating the GDP are the output approach, the income approach and the expenditure approach.
3. The output approach is also called the product method or the value added method. Here, the total value of all the final goods and services produced in an economy during a given time period are estimated in three stages.
4. The income approach is also called the factor income method or factor share method. To estimate the GDP by this approach, the total sum of factor payments received during a given period is estimated.
5. In the expenditure approach, there are four components: private consumption expenditure, investment expenditure, government purchases and net exports.
6. Net Income from abroad is to be added to the GDP to arrive at the GNI.

7. The three approaches must, theoretically, yield the same result. However, in practice there exist minor differences in the various methods due to changes in inventory levels and errors in the statistics and due to issues related to timing.

REVIEW QUESTIONS

TRUE OR FALSE QUESTIONS

1. GDP is a measure of the value of goods and services that the nationals or residents of the country produce regardless of where they are located.
2. Personal Income is the income received by the households and the non-corporate businesses.
3. Disposable personal income is the amount, which is actually available to the households and to the non-corporate businesses after they have fulfilled their tax obligations to the government.
4. Personal Income is perhaps one of the most important macroeconomic variables and one of the best measures to judge an economy' performance.
5. Three approaches to calculating the GDP are the output approach, the income approach and the expenditure approach.

VERY SHORT-ANSWER QUESTIONS

1. Explain (a) GNP and (b) GDP
2. Explain the difference between personal income and disposable personal income.
3. What are the different approaches to the calculation of the GDP? Why should the three approaches yield the same result?
4. 'Theoretically the three approaches to the calculation of the GDP must yield the same result. However, in practice there exist minor differences from the various methods for several reasons.' Comment.
5. Give the other names for the income approach. What are the five components of income?

SHORT-ANSWER QUESTIONS

1. What is personal income? How can one arrive at the personal income from the national income?
2. How is the GDP calculated by the output approach? What are the different stages involved?
3. How is the GDP calculated by the income approach? What are the different components of income?
4. How is the GDP calculated by the expenditure approach? What are the different components of expenditure?
5. Differentiate between the GNP and the GDP. In the computation of the GDP, what is the treatment given to (a) inventories, (b) intermediate goods and (c) goods not sold in the market?

LONG-ANSWER QUESTIONS

1. Write a short note on the GNP and the GDP bringing out the difference between the two national income aggregates. Is the GDP a perfect measure of economic activity? Discuss.
2. Which are the three approaches to calculating the GDP? Discuss.
3. Write short notes on the following:
   (a) GNP
   (b) GDP
   (c) Nominal GDP and Real GDP
   (d) Personal income
   (e) Disposable personal income
4. (a) How is the real GDP measured?
   (b) How can we arrive at the other measures of income in the national income accounts from the Gross Domestic Product, namely Gross National Product (GNP), Net National Product (NNP) and National Income (NI)?
5. 'A sum of all the different expenditures will give the GDP by the expenditure method.' Which are these expenditures? Discuss.

ANSWERS

TRUE OR FALSE QUESTIONS

1. **False.** GNP is a measure of the value of goods and services, which the nationals or residents of the country produce regardless of where they are located.
2. **True.** Personal Income is the income received by the households and the non-corporate businesses. It includes income from all sources.
3. **True.** Disposable personal income is the amount, which is actually available to the households and to the non-corporate businesses after they have fulfilled their tax obligations to the government. It is, in fact, the income available to the households for saving and consumption.
4. **False.** GDP is one of the most important macroeconomic variables and one of the best measures to judge an economy' performance.
5. **True.** Three approaches to calculating the GDP are the output approach, the income approach and the expenditure approach. Theoretically, the three approaches must yield the same result.

The Classical Model of Income Determination

4

After studying this topic, you should be able to understand

- ✓ Say's law states that 'supply creates its own demand'.
- ✓ The aggregate of the demand in all the markets will always be equal to the aggregate of the supply.
- ✓ The production function describes the relationship between the inputs and the output.
- ✓ The marginal product schedule is the firm's demand curve for labour.
- ✓ The classical theory had propagated a free market economy, which classical economists believed would automatically lead to full employment.

INTRODUCTION

In his book *General Theory of Employment, Interest and Money*, Keynes had pointed out that the term 'the classical economists' was invented by Marx to represent the followers of Ricardo and, in fact, those economists who had complete faith in Ricardo and his principles. J. S. Mill, Edgeworth and Marshall accepted and improved upon what can be termed as Ricardian economics.

The general opinion among the classical economists was that it was impossible to have a situation of general unemployment. They believed that an economy will always operate at full employment. Unemployment, according to the classical economists, was an exception.

Economists today believe that full employment is an exception. The situation most prevalent in any economy is that of unemployment, which is totally against what the classical economists propagated.

BOX 4.1

J. B. Say was born in Lyon to a protestant family. Say was expected to take up a commercial career. He went to England to a merchant for whom he acted as a clerk. Later, he moved to London under another employer. Then he returned to France to work in a life assurance company. Say first wrote a pamphlet on the liberty of the press in 1789. In the year 1793, Say got married to the daughter of a former lawyer. Later, he edited a periodical in which he developed the doctrines of Adam Smith. In 1831, Say became a professor of political economy at a college in France. His wife passed away in 1830 and since then his health started declining. He died in Paris on 15 November 1832.

SAY'S LAW

Say's law is one of the most important conclusions, which have been provided by the classical economists. It is named after the famous economist J. B. Say who refused to believe that general overproduction and unemployment are common occurrences. Many economists of the early nineteenth century accepted this law as a true explanation of the working of any economic system.

The most famous tenet of Say's law is 'supply creates its own demand'.

Some assumptions, which are implicit in the Say's law are as follows:

(1) The income, which the households receive, is spent on goods and services. Hence, the average propensity to consume is one. This obviously implies that savings will be zero.

(2) The government does not perform any economic functions. This implies that there are no government expenditures, no taxation or subsidies or government borrowing.

(3) The economy is a closed economy. This implies that there is no trade or any other links with the rest of the world.

(4) The prices are flexible in that they can rapidly adjust upwards or downwards.

Basically, there are only two sectors in the economy which are under consideration. These two sectors, the firms and the households, are engaged in production and consumption, respectively. There is a circular flow of money from firms to households and from households to firms.

The most famous tenet of Say's law is 'supply creates its own demand'. By the very act of production, each producer aims at either the direct satisfaction of his wants or to exchange the goods that he produces for the other goods that he needs. Thus, the production of the goods itself involves a creation of demand for them.

In a barter economy, there is no doubt that this law will function. When a producer produces a good, he does so with the specific purpose of exchanging it for another good. Thus, the production or supply of the good creates a direct demand for the good in a barter economy.

In a money economy, goods are sold in the market for a price which is expressed in terms of money. According to the classical economists the producers of the goods, once they receive the money for the goods sold, use this money to buy more factors of production. The only function of money, according to the classical school, is to facilitate the process of exchange or to solely act as a medium of exchange. Its purpose is to avoid the problems faced in a barter economy. Thus, it is obvious that in any economy the supply of any commodity implies a demand for the other commodities in the economy. Hence, the aggregate of the demand in all the markets will always be equal to the aggregate of the supply. It is possible that for an individual market, the equality between the supply and the demand may not hold. But an excess supply or overproduction in one market will necessarily be accompanied by an excess demand or underproduction in the other market for the Say's law to hold.

RECAP

- In a barter economy, there is no doubt that the Say's law will function.
- In a money economy, for the Say's law to hold, an excess supply in one market should necessarily be accompanied by an excess demand in the other market.

BOX 4.2

An important point to note is that Say had himself not used any of the short definitions of the Say's law. Some of his contemporaries and those who came after him developed this law. The 'law of markets' evolved from the work of James Mill, David Ricardo, John Stuart Mill, and many others. It formed the basic framework of macroeconomics.

OUTPUT AND EMPLOYMENT IN THE CLASSICAL MODEL

The classical model, which is being discussed here, is highly simplified. It is limited to the determination of employment, output and price level.

The Production Function

The production function describes the input-output relationship. It is being defined for the short run, here. Short run is the length of time, which is too short for the firms to be able to vary the plants and equipment that they use in production. In addition, the technology or the production method is also assumed to be constant in the short run. Thus, we can represent our short-run aggregate production function as

The production function describes the input-output relationship.

$$Y = f(L, K)$$

where, Y = real output

L = labour input

K = capital input

As already discussed, it is being assumed that:

(1) the stock of capital, or in other words, the plant and equipment are constant; and

(2) the technology is constant.

In Figure 4.1, the production function has been shown. It can be divided into the following three parts:

(1) Up to labour input L_1 is the linear portion of the production function. It indicates proportional returns or, in other words, the output varies proportionately with labour.

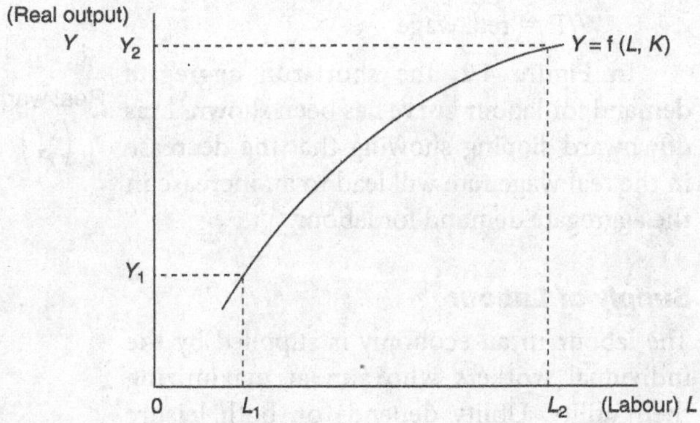

Figure 4.1 The Short-run Aggregate Production Function

(2) Between L_1 and L_2 units of labour, the output increases less than proportionately for every unit of increase in labour. This is because the increasing units of labour are applied to the fixed amounts of plant and capital equipment. Hence, this is the stage of diminishing returns as the marginal product of labour (the increase in the total product due to a unit increase in labour) decreases as the quantity of labour input increases. Thus, the diminishing returns begin at L_1 units of labour and keep diminishing to become zero at L_2 units of labour.

(3) Beyond L_2 units of labour, further additions to the labour input will not lead to an increase in the output. In fact at some higher levels of the labour input, the output may start decreasing if more labour is hired.

Given the production function, it is obvious that a firm will not hire labour beyond L_2 units.

The Labour Market in the Classical Theory

It is assumed that

(1) the workers and the firms have complete knowledge about the prices, which are prevailing in the market;

(2) the money wages adjust and thus, the market clears. There is flexibility in the wages and prices.

Demand for Labour

A perfectly competitive profit maximizing firm will go on increasing the output level till the marginal cost of producing an additional unit of the output is equal to the marginal revenue from the sale of the unit. Thus,

W/P = MPL

where, W/P = real wage

MPL = marginal product of labour

The marginal product schedule is the firm's demand curve for labour.

Thus, a profit maximizing firm will go on hiring labour till the marginal product of labour (MPL) is equal to the real wage. In other words, the marginal product schedule is the firm's demand curve for labour.

The individual firm's demand curve for labour can be summed up horizontally to arrive at the aggregate demand curve for labour. Thus, the aggregate demand schedule for labour can be expressed as

$$L^d = L^d (W/P)$$

where,

L^d = aggregate demand schedule for labour

W/P = real wage

In Figure 4.2, the short-run aggregate demand for labour curve has been shown. L^d is downward sloping showing that the decrease in the real wage rate will lead to an increase in the aggregate demand for labour.

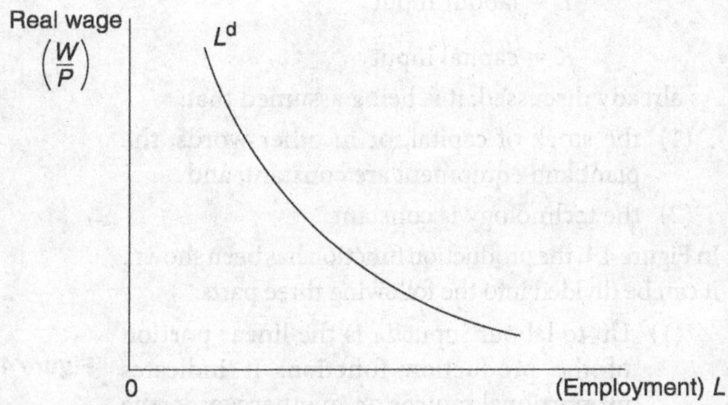

Figure 4.2 Aggregate Demand Curve for Labour

Supply of Labour

The labour in an economy is supplied by the individual workers who aim at maximizing their utility. Utility depends on both leisure and the real income. Although income can be increased by putting in more work, but work leads to a reduction in the leisure time. Hence, there appears to be a trade-off between leisure and income (or work).

The derivation of the individual's supply curve of labour has been depicted in Figure 4.3.

where,

x-axis = total number of hours available for leisure or work to an individual over a given period of time.

y-axis = real income

I_1, I_2, I_3 = indifference curves

$Z - W_1/P_1, Z - W_2/P_2, Z - W_3/P_3$ = individual's budget lines

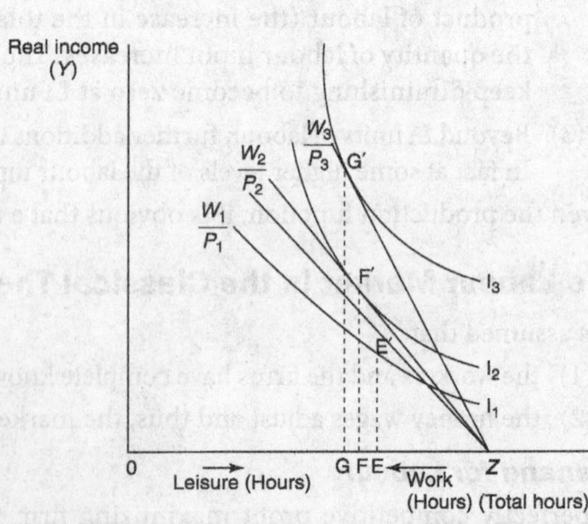

Figure 4.3 Derivation of the Individual's Supply Curve of Labour

It is important to understand that:

(1) An indifference curve shows the different combinations of income and leisure, which give the individual the same level of satisfaction. Thus, he is indifferent between these combinations. The higher the indifference curve the greater is the utility or satisfaction associated with it. The individual aims at reaching the highest possible

indifference curve. The slope of an indifference curve shows the rate at which the individual is willing to trade-off leisure for income.

(2) Real income is equal to the real wages (W/P) multiplied by the total number of hours the individual works.

(3) The slope of the budget line shows the real wage. The larger the real wage the steeper will be the budget line.

The individual aims at maximizing his utility for any given real wage. He will do so by choosing that particular point on the indifference curve where the budget line (which corresponds to that particular wage rate) is tangential to the indifference curve. At this particular point, the slope of the indifference curve is equal to the slope of the budget line. This implies that the rate at which he is willing to trade-off the leisure for income is equal to the rate at which he is actually able to trade-off.

In Figure 4.3,

(1) When the real wage rate is W_1/P_1, the individual is in equilibrium at point E' working for EZ hours, earning an income of EE' and spending OE hours on leisure.

(2) When the real wage increases to W_2/P_2, the individual is in equilibrium at point F' working for FZ hours, earning an income of FF′ and spending OF hours on leisure.

Similarly, the other points like G' can be derived. Joining these points such as E', F' and G' in Figure 4.3, we can derive the supply curve for labour as shown in Figure 4.4.

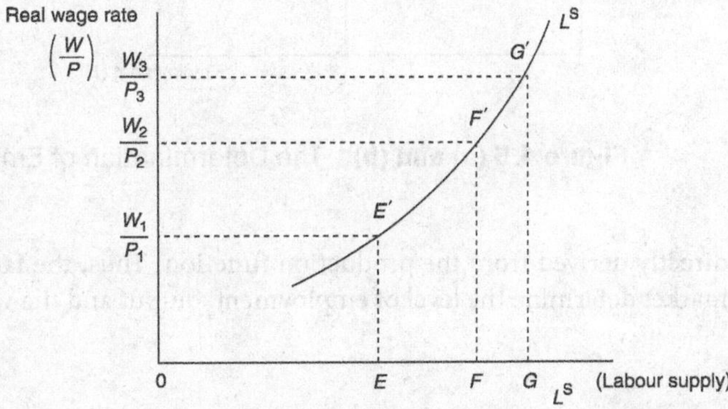

Figure 4.4 The Individual's Supply Curve of Labour

The aggregate supply curve for labour can be arrived at by summing up horizontally the individual supply curves of labour. The aggregate supply curve of labour can be expressed as $L^s = L^s\,(W/P)$.

The aggregate supply curve of labour portrays following two characteristics:

(1) The wage is the real wage rate.

(2) The curve is positively sloped showing that the supply of labour increases as the real wage rate increases. (This relationship may not exist at some very high wage rate and in that case the supply curve of labour may bend backwards.)

The Determination of Employment, Real Wage Rate and Output

The aggregate demand and aggregate supply curves of labour can now be utilized to determine the equilibrium level of output, employment and the real wage rate.

Figure 4.5(a) depicts the intersection of the aggregate demand curve for labour and aggregate supply curve for labour. The two curves intersect at point E*. Thus, the equilibrium level of employment will be L^* and the real wage rate will be $(W/P)^*$. The classical economists had proposed that this will be the full employment level, which will prevail in the long run.

Figure 4.5(b) depicts the short-run production function. Given the equilibrium level of employment at L^*, as determined in Figure 4.5(a), the corresponding equilibrium level of output can be determined from the production function at Y^*. Hence this implies that according to the classical theory, L^* amount of labour will produce an output of Y^*, given the fixed capital and the technology.

It is obvious from the above that in the classical theory, the main role in the determination of output, employment and the real wage rate is played by the supply side in the labour market. The demand for labour is

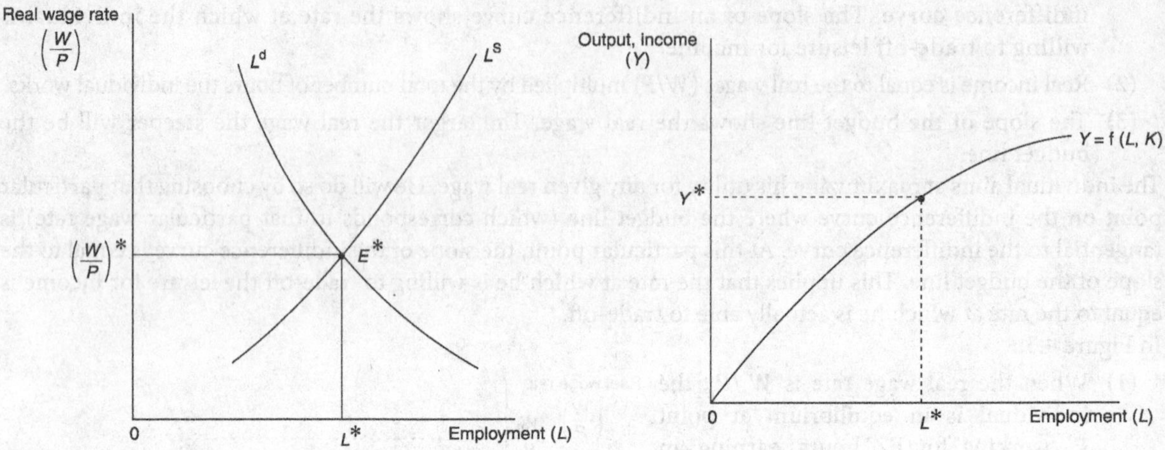

Figure 4.5 (a) and (b) The Determination of Employment, Real Wage Rate and Output

directly derived from the production function. Thus, the factors operating on the supply side in the labour market determine the level of employment, output and the wage rate.

RECAP

- One can arrive at the aggregate demand curve for labour by summing up horizontally the individual firm's demand curve for labour.
- There exists a trade-off between leisure and income.
- One can arrive at the aggregate supply curve for labour by summing up horizontally the individual supply curves of labour.
- In the classical theory in the determination of output, the most important role is that of the supply side in the labour market.

A CRITICISM OF THE CLASSICAL MODEL

The classical economists had very vehemently opposed any government interference with the market. They had propagated a free market economy, which they believed would automatically lead to full employment. It also seems that the classical equilibrium could be easily extended, with some minor adjustments, to an open economy.

BOX 4.3

It is important to note at this point that some economists are of the opinion that according to the classical theory, the aggregate supply curve is inelastic or vertical and not upward sloping. This implies that an economy will always operate at the full employment level, whatever is the wage rate.

However, some criticisms have been put forward against the classical theory. Some of them are as follows:

(1) Keynes had argued that the classical assumption of wage price flexibility is totally unrealistic. In the real world, the existence of monopolistic and oligopolistic firms, labour unions, government support programmes and minimum wage legislations are all responsible for erecting barriers in the functioning of the wage price mechanism as envisaged by the classical economists. Thus, the self-correcting mechanism of the classical school fails in its proper functioning.

(2) Keynes had no faith in the classical belief that the free enterprise system could be self-regulating. He asserted that it required periodic interventions by the authorities to evade the fluctuations and instabilities involved in the economic activities.

(3) Keynes had criticized the Say's law as a truism, which he felt could be true only under the barter system. In such a system, whatever goods are produced in the economy are either sold in the market or are used for self-consumption. Thus, supply and demand are always equal. Hence, there cannot be either a surplus or a glut. This is not true in a modern economy where every transaction involves or is carried out with money.

The Great Depression was a crucial time when the classical theory was put to test and it failed in that the classical school could not provide any solutions to the problems that the world faced at that time. This was responsible for the loss of faith in the classical economics and paved the way for the Keynesian economics.

RECAP

- The classical economists believed that voluntary and frictional unemployment were consistent with a full employment level.
- Keynes had criticized the classical assumption of wage price flexibility as totally unrealistic.
- Keynes had criticized the Say's law as a truism.

SUMMARY

INTRODUCTION

The general opinion among the classical economists was that an economy will always operate at full employment.

SAY'S LAW

1. Say's law is one of the most important conclusions, which have been provided by the classical economists. It is named after the famous economist J. B. Say who refused to believe that general overproduction and unemployment are common occurrences.
2. Some assumptions, which are implicit in the Say's law are: the average propensity to consume is one and thus savings will be zero; government does not perform any economic functions; the economy is a closed economy; and that the prices are flexible.
3. There are only two sectors in the economy—the firms and households—who are engaged in production and consumption, respectively.
4. The most famous tenet of the classical theory is the Say's law, 'supply creates its own demand'. Thus, the production of the goods itself creates a demand for them.
5. In a barter economy, there is no doubt that this law will function where the production or supply of the good creates a direct demand for the good.
6. In a money economy, goods are sold in the market for a price which is expressed in terms of money. The only function of money is to act as a medium of exchange. The aggregate of the demand in all the markets will always be equal to the aggregate of the supply.

OUTPUT AND EMPLOYMENT IN THE CLASSICAL MODEL

1. The production function describes the input—output relationship.
2. We can represent our short-run aggregate production function as $Y = f(L, K)$. A profit maximizing firm will operate in the stage of diminishing returns.
3. As far as the labour market is concerned, it is assumed that the workers and the firms have complete knowledge about the prices that are prevailing in the market and also that there exists wage price flexibility.
4. As far as the demand for labour is concerned, a perfectly competitive profit maximizing firm will go on hiring labour till the MPL is equal to the real wage. Thus, the marginal product schedule is the firm's demand curve for labour.
5. The individual firm's demand curve for labour can be summed up horizontally to arrive at the downward sloping aggregate demand curve for labour, $L^d = L^d\ (W/P)$.
6. As far as the supply of labour is concerned, there appears to be a trade-off between leisure and income.
7. The individual's supply curve of labour can be derived diagrammatically through indifference curves and budget lines where the indifference curve shows the different combinations of income and leisure, which give the individual the same level of satisfaction whereas the slope of the budget line shows the real wage.
8. The individual aims at maximizing his utility for any given real wage. He will do so by choosing that particular point on the indifference curve where the budget line (which corresponds to that particular wage rate) is tangential to the indifference curve.
9. We can derive the individual's supply curve for labour.
10. The aggregate supply curve for labour can be arrived at by summing up horizontally the individual supply curves of labour, $L^s = L^s\ (W/P)$.

THE DETERMINATION OF EMPLOYMENT, REAL WAGE RATE AND OUTPUT

1. The intersection of the aggregate demand and aggregate supply curves of labour determines the equilibrium level of output, employment and the real wage rate.
2. Given the conditions in the short run, the classical economists had proposed that this will be the full employment level.
3. Given the equilibrium level of employment, the corresponding equilibrium level of output can be determined from the production function.
4. In the classical theory, the main role in the determination of output, employment and the real wage rate is played by the supply side in the labour market.

A CRITICISM OF THE CLASSICAL MODEL

1. The classical theory had opposed any government interference with the market and had propagated a free market economy, which they believed would automatically lead to full employment.
2. However, many criticisms have been put forward against the classical theory: Keynes had argued that the classical assumption of wage price flexibility is totally unrealistic. He had criticized the Say's law as a truism only under the barter system.
3. The Great Depression was a crucial time when the classical theory was put to test and it failed. This was responsible for the loss of faith in the classical economics and paved the way for the Keynesian economics.

REVIEW QUESTIONS

TRUE OR FALSE QUESTIONS

1. The general opinion among the classical economists was that it was impossible to have a situation of full employment.
2. As of today the situation most prevalent in any economy is that of unemployment, which is totally against what the classical economists propagated.
3. The most famous tenet of Say's law is 'demand creates its own supply'.
4. The only function of money, according to the classical school, is to act as a store of value.
5. The marginal product schedule is the firm's demand curve for labour.

VERY SHORT-ANSWER QUESTIONS

1. What are the views of the classical school regarding full employment?
2. Till what stage will a profit maximizing firm go on hiring labour?
3. What are the two characteristics portrayed by the aggregate supply curve of labour?
4. Which side, the demand side or the supply side, of the labour market plays the main role in the determination of output, employment and the real wage rate?
5. What did the classical economists favour: government interference or a free market economy?

SHORT-ANSWER QUESTIONS

1. What is Say's law? Discuss in brief.
2. According to the Say's law, in a money economy 'the aggregate of the demand in all the markets will always be equal to the aggregate of the supply'. Explain.
3. Write a short note on the production function in the classical theory.
4. How does an individual maximize his utility for any given real wage?
5. Discuss any two criticisms of Keynes against the classical theory.

LONG-ANSWER QUESTIONS

1. The most famous tenet of the classical theory is the Say's law 'supply creates its own demand'. Discuss.
2. In the classical theory, 'the individual firm's demand curve for labour can be summed up horizontally to arrive at aggregate demand curve for labour'. Elaborate.
3. How can the aggregate supply curve for labour be arrived at from the individual supply curve of labour? Discuss by throwing light on the trade-off between leisure and income.
4. How are the equilibrium levels of employment, real wage rate and output determined in the classical theory? Explain.
5. What are the criticisms levelled against the classical theory of employment, real wage rate and output? Discuss.

ANSWERS

TRUE OR FALSE QUESTIONS

1. **False.** The classical economists believed that it was impossible to have a situation of unemployment.
2. **True.** In every economy, there exists at least some unemployment.
3. **False.** The most famous tenet of Say's law is 'supply creates its own demand'.
4. **False.** The only function of money, according to the classical school, is to act as a medium of exchange.
5. **True.** A profit maximizing firm will go on hiring labour till the MPL is equal to the real wage.

The Keynesian Model of Income Determination in a Two Sector Economy

5

After studying this topic, you should be able to understand

- ✓ *Aggregate demand is the total amount of goods demanded in an economy.*
- ✓ *The consumption function is a relationship between income and consumption.*
- ✓ *Saving is income that is not spent on consumption.*
- ✓ *The aggregate demand function is obtained by a vertical summation of the investment function and consumption function.*
- ✓ *In the Keynesian theory, there are two approaches to the determination of income and output: Aggregate Demand–Aggregate Supply Approach and Saving–Investment Approach.*

INTRODUCTION

This is the first of the series of four chapters, which focuses on the determination of the equilibrium level of income in the simple Keynesian model. This chapter is limited to only a two sector model, which includes only the households and the firms.

This model assumes that the aggregate supply curve is perfectly elastic (or parallel to the horizontal axis) up to the full employment level of output after which it becomes perfectly inelastic (or parallel to the vertical axis). Hence the price level, until the full employment level, will be determined solely by the height of the supply curve. Hence, the price variable gets less attention while the entire focus is on the determination of the equilibrium level of income, which is determined solely by the aggregate demand (or aggregate spending). Thus, the basic question relates to the determination of the aggregate demand.

AGGREGATE DEMAND IN A TWO SECTOR ECONOMY

The basic assumptions in this analysis are as follows.

Aggregate demand is the total amount of goods demanded in an economy.

(1) The prices are constant or do not change.

(2) Given the price level, the firms are willing to sell any amount of the output at that price level.

(3) The short-run aggregate supply curve is perfectly elastic or flat.

(4) Investment is assumed to be autonomous and thus independent of the income level.

(5) There exist only two sectors in the economy, the households and the firms.

Aggregate demand is the total amount of goods demanded in an economy. The aggregate demand function can be expressed as

$$AD = C + I \qquad (1)$$

where, C = aggregate demand for consumers goods
I = aggregate demand for investment goods

BOX 5.1

In the year 1913, Keynes published his first book, '*Indian Currency and Finance*'. In 1919, Keynes wrote '*The Economic Consequences of the Peace*', which was a controversial book but made Keynes a famous economist. In 1926, he published the book '*The End of Laissez-Faire*'. He later wrote a series of articles, '*The Means to Prosperity*' in The Times of London. In 1930, Keynes published '*A Treatise on Money*', which was his first major work in economics. In 1936, Keynes published '*The General Theory of Employment, Interest and Money*' and, in 1940, he wrote on '*How to Pay for the War*'.

As we have already assumed that investment is autonomous and independent of the income level, aggregate demand function will thus mainly depended on the consumption function. Thus, our focus will be mainly on the consumption function, which is one of the biggest sectors in any economy.

RECAP

- As investment is autonomous, aggregate demand function will depend mainly on the consumption function.

CONSUMPTION

Consumption Spending

The consumption spending or the aggregate amount of goods bought in any time period will depend upon the real income of the households. Other factors are also important but the aggregate amount of goods bought is determined only by the real income of the households.

The Consumption Function

The consumption function is a relationship between income and consumption expenditure.

The two important aspects are:

(1) Consumption expenditure varies directly with disposable income or we can say that it is a positive function of income.

(2) Keynes had stated in his 'fundamental psychological law' that, in general, an individual increases his consumption expenditure when his income increases. However, the increase in consumption is less than the increase in income.

The consumption function is a relationship between income and consumption expenditure.

Non-linear Consumption Function

The most general non-linear form of the consumption function can be expressed as

$$C = C(Y) \qquad (2)$$

where, C = consumption expenditure

Y = disposal income

The consumption function Eq. (2), which is a non-linear consumption function, has been depicted in Figure 5.1.

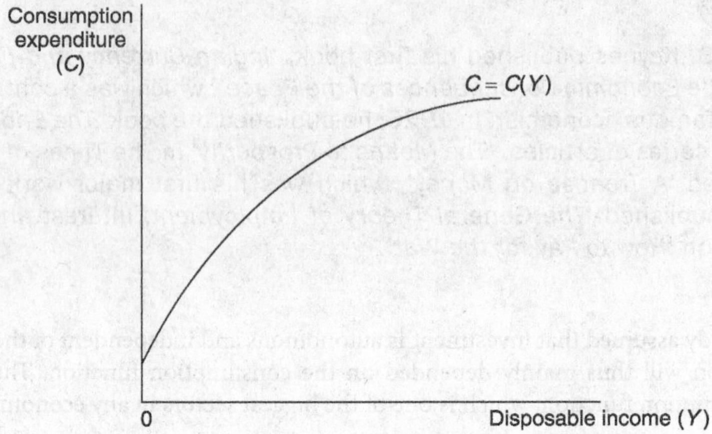

Figure 5.1 The Non-linear Consumption Function

Linear Consumption Function

The consumption function equation in a linear form can be expressed as

$$C = C_a + bY \tag{3}$$

where, C = consumption expenditure

Y = disposal income

$C_a > 0$

$0 < b < 1$

In this equation,

(1) C_a is the intercept of the consumption function on the y-axis. It shows the level of consumption at zero level of income. It is known as autonomous consumption.

(2) The constant 'b' denotes the slope of the consumption function. It is known as the marginal propensity to consume, MPC. It indicates the increase in the consumption per unit of increase in the income.

Average Propensity to Consume (APC)

The average propensity to consume (APC) is defined as the ratio of consumption to income for different levels of income.

The APC is defined as the ratio of consumption to income for different levels of income. Thus,

$$\text{APC} = \frac{C}{Y}$$

Marginal Propensity to Consume (MPC)

The marginal propensity to consume (MPC) is defined as the increase in the consumption per unit of increase in the income.

The MPC is defined as the increase in the consumption per unit of increase in the income. Thus,

$$\text{MPC} = \frac{\Delta C}{\Delta Y}$$

As b is less than 1 it implies that if income increases by a rupee, only a fraction, b, will be spent on consumption.

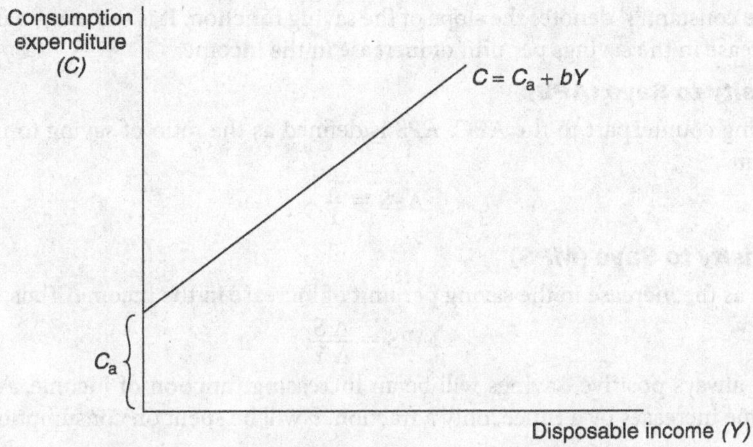

Figure 5.2 The Linear Consumption Function

Numerical Illustration 5.1

If the value of the marginal propensity to consume 'b' is 0.60, then for every rupee increase in income, what will be the increase in consumption?

Solution

For every rupee increase in income there will be an increase in consumption of 60 paisa.

Here, we will be restricting ourselves to the linear consumption function as in Figure 5.2.

RECAP

- Consumption expenditure varies directly with disposable income.

SAVING AS A COUNTERPART OF THE CONSUMPTION FUNCTION

As there are only two uses of income—consumption and saving, income that is not spent on consumption is saved.

The Saving Function

The saving function is the counterpart of the consumption function. In its most general form, the saving function can be written as

$$S = S(Y) \tag{4}$$

We know that

$$Y = C + S \tag{5}$$

or

$$S = Y - C \tag{6}$$

Equation (6) is actually the budget constraint showing that, by definition, savings will equal income net of consumption.

By substituting Eq. (3), the consumption function, in Eq. (6), which is the budget constraint, we can arrive at the saving function as shown below:

$$S = Y - C$$
$$S = Y - C_a - bY$$
$$S = -C_a + (1 - b)\,Y$$
$$S = -C_a + sY \tag{7}$$

where, $s = 1 - b$,
$s > 0$

In this equation, the constant '*s*' denotes the slope of the saving function. It is the marginal propensity to save. It indicates the increase in the savings per unit of increase in the income.

Average Propensity to Save (APS)

The APS is the saving counterpart to the APC. APS is defined as the ratio of saving to income for different levels of income. Thus,

$$\text{APS} = \frac{S}{Y}$$

Marginal Propensity to Save (MPS)

The MPS is defined as the increase in the saving per unit of increase in the income. Thus,

$$\text{MPS} = \frac{\Delta S}{\Delta Y}$$

As the MPS or s is always positive, savings will be an increasing function of income. As b is less than 1 it implies that if income increases by a rupee, only a fraction, b will be spent on consumption.

Numerical Illustration 5.2

If the value of the marginal propensity to consume, b, is 0.60, then what is the marginal propensity to save?

Solution

The marginal propensity to save = 1 − 0.60 = 0.40. This implies that of every rupee of income. 40 paisa is saved.

The saving function Eq. (7) has been shown in Figure 5.3.

Relationship between APC and APS: From Eq. (5),

$$Y = C + S$$

Dividing both sides of the equation by Y, we get

$$1 = \frac{C}{Y} + \frac{S}{Y}$$

or

$$1 = \text{APC} + \text{APS}$$

Hence, the sum of APC and APS is always equal to one.

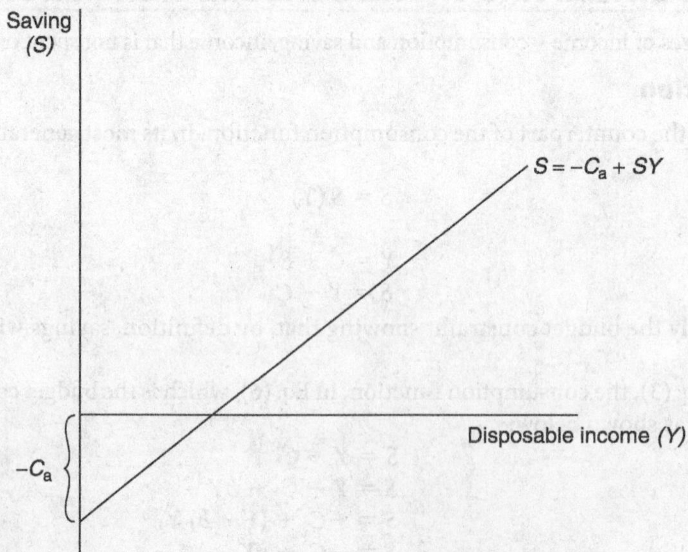

Figure 5.3 The Saving Function

Relationship between MPC and MPS: From Eq. (5),

$$Y = C + S$$

As a change in income, it can be split up into a change in consumption and a change in saving, we have

$$\Delta Y = \Delta C + \Delta S$$

Dividing both sides of the equation by ΔY, we get

$$1 = \frac{\Delta C}{\Delta Y} + \frac{\Delta S}{\Delta Y}$$

or

$$1 = \text{MPC} + \text{MPS}$$

Hence, the sum of MPC and MPS is always equal to one.

Numerical Illustration 5.3

If the consumption function is $C = 40 + 0.75Y$ then what is the saving function?

Solution

Since $S = Y - C$

$S = Y - (40 + 0.75Y)$

$S = Y - 40 - 0.75Y$

Thus, the saving function $S = -40 + 0.25\,Y$.

The Aggregate Demand Function

After having determined the consumption and the saving functions, we can now determine the aggregate demand function in a two sector economy. We are assuming that investment is constant or $I = \bar{I}$. From the aggregate demand Eq. (1) and consumption function Eq. (3), we have

$$\text{AD} = C + I \quad (1)$$

$$C = C_a + bY \quad (3)$$

Substituting for C from Eq. (3) in Eq. (1), we get

$$\text{AD} = C_a + bY + \bar{I} \quad (8)$$

Figure 5.4 depicts the derivation of the aggregate demand curve. While investment has been shown as a straight line parallel to the horizontal axis, $I = \bar{I}$, consumption has been shown as an upward sloping straight line, $C = C_a + b\,Y$. The aggregate demand function has been obtained by a vertical summation of the investment function and consumption function as $\text{AD} = C_a + b\,Y + \bar{I}$.

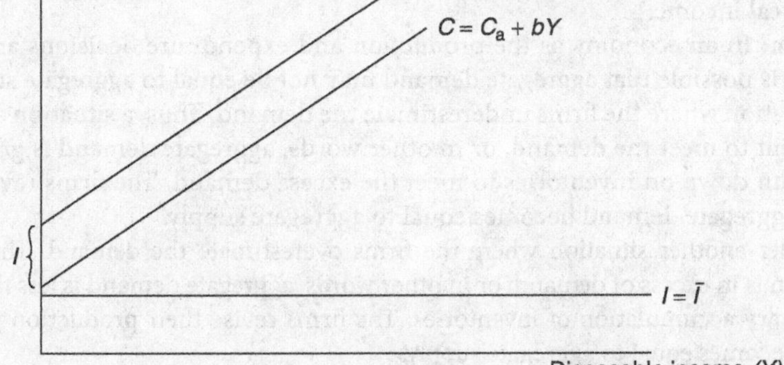

Figure 5.4 The Aggregate Demand Function

DETERMINATION OF EQUILIBRIUM INCOME OR OUTPUT IN A TWO SECTOR ECONOMY

In the most basic terms, an economy can be said to be in equilibrium when the production plans of the firms and the expenditure plans of the households are realized.

Some assumptions (already mentioned) necessary here are as follows:

(1) There exist only two sectors in the economy, the households and the firms. There is no government sector and no foreign sector.

(2) All the factors of production are owned by the households who sell the factor services to earn an income. With a part of this income, they purchase goods and services and save the rest.

(3) As there is no government in the economy, there are no taxes and subsidies and no government expenditures.

(4) As there is no foreign sector in the economy, there are no exports and imports and no external inflows and outflows.

(5) As far as the firms are concerned, there are no undistributed profits.

(6) All the prices are constant and do not change.

Investment is assumed to be autonomous and thus independent of the income level.

(7) The technology and the supply of capital are given.

According to the Keynesian theory, there are two approaches to the determination of income and output:

(1) Aggregate Demand – Aggregate Supply Approach

(2) Saving – Investment Approach

Equilibrium Income and Output: A Theoretical Explanation

Aggregate Demand – Aggregate Supply Approach

Equilibrium: The equilibrium national income is determined at that level where the aggregate demand is equal to the aggregate supply. Thus,

$$\text{Aggregate demand} = \text{Aggregate supply}$$

However, Keynes had argued that it is not necessary that aggregate demand will be always equal to aggregate supply. As far as aggregate supply is concerned, it can be assumed to be relatively stable as production depends on factors that do not change much in the short run. However, aggregate demand depends on the planned consumption expenditure of households and planned investment expenditure of firms. Aggregate demand is relatively unstable. This instability of aggregate demand can, to some extent, explain the changes in the real income.

Disequilibrium: In an economy as the production and expenditure decisions are taken by different groups of people, it is possible that aggregate demand may not be equal to aggregate supply.

Consider a situation where the firms underestimate the demand. Thus, a situation arises where the production is insufficient to meet the demand, or in other words, aggregate demand is greater than aggregate supply. There is a run down on inventories to meet the excess demand. The firms revise their production plans upwards till aggregate demand becomes equal to aggregate supply.

Now we consider another situation where the firms overestimate the demand. Thus, a situation arises where the production is in excess of demand, or in other words, aggregate demand is less than aggregate supply. There is an involuntary accumulation of inventories. The firms revise their production plans downwards till aggregate demand becomes equal to aggregate supply.

It is thus obvious that if any disequilibrium occurs, then the forces inbuilt in the system would operate in such a manner that the equilibrium is restored.

Saving–Investment Approach

Equilibrium: Before going into the depth of the saving–investment approach, it is necessary to understand the difference between *ex ante* and *ex post* saving and investment.

In the national income accounting, saving is said to be identically equal to investment. Thus,

(1) National income is equal to the sum of income generated in the production of consumer goods and investment goods, or that $Y = C + I$.

(2) National expenditure is equal to the sum of income spent on consumption and income that is saved or that $Y = C + S$.

But we know that national income = national expenditure,

or $$C + I = C + S$$

Therefore, $$I = S$$

Hence, as an identity, saving is always equal to investment.

However if we bring in the concepts of *ex ante* and *ex post*, it is not so simple. *Ex ante* (planned or desired) saving is not always equal to *ex ante* (planned or desired) investment. This is because while the households save, it is the firms who invest. There is no reason as to why the two will be the same. However, *ex post* (actual or realized) saving is always equal to *ex post* (actual or realized) investment. Thus while *ex ante* saving and investment may differ, *ex post* saving and investment are always equal.

The equilibrium national income is determined where not only the aggregate demand and the aggregate supply are equal but at that level where planned saving is also equal to planned investment. Thus,

Planned saving = Planned investment

This is possible because in a two sector economy while saving is the only leakage, investment is the only injection into the system.

Disequilibrium: Consider a situation where the firms underestimate the demand. Thus, planned saving will be less than planned investment. This implies that the consumption of goods is more than the current production. There will be a run down on inventories. Firms will expand production till the output increases to the level where planned investment is equal to planned saving.

Consider another situation where the firms overestimate the demand. Thus, planned saving will be more than planned investment. The consumption of goods is less than the current production. There will be an involuntary accumulation of inventories. Firms will cut back on production till the output decreases to the level where planned investment is equal to planned saving.

Equilibrium Income and Output: An Algebraic Explanation

Aggregate Demand–Aggregate Supply Approach

Aggregate demand = Total value of output (or income)

or $$Y = C + I$$

But the consumption function is $C = C_a + bY$ whereas investment has been assumed to be autonomous, or $I = \bar{I}$.

Thus, $$Y = C_a + bY + \bar{I}$$

Hence, equilibrium income is

$$Y - bY = C_a + \bar{I}$$

or $$Y = \frac{1}{1-b}(C_a + \bar{I}) \tag{9}$$

Saving–Investment Approach

In equilibrium,

$$AD = AS$$

or $$C + I = C + S$$

As C is common in both the sides, the equilibrium condition can be written as

$$I = S$$

But the saving function is $S = -C_a + (1-b)Y$ whereas investment has been assumed to be autonomous, or $I = \bar{I}$.

Thus, $$\bar{I} = -C_a + (1-b)Y$$

or $$Y = \frac{1}{1-b}(C_a + \bar{I})$$

This is the same equation as Eq. (9) above.

Hence, both the approaches yield the same equilibrium level of income.

Numerical Illustration 5.4

In a two sector economy when the level of the national income is Rs. 500 crores, savings are Rs. 50 crores and when the national income is Rs. 550 crores, savings are Rs. 70 crores, if planned investment is Rs. 70 crores what is the equilibrium level of the national income?

Solution

In an economy, equilibrium exists when planned saving equals planned investment. As planned investment is Rs. 70 crores, equilibrium will occur at an income level of Rs. 550 crores because at that income level alone planned investment equals planned saving of Rs. 70 crores. Thus, the equilibrium level of the national income is Rs. 550 crores.

Equilibrium Income and Output: A Graphical Explanation

Aggregate Demand–Aggregate Supply Approach

Equilibrium: The determination of the equilibrium income by the aggregate demand–aggregate supply approach in a two sector economy has been depicted in Figure 5.5(a).

where, x-axis = Disposable income

y-axis = Aggregate demand or aggregate planned expenditure

C = Aggregate consumption function, $C = C_a + bY$

C_a = The intercept of the consumption function on the y axis showing consumption spending at zero income level.

b = The MPC or the slope of the consumption function (it will remain constant as, in our analysis, the consumption function is a linear function)

AD = Aggregate demand function (which is obtained by adding the consumption function and the investment function)

AS = Aggregate supply function (also called the guideline or the 45 degree line)

Point E = Point where the aggregate demand and aggregate supply curves intersect to determine the equilibrium income at Y^*. It is also called the Keynesian cross.

Disequilibrium: Consider a situation where the firms produce an output equal to OY_1. At this level of output the aggregate demand Y_1A, consisting of consumption demand of Y_1C and investment demand of CA, is in excess of the aggregate supply of Y_1B. There is a run down on inventories to meet the excess demand. This excess demand will induce the firms to expand their output till equilibrium is reached at an income level of OY^* where aggregate demand is equal to aggregate supply.

Suppose the firms produce an output equal to OY_2. At this level of output the aggregate demand Y_2G, consisting of consumption demand of Y_2F and investment demand of FG, is insufficient to exhaust the aggregate

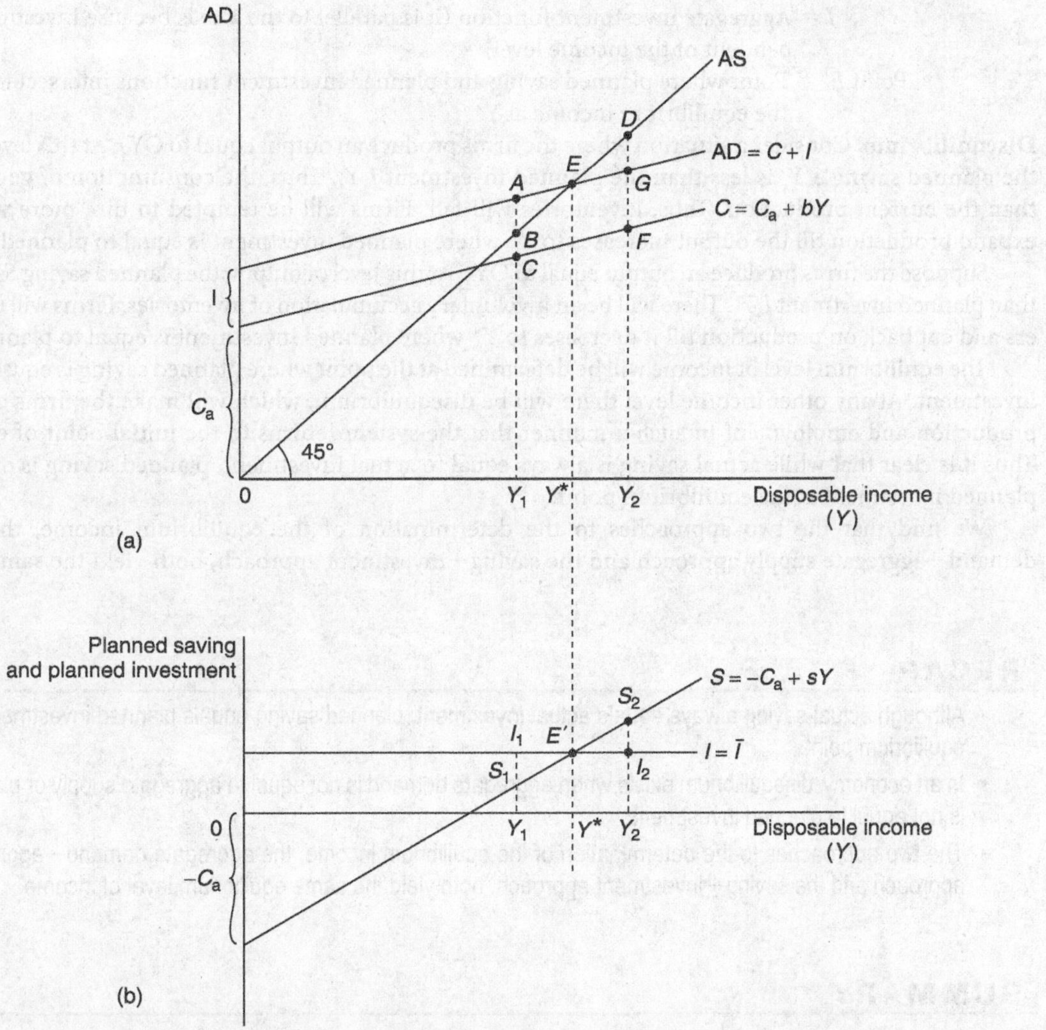

Figure 5.5 Determination of Equilibrium Income or Output in a Two Sector Economy

supply of Y_2D. There is an involuntary accumulation of inventories. Thus, the firms will cut down on production till equilibrium is reached at an income level of OY^* where aggregate demand is equal to aggregate supply.

This is a situation that arises where aggregate demand is smaller than aggregate supply.

Saving–Investment Approach

Equilibrium: The determination of the equilibrium income by the saving–investment approach in a two sector economy has been depicted in Figure 5.5(b).

where, x-axis = Disposable income

y-axis = Planned saving and planned investment

S = Aggregate saving function (it can be easily obtained from the consumption function)

$-C_a$ = The intercept of the saving function on the y-axis

s = The MPS or the slope of the saving function (it will remain constant as the saving function, in our analysis, is a linear function)

I = Aggregate investment function (it is parallel to the x-axis because investment is independent of the income level)

Point E' = Point where planned saving and planned investment functions intersect to determine the equilibrium income at Y*.

Disequilibrium: Consider a situation where the firms produce an output equal to OY_1. At this level of output, the planned saving S_1Y_1 is less than the planned investment I_1Y_1. Thus, the consumption of goods is larger than the current production. Thus, inventories will fall. Firms will be tempted to hire more workers and expand production till the output increases to Y* where planned investment is equal to planned saving.

Suppose the firms produce an output equal to OY_2. At this level of output, the planned saving S_2Y_2 is greater than planned investment I_2Y_2. There will be an involuntary accumulation of inventories. Firms will lay off workers and cut back on production till it decreases to Y* where planned investment is equal to planned saving.

The equilibrium level of income will be determined at the point where planned saving is equal to planned investment. At any other income level there will be disequilibrium, which will make the firms change their production and employment in such a manner that the system returns to the initial point of equilibrium. Thus it is clear that while actual saving is always equal to actual investment, planned saving is only equal to planned investment at the equilibrium point.

We find that the two approaches to the determination of the equilibrium income, the aggregate demand−aggregate supply approach and the saving−investment approach, both yield the same result.

RECAP

- Although actual saving always equals actual investment, planned saving equals planned investment only at the equilibrium point.
- In an economy, disequilibrium exists when aggregate demand is not equal to aggregate supply or planned saving is not equal to planned investment.
- The two approaches to the determination of the equilibrium income, the aggregate demand−aggregate supply approach and the saving−investment approach, both yield the same equilibrium level of income.

SUMMARY

INTRODUCTION

Here, we focussed on the determination of the equilibrium level of income in the simple Keynesian model in a two sector economy.

AGGREGATE DEMAND IN A TWO SECTOR ECONOMY

1. Aggregate demand is the total amount of goods demanded in an economy. The aggregate demand function can be expressed as AD = $C + I$.
2. The consumption spending or the aggregate amount of goods bought in any time period will depend upon the real income of the households.
3. The consumption function is a relationship between income and consumption expenditure.
4. The most general non-linear form of the consumption function can be expressed as $C = C(Y)$.
5. The consumption function equation in a linear form can be expressed as $C = C_a + bY$.
6. C_a also known as autonomous consumption; it is the intercept of the consumption function on the y axis whereas the constant b is known as the MPC and it denotes the slope of the consumption function.
7. The APC is defined as the ratio of consumption to income.
8. The MPC is defined as the increase in the consumption per unit of increase in the income.

SAVING AS A COUNTERPART OF THE CONSUMPTION FUNCTION

1. Income that is not spent on consumption is saved.
2. The saving function is the counterpart of the consumption function and can be written as $S = -C_a + sY$ where the constant s is the MPS and denotes the slope of the saving function.
3. The APS is the saving counterpart of the APC and is defined as the ratio of saving to income.
4. The MPS is defined as the increase in the saving per unit of increase in the income. As the MPS or s is always positive, savings will be an increasing function of income.
5. The sum of APC and APS is always equal to one.
6. The sum of MPC and MPS is always equal to one.

THE AGGREGATE DEMAND FUNCTION

1. To determine the aggregate demand function in a two sector economy, we assume that investment is constant and that $C = C_a + bY$.
2. Thus, the aggregate demand function can be written as $AD = C_a + bY + \bar{I}$.

DETERMINATION OF EQUILIBRIUM INCOME OR OUTPUT IN A TWO SECTOR ECONOMY

1. In the most basic terms, an economy can be said to be in equilibrium when the production plans of the firms and the expenditure plans of the households are realized.
2. According to the Keynesian theory, there are two approaches to the determination of income and output: Aggregate demand–Aggregate supply approach and Saving–Investment approach.

Equilibrium Income and Output

AGGREGATE DEMAND–AGGREGATE SUPPLY APPROACH

1. The equilibrium national income is determined at that level where the aggregate demand = aggregate supply.
2. Keynes had argued that it is not necessary that aggregate demand will be always equal to aggregate supply.
3. Disequilibrium occurs if aggregate demand is not equal to aggregate supply. However, if any disequilibrium occurs then the forces inbuilt in the system would operate in such a manner that equilibrium is restored.

SAVING–INVESTMENT APPROACH

1. Though *ex ante* saving and investment may differ, *ex post* saving and investment are always equal.
2. The equilibrium national income is determined where not only the aggregate demand and the aggregate supply are equal but at that level where planned saving is also equal to planned investment.
3. Disequilibrium occurs when planned saving is not equal to planned investment. However, firms expand production or cut back on production till planned investment is equal to planned saving.
4. The two approaches to the determination of the equilibrium income, the aggregate demand-aggregate supply approach and the saving–investment approach, both yield the same result.

REVIEW QUESTIONS

TRUE OR FALSE QUESTIONS

1. As investment is autonomous, aggregate demand function will depend mainly on the consumption function.
2. The MPC is defined as the ratio of consumption to income for different levels of income.
3. The APS is defined as the increase in the saving per unit of increase in the income.
4. Though planned saving always equals planned investment, actual saving equals actual investment only at the equilibrium point.
5. In an economy, disequilibrium exists when aggregate demand is not equal to aggregate supply.

VERY SHORT-ANSWER QUESTIONS

1. What is aggregate demand in the Keynesian model in a two sector economy?
2. Write a short note on the

   (a) Average propensity to consume (b) Marginal propensity to consume

3. Write a short note on the
   (a) Average propensity to save
   (b) Marginal propensity to save
4. Discuss the relationship between
   (a) APC and APS
   (b) MPC and MPS
5. Write a short note on the aggregate demand function.

SHORT-ANSWER QUESTIONS

1. Write a short note on the consumption function.
2. Write a short note on the saving function.
3. 'As an identity, saving is always equal to investment.' Comment.
4. 'If any disequilibrium occurs, then the forces inbuilt in the system would operate in such a manner that equilibrium is restored.' Comment by using the aggregate demand–aggregate supply approach to the Keynesian theory.
5. With the help of the saving–investment approach, depict equilibrium and disequilibrium in a two sector Keynesian model.

LONG-ANSWER QUESTIONS

1. Discuss the aggregate demand–aggregate supply approach to the determination of the equilibrium income and output in the Keynesian theory.
2. Discuss the saving–investment approach to the determination of the equilibrium income and output in the Keynesian theory.
3. Give the algebraic explanation to the determination of equilibrium income and output in the Keynesian theory.
4. Show the determination of equilibrium income and output in the Keynesian theory with the help of a graphical approach.
5. Discuss: (a) consumption function and (b) saving as a counterpart of the consumption function.

SOLVED NUMERICAL PROBLEMS

Numerical 1

In an economy, the basic equations are as follows: the consumption function is $C = 120 + 0.80Y$ and investment is $\bar{I} = 250$.

(a) Find the equilibrium level of income
(b) Find the equilibrium level of consumption
(c) Find the equilibrium level of saving
(d) Show that at the equilibrium level, aggregate demand equals aggregate supply and saving leakages equals investment injections.

Numerical 2

Suppose the consumption function is $C = C_a + bY$ and investment is $I = \bar{I}$, then

(a) Find an equation for the equilibrium level of output.
(b) Find the equilibrium level of output when $C_a = 150$, $b = 0.80$ and $\bar{I} = 250$.

Numerical 3

The fundamental equations in an economy are given as: consumption function $C = 200 + 0.75Y$, investment $\bar{I} = 200$.

(a) Find the equilibrium level of income.
(b) Find the equilibrium level of consumption.

Numerical 4

The fundamental equations in an economy are given as: consumption $C = 150 + 0.80Y$ and investment $\bar{I} = 200$.

(a) Derive the saving function.
(b) Find the equilibrium level of output by equating the saving leakages to the investment injections.

Numerical 5

If in an economy $C = 450 + 0.80Y$ and investment is $I = 540$, then

(a) Determine the equilibrium level of income and consumption.
(b) Derive the saving function and determine the savings at the equilibrium level.
(c) Determine the equilibrium level of income by equating planned saving and planned investment.

UNSOLVED NUMERICAL PROBLEMS (WITH ANSWERS)

1. Suppose the consumption function is $C = 50 + 0.60Y$ and the investment is $\bar{I} = 80$, then
   (a) Find the equilibrium level of income.
   (b) Find the equilibrium level of consumption.
   (c) Find the equilibrium level of saving.
   (d) Show that at the equilibrium level, aggregate demand equals aggregate supply and saving leakages equals investment injections.

2. In a two sector economy, the consumption function is $C = 60 + 0.75Y$ and investment is $\bar{I} = 60$. Find the equilibrium level of income by equating the
   (a) Output and Spending
   (b) Saving and Investment

3. Suppose the consumption function is $C = 50 + 0.8Y$ and the investment is $\bar{I} = 70$, then
   (a) Find the equilibrium level of income.
   (b) Find the equilibrium level of consumption.
   (c) Find the equilibrium level of saving.
   (d) Show that at the equilibrium level, aggregate demand equals aggregate supply and saving leakages equals investment injections.

4. If the consumption function is $C = 70 + 0.8Y$ and investment is $\bar{I} = 70$, find
   (a) The equilibrium level of income
   (b) The equilibrium level of consumption
   (c) The equilibrium level of saving
5. In an economy, planned consumption is $C = 50 + 0.60Y$ and planned investment is $\bar{I} = 70$.
   (a) Find the equilibrium level of income.
   (b) Find the equilibrium level of consumption.
   (c) Find the equilibrium level of saving.
   (d) Show that at the equilibrium level, aggregate demand equals aggregate supply and saving leakages equal investment injections.

ANSWERS

TRUE OR FALSE QUESTIONS

1. **True.** As we have assumed that investment is autonomous and independent of the income level, aggregate demand function will depend mainly on the consumption function.
2. **False.** The APC is defined as the ratio of consumption to income for different levels of income.
3. **False.** The MPS is defined as the increase in the saving per unit of increase in the income.
4. **False.** While actual saving always equals actual investment, planned saving equals planned investment only at the equilibrium point.
5. **True.** In an economy, disequilibrium exists when aggregate demand is not equal to aggregate supply or planned saving is not equal to planned investment.

SOLVED NUMERICAL PROBLEMS

Solution 1

(a) The equilibrium condition is given as $Y = C + I$.

Thus, $Y = 120 + 0.80Y + 250$

$$Y - 0.80Y = 120 + 250$$

$$0.20Y = 370$$

$$Y = \frac{370}{0.20}$$

$$Y = 1850$$

The equilibrium level of income is 1850.

(b) The consumption function is $C = 120 + 0.80Y$.

When $Y = 1850$, $C = 120 + 0.80\ (1850)$

$$C = 120 + 1480$$

$$C = 1600$$

The equilibrium level of consumption is 1600.

(c) The saving equation is $S = Y - C$.

When $Y = 1850$ and $C = 1600$, we have

$$S = 1850 - 1600$$

$$S = 250$$

The equilibrium level of saving is 250.

(d) Aggregate demand equals aggregate supply

$$C + I = C + S$$

$$1600 + 250 = 1600 + 250$$

or

$$1850 = 1850$$

Saving equals investment.

$$S = I$$

$$250 = 250$$

Solution 2

(a) The equilibrium condition is given as $Y = C + I$.

Thus, $Y = C_a + bY + \bar{I}$

$$Y - bY = C_a + \bar{I}$$

$$Y(1 - b) = C_a + \bar{I}$$

$$Y = \frac{C_a + \bar{I}}{(1 - b)}$$

The equation for the equilibrium level of output is $Y = \frac{C_a + \bar{I}}{(1 - b)}$

(b) Substituting for the values in $Y = \frac{C_a + \bar{I}}{(1 - b)}$, we get

$$Y = \frac{150 + 250}{1 - 0.80}$$

$$Y = \frac{400}{0.20}$$

$$Y = 2000$$

Thus, the equilibrium level of output is 2000.

Solution 3

(a) In a two sector economy the equilibrium level of income is $Y = \frac{1}{1-b}(C_a + \bar{I})$
In the above equation, $C_a = 200, \bar{I} = 200, b = 0.75$.
By substituting the above values, we get

$$Y = \frac{1}{1-0.75}(200 + 200)$$

$$Y = 1600$$

Thus, the equilibrium level of income is 1600.

(b) In a two sector economy, the consumption function is

$$C = C_a + bY$$

In the above equation, $C_a = 200, \bar{I} = 200, b = 0.75$.
By substituting the above values, we get

$$C = 200 + 0.75Y$$

$$C = 200 + 0.75\,(1600)$$

$$C = 1400$$

Thus, the equilibrium level of consumption is 400.

Solution 4

(a) The saving function is given by $S = Y - C$

$$S = Y - (150 + 0.80Y)$$

$$S = -150 + 0.20Y$$

Thus, the saving function is given by $S = -150 + 0.20Y$

(b) The equilibrium level of output can be determined by equating the saving leakages to the investment injections.

Thus, $-150 + 0.20Y = 200$

or $-150 + 0.20Y = 200$

$$0.20Y = 350$$

$$Y = \frac{350}{0.20}$$

$$Y = 1750$$

Thus, the equilibrium level of output is 1750.

Solution 5

(a) The equilibrium condition is given as $Y = C + I$.

Thus, $Y = 450 + 0.80Y + 540$

$$Y - 0.80Y = 450 + 540$$

$$0.20Y = 990$$

$$Y = \frac{990}{0.20}$$

$$Y = 4950$$

Thus, the equilibrium level of income is 4950.

The consumption function is $C = 450 + 0.80Y$.

When $Y = 4950$, $C = 450 + 0.80\,(4950)$

$$C = 450 + 3960$$

$$C = 4410$$

Thus, the equilibrium level of consumption is 4410.

(b) The saving function is given by $S = Y - C$.

$$S = Y - (450 + 0.80Y)$$

$$S = 0.20Y - 450$$

$$S = -\,450 + 0.20Y$$

Thus, the saving function is given by $S = -\,450 + 0.20Y$.

At the equilibrium level, $S = -450 + 0.20\,(4950)$

$$S = -450 + 990$$

$$S = 540$$

(c) The planned saving is given by $S = -450 + 0.20Y$.

In equilibrium, planned saving equals planned investment.

Thus, $-450 + 0.20Y = 540$

$$0.20Y = 540 + 450$$

$$Y = \frac{990}{0.20}$$

$$Y = 4950$$

Thus, the equilibrium level of income is 4950.

UNSOLVED NUMERICAL PROBLEMS

1. (a) $Y = 325$ (The equilibrium level of income is 325.)
   (b) $C = 245$ (The equilibrium level of consumption is 245.)
   (c) $S = 80$ (The equilibrium level of saving is 80.)
   (d) Aggregate demand equals aggregate supply or $325 = 325$.
   Saving leakages equals investment injections or $80 = 80$.
2. (a) $Y = 480$ (The equilibrium level of income is 480.)
   (b) $S = I$ (The equilibrium level of income is 480.)
3. (a) $Y = 600$ (The equilibrium level of income is 600.)
   (b) $C = 530$ (The equilibrium level of consumption is 530.)
   (c) $S = 70$ (The equilibrium level of saving is 70.)
   (d) $C + I = C + S$ $(600 = 600)$
   $S = I$ $(70 = 70)$
4. (a) $Y = 700$ (The equilibrium level of income is 700.)
   (b) $C = 630$ (The equilibrium level of consumption is 630.)
   (c) $S = 70$ (The equilibrium level of saving is 70.)
5. (a) $Y = 300$ (The equilibrium level of income is 600.)
   (b) $C = 230$ (The equilibrium level of consumption is 230.)
   (c) $S = 70$ (The equilibrium level of saving is 70.)
   (d) $C + I = C + S$ $(300 = 300)$
   Saving equals investment, $S = I$ $(300 = 300)$.

Shifts in the Aggregate Demand and the Multiplier

6

After studying this topic, you should be able to understand

- ✓ *A shift in the aggregate demand function results in a change in the equilibrium income or output. The ratio of the change in income is a multiple of the change in the investment.*
- ✓ *The concept of the investment multiplier.*
- ✓ *The importance of the multiplier in planning economic growth.*
- ✓ *The existence of certain limitations prevents the multiplier from working.*
- ✓ *The multiplier may not always work, especially in the LDCs.*
- ✓ *If the whole economy saves more, the economy's income and output may decrease.*

INTRODUCTION

In Chapter 5, we had focused on the determination of equilibrium income and output in a simple two sector economy. In this chapter, we will anaylse the changes in the equilibrium income and output in a two sector model.

A change in the equilibrium income or output is the result of a shift in the aggregate demand (or aggregate spending) function or the $C + I$ curve. The aggregate demand curve can either shift upwards or downwards. The amount of the change in the income will be a multiple of the amount of the shift in the aggregate demand curve. The multiplier is the amount by which there is a change in equilibrium income or output when autonomous aggregate expenditure (for example, autonomous investment) increases by one unit. It is this multiplier mechanism that has been discussed in the chapter. We also focus on the conditions necessary for the multiplier to work. The applicability of the multiplier to the less developed countries has also been examined in this chapter.

The multiplier can be defined as the amount by which there occurs a change in the equilibrium level of income due to a change in autonomous aggregate expenditure by one unit.

SHIFTS IN AGGREGATE DEMAND AND THE MULTIPLIER

In a two sector economy, the aggregate demand is a sum of consumption and investment expenditures. It is generally agreed that though both consumption and investment functions undergo a change from one period to another, the consumption function is relatively more stable than the investment function. Thus, the initial changes in income occur more due to the shifts in the investment function. This implies that in the Figure 6.1 it is not the consumption function or the saving function which shifts up and down, it is the investment function which shifts up and down and is responsible for the shift in the $C + I$ curve. Hence, our analysis will be in terms of the shift in the investment function (though the same analysis will apply for a shift in the consumption function).

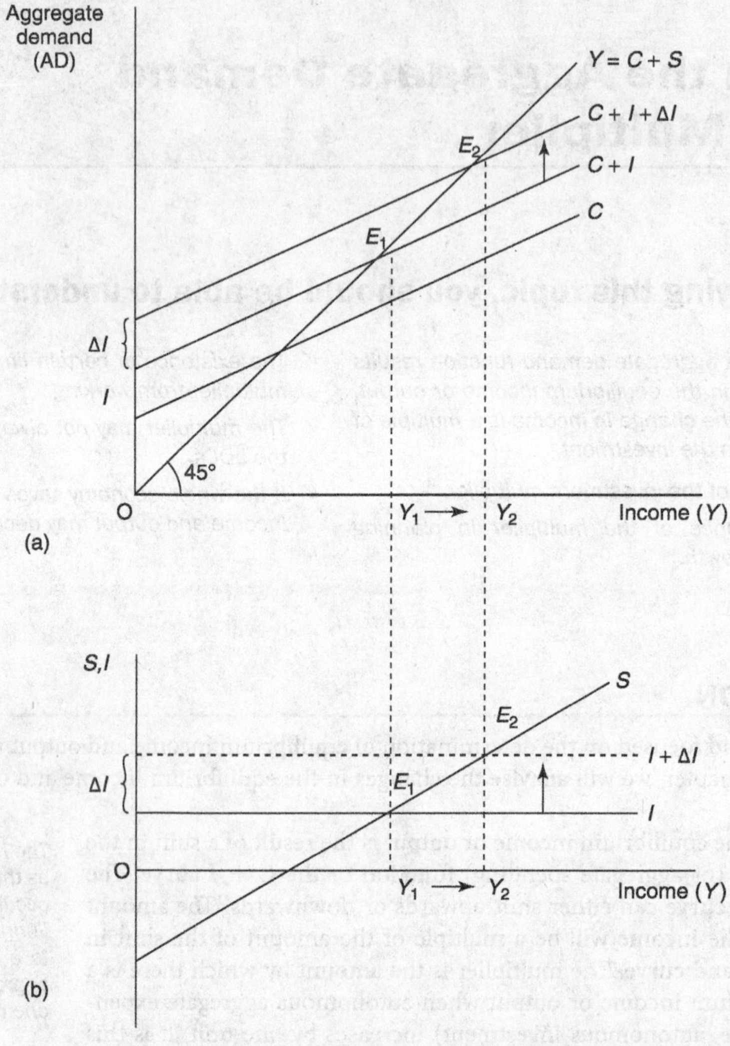

Figure 6.1 Effect of a Change in Investment on the Equilibrium Income or Output

where, x-axis = income (or output)

y-axis = aggregate demand, AD

C = consumption function

I = investment function

ΔI = change in investment

S = saving function

$Y = C + S$ is the guideline or the 45 degree line

In Figure 6.1(a) suppose that initially the $C + I$ function intersects the guideline to determine the equilibrium at point E_1 with the equilibrium level of income at Y_1. The same can be illustrated in Figure 6.1(b) where the saving function intersects the I function to determine the equilibrium at point E_1 with the equilibrium level of income at Y_1.

Assume that due to an improvement in the business expectations, there is a permanent increase in investment expenditures per time period by an amount equal to ΔI at all the levels of output. In Figure 6.1(a), this shift has been illustrated by a shift in the $C + I$ curve to $C + I + \Delta I$ whereas in Figure 6.1(b), the same shift has been illustrated by a shift in the I curve to the $I + \Delta I$ curve. In both the figures, the new equilibrium will be at point E_2 with the equilibrium level of income at Y_2.

It is of extreme importance to note that an increase in the income from Y_1 to Y_2 (national income) can occur if and only if the economy is operating at less than full employment. Otherwise, there cannot be an increase in the income.

One would expect that the increase in income from Y_1 to Y_2, say ΔY would be by the same amount as the increase in the investment expenditures, that is ΔI or that $\Delta Y = \Delta I$. However, one finds that the increase in income is much more than the increase in investment expenditure which was responsible for bringing about that increase in the income, or in other words $\Delta Y > \Delta I$. In fact, $\Delta Y = m\,\Delta I$ where m is what is known as the investment multiplier and has a value greater than 1. Thus,

$$\Delta Y = m\,\Delta I \tag{1}$$

or

$$m = \Delta Y/\Delta I \tag{2}$$

The multiplier can be defined as the amount by which there occurs a change in the equilibrium level of income due to a change in autonomous aggregate expenditure by one unit.

The Working of the Multiplier

Suppose the economy is initially in equilibrium. Let there be an increase in autonomous investment by Rs. 1 million (ΔI). If the economy is operating at less than full employment, this will be matched by an increase in production and output equal to Rs. 1 million to meet the increased demand. The increase in the production will lead to an equal increase in the income of Rs. 1 million (ΔI) in the form of wages, interest and profits. This is the first round of income generation due to the additional investment of Rs. 1 million.

Those who receive the additional income will consume only a part of it, depending on their marginal propensity to consume, and will save the rest of this income. Suppose the marginal propensity to consume, or b, is 0.8. Hence, they will spend Rs. 1 million $\times$ 0.8 = 0.80 million (or $b \times \Delta I = b\,\Delta I$) on the consumer goods and services and save Rs. 0.20 million. Thus in the second round, there is an increase in consumption and expenditure by Rs. 0.80 million (or $b\,\Delta I$). Again production and income will increase to match the increase in the expenditure.

This will lead to a third round of induced expenditures by the recipients of the income in the second round. There will be an increase in consumption and expenditure by Rs. 0.80 million $\times$ 0.8 = Rs. 0.64 million (or $b\,\Delta I \times b = b^2\Delta I$). Hence, an additional income of Rs. 0.64 million is generated in the third round.

It is important to note that the additional income generated in the second round, Rs. 0.80 million ($b\,\Delta I$), is certainly less than the additional income generated in the first round, Rs. 1 million (ΔI). Similarly the additional income generated in the third round, Rs. 0.64 million ($b^2\Delta I$), is less than the additional income generated in the second round, 0.80 million ($b\,\Delta I$). Thus, the induced expenditures in the second round are smaller than those in the first round whereas those in the third round are smaller than those in the second round. Thus the induced expenditures and, thus, the additional income generated in each round go on becoming smaller and smaller. The rounds of income generation will continue till the additional income generated falls to zero.

The total increase in the income in all the rounds can be summed up as

$$\Delta Y = \Delta I + b\Delta I + b^2\,\Delta I + b^3\,\Delta I + \cdots + b^{n-1}\,\Delta I$$

$$\Delta Y = \Delta I\,(1 + b + b^2 + b^3 + \cdots + b^{n-1}) \tag{3}$$

This is a geometric series and can be put in a simpler form as follows:

Multiplying both sides of Eq. (3) by b, we get

$$b\Delta Y = \Delta I\,(b + b^2 + b^3 + b^4 + \cdots + b^n) \tag{4}$$

Subtracting Eqs. (4) from (3), we get

$$\Delta Y - b\Delta Y = \Delta I\,(1 + b + b^2 + b^3 + \cdots + b^{n-1}) - \Delta I\,(b + b^2 + b^3 + b^4 + \cdots + b^n)$$

$$\Delta Y(1 - b) = \Delta I\,(1 - b^n)$$

Thus,

$$\frac{\Delta Y}{\Delta I} = \frac{(1 - b^n)}{1 - b} \tag{5}$$

If the multiplier process continues for a very long period, the value of n will become very large and b^n (b is a fraction with its value between zero and one) will approach zero. Hence,

$$\frac{\Delta Y}{\Delta I} = m = \frac{1}{1 - b} \tag{6}$$

Where m is the investment multiplier. Thus, we have

$$m = \frac{1}{1 - \text{mpc}} \tag{7}$$

or $$m = \frac{1}{\text{mps}}$$

(as b is the marginal propensity to consume)

Table 6.1 depicts the working of the multiplier.

An Alternative Derivation of the Multiplier

The equilibrium level of income is

$$Y = C + I \tag{8}$$

Let there be an increase in autonomous investment by ΔI. This will result in an induced increase in income, which will lead to an increase in consumption, or ΔC. Thus, now the equilibrium level of income will be

$$Y + \Delta Y = C + \Delta C + I + \Delta I \tag{9}$$

Subtracting Eq. (8) from Eq. (9), we get

$$\Delta Y = \Delta C + \Delta I \tag{10}$$

But the consumption function is $C = C_a + bY$.

Table 6.1 The Working of the Multiplier

Round	Increase in Aggregate Demand (or Aggregate Expenditure)	Total Increase in Income
1	ΔI	ΔI
2	$b\Delta I$	$\Delta I + b\Delta I = \Delta I\,(1 + b)$
3	$b^2\Delta I$	$\Delta I + b\,\Delta I + b^2\,\Delta I = \Delta I\,(1 + b + b^2)$
4	…	…
…	…	$\frac{1}{1 - b}\Delta I$

Thus,

$$\Delta C = b\Delta Y \quad (11)$$

Substituting for ΔC from Eq. (11) in Eq. (10), we get

$$\Delta Y = b\Delta Y + \Delta I$$

or,
$$\Delta Y(1-b) = \Delta I$$

or,
$$\Delta Y = \frac{\Delta I}{1-b}$$

or,
$$\frac{\Delta Y}{\Delta I} = m = \frac{1}{1-b},$$ where m is the investment multiplier.

It is obvious that the value of the multiplier depends on b, the marginal propensity to consume. The larger the marginal propensity to consume the larger will be the multiplier. When the marginal propensity to consume is 0.5, the multiplier is 2 and when the marginal propensity to consume increases to 0.9, the multiplier increases to 10.

RECAP

- A shift in the investment function results in a change in the equilibrium income or output.
- The ratio of the change in income is a multiple of the change in the investment.
- $\Delta Y = m\,\Delta I$ where m is the investment multiplier and has a value greater than 1.
- The larger the marginal propensity to consume the larger will be the multiplier.

USES AND LIMITATIONS OF THE MULTIPLIER

The importance of the multiplier is more obvious in a three sector and a four sector economy. However, it plays an important role even in a two sector economy in that it helps in evaluating the effects of an increase in the investment on the national income. Thus, it is able to determine the investment that would be required for a certain planned growth in the national income. Hence, the multiplier is of great importance in planning the economic growth of a nation.

In spite of its utility in economic planning, the multiplier has certain limitations which may prevent it from working. They are as follows:

(1) **Existence of leakages from the income stream:** Keynes was of the view that the marginal propensity to consume remains constant over time. However, empirical evidence does not lend credence to this view. It has been observed that as income increases, often, consumption may not increase proportionately and hence the value of the multiplier may be reduced. Other than consumption, individuals may utilize their increased income for different purposes as the following:
   (a) They may increase their holdings of money.
   (b) They may use a part of the increased income to pay off their old debts.
   (c) They may purchase old securities and property with the additional income.
   (d) They may purchase imported goods and services, the income spent on which will certainly be a leakage out of the economy.

(2) **The availability of the consumer goods:** For the multiplier principle to work, it is necessary that the consumer goods are available in the right quantities and at the right time. Often this may not be the case and hinder the multiplier from working properly.

(3) **There may exist time lags:** The supply of goods may increase in response to demand but only with a time gap. Also, consumption may not increase immediately in response to an increase in income.

(4) **The full employment ceiling:** When an economy is at the full employment level, any further increases in the income and output are not possible. Whatever is the marginal propensity to consume, the multiplier principle will not be able to work. In fact, any increase in the investment will trigger off inflationary expectations in the economy.

These limitations do not in any way undermine the importance of the multiplier. In fact, due to these limitations economists have time and again modified the multiplier which has further enhanced its utility in analysing the changes in income in response to an increase in the aggregate demand.

RECAP

- The multiplier plays a very important role in planning the economic growth of a nation.
- The multiplier suffers from many limitations, which may prevent it from working.
- These limitations have been responsible for the modifications in the multiplier.

APPLICABILITY OF THE MULTIPLIER TO LESS DEVELOPED COUNTRIES

In the article 'Investment, Income and the Multiplier in an Underdeveloped Economy' in the Indian Economic Review, February 1953, Dr V. K. R. V. Rao raised doubts regarding the applicability of the multiplier principle to the less developed countries.

The less developed countries (LDCs) have a lower per capita income as compared to the other countries. It is also an established fact that at low levels of income, the marginal propensity to consume is always high. According to the Keynesian theory, the higher the b or the marginal propensity to consume the higher is the value of the multiplier [$m = 1/(1 - b)$]. Thus, it is to be expected that the multiplier should apply with a stronger effect in LDCs as compared to the developed countries of the world. This would imply that even a small increase in the investment in the LDCs would result in an increase in the income and output, which would be much larger than the increase in the income and output experienced in the developed countries. However, this does not seem to be the case. The reason for this, according to Dr V. K. R. V. Rao, is that the conditions necessary for the multiplier principle to work do not exist in the LDCs. They are satisfied only in the developed countries.

The conditions necessary for the multiplier principle to work are as follows:

(1) **There should exist only involuntary unemployment and no other form of unemployment:** Such unemployment is characteristic of the developed countries where there exists wage employment in almost all the sectors of the economy. As compared to the developed countries, in the LDCs wage employment is a feature found only in the secondary sector which again is a very small sector as compared to the other sectors in the economy. Hence involuntary unemployment, which is associated with wage employment, is not so predominant in these countries.

The type of unemployment most predominant in these countries is what is known as disguised unemployment. This is a type of unemployment, which is most prevalent in agriculture in a country like India where there exist plots of land on which the whole family may be employed. The additions to the total output and the income by the last few units of labour employed may actually be zero. Yet they continue to till the land simply because they are not aware that they are actually not contributing to the total output. Hence, their unemployment is a kind of concealed one of which even they themselves are not aware. The existence of this disguised unemployment prevents the working of the multiplier principle in the LDCs.

(2) **It must be mainly an industrial economy with an upward sloping supply curve for the consumer goods:** In the developed economies, the supply curve is reasonably elastic in that an increase in demand results in an increase in the supply with not much of an inflationary increase in the prices. However, the situation is different in the LDCs where an increase in the demand is not followed by an increase in the supply. This is because due to the low incomes and poverty in the LDCs, any increase in income generates a demand largely for the agricultural goods. But agriculture is subject to the vagaries of nature. Hence, the multiplier may work in the first stage in that an increase in investment may result in a primary increase in the incomes but the increase in demand in response to an increase in these incomes may not result in an increase in the production, especially in the agricultural goods sector. The story is not any different for the non-agricultural goods sector which is characterized by outdated technology, lack of skilled workers and other problems. Thus, in the LDCs though there occurs an increase in the money incomes due to an increase in the investment, there is no perceptible increase in the output level. Thus, it is often argued that in the LDCs the multiplier principle functions only with respect to the money incomes and not with respect to the real incomes.

(3) **There should exist excess capacity in the consumer goods industries:** In the Keynesian theory, which came at the time of the Great Depression, it was not unusual to assume the existence of idle capacity in the consumer goods industry. Thus, an increase in demand could be immediately satisfied by an increase in the production. However this is not the situation in the LDCs, especially in the agriculture sector. Hence, in these countries the multiplier does not work except in that it is responsible for contributing to the inflationary fires in the economy whenever there occurs an increase in demand in response to an increase in investment.

(4) **There should exist an elastic supply of capital:** This is a necessary accompaniment to the labour if there has to occur an increase in the production in response to an increase in the demand. As the developed countries face no problem on this front, the multiplier functions quite efficiently in these countries. In the LDCs while there is not only a sufficient but in fact a surplus supply of labour as far as capital is concerned, there is a shortage of capital in these countries. Hence, again the multiplier principle does not work in the LDCs due to the acute shortage of capital that these countries face.

RECAP

- Dr V. K. R. V. Rao had raised doubts regarding the applicability of the multiplier principle to the less developed countries.
- It seems that the conditions, which are necessary for the multiplier principle to work, are not satisfied in the less developed countries.

THE MULTIPLIER AND THE PARADOX OF THRIFT

It was widely believed, especially by the classical economists, that saving or thrift was a 'virtue' for not only an individual but also for an economy. An individual has to refrain from consumption if he wishes to save. By saving, he is able to amass huge amounts of wealth. Similarly, it was believed that an economy could become rich if every individual in the economy became thrifty.

Keynes, in his General Theory, criticized these beliefs. He argued that what applies to an individual was not necessarily true for the economy. Contrary to the popular beliefs at that time Keynes argued that if the whole economy becomes thrifty, or in other words starts saving more, there will be a decrease in the total consumption in the economy. Hence there will be a decrease in the aggregate demand, and thus the income

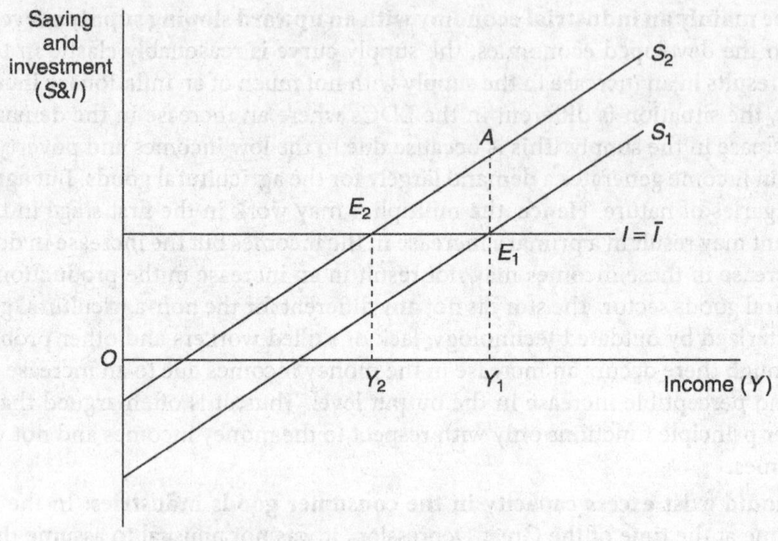

Figure 6.2 Paradox of Thrift

and output will decrease. As saving is a function of income, a decrease in income will ultimately lead to a decrease in the savings. This is what Keynes called the paradox of thrift. It is a contradiction in that what is good for an individual is not good for an economy.

where, I = Investment demand schedule where I is assumed to be constant at $\bar{I}$.

S_1 = Saving schedule where saving is positively related to income.

E_1 = The equilibrium point at which the saving schedule, S_1 and investment schedule, I intersect.

OY_1 = Equilibrium income when equilibrium is at point E_1.

S_2 = Saving schedule when the economy becomes more thrifty.

E_2 = The equilibrium point at which the saving schedule, S_2 and investment schedule, I intersect.

OY_2 = Equilibrium income when equilibrium is at point E_2.

Figure 6.2 depicts the paradox of thrift. If everyone in the economy becomes thriftier, the saving schedule will shift upwards from S_1 to S_2. The equilibrium point will move from E_1 to E_2 whereas the equilibrium income decreases from Y_1 to Y_2. This lends credence to the paradox of thrift that an increase in the thrift by one individual may be good in that it may help in increasing his fortunes in the long run but if the whole economy becomes thrifty, the economy's equilibrium income and output may in fact actually decrease, rather than increase!

Some economists describe this process, where through the paradox of thrift there is ultimately a decrease in the economy's savings, as a reverse multiplier. The increase in savings, by a reduction in consumption expenditures, will lead to a decrease in the aggregate demand. Thus, there will be a decrease in production leading to a decrease in the income which will further lead to a decrease in savings (which are a function of the income level). The economy will finally reach a new equilibrium at which saving is equal to investment. It is imperative to remember that the paradox of thrift will operate only if the increase in the economy's saving is not accompanied by an increase in the investment. If there is an increase in investment, then there will occur an increase in the income through the multiplier which will lead to additional savings and investment in the economy, rather than a decrease.

RECAP

- The classical economists believed that saving or thrift was a 'virtue' for both individual and economy.
- Keynes was of the view that an increase in the thrift by one individual may be good but if the whole economy becomes thrifty, then the economy's equilibrium income may decrease.

SUMMARY

INTRODUCTION

1. In this chapter, we anaylsed the changes in the equilibrium income and output in a two sector model.
2. A change in the equilibrium income or output is the result of a shift in the aggregate demand (or aggregate spending) function or the $C + I$ curve.
3. The multiplier is the amount by which there is a change in equilibrium income or output when autonomous investment increases by one unit.

SHIFTS IN AGGREGATE DEMAND AND THE MULTIPLIER

1. In a two sector economy, the initial changes in income occur more due to the shifts in the investment function.
2. It is to be noted that the increase in income is much more than the increase in investment expenditure, or in other words $\Delta Y > \Delta I$.
3. In fact $\Delta Y = m\ \Delta I$ where m is what is known as the investment multiplier and has a value greater than 1.

THE WORKING OF THE MULTIPLIER

1. Suppose the economy is initially in equilibrium.
2. Let there be an increase in autonomous investment by Rs. 1 million (ΔI).
3. If the economy is operating at less than full employment, this will be matched by an increase in production and output equal to Rs. 1 million, which will lead to an equal increase in income of Rs. 1 million (ΔI) in the form of wages, interest and profits. This is the first round of income generation due to the additional investment of Rs. 1 million. Similarly, there will occur other rounds of income generation.
4. The induced expenditures and thus the additional income generated in each round goes on becoming smaller and smaller.
5. We have $\frac{\Delta Y}{\Delta I} = m = \frac{1}{1-b}$

   where m is the investment multiplier and b is the marginal propensity to consume.
6. The value of the multiplier depends on b, the marginal propensity to consume. The larger the marginal propensity to consume the larger will be the multiplier.

USES AND LIMITATIONS OF THE MULTIPLIER

1. The multiplier plays an important role even in a two sector economy in that it is able to determine the investment, which would be required for a certain planned growth in the national income.
2. The multiplier suffers from many limitations, which may prevent it from working.

APPLICABILITY OF THE MULTIPLIER TO LDCS

1. Dr V. K. R. V. Rao has raised doubts regarding the applicability of the multiplier principle to the underdeveloped countries.
2. The conditions necessary for the multiplier principle to work do not exist in the LDCs.

THE MULTIPLIER AND THE PARADOX OF THRIFT

1. It was widely believed, especially by the classical economists, that saving or thrift was a 'virtue' for not only an individual but also for an economy.
2. Keynes argued that what applies to an individual was not necessarily true for the economy. This is what Keynes called the paradox of thrift.

3. An increase in the thrift by one individual may be good in that it may help in increasing his fortunes in the long run but if the whole economy becomes thrifty, the economy's equilibrium income may in fact actually decrease.

REVIEW QUESTIONS

TRUE OR FALSE QUESTIONS

1. A change in the equilibrium income is the result of a shift in the aggregate supply function.
2. The multiplier is the amount by which there is a change in autonomous investment when income or output when increases by one unit.
3. In a two sector economy, the aggregate demand is a sum of consumption and investment expenditures.
4. Keynes had pointed out that if the whole economy starts saving more, there will be an increase in the total consumption in the economy.
5. The larger the marginal propensity to consume the larger will be the multiplier.

VERY SHORT-ANSWER QUESTIONS

1. What is the multiplier?
2. Why do the initial changes in income occur due to the shifts in the investment function?
3. Why is the existence of excess capacity in the consumer goods industries necessary for the multiplier principle to work?
4. What is disguised unemployment?
5. Mention some of the limitations, which may prevent the multiplier from working?

SHORT-ANSWER QUESTIONS

1. How is the multiplier useful for an economy?
2. What were the classical views regarding thrift?
3. What was Keynes' belief as far as the thrift is concerned?
4. In the context of the paradox of thrift, discuss the reverse multiplier.
5. Describe the Paradox of Thrift graphically.

LONG-ANSWER QUESTIONS

1. Analyse the effects of a change in investment on the equilibrium income or output.
2. Discuss the working of the multiplier.
3. Mention some of the limitations of the multiplier, which prevent it from working efficiently.
4. What is the multiplier? Show the simple mathematical derivation of the multiplier.
5. What is the Paradox of Thrift? Discuss.

SOLVED NUMERICAL PROBLEMS

Numerical Problem 1

In an economy, the basic equations are as follows: the consumption function is $C = 150 + 0.80Y$ and investment is $\bar{I} = 180$ crores. Find

(a) the equilibrium level of income.

(b) the equilibrium level of income when planned investment increases from 180 to 200 crores, a total increase of 20 crores.

(c) the multiplier effect of the 20 crore increase in planned investment.

Numerical Problem 2

Suppose in an economy the marginal propensity to consume is 0.75 and the level of autonomous investment decreases by 20 crores. Find

(a) the change in the equilibrium level of income. (b) the change in consumption expenditures.

Numerical Problem 3

Calculate the value of the investment multiplier when the marginal propensity to consume is (i) 0.85, (ii) 0.70, (iii) 0.60 (iv) 0.40.

Find the effect of a decrease in the equilibrium income when autonomous investment decreases by 30 crores when the marginal propensity to consume is (i) 0.85, (ii) 0.70, (iii) 0.60 (iv) 0.40.

Numerical Problem 4

In an economy, the marginal propensity to consume is 0.50. The level of autonomous investment decreases by 30 crores. Find

(a) the change in the equilibrium level of income.

(b) the change in autonomous demand.

(c) the induced change in the consumption expenditures.

Numerical Problem 5

Assume that in a two sector economy, the income is Rs. 500 billion while the marginal propensity to consume is 40%. Suppose the government wants to increase the income to Rs. 800 billion, by an amount of Rs. 300 billion. By how much should the autonomous investment be increased?

UNSOLVED NUMERICAL PROBLEMS (WITH ANSWERS)

1. In an economy, the basic equations are as follows: the consumption function is $C = 80 + 0.75Y$ and investment is $\bar{I} = 100$ crores. Find
   (a) the equilibrium level of income.
   (b) the equilibrium level of income when planned investment increases from Rs. 100 to 120 crores, a total increase of 20 crores.
   (c) the multiplier effect of the 20 crore increase in planned investment.
2. Suppose in an economy, the marginal propensity to consume is 0.80. The autonomous investment rises by 40 crores. Find
   (a) the change in the equilibrium level of income
   (b) the change in consumption expenditures.
3. In a two sector economy, the income is Rs 200 billion whereas the marginal propensity to consume is 60%. Suppose the government wants to increase the income by 100%. By how much should the autonomous investment be increased?
4. In an economy, the marginal propensity to consume is 0.75. The level of autonomous investment decreases by Rs. 40 crores. Find
   (a) the change in the equilibrium level of income.
   (b) the change in autonomous demand
   (c) the induced change in the consumption expenditures.
5. Suppose the marginal propensity to consume is (i) 0.40, (ii) 0.50, (iii) 0.80, (iv) 1.0 and (v) 0,
   (a) Calculate the marginal propensity to save.
   (b) Calculate the value of the multiplier.
   (c) Using the values of the marginal propensity to consume, find the effect of an increase in the equilibrium income when autonomous investment increases by 40 crores.

ANSWERS

TRUE OR FALSE QUESTIONS

1. **False.** A change in the equilibrium income or output is the result of a shift in the aggregate demand or aggregate spending function or the $C+I$ curve.
2. **False.** The multiplier is the amount by which there is a change in equilibrium income or output when autonomous investment increases by one unit.
3. **True.** Consumption constitutes the demand of the household sector whereas investment is that of the firms.

4. **False.** Keynes had argued that if the whole economy becomes thrifty or in other words starts saving more, there will be a decrease in the total consumption in the economy.
5. **True.** As the value of the multiplier depends on b, the marginal propensity to consume or $m = 1/1 - b$, the larger the marginal propensity to consume the larger will be the multiplier.

SOLVED NUMERICAL PROBLEMS

Solution 1

(a) The equilibrium condition is given as $Y = C + I$

Thus,

$$Y = 150 + 0.80Y + 180$$
$$Y - 0.80Y = 150 + 180$$
$$0.20Y = 330$$
$$Y = 330/0.20$$
$$Y = 1650$$

The equilibrium level of income is 1650 crores.

(b) The equilibrium condition is given as $Y = C + I$

Thus, now

$$Y = 150 + 0.80Y + 200$$
$$Y - 0.80Y = 150 + 200$$
$$0.20Y = 350$$
$$Y = 350/0.20$$
$$Y = 1750$$

The equilibrium level of income is 1750 crores.

(c) The equilibrium level of income increases from 1650 crores to 1750 crores when planned investment increases from 180 to 200 crores. There is an increase in income by 100 crores. Hence, the multiplier effect is 5 ($m = 1/1 - b = 1/1 - 0.80 = 5$).

Solution 2

We know that $\frac{\Delta Y}{\Delta I} = m$

But m is the investment multiplier

Also, $m = \frac{1}{1 - \text{mpc}}$

Thus, $\Delta Y = \Delta I\, m = \Delta I \frac{1}{1-b} = (-20) \times \frac{1}{1 - 0.75} = -80.$

Hence, the decrease in autonomous investment causes a decrease in the equilibrium level of income by 80 crores. This effect occurs due to the reverse multiplier.

(a) $Y = C + I$

Therefore, $\Delta Y = \Delta C + \Delta S$

$$-80 = \Delta C - 20$$

(As autonomous investment decreases by 20 crores, the saving will also decrease by 20 crores)

$$\Delta C = -80 + 20 = -60 \text{ crores}$$
$$\Delta C = -60 \text{ crores}$$

The consumption expenditure decreases by 60 crores.

Solution 3

(a) The value of m, the investment multiplier is

$$m = \frac{1}{1 - \text{mpc}}$$

Hence, (i) $m = \frac{1}{1 - \text{mpc}} = \frac{1}{1 - 0.85} = 6.67$

(ii) $m = \frac{1}{1 - \text{mpc}} = \frac{1}{1 - 0.70} = 3.33$

(iii) $m = \frac{1}{1 - \text{mpc}} = \frac{1}{1 - 0.60} = 2.5$

(iv) $m = \frac{1}{1 - \text{mpc}} = \frac{1}{1 - 0.40} = 1.67$

(b) We know that

$$\frac{\Delta Y}{\Delta I} = m$$

Thus, $$\Delta Y = \Delta I\, m$$

The decrease in the equilibrium income when autonomous investment decreases by 30 crores is

(i) $\Delta Y = \Delta Im = 30 \times 6.67 = 200$

(ii) $\Delta Y = \Delta Im = 30 \times 3.33 = 100$

(iii) $\Delta Y = \Delta Im = 30 \times 2.5 = 75$

(iv) $\Delta Y = \Delta Im = 30 \times 1.67 = 50$

Solution 4

(a) We know that

$$\frac{\Delta Y}{\Delta I} = m$$

But m is the investment multiplier.

Also, $$m = \frac{1}{1 - \text{mpc}}$$

Thus, $$\Delta Y = \Delta Im = \Delta I \frac{1}{1 - b} = (-30) \times \frac{1}{1 - 0.50} = -60$$

Hence, the decrease in autonomous investment causes a decrease in the equilibrium level of income by 60 crores.

(b) The decrease in investment by 30 crores is the change in the level of autonomous demand.

(c) $Y = C + I$

Therefore, $$\Delta Y = \Delta C + \Delta S$$

$$-60 = \Delta C - 30$$

(As autonomous investment decreases by 30 crores, the saving will also decrease by 30 crores)

$$\Delta C = -60 + 30 = -30 \text{ crores}$$

$$\Delta C = -30 \text{ crores}$$

The consumption expenditure falls by 30 crores.

Solution 5

The income level = Rs. 500 billion

The planned income level = Rs. 800 billion

Change in income = $\Delta Y = 800 - 500 =$ Rs. 300 billion

But $$\frac{\Delta Y}{\Delta I} = m = m\,\Delta I = \Delta I \frac{1}{1-b}$$

$$\Delta Y = \Delta I \frac{1}{1-b}$$

Thus, $$300 = \Delta I = \frac{1}{1-0.4}$$

$$\Delta I = \text{Rs. } 180 \text{ billion}$$

Thus, autonomous investment should be increased by Rs. 180 billion for the income to increase to Rs. 800 billion, an increase in income by Rs. 300 billion.

UNSOLVED NUMERICAL PROBLEMS

1. (a) $Y = 720$

The equilibrium level of income is 720 crores.

(b) $Y = 800$

The equilibrium level of income, when planned investment increases from 100 to 120 crores, is 800 crores.

(c) The multiplier effect is 4.

$m = 4$

2. (a) $\Delta Y = 200$

The increase in autonomous investment causes an increase in the equilibrium level of income by 200 crores.

(b) $\Delta C = 160$ crores

The consumption expenditure increases by 160 crores.

3. $\Delta I =$ Rs. 80 billion

Autonomous investment should be increased by Rs. 80 billion for a 100 per cent increase in the income level.

4. (a) $\Delta Y = -160$

The decrease in autonomous investment causes a decrease in the equilibrium level of income by 160 crores. This effect occurs due to the reverse multiplier.

(b) The decrease in investment by 40 crores is the change in the level of autonomous demand.

(c) $\Delta C = -120$ crores

The consumption expenditure falls by 120 crores.

5. (a) (i) mps = 1 − mpc = 1 − 0.40 = 0.60

(ii) mps = 1 − mpc = 1 − 0.50 = 0.50

(iii) mps = 1 − mpc = 1 − 0.80 = 0.20

(iv) mps = 1 − mpc = 1 − 1.0 = 0

(v) mps = 1 − mpc = 1 − 0 = 1

(b) (i) $m = 1.67$

(ii) $m = 2$

(iii) $Nm = 5$

(iv) $m = \infty$

(v) $m = 1$

(c) (i) $\Delta Y = \Delta Im = 40 \times 1.67 = 67$

(ii) $\Delta Y = \Delta Im = 40 \times 2 = 80$

(iii) $\Delta Y = \Delta Im = 40 \times 5 = 200$

(iv) $\Delta Y = \Delta Im = 40 \times \infty = \infty$

(v) $\Delta Y = \Delta Im = 40 \times 1 = 40$

The Keynesian Model of Income Determination in a Three Sector Economy: Introduction of the Government Sector

7

After studying this topic, you should be able to understand

- ✓ *Three main activities of the government are government expenditure, transfers and taxes.*
- ✓ *Income leakages are in the form of saving and taxes, and injections are in the form of investment and government expenditure.*
- ✓ *There are two approaches to income determination in a three sector model, aggregate demand–aggregate supply approach and leakages equal injections approach.*
- ✓ *An economy can achieve a full employment output by an expansion in its budget, financing every rupee of additional expenditure with a rupee of additional taxes.*
- ✓ *Introduction of Government Transfer Payments has an expansionary effect on the income level.*
- ✓ *The expansionary effect on the income level will be smaller with a proportional income tax than with a lump sum income tax.*
- ✓ *The Government Expenditure Multiplier, Tax Multiplier and the Balanced Budget Multiplier—all have an impact on the equilibrium level of income.*

INTRODUCTION

Initial chapters have focused on income determination and the multiplier in a two sector economy, where there exist the households and the firms. This chapter focuses on extending the theory of income determination and the multiplier to a three sector model, the third sector being the government sector.

The action of the government relating to its expenditures, transfers and taxes is called the fiscal policy. Here, we focus on three fiscal policy models which are in increasing order of complexity, with the emphasis being on the government expenditure, taxation and the income level. We also discuss some of the fiscal policy multipliers, including the balanced budget multiplier.

Fiscal policy relates to the actions of the government regarding its expenditures, transfers and taxes.

DETERMINATION OF EQUILIBRIUM INCOME OR OUTPUT IN A THREE SECTOR ECONOMY

Though the government is involved in a variety of activities, three of them are of greater relevance to us in the present context. Hence, we will focus on these activities of the government, which are discussed below:

(1) **Government expenditure** (or spending) includes goods purchased by the central, state and the local governments and also the payments made to the government employees.

(2) **Transfers** are those government payments which do not involve any direct services by the recipient; for example welfare payments, unemployment insurance and others.

Direct taxes are levied directly and include personal income and corporate income taxes.

Indirect taxes are levied indirectly and include sales tax and excise tax. They are paid as a part of the price of the goods.

Transfer payments are those government payments which do not involve any direct services by the recipient, for example welfare payments, unemployment insurance and others.

(3) **Taxes** that include taxes on property, income and goods. Taxes can be classified into two categories, direct taxes and indirect taxes. Direct taxes are levied directly and include personal income and corporate income taxes. Indirect taxes are levied indirectly and include sales tax and excise tax. They are paid as a part of the price of the goods.

We simplify our analysis by making a few assumptions, which are as follows:

(1) The government purchases factor services from the household sector and goods and services from the firms.

(2) Transfer payments include subsidies to the firms and pensions to the household sector.

(3) The government levies only direct taxes on the household sector.

We here introduce the notion of an income leakage and an injection. In a two sector model, a part of the current income stream (which was not spent on consumption) 'leaked' out as saving whereas injections in the form of 'investment' were injected into the system. In a three sector model taxes, like saving, are income leakages whereas government expenditures, like investment, are injections.

First Model of Income Determination (Introducing Government Expenditure and Tax)

This model is an extension of the two sector model with the following modifications:

(1) Government expenditure is determined autonomously.

(2) There is only one kind of tax, lump sum income tax (which is independent of the income level).

(3) The government expenditure equals the tax revenue. This implies that the government follows a balanced budget.

Given the above modifications, we can now analyse the equilibrium in a three sector model.

Equilibrium Income and Output

(1) Aggregate Demand–Aggregate Supply Approach

Aggregate demand = Total value of output (or income)

or $$Y = C + I + G \tag{1}$$

where, $C = C_a + bY_d$ (consumption function)

$Y_d = Y - T$ = disposable income

$T = \bar{T}$ = tax (lump sum income tax)

$I = \bar{I}$ = investment (assumed to be autonomous)

$G = \overline{G}$ (assumed to be autonomous)

Substituting for these values in the basic Eq. (1), we get

$$Y = C_a + bY_d + \bar{I} + \overline{G}$$

$$Y = C_a + b(Y - \bar{T}) + \bar{I} + \overline{G}$$

Or $$Y - bY = C_a + \bar{I} + \overline{G} - b\,\overline{T}$$

Or $$Y(1 - b) = C_a + \bar{I} + \overline{G} - b\,\overline{T}$$

Thus, $$Y = \frac{1}{1-b}(C_a + \bar{I} + \overline{G} - b\,\overline{T}) \tag{2}$$

Equation (2) gives the equilibrium income in a three sector economy.

(2) Leakages Equal Injections Approach

In equilibrium, in a three sector model,

$$AD = AS$$

or
$$C + I + G = C + S + T$$

As C is common in both the sides, the equilibrium condition can be written as

$$I + G = S + T \tag{3}$$

where, $I = \bar{I}$ = investment (assumed to be autonomous)

$G = \overline{G}$ = government expenditure (assumed to be autonomous)

$S = Y_d - C$ = saving function

$C = C_a + bY_d$ (consumption function)

$T = \overline{T}$ = tax (lump sum income tax)

Substituting for these values in the Eq. (3), we get

$$\bar{I} + \overline{G} = S + \overline{T}$$

$$\bar{I} + \overline{G} = (Y_d - C) + \overline{T}$$

$$\bar{I} + \overline{G} = [Y - \overline{T} - (C_a + bY_d)] + \overline{T}$$

$$\bar{I} + \overline{G} = [Y - \overline{T} - C_a - b(Y - \overline{T})] + \overline{T}$$

$$Y - bY = C_a + \bar{I} + \overline{G} - b\overline{T}$$

$$Y(1 - b) = C_a + \bar{I} + \overline{G} - b\overline{T}$$

or
$$Y(1 - b) = C_a + \bar{I} + \overline{G} - b\overline{T}$$

Thus,
$$Y = \frac{1}{1-b}(C_a + \bar{I} + \overline{G} - b\overline{T})$$

The above equation is the same as Eq. (2) above. Hence, both the approaches yield the same equilibrium level of income.

Equilibrium Income and Output: A Graphical Explanation

(1) Aggregate Demand–Aggregate Supply Approach

Equilibrium: The determination of the equilibrium income by the aggregate demand–aggregate supply approach in a three sector economy has been depicted in the Figure 7.1 (a).

where, x-axis = disposable income

y-axis = aggregate demand or aggregate planned expenditure

C = aggregate consumption function, $C = C_a + bY_d = C_a + b(Y - \overline{T})$

C_a = the intercept of the consumption function on the y axis showing consumption spending at zero income level.

b = the MPC or the slope of the consumption function (it will remain constant since, in our analysis, the consumption function is a linear function.)

$I = \bar{I}$ = investment (assumed to be autonomous)

$G = \overline{G}$ = government expenditure (assumed to be autonomous)

AD_1 = aggregate demand function before a tax (which is obtained by adding the consumption function, the investment function and the government expenditures)

AS = aggregate supply function (also called the guideline or the 45 degree line)

Point E = the two sector equilibrium or the initial equilibrium where the aggregate demand curve AD ($C + I$) and aggregate supply curves intersect to determine the equilibrium income at Y*.

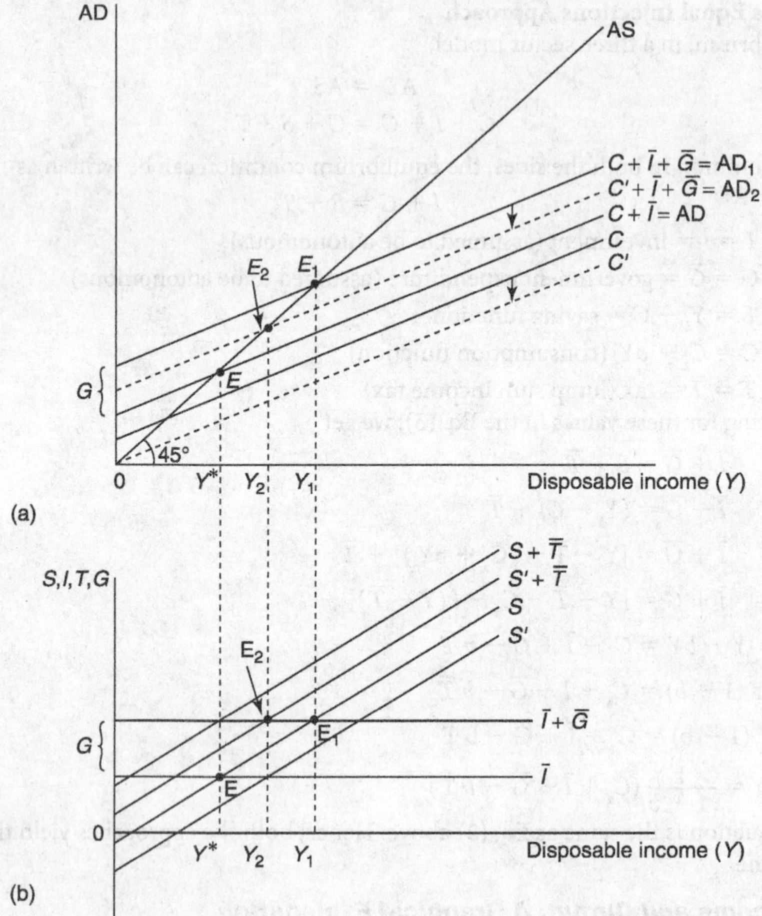

Figure 7.1 Determination of Equilibrium Income or Output in a Three Sector Economy

A balanced budget exists when the entire government expenditure is financed by taxes or that G = T.

Point E_1 = the three sector equilibrium where the aggregate demand curve AD_1 $(C + I + G)$ and aggregate supply curves intersect to determine the equilibrium income at Y_1. It is important to note that at this stage, the entire government expenditure is deficit financed and that the taxes are zero. Thus, increase in government spending will lead to an increase in income where $\Delta Y > \Delta G$ or $\Delta Y = m\Delta G$. Hence, the multiplier $m > 1$.

C' = the consumption function after the tax. As a tax is a withdrawal, it reduces the disposable income (Y_d) thus leading to a shift of the consumption function from C to C' and a shift of the aggregate demand curve from AD_1 to AD_2.

AD_2 = aggregate demand function after a tax

Point E_2 = the three sector equilibrium where the aggregate demand curve AD_2 $(C' + I + G)$ and aggregate supply curves intersect to determine the equilibrium income at Y_2. The entire government expenditure is financed by taxes or that G = T. In other words, it is a balanced budget.

(2) Leakages Equals Injections Approach

Equilibrium: The determination of the equilibrium income by the leakages and injections approach in a three sector economy has been depicted in the Figure 7.1(b).

where, x-axis = disposable income

y-axis = planned saving, planned investment, taxes and government expenditure

S = planned saving

$I = I$ = investment function

$S + \overline{T}$ = planned saving plus taxes

$I + \overline{G}$ = planned investment plus government expenditure

E = the two sector equilibrium or the initial equilibrium where the saving curve, S and the investment curve, $\overline{I}$ intersect to determine the equilibrium income at Y^*.

Point E_1 = the three sector equilibrium where the saving curve, S and the investment plus government expenditure curve, $\overline{I} + \overline{G}$ intersect to determine the equilibrium income at Y_1. Here, taxes are zero.

S' = saving after the imposition of the tax

Point E_2 = the three sector equilibrium where the planned saving and taxes curve, $S' + \overline{T}$ and investment plus government expenditure curve, $\overline{I} + \overline{G}$ intersect to determine the equilibrium income at Y_2. The entire government expenditure is financed by taxes or $\overline{G} = \overline{T}$. In other words, it is a balanced budget.

We find that the two approaches to the determination of the equilibrium income, the aggregate demand–aggregate supply approach and the leakages equals injections approach, both yield the same result.

It is important to observe that though government expenditure has an expansionary effect, taxes have a contractionary effect on the income level. However, the contractionary effect of taxes is less than the expansionary effect of government expenditure even though $\Delta G = \Delta T$. This is because though an increase in government spending is entirely an addition to the aggregate demand, an increase in T is not entirely a decrease in the aggregate demand. Some part of the increase in T involves a reduction in the savings whereas the rest is absorbed by a reduction in consumption and, hence, in aggregate demand.

Although before the imposition of the tax the equilibrium level of income was Y_1, after the tax it reduces to Y_2 and not to Y^* (even though $G = T$). Hence the imposition of a tax, given the level of government expenditure, causes a reduction in the equilibrium level of income from Y_1 to Y_2, though it is still larger than the initial income level Y^*.

An important implication for fiscal policy is that an economy can achieve full employment output by an expansion in its budget, financing every rupee of additional expenditure with a rupee of additional taxes.

RECAP

- In a three sector model, taxes and saving are the income leakages whereas government expenditures and investment are the injections.
- The First Model of Income Determination introduces government expenditure and tax.
- The two approaches to the determination of the equilibrium income, the aggregate demand–aggregate supply approach and the leakages equal injections approach, both yield the same result.
- The imposition of a tax, given the government expenditure, reduces the equilibrium level of income.
- The contractionary effect of taxes on the income level is less than the expansionary effect of government expenditure.

Numerical Illustration 1

The fundamental equations in an economy are given as:

$$C = 150 + 0.75(Y - T)$$
$$\bar{I} = 300$$
$$T = 40 + 0.2Y$$
$$\overline{G} = 150$$

Find the equilibrium level of income.

Solution

The equilibrium condition in a three sector economy is given as $Y = C + I + G$.

Thus, $Y = 150 + 0.75[Y - (40 + 0.2Y)] + 300 + 150$

$$Y = 150 + 0.75(Y - 40 - 0.2Y) + 300 + 150$$
$$Y = 600 + 0.75(-40 + 0.8Y)$$
$$Y = 600 - 30 + 0.6Y$$
$$Y - 0.6Y = 570$$
$$0.4Y = 570$$
$$Y = \frac{570}{0.4}$$
$$Y = 1425$$

The equilibrium level of income is 1600.

Second Model of Income Determination (Introducing Government Transfer Payments)

In the first model we had included only two activities of the government, namely, government expenditure and taxes. Here in this second model, we bring transfer payments also into the picture.

As already mentioned, transfer payments are those government payments which do not involve any *quid pro quo* or in other words do not involve any direct services by the recipient; for example, welfare payments. Transfer payments are, in fact, just the reverse of taxes or in other words they are negative taxes. Taxes reduce the spending capacity whereas transfer payments increase the spending capacity of the households leading to, ultimately, an increase in the equilibrium level of income.

We have our basic Eq. (1) $Y = C + I + G$

where, $C = C_a + bY_d$ = consumption function

$Y_d = Y - T + R$ = disposable income

$T = \overline{T}$ = tax (lump sum income tax)

$I = \bar{I}$ = investment (assumed to be autonomous)

$G = \overline{G}$ = government expenditure (assumed to be autonomous)

$R = \overline{R}$ = transfer payments (assumed to be autonomous)

Substituting for these values in the basic equation, we get

$$Y = C_a + b\,(Y - (\overline{T} + \overline{R}) + \bar{I} + \overline{G}$$

or $Y - bY = C_a + \bar{I} + \overline{G} - b\overline{T} + b\overline{R}$

or $Y(1 - b) = C_a + \bar{I} + \overline{G} - b\overline{T} + b\overline{R}$

Thus, $Y = \frac{1}{1-b}(C_a + \bar{I} + \overline{G} - b\overline{T} + b\overline{R})$

Similar to the first model, here also a change in any of the values within brackets will lead to a change in income which will be equal to the change in that particular value times the multiplier.

It is important to observe that both the transfer payments and the government expenditure have an expansionary effect on the income level. However, the expansionary effect of an increase in the transfer payments will be less than the effect of an increase in the government expenditure even though $\Delta G = \Delta R$ (as long as the marginal propensity to consume is less than 1). Thus,

$$\frac{1}{1-b}\Delta G > \frac{1}{1-b} b\Delta R$$

This is because while the entire increase in government spending is an addition to the aggregate demand, only a part of the increase in R will be an addition to the aggregate demand (through an increase in the consumption spending). Some part of the increase in R is directed towards savings. Hence, the increase in income

(1) in case of an increase in government expenditure is equal to the increase in the government expenditure times the multiplier;

(2) in case of an increase in transfers is equal to only b (b is the marginal propensity to consume) part of the increase in the transfers times the multiplier.

It is important to note that though a change in government expenditure affects aggregate demand directly, a change in transfer payments affects aggregate demand indirectly through a change in disposable income.

RECAP

- As long as the marginal propensity to consume is less than 1, the expansionary effect of an increase in transfer payments will be less than the effect of an increase in government expenditure even when $\Delta G = \Delta R$.
- A change in government expenditure affects aggregate demand directly.
- A change in transfer payments affects aggregate demand indirectly through a change in disposable income.

Third Model of Income Determination (Including Government Expenditures, Transfer Payments and Introducing Tax as a Function of the Income Level)

In recent years, a large part of the tax receipts of the government consists of personal and corporate income taxes. Other taxes like sales tax, excise duty and service taxes also vary indirectly with the income level though less as compared to personal and corporate income taxes. Thus, we introduce tax as a linear function of income in this model.

$$T = \overline{T} + tY + \overline{R}$$

where, T = the total tax
$T = \overline{T}$ = autonomous tax receipts (tax receipts at, theoretically, zero income level)
t = proportional income tax rate (the fraction of any income that will be taxed)
$\overline{R}$ = Transfers
$Y = C + I + G$

where, $C = C_a + bY_d$ = consumption function
$Y_d = Y - T + \overline{R}$ = disposable income
$T = \overline{T} + tY + \overline{R}$ = net tax (where the tax is a function of the income level)
$\overline{R}$ = transfer payments
$I = \overline{I}$ = investment (assumed to be autonomous)
$G = \overline{G}$ = government expenditure (assumed to be autonomous)

Substituting for these values in the Eq. (1), we get

$$Y = C_a + b[Y - (\overline{T} + tY + \overline{R})] + \overline{I} + \overline{G}$$

or $$Y - bY = C_a + \overline{I} + \overline{G} - b\overline{T} - btY + b\overline{R}$$

or $$Y - bY + btY = C_a + \overline{I} + \overline{G} - b\overline{T} + b\overline{R}$$

$$Y(1 - b + bt) = C_a + \overline{I} + \overline{G} - b\overline{T} + b\overline{R}$$

Thus, $$Y = \frac{1}{1 - b(1-t)}(C_a + \overline{I} + \overline{G} - b\overline{T} + b\overline{R}) \tag{4}$$

In the second model where the tax receipts are independent of the income level, the multiplier is larger than the multiplier in the third model where the tax receipts are dependent on the income level.

Given an increase in government expenditure, the expansion in income will be smaller with a proportional income tax than for a lump sum income tax.

RECAP

- The multiplier in the second model, where the tax receipts are independent of the income level, is larger than the multiplier in the third model where the tax receipts are dependent on the income level.
- The increase in income will be smaller in the case of a proportional income tax than for a lump sum income tax.

Numerical Illustration 2

In the Numerical Illustration 1 suppose the government transfer payments are at Rs. 60 crores. Find the equilibrium level of income.

Solution

The equilibrium condition in the three sector economy is given as $Y = C_a + b(Y - \overline{T} + \overline{R}) + \overline{I} + \overline{G}$

Thus, $Y = 150 + 0.75[Y - (40 + 0.2Y) + 60] + 300 + 150$

$Y = 150 + 0.75(Y - 40 - 0.2Y + 60) + 300 + 150$

$Y = 600 + 0.75(20 + 0.8Y)$

$Y = 600 + 15 + 0.6Y$

$Y - 0.6Y = 615$

$0.40 = 615$

$Y = \frac{615}{0.4}$

$Y = 1537.50$

The equilibrium level of income is 1537.50

MULTIPLIERS IN A THREE SECTOR ECONOMY—THE FISCAL MULTIPLIERS

Through its fiscal policy, the government is in a position to influence the economic activities in an economy. To what extent its fiscal operations have an impact on the equilibrium level of income depends on the fiscal multipliers. Here, we analyse three multipliers.

Government Sector Multipliers with Lump Sum Tax

Government Expenditure Multiplier: In the First Model, we had arrived at

$$Y = C + I + G \tag{1}$$

where, $C = C_a + bY_d$ (consumption function)

$Y_d = Y - T =$ disposable income

$T = \overline{T} =$ tax (lump sum income tax)

$I = \overline{I} =$ investment (assumed to be autonomous)

$G = \overline{G}$ (assumed to be autonomous)

Substituting for these values in the basic Eq. (1), we get the equilibrium level of income as

$$Y = \frac{1}{1-b}(C_a + \overline{I} + \overline{G} - b\overline{T}) \tag{2}$$

Assume that there is an increase in government expenditure by ΔG. Hence,

$$Y + \Delta Y = \frac{1}{1-b}(C_a + \bar{I} - b\bar{T} + \bar{G} + \Delta G) \tag{3}$$

Subtracting Eq. (2) from Eq. (3), we get

$$\Delta Y = \frac{1}{1-b}(\Delta G)$$

or

$$G_M = \frac{\Delta Y}{\Delta G} = \frac{1}{1-b}$$

where, ΔG = change in government expenditure
b = marginal propensity to consume
ΔY = change in income
G_M = government expenditure multiplier

An increase in government expenditure by ΔG leads to an increase in aggregate demand and, hence, in the equilibrium level of income by ΔY. The government expenditure multiplier has the same value as the investment multiplier in the two sector model, as discussed in Chapter 5, of $\frac{1}{1-b}$ or $\frac{1}{1-mpc}$. As the value of b is always between 0 and 1, the multiplier will always have a value greater than 1. Hence, *a change in* government expenditure by ΔG will lead to a change in the equilibrium level of income by ΔY where $\Delta Y > \Delta G$.

(1) Tax Multiplier (Lump Sum Tax)

We have Eq. (2) as

$$Y = \frac{1}{1-b}(C_a + \bar{I} + \bar{G} - b\bar{T})$$

Assume that there is a change in tax by $\Delta\bar{T}$. Hence, we get

$$Y + \Delta Y = \frac{1}{1-b}[C_a + \bar{I} - b(\bar{T} + \Delta\bar{T}) + \bar{G}] \tag{4}$$

Subtracting Eq. (2) from Eq. (4), we get

$$\Delta Y = \frac{1}{1-b}(-b\Delta\bar{T})$$

or

$$G_T = \frac{\Delta Y}{\Delta\bar{T}} = \frac{-b}{1-b}$$

where, $\Delta\bar{T}$ = change in tax
b = marginal propensity to consume
ΔY = change in income
G_T = government tax multiplier

As the tax multiplier is negative, an increase in tax leads to a decrease in the equilibrium level of income.

(Similarly, the transfer multiplier can be written as $\frac{\Delta Y}{\Delta R} = \frac{b}{1-b}$)

(2) The Balanced Budget Multiplier

The budget is in balance when the government expenditures plus transfer payments equal the gross tax receipts, or in other words, $G = T$. It follows that when there is an increase in the government expenditure, it will be financed by an increase in taxation. Thus, $\Delta G = \Delta T$.

Balanced budget multiplier is the increase in the output as a consequence of equal increases in the government expenditure and taxes.

It is important to note that an increase in the government expenditures, which is balanced by an increase in taxes of an equal amount, will not leave the income level unchanged. In fact, there will be an increase in income by the same amount as the increase in the government expenditures and the tax. This implies that it is incorrect to assert that government expenditures and taxes of an equivalent amount offset one another and that there is no increase in the income level if the budget is balanced. In fact, the increase in the income is exactly equal to the amount by which there is an increase in the government expenditures and tax. Hence the value of the 'balanced budget' multiplier, which is the increase in the output as a consequence of equal increases in the government expenditure and taxes, is equal to one. This is what is known as the 'balanced budget' or 'unit multiplier' theorem.

We have Eq. (2) as

$$Y = \frac{1}{1-b}(C_a + \bar{I} + \bar{G} - b\,\bar{T})$$

Assume that there is a change in government expenditure by ΔG and in tax by ΔT, and $\Delta G = \Delta T$; hence, we get

$$Y + \Delta Y = \frac{1}{1-b} C_a + \bar{I} - b(\bar{T} + \Delta\bar{T}) + (\bar{G} + \Delta G) \tag{5}$$

Subtracting Eq. (2) from Eq. (5), we get

$$\Delta Y = \frac{1}{1-b}(-\,b\,\Delta T + \Delta\,\bar{G}) \tag{6}$$

But $\quad \Delta G = \Delta T$

Thus, we can write

$$\Delta Y = \frac{1}{1-b}(-b\,\Delta\,\bar{G} + \Delta\,\bar{G})$$

or $\quad \Delta Y(1-b) = \Delta\,\bar{G}(-b+1)$

or $\quad \Delta Y(1-b) = \Delta\,\bar{G}(1-b)$

or $\quad \dfrac{\Delta Y}{\Delta \bar{G}} = \dfrac{1-b}{1-b} = 1$

where, ΔG = change in government expenditure
ΔT = change in tax
b = marginal propensity to consume
ΔY = change in income

Alternatively, the balanced budget multiplier can also be obtained by summing up the government expenditure multiplier and the tax multiplier to get

$$\frac{\Delta Y}{\Delta G} + \frac{\Delta Y}{\Delta T} = \frac{1}{1-b} + \frac{-b}{1-b} = \frac{1-b}{1-b} = 1$$

The budget is in balance when the government expenditures plus transfer payments equal the gross tax receipts, or in other words, G = T.

Whatever the value of b, the sum of the government expenditure multiplier and the tax multiplier will always be equal to unity.

Regardless of the value of b (the marginal propensity to consume), the government expenditure multiplier will always be one greater than the tax multiplier.

Government Sector Multipliers with Income Tax

(1) Government Expenditure Multiplier

$$G_M = \frac{\Delta Y}{\Delta G} = \frac{1}{1 - b(1-t)}$$

(2) Tax Multiplier (Lump Sum Tax)

$$G_T = \frac{\Delta Y}{\Delta T} = \frac{-b}{1 - b(1-t)}$$

RECAP

- The government expenditure multiplier has the same value as the investment multiplier, of $\frac{1}{1-b}$ or $\frac{1}{1-\text{mpc.}}$
- As the tax multiplier is negative, an increase in tax will lead to a decrease in the equilibrium level of income.
- The value of the government expenditure multiplier will always be one greater than the value of the tax multiplier.
- An increase in the government expenditures, which is balanced by an increase in taxes of an equal amount, will lead to an increase in income by the same amount as the increase in the government expenditures and the tax.

SUMMARY

INTRODUCTION

1. The present chapter focused on income determination and the multiplier to a three sector model, the third sector being the government sector.
2. The action of the government relating to its expenditures, transfers and taxes is called the fiscal policy.

DETERMINATION OF EQUILIBRIUM INCOME OR OUTPUT IN A THREE SECTOR ECONOMY

1. Three activities of the government are important: government expenditure, transfers and taxes.
2. We simplify our analysis by making a few assumptions like the government levies only direct taxes on the household sector.
3. In a three sector model, taxes are income leakages whereas government expenditures are injections.

FIRST MODEL OF INCOME DETERMINATION (INTRODUCING GOVERNMENT EXPENDITURE AND TAX)

1. This model is an extension of the two sector model in that it includes autonomous government expenditure and a lump sum income tax. Also the government follows a balanced budget, or $\overline{G} = \overline{T}$.
2. There are two approaches to the determination of equilibrium income and output: aggregate demand–aggregate supply approach and leakages equal injections approach. Both the approaches yield the same equilibrium level of income.
3. The contractionary effect of taxes is less than the expansionary effect of government expenditure, even when $G = T$.

SECOND MODEL OF INCOME DETERMINATION (INTRODUCING GOVERNMENT TRANSFER PAYMENTS)

1. In this model, in addition to the government expenditure and taxes, we bring transfer payments also into the picture.
2. Transfer payments are just the reverse of taxes or, in other words, they are negative taxes.
3. Taxes reduce the spending capacity whereas transfer payments increase the spending capacity of the households leading to, ultimately, an increase in the equilibrium level of income.
4. The expansionary effect of an increase in transfer payments will be less than the effect of an increase in government expenditure, even when $\Delta G = \Delta R$.
5. It is important to note that while a change in government expenditure affects aggregate demand directly, a change in transfer payments affects aggregate demand indirectly through a change in disposable income.

THIRD MODEL OF INCOME DETERMINATION (INCLUDING GOVERNMENT EXPENDITURES, TRANSFER PAYMENTS AND INTRODUCING TAX AS A FUNCTION OF THE INCOME LEVEL)

1. In this model, tax is a linear function of income.
2. In the model where the tax receipts are independent of the income level, the multiplier is larger than the multiplier in the model where the tax receipts are dependent on the income level.
3. Given an increase in government expenditure, the expansion in income will be smaller with a proportional income tax than for a lump sum income tax.

MULTIPLIERS IN A THREE SECTOR ECONOMY—THE FISCAL MULTIPLIERS

1. To what extent fiscal operations of the government have an impact on the equilibrium level of income depends on the fiscal multipliers.

2. Government Expenditure Multiplier:

$$G_M = \frac{\Delta Y}{\Delta G} = \frac{1}{1-b}$$

3. The government expenditure multiplier has the same value as the investment multiplier of $\frac{1}{1-b}$ or $\frac{1}{1-\text{mpc}}$.
4. Tax Multiplier:

$$G_T = \frac{\Delta Y}{\Delta T} = \frac{-b}{1-b}$$

As the tax multiplier is negative, an increase in tax leads to a decrease in the equilibrium level of income.

5. Whatever the value of b, the sum of the government expenditure multiplier and the tax multiplier will always be equal to unity.
6. The budget is in balance when $\Delta G = \Delta T$.
7. An increase in the government expenditures, which is balanced by an increase in taxes of an equal amount, will lead to an increase in income by the same amount as the increase in the government expenditures and the tax.
8. The value of the 'balanced budget' multiplier, which is the increase in the output as a consequence of equal increases in the government expenditure and taxes, is equal to one.
9. The sum of the government expenditure multiplier and the tax multiplier will always be equal to unity.

REVIEW QUESTIONS

TRUE OR FALSE QUESTIONS

1. The action of the government relating to its expenditures, transfers and taxes is called the monetary policy.
2. In a three sector model while taxes are income leakages, government expenditures are injections.
3. The contractionary effect of taxes is less than the expansionary effect of government expenditure on the income level, even though G = T.
4. Transfer payments are just the reverse of taxes or, in other words, they are negative taxes.
5. The sum of the government expenditure multiplier and the tax multiplier will always be equal to unity.

VERY SHORT-ANSWER QUESTIONS

1. Discuss the assumptions necessary for the determination of the equilibrium income in a three sector economy.
2. What are income leakages and injections?
3. Discuss the modifications in the First Model of Income Determination (including government expenditure and lump sum tax).
4. 'Whatever the value of b, the sum of the government expenditure multiplier and the tax multiplier will always be equal to unity.' Prove.
5. 'It is incorrect to assert that government expenditures and taxes of an equivalent amount offset one another and that there is no increase in the income level if the budget is balanced' Explain.

SHORT-ANSWER QUESTIONS

1. Show as to how the imposition of a tax, given the level of government expenditure, causes a reduction in the equilibrium level of income in a three sector economy.
2. The contractionary effect of taxes is less than the expansionary effect of government expenditure on the income level even though $G = T$. Explain.
3. Differentiate between the expansionary effect of an increase in transfer payments and that of an increase in government expenditure.
4. How is income determined in a model where there exists government expenditure, transfer payments and proportional income tax? Explain.
5. A change in government expenditure by ΔG will lead to a change in the equilibrium level of income by ΔY where $\Delta Y > \Delta G$. Explain.

LONG-ANSWER QUESTIONS

1. Discuss the two approaches to the First Model of income determination (including government expenditure and tax).
2. How is income determined in a model where there exists government expenditure, lump sum income taxes and transfer payments? Explain.
3. Compare the model where there exists government expenditure, transfer payments and lump sum income tax with one where there exists government expenditure, transfer payments and proportional income tax.
4. Write short notes on the following:
   (a) Government expenditure multiplier
   (b) Tax multiplier
5. What is the balanced budget multiplier? Discuss.

SOLVED NUMERICAL PROBLEMS

Numerical Problem 1

In a two sector economy, the basic equations are as follows: the consumption function is $C = 100 + 0.80Y_d$ and investment is $\bar{I} = 150$ crores. The equilibrium level of income is Rs. 1250 crores. Suppose the government sector is added to this two sector model, which then becomes a three sector economy. The government expenditure is at Rs. 50 crores.

(a) Find the equilibrium level of income in the three sector economy.
(b) What is the multiplier affect of the government expenditure? Is it of the same magnitude as the multiplier effect of a change in the autonomous investment?
(c) Suppose that there is a balanced budget in that the entire government expenditure is financed from a lump sum tax. Find the new equilibrium level of income in the three sector economy.

Numerical Problem 2

In an economy, the full employment output occurs at Rs. 1000 crores. The marginal propensity to consume is 0.80 and the equilibrium level of output is currently at Rs. 800 crores. Suppose the government aspires to achieve the full employment output, find the change in

(a) the level of government expenditures
(b) net lump sum tax
(c) the level of government expenditures and the net lump sum tax when the government aims at bringing the output to the full employment while keeping the budget balanced.

Numerical Problem 3

Suppose the consumption function is $C = 50 + 0.80Y_d$ and investment is $\bar{I} = 100$ crores. The government expenditure is at Rs. 90 crores whereas the tax function is a proportional income tax function where $T = 0.10Y$.

(a) Find the equilibrium level of income in the three sector economy.
(b) Find the revenue from taxes at the equilibrium level of income. Is the government budget balanced?
(c) Suppose there is an increase in investment from Rs. 100 crores to Rs. 120 crores; what is the equilibrium level of income?
(d) What is the revenue from taxes at the new equilibrium level of income? Is there a balanced government budget?

Numerical Problem 4

In an economy, the marginal propensity to consume is 0.80. The tax is a lump sum tax or, in other words, not related to the income level. Find the change in the equilibrium output for the following:

(a) Increase in government expenditure by 10 crores.
(b) Increase in taxes by 15 crores.
(c) Increase in transfers by 10 crores.

Numerical Problem 5

In an economy, $C = 50 + 0.80Y_d$, $\bar{I} = 100$ crores, government expenditure is at Rs. 50 crores whereas $T = 20$ crores.

(a) Find the equilibrium level of income in the three sector economy.

(b) Find the equilibrium level of consumption and saving at the equilibrium level of income.

(c) Depict the injections leakages equality at the equilibrium level.

UNSOLVED NUMERICAL PROBLEMS (WITH ANSWERS)

1. Given the proportional tax function as $t = 10\% = 0.1$ and the marginal propensity to consume as 0.75, find the change which will occur in the equilibrium level of income when there is
   (a) an increase in government expenditure by 100.
   (b) an increase in autonomous tax by 150.
   (c) an increase in transfers by 150.
2. In an economy, the full employment output occurs at Rs. 800 crores. The marginal propensity to consume is 0.75 and the equilibrium level of output is currently at Rs. 700 crores. Suppose the government aspires to achieve the full employment output, find the change in
   (a) the level of government expenditures.
   (b) net lump sum tax.
   (c) the level of government expenditures and the net lump sum tax when the government aims at bringing the output to the full employment while keeping the budget balanced.
3. In an economy, the consumption function is $C = 100 + 0.75Y_d$ and investment is $\bar{I} = 200$ crores. The government expenditure is at Rs. 180 crores whereas the tax function is a proportional income tax function where $T = 0.10Y$.
   (a) Find the equilibrium level of income in the three sector economy.
   (b) Find the revenue from taxes at the equilibrium level of income. Is the government budget balanced?
   (c) Suppose there is an increase in investment from Rs.. 200 crores to Rs. 350 crores, what is the equilibrium level of income?
   (d) What is the revenue from taxes at the new equilibrium level of income? Is there a balanced government budget?
4. Given the marginal propensity to consume as 0.75 and the proportional tax function as $t = 20\% = 0.2$. Find the change which will occur in the equilibrium level of income when there is
   (a) an increase in government expenditure by 50.
   (b) an increase in autonomous tax by 30.
   (c) an increase in transfers by 20.
5. In an economy, the consumption function is $C = 40 + 0.80Y_d$ and investment is $\bar{I} = 80$ crores. The government expenditure is at Rs. 40 crores whereas the tax is a lump sum tax where $T = 0.10$.
   (a) Find the equilibrium level of income in the three sector economy.
   (b) Find the equilibrium level of consumption and saving at the equilibrium level of income.
   (c) Depict the injections leakages equality at the equilibrium level.

ANSWERS

TRUE OR FALSE QUESTIONS

1. **False.** The actions of the government relating to its expenditures, transfers and taxes is called the fiscal policy.
2. **True.** In a three sector model, taxes and saving are income leakages whereas government expenditures and investment are injections.
3. **True.** This is because while an increase in government spending is entirely an addition to the aggregate demand, an increase in T is not entirely a decrease in the aggregate demand. Some part of the increase in T involves a reduction in the savings whereas the rest is absorbed by a reduction in consumption and hence in aggregate demand.
4. **True.** Taxes reduce the spending capacity whereas transfer payments increase the spending capacity of the households leading to, ultimately, an increase in the equilibrium level of income.
5. **False.** Whatever is the value of b, the sum of the government expenditure multiplier and the tax multiplier will always be equal to unity.

SOLVED NUMERICAL PROBLEMS

Solution 1

(a) The equilibrium condition in the three sector economy is given as $Y = C + I + G$.

Thus, $Y = 100 + 0.80Y + 150 + 50$

$$Y - 0.80Y = 100 + 150 + 50$$
$$0.20Y = 300$$
$$Y = 300/\ 0.20$$
$$Y = 1500$$

The equilibrium level of income in the three sector economy is Rs. 1500 crores, which is an increase by Rs. 250 crores over the two sector economy.

(b) Government Expenditure Multiplier: $G_M = \dfrac{\Delta Y}{\Delta G} = \dfrac{1}{1-b} = \dfrac{1}{1-0.80} = 5$

Investment Multiplier, $m = \dfrac{\Delta Y}{\Delta I} = \dfrac{1}{1-b}$

(where b is the marginal propensity to consume)

Thus, the magnitude of the multiplier effect (of a change in the autonomous investment) is the same as that of a change in government expenditure.

(c) $G = T =$ Rs. 50 crores

Thus, $C = 100 + 0.80(Y - 50)$

$$C = 100 - 40 + 0.80Y$$
$$C = 60 + 0.80Y$$

But $Y = C + I + G$

$$Y = 60 + 0.80Y + 150 + 50$$
$$Y - 0.80Y = 60 + 150 + 50$$
$$0.20Y = 260$$
$$Y = 26/0.20$$
$$Y = 1300$$

The new equilibrium level of income in the three sector economy, when there exists a balanced budget, is Rs. 1300 crores.

Solution 2

(a) We have $G_M = \dfrac{\Delta Y}{\Delta G} = \dfrac{1}{1-b}$

where, ΔG = change in government expenditure

b = marginal propensity to consume

ΔY = change in income

G_M = government expenditure multiplier

For example,

$$b = 0.80$$
$$\Delta Y = 1000 - 800 = 200$$

Thus, $\dfrac{200}{\Delta G} = \dfrac{1}{1-0.80}$

$$\Delta G = 200(0.20) = 40$$

Thus, the level of government expenditures required to achieve the full employment output is Rs. 40 crores.

(b) We have $$G_T = \frac{\Delta Y}{\Delta T} = \frac{-b}{1-b}$$

where,
ΔT = change in tax
b = marginal propensity to consume
ΔY = change in income
G_T = government tax multiplier

As the tax multiplier is negative, an increase in tax leads to a decrease in the equilibrium level of income.

For example,

$$b = 0.80$$

$$\Delta Y = 1000 - 800 = 200$$

Thus, $$\frac{200}{\Delta T} = \frac{-0.80}{1-0.80}$$

$$-0.80\Delta T = 200(0.20) = -50$$

The net lump sum tax is Rs. −50 crores. There should be a decrease in lump sum tax by Rs. 50 crores.

(c) Equation (8) is

$$\Delta Y = \frac{1}{1-b}(-b\Delta T + \Delta \overline{G})$$

But, $$\Delta G = \Delta T$$

Thus, we can write $$\Delta Y = \frac{1}{1-b}(-b\Delta\overline{G} + \Delta\overline{G})$$

or $$\Delta Y(1-b) = \Delta\overline{G}(-b+1)$$

or $$\Delta Y(1-b) = \Delta G(1-b)$$

or $$\frac{\Delta Y}{\Delta G} = \frac{1-b}{1-b} = 1$$

Thus, $$\Delta Y = \Delta G = \text{Rs. } 200 \text{ crores.}$$

The required increase in the level of government expenditures and the net lump sum tax is Rs. 200 crores.

Solution 3

(a) The equilibrium condition in the three sector economy is given as $Y = C + I + G$

Here $C = 50 + 0.80Y_d$

$C = 50 + 0.80(Y - T)$

$C = 50 + 0.80(Y - 0.10Y)$

$C = 50 + 0.80\,(0.9Y)$

$C = 50 + 0.72Y$

Thus, $Y = 50 + 0.72Y + 100 + 90$

$Y - 0.72Y = 50 + 100 + 90$

$0.28Y = 240$

$Y = 240/0.28$

$Y = 85.71$

The equilibrium level of income is Rs. 857.14 crores.

(b) The revenue from taxes at the equilibrium level of income.

The tax function is a proportional income tax function where $T = 0.10Y$.

Thus, $T = 0.10(857.14) = 85.71$ crores

Hence, the revenue from taxes at the equilibrium level of income is Rs. 85.71 crores whereas the government expenditure is at Rs. 90 crores. Therefore, there is a budget deficit of Rs. 4.29 crores.

(c) When there is an increase in investment from Rs. 100 crores to Rs. 120 crores,

$Y = 50 + 0.72Y + 120 + 90$

$Y - 0.72Y = 50 + 120 + 90$

$$0.28Y = 260$$
$$Y = 260/0.28$$
$$Y = 928.57$$

The equilibrium level of income is Rs. 928.57 crores.

(d) The revenue from taxes at the new equilibrium level of income is

$$T = 0.10(928.57) = 92.857 \text{ crores}$$

Hence, the revenue from taxes at the equilibrium level of income is Rs. 92.857crores whereas the government expenditure is at Rs. 90 crores. Therefore, there is a budget surplus of Rs. 2.857 crores. Due to the higher income level, there are larger tax revenues leading to a budget surplus.

Solution 4

(a) We have $G_M = \dfrac{\Delta Y}{\Delta G} = \dfrac{1}{1-b}$

For example, $b = 0.80$ and $\Delta G = 10$.

Thus, $\dfrac{\Delta Y}{10} = \dfrac{1}{1-0.80} = 50$

Thus for a 10 crore increase in the level of government expenditures, the equilibrium output increases by 50 crores.

(b) We have $G_T = \dfrac{\Delta Y}{\Delta T} = \dfrac{-b}{1-b}$

For example,

$b = 0.80$

$\Delta T = 15$

Thus, $\dfrac{\Delta Y}{15} = -\dfrac{0.80}{1-0.80} = -60$

Thus, for a 15 crore increase in taxes, the equilibrium output decreases by 60 crores.

(c) When transfers are at 10 crores,

$$\frac{\Delta Y}{10} = \frac{0.80}{1-0.80} = 40$$

Thus, a 10 crore increase in transfers, increases the equilibrium output by 40 crores.

Solution 5

(a) The equilibrium condition in the three sector economy is given as $Y = C + I + G$

Here $C = 50 + 0.80Y_d$

$C = 50 + 0.80(Y - T)$

$C = 50 + 0.80(Y - 20)$

$C = 50 + 0.80Y - 16$

$C = 50 + 0.80Y - 16$

Thus, $Y = 50 + 0.80Y - 16 + 100 + 50$

$Y - 0.8Y = 50 - 16 + 100 + 50$

$0.2Y = 184$

$Y = 184/0.2$

$Y = 920$

The equilibrium level of income is Rs. 920 crores.

(b) When the equilibrium level of income is Rs. 920 crores,

Equilibrium level of consumption:

$C = 50 + 0.80Y_d$

$C = 50 + 0.80(Y - T)$

$$C = 50 + 0.80(Y - 20)$$
$$C = 50 + 0.80\ Y - 16$$
$$C = 50 + 0.80Y - 16$$
$$C = 50 + 0.80\ (920) - 16$$
$$C = 770$$

The equilibrium level of consumption is 770 crores.

Equilibrium level of saving: $S = Y - C - T$

$$S = 920 - 770 - 20 = 130$$

The equilibrium level of saving is 130 crores.

(c) Injections $= I + G = 100 + 50 = 150$

Leakages $= S + T = 130 + 20 = 150$

This depicts the injections leakages equality at the equilibrium level.

UNSOLVED NUMERICAL PROBLEMS

1. (a) The equilibrium level of income increases by 307.70 when there is an increase in government expenditure by 100.
   (b) The equilibrium level of income decreases by 346.15 when there is an increase in autonomous tax by 150.
   (c) The equilibrium level of income decreases by 230.77 when there is an increase in transfers by 150.

2. (a) The level of government expenditures required to achieve the full employment output is Rs. 25 crores.
   (b) There should be a decrease in lump sum tax by Rs. 33.33 crores.
   (c) The required increase in the level of government expenditures and the net lump sum tax is Rs. 100 crores.

3. (a) The equilibrium level of income is Rs. 1476.92 crores.
   (b) The revenue from taxes at the equilibrium level of income is Rs. 147.692 crores whereas the government expenditure is at Rs. 180 crores. Therefore, there is a budget deficit of Rs. 32.31 crores.
   (c) The equilibrium level of income is Rs. 1938.46 crores.
   (d) The revenue from taxes at the equilibrium level of income is Rs. 193.846 crores whereas the government expenditure is at Rs. 180 crores. Therefore, there is a budget surplus of Rs. 13.84 crores.

4. (a) The equilibrium level of income increases by 125 when there is an increase in government expenditure by 50.
   (b) The equilibrium level of income decreases by 56.25 when there is an increase in autonomous tax by 150.
   (c) The equilibrium level of income decreases by 37.5 when there is an increase in transfers by 150.

5. (a) The equilibrium level of income is Rs. 760 crores.
   (b) The equilibrium level of consumption is 640 crores.
   The equilibrium level of saving is 130 crores.
   (c) Injections $= I + G = 80 + 40 = 120$
   Leakages $= S + T = 110 + 10 = 120$
   This depicts the injections leakages equality at the equilibrium level.

The Keynesian Model of Income Determination in a Four Sector Economy: Introduction of the Foreign Sector

8

After studying this topic, you should be able to understand

- ✓ *In a four sector economy, the export and import of goods and services affect the level of aggregate demand.*
- ✓ *There are two approaches to the determination of the equilibrium income and output, the aggregate demand–aggregate approach and supply leakages equals injections approach.*
- ✓ *Transfer payments increase the equilibrium level of income.*
- ✓ *The four sector equilibrium exists where the $C + I + G + X - M$ curve and aggregate supply curve intersect.*
- ✓ *A zero marginal propensity to import implies a multiplier, which has the same value as the ordinary multiplier.*
- ✓ *In an open economy, the value of the multiplier is less than that in a closed economy.*

INTRODUCTION

The earlier chapters have focused on income determination in two and three sector models. Thus, the economy that was analysed was a closed economy which is in isolation from the rest of the world. This chapter presents a more realistic picture in that it focuses on a four sector model, or in other words an open economy, which is engaged in trade with the rest of the world. Thus, the aggregate demand will be now determined by the spending of four sectors, namely, households, firms, government and the foreign sector. The foreign sector will include the foreign consumers, the foreign business and the foreign governments.

The chapter also discusses the foreign trade multiplier.

DETERMINATION OF EQUILIBRIUM INCOME OR OUTPUT IN A FOUR SECTOR ECONOMY

The inclusion of the foreign sector in our analysis influences the level of aggregate demand through the export and import of goods and services. Hence, it is necessary to understand the factors that influence the exports and imports.

Open economy is an economy which is engaged in trade with the rest of the world.

The volume of exports in any economy depends on the following factors:

(1) The prices of the exports in the domestic economy relative to the price in the other economies.
(2) The income level in the other economies.
(3) Tastes, preferences, customs and traditions in the other economies.
(4) The tariff and trade policies between the domestic economy and the other economies.
(5) The domestic economy's level of imports.

To simplify our analysis we assume that the exports in any economy are determined by external factors, or in other words forces which are external to the domestic economy. Thus, the level of exports is assumed to be an autonomous variable.

As far as imports are concerned, the volume of imports in any economy depends on the following factors:

(1) The prices of the imports relative to the domestic prices.
(2) The income level in the domestic economy.
(3) The tastes and preferences for imports as compared to the domestic goods.
(4) The tariff and trade policies of the domestic economy vis á vis the other economies.
(5) The domestic economy's exchange rate policies.

The marginal propensity to import is the fraction of any change in income that will be devoted to imports.

To simplify our analysis, we assume that the imports in any economy are determined by the income level in the domestic economy. This brings us to the import function, which in its simplest form can be expressed as a linear function.

$$M = M_a + mY$$

Figure 8.1 depicts the import function as an upward sloping line and the exports function as a line parallel to the *x*-axis (as they are assumed to be determined autonomously).

where, x-axis = income or output
y-axis = level of exports and imports
M = imports
M_a = autonomous imports (imports at a theoretically zero level of income)
$m = \Delta M/\Delta Y$ = marginal propensity to import (fraction of any change in income that will be devoted to imports)
Y = income level

In Figure 8.1,

(1) At all the income levels below Y_1, as exports are greater than imports, there exists a net export balance or a favourable balance of trade.
(2) At all the income levels above Y_1, as exports are less than imports, there exists a net import balance or an unfavourable balance of trade.

It is important to note that:

(1) A change in the factors that influence the exports such that there is an upward shift in the exports function will lead to an increase in the net export balance or a decrease in the net import balance at each income level.

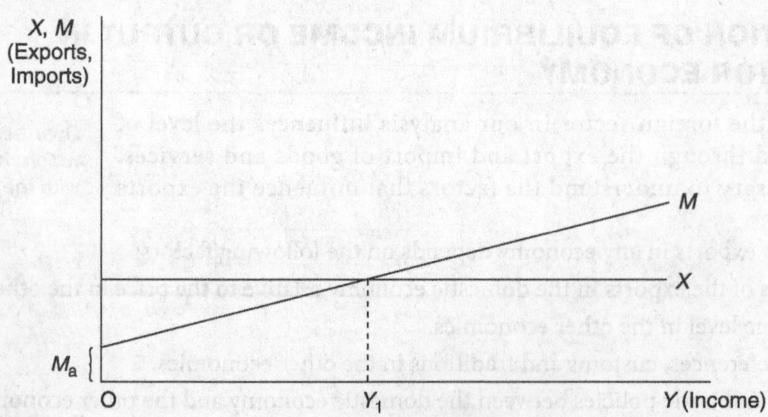

Figure 8.1 The Import and Export Functions

(2) A change in the factors that influence the imports such that there is a downward shift in the imports function (a decrease in M_a) or a decrease in the slope of the import function (decrease in m) will lead to an increase in the net export balance or a decrease in the net import balance at each income level.

Exports, imports and aggregate demand: While exports must be added to the total final expenditures to arrive at the aggregate demand, all the spending on imports do not contribute to the domestic demand, and thus must be deducted from the total final expenditures to arrive at the aggregate demand.

RECAP

- The level of exports is assumed to be an autonomous variable.
- The imports in any economy are determined by the income level in the domestic economy.
- When exports are greater than imports, there exists a net export balance or a favourable balance of trade.
- While exports need to be added to the total final expenditures, imports need to be deducted from the total final expenditures to arrive at the aggregate demand.

EQUILIBRIUM INCOME AND OUTPUT

(1) **Aggregate Demand–Aggregate Supply Approach**

Aggregate demand = Total value of output (or income)

or $$Y = C + I + G + X - M \quad (1)$$

where $C = C_a + b\,Y_d$ = consumption function

$Y_d = Y - T$ = disposable income

$T = \overline{T}$ = tax (lump sum income tax)

$I = I$ = investment (assumed to be autonomous)

$G = \overline{G}$ goverment expenditure (assumed to be autonomous)

$X = \overline{X}$ = exports (assumed to be autonomous)

$M = M_a + mY$ =imports function

Substituting for these values in the basic Eq. (1), we get

$$Y = C_a + bY_d + \bar{I} + \overline{G} + \overline{X} - (M_a + mY)$$

$$Y = C_a + b(Y - T) + \bar{I} + \overline{G} + \overline{X} - M_a - mY$$

or $$Y - bY + mY = C_a + \bar{I} + \overline{G} + \overline{X} - b\,\overline{T} - M_a$$

or $$Y(1 - b + m) = C_a + \bar{I} + \overline{G} + \overline{X} - b\,\overline{T} - M_a$$

Thus, $$Y = \frac{1}{1 - b + m}(C_a + \bar{I} + \overline{G} + \overline{X} - b\,\overline{T} - M_a) \quad (2)$$

(2) **Leakages Equal Injections Approach**

In equilibrium in a four sector model,

$$AD = AS$$

or $$C + I + G + X = C + S + T + M$$

(In a four sector model, the injections include investment, government expenditures and exports whereas the leakages include saving, taxes and imports.)

As C is common in both the sides, the equilibrium condition can be written as

$$I + G + X = S + T + M \quad (3)$$

where, $I = \bar{I}$ = investment (assumed to be autonomous)

$G = \bar{G}$ = government expenditure (assumed to be autonomous)

$X = \bar{X}$ = exports (assumed to be autonomous)

$S = Y_d - C$ = saving function

$C = C_a + b\,Y_d$ (consumption function)

$T = \bar{T}$ = tax (lump sum income tax)

$M = M_a + mY$ (imports function)

Substituting for these values in the Eq. (3), we get

$$\bar{I} + \bar{G} + \bar{X} = S + \bar{T} + M_a + mY$$

$$\bar{I} + \bar{G} + \bar{X} = (Y_d - C) + \bar{T} + M_a + mY$$

$$\bar{I} + \bar{G} + \bar{X} = \{Y - \bar{T} - [C_a + b\,Yd\} + \bar{T} + M_a + mY$$

$$\bar{I} + \bar{G} + \bar{X} = \{Y - \bar{T} - C_a - b(Y - \bar{T})\} + \bar{T} + M_a + mY$$

$$Y - b\,Y + mY = C_a + \bar{I} + \bar{G} + \bar{X} - b\,\bar{T} + M_a$$

$$Y(1 - b + m) = C_a + \bar{I} + \bar{G} + \bar{X} - b\,\bar{T} - M_a$$

Thus,
$$Y = \frac{1}{1 - b + m}(C_a + \bar{I} + \bar{G} + \bar{X} - b\,\bar{T} - M_a)$$

The above equation is the same as Eq. (2) above. Hence, both the approaches yield the same equilibrium level of income.

RECAP

- Both the approaches to income determination yield the same equilibrium level of income.

INTRODUCTION OF GOVERNMENT TRANSFER PAYMENTS IN A FOUR SECTOR MODEL

Till now, we have not included transfer payments in our analysis. As already mentioned transfer payments increase the spending capacity of the households, leading to an increase in the equilibrium level of income.

We have our basic Eq. (1)

$$Y = C + I + G + X - M$$

where, $C = C_a + bY_d$ = consumption function

$Y_d = Y - T + R$ = disposable income

$T = \bar{T}$ = tax (lump sum income tax)

$I = \bar{I}$ = investment (assumed to be autonomous)

$G = \bar{G}$ = government expenditure (assumed to be autonomous)

$X = \bar{X}$ = exports

$M = M_a + mY$ = imports

$R = \bar{R}$ = transfer payments (assumed to be autonomous)

Substituting for these values in the basic equation, we get

$$Y = C_a + b\,(Y - \overline{T} + \overline{R}) + \overline{I} + \overline{G} + \overline{X} - M_a - mY$$

or $$Y - bY + mY = C_a + \overline{I} + \overline{G} + \overline{X} - b\,\overline{T} + bR + M_a$$

or $$Y(1 - b + m) = C_a + \overline{I} + \overline{G} + \overline{X} - b\,\overline{T} + bR + M_a$$

Thus, $$Y = \frac{1}{1 - b + m}(C_a + \overline{I} + \overline{G} + \overline{X} - b\,\overline{T} + bR + M_a) \tag{4}$$

Determination of Equilibrium Income and Output: A Graphical Explanation

Aggregate Demand–Aggregate Supply Approach

Equilibrium: The determination of the equilibrium income by the aggregate demand–aggregate supply approach in a four sector economy has been depicted in the Figure 8. 2(a).

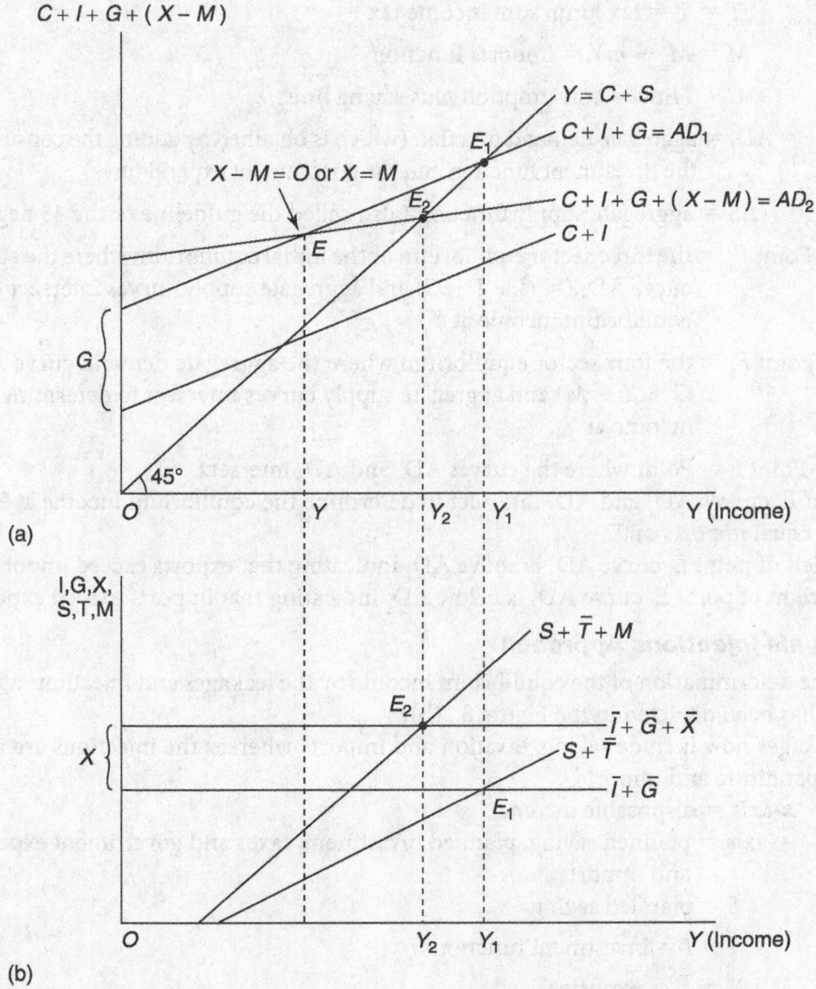

Figure 8.2 Determination of Equilibrium Income or Output in a Four Sector Economy

where, x-axis = disposable income

y-axis = aggregate demand or aggregate planned expenditure

C = aggregate consumption function, $C = C_a + b\,Y_d = C_a + b(Y - \overline{T})$

C_a = the intercept of the consumption function on the y-axis showing consumption spending at zero income level.

b = the MPC or the slope of the consumption function (it will remain constant as, in our analysis, the consumption function is a linear function).

$I = \overline{I}$ = investment (assumed to be autonomous)

$G = \overline{G}$ = government expenditure (assumed to be autonomous)

$X = \overline{X}$ = exports (assumed to be autonomous)

$S = Yd - C$ = saving function

$C = C_a + b\,Y_d$ = consumption function

$T = \overline{T}$ = tax lump sum income tax

$M = M_a + mY$ = imports function

$C + I$ line = consumption plus saving line

AD_1 = aggregate demand function (which is obtained by adding the consumption function, the investment function and the government expenditures)

AS = aggregate supply function (also called the guideline or the 45 degree line)

Point E_1 = the three sector equilibrium or the initial equilibrium where the aggregate demand curve AD_1 $(= C + I + G)$ and aggregate supply curves intersect to determine the equilibrium income at Y_1

Point E_2 = the four sector equilibrium where the aggregate demand curve AD_2 $(= C + I + G + X - M)$ and aggregate supply curves intersect to determine the equilibrium income at Y_2

Point E = Point where the curves AD_1 and AD_2 intersect

At point E, curves AD_1 and AD_2 intersect to determine the equilibrium income at Y. At this level of income, exports equal imports or $X = M$.

To the left of point E, curve AD_2 is above AD_1 indicating that exports exceed imports or $X > M$.

To the right of point E, curve AD_2 is below AD_1 indicating that imports exceed exports or $X < M$.

Leakages Equals Injections Approach

Equilibrium: The determination of the equilibrium income by the leakages and injections approach in a four sector economy has been depicted in the Figure 8.2(b).

The leakages now include saving, taxation and imports whereas the injections are investment, government expenditure and imports.

where, x-axis = disposable income

y-axis = planned saving, planned investment, taxes and government expenditure, exports and imports

S = planned saving

$I = \overline{I}$ = investment function

$X = \overline{X}$ = exports

M = imports function

$S + \overline{T} + M$ = planned saving plus taxes plus imports

$\bar{I} + \overline{G} + \overline{X}$ = planned investment plus government expenditure plus exports

Point E_1 = the three sector equilibrium where the planned saving and taxes curve, $S + \overline{T}$ and investment plus government expenditure curve, $\bar{I} + \overline{G}$ intersect to determine the equilibrium income at Y_1

Point E_2 = the four sector equilibrium where the planned saving, taxes and imports curve, $S + \overline{T} + M$ and investment plus government expenditure plus exports curve, $\bar{I} + \overline{G} + \overline{X}$ intersect to determine the equilibrium income at Y_2

We find that in a four sector economy the two approaches to the determination of the equilibrium income, the aggregate demand–aggregate supply approach and the leakages equal injections approach, both yield the same result.

The introduction of foreign trade has the affect of reducing the equilibrium level of income from Y_1 to Y_2.

RECAP

- In an economy, the exports are assumed to be exogenous whereas the imports are assumed to be a linear function of the income level.
- At the level of income where the $C + I + G$ and $C + I + G + X - M$ curves intersect, exports equal imports or $X = M$.
- The introduction of foreign trade has the affect of reducing the equilibrium level of income.

MULTIPLIER IN A FOUR SECTOR ECONOMY—THE FOREIGN TRADE MULTIPLIER

To have an understanding of the multiplier in the foreign sector, we assume that due to an increase in the income level in the other countries there occurs an increase in the exports of the domestic country. To meet this increased demand for exports, there is an increase in the domestic production which leads to an increase in the income and hence in the consumption expenditure (depending on the marginal propensity to consume). A part of this increase in the consumption expenditure will be directed towards imports, depending on the marginal propensity to import. This will further lead to a second stage of expansion; though due to the leakage from the economy in the form of imports, there will occur only a restricted increase in the income. Further increases in the income will become smaller and smaller. The size of the multiplier will be lower when the marginal propensity to import is positive.

In a four sector economy, the equilibrium level of income is

$$Y = \frac{1}{1 - b + m}(C_a + \bar{I} + \overline{G} + \overline{X} - b\overline{T} - M_a) \tag{2}$$

Assume that there is an increase in exports by ΔX. Hence,

$$Y + \Delta Y = \frac{1}{1 - b + m}(C_a + \bar{I} - b\overline{T} + \overline{G} - M_a G + \overline{X} + \Delta X) \tag{5}$$

Subtracting Eq. (2) from Eq. (5), we get

$$\Delta Y = \frac{1}{1 - b + m}(\Delta X)$$

$$\frac{\Delta Y}{\Delta X} = \frac{1}{1 - b + m}$$

where, ΔX = change in exports

b = marginal propensity to consume

ΔY = change in income

$\frac{\Delta Y}{\Delta X} = \frac{1}{1 - b + m}$ = foreign trade multiplier

The value of the multiplier in an open economy is less than that in a closed economy. This is because in the open economy, there is an additional leakage in the form of imports. Thus as long as the marginal propensity to import is positive, the size of the multiplier gets reduced. A zero marginal propensity to import implies a multiplier, which is the same as the ordinary multiplier, $1/1 - b$.

Another way of analysing the effect of the marginal propensity to import on the multiplier is by expressing the multiplier as $1/1 - (b - m)$.

Here, we can write

b = marginal propensity to purchase both domestically and foreign produced goods
m = marginal propensity to purchase foreign produced goods
$b - m$ = marginal propensity to purchase domestically produced goods

It is to be observed that

(a) If $b = m$, the value of the multiplier is equal to 1.
(b) If $b < m$, the value of the multiplier would be greater than 1.
(c) If the value of m were zero, then the multiplier would become equal to the ordinary multiplier.

RECAP

- When the marginal propensity to import is positive, the size of the multiplier will be lower.
- When the marginal propensity to import is zero, then the multiplier would become equal to the ordinary multiplier.

SUMMARY

INTRODUCTION

1. The chapter focused on a four sector model or, in other words, an open economy which is engaged in trade with the rest of the world.
2. The aggregate demand will be determined by the spending of four sectors, namely, households, firms, government and the foreign sector.

DETERMINATION OF EQUILIBRIUM INCOME OR OUTPUT IN A FOUR SECTOR ECONOMY

1. The inclusion of the foreign sector influences the level of aggregate demand through the export and import of goods and services.
2. The volume of exports in any economy depends on many factors including prices of the exports and income level in the other economies.
3. The level of exports is assumed to be an autonomous variable.
4. The volume of imports in any economy depends on many factors including the prices of the imports and the income level in the domestic economy.
5. We assume that the imports in any economy are determined by the income level in the domestic economy with the import function as $M = M_a + mY$.
6. When exports are greater than imports, there exists a net export balance or a favourable balance of trade. When exports are less than imports, there exists a net import balance or an unfavourable balance of trade.
7. Although exports must be added to the total final expenditures to arrive at the aggregate demand, all spending on imports does not contribute to the domestic demand and thus must be deducted from the total final expenditures to arrive at the aggregate demand.

EQUILIBRIUM INCOME AND OUTPUT

1. There are two approaches to the determination of the equilibrium income and output, the aggregate demand–aggregate supply approach where $Y = C + I + G + X - M$ and leakages equals injections approach where $I + G + X = S + T + M$.

2. Both the approaches yield the same equilibrium level of income.

$$Y = \frac{1}{1-b+m}(C_a + \bar{I} + \bar{G} + \bar{X} - b\bar{T} - M_a)$$

INTRODUCTION OF GOVERNMENT TRANSFER PAYMENTS IN A FOUR SECTOR MODEL

1. Transfer payments increase the spending capacity of the households leading to an increase in the equilibrium level of income.
2. The equilibrium level of income is thus

$$Y = \frac{1}{1-b+m}(C_a + \bar{I} + \bar{G} + \bar{X} - b\bar{T} + bR + M_a)$$

EQUILIBRIUM INCOME AND OUTPUT: A GRAPHICAL EXPLANATION

1. According to the aggregate demand–aggregate supply approach, in the Figure 8.2(a) the four sector equilibrium exists at point E_2 where the aggregate demand curve AD_2 $(= C + I + G + X - M)$ and aggregate supply curves intersect to determine the equilibrium income at Y_2.
2. At point E, the curves AD_1 and AD_2 intersect to determine the equilibrium income at Y. At this level of income, exports equal imports or $X = M$.
3. According the leakages equals injections approach, in the Figure 8.2(b) the four sector equilibrium exists at point E_2 where the $S + \bar{T} + M$ curve and $\bar{I} + \bar{G} + \bar{X}$ curve intersect to determine the equilibrium income at Y_2.
4. The introduction of foreign trade has the affect of reducing the equilibrium level of income.

MULTIPLIER IN A FOUR SECTOR ECONOMY — THE FOREIGN TRADE MULTIPLIER

1. The size of the multiplier will be lower when the marginal propensity to import is positive.
2. The foreign trade multiplier can be expressed as

$$\frac{\Delta Y}{\Delta X} = \frac{1}{1-b+m}$$

3. The value of the multiplier in an open economy is less than that in a closed economy.
4. A zero marginal propensity to import implies a multiplier which is the same as the ordinary multiplier, $1/1-b$.
5. It is to be observed that if $b = m$, the value of the multiplier is equal to 1; if $b < m$, the value of the multiplier would be greater than 1; if the value of m were zero, then the value of the multiplier would become equal to the ordinary multiplier.

REVIEW QUESTIONS

TRUE OR FALSE QUESTIONS

1. The level of imports is assumed to be an autonomous variable.
2. The imports in any economy are determined by the income level in the domestic economy.
3. When exports are greater than imports, there exists a net import balance or an unfavourable balance of trade.
4. While exports must be added to the total final expenditures, imports must be deducted from the total final expenditures to arrive at the aggregate demand.
5. The introduction of foreign trade has the affect of increasing the equilibrium level of income

VERY SHORT-ANSWER QUESTIONS

1. Discuss the factors that influence the volume of exports in an economy.
2. Discuss the factors that influence the volume of imports in an economy.
3. Which are the two approaches to the determination of the equilibrium income and output?
4. Show, diagrammatically, the significance of the point at which the level of exports equal the level of imports.
5. 'The value of the multiplier in an open economy is less than that in a closed economy.' Explain.

SHORT-ANSWER QUESTIONS

1. Describe the imports function and the exports function.
2. What is the impact on the export or import balance of
   (a) an upward shift in the exports function?
   (b) a downward shift in the imports function?
3. How does the introduction of government transfer payments affect a four sector model.
4. 'The size of the multiplier will be lower when the marginal propensity to import is positive'. Explain.
5. In the foreign trade multiplier $\frac{\Delta Y}{\Delta X} = \frac{1}{1 - b + m}$.
   What is the relationship between b and m? Discuss.

LONG-ANSWER QUESTIONS

1. What are the assumptions necessary for the determination of equilibrium income or output in a four sector economy? Discuss.
2. How is the equilibrium level of income and output determined in a four sector model? Explain using both the aggregate demand–aggregate supply and leakages equals injections approach.
3. Show a graphical explanation to the determination of the equilibrium income and output in a four sector model.
4. Write a short note on the foreign trade multiplier.
5. Compare the equilibrium income

$$Y = \frac{1}{1 - b + m}(C_a + \bar{I} + \bar{G} + \bar{X} - b\bar{T} + M_a)$$

With $Y = \frac{1}{1 - b + m}(C_a + \bar{I} + \bar{G} + \bar{X} - b\bar{T} + bR + M_a)$

What is the difference between the two equations? Comment.

SOLVED NUMERICAL PROBLEMS

Numerical Problem 1

The fundamental equations in an economy are given as:

Consumption function $C = 100 + 0.80Y_d$

Investment function $\bar{I} = 150$

Tax $T = 60$

Government expenditure $G = 100$

Exports $X = 50$

Imports $M = 0.05Y$.

Find the following:

(a) the equilibrium level of income.

(b) the net exports.

Numerical Problem 2

For the credentials of the Numerical Problem 1, find

(a) the increase in the income if both government expenditure and tax increased by an amount of 10 each.

(b) the net exports, if exports increased by an amount of 30.

(c) the increase in the government expenditure if the economy were to achieve the full employment income level of 1600.

Numerical Problem 3

In an economy, the following information is given:

(a) The level of consumption is 50 crores plus 50 per cent of each increment of the disposable income.

(b) Investment is fixed at 200 crores.

(c) Tax is fixed at 120 crores.

(d) Government expenditure is also fixed at 150 crores.

(e) Exports are at 70 crores whereas imports are at 50 crores.

Find the equilibrium level of the national income.

Numerical Problem 4

Suppose the basic functions in an economy are as follows:

$$C = 130 + 0.80Y_d$$

$$\bar{I} = 160$$

$$T = 150$$

$$G = 150$$

$$X = 150 - 0.05Y$$

(a) Find the equilibrium level of income.

(b) Find the net exports at equilibrium level of income.

(c) Find the equilibrium level of income and the net exports when there is an increase in investment from 160 to 170.

(d) Find the equilibrium level of income and the net exports when the net export function becomes $140 - 0.05Y$.

Numerical Problem 5

The equations in an economy are given as:

Consumption function $C = 200 + bY_d$

Investment function $\bar{I} = 70$

Tax $T = 60$

Government expenditure $G = 70$

Exports $X = 20$

Imports $M = 10 + 0.1Y$

Marginal propensity to consume, $b = 0.8$.

Find

(a) the equilibrium level of income.

(b) the value of the foreign trade multiplier.

(c) the equilibrium level of imports.

UNSOLVED NUMERICAL PROBLEMS (WITH ANSWERS)

1. The fundamental equations in an economy are given as follows:

Consumption function $C = 50 + 0.50Y_d$

Investment function $\bar{I} = 350$

Tax $T = 60$

Government expenditure $G = 200$

Exports $X = 90$

Imports $M = 0.05Y$

Find

(a) the equilibrium level of income.

(b) the net exports.

2. In Numerical Problem 1, find

(a) the increase in the income if government expenditure increased by an amount of 130 and tax increased by an amount of 40.

(b) the net exports if exports increased by an amount of 22.

(c) the increase in the government expenditure if the economy were to achieve the full employment income level of 1500.

3. The fundamental equations in an economy are given as:

Consumption function $C = 100 + 0.60Y_d$

Investment function $\bar{I} = 400$

Tax $T = 200$

Government expenditure $G = 300$

Exports $X = 300$

Imports $M = 200$.

Find

(a) the equilibrium level of income.

(b) the net exports.

4. The following information is given in an economy:

(a) The level of consumption is 100 crores plus 60 per cent of each increment of the disposable income.

(b) Investment is fixed at 400 crores.

(c) Tax is fixed at 200 crores.

(d) Government expenditure is also fixed at 300 crores.

(e) Exports are at 300 crores whereas imports are at 200 crores.

Find the equilibrium level of the national income.

5. Suppose the basic functions in an economy are as follows:

$C = 50 + 0.60Y_d$

$\bar{I} = 60$

$T = 30$

$G = 28$

$X = 20 + 0.05Y$

(a) Find the equilibrium level of income.

(b) Find the net exports at equilibrium level of income.

(c) Find the equilibrium level of income and the net exports when there is an increase in investment from 60 to 95.

(d) Find the equilibrium level of income and the net exports when the net export function becomes $6 + 0.05Y$.

6. The equations in an economy are given as:

Consumption function $C = 50 + bY_d$

Investment function $\bar{I} = 40$

Tax $T = 20$

Government expenditure $G = 40$

Exports $X = 20$

Imports $M = 20 + 0.1Y$

Marginal propensity to consume, $b = 0.75$.

Find the following:

(a) the equilibrium level of income.

(b) the value of the foreign trade multiplier.

(c) the equilibrium level of imports.

ANSWERS

TRUE OR FALSE QUESTIONS

1. **False.** The level of exports is assumed to be an autonomous variable.
2. **True.** The import function in its simplest form can be expressed as a linear function $M = M_a + mY$.
3. **False.** When exports are greater than imports, there exists a net export balance or a favourable balance of trade. When exports are less than imports, there exists a net import balance or an unfavourable balance of trade.
4. **True** While exports must be added to the total final expenditures to arrive at the aggregate demand, all spending on imports does not contribute to the domestic demand, and thus must be deducted from the total final expenditures to arrive at the aggregate demand.
5. **False.** The introduction of foreign trade has the affect of reducing the equilibrium level of income.

SOLVED NUMERICAL PROBLEMS

Solution 1

(a) The consumption function is

$$C = 100 + 0.8Y_d$$
$$C = 100 + 0.8\,(Y - T)$$
$$C = 100 + 0.8\,(Y - 60)$$

The equilibrium condition is given as $Y = C + I + G + X - M$

Thus,
$$Y = 100 + 0.8\,(Y - 60) + 150 + 100 + (50 - 0.05Y)$$
$$Y = 100 + 0.8\,Y - 48 + 300 - 0.05Y$$
$$Y - 0.8Y + 0.05Y = 352$$
$$0.25Y = 352$$
$$Y = \frac{352}{0.25}$$
$$Y = 1408$$

The equilibrium level of income is 1408.

Checking the answer

In equilibrium in a four sector model, leakages equal injections or $C + I + G + X = C + S + T + M$.

The consumption function is $C = 100 + 0.8\,Y_d$

$$C = 100 + 0.8\,(1408 - 60)$$
$$C = 100 + 0.8\,(1348)$$
$$C = 1178.4$$

The saving function is $S = Y_d - C$

$$S = (Y - 60) - 1178.4$$
$$S = (1408 - 60) - 1178.4 = 169.6$$
$$S = 169.6$$

Thus,
$$I + G + X = S + T + M$$
$$150 + 100 + 50 = 169.6 + 60 + 0.05Y$$
$$300 = 229.6 + 0.05\,(1408)$$
$$300 = 300$$

(b) Imports $M = 0.05Y = 0.05\ (1408) = 70.4$

Net Exports: $X - M = 50 - 70.4 = -20.4$

$$X - M = -20.4$$

There is a deficit in the balance of trade.

Solution 2

(a) If both government expenditure and tax increased by an amount of 10 each, $G = 110$ and $T = 70$.

The equilibrium condition is given as $Y = C + I + G + X - M$

Thus,

$$Y = 100 + 0.8\ (Y - 70) + 150 + 110 + (50 - 0.05Y)$$

$$Y = 100 + 0.8\ Y - 56 + 310 - 0.05Y$$

$$Y - 0.8Y + 0.05Y = 354$$

$$0.25Y = 354$$

$$Y = \frac{354}{0.25}$$

$$Y = 1416$$

The equilibrium level of income is 1416. Hence, there is an increase in the income level by 8.

(b) If exports increased by an amount of 30, $X = 80$.

The equilibrium condition is given as $Y = C + I + G + X - M$.

Thus,

$$Y = 100 + 0.8\ (Y - 60) + 150 + 100 + (80 - 0.05Y)$$

$$Y = 100 + 0.8\ Y - 48 + 330 - 0.05Y$$

$$Y - 0.8Y + 0.05Y = 382$$

$$0.25Y = 382$$

$$Y = \frac{382}{0.25}$$

$$Y = 1528$$

The equilibrium level of income is 1528.

Imports $M = 0.05Y = 0.05\ (1528) = 76.4$

Net Exports: $X - M = 80 - 76.4 = 3.6$

$$X - M = 3.6$$

There is a surplus in the balance of trade.

(c) We have $G_M = \frac{\Delta Y}{\Delta G} = \frac{1}{1 - b + m}$

Where, ΔG = change in government expenditure

b = marginal propensity to consume

ΔY = change in income

G_M = government expenditure multiplier

m = marginal propensity to import

In the present example,

$$b = 0.80$$

$$\Delta Y = 1600 - 1408 = 192$$

Thus,

$$\frac{192}{\Delta G} = \frac{1}{1 - 0.80 + 0.05}$$

$$\Delta G = 192\ (0.25) = 48$$

$$\Delta G = 48$$

The level of government expenditures required to achieve the full employment output is 48.

Solution 3

Here, we have the consumptisubon function as

$$C = 50 + 0.5\,Y_d$$
$$C = 50 + 0.5\,(Y - T)$$
$$C = 50 + 0.5\,(Y - 120)$$

The equilibrium condition is given as $Y = C + I + G + X - M$

Thus,
$$Y = 50 + 0.5\,(Y - 120) + 200 + 150 + (70 - 50)$$
$$Y = 50 + 0.5\,Y - 60 + 350 + 20$$
$$Y - 0.5Y = 360$$
$$0.5Y = 360$$
$$Y = \frac{360}{0.5}$$
$$Y = 720$$

The equilibrium level of income is 720.

Checking the answer

In equilibrium in a four sector model, leakages equal injections

or
$$C + I + G + X = C + S + T + M$$

The consumption function is $C = 50 + 0.5\,Y_d$

$$C = 50 + 0.5\,(720 - 120)$$
$$C = 50 + 0.5\,(600)$$
$$C = 350$$

The saving function is $S = Y_d - C$

$$S = (Y - T) - C$$
$$S = (720 - 120) - 350 = 250$$
$$S = 250$$

Thus,
$$I + G + X = C + S + T + M$$
$$200 + 150 + 70 = 250 + 120 + 50$$
$$420 = 420$$

Solution 4

(a) The consumption function is

$$C = 130 + 0.8Y_d$$
$$C = 130 + 0.8\,(Y - T)$$
$$C = 130 + 0.8\,(Y - 150)$$

The equilibrium condition is given as $Y = C + I + G + X - M$.

Thus,
$$Y = 130 + 0.8\,(Y - 150) + 160 + 150 + (150 - 0.05Y)$$
$$Y = 130 + 0.8\,Y - 120 + 460 - 0.05Y$$
$$Y - 0.8Y + 0.05Y = 470$$
$$0.25Y = 470$$
$$Y = \frac{470}{0.25}$$
$$Y = 1880$$

The equilibrium level of income is 1880.

(b) Imports $M = 0$

Net Exports: $X - M = 150 - 0.05\,(1880) - 0$

$X - M = 56$

There is a surplus in the balance of trade.

(c) $Y = 130 + 0.8\,(Y - 150) + 170 + 150 + (150 - 0.05Y)$

$Y = 130 + 0.8\,Y - 120 + 470 - 0.05Y$

$Y - 0.8Y + 0.05Y = 480$

$0.25Y = 480$

$Y = \dfrac{480}{0.25}$

$Y = 1920$

The equilibrium level of income is 1920 which is an increase by 40.

Imports $M = 0$

Net Exports: $X - M = 150 - 0.05\,(1920) - 0$

$X - M = 54$

(d) There is a surplus in the balance of trade.

$Y = 130 + 0.8\,(Y - 150) + 160 + 150 + (140 - 0.05Y)$

$Y = 130 + 0.8\,Y - 120 + 450 - 0.05Y$

$Y - 0.8Y + 0.05Y = 460$

$0.25Y = 460$

$Y = \dfrac{460}{0.25} = 1840$

$Y = 1840$

The equilibrium level of income is 1840, which is a decrease by 40.

Imports $M = 0$

Net Exports: $X - M = 140 - 0.05\,(1840) - 0$

$X - M = 48$

There is a surplus in the balance of trade.

Solution 5

(a) The consumption function is

$$C = 200 + 0.8Y_d$$

$$C = 200 + 0.8\,(Y - T)$$

$$C = 200 + 0.8\,(Y - 60)$$

The equilibrium condition is given as $Y = C + I + G + X - M$

Thus, $Y = 200 + 0.8\,(Y - 60) + 70 + 70 + 20 - 10 - 0.1Y$

$Y = 200 + 0.8Y - 48 + 150 - 0.1Y$

$Y - 0.6Y - 0.1Y = 302$

$0.3Y = 302$

$Y = \dfrac{302}{0.3}$

$Y = 1006.67$

The equilibrium level of income is 1006.67.

(b) Foreign trade multiplier $\dfrac{\Delta Y}{\Delta X} = \dfrac{1}{1 - b + m} = \dfrac{1}{1 - 0.80 + 0.1} = 3.33$

(c) Imports at the equilibrium level: $M = 10 + 0.1Y = 10 + 0.1\ (1006.67)$

$$M = 110.67$$

The equilibrium level of imports is 110.67.

UNSOLVED NUMERICAL PROBLEMS

1. (a) $Y = 1200$

   The equilibrium level of income is 1200.

   (b) $X - M = 30$

   There is a surplus in the balance of trade.

2. (a) $Y = 1400$

   The equilibrium level of income is 1400.

   (b) $Y = 1240$

   The equilibrium level of income is 1240.

   $X - M = 50$

   There is a surplus in the balance of trade.

   (c) $\Delta G = 165$

   The level of government expenditures required to achieve the full employment output is 165.

3. (a) $Y = 1950$

   The equilibrium level of income is 1950.

   (b) $X - M = 100$

   There is a surplus in the balance of trade.

4. $Y = 1950$

   The equilibrium level of income is 1950.

5. (a) $Y = 400$

   The equilibrium level of income is 400.

   (b) $X - M = 40$

   There is a surplus in the balance of trade.

   (c) $Y = 500$

   The equilibrium level of income is 500, which is an increase by 100.

   $X - M = 45$

   There is a surplus in the balance of trade.

   (d) $Y = 360$

   The equilibrium level of income is 360.

   $X - M = 24$

   There is a surplus in the balance of trade.

6. (a) $Y = 328.57$

   The equilibrium level of income is 328.57.

   (b) Foreign trade multiplier = 2.86

   (c) $M = 52.86$

   The equilibrium level of imports is 52.86.

UNIT III THEORIES OF CONSUMPTION AND INVESTMENT SPENDING

9 Theories of Consumption

After studying this topic, you should be able to understand

- ✓ *The basic principle of absolute income hypothesis is that the individual consumer will determine the fraction of his current income that he will allocate to consumption on the basis of his absolute income level.*
- ✓ *According to the relative income hypothesis, the fraction of a family's income that will be allocated to consumption will depend on its income level relative to the income level of the other families with which it classifies itself.*
- ✓ *The permanent income hypothesis puts forward the view that consumption is related to the permanent income.*
- ✓ *The average propensity to consume, expressed in terms of the permanent income, is the same on an average for all families whether rich or poor.*
- ✓ *The life cycle hypothesis puts forward the view that consumption is related to the present value of the individual's income or wealth.*
- ✓ *Besides income, there are many other factors like the rate of interest, price level, price expectations, income distribution and financial assets, which influence the consumption levels.*

INTRODUCTION

In Chapter 5, we had introduced the relationship between consumption and income in a simplified form. This chapter analyses the relationship more closely by looking at four hypotheses, which focus on the influence of income on consumption, namely, the absolute income hypothesis, relative income hypothesis, permanent income hypothesis and the life cycle hypothesis.

It was with Keynes' theory of the consumption function that optimism was felt that perhaps it was possible to predict consumption expenditures. However, this optimism was short lived and the predictions in the post World War II period proved to be off the mark. Hence, economists came up with different theories to explain the factors, which in addition to income, determine the consumption expenditures. These factors could range from age size of the family, demographic characteristics, wealth, and rate of interest to the income distribution.

ABSOLUTE INCOME HYPOTHESIS

The basic principle of absolute income hypothesis is that the individual consumer will determine the fraction of his current income that he will allocate to consumption on the basis of his absolute income level.

The absolute income hypothesis is associated with Keynes and later with James Tobin and Arthur Smithies. The basic principle of this hypothesis is that the individual consumer will determine the fraction of his current income that he will allocate to consumption on the basis of his absolute income level. Thus, the individual consumer's consumption expenditure depends on his absolute income level. Everything else remaining unchanged, an increase in the income will lead to a decrease in the fraction of the income allocated to consumption.

BOX 9.1

The study of the relationship between consumption and income has gained importance in the last 10 to 15 years. It has created interest among sociologists, anthropologists, historians and philosophers also. However, in spite of the vital role played by consumption in economic theory, economists have not contributed much in the new wave of research which has accompanied the dynamic changes in this field. This is a reflection of the rigidity in the conventional theory of consumer behaviour. This theory assumes that consumption depends on income, prices and tastes only. It is not in any way influenced by the culture, society, economic institutions and the choices of the others. Hence, economists feel that there is little point in discussing any of these other social factors which are said to influence consumption.

Figure 9.1 depicts the relationship between income and consumption as in the absolute income hypothesis.

The straight line through the axis is the 45° line showing the hypothetical relationship between consumption and income that the current consumption is always equal to the current income. Thus, when income is zero consumption is always zero.

The curve *C* illustrates Keynes' absolute income hypothesis. It can be analysed in three parts:

(1) Until point *E* on the curve *C* corresponding to the income level before Y_1, the consumption expenditure exceeds the current income level. This clearly shows that families with low incomes have a high marginal propensity to consume as they spend a large proportion of their incomes on consumption.

(2) At point *E* on the curve *C* corresponding to the income level Y_1, the consumption expenditure equals the current income level.

Thus, current consumption and current income break even at the income Y_1.

(3) Beyond point *E* on the curve *C* corresponding to the income level greater than Y_1, the consumption expenditure is *less* than the current income level. Hence, the consumption increases with income but at a lesser rate. This explains why families with high incomes have a low marginal propensity to consume as they spend a small proportion of their incomes on consumption and save a larger proportion of their incomes.

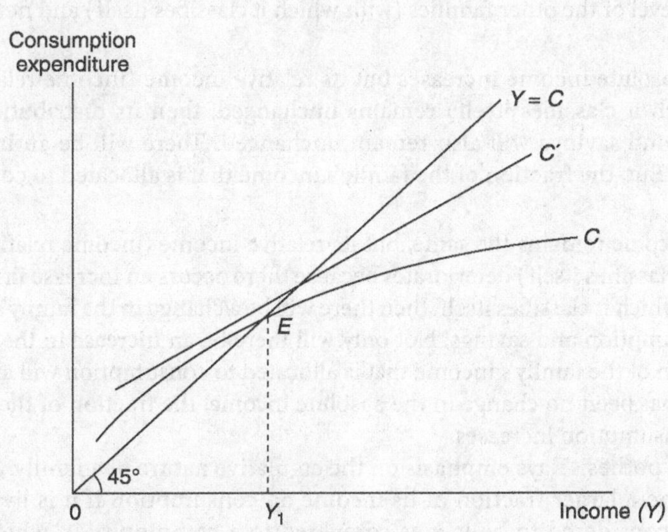

Figure 9.1 Relationship Between Income and Consumption: The Absolute Income Hypothesis

The above analysis gives rise to an income consumption curve, which is upward sloping but with a downwards bend.

Some conclusions, which can be drawn, are:

(1) The high income families save a large proportion of their incomes as compared to the low income families as they are left with a large proportion of their incomes after fulfilling their consumption needs. Thus, the marginal propensity to consume of high income groups will be low.

(2) As families climb up the income scale, the proportion of income that they can save increases.

(3) For the average family, there is a decrease in the average propensity to consume when it climbs up the income scale.

In the initial years, the absolute income hypothesis was widely accepted. Later on, the Keynesians modified the relationship.

Criticisms: The absolute income hypothesis assumes that there is no change in any of the factors that influence consumption, which is incorrect. Also, as already mentioned, empirical data in the post World War II period does not support Keynes' absolute income hypothesis. Yet, we cannot deny the importance of Keynes' work which marked the beginning of an era due to which attempts were made and researches were conducted to analyse the relationship between consumption and income, which initiated the different theories which came up post Keynes.

RECAP

- Everything else remaining unchanged, an increase in the income will lead to a decrease in the fraction of the income allocated to consumption.
- Families with high incomes have a low marginal propensity to consume.

RELATIVE INCOME HYPOTHESIS

The 'relative income hypothesis' was put forward by J. S. Duesenberry in the 1940s. According to this hypothesis, the fraction of a family's income that will be allocated to consumption will depend on its income level relative to the income level of the other families (with which it classifies itself) and not on its absolute income level. Thus,

(1) If a family's absolute income increases but its relative income (income relative to the other families with which it classifies itself) remains unchanged, then its distribution of income between consumption and savings will also remain unchanged. There will be an increase in the absolute consumption. But, the fraction of the family's income that is allocated to consumption will remain the same.

(2) If a family's income remains the same, but its relative income (income relative to the other families with which it classifies itself) deteriorates because there occurs an increase in the income of the other families with which it classifies itself, then there will be a change in the family's distribution of income between consumption and savings. Not only will there be an increase in the absolute consumption, but the fraction of the family's income that is allocated to consumption will also increase. Thus, even though there has been no change in the absolute income, the fraction of the family's income that is devoted to consumption increases.

The 'relative income hypothesis' lays emphasis on the emulative nature of a family. A family with a certain given income will spend a larger fraction of its income on consumption if it is living in a community in which that income is considered to be low as compared to a community in which that income is considered to be high. This is due to what Duesenberry called the 'demonstration effect' where families are influenced by the other family's standard of living and thus try to 'keep up with the Joneses'. Hence, the absolute income becomes less important and the family's relative income in the community that it lives in becomes more important.

In Figure 9.1, suppose that there is a doubling-up of the absolute incomes of all the families between a certain time period. It is important to note that this does not lead to any change in the distribution of the income. Hence, the relative position of each family on the income scale remains unchanged. According to the relative income hypothesis, for the average family there will be no change in the fraction of the income devoted to consumption. Thus as long as the relative income remains unchanged, the fraction of a family's income devoted to consumption will also remain unchanged, even though there may be a change in the family's absolute income.

Each family will, thus, move along the consumption function C' in Figure 9.1 which is a straight line depicting that the fraction of income devoted to consumption remains unchanged. Hence, the average propensity to consume will remain the same before and after the change in the income. An average family will not feel that it is better off as its relative position on the income scale has not changed and thus it will continue to consume the same proportion of its income that it was consuming earlier. Hence, its average propensity to consume will remain as earlier and it will not move along the curve C as predicted by the absolute income hypothesis where as the family's absolute income increases there is a decrease in the average propensity to consume.

Similar to the absolute income hypothesis, the relative income hypothesis also assumes that there is no change in any of the factors which influence consumption.

Criticisms

(1) According to the relative income hypothesis, upward changes in income and consumption are proportional where as empirical evidence suggests that unexpected gains in the income levels are linked to less than proportional increases in consumption levels.

(2) The view that consumption standards once maintained are permanent and thus irreversible is also not correct.

RECAP

- The 'relative income hypothesis' lays emphasis on the emulative nature of a family.

PERMANENT INCOME HYPOTHESIS

The permanent income hypothesis was developed by Milton Friedman in 1957. It is a departure from the earlier two analyses in that it focused on the concept of the permanent income. It puts forward the view that consumption is related to the permanent income. The absolute income hypothesis and the relative income hypothesis related consumption to the individual family's current income. Both the absolute and relative incomes are current incomes.

A family's permanent income is not in any way indicated by its current income. It is, in fact, determined by the expected income over the next few years and is thus a long-term estimate of income. It is determined by the family's wealth, both physical and human wealth. Thus the permanent income is the average income, which is regarded as permanent by the individual family. It will determine the steady pace of expenditure, which the family could maintain for the rest of their life.

The family's measured income or the observed income may be different from the permanent income. Friedman has split up the measured income into two components, the permanent income and the transitory income. The difference between the measured income and the permanent income is, thus, related to whether the transitory income is positive or negative, that is:

(1) If a wage earner in a family receives an unexpected bonus in a particular year, then in that case the transitory income is positive and thus the measured income is greater than the permanent income.

(2) If a wage earner in a family suffers an unanticipated loss in his income in a particular year, say due to a fire, then in that case the transitory income is negative and thus the measured income is lesser than the permanent income.

Friedman has similarly split up consumption into two components, permanent consumption and transitory consumption. Permanent income is what households expect to receive over a certain period in the future where as the transitory income forms the unanticipated addition or subtraction in the permanent income. His main argument is that permanent consumption depends on the permanent income. In fact, it is a constant fraction of the permanent income. Permanent consumption is determined by different factors like the ratio of human wealth to the total wealth, the rate of interest and tastes which are influenced by factors like age and the composition of the family. If these factors do not vary much, then in that case, the average ratio of consumption to the permanent income will turn out to be the same even for families at different income levels. According to the hypothesis, the average fraction of the permanent income of a family that is allocated to consumption is the same whether they are at the top or the bottom of the income scale, or in other words, whether they are rich or poor. Thus the average propensity to consume expressed in terms of the permanent income is the same on an average for all families, whether rich or poor.

The above analysis implies that the average propensity to save, when expressed in terms of the permanent income, is the same for all families whether rich or poor. The main purpose of saving is to provide for the future by smoothening out consumption over a period of time. Economists raise doubts about whether this is a correct depiction of the behaviour, which exists in reality. There is no doubt that the low income families try to prevent a situation where consumption in the future is lower than what it is at the present. However, this does not in any way overcome their need for the present consumption. For these families with small and insufficient incomes, the present seems to be more important than the future and hence their inclination would be towards the present consumption rather than saving for an uncertain future. This would imply behaviour where the low income families would be consuming a large part of their income where as the high income families would be saving a large part of their income.

Another argument put forward by Friedman here is that transitory consumption is not related, in any way, to transitory income. This implies that any unanticipated increases or decreases in the income level lead to comparable increases or decreases in the saving (and not in consumption). Whenever there are any windfalls or losses the consumption level remains the same; or in other words, the marginal propensity to consume out of transitory income is zero. Economists have raised doubts about this argument put forward by Friedman questioning the proximity of this behaviour to actual behaviour. However, this will imply that the marginal propensity to consume expressed in terms of the permanent income will be unstable because the individual family's perception of the changes in their income, whether transitory or permanent, will ultimately determine their marginal propensity to consume. The larger the transitory income as perceived by the individual families the lower is the marginal propensity to consume and vice versa.

The permanent income hypothesis has been criticized for many reasons. Some of them are as follows:

(1) It assumes that the average propensity to consume is the same on an average for all families whether they are rich or poor. This seems questionable as the low income families consume more than the high income families. Empirical data also do not support this argument.

(2) Friedman has argued that transitory consumption is not related to transitory income. This, again, is not supported by empirical data as individuals always alter their consumption when there is a windfall gain or a sudden loss.

BOX 9.2

Franco Modigliani and his student Richard Brumberg had in the 1950s come up with the life cycle hypothesis. This was a theory whose basis was that people are intelligent in making choices about their future consumption expenditures and their diverse consumption patterns according to their age. They make their decisions keeping in mind the resources available to them during their lifetime. The theory comes to the conclusion that the level of the national savings depends not on the level of the national income but on the rate of growth of national income. Also, the wealth in the economy is related to the length of the retirement period. Empirical evidence also seems to support the work by Modigliani and Brumberg. In spite of the numerous criticisms and challenges that it has been subjected to, the life cycle hypothesis continues to play an essential role in economics. It is due to this theory that we are able to analyse many important issues like the effects of demographic changes on the level of the national savings, the role played by savings in economic growth and the influence of the stock market on the economy.

RECAP

- The average propensity to save, when expressed in terms of the permanent income, is the same for all families whether rich or poor.
- Transitory consumption is not related, in any way, to transitory income.

LIFE CYCLE HYPOTHESIS

The life cycle hypothesis was developed by Franco Modigliani, Albert Ando and Richard E. Brumberg in the 1960s. It focuses on the concept of the present value of the individual's income or wealth. It puts forward the view that consumption is related to the present value of the individual's income or wealth. Hence, to some extent, it is similar to Friedman's permanent income hypothesis in that it does not relate the consumption to the individual family's current income. This suggests that the individual sustains a constant or slightly increasing level of consumption over his entire life cycle. It maintains that individuals stabilize their consumption levels over a period of time as they relate their consumption streams to the expected lifetime income stream.

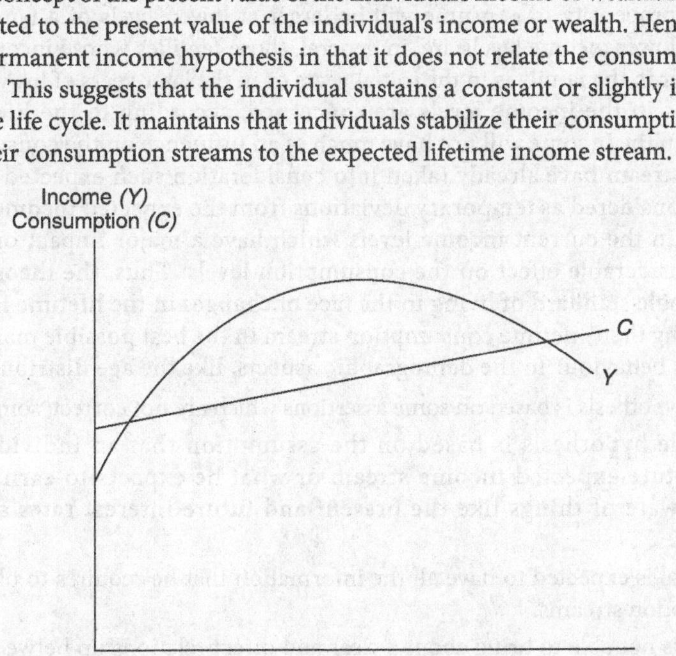

Figure 9.2 Relationship Between Income and Consumption: The Life Cycle Hypothesis

Figure 9.2 depicts the relationship between income and consumption based on the life cycle hypothesis where,
x-axis = time, in say, years
y-axis = income and consumption streams
Curve Y = a profile of the income stream earned by an individual during his entire life
Curve C = the consumption stream during his entire life

The curve Y depicts the income stream of the individual in each year. It starts from the year when the individual begins with full time employment, reaches a maximum when he approaches his middle years and falls thereafter. The curve C, which depicts the consumption stream, curves as an upward sloping line showing consumption level that increases steadily from year to year. If an individual decides not to make any bequests, then he will attempt at making the present value of his income stream equal to the present value of his consumption stream. In simpler terms, it implies that he would spend his entire income on consumption over the entire period of his life.

Figure 9.2 shows that:

(1) In the initial years of his working life, the individual is a dissaver or in other words a net borrower and thus his consumption curve is above the income curve.
(2) In the middle years of his working life, the individual is a saver and thus his consumption curve is below the income curve. He may be paying back his earlier debts and also investing his savings in interest-earning assets.
(3) In the later years of his working life, the individual is once again a dissaver and his consumption curve is above the income curve. However, the difference now is that he finances his dissavings not through borrowing but through the savings that he built up in the earlier years of his life.

From the above analysis, the following are analysed.

(1) The average propensity to consume will be smaller at higher levels of a family's income. The families with the higher income levels are, in general, those families whose incomes are high because the income earner in the family is in the middle years of his working life.
(2) The average propensity to consume will be larger at lower levels of a family's income. The families with the lower income levels are, in general, those families whose incomes are low because the income earner in the family is in the initial years or in the later years of his working life.

As far as the changes in the income levels are concerned, according to the life cycle hypothesis, any increase or decrease in the income will not have much of an influence on the consumption level as the life cycle consumptions stream have already taken into consideration such expected changes in the income levels. They will be considered as temporary deviations from the expected income in one's life. However, unexpected changes in the current income levels which have a major impact on the expected income levels will have a considerable effect on the consumption levels. Thus, the theory lays an emphasis on how to maintain a stable standard of living in the face of changes in the lifetime income stream. It views individuals as planning their lifetime consumption stream in the best possible manner. It links consumption and thus savings behaviour to the demographic aspects, like the age distribution of the population.

Criticisms: The hypothesis is based on some assertions which are not correct; some of them are as follows:

(1) The life cycle hypothesis is based on the assumption that an individual has a clear vision about his future expected income stream or what he expects to earn in his entire lifetime. He is also aware of things like the present and future interest rates and the returns on his investments.
(2) The individual is expected to have all the information that he requires to plan his life cycle income and consumption streams.
(3) The analysis is not able to bring about a clear and direct relationship between current consumption and current income.
(4) The empirical evidence does not support the life cycle hypothesis.

RECAP

- The life cycle hypothesis maintains that individuals stabilize their consumption levels over a period of time as they relate their consumption streams to the expected lifetime income stream.
- The average propensity to consume will be smaller at higher levels of a family's income.
- The average propensity to consume will be larger at lower levels of a family's income.
- Any increase or decrease in the income will not have much of an influence on the consumption level.

OTHER FACTORS INFLUENCING CONSUMPTION

Besides income, there are many other factors that have an affect on the consumption levels. These include:

(1) **Rate of interest:** Though it is quite certain that the rate of interest influences the allocation of the aggregate disposable income between saving and consumption, it is highly uncertain as to the whether a high rate of interest implies that less of the disposable income will be devoted to consumption and more to saving. Any change in the interest rate may effect saving in either way for an individual's saving is directly related to the interest rate.

An increase in the rate of interest has a two-fold effect:

(a) **Substitution effect**: It produces a substitution of present consumption to future consumption. This implies that due to the substitution effect, more will be saved at high interest rates (to be able to consume more in the future).

(b) **Income effect:** It increases the individual's future income as compared to the present income. This may, in fact, encourage him to take a part of this increased future income in the form of increased present consumption. Hence, this implies less saving at high interest rates due to the income effect.

For individuals with high incomes, there is a tendency to save a large part of their incomes. Therefore, the income effect may outweigh the substitution effect. The high rate of interest may lead to a reduction in the current saving. The supply curve showing the relationship between the rate of interest and saving will initially have an upward slope to the right but may bend backwards at some very high rate of interest implying that savings decrease for all higher rates.

For individuals with low incomes, even at high interest rates saving is only a small part of the income. Therefore, the substitution effect may outweigh the income effect. The saving will fluctuate directly with the interest rate. The supply curve showing the relationship between the rates of interest and saving will slope upwards towards the right.

We find that at a high rate of interest while some individuals save more, others save less. However, this is applicable only to those individuals who save. As far as the dissavers are concerned, they finance their current consumption requirements out of their current income. Any excess of current consumption will have to be financed either by borrowing or by drawing from the past saving. High interest rates will discourage them from borrowing and, thus, reduce on dissavings. In other words, this implies that the there is direct relationship between saving and interest rate.

It appears that for some savers, the supply curve showing the relationship between the rates of interest and saving may slope upwards towards the right, depicting a direct relationship with the rate of interest. For the other savers, the supply curve may ultimately bend backwards at some very high rate of interest implying that savings are inversely related to the interest rate. As far as the dissavers are concerned, the supply curve will vary directly with the interest rate. The problem that arises is that the general aggregate supply curve, which is a summation of all these individual supply curves, cannot be specified. A simple relationship between the interest rate and aggregate personal saving (and hence, consumption) cannot be specified under these circumstances.

(2) **The price level:** To analyse the influence of the price of the consumer goods and services on consumption, it is first important to understand that we are here interested in aggregate consumption expenditures (and not the expenditures on a single good). When there is an increase or a decrease in the price level of the consumer goods, the consumer will react by either spending more or less of his income on goods and services.

It is important to understand that if the current disposable income rises or falls in proportion to the consumer price level, then the real disposable income will not change. If it rises or falls disproportionately, then the real disposal income will also rise or fall accordingly.

Money illusion: Consumers may often be subjected to money illusion. Suppose that during a certain time period the price level increases by 20 per cent and the current disposable income also increases by 20 per cent, there may be some families who realize that their real income is unchanged and thus they do not suffer any money illusion. They increase their current consumption and current saving by 20 percent and, thus, their real consumption and real saving remains unchanged.

However, there may be families of a different kind who may be subject to a money illusion. They are of two kinds which are as follows:

(1) Those families who may consider only the increase in the prices and may fail to notice the increase in their current incomes. These families feel that they are worse off as their real income has reduced. Thus, they react to the situation by cutting down on their saving and increasing their consumption. There is an increase in their real consumption.

(2) Those families who may consider only the increase in their current incomes and may fail to notice the increase in the price level. These families feel that they are better off. They react to the situation by increasing their saving and decreasing their consumption. There is a decrease in their real consumption.

If the consumers are not subject to a money illusion, then:

(1) If the change in the price level is accompanied by a proportionate change in the income, there will be no change in the consumer's real income. Hence, his real consumption will remain unchanged.

(2) If the change in the price level is accompanied by a disproportionate change in the income, there will be a change in the consumer's real income. Hence, his real consumption will change. When there is an increase in the price level, there will be a decrease in the real income. Hence, the individual will reduce his real consumption but it is to be noted that the fraction of his real income devoted to consumption may actually increase. When there is a decrease in the price level, there will be an increase in the real income. The individual will increase his real consumption but the fraction of his real income devoted to consumption may actually decrease.

Price expectations: Till now, we have focused on the realized changes in the consumer price level and the effects which follow from it. However, it is possible that real consumption may change due to the mere expectations of a change in the price level.

If the price level has been increasing for some time, then it is possible that the consumers may expect an even higher price level tomorrow. Hence, they may increase their real consumption by spending a large fraction of their real income on consumption.

If the price level has been decreasing for some time, then it is possible that the consumers may expect an even lower price level tomorrow. Hence, they may decrease their real consumption by spending a smaller fraction of their real income on consumption. They prefer to postpone their consumption to the future in which they expect lower prices.

The expectations of a price change are crucial in determining the consumption expenditures of an individual. In fact, consumer expectations can undergo a change even due to social, political and economic changes leading to a change in the consumption.

(4) **Income distribution:** The distribution of income plays an important role in determining the consumption expenditures. The fraction of the income, which is allocated to consumption, is lower at the higher levels of a family's income and higher at the lower levels of a family's income. It follows that the more equal is the income distribution the larger is the fraction of the income that is devoted to consumption. However, it is not necessary that a redistribution of the income in favour of the low income families will increase the fraction of the income that is devoted to consumption. This is due to many reasons; some of them are:

(a) In the short period, the changes in the distribution of income may be moderate and yearly changes are very insignificant. The government may, to some extent, try to make the income distribution more equal through a progressive tax. But even then, past experience shows that such changes in the income distribution do not bring about much of a change in the consumption expenditures.

(b) A redistribution of the income will involve additions to the income of some and deductions from the income of the others. It is important to observe that while consumption expenditures from the total income depend on the average propensity to consume, the consumption expenditures from the additions to or deductions from the total income depend on the marginal propensity to consume. Thus, the immediate impact of any additions or reductions will depend on the marginal propensity to consume. But the marginal propensity to consume (as compared to the average propensity to consume) is more or less the same at different levels of a family's income. Thus, it seems that a redistribution of the income does not lead to much of an increase in the fraction of the income devoted to consumption.

(5) **Financial assets:** The volume of the financial assets accumulated by the individual is also important in determining his consumption expenditures. These assets may include cash, demand and time deposits, saving deposits, stocks and bonds. A family, which has amassed larger amounts of such assets, will spend more on consumption as it does not feel any need to add to its already large accumulation of the financial assets. Hence, it will devote a smaller fraction of its income to saving and a larger one to consumption. On the other hand, a family with a smaller accumulation of the financial assets will devote a larger fraction of its income to saving and a smaller one to consumption.

The above analysis is subject to some qualifications; these are:

(1) The increase in the consumption will depend on the ownership of the financial assets. If the increase in the financial assets is concentrated among the upper class, the consumption may not increase much because the rich save a large part of their income.

(2) For many families, the acquisition of a few financial assets may simply stimulate their appetite for more of these assets. Hence, they may cut down on consumption in favour of savings which will facilitate them to acquire more financial assets.

Though these assets are one of the most important non-income factors, which influence consumption but evidence seems to support the view that these assets do not have a major influence on the consumption expenditures.

RECAP

- The other factors, which influence consumption, do play an important role but the income level continues to be the most important factor that influences consumption.

SUMMARY

INTRODUCTION

The present chapter analyses the relationship between consumption and income by looking at four hypotheses—absolute income hypothesis, relative income hypothesis, permanent income hypothesis and the life cycle hypothesis.

ABSOLUTE INCOME HYPOTHESIS

1. The basic principle of absolute income hypothesis is that the individual consumer will determine the fraction of his current income that he will allocate to consumption on the basis of his absolute income level.
2. Everything else remaining unchanged, an increase in the income will lead to a decrease in the fraction of the income allocated to consumption.
3. Families with low incomes have a high marginal propensity to consume as they spend a large proportion of their incomes on consumption where as families with high incomes have a low marginal propensity to consume as they spend a small proportion of their incomes on consumption.
4. For the average family, there is a decrease in the average propensity to consume when it climbs up the income scale.

RELATIVE INCOME HYPOTHESIS

1. According to the relative income hypothesis, the fraction of a family's income that will be allocated to consumption will depend on its income level relative to the income level of the other families with which it classifies itself.
2. If a family's absolute income increases but its relative income (income relative to the other families with which it classifies itself) remains unchanged, then its distribution of income between consumption and savings will also remain unchanged.
3. If a family's income remains the same but its relative income (income relative to the other families with which it classifies itself) deteriorates because there occurs an increase in the income of the other families with which it classifies itself, then there will be a change in the family's distribution of income between consumption and savings.
4. The 'relative income hypothesis' lays emphasis on the emulative nature of a family and on what Duesenberry called the 'demonstration effect'.

PERMANENT INCOME HYPOTHESIS

1. The permanent income hypothesis puts forward the view that consumption is related to the permanent income.
2. The average propensity to consume expressed in terms of the permanent income is the same on an average for all families whether rich or poor.
3. Friedman has split up the measured income into two components, the permanent income and the transitory income. His main argument is that the permanent consumption depends on the permanent income.
4. Another argument put forward by Friedman here is that transitory consumption is not related, in any way, to transitory income. This implies that any unanticipated increases or decreases in the income level lead to comparable increases or decreases in the saving (and not in consumption).

LIFE CYCLE HYPOTHESIS

1. The life cycle hypothesis puts forward the view that consumption is related to the present value of the individual's income or wealth.
2. It argues that consumption is related to the present value of the individual's income or wealth. This suggests that the individual sustains a constant or slightly increasing level of consumption over his entire life cycle.
3. The average propensity to consume will be smaller at higher levels of a family's income.
4. The average propensity to consume will be larger at lower levels of a family's income.
5. As far as the changes in the income levels are concerned, according to the life cycle hypothesis, any increase or decrease in the income will not have much of an influence on the consumption level.

OTHER FACTORS INFLUENCING CONSUMPTION

1. Besides income, there are many other factors like the rate of interest, price level, price expectations, income distribution and financial assets, which influence the consumption levels.
2. Rate of interest: It is highly uncertain whether a high rate of interest implies that less of the disposable income will be devoted to consumption and more to saving.
3. The price level: When there is an increase or a decrease in the price level of the consumer goods, the consumer will react by either spending more or less of his income on goods and services. Consumers may often be subject to money illusion.
4. Price expectations: It is possible that real consumption may change due to the mere expectations of a change in the price level. If the price level has been increasing for some time, then it is possible that the consumers may expect an

even higher price level tomorrow. Hence, they may increase their real consumption by spending a large fraction of their real income on consumption.

5. Income distribution: The distribution of income plays an important role in determining the consumption expenditures. The fraction of the income, which is allocated to consumption, is lower at the higher levels of a family's income and higher at the lower levels of a family's income. It follows that the more equal is the income distribution the larger is the fraction of the income that is devoted to consumption. It seems that a redistribution of the income does not lead to much of an increase in the fraction of the income devoted to consumption.
6. Financial assets: The volume of the financial assets accumulated by the individual is also important in determining his consumption expenditures. These assets may include cash, demand and time deposits, saving deposits, stocks and bonds. A family, which has amassed larger amounts of such assets, will spend more on consumption as it does not feel any need to add to its already large accumulation of the financial assets.

REVIEW QUESTIONS

TRUE OR FALSE QUESTIONS

1. According to the absolute income hypothesis, everything else remaining unchanged, an increase in the income will lead to a decrease in the fraction of the income allocated to consumption.
2. Families with high incomes have a high marginal propensity to consume as they spend a large proportion of their incomes on consumption.
3. The high income families save a large proportion of their incomes as compared to the low income families.
4. The permanent income hypothesis puts forward the view that consumption is related to the relative income.
5. The 'relative income hypothesis' lays emphasis on what Duesenberry called the 'demonstration effect'.

VERY SHORT-ANSWER QUESTIONS

1. Why do families with high incomes have a low marginal propensity to consume?
2. Give a brief criticism of Keynes' absolute income hypothesis.
3. According to the life cycle hypothesis, the average propensity to consume will be smaller at higher levels of a family's income and larger at lower levels of a family's income. Why?
4. What is money illusion? How does it affect consumption?
5. How do price expectations influence consumption? Discuss.

SHORT-ANSWER QUESTIONS

1. What is Duesenberry's 'demonstration effect'? Explain.
2. What is the permanent income according to Friedman?
3. What are permanent consumption and transitory consumption? How are they related to the permanent income and transitory income? Explain.
4. What is the relationship between income and consumption according to the life cycle hypothesis? Explain.
5. Analyse the effects of income distribution and a change in the holding of financial assets on consumption.

LONG-ANSWER QUESTIONS

1. 'The basic principle of absolute income hypothesis is that the individual consumer will determine the fraction of his current income that he will allocate to consumption on the basis of his absolute income level.' Comment.
2. Depict the relationship between income and consumption in the absolute income hypothesis with the help of a diagram.
3. 'According to the relative income hypothesis, the fraction of a family's income that will be allocated to consumption will depend on its income level relative to the income level of the other families with which it classifies itself.' Comment.
4. What is the permanent income hypothesis? Explain.
5. 'The life cycle hypothesis puts forward the view that consumption is related to the present value of the individual's income or wealth.' Is this correct? Comment.

ANSWERS

TRUE OR FALSE QUESTIONS

1. **True.** The basic principle of the absolute income hypothesis is that the individual consumer will determine the fraction of his current income that he will allocate to consumption on the basis of his absolute income level. Everything else remaining unchanged, an increase in the income will lead to a decrease in the fraction of the income allocated to consumption.
2. **False.** Families with low incomes have a high marginal propensity to consume as they spend a large proportion of their incomes on consumption.
3. **True.** The high income families save a large proportion of their incomes as compared to the low income families as they are left with a large proportion of their incomes after fulfilling their consumption needs.
4. **False.** The permanent income hypothesis puts forward the view that consumption is related to the permanent income.
5. **True.** The 'relative income hypothesis' lays emphasis on the emulative nature of a family and on what Duesenberry called the 'demonstration effect' where families are influenced by the other family's standard of living and thus try to 'keep up with the Joneses'.

Theories of Investment Spending

10

After studying this topic, you should be able to understand

- ✓ *Investment can be defined as the value of that portion of an economy's output for any period of time that takes the form of new producer's durable equipment, new structures and the change in inventories.*
- ✓ *To arrive at net investment, a deduction is made from gross investment for producer's durable equipment and the existing structures that are used in the production process.*
- ✓ *The decision to invest is different as compared to the decision to buy consumer goods.*
- ✓ *Once the marginal efficiency of capital (MEC) is determined, a comparison of the market rate of interest with the MEC will enable one to make a decision as to whether the vestment in the capital asset is profitable or not.*
- ✓ *The marginal efficiency of investment (MEI) schedule depicts the relationship between the economy's investment and rate of interest when the change in the price of capital goods is taken into consideration.*
- ✓ *MEI schedule represents the true investment demand schedule for the economy as a whole.*
- ✓ *The concavity of the MEI schedule is due to the increasing cost of the capital goods.*
- ✓ *Given the MEC schedule, net investment is determined by the rate of interest and the size of the capital stock.*
- ✓ *An upward shift in the MEC schedule leads to an increase in the profit maximizing capital and thus to capital accumulation.*
- ✓ *According to the accelerator theory, the desired stock of capital depends on the economy's output level.*
- ✓ *The main idea in the flexible accelerator model is that whenever there exists a large gap between the firm's existing capital stock and the desired capital stock, the firm's investment is swifter.*

INTRODUCTION

One of the most important components of the GNP is investment. In the earlier chapters of the simple model of income determination, investment was assumed to be given at some particular level. This chapter analyses the relationship between investment and the rate of interest and also the responsiveness of investment to the rate of interest.

Capital is the accumulated stock of plant and equipment, which is held by the business firms.

Investment expenditure constitutes an extremely volatile component of the aggregate demand. The fluctuations in investment cause fluctuations in the production and income levels. They are responsible for much of the business cycles. In this chapter, we attempt at determining the factors that influence the investment decisions. We also examine some of the theories of investment spending.

Investment can be defined as the value of that portion of an economy's output for any period of time that takes the form of new producer's durable equipment, new structures and the change in inventories.

BOX 10.1

All human beings attempt to increase their wealth. But they try to do so in a way that their savings, wealth and investments are not put at an undue risk. Though all investments involve some element of risk, however, through cautious investments one can attempt to reduce such risk. This has over time given rise to many theories of investment. These investment theories attempt at explaining and supporting the different types of investment strategies. Some of these popular investment theories include Diversification Theory, Bernstein's Psychology of Successful Investing, Efficient Market Theory and Life Cycle Investment Theory.

BASIC CONCEPTS

Before we embark on our analysis of investment, we will discuss some of the concepts relating to investment.

Investment

Capital is the accumulated stock of plant and equipment, which is held by the business firms. It is the stock of the productive facilities, which are available to produce the output. Hence, capital is a stock concept. On the other hand, investment is a flow concept. In the simplest terms, investment can be defined as the value of that portion of an economy's output for any period of time that takes the form of new producer's durable equipment, new structures and the change in inventories. It is the flow of spending, which makes an addition to the physical stock of capital. In the long run, it is investment that determines the stock of capital and hence the long-run growth in the economy. It is to be noted that compared to the stock of capital, the flow of investment is quite small.

In Chapter 3, investment expenditure was defined as consisting of goods and services bought for use in the future. It was grouped into three categories: (i) business fixed investment is the purchase of new plant and equipment by firms, (ii) residential investment is the purchase of new housing by households and others, and (iii) inventory investment is the change in the inventory of goods by the firm. The present chapter focuses on, specifically, the business fixed investment.

It is obvious that different factors influence the different types of investment. Thus, there can be no single investment theory which is applicable to all the different types of investment.

Gross and Net Investment

Investment can be in net terms or in gross terms. Gross investment consists of two parts: the replacement investment, which is required to keep the capital stock intact and the net investment that is required to expand the existing capital stock. To arrive at net investment, a deduction is made from gross investment for producer's durable equipment and the existing structures that are used in the production process. Net investment is equal to gross investment minus depreciation. In fact, net investment is an accretion to the stock of capital.

Net investment is an accretion to the stock of capital.

If in a particular period of time,

(1) the gross investment is equal to the amount of capital that is used up in that particular period, (in other words the cumulative depreciation thereon) then there will no net investment.
(2) the gross investment is greater than the amount of capital that is used up in that particular period, then there will be positive net investment that involves an increase in the stock of capital.
(3) the gross investment is smaller than the amount of capital that is used up in that particular period, then there will be negative net investment or in other words there will be a disinvestment. This involves a reduction in the stock of capital.

Other things remaining unchanged, for example, given the labour force, technology and natural resources, an accretion to the stock of capital increases the economy's productive capacity. However, in practice as the stock of capital increases the other things do not remain unchanged. But it is necessary to separate the growth in the other factors if one wishes to isolate the effect of the growth of capital stock on the potential output. Thus, for the sake of convenience we assume that all the variables like labour force, technology and natural resources are assumed to be constant. Hence, we can associate all the increases in the capital stock with increases in the productive capacity of an economy.

Public and Private Investment

It is important to differentiate between public investment and private investment. Public investment refers to the investment in the public sector and private investment refers to the investment in the private sector. The motivating factor behind public investment is social welfare where as private investment is guided by the profit motive. Our analysis primarily relates to the private investment.

Public investment refers to the investment in the public sector whereas private investment refers to the investment in the private sector.

Induced and Autonomous Investment

Investment can be divided into two categories:

Induced Investment

In general, the investment function can be expressed as

Investment that changes due to a change in income and the interest rate is called induced investment.

$$I = I(Y, i)$$

where, I = investment

Y = income level

i = rate of interest

While investment is positively related to the income level, there is a negative relationship between investment and the rate of interest. Investment that changes due to a change in income and the interest rate is called induced investment.

In the short run as income remains more or less constant, the investment function can be expressed as

$$I = I(i)$$

Autonomous Investment

Investment that does not change due to a change in income and the interest rate is called autonomous investment. This is the investment that depends on the other factors like inventions, population and future expectations. While most of the investments in the public sector are autonomous as they are made for considerations other than profit, some of the investments in the private sector may also be autonomous.

Investment that does not change due to a change in income and the interest rate is called autonomous investment.

RECAP

- In the long run, it is the investment that determines the stock of capital and hence the long-run growth in the economy.
- We can associate all the increases in the capital stock with increases in the productive capacity of an economy.
- Most of the investments in the public sector are autonomous as they are made for considerations other than profit, some of the investments in the private sector may also be autonomous.

BOX 10.2

It is only recently that there has arisen some interest in the theory of finance. This is because the theory of finance was a neglected part of the theories of investment. According to the traditional theory, investment depends on the marginal efficiency of capital and also the purchase price of the capital good. As far as finance is concerned, these theories assumed that there is a perfect capital market from which funds will be forthcoming. Thus, finance has been given a back seat as it was assumed that finance presented no problem. It was only later on that work was done by the different economists to remedy the neglect, which the theory of finance had suffered.

THE DECISION TO INVEST

The decision to invest is different as compared to the decision to buy consumer goods. This is due to the following reasons:

(1) A firm must make a decision whether to go for capital expansion or buy an existing asset like equity in another company.

(2) Most of the capital goods have a long life and one can learn only several years later as to whether the investment in these capital goods has been profitable or not.

(3) When a firm has decided to expand, it will have to decide as to whether the cost of borrowing is greater than the return expected on the new investment undertaken by the firm.

A firm's investment decision is based on the relationship between three elements:

(1) Expected income flow from capital good under consideration: As the future is uncertain, a crucial decision for the firm in making its investment decision is regarding two aspects:

  (a) An estimate of the future flow of income that the capital asset under consideration is expected to yield over its entire life.

  (b) The expected life of the capital good, which may last more than expected or may become obsolete before its lifetime due to technological advancements.

(2) The purchase price of the good in question: Often, there exists an uncertainty regarding the price at which the good is to be purchased. This is more for projects where new machines and equipment are involved and where the cost may undergo change over time.

(3) The rate of interest prevailing in the market which again is subject to fluctuations.

It is important to note that any calculations that relate to the future must take into consideration the fact that the returns over the future have a much lower worth as compared to the same returns today. While making an investment decision relating to the future, a calculation may be made regarding the present value of the capital asset and the discounted rate of return on the asset.

Present Value of a Capital Asset and Discounting

To make its investment decision, a firm compares the present value of the capital asset with its purchase price or the supply price.

The supply price of a capital asset is the cost of replacing the capital asset, which is under consideration, with a new one.

The supply price of a capital asset is the cost of replacing the capital asset, which is under consideration, with a new one.

The present value of a capital asset is the sum obtained after discounting the expected future yields over its entire life at the market rate of interest. The higher is the market rate of interest the lower is the present value. In the extreme case if the market rate of interest is zero, then the present value is equal to the expected future yield.

The discounting process is the process by which a future sum is converted into its present value. It is just the reverse of the process by which a sum of money grows as it is invested in the future.

The present value of a capital asset is the sum obtained after discounting the expected future yields over its entire life at the market rate of interest.

Suppose that an amount R_0 is invested for a period of one year at a market rate of interest, r. The amount the individual will receive at the end of year 1:

$$R_1 = R_0 (1 + r) \tag{1}$$

Suppose that the amount R_1 is invested for a period of another year.

The amount the individual will receive at the end of year 2:

$$R_2 = R_1 (1 + r)$$

But
$$R_1 = R_0 (1 + r)$$

Thus,
$$R_2 = R_0 (1 + r)(1 + r) = R_0 (1 + r)^2$$

If R_2 is invested for a period of another year, then at the end of year 3 the individual will receive:

$$R_3 = R_0 (1 + r)^3$$

In general if an amount R_0 is invested for a period of n years at a market rate of interest, r, the amount the individual will receive at the end of the n years:

$$R_n = R_0 (1 + r)^n \tag{2}$$

Equation (1) can be written as
$$R_0 = \frac{R_1}{(1 + r)}$$

where,
$$(1 + r) = \text{discount rate}$$

$$\frac{R_1}{(1 + r)} = \text{the discounted present value of } R_1$$

Numerical Illustration 1

Suppose that Rs. 100 is to be received by an individual after a period of 1 year. The market rate of interest is 10 per cent. How much must he invest today.

Solution

The discounted present value of Rs. 100 is

$$R_0 = \frac{100}{(1 + 0.10)} = 90.91$$

This implies that to get a sum of Rs. 100 at the end of 1 year, Rs. 90.91 must be invested today at an interest rate of 10 per cent.

Equation (2) can be written as

$$R_0 = \frac{R_n}{(1 + r)^n}$$

where,
$$(1 + r) = \text{discount rate}$$

$$\frac{R_n}{(1 + r)^n} = \text{the discounted present value of } R_n$$

We consider the determination of the present value of a bond. A bond yields a yearly income, say R, until it reaches maturity at the end of n years when it returns the principal amount, P. the present value of the bond is

$$V = \frac{R}{(1 + r)} + \frac{R}{(1 + r)^2} + \frac{R}{(1 + r)^3} + \cdots + \frac{R}{(1 + r)^n} + \frac{P}{(1 + r)^n}$$

Alternatively, a machine is expected to yield an income stream of $R_1, R_2, R_3, \ldots, R_n$ over a period of its entire life. At the end, it has a scrap value of J. The market rate of interest is r. The present value of the returns from the machine is

$$V = \frac{R_1}{(1 + r)} + \frac{R_2}{(1 + r)^2} + \frac{R_3}{(1 + r)^3} + \cdots + \frac{R_n}{(1 + r)^n} + \frac{J}{(1 + r)^n}$$

Numerical Illustration 2

Suppose the annual expected returns from a machine are Rs. 35,000 over a period of 5 years, which is the expected economic life of the machine. The scrap value of the machine is Rs. 20,000. The market rate of interest is 10 per cent. The cost of the machine is Rs. 100,000. Find the present value of the expected returns from the machine. Is it profitable to invest in the machine.

Solution

The present value of the expected returns from the machine is

$$V = \frac{R_1}{(1+r)} + \frac{R_2}{(1+r)^2} + \frac{R_3}{(1+r)^3} + \cdots + \frac{R_n}{(1+r)^n} + \frac{J}{(1+r)^n}$$

$$V = \frac{35{,}000}{1.10} + \frac{35{,}000}{(1.10)^2} + \frac{35{,}000}{(1.10)^3} + \frac{3{,}50{,}000}{(1.10)^4} + \frac{35{,}000}{(1.10)^5} + \frac{20{,}000}{(1.10)^5}$$

$$V = 31{,}818 + 28{,}925 + 26{,}296 + 23{,}905 + 21{,}732 + 12{,}418 = 1{,}45{,}904$$

As the discounted present value of the returns from the machine is Rs. 1,45,904 which is greater than the cost of the machine, Rs. 1,00,000 the investment in the machine is profitable.

The Marginal Efficiency of Capital

Till now we have focused on the determination of the present value of a given income stream and the market rate of interest. We now assume that we are given the following:

(1) The income stream from the capital asset, $R_1, R_2, R_3, \ldots, R_n$

(2) The cost or purchase price of the capital asset, C.

We wish to find the rate of interest that will make the cost or purchase price of the capital asset equal to the present value of a given income stream. Thus, given C and $R_1, R_2, R_3, \ldots R_n$ we wish to find i, which is the rate of return expected from a particular capital asset. It is also called the marginal efficiency of capital, MEC. Thus,

$$C = \frac{R_1}{(1+i)} + \frac{R_2}{(1+i)^2} + \frac{R_3}{(1+i)^3} + \cdots + \frac{R_n}{(1+i)^n} + \frac{J}{(1+i)^n}$$

Numerical Illustration 3

Suppose the income stream from an investment project is R_1 = Rs. 500 million, R_2 = Rs. 600 million, R_3 = Rs. 600 million, R_4 = Rs. 400 million and R_5 = Rs. 400 million. The cost of the machine is Rs. 2000 million. Find the internal rate of return.

Solution

The marginal efficiency of capital is

$$C = \frac{R_1}{(1+i)} + \frac{R_2}{(1+i)^2} + \frac{R_3}{(1+i)^3} + \cdots + \frac{R_n}{(1+i)^n}$$

We get the internal rate of return (IRR), i = 8.397 per cent, or in other words, the MEC as 8.397 per cent. Hence, if market rate of interest is greater than 8.397 per cent, the project is not profitable and hence not acceptable. If the cost of borrowing funds is lower than the IRR threshold of 8.397 per cent, the project can be taken up.

It is important to note that:

(1) For a given level of the income stream the higher the cost or purchase price of the capital asset, C the lower is the value of i, the marginal efficiency of capital.

(2) For a given level of the income stream the lower the cost or purchase price of the capital asset, C the higher is the value of i, the marginal efficiency of capital.

Once the MEC is determined, a comparison of the market rate of interest with the MEC will enable one to make a decision whether the investment in the capital asset is profitable or not. The level of *r* determines whether the capital asset will be purchased or not, given the MEC. However, r does not, in any way, determine the MEC of the capital asset.

The difference between the MEC and the market rate of interest is the net rate of return expected after allowance is made for all costs. Though both the MEC and *r* are percentages, they are totally different.

The MEC will increase when:

(1) Given an unchanged price of the capital good, business expectations improve leading to an upward revision of the expected income flow from the capital asset.
(2) There is a decrease in the purchase price of the capital asset, and no change in the expected income flow from the capital asset.

The MEC will decrease when:

(1) Given an unchanged price of the capital good, business expectations worsen leading to a downward revision of the expected income flow from the capital asset.
(2) There is an increase in the purchase price of the capital asset, and no change in the expected income flow from the capital asset.

Hence, we find that the basic rule for making a decision is that:

(1) If the MEC is greater than the market rate of interest, then the purchase of the capital asset is worthwhile.
(2) If the MEC is smaller than the market rate of interest, then the purchase of the capital asset is not worthwhile.

The Marginal Efficiency of Capital Schedule and the Rate of Investment

A firm has, often, variety of investment projects among which it has to make a choice. These may involve new projects or even the expansion of existing buildings and purchase of more equipment of a similar type. In making its decision, a firm will compare the MEC of the capital asset with the current market rate of interest. Once it has estimated the MEC from all the projects, the firm's MEC would be as shown in Figure 10.1.

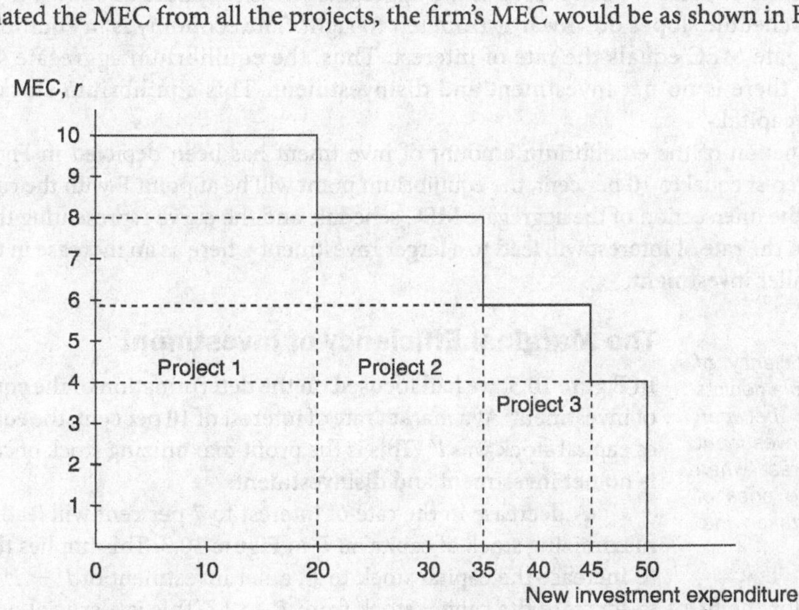

Figure 10.1 The Marginal Efficiency of Capital Schedule

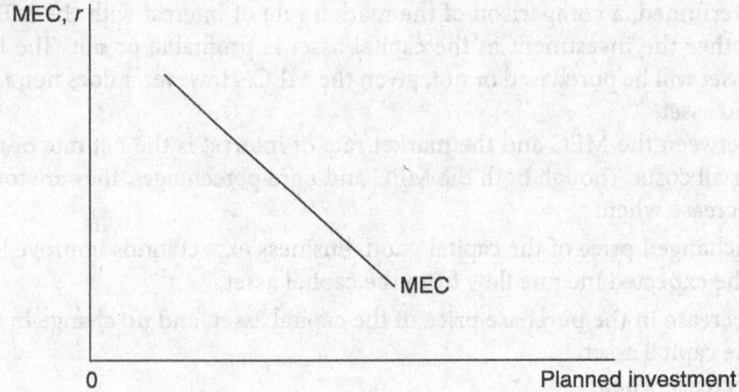

Figure 10.2 The Aggregate Marginal Efficiency of Capital Schedule

In Figure 10.1, a firm can invest in four different projects. Project 1 requires an investment of 20 crores with an MEC of 10 per cent. Project 2 involves an investment of 15 crores with an MEC of 8 per cent. Project 3 requires an investment of 10 crores with an MEC of 6 per cent. Project 4 involves an investment of 5 crores with an MEC of 4 per cent. If the market rate of interest is 6 per cent the firm will invest in projects 1, 2 and 3 a total investment of 45 crores. Once the investment has increased to the point where the last project yields an MEC that equals the market rate of interest the firm will stop with its expansion drive unless there is a further change in the market rate of interest. The firm has achieved its desired capital stock. For an individual firm, the lower is the rate of interest the higher is its investment expenditures.

For every firm, the MEC schedule will resemble the stair like curve shown in Figure 10.1 with an obvious difference in the heights and the lengths of the steps depending on the investment opportunities available to the firm. However once the MEC's for all the firms are added together horizontally, the steps would all even out and we can arrive at the aggregate MEC schedule as shown in Figure 10.2. The aggregate MEC schedule slopes downwards from left to right. The economy is in equilibrium at the point where the aggregate MEC equals the rate of interest. Thus, the equilibrium aggregate stock of capital is determined and there is no net investment and disinvestment. This equilibrium stock of capital is the desired stock of capital.

The determination of the equilibrium amount of investment has been depicted in Figure 10.3. Given a market rate of interest equal to 10 per cent, the equilibrium point will be at point E with the capital stock at I^*. It is determined at the intersection of the aggregate MEC schedule and the curve representing the rate of interest.

A decrease in the rate of interest will lead to a larger investment where as an increase in the rate of interest will lead to a smaller investment.

The Marginal Efficiency of Investment

The marginal efficiency of investment schedule depicts the relationship between the economy's investment and rate of interest when the change in the price of capital goods is taken into consideration.

In Figure 10.3, we had focused on the determination of the equilibrium amount of investment. At a market rate of interest of 10 per cent, the equilibrium amount of capital stock was I^*. This is the profit maximizing stock of capital where there is no net investment and disinvestment.

A decrease in the rate of interest to 7 per cent will lead to a larger profit, maximizing stock of capital at I_1 in Figure 10.3. This implies that there is a need to increase the capital stock to I_1, a net investment of $I_1 - I^*$. How much time will be required for the firms to increase the capital stock from I^* to I_1? This is a crucial question and needs considerable attention.

There can be two totally diverse situations:

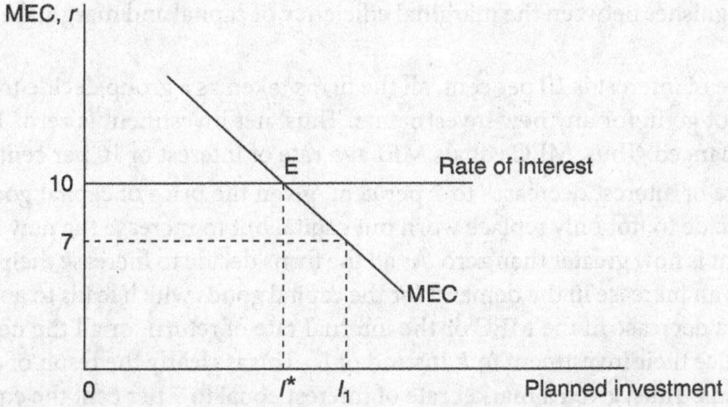

Figure 10.3 Determination of the Equilibrium Investment

(1) The capital goods industry has unlimited capacity with a supply curve, which is perfectly elastic. In such a case, the net investment will increase at a faster rate and the optimum capital stock will be achieved quickly.

(2) The capital goods industry has limited capacity with a supply curve, which is upward sloping. The marginal costs increase as the level of output increases, which leads to increasing prices of the capital goods. In such a case due to the increasing prices of the capital goods, the rate of investment will slow down and thus more time will be taken to achieve the optimum capital stock.

When we were analysing the investment expenditures by a single firm, we could increase the capital stock overnight because the capitals goods industry may be able to cater to the increased demands of a single firm at short notice and without much increase in the price of the capital goods. However, when all the firms in the industry increase their stock of capital the capitals goods industry will not only take a long time to produce the additional output but it may have to install extra capacity which may lead to increased costs and thus increase in price of the capital goods.

It is necessary at this stage of our analysis to distinguish between the marginal efficiency of capital and marginal efficiency of investment. The marginal efficiency of investment schedule depicts the relationship between the economy's investment and rate of interest when the change in the price of capital goods is taken into consideration.

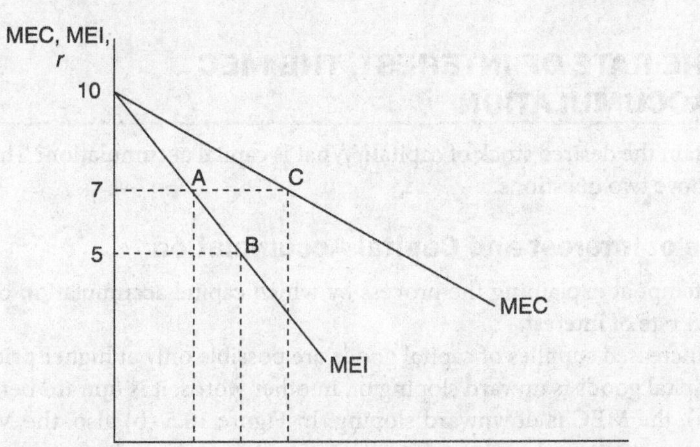

Figure 10.4 Marginal Efficiency of Capital Schedule and Marginal Efficiency of Investment Schedule

Figure 10.4 distinguishes between the marginal efficiency of capital and marginal efficiency of investment schedules.

(1) When the rate of interest is 10 per cent, all the firms taken as a group decide to only replace worn out capital and not go in for any new investments. Thus, net investment is zero. The capital goods price remains unchanged. Thus, MEC equals MEI at a rate of interest of 10 per cent.

(2) When the rate of interest decreases to 7 per cent, given the price of capital goods, all the firms taken as a group decide to not only replace worn out capital but to increase the new investment to I_1'. Thus, net investment is now greater than zero. As all the firms decide to increase their investment simultaneously, there is an increase in the demand for the capital goods which leads to an increase in their price. This leads to a decrease in the MEC or the internal rate of return for all the new investments. Hence, the firms reduce their investment to I_1 instead of I_1'. This is clearly the result of an increase in the price of capital goods. Thus, given a market rate of interest equal to 7 per cent the equilibrium point will be at point A (and not point C) with the capital stock at I_1. This gives one point on the MEI schedule.

(3) Similarly, if the rate of interest falls to 5 per cent the equilibrium point will be at point B with the capital stock at I_2. This gives another point on the MEI schedule.

By joining such points we can arrive at the MEI schedule, which represents the true investment demand schedule for the economy as a whole. The MEI schedule is downward sloping showing a negative relationship between the level of investment and the rate of interest.

RECAP

- A firm's investment decision is based on the relationship between three elements which are the expected income flow from capital good under consideration, purchase price of the good in question and the rate of interest prevailing in the market.
- For every firm, the MEC schedule is a stair like curve where as the aggregate MEC schedule is downward sloping and a smooth curve.
- When all the firms in the industry increase their stock of capital, there will be increases in the price of the capital.
- The MEI schedule is downward sloping showing a negative relationship between the level of investment and the rate of interest.

CHANGES IN THE RATE OF INTEREST, THE MEC AND CAPITAL ACCUMULATION

When do the firms attain the desired stock of capital? What is capital accumulation? This section is concerned with answering the above two questions.

A Fall in the Rate of Interest and Capital Accumulation

In this section, we attempt at explaining the process by which capital accumulation occurs in response to a decrease in the market rate of interest.

We assume that increased supplies of capital goods are possible only at higher prices. In such a scenario, the supply curve of capital goods is upward sloping or, in other words, it is upward bending.

In Figure 10.5 (a), the MEC is downward sloping. In Figure 10.5 (b) also, the MEI slopes downwards from left to right because the supply curve of capital is upward sloping. In fact, the concavity of the MEI schedule is due to the increasing cost of the capital goods. It is important to note that with a given stock of capital there is only one MEI.

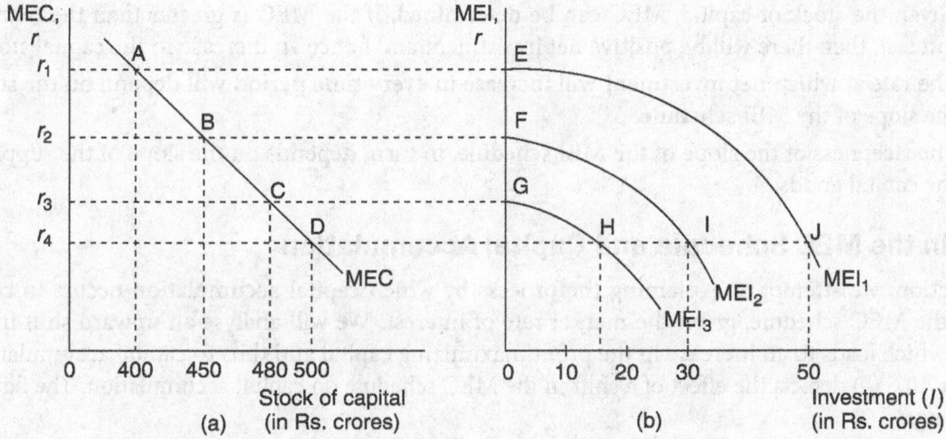

Figure 10.5 A Fall in the Rate of Interest and Capital Accumulation

In Figure 10.5 (a), assume that:

(1) At point A on the MEC, the economy's actual stock of capital is of 400 crores. This is also the desired stock of capital as the MEC equals the market rate of interest, r_1. Thus the net investment is zero.

(2) There is a decrease in the market rate of interest to r_4. At this rate of interest, the equilibrium occurs at point D (as the MEC equals the market rate of interest). The desired stock of capital increases to 500 crores. This is difference of 100 crores from the existing actual stock. Thus, 100 crores of net investment is required to increase the capital stock to the desired level.

The important question here is how long will it take the firms to increase the capital stock by 100 crores? If the production capacity of the capital goods industry were unlimited, the firm could increase its capital goods to 500 crores in just one time period. However, the production capacity of the capital goods industry is limited and increasing the capital goods to the desired level will take more than one time period.

Figure 10.5 (b) shows that:

(1) In period 1, given MEI$_1$, due to the decrease in the rate of interest to r_4, net investment will increase but only by 50 crores. This is because the horizontal line, which corresponds to the rate of interest r_4 meets MEI$_1$ at point *J*. Hence, the stock of capital increases to 450 crores at the end of period 1.

(2) In period 2, the actual stock of capital in the beginning of the period is 450 crores. In Figure 10.5 (a), corresponding to this stock of capital of 450 crores, the equilibrium occurs at point B where the MEC equals the market rate of interest which is r_2. The corresponding MEI curve is MEI$_2$. The net investment will increase by 30 crores. Again this is because the horizontal line, which corresponds to the rate of interest r_4, meets MEI$_2$ at point *I*. The stock of capital increases to 480 crores at the end of period 2.

Similarly in the next period, there will be a further increase in the capital stock and the process will continue till the actual stock of capital gradually increases over time to 500 crores, which is the desired capital stock. It is obvious from the above analysis that in each period the net investment is smaller as compared to the previous period.

Thus,

(1) Given the MEC schedule (which does not shift), net investment is determined by the rate of interest and the size of the capital stock.

(2) Given the stock of capital, MEC can be determined. If the MEC is greater than the market rate of interest, then there will be positive net investment and hence an increase in the capital stock.
(3) The rate at which net investment will increase in every time period will depend on the steepness of the slope of the MEI schedule.
(4) The steepness of the slope of the MEI schedule, in turn, depends on the slope of the supply curve of the capital goods.

A Shift in the MEC Schedule and Capital Accumulation

In this section, we attempt at explaining the process by which capital accumulation occurs in response to a shift in the MEC schedule, given the market rate of interest. We will analyse an upward shift in the MEC schedule, which leads to an increase in the profit maximizing capital and thus to capital accumulation.

Figure 10.6 (a) depicts the effect of a shift in the MEC schedule on capital accumulation. The figure depicts the following:

(1) The original MEC schedule is MEC_1. At a rate of interest of r_1, the profit maximizing or the desired capital stock is at 400 crores. As the actual capital stock is also 400 crores, net investment is zero.
(2) Suppose the MEC schedule shifts upwards to MEC_2. At a rate of interest of r_1, the profit maximizing or the desired capital stock is now at 500 crores. As the actual capital stock is at 400 crores, there is a difference of 100 crores from the optimum or desired capital stock. Thus, 100 crores of net investment is required implying that net investment is positive or greater than zero.
The important question here again is how long will it take the firms to increase the capital stock by 100 crores? As the production capacity of the capital goods industry is limited, increasing the capital goods to the desired level will take more than one time period.

Figure 10.6 (b) shows that:

(1) In time period 1, given MEI_1, net investment will increase but only by 50 crores. This is because the horizontal line, which corresponds to the rate of interest r_1, meets MEI_1 at point *J*. Thus, the stock of capital increases to 450 crores at the end of period 1.
(2) In period 2, the actual stock of capital in the beginning of the period is 450 crores. In Figure 10.6 (a), corresponding to this stock of capital of 450 crores is point B on MEC_2. The corresponding MEI curve is MEI_2. The net investment will increase by 25 crores. Again this is because the horizontal line, which

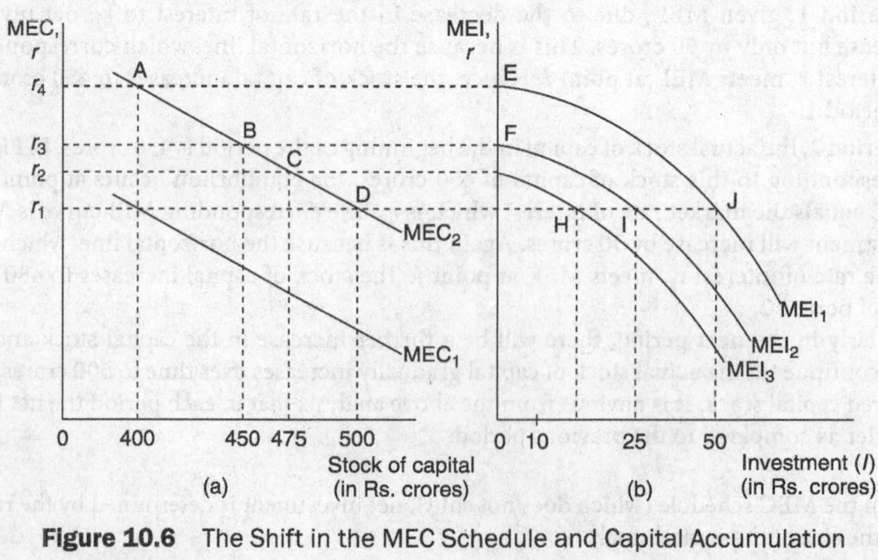

Figure 10.6 The Shift in the MEC Schedule and Capital Accumulation

corresponds to the rate of interest r_1, meets MEI_2 at point I. The stock of capital increases to 475 crores at the end of period 2. However, the actual stock of capital is still less than the desired stock of capital. Thus in the next period, there will be a further increase in the capital stock and the process of capital accumulation will continue till the actual stock of capital gradually increases over time to 500 crores, which is the desired capital stock.

Thus,

(1) Given the rate of interest, an upward shift in the MEC schedule generates conditions which are apt for investment.

(2) Due to the upward shift in the MEC schedule, the MEC becomes greater than the current market rate of interest (given the actual capital stock). This leads to a situation, which initiates the investment activity or the net investment is greater than zero. The process of investment, or in other words the process of capital accumulation, will continue till the actual capital stock is equal to the desired capital stock. At this level, investment activity will cease as the MEC is equal to the market rate of interest.

RECAP

- In each period, the net investment is smaller as compared to the previous period.
- The rate at which net investment will increase in every time period will depend on the steepness of the slope of the MEI schedule.
- Given the rate of interest, an upward shift in the MEC schedule generates conditions which are apt for investment.

THEORIES OF INVESTMENT

Many theories have been put forward to explain investment demand. It is a difficult and complex subject and one of the most controversial subjects. We throw light on some of these theories.

Accelerator Theory of Investment

The simple accelerator model states that investment is proportional to the change in the level of output and is not influenced by the cost of capital.

According to the accelerator theory, the desired stock of capital depends on the economy's output level. An increase in the output leads to an outward shift in the MEC schedule implying that at each interest rate a larger capital stock is desired. Thus, changes in investment can be explained in terms of shifts in the MEC schedule. The increases in the output puts pressures on the existing stock of capital, or in other words on the existing productive capacity. An increase in the productive capacity is possible only by an expansion of the existing capital stock thus providing the incentive to the firm to obtain more capital goods and a higher rate of investment.

According to this approach, the rate of investment spending depends on the output level. To produce more output, more capital is required. Within limits it is possible to increase the output by using the existing capacity more intensively. But there exists a particular capital output ratio, which the firms consider to be the ideal ratio. This ratio differs from industry to industry being higher in some industries and lower in the others. However, at a particular point in time there exists a particular capital output ratio which is considered to be the desired ratio for the economy as a whole. As there occur technological and other changes in the economy, this ratio will undergo a change. However, for simplifying our analysis we assume that the ratio remains unchanged over time.

We have,

$$K = kY$$

where, K = capital stock

k = capital output ratio

Y = output level

Given an unchanged capital output ratio, as the output changes, the desired stock of capital will also change. Suppose,

$$K_{t-1} = k\,Y_{t-1}$$

where, t = some particular time period

$t-1, t-2$ = preceding time periods

$t+1, t+2$ = subsequent time periods

Suppose there is an increase in the output level in period t. Hence,

$$K_t = k\,Y_t$$

The increase in the desired stock of capital $= K_t - K_{t-1}$.

The capital will increase only when net investment equals the increase in the capital stock, or

$$I_t = K_t - K_{t-1}$$

where, I_t = net investment in period t

We can also write,

$$I_t = K_t - K_{t-1} = kY_t - kY_{t-1} = k\,(Y_t - Y_{t-1})$$

The above equation indicates that the net investment in time period t depends on the change in the output level between time periods t and $t-1$ multiplied by the capital output ratio. It is clear that:

(a) If $Y_t > Y_{t-1}$, there is a positive net investment in period t.

(b) If $Y_t < Y_{t-1}$, there is a negative net investment or disinvestment in period t.

(c) If $Y_t = Y_{t-1}$, there is a zero net investment in period t.

If replacement investment (which we assume to be equal to depreciation) is added to net investment, we get gross investment. Thus, we have

$$I_t + D_t = k\,(Y_t - Y_{t-1}) + D_t$$

where, D_t = depreciation in period t

Thus,

$$I_{gt} = k\,(Y_t - Y_{t-1}) + D_t$$

where, I_{gt} = gross investment

Investment will change if there is a change in the output level. However, it is assumed that there is no excess capacity. We allow for excess capacity by including X_t, which is the excess capacity in period t, in our analysis. Thus,

$$I_{gt} = k(Y_t - Y_{t-1}) + D_t - X_t$$

where, X_t = excess capacity in period t

If $k(Y_t - Y_{t-1}) + D_t$ is equal to or less than X_t, then I_{gt} will be zero.

The basic relationship that exists between the investment and the change in the output level is known as the accelerator principle. The capital output ratio, *k*, is known as the accelerator. The investment theory that is based on the above relationship is known as the accelerator theory.

The basic relationship that exists between the investment and the change in the output level is known as the accelerator principle.

The following points are important in the context of the theory:

(1) If the economy is in a position where the existing capital stock is fully utilized and there is no excess capacity, and the capital output ratio is constant, then in that case an expansion of output is possible only with an expansion in the existing stock of capital.

(2) If the accelerator is greater than one, then the increase in the capital stock will be greater than the increase in the output. Thus, the increase in the investment is greater than the increase in the output.

For the accelerator principle to work certain conditions must be satisfied as follows:

(1) The firms must operate without any excess capacity. During periods of excess capacity, the accelerator principle is temporarily inactive.

(2) The firms increase their capacity to be able to meet every increase in the level of real spending. This implies that whenever there is an increase in the quantity of goods sold there is an increase in investment by the firms and whenever there is a decrease in the quantity of goods sold there is a decrease in investment by the firms.

(3) The capital output ratio, *k*, or in other words, the accelerator must be constant.

The capital output ratio, k, is known as the accelerator.

(4) The gap between the desired output and the actual output of the firms is closed within a single time period. In practice, this will depend on the production capacity of the capital goods industries.

Criticism: Due to its rigid assumptions, the accelerator theory has been subject to severe criticisms. Also, it appears that the accelerator principle does not work during periods of recession when there exists excess capacity. The accelerator principle is based on calculations about the future, which are not necessarily accurate. Thus, doubts have been raised about the validity of the accelerator principle. However, its basic idea remains that investment depends upon changes in the level of output. It does not depend upon changes in the cost of capital.

The Flexible Accelerator Model

Many theories have been put forward regarding the speed at which firms fine tune their stock of capital over time. The main idea in the flexible accelerator model is that whenever there exists a large gap between the firm's existing capital stock and the desired capital stock, the firm's investment is swifter.

According to the model the firm, in each period, plans on bridging only a fraction of the gap that exists between the desired and the actual capital stocks.

At the end of current period, the actual stock of capital is

$$K_0 = K_{-1} + \beta(K^* - K_{-1})$$

where, K_{-1} = capital stock at the end of preceding period

K^* = desired capital stock

$(K^* - K_{-1})$ = gap between the desired and the actual capital stock

Net investment to be achieved by the firm is

$$I = K_0 - K_{-1}$$

$$I = \beta (K^* - K_{-1})$$

The larger is the value of β, the quicker is the reduction in the gap between the desired and the actual capital stock. The investment function shows that the desired stock of capital, K^*, and the actual stock of capital, K_{-1}, together determine the level of current spending. Any factor that is responsible for an increase in the desired capital stock also leads to an increase in the rate of investment.

The factors that are responsible for an increase in the rate of investment are as follows:

(1) An increase in the investment tax credit.

(2) An increase in the expected level of output.

(3) A decrease in the real rate of interest.

The flexible accelerator theory emphasizes that:

(1) Net investment adjusts gradually over a period of time.

(2) Investment shows the various aspects of a firm's dynamic behaviour.

The *q* Theory of Investment

This theory is based on the relationship between investment and the stock market. The relationship between the stock market and investment was first put forward by James Tobin.

According to the theory, q is the ratio of a firm's market value (capitalization) to the replacement cost of capital. Hence, it is an assessment of the value placed on the firm's assets by the stock market in comparison to the cost of producing those assets.

A high q ratio implies that a firm will like to increase the production. Thus, there will be an increase in investment. Hence, a high q indicates a high investment. For example, if the value of q is larger than one it implies that a firm should increase the investment level. For every rupee worth of new machinery, a firm will be able to sell rupee q worth of stocks and hence make a profit equal to $q - 1$. Hence, when the value of q is greater than one it implies a flurry of investment.

RECAP

- According to the accelerator theory, given an unchanged capital output ratio, as the output changes the desired stock of capital will also change.
- If the accelerator is greater than one, then the increase in the capital stock will be greater than the increase in the output.
- The flexible accelerator theory emphasizes that net investment adjusts gradually over a period of time.
- The *q* theory of investment is based on the relationship between investment and the stock market

SUMMARY

INTRODUCTION

1. The chapter analyses the relationship between investment and the rate of interest and also the responsiveness of investment to the rate of interest.
2. We attempt at determining the factors that influence the investment decisions. We also examine some of the theories of investment spending.

BASIC CONCEPTS

1. Capital is the accumulated stock of plant and equipment, which is held by the business firms.

2. Investment can be defined as the value of that portion of an economy's output for any period of time that takes the form of new producer's durable equipment, new structures and the change in inventories. In the long run, it is the investment that determines the stock of capital and hence the long-run growth in the economy.
3. As different factors influence the different types of investment, there can be no single investment theory which is applicable to all the different types of investment.

GROSS AND NET INVESTMENT

1. Gross investment consists of two parts: the replacement investment, which is required to keep the capital stock intact and the net investment which is required to expand the existing capital stock.
2. Net investment is equal to gross investment minus depreciation. In fact, net investment is an accretion to the stock of capital.
3. Other things remaining unchanged, for example, given the labour force, technology and natural resources, an accretion to the stock of capital increases the economy's productive capacity.

PUBLIC AND PRIVATE INVESTMENT

1. Public investment refers to the investment in the public sector and private investment refers to the investment in the private sector.
2. The motivating factor behind public investment is social welfare where as private investment is guided by the profit motive.

INDUCED AND AUTONOMOUS INVESTMENT

1. Investment that changes due to a change in income and the interest rate is called induced investment.
2. In general, the investment function can be expressed as $I = I(Y, i)$. While investment is positively related to the income level, there is a negative relationship between investment and the rate of interest.
3. Investment that does not change due to a change in income and the interest rate is called autonomous investment.
4. Most of the investments in the public sector are autonomous as they are made for considerations other than profit, some of the investments in the private sector may also be autonomous.

THE DECISION TO INVEST

1. The decision to invest is different as compared to the decision to buy consumer goods.
2. Most capital goods have a long life and one can learn only several years later as to whether the investment in these capital goods has been profitable or not.
3. A firm's investment decision is based on the relationship between three elements: (i) expected income flow from capital good under consideration, (ii) the purchase price of the good in question and (iii) the rate of interest prevailing in the market.

PRESENT VALUE OF A CAPITAL ASSET AND DISCOUNTING

1. To make its investment decision, a firm compares the present value of the capital asset with its purchase price or the supply price.
2. The supply price of a capital asset is the cost of replacing the capital asset, which is under consideration, with a new one.
3. The present value of a capital asset is the sum obtained after discounting the expected future yields over its entire life at the market rate of interest. The higher the market rate of interest the lower is the present value.
4. The discounting process is the process by which a future sum is converted into its present value.
5. In general if an amount if an amount R_0 is invested for a period of n years at a market rate of interest, r, the amount the individual will receive at the end of the n years: $R_n = R_0 (1 + r)^n$
6. $\frac{R_n}{(1+r)^n}$ = the discounted present value of R_n
7. The present value of the bond is
$$V = \frac{R}{(1+r)} + \frac{R}{(1+r)^2} + \frac{R}{(1+r)^3} + \cdots + \frac{R}{(1+r)^n} + \frac{P}{(1+r)^n}$$
8. The present value of a machine is
$$V = \frac{R_1}{(1+r)} + \frac{R_2}{(1+r)^2} + \frac{R_3}{(1+r)^3} + \cdots + \frac{R_n}{(1+r)^n} + \frac{J}{(1+r)^n}$$

THE MARGINAL EFFICIENCY OF CAPITAL

1. We assume that we are given the following: the income stream from the capital asset, R_1, R_2, R_3, ..., R_n and; cost or purchase price of the capital asset, C.

2. Given C and $R_1, R_2, R_3, \ldots, R_n$ we wish to find i, which is the rate of return expected from a particular capital asset. It is also called the marginal efficiency of capital, MEC.
3. Once the MEC is determined, a comparison of the market rate of interest with the MEC will enable one to make a decision as to whether the investment in the capital asset is profitable or not.
4. The difference between the MEC and the market rate of interest is the net rate of return expected after allowance is made for all costs.
5. The basic rule for making a decision is that if the MEC is greater than the market rate of interest, then the purchase of the capital asset is worthwhile and if the MEC is smaller than the market rate of interest, then the purchase of the capital asset is not worthwhile.

THE MARGINAL EFFICIENCY OF CAPITAL SCHEDULE AND THE RATE OF INVESTMENT

1. A firm, often, has variety of investment projects among which it has to make a choice.
2. In making its decision, a firm will compare the MEC of the capital asset with the current market rate of interest.
3. For every firm, the MEC schedule will resemble the stair like curve in Figure 10.1.
4. Once the MECs for all the firms are added together horizontally, the steps would all even out and we can arrive at the downward sloping and a smooth aggregate MEC schedule.
5. The equilibrium amount of investment is determined at the intersection of the aggregate MEC schedule and the curve representing the rate of interest.

THE MARGINAL EFFICIENCY OF INVESTMENT

1. When all the firms in the industry increase their stock of capital, the capitals goods industry will not only take a long time to produce the additional output but it may have to install extra capacity which may lead to increased costs and thus increasing price of the capital goods.
2. The marginal efficiency of investment (MEI) schedule depicts the relationship between the economy's investment and rate of interest when the change in the price of capital goods is taken into consideration.
3. The MEI schedule represents the true investment demand schedule for the economy as a whole. The MEI schedule is downward sloping showing a negative relationship between the level of investment and the rate of interest.

CHANGES IN THE RATE OF INTEREST, THE MEC AND CAPITAL ACCUMULATION

FALL IN THE RATE OF INTEREST AND CAPITAL ACCUMULATION

1. Here we attempt at explaining the process by which capital accumulation occurs in response to a decrease in the market rate of interest.
2. We assume that the supply curve of capital goods is upward sloping.
3. The concavity of the MEI schedule is due to the increasing cost of the capital goods.
4. There is a decrease in the market rate of interest. The desired stock of capital increases.
5. The important question here is how long it will take the firms to increase the capital stock to the desired level.
6. In each period, there is an increase in the capital stock and the process will continue till the actual stock of capital gradually increases over time to the optimum level.
7. In each period, the net investment is smaller as compared to the previous period.
8. Given the MEC schedule (which does not shift), net investment is determined by the rate of interest and the size of the capital stock.

A SHIFT IN THE MEC SCHEDULE AND CAPITAL ACCUMULATION

1. In this section, we attempt at explaining the process by which capital accumulation occurs in response to an upward shift in the MEC schedule, given the market rate of interest.
2. Suppose the MEC schedule shifts upwards. Given the market rate of interest, there is an increase in the profit maximizing or the desired capital stock.

3. The important question here again is how long it will take the firms to increase the capital stock.
4. In each period, there is an increase in the capital stock and the process will continue till the actual stock of capital gradually increases over time to the optimum level.
5. Thus given the rate of interest, an upward shift in the MEC schedule generates conditions which are apt for investment.
6. The process of investment, or in other words the process of capital accumulation, will continue till the actual capital stock is equal to the desired capital stock. At this level, investment activity will cease as the MEC is equal to the market rate of interest.

THEORIES OF INVESTMENT

ACCELERATOR THEORY OF INVESTMENT

1. The simple accelerator model states that investment is proportional to the change in the level of output and is not influenced by the cost of capital.
2. According to this approach, the rate of investment spending depends on the output level. At a particular point in time, there exists a particular capital output ratio which is considered to be the desired ratio for the economy as a whole.
3. The net investment in time period, *t*, depends on the change in the output level between time periods t and $t-1$ multiplied by the capital output ratio.
4. Investment will change if there is a change in the output level. However, it is assumed that there is no excess capacity.
5. The basic relationship that exists between the investment and the change in the output level is known as the accelerator principle. The capital output ratio, *k*, is known as the accelerator. The investment theory that is based on the above relationship is known as the accelerator theory.
6. If the accelerator is greater than one, then the increase in the capital stock will be greater than the increase in the output. Thus, the increase in the investment is greater than the increase in the output that is responsible for the increase in it.
7. Due to its rigid assumptions, the accelerator theory has been subject to severe criticisms. Also it appears that the accelerator principle does not work during periods of recession when there exists excess capacity. The accelerator principle is based on calculations about the future, which are not necessarily accurate.

THE FLEXIBLE ACCELERATOR MODEL

1. The main idea in the flexible accelerator model is that whenever there exists a large gap between the firm's existing capital stock and the desired capital stock, the firm's investment is swifter.
2. According to this model the firm, in each period, plans on bridging only a fraction of the gap that exists between the desired and the actual capital stocks.
3. The investment function shows that the desired stock of capital and the actual stock of capital together determine the level of current spending.
4. qThe flexible accelerator theory emphasizes that net investment adjusts gradually over a period of time.

THE *q* THEORY OF INVESTMENT

1. This theory is based on the relationship between investment and the stock market. The relationship between the stock market and investment was first put forward by James Tobin.
2. According to this theory, *q* is the ratio of a firm's market value (capitalization) to the replacement cost of capital.
3. A high *q* indicates a high investment.

REVIEW QUESTIONS

TRUE OR FALSE QUESTIONS

1. Investment that changes due to a change in income and the interest rate is called autonomous investment.
2. The present value of a capital asset is the sum obtained after discounting the expected future yields over its entire life at the market rate of interest.

3. The supply price of a capital asset is the cost of replacing the capital asset, which is under consideration, with an old one.
4. For every firm, the MEC schedule is a stair like curve where as the aggregate MEC schedule is a downward sloping curve.
5. The MEC schedule represents the true investment demand schedule for the economy as a whole.

VERY SHORT-ANSWER QUESTIONS

1. What is the difference between induced and autonomous investment?
2. Differentiate between public and private investment.
3. Which are the three elements, which determine a firm's investment decision?
4. What is the difference between a firm's MEC schedule and the aggregate MEC schedule? Discuss.
5. What is the marginal efficiency of investment schedule?

SHORT-ANSWER QUESTIONS

1. What is capital? How is it different from investment?
2. Distinguish between gross investment and net investment.
3. 'The decision to invest is different as compared to the decision to buy consumer goods.' Comment.
4. On which three factors does a firm's investment decision depend? Discuss.
5. 'MEI schedule represents the true investment demand schedule for the economy as a whole.' Comment.

LONG-ANSWER QUESTIONS

1. Write short notes on the following:
   (i) Capital and Investment
   (ii) Gross and Net Investment
   (iii) Public and Private Investment
   (iv) Induced and Autonomous Investment
2. What is the present value of a capital asset? How is it related to discounting? Explain.
3. What is the marginal efficiency of capital? How can we arrive at the aggregate marginal efficiency of capital schedule?
4. (a) Analyse the effect of a decrease in the rate of interest on capital accumulation.
   (b) Analyse the effect of an upward shift in the MEC schedule on capital accumulation.
5. Write short notes on the following theories of investment:
   (i) Accelerator Theory of Investment
   (ii) The Flexible Accelerator Model
   (iii) The *q* Theory of Investment

ANSWERS

TRUE OR FALSE QUESTIONS

1. **False.** Investment that changes due to a change in income and the interest rate is called induced investment.
2. **True.** The higher is the market rate of interest the lower is the present value. In the extreme case if the market rate of interest is zero, then the present value is equal to the expected future yield.
3. **False.** The supply price of a capital asset is the cost of replacing the capital asset, which is under consideration, with a new one.
4. **True.** For every firm, the MEC schedule will resemble the stair like curve. However, once the MEC's for all the firms are added together horizontally the steps would all even out and we can arrive at the aggregate MEC schedule which is a downward sloping and smooth curve.
5. **False.** The MEI schedule represents the true investment demand schedule for the economy as a whole.

Money

After studying this topic, you should be able to understand

- ✓ *Money evolved in a set pattern in the different societies as commodity money, metallic money, paper money and deposit money.*
- ✓ *The conventional approach to the definition of money lays emphasis on the medium of exchange, function of money and the importance of money as a measure of value.*
- ✓ *The Gurley and Shaw school of thought argues that the definition of money should be a weighted sum of the different financial assets.*
- ✓ *The Central Bank view is to include in the definition of money not only all the existing means of payment but also the credit flowing to the borrowers.*
- ✓ *Traditionally, only currency and demand deposits were included under money.*
- ✓ *The primary functions of money include money as a medium of exchange and as a measure of value.*
- ✓ *The secondary functions of money include money as a standard of deferred payments and as a store of value.*
- ✓ *If money had not been invented, we perhaps would have been still in the ancient ages moving at a very slow rate of growth.*

INTRODUCTION

There was no money in any economy in the initial stages of development. The system which was prevalent was the barter system in which there was a direct exchange of one commodity for the other. The barter system, to be successful, requires a double coincidence of wants; for each party involved in the exchange must not only have the commodity which the other party requires, but it must also be in the right quantity and at the right time.

Barter can be successful in the initial stages of development. However, later on when man's wants multiply and there are a large number of people, each engaged in a different profession, then the barter system is inadequate to cater to the variety of needs of the economy. What is required is a convenient form of exchange, which is possible only with money.

EVOLUTION AND FORMS OF MONEY

As to the evolution of money, there are no certain answers. However, it is of great interest to note that there seems to be a set pattern in which money evolved in the different societies. Let's learn about its evolutionary stages:

Commodity Money

In the earlier stages, money took the form of commodity money. There were amazing varieties like seashells, furs, skins, rice, wheat, utensils and weapons. They certainly did not possess the essential qualities of money, namely divisibility, portability, durability and homogeneity.

BOX 11.1

Evidence does not support the existence of any economy that solely relied and functioned through the barter system. It is quite possible that barter like methods were used even 1,00,000 years ago. Mostly, the societies which existed functioned along the system of gift economics to the extent that though barter existed, it was mostly between strangers.

Metallic Money

As society progressed, money left its earlier abode in the form of commodities to move to metals. Initially pieces of iron, copper, brass, silver and gold were money. Later on, coins were issued which were initially very crude but as time progressed there was an improvement in their quality. Coins now are only token money because the intrinsic (metallic) value of a token coin is less than its face value.

Paper Money

It is believed that paper money originated with the advent of the receipts given by the goldsmiths to those who deposited their money with them for purposes of safe keeping. As time progressed, these receipts took the form of bank notes. Much later, it acquired the form of paper money issued by the government/banking institutions.

Deposit Money

Deposit money or chequeable deposits are entries in the ledgers of the bank to the credit of the holder.

As the banking system evolved, a development took place in the form of deposit money. Unlike coins and currency notes, deposit money cannot be passed on from hand to hand to transfer purchasing power. Deposit money or chequeable deposits are entries in the ledgers of the bank to the credit of the holder. These deposits can be transferred by cheques. It is in this respect that they serve as a medium of exchange or as a means of payment.

As both currency notes and coins are legal tender under the law, no one can refuse the same in the course of settlement of transactions. This is not the case for demand deposits, which are not legal tender money and are accepted on trust. A person has a right to refuse to accept a payment made through a cheque and can insist on a cash payment (though income-tax related laws in a country may penalize cash payments for transactions above a certain limit, as a means to counter black money).

RECAP

- Deposit money are entries in the ledgers of the bank to the credit of the holder.
- Deposits can be transferred by cheques and it is in this respect that they serve as a medium of exchange.

BOX 11.2

Paper money or currency notes are simply pieces of paper with no intrinsic value. Then what is the implication of the legend on the RBI's currency note of, say, a hundred rupees, signed by the Governor of the RBI that 'I promise to pay the bearer the sum of one hundred rupees'? It is interesting to note that this is in fact a legacy of the past when the currency notes were convertible into silver rupees. Today, it means that the notes can be converted into coins or other notes of some other denominations only.

DEFINITION OF MONEY

Economists have come up with innumerable definitions of money, emphasizing different aspects of money. Broadly speaking, we can group them under two different approaches:

The Conventional Approach

This is perhaps one of the oldest approaches to the definition of money. It basically lays emphasis on the most important functions of money, namely, the medium of exchange function and the importance of money as a measure of value.

According to this approach, any commodity that satisfies these two functions would be termed as money, irrespective of the fact that it may not have any backing of the government. Thus, various things which have served as money include courie shells, cows, goats, rice, silver and gold pieces, etc. They were treated as money as long as they satisfied the two functions, which money was supposed to perform.

The Modern Approach

Lately, it has been felt that the conventional approach to the definition of money is too restrictive. Money certainly does much more than being just a medium of exchange and a measure of value. It performs many other functions and any definition of money, it is felt, should reflect these functions of money.
Broadly speaking, there can be three schools of thought:

The Chicago School of Thought

Associated with the monetarists led by Milton Friedman, Schwartz and many others, this approach lays emphasis on extending the conventional definition of money to include not only currency and demand deposits but time deposits also. The traditional approach is against the inclusion of time deposits in the definition of money because, according to the protagonists of this approach, time deposits cannot be spent directly and hence are not money.

This group has put forward two arguments in support of the inclusion of time deposits in the definition of money, which are as follows:

(1) There exists a correlation between the national income and money. This correlation is higher if time deposits are included in the definition of money.
(2) The definition of money should include the close substitutes of money and time deposits certainly fall in this category.

Gurley and Shaw School of Thought

Attributed to John G. Gurley and Edward S. Shaw, this approach goes a step ahead in that it attempts to include the liabilities of non-bank financial intermediaries in the definition of money.

The approach argues that these are alternative stores of value but differ in the degree of their substitutability to currency and demand deposits. Thus, the definition of money should be a weighted sum of these different financial assets including currency, demand deposits, time deposits and the liabilities of non-bank financial intermediaries like post office saving deposits. The weights should be assigned to the financial assets on the basis of their substitutability to money. In spite of the theoretical superiority of this approach, its practicality is very limited as it is very difficult to assign weights to the different assets as it is difficult to determine and assess their closeness to money.

The Central Bank View

This is a much broader view of the whole concept. The Radcliffe Committee of the United States had put forward this approach to include in the definition of money not only all the existing means of payment but the credit flowing to the borrowers also. Thus, under this definition all credit funds which are lent to the borrowers is a part of money. The committee argued that as credit can be substituted for money without any limit, all credit outstanding is relevant in the definition of money.

This approach is more practical as it realizes the importance and the influence of the varied financial assets in the formulation of the monetary policy of an economy. On the basis of this approach, depending on the economy's objectives and the monetary policy, the central bank of a country may come up with different measures of money supply. In India, the RBI publishes data on M_1, M_2, M_3 and M_4, which quantify the money supply in the economy under four escalating categories.

Money is anything that is generally accepted as a means of payment in the settlement of transactions.

For the sake of convenience, we can define money simply as anything that is generally accepted as a means of payment in the settlement of transactions. Money is acceptable in any transaction because of the conviction that later on in the course of any another transaction the same would be accepted in payment by others. This implies that money can take any form starting from courie shells to goats to gold and silver pieces to currency notes. One of the most important features of money is that it is generally acceptable. Money alone is acceptable by all in the settlement of transactions. It does not need to be converted into something else.

RECAP

- The conventional approach is against the inclusion of time deposits in the definition of money.
- The Chicago school of thought extends the conventional definition of money to include not only currency and demand deposits but time deposits also.
- The Gurley and Shaw school of thought goes a step further in that it attempts to include the liabilities of non-bank financial intermediaries in the definition of money.
- The Central Bank view is that all credit outstanding is relevant in the definition of money.

MONEY AND NEAR MONEY

Traditionally, economists often differentiated between money and near money assets. Only those monetary assets—namely, currency and demand deposits—which could be used as a medium of exchange and in addition as a store of value were included under money. Non-monetary assets like stocks, bonds, time deposits and treasury bills, which are stores of value but do not circulate as a medium of exchange and are not used for making payments were all treated as near money. It was felt that as near money is just a claim over money, they should be treated separately from money.

Recent innovations in the financial sector, however, portray a different scenario. The non-monetary assets like stocks, bonds, time deposits and others have, over time, become quite liquid just like the monetary assets. On the other hand, monetary assets are gaining popularity as stores of value and, hence, are in no way less than non-monetary assets as stores of value.

The public often finds it easy to switch from one type of asset to another. This has implications for the policy makers in that it dilutes the effect of the policy. As these non-monetary assets are not subject to the same stringent requirements as the monetary assets, they may often complicate matters for the policy makers.

BOX 11.3

Fiat money is the money the value for which is determined legally. It serves as money on the fiat or order of the government. In India, coins and currency are the fiat money because they serve as money on the order or fiat of the Government of India.

RECAP

- Non-monetary assets like stocks, bonds, time deposits and treasury bills were all treated as near money.

FUNCTIONS OF MONEY

The functions of money can be, broadly speaking, grouped into two categories, which are as follows:

Primary Functions of Money

These refer to the basic functions or what we can call the original functions of money. These include:

Money as a Medium of Exchange

This is the primary function of money. Money alone can perform this function, which is a distinguishing characteristic of money and which differentiates it from near money. In fact, all the other functions of money can be derived from this basic function of money.

The use of money as a medium of exchange has certain advantages. Some of them are as follows:

(1) It avoids the wastage of time and resources involved in exchange and are thus an essential ingredient of a barter economy. Hence, it promotes a transactional efficiency in the exchange of goods and services.

(2) It promotes an allocational efficiency in that there exists specialization in the trade and production of goods and services.

Money as a Measure of Value or as a Unit of Account

Money serves as a common denominator in terms of which the value of all other commodities is expressed. All the prices are quoted in terms of money. These values, per unit of the good or service, expressed in terms of money are what we call the price of a good or service.

The use of money as a measure of account has certain advantages. Some of them are as follows:

(1) As price of the goods and services are expressed in terms of a common denominator, money, it is easy to compare them and calculate the rate of exchange between the two goods. In a system where money does not exist, there will be an innumerable number of such ratios between the different goods.

(2) The use of money makes it possible to have meaningful accounting systems by adding up the value of goods and services, which are of a wide variety and measured in terms of different units.

(3) Important estimates of value totals like the national income can be compared across time and between nations by comparing the different exchange rates that are all expressed in terms of a common denominator, money.

(4) Production, consumption and distribution all can be expressed in terms of money, which facilitates a comparison between them.

The disadvantage of money as a measure of value is that it may not be very accurate. This is because the value of money is itself subject to change and keeps varying over time. This is not so with the physical measures like meter, kilogram, etc.

Secondary Functions of Money

These, though important functions of money, are actually derived from the primary functions of money.

Money as a Standard of Deferred Payments

Deferred or future payments include payment of interest, rents, salaries, insurance premium, pensions and loans. All these are expressed in terms of money. Thus, money is used in long-term transactions. During the barter system such payments did exist, but they lacked the general acceptability, durability and homogeneity of money.

It is to be noted that the use of money as a standard of deferred payments is laden with problems in that its value itself is subject to fluctuations through inflation or deflation.

Money as a Store of Value

Liquidity can be defined as the ease with which an asset can be converted into cash at short notice and without any/least loss. It is obvious that money is the only asset, which is perfectly liquid.

The public holds or stores its wealth in the form of money. Thus, money is an asset that retains value over time. This function of money has actually been derived from the function of money as a medium of exchange.

In a barter system there existed only one transaction, a simultaneous purchase and sale. However, under a money economy this gets split up into two separate transactions consisting of a sale and a purchase. This is possible only if money can not only serve as a medium of exchange but also serve as a store of value.

Salaries, rents and loans are payments all of which are a part of a money using economy. They are received in the form of money at time intervals and are spent gradually. This is possible only if money is a store of value.

Money is able to store value only because it is a medium of exchange and acceptable to all as a general purchasing power and the only asset, which is perfectly liquid. Other assets like bonds and stocks also serve as store of value. However, the unique feature of money that differentiates it from other such assets is that it alone is perfectly liquid, unlike the other assets which must be converted into money first.

Liquidity can be defined as the ease with which an asset can be converted into cash at short notice and without any/least loss. It is obvious that money is the only asset, which is perfectly liquid.

However, it is to be noted that the use of money as a store of value is again subject to the same problems in that its value itself is subject to fluctuations that may strongly influence it in performing its role as a store of value.

RECAP

- The unique feature of money is that it alone is perfectly liquid.
- The main problem in the use of money is that its value itself is subject to fluctuations.

SIGNIFICANCE OF MONEY

In today's world, money plays an important role. It is not true to say that an economy cannot survive without money. The so-called mythical barter economy where every transaction involved an exchange of goods for goods did survive for years and years without money. However, what is to be emphasized is that had money not been invented we perhaps would have been still in the ancient ages moving at a very slow growth rate.

In a modern economy, money performs several functions; some of them are as follows:

(1) **Resource allocation in an economy:** In a modern economy, it has been possible to produce the large variety of goods only with the advent of money. The role of money starts right from the purchase of the factors of production and the raw materials to the evaluation of the cost of production and the estimates of profits. Thus, money plays a crucial role in solving the three basic economic problems of what, how and for whom to produce.

(2) **Consumption in an economy:** In a barter economy, due to the double coincidence of wants, the consumer could not get all that he desired. However, the existence of money makes it possible for the consumer to maximize his utility, given his income and the prices of the goods. He is able to assert the full power of money by satisfying his needs to the utmost within the constraints of the money he has at his disposal. Certainly with the power of money, the consumer feels no less than a king.

(3) **Distribution in an economy:** The distribution of incomes to the different factors of production—wages to labour, rent to land, interest to capital and profits to the entrepreneur—are all possible because money is there to reward each according to his marginal productivity.

(4) **Development of an organized credit and money market in an economy:** In a barter economy, borrowing was possible in the form of goods. This limited the borrowings and prevented a credit market from emerging. The arrival of money encouraged and provided the avenue for some to borrow and others to lend.

(5) **Introducing dynamism in an economy:** To some extent the credit for bringing dynamism in any economy goes to the monetary authorities, which by the efficient utilization of their credit and monetary policies, are able to not only trigger growth but are also able to sustain this growth. The different economies of the world are, at present, trying to experiment with their credit and monetary policies to try to come out of the recession, which is affecting the growth of almost all the economies of the world.

RECAP

- In a modern economy, money performs several functions like resource allocation in an economy and distribution of incomes among the different factors of production.

SUMMARY

INTRODUCTION

1. The barter system was prevalent in the initial stages of development.
2. The barter system to be successful requires a double coincidence of wants.

EVOLUTION AND FORMS OF MONEY

1. There seems to be a set pattern in which money evolved in the different societies.
2. In the earlier stages, money took the form of commodity money.
3. As society progressed, money left its earlier abode in the form of commodities to move to metallic money.
4. It is believed that paper money originated with the advent of the receipts given by the goldsmiths to those who deposited their money with them for purposes of safe keeping. As time progressed, these receipts took the form of bank notes.
5. As the banking system evolved, a development took place in the form of deposit money.

DEFINITION OF MONEY

1. Economists have come up with innumerable definitions of money. We can group them under two different approaches.
2. The Conventional Approach is perhaps one of the oldest approaches to the definition of money and lays emphasis on the most important functions of money, namely, the medium of exchange function and the importance of money as a measure of value.
3. The Modern Approach where there can be three schools of thought.
4. The Chicago school of thought lays emphasis on extending the conventional definition of money to include not only currency and demand deposits but time deposits also.
5. Gurley and Shaw school of thought goes a step ahead in that it attempts to include the liabilities of non-bank financial intermediaries in the definition of money.
6. Central Bank view includes in the definition of money not only all the existing means of payment but also the credit flowing to the borrowers.

MONEY AND NEAR MONEY

1. Traditionally, economists often differentiated between money and near money assets.
2. Money includes currency and demand deposits.

3. Non-monetary assets like stocks, bonds, time deposits and treasury bills were all treated as near money.
4. Recent innovations in the financial sector portray that though the non-monetary assets have, over time, become quite liquid, the monetary assets are gaining popularity as stores of value.

FUNCTIONS OF MONEY

1. Primary functions of money include medium of exchange and measure of value or a unit of account.
2. Medium of exchange is the primary function of money, which differentiates it from near money.
3. Measure of value or a unit of account is where money serves as a common denominator in terms of which the value or price of all other commodities are expressed.
4. Secondary functions of money are derived from the primary functions of money. They include money as a standard of deferred payments and as a store of value.
5. Deferred or future payments include payment of interest, rents, salaries, insurance premium, pensions and loans, all of which are expressed in terms of money.
6. The public holds or stores its wealth in the form of money. Salaries, rents and loans are received in the form of money at certain time intervals and are spent gradually.
7. The unique feature of money that differentiates it from other such assets is that it alone is perfectly liquid.

SIGNIFICANCE OF MONEY

1. Money performs the function of allocation of resources in a modern economy and helps in solving the three basic economic problems of what, how and for whom to produce.
3. It performs the function of consumption in an economy. The consumer is able to assert the full power of money by satisfying his needs to the utmost within the constraints of the money he has at his disposal.
4. It performs the function of distribution of incomes to the different factors of production in an economy rewarding each according to its marginal productivity.
5. It leads to the development of an organized credit and money market in an economy.
6. It introduces dynamism in an economy by the efficient utilization of credit and monetary policies.

REVIEW QUESTIONS

TRUE OR FALSE QUESTIONS

1. The barter system, to be successful, requires a double coincidence of wants.
2. Commodity money had the essential qualities of money, namely divisibility, portability, durability and homogeneity.
3. Coins now are only token money.
4. Traditionally, non-monetary assets like stocks, bonds and time deposits were all treated as money.
5. Had money not been invented, we perhaps would have been still in the ancient ages.

VERY SHORT-ANSWER QUESTIONS

1. What is the barter system of direct exchange?
2. Name the different forms in which money has evolved over time.
3. What are the views of the Chicago school of thought regarding the definition of money?
4. Why is the function of money as a medium of exchange said to be the primary function of money?
5. Name the five functions performed by money in a modern economy.

SHORT-ANSWER QUESTIONS

1. Write short notes on commodity money and metallic money?
2. What is the conventional approach to the definition of money?
3. Write a short note on the primary functions of money.
4. Write a short note on the secondary functions of money.
5. Write a short note on the Central Bank view to the definition of money.

LONG-ANSWER QUESTIONS

1. Discuss the evolution of money throwing light on the different forms of money, which have emerged at different periods of time.
2. Define money by using the different approaches that economists have put forward.
3. What are money and near money assets? Differentiate between the two.
4. What are the primary and secondary functions of money? Which among the two are the more important functions of money?
5. What is the significance of money in an economy? How important is money for an economy to function?

ANSWERS

TRUE OR FALSE QUESTIONS

1. **True.** Each party, which is involved in the exchange must not only have the commodity which the other party requires, but it must also be in the right quantity and at the right time.
2. **False.** Commodity money certainly did not posses the essential qualities of money, namely divisibility, portability, durability and homogeneity.
3. **True.** Coins now are only token money as the intrinsic metallic value of a token coin is less than its face value.
4. **False.** These non-monetary assets like stocks, bonds and time deposits that are stores of value but do not circulate as a medium of exchange were all treated as near money.
5. **True.** Had money not been invented, we perhaps would have been still in the ancient ages moving at a very slow growth rate.

12 Supply of Money

After studying this topic, you should be able to understand

- ✓ *In India, the RBI publishes data on the alternative measures of money supply.*
- ✓ *In fractional reserve banking system, banks utilize some of their deposits for making loans and keep some as reserves for withdrawals by the depositors.*
- ✓ *High-powered money is money produced by the government and the central bank and held in the hands of the public and the banks.*
- ✓ *The lending and the borrowing activities of the commercial banks lead to credit creation.*

INTRODUCTION

As already discussed in the previous chapter, there is no single definition of what constitutes money in any economy. But the problem is that money is a very important variable and, hence, cannot be just ignored. In this chapter, we discuss the theory of money supply or what is often called the *H* theory of money supply. We also examine the measures of money supply in India. We will discuss in detail that the money supply in an economy is determined not only by the monetary authorities but also by the banking system through the creation of credit.

MEASURES OF MONEY SUPPLY IN INDIA

Before we embark on the measures of money supply, it is imperative to make certain important observations regarding money:

(1) The supply of money is a stock variable (as compared to, say income which is a flow variable) and refers to the stock of money at a point in time.

(2) When we measure the supply of money, it is the money in the hands of the 'public', by which we mean the households, firms and institutions (like the non-bank financial institutions).The government (including the Central and the State governments) and the banking system are not a part of the 'public', and are in fact the producers of money. The Central Bank and all banks that accept demand deposits form a part of the banking system.

As the measurement of money may differ from country to country, we here analyse the different measures of money supply published by the Reserve Bank of India, the RBI.

Until the year 1967–68, the RBI used to publish data only on what is called the narrow measure of money supply. As this definition laid emphasis on the medium of exchange function of money, only currency and demand deposit held by the public were included in the narrow measure of money supply.

From the year 1967–68, RBI started publishing data on the broader measure of money supply in addition to the earlier narrow measure. This is also known as 'aggregate monetary resources' or the AMR. The AMR is based on the liquidity approach, which emphasizes the store of value function of money.

Hence, the AMR includes the time deposits of commercial banks held by the public, in addition to currency and demand deposits.

The RBI publishes data on the following four alternative measures of money supply:

$M_1 = C + DD + OD$

$M_2 = M_1$ + Saving Deposits with Post Offices

$M_3 = M_1$ + Net Time Deposits of Banks

$M_4 = M_3$ + Total Deposits with Post Office Savings Organization (including NSC)

where, C = Currency

DD = Demand deposits of banks

OD = Other deposits of the RBI

NSC = National saving certificates

Before analysing the above measures of money supply, it is necessary to throw some light on the different components included in the measures of money supply. They are:

Currency: Currency includes both the coins and paper notes, though paper notes are the more predominant of the two. Coins and one rupee notes are issued by the Government of India whereas the currency notes of rupees two and higher denominations (including rupees five, ten, twenty, fifty, hundred, five hundred and thousand notes) are issued by the RBI. However, all the currency is put into circulation by the RBI.

Currency includes both the coins and paper notes, though paper notes are the more predominant of the two.

Demand deposits of banks: These are current account deposits, which are payable on demand either by cheque (with no restrictions) or otherwise. There is no interest payment on these deposits, which are generally held by the business firms for their transactions. However, the banks do provide various kinds of services to their account holders. Hence, they serve as a medium of exchange and are therefore included under the narrow definition of money side by side with currency.

Demand deposits of banks are current account deposits, which are payable on demand either by cheque (with no restrictions) or otherwise.

Time deposits of banks: These are fixed term deposits where the term of the deposit may vary. Unlike demand deposits, time deposits are not payable on demand. Also, cheques cannot be issued against them. They are interest earning deposits where the interest rises as the term of the deposit increases. They can be withdrawn before the maturity period but only with a loss of interest.

Time deposits of banks are fixed term deposits where the term of the deposit may vary and, in addition, they are not payable on demand.

Savings account deposits: These combine features of both the demand deposits and the time deposits. Like demand deposits, they are payable on demand and withdrawable by cheques, though the chequing facilities are limited. Like time deposits, they earn an interest. Because of these very characteristics that they possess, saving deposits are held only by households for their short term savings. Business firms cannot hold a savings account.

Savings account deposits are payable on demand and withdrawable by cheques, though the chequing facilities are limited and in addition they earn an interest.

Time deposits with post offices: These include recurring deposits and cumulative time deposits. The depositor makes a regular deposit of a fixed sum for over a certain time period.

Saving deposits with post offices: These are deposits with the post offices, which are withdrawable on demand though that can only be done by withdrawal slips on which there are restrictions and also limits. Hence, the encashability of these deposits is very restricted and therefore they do not serve as a medium of exchange.

Other deposits of the RBI: These are deposits of the RBI other than those held by the government (both the Central and the State governments) and the banks. These deposits include demand deposits of quasi government institutions, IMF, World Bank, foreign central banks and governments, and others. As these other deposits form a very small proportion of the total money supply, they are often ignored.

National saving certificates is a tax saving instrument for purposes of investing long-term savings available at all post offices in India being a combination of both high safety and adequate returns.

National Saving Certificates (NSC): NSC is a tax saving instrument available at all post offices in India. It is a saving instrument for purposes of investing long-term savings. It is a combination of both high safety and adequate returns. It is also often used by the middle class families in India for saving on their tax. NSCs are available in denominations of Rs. 100, Rs. 500, Rs. 1000, Rs. 5000 and Rs. 10,000. There are no maximum limits on the purchase of the NSCs.

A look at the new series by the RBI brings us to certain conclusions:

(1) What we call M_1 in the new series is actually the old M or what we called the narrow measure of money supply. The only difference between the two is that the new series includes into the picture the net demand deposits of state co-operative banks, central co-operative banks and a part of primary co-operative banks.

(2) What we call M_3 in the new series is actually the AMR or what we called the broad measure of money supply. The only difference between the two is that the new series gives a better treatment to the co-operative banking sector.

(3) In the new series, M_2 and M_4 aim at including into the picture the post office deposits. M_2 includes only the saving deposits with post offices whereas M_4 includes total (saving and time) deposits with post offices.

(4) It is interesting to note that in the new series, the four measures of money supply are in descending order of liquidity with M_1 having the highest liquidity and M_4 having the lowest liquidity.

The RBI publishes data on all the four measures of money supply as they all are useful for purposes of monetary policy.

RECAP

- When we measure the supply of money, it is the money in the hands of the 'public'.
- The new series on the four measures of money is in descending order of liquidity.

THE THEORY OF MONEY SUPPLY

We have assumed till now that the supply of money in any economy is policy determined. But, actually, the supply of money is determined not only by the monetary authorities but also the public and the banks that play an important, if not the major, role in the determination of the supply of money. To simplify the analysis, we assume that there exists a fractional reserve system.

In a hundred per cent reserve banking system (which is just a theoretical concept), banks do not make any loans; in a fractional reserve banking system, banks utilize some of their deposits for making loans on which they charge an interest and keep some as reserves for withdrawals by the depositors. This system is based on the presumption that not all the depositors come at the same time to withdraw their deposits and also in case there are outflows there are inflows also. Hence, a bank needs to keep aside only a fraction of the total deposits as reserves and it gives out the rest in the form of loans.

To understand the theory of money supply (also called the *H* theory of money supply or the money multiplier theory of money supply), it is imperative to understand the difference between money and what we call high-powered money (or the monetary base).

We can define money by using the narrow definition of money as

$$M = C + DD \tag{1}$$

BOX 12.1

In the US, the money supply is measured as four categories in ascending order *M0*, *M1*, *M2* and *M3*. *M0* represents base money and includes coins, bills and deposits of the central bank whereas *M3* represents all the different forms of money, including credit. In the US, the Federal Reserve is responsible for controlling the money supply, in Japan it is the Bank of Japan, in China the People's Bank of China and in UK the Bank of England are the central banks of the respective countries.

where, M = Money
C = Currency
DD = Demand deposits of banks

High-powered money is the money, which is produced by the government and the central bank and held in the hands of the public and the banks. It can be defined as:

High-powered money is the money, which is produced by the government and the central bank and held in the hands of the public and the banks. It can be defined as H = C + R.

$$H = C + R \qquad (2)$$

where, H = High-powered money
C = Currency held by the public
R = Cash reserves held by banks

(We are not including OD, other deposits of the central bank in our analysis as they are a very small proportion of the total money supply.)

A comparison of the above two equations, Eqs. (1) and (2), reveals that currency (C) is common to both the equations, the difference is due to the presence of DD in the equation of money and that of R in the equation of high-powered money. This difference is of great importance in the theory of money supply. DD are created by the banks. But to be able to create them, banks have to maintain an R. In fact in a fractional reserve system, DD are a certain multiple of R. It is this, which gives H a quality of high power, because of which it serves as the basis for the creation of demand deposits.

Dividing Eqs. (1) by (2), we get

$$\frac{M}{H} = \frac{C + \text{DD}}{C + R} \qquad (3)$$

Dividing both the numerator and the denominator of the above equation on the right hand side by DD, we get

$$\frac{M}{H} = \frac{C/\text{DD} + \text{DD}/\text{DD}}{C/\text{DD} + R/\text{DD}}$$

$$\frac{M}{H} = \frac{c + 1}{c + r}$$

$$M = mH$$

where, $m = \frac{c+1}{c+r}$ is the money multiplier

$c = \frac{C}{\text{DD}}$ is the currency demand deposit ratio

$r = \frac{R}{\text{D}}$ is the reserve deposit ratio

Currency deposit ratio: It is the currency held by the public as a fraction of their demand deposits. Both the currency and the demand deposits are a function of the income level and the rate of interest. Hence, they are highly correlated. The currency deposit ratio is determined by the payment practices of the public, and the cost and convenience with which cash can be made available. In addition, this ratio is affected to a large extent by the seasonal patterns; for example, in India it is highest around the Diwali festival.

Currency deposit ratio is the currency held by the public as a fraction of their demand deposits.

Reserve deposit ratio: It is the reserves held by the banks as a fraction of their deposits. (As here D = DD, the reserves will be a fraction of demand deposits.) These reserves of the banks are usually divided under two headings which are as follows:

Reserve deposit ratio is the reserves held by the banks as a fraction of their deposits.

(1) Required reserves: These are those reserves, which every bank is statutorily required to hold. They are also called the Cash Reserve Ratio (CRR).

(2) Excess reserves: These are reserves in excess of the required reserves. Banks hold them voluntarily as 'cash on hand' or 'vault cash' for purposes of meeting currency drains and clearing drains. As these reserves do not earn any interest banks, try to minimize them.

Introduction of Time Deposits: A Broader View

Until now we have only included demand deposits in our analysis, while in practice time deposits are also very important. Hence, we define

$$D = \text{DD} + \text{TD}$$

where,

$$\text{TD} = \text{time deposits}$$

$$t = \frac{\text{TD}}{\text{DD}} \text{ is the time deposit ratio}$$

Time deposit ratio This is the ratio of time deposits to demand deposit. The division between these two deposits is a decision, which is made by the public depending on the terms and conditions offered by the banks on the two deposits.

Time deposit ratio is the ratio of time deposits to demand deposit.

We have

$$D = \text{DD} + \text{TD}$$

Thus,

$$\begin{aligned} R &= r(\text{DD} + \text{TD}) \\ &= r(\text{DD} + t\,\text{DD}) \\ &= r(1 + t)\,\text{DD} \end{aligned}$$

We have Eq. (3) as,

$$\frac{M}{H} = \frac{C + \text{DD}}{C + R}$$

Substituting for R, we get

$$\frac{M}{H} = \frac{C + \text{DD}}{C + r(1 + t)\,\text{DD}} \qquad (4)$$

Dividing both the numerator and the denominator of the above Eq. (4) on the right-hand side by DD, we get

BOX 12.2

In the UK, the behaviour of the money multiplier has undergone a spectacular change in the recent years. During the period 1870–1970, it was quite stable and fluctuated within very narrow limits. However, from the 1970s, the magnitude of the money multiplier has more than doubled.

$$\frac{M}{H} = \frac{C/DD + DD/DD}{C/DD + r(1 + t)\ DD/DD} \quad (5)$$

$$\frac{M}{H} = \frac{c + 1}{c + r(1 + t)} \quad (6)$$

We get the final equation of the *H* theory of money supply as

$$M = \frac{c + 1}{c + r(1 + t)} H \quad (7)$$

We can put it in the form $M = mH$

where, $$m = \frac{c + 1}{c + r(1 + t)}$$

This is the money multiplier equation when time deposits are included in the analysis.

We can put it in the form $M = m(c, t, r)\ H$.

The above equation shows that the determinants of money supply can be grouped under the following two headings:

Those That Influence The High-Powered Money, H

It is important to realize that the changes in *H* are mainly controlled through policies and determined by the public and the banks.

As already discussed, *H* or high-powered money is the money which is produced by the monetary authorities and held by the public and the banks. In India, the central government and the RBI constitute the monetary authorities. Thus money produced by the government, or government currency and money produced by the RBI, or Reserve Bank money constitute the supply of high-powered money. Among the two, government currency and reserve bank money, the more important component of high-powered money is the latter, namely, Reserve Bank money. Hence, the changes in the Reserve Bank money (RBM) are largely responsible for the changes in high-powered money.

Changes in the RBM occur due to changes in the following factors:

(1) Net reserve bank credit to the government
(2) Reserve Bank credit to banks
(3) Reserve Bank credit to development banks
(4) Net foreign exchange assets of the Reserve Bank
(5) Net non-monetary liabilities of the Reserve Bank

Of the above, an increase in the first four factors leads to an increase in the RBM whereas an increase in the last factor will lead to a decrease in the RBM.

Those That Influence The Money Multiplier, m

The changes in '*m*' are mainly endogenous as *c*, *t* and *r* all are behavioural ratios.

The determinants of the money multiplier can be divided under two heads:

(1) The proximate determinants of the money multiplier include the behavioural ratios *c*, *t* and *r*.
In general, there will occur an increase in the money multiplier and hence the money supply when:
   (a) there is a decrease in the *c*, currency deposit ratio. This means that if the public prefers to hold a smaller proportion of *H* in the form of currency and a larger proportion as deposits, then the banks will be able to hold more in the form of reserves and hence they will be able to create more money.
   (b) there is a decrease in the *r*, reserve deposit ratio. This implies that with a lower reserve deposit ratio, the ability of the banks to extend credit increases and hence they will be able to create more money.
   (c) there is a decrease in *t*, time deposit to demand deposit ratio.

(2) The ultimate determinants of the money multiplier include those factors, which influence the proximate determinants of the money multiplier. They are as follows:

(a) As far as the c and t ratios are concerned, they are determined by the public's preferences between currency, demand deposits and time deposits. These factors further depend on the income level, the interest rate, development of the banking system, payments habit of the public and many more factors.

(b) As far as the r ratio is concerned, while the fixation of the cash reserve ratio is a policy decision at the behest of the central bank, the maintenance of excess reserves is an internal decision made by the banks themselves.

The Money Multiplier Process

A discussion relating to the H theory would be incomplete if the actual money multiplier process is not discussed in detail.

Here we discuss as to how a given increase in H leads, over time, to a multiple expansion in bank credit and in the supply of money in the economy.

To analyse the process, some assumptions are necessary, which are as follows:

(1) The only type of deposits with the banks are demand deposits, i.e., $D = DD$.

(2) Commercial banks assets take the form of loans and advances only.

(3) The c ratio is 0.5 whereas the r ratio is 0.1 (where the r ratio includes both the required reserve ratio and the excess reserve ratio).

(4) At the going rate of interest, there is a large demand for bank loans.

(5) There exists a fractional reserve system because of which banks have to maintain only a fraction of its total deposits as cash reserves while the rest can be used for making loans.

Suppose that the government purchases goods worth Rs 600 crores from the public. The payment is made through cheques drawn on the RBI. The public on receipt of the cheques deposits them with their banks, who after the collection, credit the accounts of the depositors. Hence, there is an increase in the deposits of the public as also in the reserves of the banks of an amount of Rs 600 crores. The public withdraws Rs 200 crores as currency (the c ratio is 0.5) and leaves the rest with the banks whose reserves go up by Rs 400 crores. These new reserves are known as primary deposits and it is with these reserves that the credit creation commences.

Out of these additional reserves, the banks keep aside just the required reserves and lends out the rest (the r ratio is 0.1). The process of expansion continues leading to a multiple creation of deposits, credit and money.

The crucial question is to what will be the total increase in the supply of money. To calculate it, we need to first find the value of the money multiplier.

We know that m $= \dfrac{c + 1,}{c + r}$

but $c = 0.5$ and $r = 1.$

BOX 12.3

Since the year 1995, the money multiplier in China showed an upward trend. However, in 1998 there occurred some major financial reforms which led to significant changes. Though initially the money multiplier remained stable, later on it became unstable and difficult to control, with the money multiplier and high-powered money moving in opposite directions. An attempt at increasing the high-powered money to bring about changes in the money supply was accompanied by a decrease in the money multiplier. These developments presented immense challenges and opportunities to the central bank and the framers of the monetary policy.

Hence, $$M = \frac{0.5 + 1}{0.5 + 0.1} = 2.5$$

The total increase in the supply of money = 2.5 × ΔH
= 2.5 × Rs. 600 crores
= Rs. 1500 crores.

It is important to note that the smaller are the *c* and the *r* ratios the larger is the value of the multiplier.

RECAP

- The determinants of money supply can be grouped under two headings: those that influence high-powered money and those that influence the money multiplier.
- A given increase in *H* leads, over time, to a multiple expansion in bank credit and in the supply of money in the economy.

THE PROCESS OF CREDIT CREATION AND THE DEPOSIT MULTIPLIER

One of the most important functions performed by a commercial bank is the creation of credit. In fact, it is the lending and the borrowing activities of the commercial banks that lead to the credit creation.

Bank deposits can be grouped into two categories:

(1) **Primary deposits:** These are deposits that bring in new reserves to the banks.

(2) **Secondary deposits:** They are also called derivative deposits; they are deposits that do not bring in new reserves to the banks. They are created out of the credit extended by the banks.

Credit Creation in a Single Bank Model

We assume that:

(1) There exists a single bank in the banking system.

(2) The bank is only accepting demand deposits.

(3) The *c* ratio is 0.5 whereas the *r* ratio is 0.1 (where the *r* ratio includes both the required reserve ratio and the excess reserve ratio).

(4) The bank's assets include reserves and the loans on which they charge an interest.

In continuation of the earlier example, the government purchases goods worth Rs. 600 crores from the public and makes a payment by a cheque drawn on the RBI. This cheque is deposited by the public with the bank, which collects the payment. The deposits of the public and the reserves of the bank increase by an amount of Rs. 600 crores.

As we have assumed that the currency deposit ratio is 0.5, the public makes a withdrawal of only Rs. 200 crores and leaves the rest Rs. 400 crores with the bank. Thus, Rs. 400 crores worth of deposits is created with the bank. As these deposits bring in new reserves to the bank, they are called primary deposits.

These do not earn any interest. Thus as per the desired reserve ratio of 0.1, the bank keeps aside an amount of Rs. 40 crores and lends out the rest Rs. 360 crores to the borrowers at an interest. Actually, this lending is not in the form of cash. All that happens is that the borrower's account is credited for this particular amount and he can draw cheques for that amount. This is the first round of credit creation.

When the borrower spends the amount, he actually withdraws only a part of the total amount (as per the *c* ratio). Thus, the borrower withdraws Rs. 120 crores and Rs. 240 crores continue to remain with the bank representing an addition to the secondary deposits. It represents a second round increase in deposits and in money.

Out of this amount, the bank again keeps aside a certain amount and lends out the rest. As the proceeds of the loans are spent, the recipients of the payments again deposit them with the bank, leading to another round of credit creation and deposits and money. However, it is to be noted that in each successive round the amount of money involved becomes smaller and smaller. This can be put in the form of an infinite geometric series, which is the same as in the case of the multiple bank model discussed below.

BOX 12.4

It is felt that the economic growth in the recent years all over the world has occurred due to the liberal creation of credit and the liquidity injects at low rates of interests by the central banks. The lenders have been no less instrumental in perpetuating the lending aggressively by offering innovative credit instruments such as credit default swaps (CDS), commercial mortgage backed securities (CMBS), residential mortgage backed securities (RMBS) and others. However, the recent spurt in defaults in the mortgage market, erratic rating issues, etc. have led to a fall in the demand for these instruments and the potential investors no longer take fancy to such investments. This may perhaps be the start of a vicious cycle of liquidity crisis and credit reversal and is capable of significantly impacting the economic growth of the different nations.

Credit Creation in a Multiple Bank Model

Till now, we have assumed that there exists a single bank. However, in reality there exist several banks in the banking system.

Suppose the first bank receives Rs. 10,000 as primary deposits. With a reserve ratio of 10 per cent, the bank will make a loan of Rs. 9000 and keep Rs. 1000 of the deposits as reserves. Hence, there will be a creation of credit. The balance sheet of the first bank will be as shown below:

Balance sheet of the first bank

Liabilities	Amount (Rs.)	Assets	Amount (Rs.)
Deposits	10,000	Cash Balances (Reserves)	1,000
		Loans	9,000
Total	10,000	Total	10,000

The credit creation process will continue as the borrowers deposit the loan amount of Rs. 9,000 with another bank and make use of the loan amount of Rs. 9,000 to make a payment to a creditor who then deposits it with another bank, the second bank. The balance sheet of the second bank will be as shown below:

Balance sheet of the second bank

Liabilities	Amount (Rs.)	Assets	Amount (Rs.)
Deposits	9,000	Cash Balances (Reserves)	900
		Loans	8100
Total	9,000	Total	9000

The amount of Rs. 8100, which is given out as loan by the second bank may eventually get deposited in a third bank whose balance sheet will be as shown below:

Balance sheet of the third bank

Liabilities	Amount (Rs.)	Assets	Amount (Rs.)
Deposits	8100	Cash Balances (Reserves)	810
		Loans	7290
Total	8100	Total	8100

This process continues in the same manner as in the case of the single bank model. The total amount of money created by the banking system can be calculated as follows:

Original Deposit with the first bank = Rs. 10,000
Lending by the first bank $= (1-r) \times 10{,}000$
Lending by the second bank $= (1-r)^2 \times 10{,}000$
Lending by the third bank $= (1-r)^3 \times 10{,}000$

Total money supply

$$= 10{,}000 + (1-r) \times 10{,}000 + (1-r)^2 \times 10{,}000 + (1-r)^3 \times 10{,}000 + \cdots$$
$$= [\,1 + (1-r) + (1-r)^2 + (1-r)^3 + \ldots] \times 10{,}000$$

This is the sum of an infinite geometric series and can be expressed as

$$\text{Total money supply} = \frac{1}{r} \times 10{,}000 = \frac{1}{0.1} \times 10{,}000 = 100{,}000$$

(as we have assumed $r = 10\% = 0.1$)

Thus, the original deposit of Rs. 10,000 will generate a total amount of money equal to Rs. 100,000. It is of extreme importance to understand that under the fractional reserve system, although there is creation of money, there is no creation of wealth as such. Thus there is an increase in the liquidity in the economy, but there is certainly no increase in the economy's wealth.

The Deposit and the Credit Multipliers (in a Simple Model Where There are Only Demand Deposits)

Deposit Multiplier

We have observed that starting with a primary deposit, the banking system is able to create secondary deposits, which are in fact a multiple of the primary deposits. This multiple will depend on the value of the deposit multiplier, D_m.

The deposit multiplier is the ratio of the change in deposits to the change in reserves. Thus

Deposit multiplier is the ratio of the change in deposits to the change in reserves.

$$D_m = \frac{\Delta D}{\Delta R}$$

where,
ΔD = change in deposits
ΔR = change in reserves

Thus, we have

Deposit Multiplier, $$D_m = \frac{1}{c + r}$$

In our example, as c is 0.5 and r is 0.1, the value of the deposit multiplier will be

$$D_m = \frac{1}{0.5 + 0.1} = \frac{1}{0.6} = 1.67$$

The value of the deposit multiplier depends on the following factors:

(1) **The reserve ratio:** Given the currency deposit ratio, the higher the reserve ratio the lower will be the value of the deposit multiplier.

(2) **The currency deposit ratio:** Given the reserve deposit ratio, the higher the currency deposit ratio the lower will be the value of the deposit multiplier. In the extreme case, where there is no currency drain, then the whole of the initial amount of Rs. 600 crores will be deposited with the banking system and the deposit multiplier will be

$$D_m = \frac{1}{0.1} = 10$$

Credit multiplier is the ratio of the change in the amount of credit to the change in reserves.

Credit Multiplier

This is a concept, which is akin to the deposit multiplier. The credit multiplier is the ratio of the change in the amount of credit to the change in reserves. Thus,

$$C_m = \frac{\Delta C_r}{\Delta R}$$

where, ΔC_r = change in credit

ΔR = change in reserves

Thus, we have

Credit Multiplier, $$C_m = \frac{1-r}{c+r}$$

In our example, as c is 0.5 and r is 0.1, the value of the deposit multiplier will be

$$C_m = \frac{1-0.1}{0.5+0.1} = \frac{0.9}{0.6} = 1.5$$

The value of the credit multiplier also depends on the two ratios, the reserve ratio and the currency deposit ratio.

A comparison of the deposit and the credit multiplier shows that while the denominator is the same in both of them, the deposit multiplier has a change in deposits, ΔD in the numerator and the credit multiplier has a change in credit, ΔC in the numerator. Thus what is required is to distinguish between a change in deposits, ΔD and change in credits, ΔC. Although a change in deposits can occur due to change in both the primary deposits and in the secondary deposits, a change in credit occurs only when there is a change in the secondary deposits.

RECAP

- Bank deposits can be grouped into two categories: primary deposits and secondary deposits.
- By starting with a primary deposit the banking system is able to create secondary deposits, which are in fact a multiple of the primary deposits.

SUMMARY

INTRODUCTION

In this chapter, we discussed the theory of money supply or what is often called the *H* theory of money supply, the measures of money supply in India and the creation of credit.

MEASURES OF MONEY SUPPLY IN INDIA

1. The supply of money is a stock variable.
2. When we measure the supply of money, it is the money in the hands of the 'public'.
3. Until the year 1967–68, the RBI used to publish data only on what is called the narrow measure of money supply.
4. From the year 1967–68, RBI started publishing data on the broader measure of money supply or the AMR in addition to the earlier narrow measure.
5. Since April 1977, the RBI has started publishing data on four alternative measures of money supply:

   $M_1 = C + DD + OD$

   $M_2 = M_1 +$ Saving deposits with post offices

   $M_3 = M_1 +$ Net time deposits of banks

   $M_4 = M_3 +$ Total deposits with post office savings organization (including NSC)

6. What we call M_1 in the new series is actually the narrow measure of money supply; what we call M_3 in the new series is actually the AMR.
7. In the new series, the four measures of money supply are in descending order of liquidity.

THE THEORY OF MONEY SUPPLY

1. The supply of money is determined by the monetary authorities, the public and the banks.
2. In a fractional reserve banking system, banks need to keep aside only a fraction of the total deposits as reserves and give out the rest in the form of loans.
3. The theory of money supply is also called the *H* theory of money supply or the money multiplier theory of money supply, where $m = \frac{c+1}{c+r}$ is the money multiplier.
4. With the introduction of time deposits, $D = DD + TD$. The money multiplier equation becomes $m = \frac{c+1}{c+r(1+t)}$
5. In the money multiplier equation, *c* is the currency demand deposit ratio, *r* is the reserve deposit ratio and *t* is the time deposit ratio.
6. The equation $M = m\ (c, t, r)\ H$ shows that the determinants of money supply can be grouped under two headings: those that influence the high-powered money, *H* and those that influence the money multiplier, *m*.
7. *H* or High-powered money is money, which is produced by the monetary authorities and held by the public and the banks. Changes in the RBM are largely responsible for the changes in high-powered money.
8. The determinants of the money multiplier can be divided under two heads: the proximate determinants and the ultimate determinants.

THE PROCESS OF CREDIT CREATION AND THE DEPOSIT MULTIPLIER

1. It is the lending and the borrowing activities of the commercial banks that lead to the credit creation.
2. Bank deposits can be grouped into two categories: primary deposits, which are deposits that bring in new reserves to the banks and secondary deposits, which are deposits that do not bring in new reserves to the banks. They are created out of the credit extended by the banks.
3. Credit creation in a single bank model shows the process of how, with successive rounds of credit creation, the single bank is able to create credit.
4. Credit creation in a multiple bank model shows the process of how, with successive rounds of credit creation, the several banks in the banking system are able to create credit.
5. The deposit multiplier is the ratio of the change in deposits to the change in reserves and given as $D_m = \frac{1,}{c+r}$ and the credit multiplier is the ratio of the change in the amount of credit to the change in reserves and given as, $C_m = \frac{1-r.}{c+r}$

REVIEW QUESTIONS

TRUE OR FALSE QUESTIONS

1. The supply of money is a flow variable.
2. Until the year 1967–68, the RBI used to publish data only on what is called the broad measure of money supply.
3. Coins and one rupee notes are issued by the RBI.
4. High-powered money is money, which is produced by the government and the central bank.
5. New reserves are known as secondary deposits.

VERY SHORT-ANSWER QUESTIONS

1. What is the meaning of money in the hands of the 'public'?
2. What are 'aggregate monetary resources' or the AMR?
3. What is high-powered money?
4. What is the fractional reserve banking system?
5. Explain the difference between money and high-powered money.

SHORT-ANSWER QUESTIONS

1. Mention the four measures of money supply (with their components) published by the RBI.
2. Write short notes on the following:
   (i) Time deposits of banks
   (ii) Savings account deposits
3. What is the money multiplier? Explain.
4. Write short notes on the following:
   (i) Currency deposit ratio
   (ii) Reserve deposit ratio
5. What is the difference between the deposit and the credit multipliers?

LONG-ANSWER QUESTIONS

1. Discuss the various measures of money supply in India.
2. The theory of money supply is also called the *H* theory of money supply or the money multiplier theory of money supply. Discuss.
3. Write a short note on the working of the money multiplier process.
4. Elucidate the process of credit creation when there exists only a single bank in the banking system.
5. Credit creation in a multiple bank model shows how, with successive rounds of credit creation, the several banks in the banking system are able to create credit. Discuss.

ANSWERS

TRUE OR FALSE QUESTIONS

1. **False.** The supply of money is a stock variable and refers to the stock of money at a point in time.
2. **False.** Until the year 1967–68, the RBI used to publish data only on the narrow measure of money supply.
3. **False.** Coins and one rupee notes are issued by the Government of India whereas currency notes of rupees two and higher denominations are issued by the RBI.
4. **True.** High-powered money is money, which is produced by the government and the central bank and held in the hands of the public and the banks.
5. **False.** New reserves are known as primary deposits and it is with these reserves that the credit creation commences.

Demand for Money and the Rate of Interest: The Classical Approach

13

After studying this topic, you should be able to understand

- ✓ *The crux of Fisher's quantity theory is his famous equation of exchange, $MV_T = P_T T$.*
- ✓ *The most important feature of the Cambridge cash balance approach is that the demand for money is a function of money income.*
- ✓ *According to the classical theory, the rate of interest is determined by the demand and the supply of capital.*
- ✓ *In contrast to the classical theory, the loanable funds theory incorporates both the monetary and the non-monetary factors in the determination of the rate of interest.*

INTRODUCTION

This section of the book is devoted to the monetary sector. The last two chapters analysed money and the determinants of the theory of money supply. In the next three chapters, we examine the theories of demand for money. The present chapter examines the classical approach to the demand for money, known as the quantity theory of money (QTM). The QTM has several versions. Two versions, which have gained importance, are Irving Fisher's transaction approach and the Cambridge cash balance approach. In the chapter, we also focus on the determination of the rate of interest in the classical theory.

FISHER'S TRANSACTIONS APPROACH TO THE QUANTITY THEORY OF MONEY

This approach was formulated by the famous American economist Irving Fisher. The crux of Fisher's quantity theory is his famous equation of exchange,

$$MV_T = P_T T \tag{1}$$

where, M = total quantity of money in circulation

V_T = transactions velocity of money or the average number of times a unit of money changes hands to perform transactions during a given period of time

P_T = average price of all kinds of market transactions

T = aggregate or sum of all transactions of goods and services during a given time period

The equation of exchange is a truism in that it depicts something that is self evident and holds at all times. Each side of the above equation depicts the value (in terms of money) of the total transactions during a given period of time.

A look at the left hand side of the equation shows that while M is the total quantity of money in the economy, V_T is the transactions velocity of money. Thus, MV_T is the money value of the total transactions during the given period of time.

BOX 13.1

The beginning of classical economics is associated with the publication of Adam Smith's '*The Wealth of Nations*' in the year 1776. The proponents of classical economics include Adam Smith, Thomas Malthus, David Ricardo and John Stuart Mill. All of them were in favour of free markets, which they believed can regulate themselves. They came up with their views at a time when there occurred the advent of capitalism and the industrial revolution was bringing about changes in the society. The classical school of thought was active with their views till the middle of the nineteenth century. Since the 1870s, the views of the neoclassical school gained prominence.

A look at the right hand side of the equation shows that for a single transaction *i*, the price is p_i while the quantity is t_i. Thus, $p_i t_i$ is the money value of the transaction *i*. The total money value of all transactions will be $\Sigma\, p_i t_i$, which can be denoted as $P_T T$.

Fisher's QTM is a tautology and does not make any assertions about the relationships among the variables in the real world. It is unable to express as to what the cause is and what the effect is. In spite of all these criticisms, it is called a theory. The reason is because the equation of exchange is one equation with four variables. It is possible to express the value of one variable in terms of the other three variables. To develop the theory, certain assumptions are necessary; which are as follows:

Transactions, *T*: It is assumed that the total volume of transactions is a function of the basic physical and operational characteristics of the economy, namely capital, labour, the factors of production and technology which are all independent of M, V_T and P_T.

Money, *M*: The assumption here is that the stock of money is determined by the monetary system.

Velocity of circulation, V_T: V_T is assumed to be constant because payment practices (including the frequency with which people are paid and the irregularity in payments, etc.) change quite slowly.

Prices, P_T: In the QTM, P_T is the only variable that is influenced by the changes in *M*. Hence, we get from Eq. (1)

$$P_T = \frac{MV_T}{T} \tag{2}$$

The above analysis shows that

(1) Given V_T and *T*, changes in *M* lead to changes in P_T.
(2) A doubling of *M* will lead to a doubling of P_T. Thus, changes in *M* lead to equiproportionate changes in P_T.

The Quantity Theory: The Income Version

Due to the dissatisfaction with the transactions approach to the quantity theory, a modified form of the theory was put forward where the quantity equation was expressed in terms of the real income. The other variables in the equation got a similar treatment.

The income version of the quantity theory can be expressed as:

$$MV = Py \tag{3}$$

where, M = total quantity of money in circulation

V = income velocity of money or the average number of times a unit of money changes hands to perform income transactions or transactions relating to final goods and services, during a given period of time

P = average level of prices of only the final goods and services

y = real income

Similar to the earlier version of the quantity theory, the income version is also an identity. However, it is a genuine equation where the variable P can be determined, given y, V and M. Assuming that V is a constant, and that y is determined by the forces in the real sector, the theory arrives at the conclusion that autonomous changes in the supply of money, M lead to equiproportionate changes in the price level, P.

Demand for Money

The focus of this chapter is on the demand for money. Though Fisher had as such not expressed it, the demand for money in an economy is determined by the value of transactions (since money is demanded for the very purpose of carrying on transactions). It is a constant fraction of the value of the transactions. Thus,

$$M^d = kP_T \tag{4}$$

In equilibrium, the supply of money is equal to the demand for money.

Thus,

$$M^s = M^d \tag{5}$$

Combining the Eqs. (4) and (5), we get

$$M^s = kP_T T$$

or

$$M^s \frac{1}{k} = P_T T$$

or

$$M^s \frac{1}{k} = M^s V_T = P_T T$$

where

$$V_T = \frac{1}{k}$$

The transactions approach leads to the hypothesis that the demand for money is a constant proportion of the level of transactions.

Shortcoming of the QTM Approach

The variables T and P_T are ambiguous, and difficult to measure with the given data. Also V_T, the velocity of circulation, is influenced by consumer and business spending which are not constant.

RECAP

- According to Fisher's transactions approach, changes in M lead to equiproportionate changes in P_T.
- The equation of exchange is a truism as it depicts something that is self evident and holds at all times.
- The transactions approach leads to the hypothesis that the demand for money is a constant proportion of the level of transactions.

BOX 13.2

In some major economies of the world, the QTM gained immense popularity in the 1980s. In the United States under Ronald Reagan and in the UK under Margaret Thatcher, the QTM became so popular that the leaders attempted to apply the main principles of the theory to achieve the targets in the growth rate of money. However, later on it was realized that it was perhaps not the solution to the problems faced by the economy.

THE CAMBRIDGE CASH BALANCE APPROACH

Given by the economists Marshall and Pigou, this early neoclassical theory hypothesized the following demand function for money:

$$M^d = KY \quad (6)$$

where, M^d = the amount of money demanded

K = a constant

Y = national income in money terms

Now, $K = \frac{M^d}{Y}$

Thus, K gives the demand for money for every rupee of income per unit time. In fact, K depicts the proportion of money income, which the public likes to hold as money. This is, in fact, the most important feature of the Cambridge theory in that the demand for money is a function of money income.

We have

$$y = \frac{Y}{P} \quad (7)$$

where, y = the real national income

P = general price level

Combining Eqs. (6) and (7), we get

$$M^d = KPy \quad (8)$$

The equilibrium condition for the money market is

$$M^d = M^s \quad (9)$$

Thus, we get from Eqs. (8) and (9),

$$M^s = KPy$$

Hence,

$$M^s\frac{1}{K} = M^sV = Py$$

The above equation looks very similar to the Fisher's equation, except for V, which represents the income velocity (and not the transactions velocity).

A comparison of the two approaches depicts the conceptual differences between the two approaches, which are as follows:

(1) The transactions approach lays emphasis on the medium of exchange function of money and thus defines money in terms of whatsoever is included as the medium of exchange. On the other hand, the cash balance approach lays emphasis on the store of value function of money and is therefore consistent with the broader meaning of money.

(2) The transactions approach lays stress on the mechanical aspects of the payments practices while examining the determinants of the transactions velocity of money. In contrast, the cash balance approach is influenced by K, which is a behavioural ratio.

(3) The cash balance approach can be easily expressed in terms of the simple demand supply analysis whereas the same cannot be said for the transactions approach.

RECAP

- The cash balance approach lays emphasis on the store of value function of money.
- The cash balance approach can be easily expressed in terms of the simple demand supply analysis.

THE CLASSICAL THEORY OF INTEREST

Interest is the price, which is paid by the borrower to the lender of borrowed funds.

Interest is the price, which is paid by the borrower to the lender of borrowed funds. When this price is expressed in terms of a rate per cent per unit time, it becomes a rate of interest. The interest rate exercises a strong influence on all economic activities like investment, saving and international capital flows.

The reason for discussing it here in the present chapter (with the demand for money) is the influence of Keynes, who had argued that the rate of interest is determined by the demand and supply of money.

Before the advent of Keynes on the economic scenario, the classical theory was considered to be a satisfactory theory for the determination of the rate of interest. According to the classical theory, the rate of interest is determined by the demand and the supply of capital.

Demand for Capital

The proponents of the classical theory believed that capital is demanded only for purposes of investment. It is inversely related to the rate of interest. Other things being equal, the lower the rate of interest higher will be the investment. For every new investment project that a firm undertakes, the firm will have to first estimate the rate of return and then compare it with the interest rate. At a higher interest rate, relatively fewer projects will be undertaken unless they yield a return at least equal to, if not greater than, the interest rate. Thus, at higher rates of interest investment is low. In contrast, at lower rates of interest investment is comparatively high. Hence, there exists an inverse relationship between the investment and the rate of interest.

In Figure 13.1, the investment demand schedule, I is downward sloping from left to right. Keynes had accepted that investment is a function of the rate of interest.

Supply of Capital

As far as the supply of capital is concerned, its source is saving. Saving is income that is withheld from consumption. According to the classical theory, saving is a function of the rate of interest. The classical theory had emphasized that the normal state for an economy is full employment. Hence, income cannot be taken as a variable and it cannot have an influence on savings in the short run. Therefore at the full employment level of income, saving is a direct function of the rate of interest. The higher the rate of interest, the larger is the amount of the income that is saved. In Figure 13.1, the saving schedule, S is upward sloping.

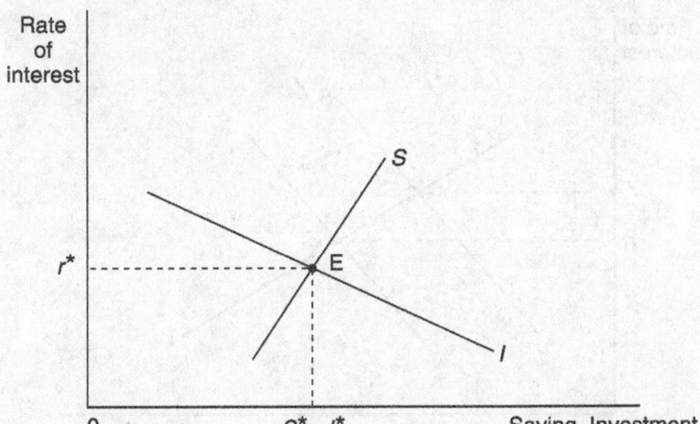

Figure 13.1 Determination of the Rate of Interest: The Classical Theory

Interest Rate Determination

In Figure 13.1, saving and investment curves are represented by curves *S* and *I*. They intersect each other at point E. Thus, the equilibrium rate of interest is r^*. At all other rates of interest, there will exist disequilibrium and forces will be at work to push the rate of interest back until the equilibrium rate of interest is achieved at r^*.

If the rate of interest were above r^*, the funds supplied by the savers would be more than those demanded by the investors and this would push down the rate of interest. If the rate of interest were below r^*, demand for funds from the investors would be more than those supplied by the savers and this would push up the rate of interest. It is only at the equilibrium rate r^* that every rupee of saving is matched by a rupee of investment.

Changes in Saving and Investment

A shift in either the saving or the investment curves will move the economy to a new equilibrium. Suppose that the recipients of the income become thriftier and save more of their income at each rate of interest. The saving curve in Figure 13.2 will shift outwards from *S* to S_1. The equilibrium would change from E^* to E_1 and there would occur a decrease in the interest rate from r^* to r_1. A shift of the saving function in the opposite direction, indicating that less is saved at each rate of interest, would lead to a rise in the interest rate.

The effects of a shift in the investment curve can be analysed in a similar manner.

The Classical Theory: A Critical Appraisal

The negative points of the classical theory are:

(1) Keynes had criticized the classical theory in classicists' belief that saving is a unique function of the interest rate. According to Keynes, there does not exist a significant relationship between savings and the interest rate. He also emphasized that savings function will shift whenever there is a change in the income level.

(2) The classical theory assumed that a shift in the investment curve can take place without causing a change in the income level. Thus, the classical theory fails to recognize the relationship between investment and income.

However, in spite of all these shortcomings, we do study the classical theory for many reasons, which are as follows:

(1) It is incorrect to say that the classical theory is unacceptable or wrong. Without the refinements in the theory which would give us a more correct picture, it is wrong to categorize the theory as correct or incorrect.

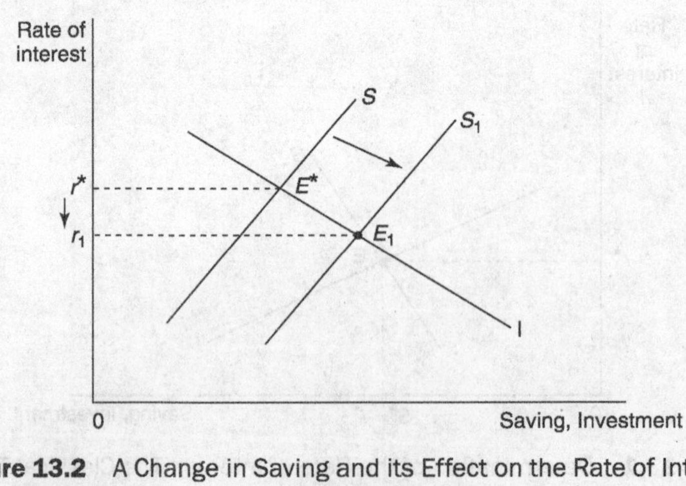

Figure 13.2 A Change in Saving and its Effect on the Rate of Interest

(2) To be able to understand a new theory in a better way, it is necessary to study even an old theory which is not totally incorrect but nevertheless which was accepted world wide for over a hundred years.
(3) Even today despite the success faced by the Keynesian theory, many people still have faith in the classical theory.

RECAP

- The proponents of the classical theory believed that capital is demanded only for purposes of investment, which is inversely related to the rate of interest.
- As far as the supply of capital is concerned, its source is saving, which, according to the classical theory is a direct function of the rate of interest.
- The intersection of the saving and investment curves determines the equilibrium rate of interest.
- A shift in either the saving or the investment curves will move the economy to a new equilibrium position.

THE LOANABLE FUNDS THEORY

Till Keynes had arrived on the scene, the classical theory of the rate of interest was the accepted theory for the determination of the interest rate. Later, it was reconstructed as the loanable funds theory. Hence, the theory can be said to be an extension of the classical saving investment theory.

While the classical theory had incorporated only the non-monetary (real) factors, the loanable funds theory incorporates both the monetary as well as the non-monetary factors in the analysis. It is associated with Wicksell, D. H. Robertson and others.

The theory is based on the following assumptions:

(1) The market for loanable funds is fully integrated with perfect mobility of funds.
(2) There exists perfect competition in the market and so each borrower and lender is a price taker. There will be only one rate of interest and that will be the market clearing rate of interest.
(3) All factors, other than the rate of interest, are assumed to be constant. The rate of interest does not respond to or interfere with the other macroeconomic variables. In other words, the theory uses a partial equilibrium analysis.
(4) The theory is in 'flow' terms where the flow demand and supply of loanable funds are analysed to determine the rate of interest.

The rate of interest is determined by standard demand supply analysis. According to the loanable funds theory, the rate of interest, which is the price of loanable funds, is determined by the demand for and supply of loanable funds.

Demand for Loanable Funds, LD

The demand for loanable funds can be expressed as

$$\text{LD} = I + \Delta\text{MD}$$

where,

$$\text{LD} = \text{Demand for loanable funds}$$
$$I = \text{Gross investment expenditure}$$
$$\Delta\text{MD} = \text{Incremental demand for money}$$

Since both, I and ΔMD are a decreasing function of the rate of interest so LD is also a decreasing function of the rate of interest. Investment (which was present in the classical theory also) is a real factor whereas the incremental demand for money is a monetary factor. Hence, both real and monetary factors are included in the demand for money.

Supply of Loanable Funds, LS

The sources of supply of loanable funds are

$$\text{LS} = S + \text{DH} + \Delta M$$

$$\text{LS} = \text{Supply of loanable funds}$$

S = Aggregate saving of all the households and firms in the economy, net of their dissaving
DH = Aggregate dishoarding of previously accumulated cash balances
ΔM = Incremental supply of money

Since both S and DH are increasing functions of the rate of interest, while ΔM is given autonomously, LS is also an increasing function of the rate of interest. While S, the aggregate saving of all the households and firms (which was present in the classical theory also) is a real factor, DH the aggregate dishoarding of previously accumulated cash balances and ΔM, the incremental supply of money are both monetary factors. Hence, both real and monetary factors are included in the supply of money.

Interest Rate Determination

In Figure 13.3, S represents the saving curve and LS represents the supply of loanable funds. The horizontal distance between the S and LS curves is the sum of DH and ΔM. This distance increases as r increases because while ΔM is given exogenously, DH is an increasing function of r. Similarly, I represents the investment curve and LD represents the demand for loanable funds. The horizontal distance between I and LD curves is ΔMD. This distance increases as r decreases because ΔMD is a decreasing function of r.

According to the standard demand supply theory, equilibrium is determined at the level where
Demand for loanable funds = Supply of loanable funds

or $$\text{LD} = \text{LS}$$

or $$I + \Delta \text{MD} = S + \text{DH} + \Delta M$$

On the other hand, in the classical theory equilibrium is determined at the level where

$$I(r) = S(r)$$

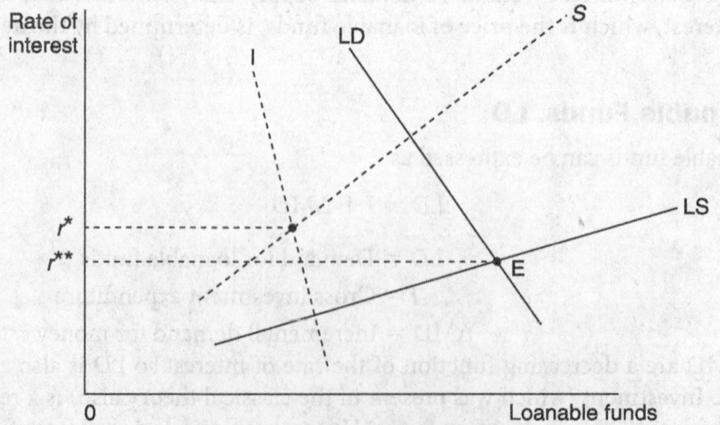

Figure 13.3 Interest Rate Determination in the Loanable Funds Theory

BOX 13.3

Wicksell had differentiated between the money rate of interest and the market rate of interest. While the money rate of interest is determined by the intersection of the LD and LS curves, the natural rate is determined by the intersection of the S and *I* curves. He had emphasized that prices will continuously increase or decrease when the market rate is different from the natural rate.

In Figure 13.3, the LD and LS curves intersect each other at point E. The equilibrium rate of interest is r^{**}. The *S-I* equilibrium of the classical theory yields r^* as the equilibrium rate of interest.

The Loanable Funds Theory: A Critical Appraisal

The positive points of the loanable funds theory are as follows.

(1) It is an improvement over the classical theory in that it recognizes the fact that loanable funds are demanded for purposes other than investment expenditures and also that besides saving there exist other sources of loanable funds also.

(2) The classical theory considers only the real factors in the determination of the interest rate whereas the loanable funds theory takes into consideration both the real and the monetary factors.

(3) The theory recognizes that like saving and investment, the aggregate dishoarding of previously accumulated cash balances and the incremental demand for money also exercise a strong influence on the rate of interest.

The negative points of the loanable funds theory are mentioned below. The theory is unable to specify in a clear manner the different sources of the supply and demand for loanable funds.

On the supply side:

(1) Some savings may not come through the loan market. Firms and households may invest their savings directly into physical assets.

(2) Not all dishoarding of cash balances are lent out. The dishoarders may spend them directly.

On the demand side:

(1) Investments or hoardings may be financed from owned funds and not necessarily from borrowed funds.

(2) Funds may be borrowed not only for investment and hoarding but also for the buying of old financial and non-financial assets, and for consumption spending.

(3) The flow equilibrium approach of the theory has also been subjected to a lot of criticism. In the bond market at least in the short period, the amount of outstanding bonds (a stock concept) is much more than the demand and supply of bonds (a flow concept). Hence, in the short period the stock equilibrium exercises a strong influence on the behaviour of the interest rate. What is required is a stock flow analysis to determine the interest rate.

(4) The rate of interest not only has a strong influence on the different macro variables like savings, investment, prices, supply and demand for money, but in turn, it is also affected by these variables. So what is required is a general equilibrium approach, and not a partial equilibrium approach, for the determination of the interest rate.

(5) Like all other theories, the basic tenet of the loanable funds theory is that there exists a fully integrated market where all the lending and borrowing activities are performed through perfectly homogenous bonds at a single rate of interest. This does not present a true picture of even the most well developed financial markets where there exists a variety of interest rates.

RECAP

- The demand for loanable funds is a decreasing function of the rate of interest.
- The supply of loanable funds is an increasing function of the rate of interest.
- The equilibrium rate of interest is determined by the intersection of the demand for loanable funds schedule and the supply of loanable funds schedule.

SUMMARY

INTRODUCTION

The chapter examines the quantity theory of money (QTM) and its two versions, Irving Fisher's transaction approach and the Cambridge cash balance approach.

FISHER'S TRANSACTIONS APPROACH TO THE QUANTITY THEORY OF MONEY

1. The crux of Fisher's quantity theory is his famous equation of exchange, $MV_T = P_T T$.
2. The equation of exchange is a truism. In spite of all these criticisms, it is called a theory. To develop the theory, certain assumptions are necessary: T is assumed to be a function of the basic physical and operational characteristics of the economy; M is assumed to be determined by the monetary system; and V_T is assumed to be constant.
3. P_T is the only variable that is influenced by the changes in M. Hence, we get the equation $P_T = \frac{MV_T}{T}$
4. The analysis shows that given V_T and T, changes in M lead to equiproportionate changes in P_T.
5. The main shortcoming of the QTM approach is that the variables T and P_T are ambiguous and with the given data it is difficult to measure them.

THE QUANTITY THEORY: THE INCOME VERSION

1. Here, the quantity equation is expressed in terms of the real income.
2. The income version of the quantity theory can be expressed as:

$$MV = Py$$

3. Similar to the earlier version of the quantity theory, the income version is also an identity.
4. It is a genuine equation where the variable P can be determined, given y, V and M.
5. The theory arrives at the conclusion that autonomous changes in the supply of money lead to equiproportionate changes in the price level.

DEMAND FOR MONEY

1. The demand for money in an economy is determined by the value of transactions and is a constant fraction of the value of the transactions.
2. Thus, $M^d = kPT$

SHORTCOMING OF THE QTM APPROACH

The variables T and P_T are ambiguous, and V_T is influenced by consumer and business spending.

THE CAMBRIDGE CASH BALANCE APPROACH

1. Given by the economists Marshall and Pigou, this early neoclassical theory hypothesized the following demand function for money: $M^d = \frac{K}{Y}$
2. Here K depicts the proportion of money income, which the public likes to hold as money. This is, in fact, the most important feature of the Cambridge theory in that the demand for money is a function of money income.
3. The equation $M^s \frac{1}{K} = M^S V = Py$

   The above equation looks very similar to the Fisher's equation, except for V which represents the income velocity.

A COMPARISON OF THE TWO APPROACHES:

1. The transactions approach lays emphasis on the medium of exchange function of money whereas the cash balance approach lays emphasis on the store of value function of money.
2. The transactions approach lays stress on the mechanical aspects of the payments practices while examining the determinants of the transactions velocity of money. In contrast, in the cash balance approach K is more of a behavioural ratio.
3. While the cash balance approach can be easily expressed in terms of the simple demand supply analysis, the same cannot be said for the transactions approach.

THE CLASSICAL THEORY OF INTEREST

1. Interest is the price, which is paid by the borrower to the lender of borrowed funds. When this price is expressed in terms of a rate per cent per unit time, it becomes a rate of interest.
2. The rate of interest is determined by the demand and the supply of capital.
3. As far as the demand for capital is concerned, it is demanded only for purposes of investment.
4. There exists an inverse relationship between investment and the rate of interest. Thus, the investment demand schedule is downward sloping.
5. As far as the supply of capital is concerned, its source is saving that is income withheld from consumption.
6. Saving is a direct function of the rate of interest. Thus, the saving schedule, S is upward sloping.

INTEREST RATE DETERMINATION

1. Saving and investment curves intersect to determine the equilibrium rate of interest at r^*.
2. At all other rates of interest there will exist disequilibrium and forces will be at work to push the rate of interest back until the equilibrium rate of interest is achieved at r^*.

CHANGES IN SAVING AND INVESTMENT

1. A shift in either the saving or the investment curves will move the economy to a new equilibrium.
2. Suppose that the recipients of the income become thriftier and save more of their income at each rate of interest, the saving curve will shift outwards and there would occur a decrease in the interest rate.
3. The effects of a shift in the investment curve can be analysed in a similar manner.

THE CLASSICAL THEORY: A CRITICAL APPRAISAL

The negative points of the classical theory are as follows:

1. According to Keynes, there does not exist a significant relationship between savings and the interest rate.
2. The classical theory fails to recognize the relationship between investment and income.
3. In spite of all these shortcomings, we do study the classical theory because to be able to understand a new theory in a better way it is necessary to study even an old theory which may not be totally correct.

THE LOANABLE FUNDS THEORY

1. The theory can be said to be an extension of the classical saving investment theory.
2. While the classical theory had incorporated only the non-monetary (real) factors, the loanable funds theory incorporates both the monetary as well as the non-monetary factors in the analysis.
3. The theory is based on the following assumptions:
   (a) The market for loanable funds is fully integrated with perfect mobility of funds.
   (b) There exists perfect competition in the market and so each borrower and lender is a price taker.
   (c) There will be only one rate of interest and that will be the market clearing rate of interest.
   (d) All factors, other than the rate of interest, are assumed to be constant.
   (e) The theory is in 'flow' terms.
4. The rate of interest, which is the price of loanable funds, is determined by the demand for and supply of loanable funds.

DEMAND FOR LOANABLE FUNDS, LD

1. The demand for loanable funds can be expressed as

$$\text{LD} = I + \Delta\text{MD}$$

2. Since both I and ΔMD are a decreasing function of the rate of interest, so LD is also a decreasing function of the rate of interest.

SUPPLY OF LOANABLE FUNDS, LS

1. The sources of supply of loanable funds are

$$LS = S + DH + \Delta M$$

2. Since both S and DH are increasing functions of the rate of interest, while ΔM is given autonomously, LS is also an increasing function of the rate of interest.

INTEREST RATE DETERMINATION

1. The horizontal distance between the S and LS curves is the sum of DH and ΔM. This distance increases as r increases.
2. The horizontal distance between I and LD curves is ΔMD. This distance increases as r decreases.
3. Equilibrium is determined at the level where the demand for loanable funds is equal to the supply of loanable funds.

THE LOANABLE FUNDS THEORY: A CRITICAL APPRAISAL

1. The positive points of the loanable funds theory are as follows:
   (a) It recognizes the fact that loanable funds are demanded for purposes other than investment expenditures and also that besides saving, there exist other sources of loanable funds also.
   (b) The loanable funds theory takes into consideration both the real and the monetary factors.
2. The negative points of the loanable funds theory are as follows:
   (a) The theory is unable to specify in a clear manner the different sources of the supply and demand for loanable funds.
   (b) The flow equilibrium approach of the theory has also been subjected to a lot of criticism. What is required is a stock flow analysis to determine the interest rate.
   (c) For the determination of the interest rate, a general equilibrium approach and not a partial equilibrium approach is required.
   (d) The basic tenet of the loanable funds theory is that there exists a fully integrated market, which does not present a true picture of reality.

REVIEW QUESTIONS

TRUE OR FALSE QUESTIONS

1. According to Fisher's transactions approach to the quantity theory of money, changes in M lead to equiproportionate changes in P_T.
2. The most important feature of the Cambridge cash balance approach is that the demand for money is a constant fraction of the value of the transactions.
3. The demand for loanable funds is an increasing function of the rate of interest.
4. The classical theory had incorporated only the monetary factors in the determination of the rate of interest.
5. The loanable funds theory incorporated both the monetary as well as the non-monetary factors in the determination of the rate of interest.

VERY SHORT-ANSWER QUESTIONS

1. 'The transactions approach leads to the hypothesis that the demand for money is a constant proportion of the level of transactions.' Comment.
2. Discuss the income version of the quantity theory of money.
3. Compare Fisher's transactions approach and the Cambridge cash balance approach.
4. What is interest? Discuss.
5. How does a shift in either the saving or the investment curves move the economy to a new equilibrium? Explain.

SHORT-ANSWER QUESTIONS

1. 'Fisher's quantity theory of money is a tautology and does not make any assertions about the relationships between the variables in the real world.' Explain.
2. Give a critical appraisal of the loanable funds theory.
3. 'According to the classical theory, the rate of interest is determined by the demand and the supply of capital.' Explain.
4. Discuss briefly the Cambridge cash balance approach to the demand for money.
5. Discuss briefly the following approaches to the demand for money bringing out the special features of each approach:
   (i) Fisher's transactions approach to money
   (ii) The Cambridge cash balance approach
   (iii) The classical theory of interest
   (iv) The loanable funds theory

LONG-ANSWER QUESTIONS

1. What is the rate of interest? How is it determined in the classical theory of interest?
2. How is the rate of interest determined in the loanable funds theory? Explain.
3. Give a critical appraisal of the loanable funds theory.
4. Compare the loanable funds theory with the classical theory of the determination of the rate of interest.
5. Write a short note on Fisher's transactions approach to money.

ANSWERS

TRUE OR FALSE QUESTIONS

1. **True.** A doubling of M will lead to a doubling of P_T. Thus, changes in M lead to equiproportionate changes in P_T.
2. **False.** The most important feature of the Cambridge cash balance approach is that the demand for money is a function of money income.
3. **False.** The demand for loanable funds is a decreasing function of the rate of interest.
4. **False.** The classical theory had incorporated only the non-monetary (real) factors in the determination of the rate of interest.
5. **True.** Unlike the classical theory, the loanable funds theory incorporated both the monetary as well as the non-monetary or real factors in the determination of the rate of interest.

Demand for Money: The Keynesian Approach

14

After studying this topic, you should be able to understand

- ✓ *The transactions demand for money is the money demanded by the public for carrying on its various current transactions.*
- ✓ *The precautionary demand for money is the demand for cash by the public for contingencies, which may involve unexpected expenditures and opportunities.*
- ✓ *The existence of an uncertainty about the future gives rise to the speculative demand for money.*
- ✓ *In Keynes' theory, the rate of interest is a monetary phenomenon determined by the equality between the demand for and supply of money.*
- ✓ *Given the demand for money, an increase in the supply of money leads to a decrease in the interest rate and vice versa.*
- ✓ *There can occur a change in the demand for money either due to a change in the transactions demand for money or due to change in the speculative demand for money.*
- ✓ *It can be argued that Keynes' theory is indeterminate.*

INTRODUCTION

In Chapter 13, we had focused on the classical theory of demand for money. According to the classical theory, money is demanded as a medium of exchange or in other words for conducting transactions. But according to J. M. Keynes, who formulated his theory of demand for money in his well known book *The General Theory of Employment, Interest and Money* in 1936, money is demanded due to three motives which we discuss at length in the present chapter. We go on to determinc the rate of interest in this Keynesian model through the supply and demand for money. We also analyse how changes in the supply of money, the income level and the speculative demand for money lead to changes in the rate of interest.

THE KEYNESIAN THEORY OF THE DEMAND FOR MONEY

The transactions demand for money is the demand for cash by the public for carrying on its various current transactions.

Unlike the classical economists who recognized only the medium of exchange function of money, Keynes emphasized the store of value function of money also. Thus, he had put forward that money was demanded due to three motives: transactions motive, precautionary motive and speculative motive.

Transactions Demand

The transactions demand for money is the demand for cash by the public for carrying on its various current transactions. The transactions motive creates transactions demand for money. Everyone needs to hold some amount of money to facilitate their day-to-day transactions in goods and services. Thus money is needed as a medium of exchange, as has also been emphasized by the classical economists.

BOX 14.1

John Maynard Keynes is largely recognized for having created the shape and terminology of modern macroeconomics. His book, *General Theory of Employment, Interest and Money* brought about a revolution in the thinking of economists. The book is the foundation of Keynesian thought. It provided a great challenge for the classical school of thought by introducing some new and revolutionary concepts. Keynes is perhaps one of the greatest and most prominent economists of the twentiethth century. He is often known as the father of modern economics.

The reason why this money is held is due to the time gap involved between which the income is received and the payments are made out. In other words, it is required to bridge the gap between the receipts and the regular payments to be made. The closer is this gap the smaller will be the transactions demand for money.

Often, individuals do not find their time patterns for payments identical. Also it is very rare for these payments to be evenly distributed over the entire month. However, for simplicity we assume that these payments are evenly distributed over the entire month. We find that

(1) A person whose receipts arrive on the first day of the month will be required to hold on an average larger amount of transactions balances as shown in Figure 14.1 (a).

(2) A person whose receipts arrive at regular intervals in the month will be required to hold on an average smaller amount of transactions balances as shown in Figure 14.1 (b).
(It is important to note that the total amount of receipts is the same in the above two cases and, therefore, a comparison is possible.)

Thus, as the frequency of the receipts increase the average holdings of transactions balances by the individual decreases.

Transactions demand for money as a function of income

It is believed that there exists a stable and direct relationship between income and transactions money balances. This relationship can expressed as

$$M_t = k\,(PY) \tag{1}$$

where,
M_t = amount of money balances demanded for transactions
k = fraction of money income, which the public likes to hold as money balances for transactions
P = price level
Y = income level

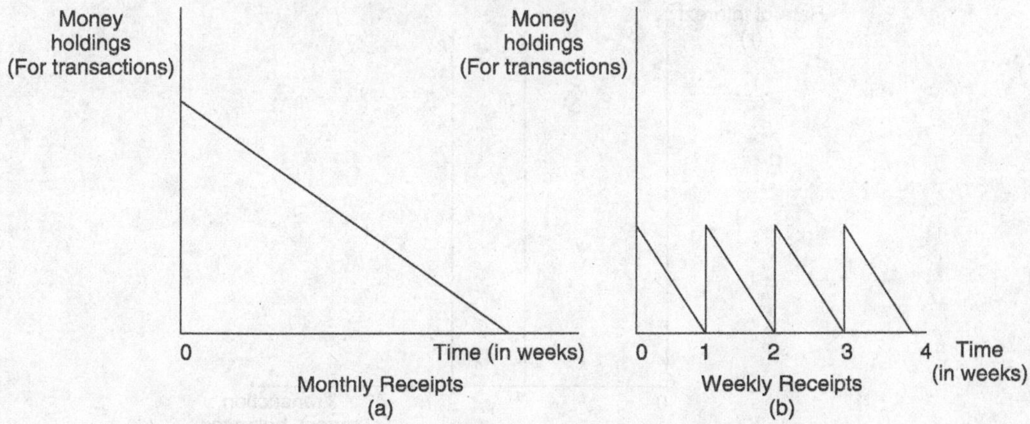

Figure 14.1 Individual's Money Holdings for Transactions

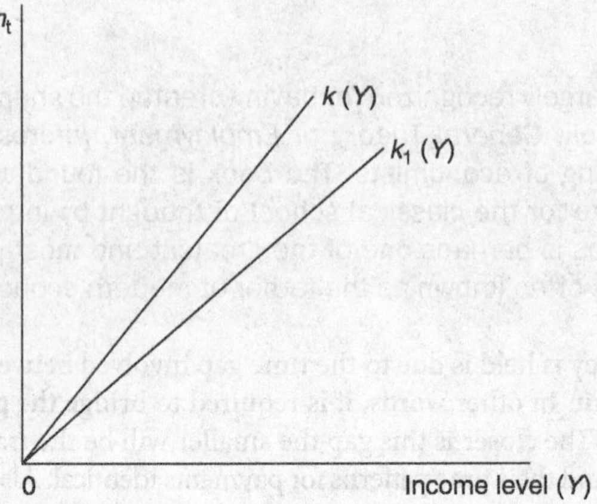

Figure 14.2 Transactions Demand for Money as a Function of the Income Level

Equation (1) specifies the existence of a direct relationship between the transactions balances and the income level. The equation, which is in nominal terms, can be expressed in real terms by dividing throughout by P to get

$$M_t/P = k(Y)$$

or $$m_t = k(Y) \quad (2)$$

where m_t = amount of real balances demanded for transactions

The relationship between transactions demand for money and income can be depicted through Figure 14.2. The line $k(Y)$ shows the amount of transactions balances, m_t for different levels of income, Y with k at say 1/4. Thus if Y were Rs. 4000, m_t would be 1000. If k were 1/5 we would have the line $k_1(Y)$ in the figure. Hence with Y at Rs. 4000, m_t would be 800.

The size of k will be a function of the institutional and the structural conditions in the economy. This includes the time gap between receipts and payments for each individual, speed for movement of money, etc. However for simplicity sake k is assumed to be stable, at least in the short run.

Transactions Demand for Money as a Function of the Rate of Interest

According to Keynes, the transactions demand for money is perfectly interest inelastic as shown in Figure 14.3. A change in income will lead to a shift of the curve from Y_1 to Y_2, but the curve remains inelastic throughout.

Figure 14.3 Transactions Demand for Money as Interest Inelastic

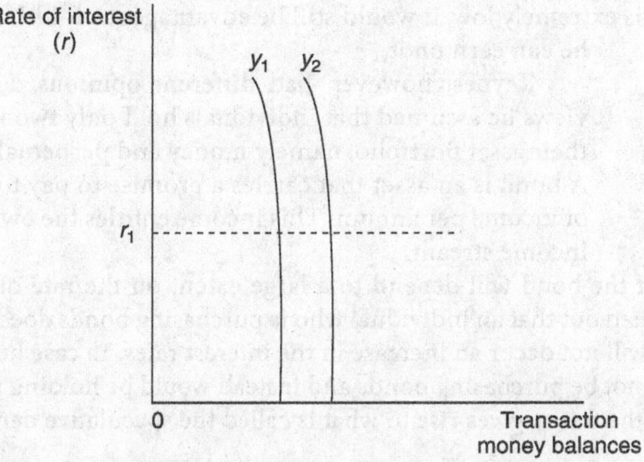

Figure 14.4 Transactions Demand for Money as Interest Elastic

However, some economists are of the opinion that in practice there may exist some rate of interest r_1 at which the transaction demand for money curve may slope backwards as in Figure 14.4. The curve indicates that at low rates of interest, the transactions demand for money may be interest inelastic. But at higher rates of interest, the opportunity cost in terms of holding transactions balances, rather than some interest earning assets, may be too high.

Precautionary Demand

The precautionary demand for money is the demand for cash by the public for contingencies, which may involve unexpected expenditures and opportunities. Thus, precautionary demand for money exists due to uncertainties. It is for those payments, which are neither regular nor planned. Hence, it enables individuals to meet unexpected increases in expenditure or unexpected delays in receipts.

The precautionary demand for money is the demand for cash by the public for contingencies, which may involve unexpected expenditures and opportunities.

The precautionary demand for money varies with the income level. At higher levels of income, individuals certainly need more money and are in a position and have the means to keep aside more money for emergencies and contingencies. The other factor, which influences precautionary demand for money, is the rate of interest. At high rates of interest, one may feel tempted to hold smaller precautionary balances rather than forego the high interests which could be earned by putting these balances in interest-earning assets.

For the sake of convenience and following the conventional procedure, transactions and precautionary balances are often put together as a function primarily of the income level and as being interest inelastic.

Speculative Demand

While the transactions demand and precautionary demand for money do not in any way conflict with the views of the classical theory, the speculative demand for money (also called asset demand for money) represents a complete break from the classical theory. It is one of the most important contributions made by Keynes to the theory of demand for money. It is the speculative motive, which gives rise to the speculative demand for money.

Speculative demand for money arises due to the existence of an uncertainty about the future.

The classical economists had put forward the view that an individual would not hold money in excess of what he requires for transactions and precautionary purposes. For in doing so, he would be losing the interest which he could have earned by putting that amount of money in a bond.

Even if the interest rate is extremely low, it would still be advantageous for him to earn whatever interest he can earn on it.

A bond is an asset that carries a promise to pay to its owner a fixed amount of income per annum. This income entitles the owner of the bond to a future income stream.

Keynes, however, had different opinions. First of all, to present his views he assumed that individuals hold only two kinds of financial assets in their asset portfolio, namely money and perpetual (or irredeemable) bonds. A bond is an asset that carries a promise to pay to its owner a fixed amount of income per annum. This income entitles the owner of the bond to a future income stream.

The market price of the bond will depend to a large extent on the rate of interest fixed in terms of money. Keynes had pointed out that an individual who is purchasing bonds does so because he expects that in the near future there will not occur an increase in the interest rates. In case he expects an increase in the interest rates, he should not be purchasing bonds and instead would be holding money. Thus, the existence of an uncertainty about the future gives rise to what is called the speculative demand for money.

Interest Rates and Bond Prices

For an understanding of the speculative demand for money, it is fruitful to understand the relationship between the rate of interest and the price of a bond. We assume on one hand that the bond is totally risk free, or in other words it does not involve any kind of risk, but it does yield an interest income; on the other hand, the holders of money do not earn any interest but the capital value of money remains unchanged.

The price of a perpetual bond is equal to the reciprocal of the market rate of interest multiplied with the coupon rate of interest, where the coupon rate of interest is the interest payable on a bond. For example, suppose the coupon rate of interest is Rs. 1 per annum (1 per cent on the Rs. 100 face value bond) and the market rate of interest is 5 per cent per annum, then the market price of the bond will be Rs. $1/0.05 \times 1 = 20$. If there is an increase in the market rate of interest to 6 per cent per annum, then the market price of the bond will be Rs. $1/0.06 \times 1 = 16.67$. Thus, a rise in the market rate of interest implies a decrease in the price of a bond and vice versa. Thus, there exists an inverse relationship between the market rate of interest and the price of a bond.

In addition, the price of a bond is subject to capital gain and losses. Hence, the return from a bond will be the sum of the rate of interest and the capital gains and losses per annum. At the time of the purchase of the bond the market rate of interest is given, but the future rate of interest and hence the price of the bond will keep fluctuating leading to an element of uncertainty and thus a speculation in the money and bond markets.

Speculation in the Money Market and Bond Market

The speculators can be grouped into two categories:

Bulls are those who expect that the price of bonds will rise in the future.

(1) Bulls are those who expect that the price of bonds will rise in the future. Hence, they move out of money into bonds by investing all their idle cash in bonds.

Bears are those who expect that the price of bonds will fall in the future.

(2) Bears are those who expect that the price of bonds will fall in the future. Hence, they move out of bonds into money if they expect capital losses on bonds. Hence, they attempt to minimize on their losses. It is from these bears that the speculative demand for money arises. The bears build up on their cash balances to purchase bonds whenever they expect an increase in the price of bonds in the future.

From the above analysis it is obvious that as far as the asset holders are concerned, they either hold only bonds (and are thus bulls) or they hold only money (and are thus bears). Hence, they do not have a diversified portfolio.

BOX 14.2

Keynes was of the opinion that the depressions could be thought of in terms of recessions, which had fallen into a liquidity trap. In a liquidity trap since the public prefers to hoard money, the government can do just the opposite, that is, spend to restore the circular flow of money. It is a different matter that Keynes' advice on how to end the Great Depression was not put into practice. In fact, it was the World War II that was to some extent responsible in curing the Great Depression. This was because of the huge amounts of public spending on defense. Could this be the reason for the views that wars are good for the economy and are an economic boon?

Speculative Demand Curve for Money

Keynes had assumed that there are many asset holders, each with a different expectation regarding the interest rate. At some very high rate of interest (low price of bonds), all may expect an increase in the price of bonds and hence they may all be bulls. Here, the speculative demand for money will be zero. At a slightly lower rate of interest, expectations may change with some bulls now becoming bears and with there appearing a positive demand for speculative money balances. At a still lower interest rate, some more of the bulls may become bears with a higher speculative demand for money. Hence, Keynes arrived at a downward sloping speculative demand curve for money as shown in Figure 14.5.

The speculative demand curve for money depicts the inverse relationship between the interest rate and the speculative demand for money. A very significant contribution of Keynes is what he called the liquidity trap. The liquidity trap is a situation when at some very low rate of interest all asset holders become bears. The demand for money becomes what can be called to be perfectly elastic. In such a situation, any amount of expansion of money supply cannot lower the interest rate any further. At this interest rate, the public is willing to hold only money. We often say that the extra liquidity gets sucked in the asset portfolio of the public in the form of money and no additions to the money supply can succeed in lowering the interest rates any further. Thus, r_1 in Figure 14.5 is the minimum interest rate and cannot fall any further.

A very important feature here without which a discussion on Keynes' theory of speculative demand will be incomplete is the normal rate of interest. Keynes had emphasized that at any point in time there will exist a certain r which can be said to be that rate of interest which will prevail under normal circumstances.

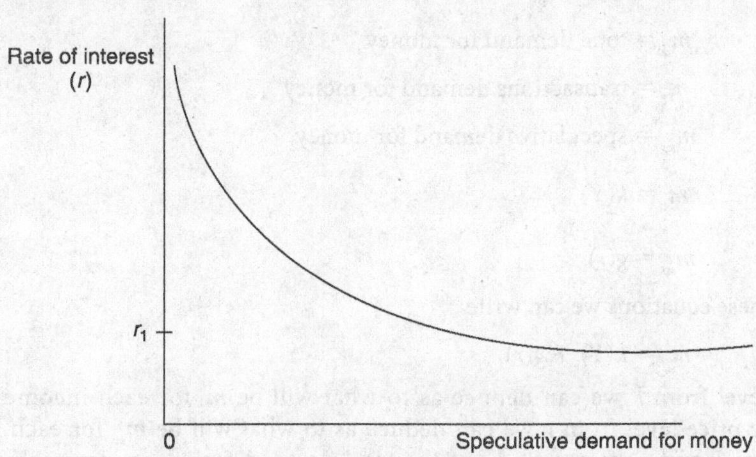

Figure 14.5 Speculative Demand Curve for Money

For the asset holders, this 'normal' r is the benchmark or yardstick with which they compare any actual r in making their decisions. Thus if at any point of time the interest rate were above the normal level, people would expect it to fall and thus expect capital gains and interest income from holding bonds and will continue to hold bonds. If it were below this normal rate, people would expect it to rise and expect capital losses on holding bonds.

In the case of an individual with given expectations about the future rate of interest, the speculative demand for money is a discontinuous curve. However for the aggregate economy, different individuals have different expectations regarding the rate of change of the actual rate of interest. Hence, the aggregate speculative demand for money curve becomes a smooth downward sloping curve showing an inverse relationship between the speculative demand for money and the current rate of interest.

Speculative Demand for Money as a Function of the Rate of Interest

Unlike the direct relationship between income and transactions money balances, there exists an inverse relationship between the speculative balances and the rate of interest. This relationship can be expressed as

$$M_{sp} = P_g(r) \tag{3}$$

where, M_{sp} = amount of money balances demanded for speculative purposes

P = price level

Equation (3) specifies the existence of an indirect relationship between the speculative balances and the rate of interest. The equation, which is in nominal terms, can be expressed in real terms by dividing throughout by P to get

$$M_{sp}/P = g(r)$$

or

$$m_{sp} = g(r) \tag{4}$$

where m_{sp} = amount of real balances demanded for speculative purposes.

The Total Demand for Money

The total demand for money can be expressed as follows:

$$m_d = m_t + m_{sp} \tag{5}$$

where, m_d = total demand for money

m_t = transactions demand for money

m_{sp} = speculative demand for money

But from Eq. (2), $m_t = k(Y)$

and from Eq. (4), $m_{sp} = g(r)$

Thus, combining these equations we can write

$$m_d = k(Y) + g(r) \tag{6}$$

Given any price level from k we can deduce as to what will be m_t for each income level. In a similar manner, given any price level from g we can deduce as to what will be m_{sp} for each level of the rate of interest. Thus, from k and g we can find out the total demand for money for each and every possible combination of Y and r.

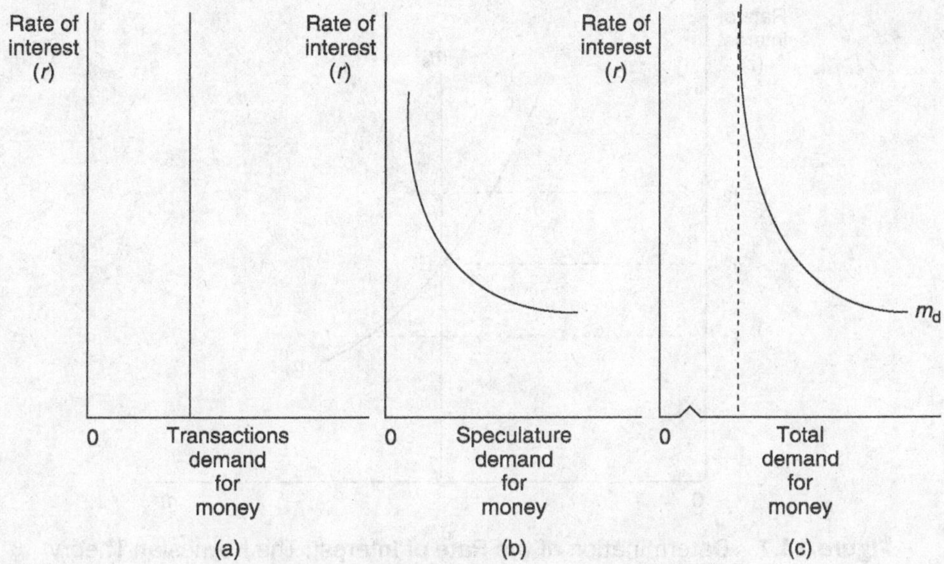

Figure 14.6 The Total Demand for Money

Figure 14.6 attempts at determining the total demand for money. It has been divided into three parts: part (a) shows the transactions demand for money as vertical (since it is interest inelastic); part (b) shows the speculative demand for money as a downward sloping curve (since it is inversely related to the interest rate); part (c) shows the total demand for money as the sum of m_t and m_{sp}. Thus, m_d is the Keynesian demand curve for money and is downward sloping.

Criticism of Keynes's Theory of Demand for Money

(1) As pointed out by Tobin, in reality, individuals do not hold either just money or only bonds. They, in fact, hold a diversified asset portfolio with a blend of both bonds and money and other financial assets.

(2) It has also been pointed out that Keynes' theory treats all non-money financial assets as bonds while in reality there exists a variety of assets, which have characteristics which are far removed from those of bonds.

(3) As Keynes himself had also accepted like the other economists, the possibilities of the occurrence of a liquidity trap are quite far-flung. However, it seems that what is occurring in the world today may be something akin to a liquidity trap.

(4) Keynes' division of money into transaction, precautionary and speculative demands is not realistic. The same unit of money can be used to serve all the three motives.

(5) Many economists like Baumol and Tobin had emphasized that the transactions demand for money is interest elastic.

RECAP

- As the frequency of the receipts increase, the average holding of transactions balances by the individual decreases.
- There exists a stable and direct relationship between income and transactions money balances.

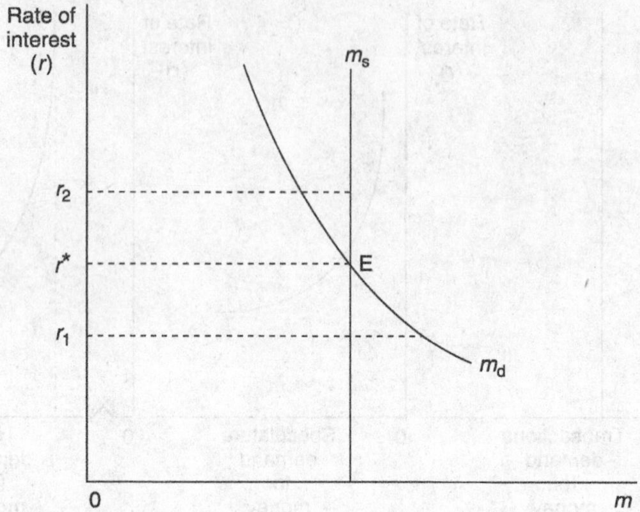

Figure 14.7 Determination of the Rate of Interest: The Keynesian Theory

- According to Keynes, the transactions demand for money is perfectly interest inelastic.
- There exists an inverse relationship between market rate of interest and the price of a bond.
- The liquidity trap is a situation when at some very low rate of interest all asset holders become bears.

THE KEYNESIAN THEORY OF INTEREST

The liquidity trap is a situation when at some very low rate of interest all asset holders become bears.

In the classical theory, the rate of interest is a real phenomenon determined by the equality between savings and investment in the commodity market. In contrast in Keynes theory, the rate of interest is a monetary phenomenon determined by the equality between the demand for and supply of money. It is in fact a compensation for parting with liquidity.

As far as the total demand for money is concerned from Eq. (6), we have

$$m_d = k(Y) + g(r)$$

Regarding the supply of money, Keynes assumed that the supply of money is exogenously determined by the monetary authorities. Hence in Figure 14.7, it is shown by a vertical line parallel to the vertical axis and is interest inelastic.

The money market will be in equilibrium when the demand for money is equal to the supply of money.

In nominal terms, $$M_d = M_s$$

In real terms, $$m_d = m_s$$

or $$k(Y) + g(r) = m_s$$

At a higher rate of interest rate r_2, the demand for money will be less than the supply of money. In other words, there is an excess supply of money in the money market. This implies an excess demand for bonds in the bond market. Thus, there will be an increase in the price of bonds and a decrease in the rate of interest till r^* is achieved.

According to Keynes, r^* represents a stable equilibrium value of r which is determined by the monetary forces of demand and supply of money. Variations in r alone act as the adjustment mechanism for bringing

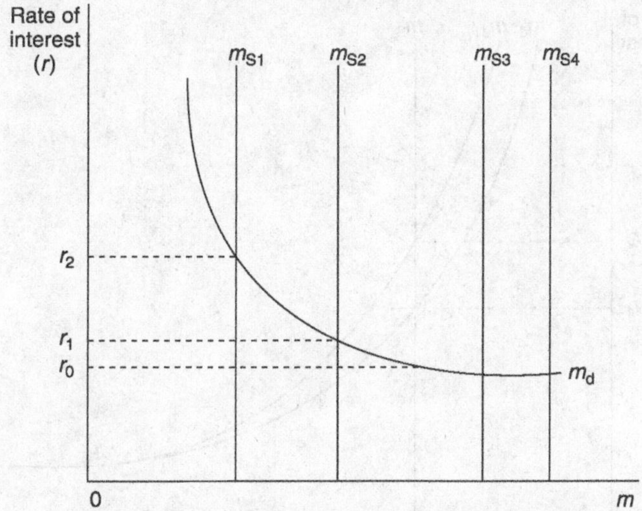

Figure 14.8 Effect of Changes in the Money Supply on the Interest Rate

about equilibrium in the money market whenever disequilibrium occurs. Variations in r will occur due to changes in the supply of money and the demand for money.

RECAP

- Variations in the rate of interest alone act as the adjustment mechanism for bringing about equilibrium in the money market whenever disequilibrium occurs.

VARIATIONS IN THE INTEREST RATE

Changes in the Supply of Money and their Effects on the Interest Rate

We now analyse the effects of a change in the supply of money and its influence on the interest rate. Given the demand for money curve, an increase in the supply of money leads to a decrease in the interest rate and vice versa.

In Figure 14.8 given the demand for money curve m_d and supply of money as m_{s1}, the money market is in equilibrium at only one rate of interest, r_2. Suppose that while the demand for money remains unchanged, the supply of money is increased from m_{s1} to m_{s2}. The equilibrium value of the rate of interest will fall from r_2 to r_1.

As the money supply is increased further to m_{s3}, the equilibrium value of the rate of interest will fall from r_1 to r_0. Any further increases in the supply of money, say to m_{s4} will not lower the rate of interest any further because at r_0 it is caught in what is called the liquidity trap. Thus, r_0 is the absolute minimum below which there cannot be a fall in the rate of interest. This is that rate of interest at which, according to the liquidity trap hypothesis, the public is willing to hold only money and no bonds.

Changes in the Demand for Money and their Effects on the Interest Rate

There can occur a change in the demand for money either due to a change in the transactions demand for money or due to change in the speculative demand for money.

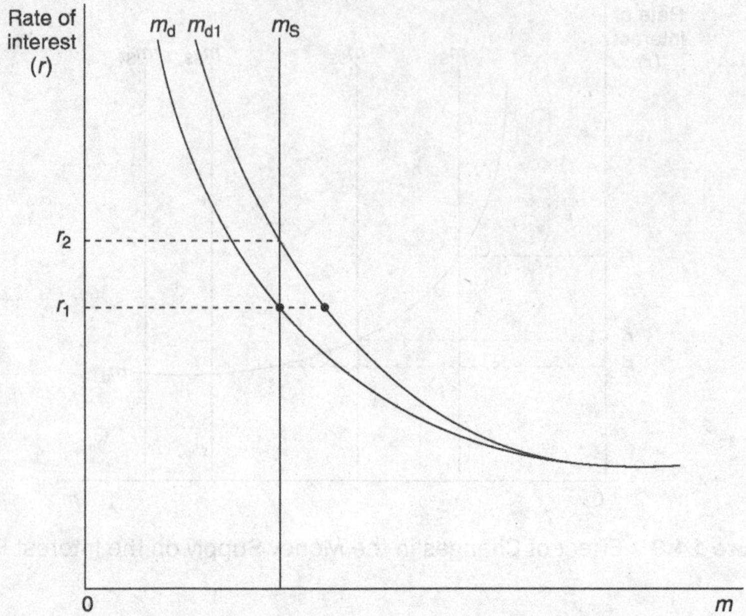

Figure 14.9 Effect of Changes in the Transactions Demand for Money on the Interest Rate

Changes in the Transactions Demand for Money and their Effects on the Interest Rate

Given the money supply and the speculative demand for money, the rate of interest will vary directly with the income level.

An Increase in the Income Level

In Figure 14.9, initial equilibrium in the money market is determined at the intersection of m_s and m_d with the equilibrium rate of interest at r_1. Given the value of k (fraction of money income which the public likes to hold as money balances for transactions), an increase in the income will raise the transactions demand for money and hence the total demand for money curve will shift outwards at each rate of interest to give the new demand curve m_{d1}. Given the supply of money and an increase in the demand for money, the rate of interest will rise to new equilibrium rate of r_2.

The underlying process here involves a diversion of money from speculative balances to transactions balances. With an increase in their incomes, individuals realize that they need more money for transactions. As the supply of money is unchanged, the additional demand for transactions balances can be satisfied only by selling bonds leading to a decrease in the price of bonds and an increase in the rate of interest from r_1 to r_2.

A Decrease in the Income Level

Initial equilibrium in the money market exists with m_s and m_{d1} with the equilibrium rate of interest at r_2. Given the value of k, a decrease in the income will reduce the transactions demand for money and hence the total demand curve will shift inwards at each rate of interest to give the new demand curve m_d. Given the supply of money and a decrease in the demand for money, the rate of interest will fall to new equilibrium rate of r_1.

Changes in the Speculative Demand for Money and their Effects on the Interest Rate

We assume that the money supply and the transactions demand for money are given and there is a change in the speculative demand for money.

The question arises how does the speculative demand for money change? This particular demand for money is based on the wealth holder's expectations regarding the normal rate of interest. The change in the expectations regarding the normal rate of interest occurs if there are expected changes in the domestic and international factors, which have an influence on the business forecasts and also the response expected from the Central Bank to such changes.

Suppose in Figure 14.9, money supply is given as m_s while the demand for money is given as m_d and the normal rate of interest is r_1. With no decrease in the supply of money and no increase in the income level, suppose the wealth holders' views undergo a change and they now regard a higher rate r_2 as the normal rate of interest. Thus rates above r_2 will be viewed as high while rates below r_2 will be viewed as low. This will amount to an outward shift in the demand curve from m_d to m_{d1}.

On the other hand, with no increase in the money supply and no decrease in the income level, suppose the wealth holders now regard a rate below r_1 as the normal rate of interest. Thus, rates above r_1 will be viewed as high while rates below r_1 will be viewed as low. This will amount to an inward shift in the demand curve.

RECAP

- Given the money supply and the speculative demand for money, the rate of interest will vary directly with the income level.

A CRITICISM OF THE KEYNESIAN APPROACH

(1) The money market equilibrium equation of Keynes $k(Y) + g(r) = m_s$, is actually one equation and two unknowns, r and Y. Only if the value of Y is known can $k(Y)$ be taken as known and then the above equation can be used to calculate r. However, the problem is that while Y not only affects r through $k(Y)$ but that itself is affected by r through investment, I. Thus, r and Y are interdependent variables. Hence, it can be argued that Keynes theory is indeterminate.

(2) Keynes had denied the influence of the real factors, saving and investment, in the determination of the rate of interest. This is perhaps a view which is too extreme as the influence of these real factors cannot be ignored.

RECAP

- Keynes had denied the influence of the real factors in the determination of the rate of interest, a view which is too extreme as the influence of these real factors cannot be ignored.

SUMMARY

INTRODUCTION

The chapter discusses the three motives for holding money and the determination of the rate of interest in the Keynesian model through the supply and demand for money.

THE KEYNESIAN THEORY OF THE DEMAND FOR MONEY

1. Unlike the classical economists who recognized only the medium of exchange function of money, Keynes emphasized the store of value function of money also.
2. According to Keynes, money was demanded due to three motives: transactions motive, precautionary motive and speculative motive.

TRANSACTIONS DEMAND

1. The transactions demand for money is the demand for cash by the public for carrying on its various current transactions.
2. The reason why this money is held is due to the time gap involved between which the income is received and the payments are made out.
3. As the frequency of the receipts increase, the average holding of transactions balances by the individual decreases.
4. There exists a stable and direct relationship between income and transactions money balances.
5. Keynes had argued that the transactions demand for money is perfectly interest inelastic.

PRECAUTIONARY DEMAND

1. The precautionary demand for money is the demand for cash by the public for contingencies, which may involve unexpected expenditures and opportunities.
2. The precautionary demand for money varies directly with the income level.
3. The other factor which influences precautionary demand for money is the rate of interest. At high rates of interest, one may feel tempted to hold smaller precautionary balances.
4. For the sake of convenience and following the conventional procedure, transactions and precautionary balances are often put together as a function primarily of the income level and as being interest inelastic.

SPECULATIVE DEMAND

1. The speculative demand for money represents a complete break from the classical theory and it is one of the most important contributions made by Keynes.
2. Keynes assumed that individuals hold only two kinds of financial assets in their asset portfolio, namely money and perpetual (or irredeemable) bonds.
3. The existence of an uncertainty about the future gives rise to what is called the speculative demand for money.
4. There exists an inverse relationship between market rate of interest and the price of a bond. In addition, the price of a bond is subject to capital gain and losses.
5. The speculators can be grouped into two categories: bulls who expect that the price of bonds will rise in the future and bears who expect that the price of bonds will fall in the future.
6. It is from the bears that the speculative demand for money arises.
7. The asset holders either hold only bonds or they hold only money. They do not have a diversified portfolio.
8. A very significant contribution of Keynes is the liquidity trap, which is a situation when at some very low rate of interest all asset holders become bears. No additions to the money supply can succeed in lowering the interest rates any further.
9. Keynes had emphasized that at any point in time there will exist a certain r which can be said to be that rate of interest which will prevail under normal circumstances and which is the benchmark or yardstick with which any actual r is compared in making decisions.
10. The aggregate speculative demand for money curve is a smooth downward sloping curve showing an inverse relationship between the speculative demand for money and the current rate of interest.

THE TOTAL DEMAND FOR MONEY

The total demand for money can be written as $m_d = m_t + m_{sp}$ or $m_d = k(Y) + g(r)$. It represents the Keynesian demand curve for money and is downward sloping.

CRITICISM OF KEYNES' THEORY OF DEMAND FOR MONEY

1. In reality, individuals do not hold either just money or only bonds and in fact hold a diversified asset portfolio.
2. The possibilities of the occurrence of a liquidity trap are quite far-flung.
3. Keynes' division of money into transaction, precautionary and speculative demands is not realistic and the same unit of money can be used to serve all the three motives.

THE KEYNESIAN THEORY OF INTEREST

1. In Keynes' theory, the rate of interest is a monetary phenomenon determined by the equality between the demand for and supply of money. Thus, $k(Y) + g(r) = m_s$.

2. Variations in *r* alone act as the adjustment mechanism for bringing about equilibrium in the money market whenever disequilibrium occurs.

VARIATIONS IN THE INTEREST RATE

CHANGES IN THE MONEY SUPPLY AND THEIR EFFECTS ON THE INTEREST RATE

1. Given the demand for money curve, an increase in the supply of money leads to a decrease in the interest rate and vice versa.
2. However in the liquidity trap, any increases in the supply of money will not lower the rate of interest any further.

CHANGES IN THE DEMAND FOR MONEY AND THEIR EFFECTS ON THE INTEREST RATE

1. There can occur a change in the demand for money either due to a change in the transactions demand for money or due to change in the speculative demand for money.
2. As far as changes in the transactions demand for money are concerned, given the money supply and the speculative demand for money, the rate of interest will vary directly with the income level.
3. As far as changes in the speculative demand for money are concerned, given the money supply and the transactions demand for money a change in the speculative demand for money will lead to a change in the interest rate.

CRITICISM OF THE KEYNESIAN APPROACH

1. The money market equilibrium equation of Keynes is actually one equation and two unknowns. Hence, it can be argued that Keynes theory is indeterminate.
2. Keynes had denied the influence of the real factors, saving and investment, in the determination of the rate of interest.

REVIEW QUESTIONS

TRUE OR FALSE QUESTIONS

1. The precautionary demand for money is the demand for cash by the public for carrying on its various current transactions.
2. Keynes had laid emphasis on the store of value function of money.
3. The average holdings of transactions balance by the individual increases as the frequency of the receipts increases.
4. The speculative demand for money arises due to the existence of an uncertainty about the future.
5. The liquidity trap is a situation when at some very low rate of interest all asset holders become bulls.

VERY SHORT-ANSWER QUESTIONS

1. Is the transactions demand for money interest elastic? Explain.
2. What is the precautionary demand for money?
3. Bulls and bears are the two categories of speculators in the market? How do they function? Explain.
4. 'The liquidity trap is a situation when at some very low rate of interest all asset holders become bears.' Explain.
5. The speculative demand for money represents a complete break from the classical theory and it is one of the most important contributions made by Keynes. Comment.

SHORT-ANSWER QUESTIONS

1. Analyse the transactions demand for money as a function of the income level.
2. What is the precautionary demand for money? What are the factors that influence it? Discuss.
3. Derive Keynes' total demand for money curve.
4. (a) What is normal rate of interest in the Keynesian speculative demand for money? Explain.

   (b) Give a criticism of Keynes' theory of demand for money.
5. In the Keynesian theory of interest, 'there can occur a change in the demand for money either due to a change in the transactions demand for money or due to change in the speculative demand for money'. Explain.

LONG-ANSWER QUESTIONS

1. What is the transactions demand for money? Explain
2. 'According to Keynes, money is demanded due to three motives: transactions motive, precautionary motive and speculative motive.' Briefly discuss the three motives.
3. What is the speculative demand for money? What are the factors that influence it? Discuss.
4. How is the rate of interest determined in the Keynes theory? Is it a real or a monetary phenomenon?
5. 'In Keynes theory, variations in *r* will occur due to changes in the supply of money and the demand for money.' Explain.

ANSWERS

TRUE OR FALSE QUESTIONS

1. **False.** The transactions demand for money is the demand for cash by the public for carrying on its various current transactions.
2. **True.** Unlike the classical economists who recognized only the medium of exchange function of money, Keynes emphasized the store of value function of money also.
3. **False.** The average holdings of transactions balance by the individual decreases as the frequency of the receipts increases.
4. **True.** The existence of an uncertainty about the future gives rise to the speculative demand for money.
5. **False.** The liquidity trap is a situation when at some very low rate of interest all asset holders become bears.

Demand for Money: The Post-Keynesian Approach

15

After studying this topic, you should be able to understand

- ✓ *The post Keynesian theories like the portfolio theories lay emphasis on the store of value function of money.*
- ✓ *The transactions theories lay more emphasis on the medium of exchange function of money.*
- ✓ *The Baumol-Tobin model of transactions demand for money lays stress on the fact that the holding of money by the individual transactor in his asset portfolio involves both a cost and a benefit.*
- ✓ *Friedman's theory of demand for money is partly Keynesian and partly non-Keynesian.*
- ✓ *Friedman ignores the motives for holding money and takes it for granted that people will certainly hold money.*

INTRODUCTION

As already discussed in Chapter 14 that Keynes believed that there exist only two kinds of assets between which individuals make a choice: money and bonds. One of the most important post Keynesian developments was the realization that besides money and bonds, there exist a variety of assets between which the individual chooses. This chapter makes an attempt at analysing some of these theories, which came after Keynes had presented his theory.

PORTFOLIO THEORIES OF DEMAND FOR MONEY: TOBIN'S PORTFOLIO BALANCE THEORY

Money is demanded because it performs many functions. While the classical economists had laid emphasis on the medium of exchange function of money (as in the QTM), Keynes had realized the importance of both the medium of exchange function and the store of value function of money. The post Keynesian theories like the portfolio theories lay emphasis on the store of value function of money.

In comparison to other assets, money offers a different combination of risk and return. While bonds and stocks are subject to price fluctuations money is at least safe in comparison. Hence, according to some economists like James Tobin, people have a preference for money in their optimal asset portfolio.

As per the portfolio theories, the demand for money is influenced by many factors; some of them are as follows:

(1) The total amount of wealth to be divided between money and the other assets.

(2) The risk and return on money in comparison to the other assets a household holds.

The demand function for money can be written as:

$$(M/P)^d = L(r_s, r_b, \pi^e, W)$$

where, $(M/P)^d$ = demand for real money

r_s = expected real return on stocks

r_b = expected real return on bonds

π^e = the expected rate of inflation in the economy

W = real wealth

A look at the demand for money function shows that:

(1) A decrease in r_s or r_b leads to an increase in the demand for money as the other assets are now less attractive.

(2) A decrease in π^e will lead to an increase in demand for money because money is now more attractive.

(3) An increase in W will lead to an increase in the demand for money because a larger wealth is associated with a larger asset portfolio.

Thus, according to the portfolio theories, the demand for money, which is the safest asset, depends not only on the expected yields from the other assets but also on the risk on the yields expected from these other assets. Thus, the demand for money is a function of the expected returns on the other assets, the expected rate of inflation and the real wealth. In general, an increase in the risk perception of the yields accruing on the other assets will result in an increase in the demand for money as this will decrease the opportunity cost of holding money.

The usefulness of the portfolio theories in evaluating the demand for money will depend on the definition of money which is under consideration:

(1) The narrow measure of money is M_1,

$$M_1 = C + DD$$

It is clear as since currency and demand deposits are safe assets but earn zero or very low rates of interest, M_1, as a store of value is much below the other assets.

Thus portfolio theories are not able to explain the demand for currency and demand deposits, which form a part of M_1.

(2) The broad measure of money is M_2

$$M_2 = C + DD + \text{Saving Deposits with Post Offices} + \text{Net Time Deposits of Banks}$$

Since saving deposits and time deposits have the same risk but pay a higher yield than currency and demand deposits, portfolio theories are able to explain the demand for such assets like saving deposits and time deposits.

The portfolio theories, thus, are able to explain the demand for M_2 better than M_1.

Tobin's Portfolio Balance Theory

In the year 1958 in his famous article *Liquidity Preference as Behaviour towards Risk*, Tobin had put forward the view that the individual wealth holder in his asset portfolio, in addition to other capital assets, always prefers to hold money which is a safe asset with a nominal value which is certain. He does so as an insurance against those capital assets whose prices tend to fluctuate in an uncertain manner.

Tobin's portfolio balance theory analyses the behaviour of such an individual wealth holder. Keynes had emphasized that the individual wealth holder will hold either nothing or bonds or nothing but money in his asset portfolio. However, empirical evidence goes against Keynes' beliefs. People prefer to hold a diversified asset portfolio, where they hold money, bonds, and many other assets. They do so because they are uncertain about the future. If the individual wealth holder had been certain regarding the future he would hold only that asset from which he expects the highest returns.

We consider an individual who gets a certain income once in a time period. A part of this income is put aside as savings to be invested in assets. Tobin's analysis is based on certain assumptions which are as follows:

(1) The assets that are available to him for his asset portfolio are only bonds and money.

(2) The individual treats wealth as a good, which increases his utility and risk as a bad which decreases his utility.

(3) Money involves no risk and does not give any returns.

(4) Bonds are subject to price fluctuations. They do yield an income but which is subject to uncertainty. This income has two parts:

  (a) The interest on the bond, which is a certain amount.

  (b) The capital gains and losses, which are subject to risks and uncertainty.

(5) There exists a trade-off between risk and return. Thus, an individual with a higher proportion of bonds in his portfolio is expecting to earn more wealth but is at a higher risk.

Figure 15.1 depicts the utility maximization by an individual wealth holder where

Vertical axis = expected wealth in the next period, w

Horizontal axis = risk, σ

I_0, I_1 = indifference curves where each curve represents the different combinations of risk and expected wealth between which the individual is indifferent.

Unlike the standard indifference curve, here each curve slopes upwards towards the right because while wealth is a good which increases the individual's utility, risk is a bad which decreases his utility. Thus as an individual's wealth increases, he will be better off unless there occurs an increase in the risk.

A movement upwards and towards the left represents indifference curves with higher levels of utility indicating that the individual is in a better position.

As against the standard convex to the origin indifference curves, the indifference curves here are convex downwards. The larger the wealth the individual has, lesser would be the importance of each incremental unit. Thus, the smaller will be the additional risk that he will be willing to undertake to add to his wealth.

$w - w(1 + i_0)$ = line depicting the budget constraint of the individual. It shows the different combinations of risk and expected wealth among which he makes a choice while he is arranging his asset portfolio.

Along this line, the options available to the individual are as follows:

(1) Point w, which represents the wealth he begins with. If he continues to hold his entire wealth in the form of money, he would have the same wealth in the end.

(2) Point $w(1 + i_0)$, which represents the situation when he holds his entire wealth in form of bonds. At this particular point,

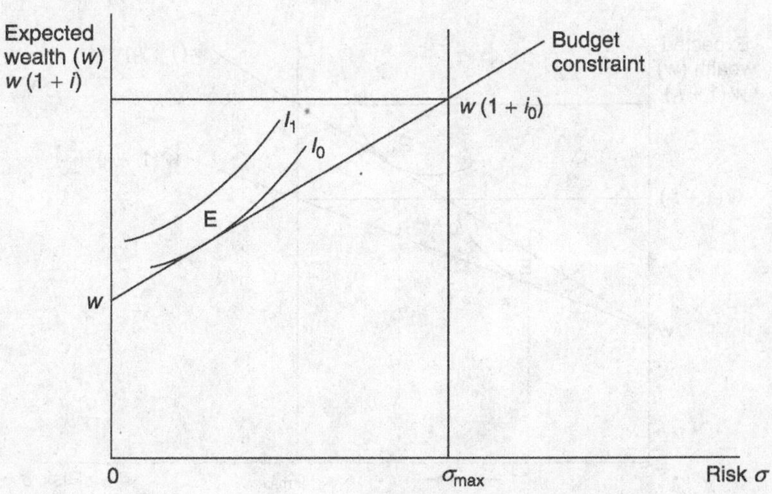

Figure 15.1 Maximization of Utility by the Individual Wealth Holder

BOX 15.1

The main difference between Keynes and Friedman exists in their opinion with respect to the sensitivity of the demand for money to the rate of interest and regarding the stability of the demand for money function over time. Tobin on the basis of his research had concluded that the demand for money is sensitive to the rate of interest. Others also came up with similar conclusions. However, as far as the stability of the demand for money in the US is concerned, while it was stable initially but later on from the 1970s it became quite unstable and created problems for the Federal Reserve.

(a) If the rate of interest is i_0, his expected wealth will be $w(1 + i_0)$.

(b) Since he would be holding all his assets in the form of bonds, he would be undertaking the maximum risk, σ_{Max}.

(3) Any point on the line $w - w(1 + i_0)$ which represents a combination of money and bonds in his asset portfolio.

Given the interest rate and the risk on the bonds, the individual wealth holder aims at maximizing his utility from his asset portfolio. Such a point is E where the indifference curve I_0 is tangential to the budget constraint. At this point, his portfolio consists of a combination of both money and bonds.

Effects of a Change in the Interest Rate on the Individual Wealth Holder's Asset Portfolio

Suppose while the risk remains the same, there is an increase in the interest rate on the bonds, from i_0 to i_1. In Figure 15.2, there is a shift in the budget line and the individual wealth holder is now in equilibrium at point E_1 which is on a higher indifference curve than point E. At point E_1, the individual is earning more returns as compared to point E but he is able to do so by undertaking greater risk. More risk implies that the individual is holding more bonds and thus less of money. Therefore, it is obvious that an increase in the interest rate leads to a decrease in the demand for money. This analysis helps in the derivation of what Keynes called the speculative demand for money, showing the inverse relationship between the rate of interest and the demand for money.

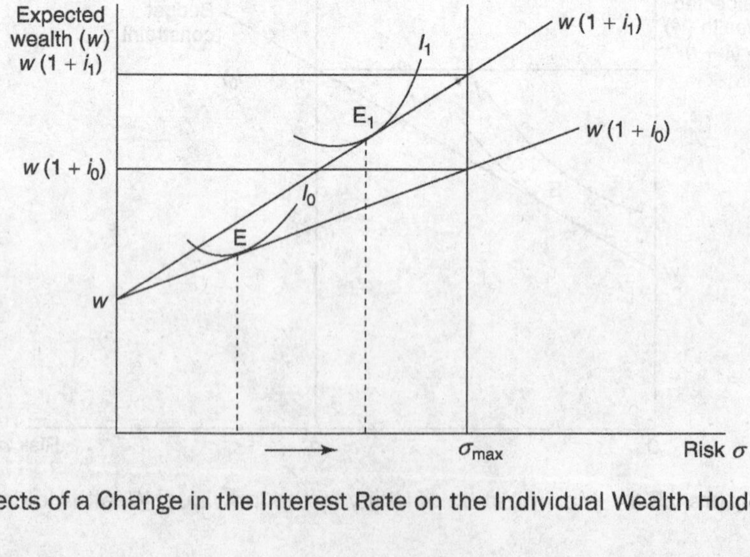

Figure 15.2 Effects of a Change in the Interest Rate on the Individual Wealth Holder's Asset Portfolio

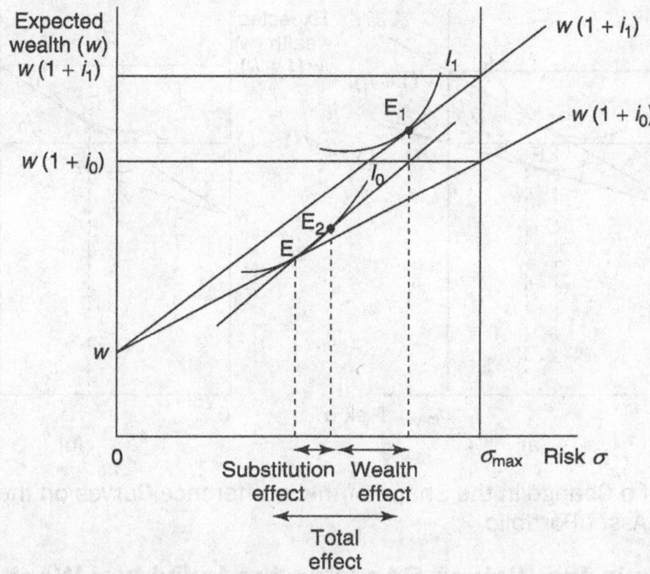

Figure 15.3 Effects of a Change in the Interest Rate on the Individual Wealth Holder's Asset Portfolio: The Substitution Effect and the Wealth Effect

Effects of a Change in the Interest Rate on the Individual Wealth Holder's Asset Portfolio: The Substitution Effect and the Wealth Effect

In Figure 15.2, we had analysed the effect of a change in the interest rate leading to a shift in the budget line with the individual wealth holder in equilibrium at point E_1. Figure 15.3 splits up the movement from E to E_1 into the substitution effect and the wealth effect:

(1) A movement from E to E_2 is the substitution effect. Due to this effect there occurs a movement along the indifference curve I_0, leading to an increase in risk undertaken and thus in the holding of bonds. Thus, there is a decrease in the demand for money.

(2) A movement from E_2 to E_1 is the wealth effect. This effect can take any direction. With an increase in the individual's wealth if his bond holding increases, then in that case the substitution effect gets reinforced by the wealth effect. Hence, with an increase in the rate of interest the individual wealth holder increases his holdings of bonds and decreases his demand for money.

Effects of a Change in the Shape of the Indifference Curves on the Individual Wealth Holder's Asset Portfolio

Figure 15.4 (a) shows an indifference curve map where an increase in the rate of interest rate leads to situation where the individual is willing to undertake less risk. Less risk implies that the individual is reducing his holding of bonds and increasing the demand for money.

Figure 15.4 (b) shows an indifference curve map where an increase in the rate of interest rate leads to situation where the individual is willing to undertake the same amount of risk, and thus his holding of bonds and the demand for money remains unchanged.

Thus, it is important to note that the shape of the indifference curves plays an important role in determining the demand for money.

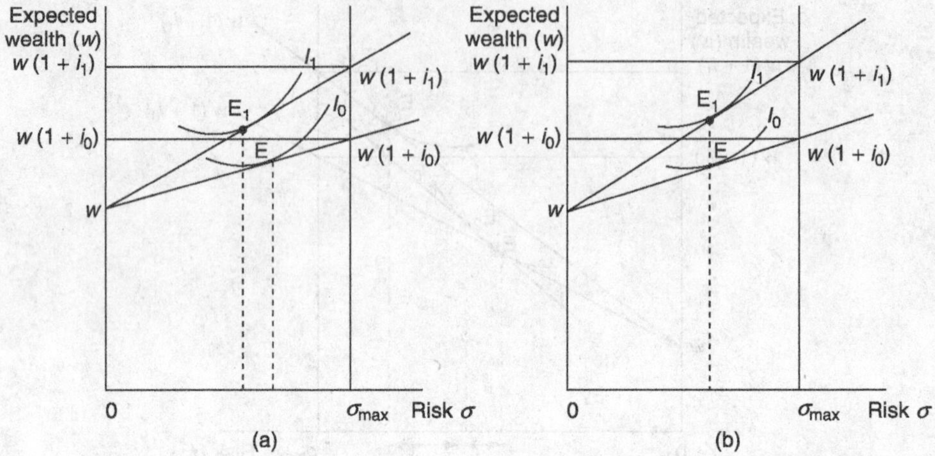

Figure 15.4 Effects of a Change in the Shape of the Indifference Curves on the Individual Wealth Holder's Asset Portfolio

Effects of a Change in the Risk on Bonds on the Individual Wealth Holder's Asset Portfolio

In Figure 15.5, an increase in the risk on bonds leads to a downward shift of the budget constraint. There is a change in equilibrium from E_1 to E. Thus with the increase in risk on bonds, the individual is less willing to hold bonds and thus his demand for money goes up.

Similarly with a decrease in the risk on bonds, there will be an upward shift of the budget constraint with a change in equilibrium. The individual is now more willing to hold bonds and thus his demand for money goes down.

Thus we find that the demand for money, according to Tobin, depends on the following factors:

(1) the individual's wealth;

(2) the interest rate or the expected yield on the bonds;

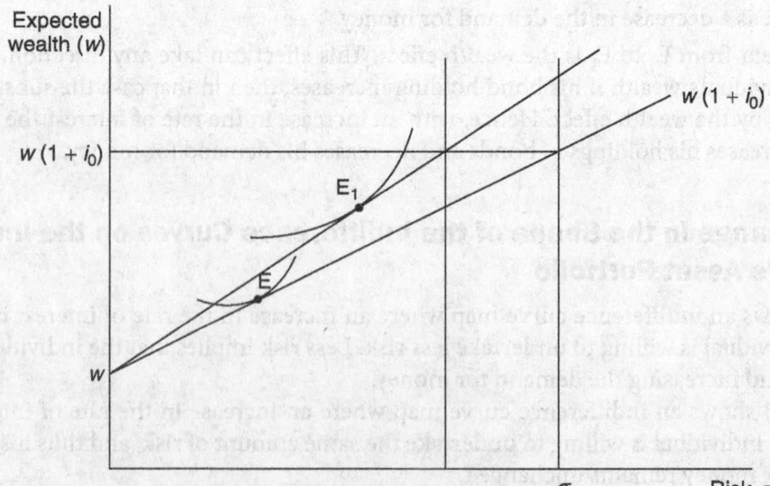

Figure 15.5 Effects of an Increase in the Risk on Bonds on the Individual Wealth Holder's Asset Portfolio

(3) the risk on the bonds;
(4) the price level; and
(5) shape of the indifference curves.

RECAP

- The demand for money is a function of the expected returns on the other assets, the expected rate of inflation and the real wealth.
- The portfolio theories are able to explain the demand for M_2 better than M_1.
- When there is an increase in the rate of interest, the individual wealth holder increases his holdings of bonds and decreases his demand for money.
- When there is a decrease in the risk on bonds, the individual is more willing to hold bonds and thus his demand for money goes down.

TRANSACTIONS THEORIES OF DEMAND FOR MONEY: BAUMOL–TOBIN MODEL OF CASH MANAGEMENT

Unlike some of the post Keynesian theories like the portfolio theories which lay emphasis on the store of value function of money, the transactions theories lay more emphasis on the medium of exchange function of money. According to these theories, even though money does not yield any returns people continue to hold it because it has the advantage of making it more convenient to conduct transactions. Hence, they are in a position to explain the demand for even the narrow measure of money M_1. Of the many transactions theories, one theory which became quite popular is the Baumol-Tobin model.

Baumol–Tobin Model of Transactions Demand for Money

The model was developed in the 1950s by William Baumol and James Tobin. The model analyses the behaviour of an individual transactor (who may be a firm or even a household) who continues to hold money in his asset portfolio. This holding of money involves both a cost and a benefit:

(1) The cost of holding money has two components :
   (a) An opportunity cost in terms of the interest that would have accrued had the money been deposited in some saving deposits.
   (b) The cost, which is involved per transaction of moving between bonds and money.

(2) The benefit of holding money is the ease with which the transactions can be conducted with the money.

The model is based on certain assumptions, which are as follows:
   (a) An individual receives an income Y once in a certain time period but spends it gradually over a year.
   (b) The individual's cash purchases (or expenditures) are spread evenly throughout the year.
   (c) The individual holds a combination of money and risk free income yielding bonds in his portfolio.
   (d) There is a given cost involved per transaction of moving between bonds and money.

The individual will aim at achieving an optimal size of his money holding. This will further depend on the number of trips he makes to the bank in a year:

(1) He makes one trip to the bank in a year. He withdraws the entire income Y at the beginning of the year and then spends it uniformly over the year. Figure 15.6(a) shows that his money holdings:
   (a) At the beginning of the year is Y;
   (b) At the end of the year are zero.
   (c) Average money holdings over the whole year are $Y/2$.

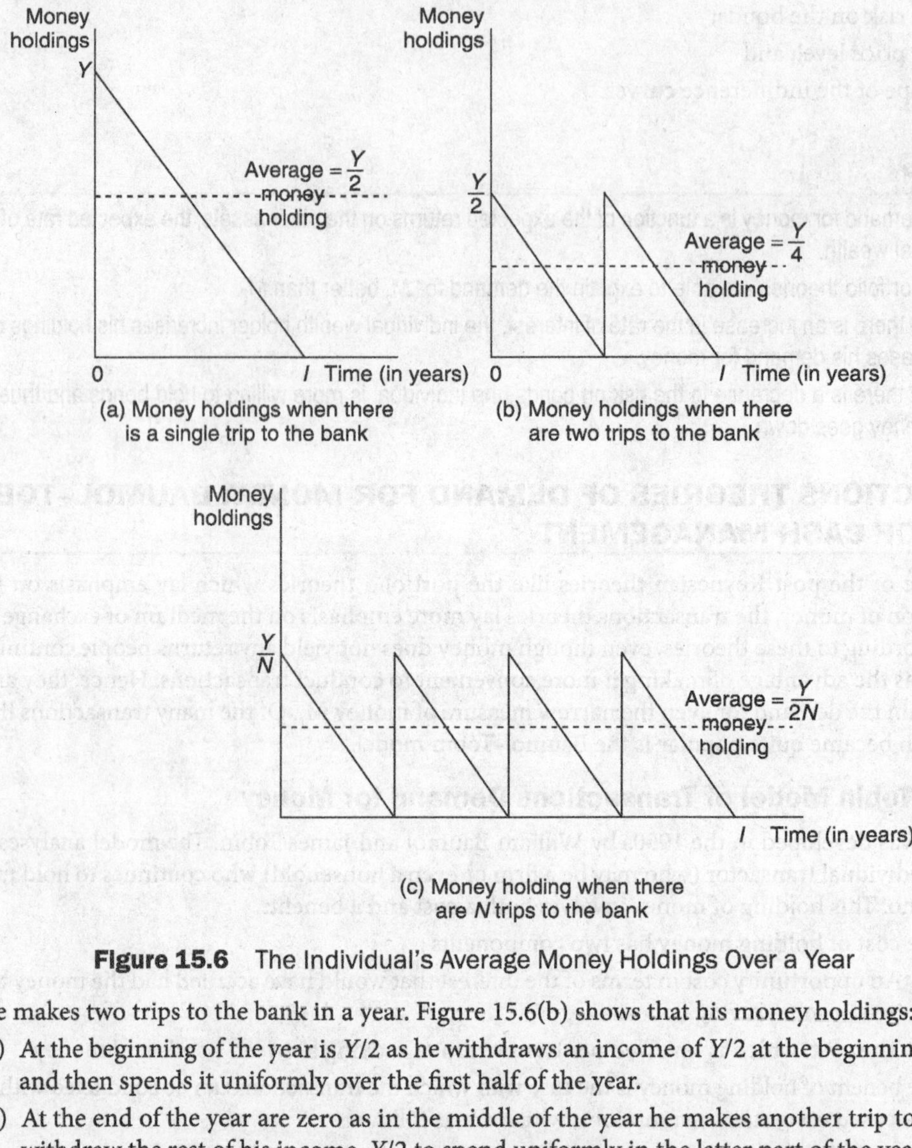

Figure 15.6 The Individual's Average Money Holdings Over a Year

(2) He makes two trips to the bank in a year. Figure 15.6(b) shows that his money holdings:

(a) At the beginning of the year is $Y/2$ as he withdraws an income of $Y/2$ at the beginning of the year and then spends it uniformly over the first half of the year.

(b) At the end of the year are zero as in the middle of the year he makes another trip to the bank to withdraw the rest of his income, $Y/2$ to spend uniformly in the latter part of the year.

(c) Average money holdings over the whole year are $Y/4$.

(3) He makes N number of trips to the bank in a year. Figure 15.6 (c) shows that his money holdings:

(a) At the beginning of the year is Y/N.

(b) At the end of the year are zero.

(c) Average money holdings over the whole year are $Y/2N$ since in every trip that he makes to the bank he withdraws an income Y/N to spend uniformly over the year.

The smaller is N (that is, the fewer the number of trips that he makes to the bank).

(1) The more is the money holding of the individual (on an average).

(2) The higher is the loss of interest.

(3) The less are the hassles involved in making frequent trips to the bank.

Optimal Level of Transactions Demand for Money

To determine this, we first need to determine the optimal value of N. We assume

i = interest rate

T = the fixed cost per transaction involved in moving between bonds and money

Total cost of N trips = Costs of trips + Interest forgone

or $$C = TN + \frac{iY}{2N}$$

where, TN = the total cost of making N trips to the bank

$\frac{iY}{2N}$ = the interest forgone by holding money instead of bonds from the N trips [where $\frac{Y}{2N}$ is the average cash balance for N trips]

Now since $C = TN + \frac{iY}{2N}$,

to find the optimal number of transactions we minimize the total cost with respect to N

$$\frac{dC}{dN} = T + \left(\frac{-iYN^{-2}}{2}\right)$$

But at the optimum $$\frac{dC}{dN} = 0$$

Thus, $$T + \left(\frac{-iYN^{-2}}{2}\right) = 0$$

or $$T = \left(\frac{iYN^{-2}}{2}\right)$$

or $$iY = 2TN^2$$

or, $$N^* = \text{square root } \sqrt{iY/2T}$$

where N^* is the optimal number of transactions.

Thus, an individual would make more transactions if

(1) the lower is the transactions cost.

(2) the higher is the income.

(3) the higher is the interest rate.

The theory arrives at the following conclusions:

(1) The transactions demand for money increases less than proportionately with the increases in income. This is because there exist economies of scale in an individual's transactions demand for money.

(2) The transactions demand for money varies inversely with the interest rate.

Empirical evidence suggests that while the income elasticity seems to be between 1/2 and 1, the interest elasticity seems to be between 0 and 1/2.

BOX 15.2

Milton Friedman is one of the most well known and influential political commentators and economist of the century. He was a very strong opponent of the Keynesian economics and the Keynesian orthodoxy. He attacked the Keynesian theory with his article. The Quantity Theory of Money, A Restatement (1956), followed by a historical study on the Monetary History of the United States, in 1963 with Anna J. Schwartz. Friedman also wrote on the different aspects of economic policy. In general, he advocated laissez-faire policies. In the year 1976, Friedman won the Nobel Prize.

RECAP

- According to the Baumol–Tobin model of transactions demand for money, the transactions demand for money increases less than proportionately with the increases in income and inversely with the interest rate.

MODERN QUANTITY THEORY OF MONEY: FRIEDMAN'S MODEL

The main proponent of the modern quantity theory of money is Milton Friedman who has developed his own version of the quantity theory of money (QTM). Friedman's theory of demand for money is partly Keynesian and partly non-Keynesian. Unlike Keynes, he ignores the motives for holding money and takes it for granted that people will certainly hold money. The crux relates to the question as to how much money people will hold.

To identify the determinants of the demand for money, Friedman divides the holders of money into two categories:

(1) The ultimate wealth holders
(2) The business firms

However in putting forward his theory, Friedman has laid more emphasis on the ultimate wealth holders as compared to the business firms.

Demand for Money by the Ultimate Wealth Holders

It is important to note the following:

(1) The ultimate wealth holders are the households.
(2) For the households, money is just like any other durable good; hence, we can apply the standard theory of demand for consumer durable goods to the demand or money.
(3) Households are interested in real (and not nominal) money and its command over the goods and services.

According to Friedman, the key determinants of the demand for money are as follows:

(1) **Wealth:** The concept of wealth is similar to the budget constraint of the standard consumer theory. Friedman defines wealth to include both physical wealth (non-human wealth) and human wealth. While estimates are available for the former, it is extremely difficult to measure human wealth, which can be taken as the present value of the expected future flow of labour income.
The solution to the problem of measuring wealth is to use income, which includes both labour income and physical income, as a proxy for wealth. But as far as income is concerned, Friedman had suggested the use of the 'permanent income' rather than the current income. Thus in Friedman's analysis, income is a proxy for wealth and is not money earned for work done.

(2) **The division of wealth between human wealth and physical wealth:** While physical wealth can be easily bought and sold, there is no market for human wealth and thus there cannot be substitution between human and physical wealth in the asset portfolio.
Friedman suggests that the ratio of human wealth to physical wealth should be considered as an important variable. Given the total wealth, the higher the component of human wealth, the higher will be the demand for money to make up for the lack of a market in human wealth.

(3) **Expected rate of return on money and other assets:** This is similar to the concept of the price of the good under consideration and the price of substitutes and complements in the standard consumer theory of demand.

As far as the nominal rate of return is concerned, it may be:

(1) positive as in the case of saving deposits,
(2) zero as in the case of currency or
(3) negative (only theoretically) when there are net service charges on the current account deposits.

In general, the nominal rate of return on assets can be divided into two components, which are as follows:

(i) The interest income on the assets.

(ii) Expected change in the nominal price of these assets.

Although we have taken the rates of returns on the different assets as separate variables, in reality, a change in any one of them will have an impact on others as well.

(4) **Price level:** An increase in the price level will lead to a decrease in real value of the nominal money holdings. Hence, the expected rate of change in prices is an important variable as it exercises an influence on the expected rate of return to money.

(5) **Other variables:** This includes variables like the extent to which economic stability is expected to prevail in the economy in the future. Wealth holders will prefer to hold more liquidity during unstable economic conditions.

Friedman's theory of demand for money can be expressed in the form of the following function:

$$\left(\frac{M}{P}\right)^d = (y, w, r_m, r_b, r_e, p^e, u)$$

where, M = Demand for nominal money

P = Price level

$\left(\frac{M}{P}\right)^d$ = Demand for real money

y = Real income

w = Ratio of human wealth to non-human wealth

r_m = Expected rate of return on money

r_b = Expected rate of return on fixed value securities

r_e = Expected return on equities

p^e = Expected rate of change of prices of goods

u = variables other than income, which influence the utility of money

Thus, we have Friedman's demand function for money. However, this equation is subject to certain qualifications which are as follows:

(1) It is the aggregate demand for money function.

(2) M, y and w refer to aggregate magnitudes.

(3) We are ignoring the distribution of income among the households and the firms.

RECAP

- According to Friedman, the key determinants of the demand for money are wealth, the division of wealth between human wealth and physical wealth, and the expected rate of return on money and other assets.

SUMMARY

INTRODUCTION

The chapter makes an attempt at analysing some of those theories, which came after Keynes had presented his theory.

PORTFOLIO THEORIES OF DEMAND FOR MONEY: TOBIN'S PORTFOLIO BALANCE THEORY

1. The post Keynesian theories like the portfolio theories lay emphasis on the store of value function of money.
2. According to some economists like James Tobin, people have a preference for money in their optimal asset portfolio.
3. As per the portfolio theories, the demand function for money can be written as:

$$\left(\frac{M}{P}\right)^d = L\,(r_s, r_b, \pi^e, W)$$

Thus, the demand for money is a function of the expected returns on the other assets, the expected rate of inflation and the real wealth.

4. As to the usefulness of the portfolio theories in evaluating the demand for money, the portfolio theories are able to explain the demand for M_2 better than M_1.

TOBIN'S PORTFOLIO BALANCE THEORY

1. Tobin's portfolio balance theory analyses the behaviour of an individual wealth holder who is uncertain about the future and thus holds a diversified asset portfolio, where he holds money, bonds, and many other assets.
2. The individual wealth holder aims at maximizing his utility. His indifference curves slope upward with wealth as a good and risk as a bad. His budget constraint shows the different combinations of risk and expected wealth among which he makes a choice while he is arranging his asset portfolio.
3. Given the interest rate and the risk on the bonds, the individual wealth holder will be in equilibrium at a point where the indifference curve is tangential to the budget constraint. At this point, his portfolio consists of a combination of both money and bonds.

EFFECTS OF A CHANGE IN THE INTEREST RATE ON THE INDIVIDUAL WEALTH HOLDER'S ASSET PORTFOLIO

1. Suppose while the risk remains the same, there is an increase in the interest rate on the bonds.
2. There occurs a shift in the budget line and the individual wealth holder moves to new equilibrium, which is on a higher indifference curve.
3. At this point he is undertaking a greater risk that he can do only by holding more bonds and less of money.
4. Thus, an increase in the interest rate leads to a decrease in the demand for money.
5. The effects of a change in the interest rate can be discussed in terms of the substitution effect and the wealth effect.

EFFECTS OF A CHANGE IN THE SHAPE OF THE INDIFFERENCE CURVES ON THE INDIVIDUAL WEALTH HOLDER'S ASSET PORTFOLIO

Depending on the shape of the indifference curves, it is possible for an increase in the rate of interest to lead to a situation where

1. The individual is willing to undertake less risk and he thus reduces his holding of bonds thereby increasing the demand for money.
2. The individual is willing to undertake the same amount of risk and, thus, his holding of bonds and the demand for money remains unchanged.

EFFECTS OF A CHANGE IN THE RISK ON BONDS ON THE INDIVIDUAL WEALTH HOLDER'S ASSET PORTFOLIO

1. An increase in the risk on bonds leads to a downwards shift of the budget constraint and thus a change in equilibrium. The individual is less willing to hold bonds and thus his demand for money goes up.
2. A decrease in the risk on bonds leads to an upwards shift of the budget constraint with a change in equilibrium. The individual is now more willing to hold bonds and thus his demand for money goes down.

TRANSACTIONS THEORIES OF DEMAND FOR MONEY: BAUMOL–TOBIN MODEL OF CASH MANAGEMENT

The transactions theories lay more emphasis on the medium of exchange function of money. Hence, they are in a position to explain the demand for even the narrow measure of money M_1.

BAUMOL–TOBIN MODEL OF TRANSACTIONS DEMAND FOR MONEY

1. The model analyses the behaviour of an individual transactor who continues to hold money in his asset portfolio.
2. The holding of money involves both a cost (opportunity cost in terms of the loss of interest and the cost per transaction of moving between bonds and money) and a benefit (in terms of the ease with which the transactions can be conducted with the money).

3. The individual will aim at achieving an optimal size of his money holding. This will depend on the number of trips he makes to the bank in a year.
4. In general, the fewer the number of trips that he makes to the bank.
   (a) the more is the money holding of the individual (on an average).
   (b) the higher is the loss of interest.
   (c) the less are the hassles involved in making frequent trips to the bank.
5. Thus, an individual would make more transactions if.
   (a) the lower is the transactions cost.
   (b) the higher is the income.
   (c) the higher is the interest rate.
6. The theory arrives at the conclusions that transactions demand for money increases less than proportionately with the increases in income and also that it varies inversely with the interest rate.

MODERN QUANTITY THEORY OF MONEY: FRIEDMAN'S MODEL

1. Friedman's theory of demand for money is partly Keynesian and partly non-Keynesian.
2. To identify the determinants of the demand for money, Friedman divides the holders of money into two categories: the ultimate wealth holders and the business firms.
3. The ultimate wealth holders are the households who hold money like any other durable good and are interested in only real money.
4. According to Friedman, the key determinants of the demand for money are as follows:
   (a) Wealth where Friedman defines wealth to include both physical wealth (non-human wealth) and human wealth. He uses income, which includes both labour income and physical income, as a proxy for wealth.
   (b) The division of wealth between human wealth and physical wealth is important in that, given the total wealth, the higher is component of human wealth the higher will be the demand for money.
   (c) Expected rate of return on money and other assets play an important role. In general, the nominal rate of return on assets can be divided into two components: interest income on the assets and expected change in the nominal price of these assets.
   (d) An increase in the price level will lead to a decrease in real value of the nominal money holdings.
   (e) Other variables include extent to which economic stability is expected to prevail in the economy in the future.
5. Friedman's demand for money function can be expressed in the form of the following function: $\left(\frac{M}{P}\right)^d = (y, w, r_m, r_b, r_e, p^e, u)$

REVIEW QUESTIONS

TRUE OR FALSE QUESTIONS

1. The post Keynesian theories like the portfolio theories lay emphasis on the store of value function of money.
2. The portfolio theories are able to explain the demand for M_1 better than M_2.
3. Tobin's portfolio balance theory analyses the behaviour of such an individual wealth holder who holds either nothing or bonds or nothing but money in his asset portfolio.
4. When there is a decrease in the risk on bonds, the individual demand for money goes down.
5. The transactions theories lay more emphasis on the medium of exchange function of money.

VERY SHORT-ANSWER QUESTIONS

1. Why do people have a preference for money in their optimal asset portfolio?
2. Even though money does not yield any returns, why do people continue to hold it? Explain with the help of the transactions theories of demand.
3. What are the main conclusions of Baumol—Tobin Model of transactions demand for money?

4. Discuss Friedman's demand for money function explaining its variables.
5. Compare the transactions theories of demand for money with the portfolio theories of demand for money.

SHORT-ANSWER QUESTIONS

1. Discuss the effects of a change in the interest rate on the individual wealth holder's asset portfolio. What are the substitution effect and the wealth effect?
2. Analyse the effects of a change in the risk on bonds on the individual wealth holder's asset portfolio.
3. What are the key determinants of the demand for money in the Friedman's theory of demand for money? Explain.
4. How does the individual wealth holder maximize his utility? Show with the help of the upward sloping indifference curves where wealth is a good and risk is a bad.
5. Discuss in brief
   (a) Tobin's portfolio balance theory
   (b) Baumol–Tobin model of transactions demand for money

LONG-ANSWER QUESTIONS

1. (a) Write a short note on the demand function for money.
   (b) Discuss the usefulness of the portfolio theories in evaluating the demand for money.
2. Discuss Tobin's portfolio balance theory.
3. Explain with diagrams:
   (a) Effects of a change in the interest rate on the individual wealth holder's asset portfolio.
   (b) Effects of a change in the shape of the indifference curves on the individual wealth holder's asset portfolio.
   (c) Effects of a change in the risk on bonds on the individual wealth holder's asset portfolio.
4. Explain Baumol–Tobin model of transactions demand for money
5. Discuss modern quantity theory of money: Friedman's model.

ANSWERS

TRUE OR FALSE QUESTIONS

1. **True.** While the classical economists had laid emphasis on the medium of exchange function of money, Keynes emphasized the medium of exchange function and the store of value function of money and the post Keynesian theories lay emphasis on the store of value function of money.
2. **False.** The portfolio theories are able to explain the demand for M_2 better than M_1.
3. **False.** Tobin's portfolio balance theory analyses the behaviour of an individual wealth holder whose asset portfolio consists of a combination of both money and bonds.
4. **True.** When there is a decrease in the risk on bonds, the individual is more willing to hold bonds and thus his demand for money goes down.
5. **True.** Unlike some of the post Keynesian theories like the portfolio theories which lay emphasis on the store of value function of money, the transactions theories lay more emphasis on the medium of exchange function of money.

UNIT V THE IS–LM FRAMEWORK: EQUILIBRIUM IN THE GOODS AND MONEY MARKETS

The IS–LM Model for a Two Sector Economy

16

After studying this topic, you should be able to understand

- ✓ *The IS curve represents the goods market equilibrium.*
- ✓ *The LM curve represents the money market equilibrium.*
- ✓ *The simultaneous equilibrium in the goods and money markets exists where the IS curve intersects the LM curve.*
- ✓ *At all points, other than the point where the IS and LM curves intersect, there will exist disequilibrium.*
- ✓ *The equilibrium is disturbed due to a shift in the IS or LM curves.*

INTRODUCTION

This chapter is a synthesis of the theory of income and output and the theory of money and interest. It analyses the linkages and the interactions between the goods and money markets to determine that level of income and the interest rate which bring about a simultaneous equilibrium in both the markets. The focus of this chapter is limited to a two sector economy which is later, in other chapters, extended to three sector and four sector economies.

The IS–LM model, which is the foundation of the short-run macroeconomics, was first introduced by J. R. Hicks in his famous article 'Mr. Keynes and the Classics' in 1937. While the IS curve represents the goods market equilibrium, investment (*I*) equals saving (*S*), the LM curve represents the money market equilibrium, demand for money (*L*) equals the supply of money (*M*).

Even today, after a period of more than 70 years since its inception, the IS–LM model continues to be popular because it is a useful tool for analysing the effects of monetary and fiscal policy on the level of output and the rate of interest.

We can analyse the IS–LM model in two ways. The earlier books on macroeconomics follow a four figure quadrants approach to derive the IS and LM curves while the recent books on the subject follow a different approach. It is difficult to say as to which of the two approaches is more correct. While most books on the subject deal with only one of the two approaches, here we attempt at dealing with both the approaches to have a complete picture (Refer to Appendix A).

THE IS–LM MODEL IN A TWO SECTOR ECONOMY

Many authors prefer the approach discussed in the chapter as compared to the recent approach to determine the simultaneous equilibrium in the goods and money markets.

The analysis is based on certain assumptions:

(1) The price level is not a variable or is constant.

(2) At that price level, the firms are willing to supply whatever output is demanded.

(3) The short-run aggregate supply curve is perfectly elastic till the full employment level of output. Thus, changes in aggregate demand alone can influence the output.

BOX 16.1

In the year 1936 at the Econometric Conference which was held in Oxford, the IS–LM model was born. Many economists like James Meade, Roy Harrod and John R. Hicks presented papers aimed at summarizing Keynes' general theory of employment, interest and money. It was here that Hicks presented the IS–LM model which was later formed as 'Mr Keynes and the Classics: A Suggested Interpretation'. Later, Hicks accepted that the model missed some important points relating to the Keynesian theory. Economists today accept the model as a not perfect one and, at the most, as an approximation to reality. In spite of all the problems associated with it, the model is used widely to understand macroeconomics.

THE GOODS MARKET EQUILIBRIUM IN A TWO SECTOR ECONOMY: THE IS CURVE

In Chapter 4, we had seen that there are two approaches to determine the equilibrium level of income or in other words the goods market equilibrium:

(1) Aggregate demand–Aggregate supply approach where

$$\text{Aggregate demand} = \text{Total value of output (or income)}$$

or

$$Y = C + I$$

(2) Saving–Investment approach where

$$I = S$$

From the Aggregate demand–Aggregate supply approach, we have

$$\text{Consumption function as } C = C(Y)$$

$$\text{Investment function as } I = I(r)$$

$$\text{Equilibrium condition as } Y = C(Y) + I(r)$$

From the Saving–Investment approach, we have

$$\text{Saving function as } S = S(Y)$$

$$\text{Investment function as } I = I(r)$$

$$\text{Equilibrium condition as } S(Y) = I(r)$$

The two equilibrium conditions can be used to develop a graphical approach to the derivation of the IS curve as in Figure 16.1.

In Figure 16.1, there are four quadrants. Quadrant A depicts the investment function showing an inverse relationship between investment and the rate of interest.

Quadrant B gives the saving investment equality in the form of a 45 degree line drawn through the origin. At all points along this 45 degree line, saving equals investment.

Quadrant C depicts the saving function showing a direct relationship between saving and the income level.

Quadrant D shows the goods market equilibrium where the IS curve depicts the different combinations of the output levels and the interest rates at which planned investment equals saving (or planned spending is equal to income).

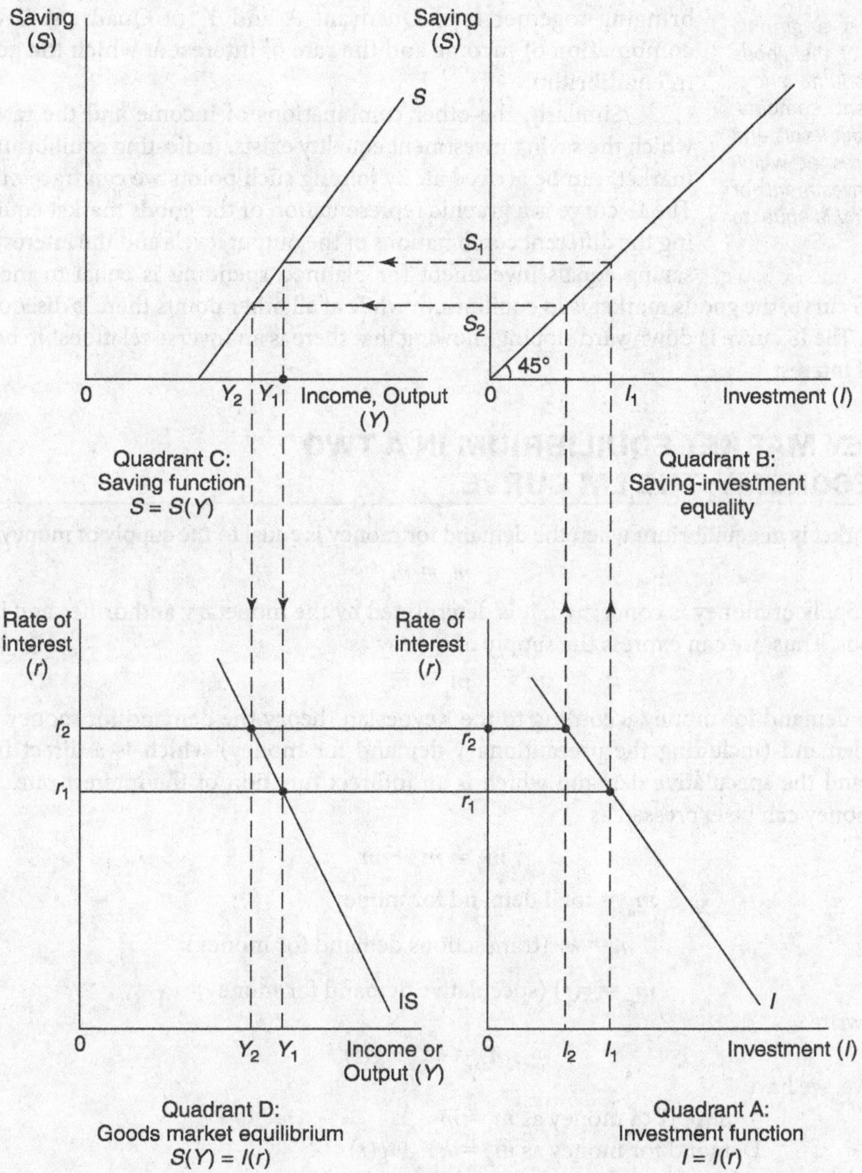

Figure 16.1 The Goods Market Equilibrium in a Two Sector Economy: The IS Curve

To understand the derivation of the IS curve in Quadrant D, we start in Quadrant A. Assume that the interest rate is r_1 indicating an investment at the level of I_1. Quadrant B shows that for saving investment equality to be maintained, saving must be equal to S_1 (where because of the 45 degree line $I_1 = S_1$). Quadrant C shows that saving will be S_1 only when the income level is Y_1. Bringing together r_1 of Quadrant A and Y_1 of Quadrant C gives one combination of income and the rate of interest at which the goods market is in equilibrium.

Now assume that the interest rate increases to r_2 indicating an investment at I_2. Quadrant B shows that saving must be equal to S_2. Quadrant C depicts that saving will be S_2 when income is Y_2. Once again

The IS curve is a graphic representation of the goods market equilibrium showing the different combinations of the output levels and the interest rates at which saving equals investment (or planned spending is equal to income).

bringing together r_2 of Quadrant A and Y_2 of Quadrant C yields another combination of income and the rate of interest at which the goods market is in equilibrium.

Similarly, the other combinations of income and the rate of interest at which the saving investment equality exists, indicating equilibrium in the goods market, can be arrived at. By joining such points we can trace out the IS curve. The IS curve is a graphic representation of the goods market equilibrium showing the different combinations of the output levels and the interest rates at which saving equals investment (or planned spending is equal to income). At each point on the IS curve, the goods market is in equilibrium while at all other points there is disequilibrium in the goods market. The IS curve is downward sloping showing that there is an inverse relationship between income and the rate of interest.

THE MONEY MARKET EQUILIBRIUM IN A TWO SECTOR ECONOMY: THE LM CURVE

The money market is in equilibrium when the demand for money is equal to the supply of money. Thus, we have

$$m_s = m_d$$

As far as the supply of money is concerned, it is determined by the monetary authorities and hence assumed to be exogenous. Thus, we can express the supply of money as

$$m_s = \overline{m}_s$$

Regarding the demand for money,according to the Keynesian theory the demand for money consists of the transactions demand (including the precautionary demand for money) which is a direct function of the income level and the speculative demand which is an indirect function of the interest rate. Thus, the total demand for money can be expressed as

$$m_d = m_t + m_{sp}$$

where m_d = total demand for money

$m_t = ky$ (transactions demand for money)

$m_{sp} = g(r)$ (speculative demand for money)

Thus, we can write

$$m_d = kY + g(r)$$

From the above, we have

Supply of money as $m_s = \overline{m}_s$

Demand for money as $m_d = kY + g(r)$

Money market equilibrium condition as $\overline{m}_s = kY + g(r)$

BOX 16.2

Economists have attempted to analyse the world around them by using different frameworks. The quantity-theory framework followed by the Keynesian framework of the income-expenditure model, the IS-LM framework which brings together the Keynesian framework and the quantity theory framework, the business-cycle framework which accepts the existence of a disequilibrium, and the aggregate supply-aggregate demand framework which attempts to develop the IS-LM model. Though each framework carries an element of truth, none of them can be said to be perfect and satisfactory on its own.

The money market equilibrium condition can be used to develop a graphical approach to the derivation of the LM curve as in Figure 16.2.

In Figure 16.2, there are four quadrants. Quadrant A depicts the speculative demand for money showing an inverse relationship between speculative demand for money and the rate of interest.

Quadrant B shows the supply of money as a straight line meeting the two axes. At point A where it is meeting the y axis indicates that the entire supply of money is used for transactions demand while at point B where it is meeting the x axis indicates that the entire supply of money is used for purposes of speculative demand. All points along the line AB show the different ways in which the supply of money can be divided between the transactions demand and the speculative demand.

Quadrant C depicts the income level that will support the transactions demand determined in Quadrant B [given the transactions demand function as $m_t = k(Y)$].

Quadrant D shows the money market equilibrium where the LM curve shows the different combinations of the output levels and the interest rates at which the demand for money is equal to the supply of money.

To understand as to how the LM curve has been derived in Quadrant D we start in Quadrant A. Assume that the interest rate is r_1 indicating that the public wants to hold a speculative demand for money equal to m_{sp1}.

Quadrant B shows that when the speculative demand is m_{sp1} the amount of money left as transactions balances will be m_{t1}. Quadrant C shows that transactions balances of m_{t1} will be consistent with an income level

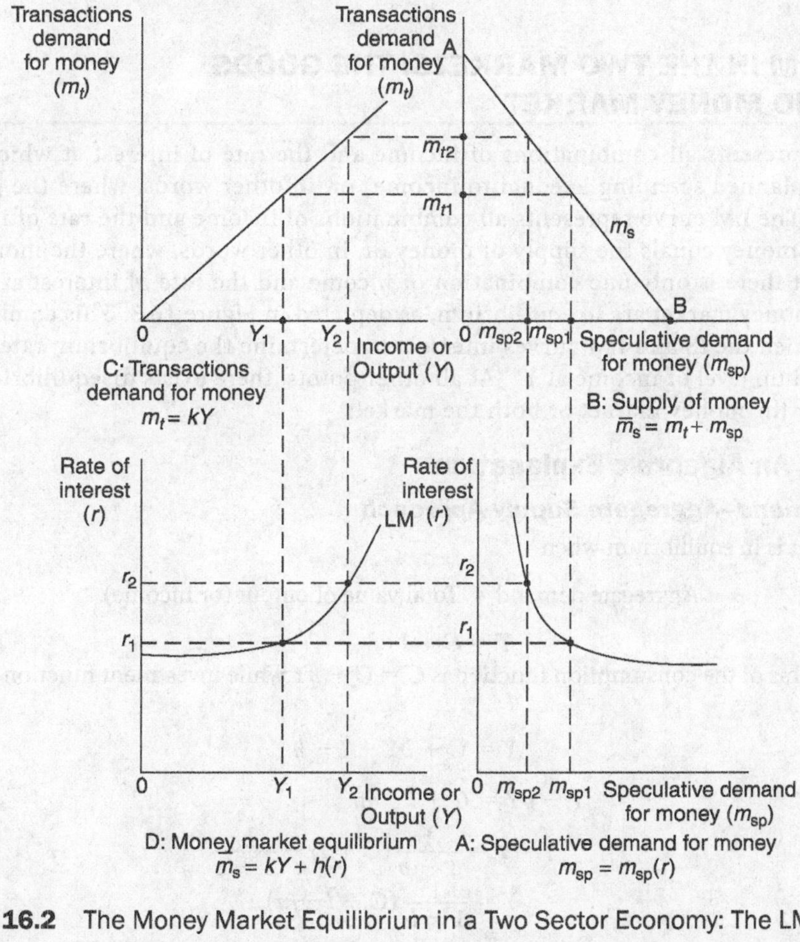

Figure 16.2 The Money Market Equilibrium in a Two Sector Economy: The LM Curve

of Y_1. Hence, combining together r_1 of Quadrant A and Y_1 of Quadrant C gives one combination of income and the rate of interest at which the money market is in equilibrium.

Next assume that the interest rate increases to r_2 indicating that the speculative demand must be m_{sp2}. Quadrant B shows that the money available for transactions will be equal to m_{t2}. Quadrant C depicts that transactions balances of m_{t2} will be consistent with an income level of Y_2. Once again bringing together r_2 of Quadrant A and Y_2 of Quadrant C yields another combination of income and the rate of interest at which the money market is in equilibrium.

The LM curve is a graphic representation of the money market equilibrium showing the different combinations of the output levels and the interest rates at which the demand for money is equal to the supply of money.

In a similar manner, the other combinations of income and the rate of interest at which the demand for money equals the supply of money indicating equilibrium in the money market can be arrived at. By joining all such points we can trace out the LM curve. The LM curve is a graphic representation of the money market equilibrium showing the different combinations of the output levels and the interest rates at which the demand for money is equal to the supply of money. It is important to note that at each point on the LM curve, the money market is in equilibrium and at all other points there exists disequilibrium in the money market. The LM curve is upward sloping showing that there is a direct relationship between income and the rate of interest. This is because when the rate of interest increases, individuals demand less for speculative purposes and more for transactions which is consistent only with a higher level of income.

EQUILIBRIUM IN THE TWO MARKETS: THE GOODS MARKET AND MONEY MARKET

The IS curve represents all combinations of income and the rate of interest at which saving equals investment (or planned spending is equal to income) or, in other words, where the goods market is in equilibrium. The LM curve represents all combinations of income and the rate of interest at which the demand for money equals the supply of money or, in other words, where the money market is in equilibrium. But there is only one combination of income and the rate of interest at which both the goods and the money market are in equilibrium, as depicted in Figure 16.3. This combination is given by point E at which the IS and LM curves intersect to determine the equilibrium rate of interest at r^* and the equilibrium level of income at Y^*. At all other points, there exists disequilibrium in either the goods market or the money market or both the markets.

The IS Curve: An Algebraic Explanation

Aggregate Demand–Aggregate Supply Approach

The goods market is in equilibrium when

$$\text{Aggregate demand} = \text{Total value of output (or income)}$$

or

$$Y = C + I$$

But the linear forms of the consumption function is $C = C_a + bY$ while investment function can be expressed as $I = \bar{I} - \text{hr}$.

Thus,

$$Y = C_a + bY + \bar{I} - hr$$

Hence,

$$Y - bY = C_a + \bar{I} - hr$$

or

$$Y = \frac{1}{1-b}(C_a + \bar{I}) - \frac{hr}{1-b}$$

$$Y = \frac{1}{1-b}(C_a + \bar{I} - hr) \quad (1)$$

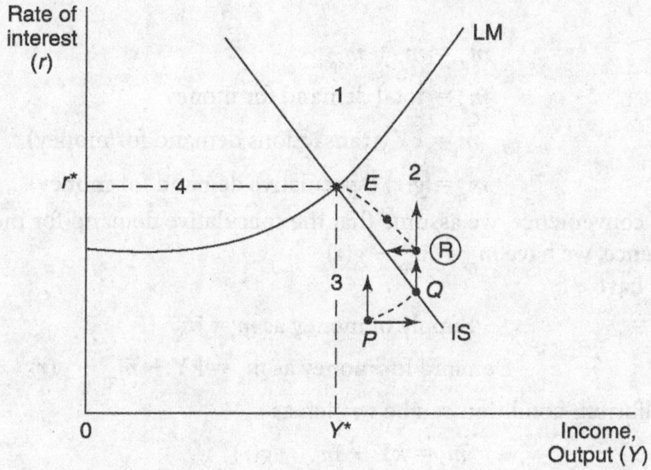

Figure 16.3 Equilibrium in the Two Markets: The Goods Market and Money Market

Equation (1) represents the IS curve.

Saving–Investment Approach

In equilibrium,

$$I = S$$

But the saving function is $S = -C_a + (1 - b)Y$ while investment function is taken as $I = \bar{I} - hr$.

Thus,
$$\bar{I} - hr = -C_a + (1 - b)Y$$

or
$$Y = \frac{1}{1-b}(C_a + \bar{I} - hr)$$

This is the same equation as Eq. (1) above.

Hence, both the approaches yield the same equation for the IS curve.

Numerical Illustration 1

Suppose the consumption and investment functions are as follows:

$$C = 100 + 0.75\,Y$$

$$I = 250 - 5r$$

Find the equation of the IS curve.

Solution

The equation of the IS curve is

$$Y = C + I$$

$$Y = 100 + 0.75Y + 250 - 5r$$

$$Y - 0.75Y = 350 - 5r$$

$$0.25Y = 350 - 5r$$

$$Y = 1400 - 20r$$

Figure16.4 shows the IS curve $Y = 1400 - 20r$.

The LM Curve: An Algebraic Explanation

The money market is in equilibrium when

$$m_d = m_s$$

But

$$m_d = m_t + m_{sp}$$

where m_d = total demand for money

$m_t = kY$ (transactions demand for money)

$m_{sp} = g(r)$ (speculative demand for money)

However for the sake of convenience, we assume that the speculative demand for money is a linear function (rather than a curve). Hence, we have $m_{sp} = \overline{m}_{sp} - g(r)$

From the above, we have

Supply of money as $m_s = \overline{m}_s$

Demand for money as $m_d = kY + \overline{m}_{sp} - g(r)$

The money market equilibrium condition can be written as

$$\overline{m}_s = kY + \overline{m}_{sp} - g(r)$$

Thus,
$$Y = \frac{1}{k}[\overline{m}_s - \overline{m}_{sp} + g(r)] \quad (2)$$

Equation (2) represents the LM curve.

Numerical Illustration 2

Suppose that the supply of money is Rs. 400. The transactions and speculative demand for money functions are as follows:

$$m_t = 0.25Y$$

$$m_{sp} = 100 - 4r$$

Find the equation of the LM curve.

Solution

$$m_d = m_t + m_{sp}$$

$$m_d = 0.25Y + 100 - 4r$$

In equilibrium, $m_d = m_s$

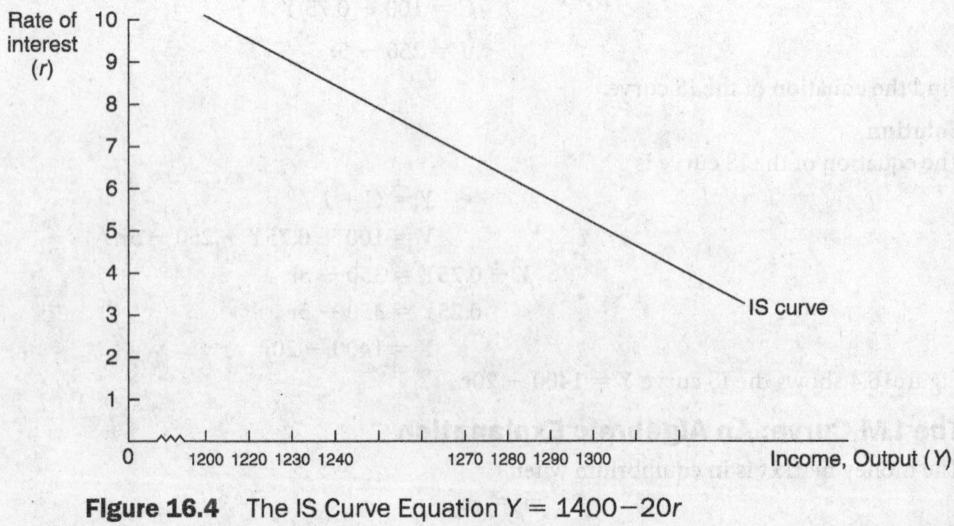

Figure 16.4 The IS Curve Equation $Y = 1400-20r$

Thus, $$0.25Y + 100 - 4r = 400$$

$$0.25Y = 300 + 4r$$

$$Y = 1200 + 16r$$

Figure16. 5 shows the LM curve $Y = 1200 + 16r$.

Equilibrium in the Two Markets: The Goods Market and Money Market: An Algebraic Explanation

A simultaneous equilibrium in both the goods and money markets can be determined by solving the equations for the IS and LM curves.

Equation of the IS curve: $Y = \frac{1}{1-b}(C_a + \bar{I} - hr)$

Equation of the LM curve: $Y = \frac{1}{k}[\overline{m}_s - \overline{m}_{sp} + g(r)]$

These are a set of simultaneous equations which can be solved to determine the equilibrium values of Y and r.

Numerical Illustration 3

Suppose the consumption and investment functions are as follows:

$$C = 100 + 0.75Y$$

$$I = 250 - 5r$$

Also assume that the supply of money is Rs. 280. The demand for money function is as follows:

$$m_d = 0.25Y - 2r$$

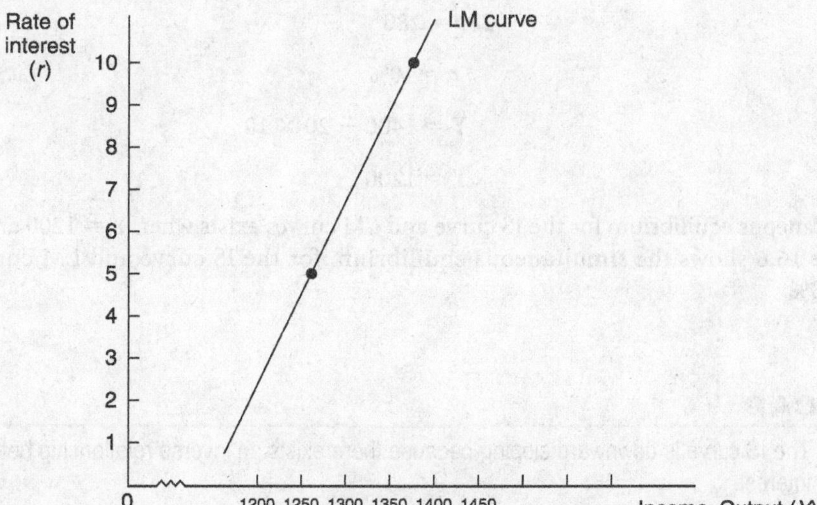

Figure 16.5 The LM Curve Equation $Y = 1200 + 16r$

(1) Find the equation of the IS curve.

(2) Find the equation of the LM curve.

(3) Find the simultaneous equilibrium for the IS curve and LM curves.

Solution

(1) IS equation:

$$Y = C + I$$

$$Y = 100 + 0.75\,Y + 250 - 5r$$

$$Y - 0.75Y = 350 - 5r$$

$$0.25Y = 350 - 5r$$

$$Y = 1400 - 20r$$

(2) LM equation:

$$m_d = 0.25Y - 2r$$

$$m_s = 280$$

In equilibrium, $m_d = m_s$

Thus, $0.25Y - 2r = 280$

$$0.25Y = 280 + 2r$$

$$Y = 1120 + 8r$$

(3) Simultaneous equilibrium for the IS curve and LM curves:

$$\text{IS} = \text{LM}$$

$$1400 - 20r = 1120 + 8r$$

$$28r = 280$$

$$r = 10\%$$

$$Y = 1400 - 20 \times 10$$

$$Y = 1200$$

Simultaneous equilibrium for the IS curve and LM curves exists when $Y = 1200$ and $r = 10\%$.
Figure 16.6 shows the simultaneous equilibrium for the IS curve and LM curves when $Y = 1200$ and $r = 10\%$.

RECAP

- The IS curve is downward sloping because there exists an inverse relationship between income and the rate of interest.
- The LM curve is upward sloping because there is a direct relationship between income and the rate of interest.
- It is only at the intersection of the IS and LM that both the goods and the money market are in equilibrium.

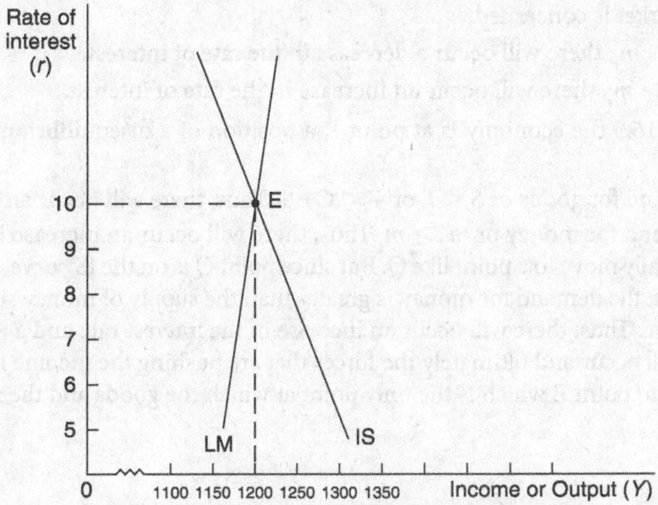

Figure 16.6 Simultaneous Equilibrium for IS and LM Curves When $Y = 1200$ and $r = 10\%$

DISEQUILIBRIUM TO EQUILIBRIUM: THE PROCESS OF ADJUSTMENT

In Figure 16.3, we have already observed that at points, other than point E*, there will exist disequilibrium in either the goods market or the money market or in both the markets.

As far as the IS curve is concerned, any combination of income and interest that lies on the IS curve represents a goods market equilibrium. However, at all other points there exists goods market disequilibrium.

(1) All combinations of income and interest that lie above and towards the right of the IS curve indicate a situation where $Y > C + I$ or saving is greater than planned investment. Hence, the level of income will fall.

(2) All combinations of income and interest that lie below and towards the left of the IS curve indicate a situation where $Y < C + I$ or saving is less than planned investment. Hence, the level of income will rise. It has been divided into four spaces.

Space	Goods Market	Money Market
Space 1	$S > I, Y > C + I$	$m_d < m_s$
Space 2	$S > I, Y > C + I$	$m_d > m_s$
Space 3	$S > I, Y < C + I$	$m_d > m_s$
Space 4	$S < I, Y < C + I$	$m_d < m_s$

Regarding the LM curve, any combination of income and interest that lies on the LM curve represents money market equilibrium. However, at all other points there exists money market disequilibrium.

(1) All combinations of income and interest that lie below and towards the right of the LM curve indicate a situation where the demand for money is greater than the supply of money or there is an excess demand for money. Hence, the rate of interest will rise.

(2) All combinations of income and interest that lie above and towards the left of the LM curve indicate a situation where the demand for money is less than the supply of money or there is an excess supply of money. Hence, the rate of interest will fall.

As far as the goods market is concerned,

(i) When $S > I$ or $Y > C + I$, there will occur a decrease in income.

(ii) When $S < I$ or $Y < C + I$, there will occur an increase in income.

As far as the money market is concerned,

(i) When $m_d < m_s$, there will occur a decrease in the rate of interest.

(ii) When $m_d > m_s$, there will occur an increase in the rate of interest.

Suppose that in Figure 16.3 the economy is at point P, a position of a disequilibrium located in the space 3. Here, there exists

(1) an excess demand for goods or $S < I$, or $Y < C + I$. Thus, there will occur an increase in the income.

(2) an excess demand for money or $m_d > m_s$. Thus, there will occur an increase in the rate of interest.

The economy will gradually move to a point like Q. But since point Q is on the IS curve, the goods market will be in equilibrium. However, the demand for money is greater than the supply of money since point Q is located to the right of the LM curve. Thus, there will occur an increase in the interest rate and a movement to a point like R. Thus, adjustments will occur and ultimately the forces that are pushing the income level and the interest rate will move the economy to point E which is the only point at which the goods and the money markets are both in equilibrium.

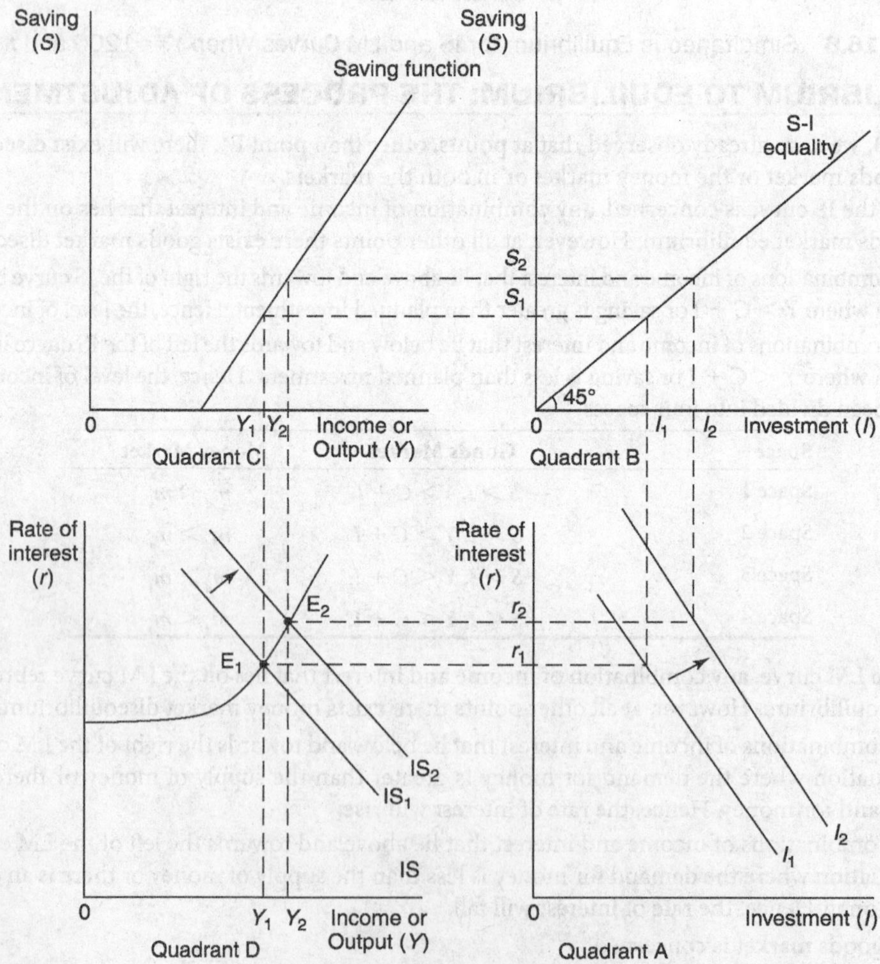

Figure 16.7 A Shift in the IS Curve

The economy could be anywhere in the system in any of the different spaces. However, it is important to remember that the forces which are at work will go on till the final equilibrium is attained at point E. Once point E is reached, the income level and the rate of interest will remain unchanged until there occurs a shift in the IS or LM curve or in both of them which can disturb the equilibrium and start off a new round of adjustments.

RECAP

- If there exists disequilibrium in the economy, then the forces will be at work till the final equilibrium is attained at the intersection of the IS–LM curves.

A SHIFT IN THE IS–LM CURVES

A shift in the IS or LM curve or in both of them will disturb the equilibrium; Hence, it is imperative to examine these shifts.

A Shift in the IS Curve

The shifts in the IS curve can occur due to a shift in the investment function or the saving function or due to a change in any of the factors which are responsible for a shift in these functions.

In Figure. 16.7, the IS_1 curve has been derived diagrammatically from the investment curve I_1in Quadrant A, the saving–investment equality in Quadrant B and the saving function in Quadrant C. The intersection of IS_1 and the LM curves at point E_1 determines the equilibrium income as Y_1 and the equilibrium interest rate at r_1.

Assume there is rightward shift in the investment function from I_1 to I_2 in Quadrant A of the Figure 16.7. This implies an increase in investment at all interest rates. Given the interest rate at r_2, to match the increase in the investment, the equilibrium level of saving in Quadrant B will also increase from S_1 to S_2 leading to an increase in the income level from $Y_1$to Y_2 in the Quadrant C. Thus, combining the income Y_2 with the interest rate, r_2 we can trace out the new IS curve IS_2. The intersection of IS_2 and the LM curves at point E_2 determines the new equilibrium income as Y_2 and the equilibrium interest rate at r_2.

For a leftward shift in the investment function, the results that follow will be just the opposite.

A shift in the consumption function also leads to a shift in the IS curve. An upward shift in the consumption function (or in other words a downward shift in the saving function) implies a decrease in the saving at any income level. To maintain the saving investment equality, the income level would have to increase leading to eventually a rightward shift in the IS curve. For a downward shift in the consumption function, the results that follow will just be the opposite.

A Shift in the LM Curve

The shift in the LM curve can occur due to a shift in the transactions demand, speculative demand or the money supply function.

In Figure 16.8, LM_1 has been derived diagrammatically from the transactions demand and speculative demand for money functions. The intersection of IS and the LM_1 curves at point E_1 determines the equilibrium income as Y_1 and the equilibrium interest rate at r_1.

Assume there is an increase in the money supply. Hence, there is a rightward shift in the money supply curve from m_{s1} to m_{s2} in Quadrant B of Figure 16.8. Given the rate of interest at r_2, this will lead to an increase in the transactions demand for money from m_{t1} to m_{t2}. Since a larger transactions demand for money is consistent only at a higher income level, this will involve an increase in the income level from Y_1 to Y_2. Hence, combining the change in income Y_2 with the change in the interest rate, r_2 we can

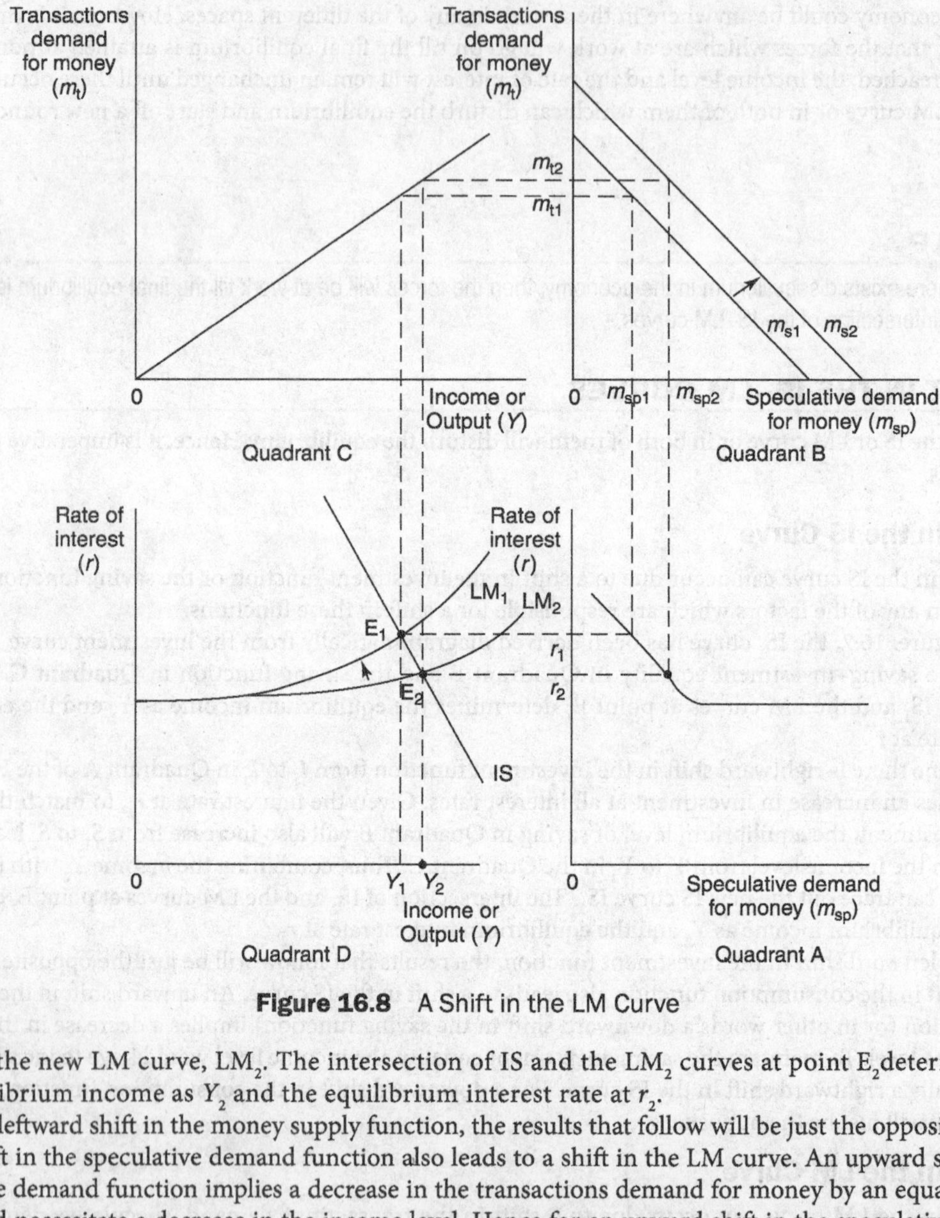

Figure 16.8 A Shift in the LM Curve

trace out the new LM curve, LM$_2$. The intersection of IS and the LM$_2$ curves at point E$_2$determines the new equilibrium income as Y_2 and the equilibrium interest rate at r_2.

For a leftward shift in the money supply function, the results that follow will be just the opposite.

A shift in the speculative demand function also leads to a shift in the LM curve. An upward shift in the speculative demand function implies a decrease in the transactions demand for money by an equal amount. This would necessitate a decrease in the income level. Hence for an upward shift in the speculative demand function, the LM curve will shift to the left. Similarly, a shift in the transactions demand for money function will lead to a shift in the LM curve.

A Simultaneous Shift in Both IS and LM Curves

Till now we have analysed the shifts in the IS and LM curves separately. Now we analyse the two shifts simultaneously.

In Figure 16.9, suppose the initial IS and LM curves are given as IS$_1$ and LM$_1$. They intersect at point E$_1$ to determine the equilibrium income at Y_1 and the rate of interest at r_1.

Next suppose there is:

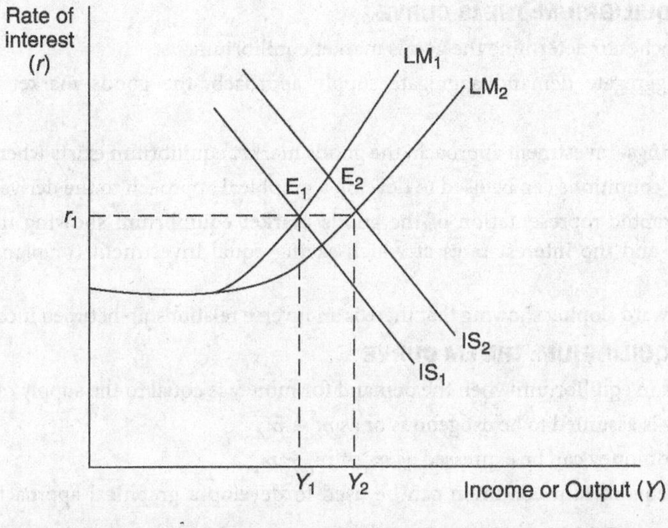

Figure 16.9 A Simultaneous Shift in Both IS and LM Curves

(1) an increase in investment (or a rightward shift in the investment function) which shifts the IS curve from IS_1 to IS_2.

(2) an increase in the money supply (or a rightward shift in the money supply function) which shifts the LM curve from LM_1 to LM_2.

The curves IS_2 and LM_2 intersect at point E_2 to determine the equilibrium income at Y_2 while the rate of interest remains unchanged at r_1. The reason why there is no change in the interest rate is that the extent of the shifts in the IS and LM curves are equal. However, in reality the extent of the shifts may not be equal in which case there will not only be a change in the income level but also a change in the interest rate.

RECAP

- The shifts in the IS curve occur due to a shift in the investment function or the saving function.
- The shift in the LM curve occur due to a shift in the transactions demand, speculative demand or the money supply function.

SUMMARY

INTRODUCTION

1. The chapter analyses the linkages and the interactions between the goods and money markets to determine that level of income and the interest rate which bring about a simultaneous equilibrium in both the markets.
2. The IS–LM model, which is the foundation of the short-run macroeconomics, was first introduced by J. R. Hicks.
3. The IS curve represents the goods market equilibrium.
4. The LM curve represents the money market equilibrium.
5. We can analyse the IS–LM model in two ways.

THE IS–LM MODEL FOR A TWO SECTOR ECONOMY

The analysis is based on certain assumptions: price level is constant; at that price level, the firms are willing to supply whatever output is demanded; short-run aggregate supply curve is perfectly elastic till the full employment level of output.

THE GOODS MARKET EQUILIBRIUM: THE IS CURVE

1. There are two approaches to determine the goods market equilibrium.
2. According to the aggregate demand–aggregate supply approach, the goods market equilibrium exists where $Y = C(Y) + I(r)$.
3. According to the savings–investment approach, the goods market equilibrium exists where $S(Y) = I(r)$.
4. The two equilibrium conditions can be used to develop a graphical approach to the derivation of the IS curve.
5. The IS curve is a graphic representation of the goods market equilibrium showing the different combinations of the output levels and the interest rates at which saving equal investment (or planned spending is equal to income).
6. The IS curve is downward sloping showing that there is an inverse relationship between income and the rate of interest

THE MONEY MARKET EQUILIBRIUM: THE LM CURVE

1. The money market is in equilibrium when the demand for money is equal to the supply of money or $m_s = m_d$.
2. The supply of money is assumed to be exogenous or as $m_s = \overline{m}_s$.
3. The total demand for money can be expressed as $m_d = m_t + m_{sp}$.
4. The money market equilibrium condition can be used to develop a graphical approach to the derivation of the LM curve.
5. The LM curve is a graphic representation of the money market equilibrium showing the different combinations of the output levels and the interest rates at which the demand for money is equal to the supply of money.
6. The LM curve is upward sloping showing that there is a direct relationship between income and the rate of interest. This is because when the rate of interest increases, individuals demand becomes less for speculative purposes and more for transactions which is consistent only with a higher level of income.

EQUILIBRIUM IN THE TWO MARKETS: THE GOODS MARKET AND MONEY MARKET

1. The IS curve represents all combinations of income and the rate of interest at which the goods market is in equilibrium.
2. The LM curve represents all combinations of income and the rate of interest at which the money market is in equilibrium.
3. There is only one combination of income and the rate of interest at which both the goods and the money market are in equilibrium, point E at which the IS and LM curves intersect.

THE IS CURVE: AN ALGEBRAIC EXPLANATION

Both the aggregate demand–aggregate supply approach and the saving–investment approach yield

$$Y = \frac{1}{1-b}(C_a + \overline{I} - r) \text{ as the equation of the IS curve.}$$

THE LM CURVE: AN ALGEBRAIC EXPLANATION

$$Y = \frac{1}{k}[\overline{m}_s - \overline{m}_{sp} + g(r)] \text{ is the equation of the LM curve.}$$

EQUILIBRIUM IN THE TWO MARKETS: THE GOODS MARKET AND MONEY MARKET: AN ALGEBRAIC EXPLANATION

A simultaneous equilibrium in both the goods and money markets can be determined by solving the equations for the IS and LM curves and thus the equilibrium values of Y and I can be determined.

A SHIFT IN THE IS–LM CURVES

1. A shift in the IS or LM curve or in both of them will disturb the equilibrium; hence, it is imperative to examine these shifts.
2. The shifts in the IS curve can occur due to a shift in the investment function or the saving (or consumption) function.
3. A rightward shift in the investment function leads to a rightward shift in the IS curve. For a leftward shift in the investment function, the results that follow will be just the opposite.
4. The shift in the LM curve can occur due to a shift in the transactions demand, speculative demand or the money supply function.
5. A rightward shift in the money supply curve leads to a leftward shift in the LM curve. For a leftward shift in the money supply function, the results that follow will be just the opposite.

6. A simultaneous shift in both IS and LM curves bring about a change in the income level and also a change in the interest rate.

REVIEW QUESTIONS

TRUE OR FALSE QUESTIONS

1. The IS–LM model is the foundation of long run macroeconomics.
2. The IS curve is upward sloping showing that there is a direct relationship between income and the rate of interest.
3. The LM curve is upward sloping showing that there is a direct relationship between income and the rate of interest.
4. There is only one combination of income and the rate of interest at which both the goods and the money market are in equilibrium.
5. The shift in the LM curve can occur due to a shift in the investment function or the saving function.

VERY SHORT-ANSWER QUESTIONS

1. Which are the two approaches to determine the goods market equilibrium?
2. Why does the LM curve slope upward? Explain.
3. At which point does a simultaneous equilibrium occur in both the goods and money markets?
4. Give the equations for the IS and LM curves.
5. How is simultaneous equilibrium in the two markets determined? Give an algebraic explanation.

SHORT-ANSWER QUESTIONS

1. Write a short note on the IS curve.
2. Write a short note on the LM curve
3. 'There is only one combination of income and the rate of interest at which both the goods and the money market are in equilibrium.' Explain.
4. Show the algebraic derivation of
   (a) IS Curve
   (b) LM Curve
5. Examine the effects of a simultaneous shift in both the IS and LM curves.

LONG-ANSWER QUESTIONS

1. 'The two equilibrium conditions aggregate demand–aggregate supply approach and S–I approach can be used to develop a graphical approach to the derivation of the IS curve.' Explain.
2. 'The money market equilibrium condition can be used to develop a graphical approach to the derivation of the LM curve'. Explain.
3. How is simultaneous equilibrium in the goods and money market achieved? Explain with the help of diagram/diagrams.
4. Examine the effects of a shift in the IS curve.
5. Examine the effects of a shift in the LM curve.

SOLVED NUMERICAL PROBLEMS

Numerical Problem 1

Suppose the consumption and investment functions are as follows:

$$C = 50 + 0.75Y$$

$$I = 80 \text{ crore} - 2r$$

Find

(1) The equation of the IS curve and plot it.

(2) The equation of the IS curve when investment increases by Rs. 20 crore.

(3) By how much does the IS curve shift?

Numerical Problem 2

Suppose that the supply of money is Rs. 240 crore. The demand for money is $m_d = 0.20Y - 5r$. Find

(1) The equation of the LM curve and plot it.

(2) The equation of the LM curve when the supply of money increases by Rs. 60 crore to Rs. 300 crore.

(3) By how much does the LM curve shift?

Numerical Problem 3

Suppose the consumption, investment, demand for money and supply of money functions are as follows:

$$C = 0.75\,Y$$

$$I = 107.5 \text{ crore} - 0.25r$$

$$m_d = 0.25Y - 2.5r$$

$$m_s = 80 \text{ crore}$$

Find

(1) The equilibrium income and the rate of interest.

(2) The equilibrium income and the rate of interest when autonomous investment increases to Rs. 135 crore.

Numerical Problem 4

Suppose autonomous consumption is Rs. 60 crore, investment is Rs. 120 crore, marginal propensity to consume is 0.75 and the value of *h*, the behavioral coefficient which measures the sensitivity of investment to the rate of interest, is 4. Find

(1) The equation of the IS curve and plot it.

(2) The equation of the IS curve when *h* increases to 8.

(3) What is the effect on the slope of the IS curve when the value of *g* increases?

Numerical Problem 5

Suppose that the value of *k* is 0.25. Find the direction and the amount of shift in the LM curve when

(1) the increase in the money supply is Rs. 10 crore.

(2) the decrease in the money supply is Rs. 25 crore.

UNSOLVED NUMERICAL PROBLEMS (WITH ANSWERS)

1. Suppose the saving and investment functions are as follows:

$$S = -50 + 0.5\,Y$$

$$I = 120 \text{ crore} - 5r$$

Find the equation of the IS curve and plot it.

2. Suppose the consumption and investment functions are as follows:

$$C = 20 + 0.5Y$$

$$I = 120 \text{ crore} - 5r$$

Find

(1) The equation of the IS curve and plot it.

(2) The equation of the IS curve when the investment function changes to $I = 120$ crore $- 10r$

3. Suppose the consumption and investment functions are as follows:

$$C = 20 + 0.75Y$$

$$I = 400 - 2500r$$

Find

(1) The equation of the IS curve by the aggregate demand–aggregate supply approach.

(2) The equation of the IS curve by the saving–investment approach.

4. In a two sector model, assume that the consumption and investment functions are as follows:

$$C = 100 + 0.75Y$$
$$I = 1500 - 10r$$

Find

(1) The equation of the IS curve

(2) The equation of the IS curve when the investment function changes to $I = 1500 - 5r$ while the consumption function remains the same.

5. Suppose in a two sector model consumption and investment functions are as follows:

$$C = 600 + 0.80Y$$
$$I = 1160 - 20r$$

The demand for money and the supply of money are

$$L = 0.20Y - 50r$$
$$M = 1200$$

(1) Find the equation of the IS curve

(2) Find the equation of the LM curve

(3) Find the simultaneous equilibrium for the IS and LM curves.

ANSWERS

TRUE OR FALSE QUESTIONS

1. **False.** The IS–LM model is the foundation of the short run macroeconomics and was first introduced by J. R. Hicks.
2. **False.** The IS curve is downward sloping showing that there is an inverse relationship between income and the rate of interest.
3. **True.** The LM curve is upward sloping showing that there is a direct relationship between income and the rate of interest. This is because when the rate of interest increases, individuals demand less for speculative purposes and more for transactions which is consistent only with a higher level of income.
4. **True.** There is only one combination of income and the rate of interest at which both the goods and the money market are in equilibrium and that is the point at which the IS and LM curves intersect. At all other points, there exists disequilibrium.
5. **False.** The shift in the LM curve can occur due to a shift in the transactions demand, speculative demand or the money supply function

SOLVED NUMERICAL PROBLEMS

Solution 1

(1) Equation of the IS curve:

$$Y = C + I$$
$$Y = 50 + 0.75Y + 80 - 2r$$
$$Y - 0.75Y = 130 - 2r$$
$$0.25Y = 130 - 2r$$
$$Y = 520 - 8r$$

(2) Equation of the IS curve when investment increases by Rs. 20 crore:

$$Y = C + I$$
$$Y = 50 + 0.75\,Y + 100 - 2r$$
$$Y - 0.75\,Y = 150 - 2r$$
$$0.25Y = 150 - 2r$$
$$Y = 600 - 8r$$

(3) When investment increases by Rs. 20 crore, the IS curve shifts horizontally by Rs. 80 crore, which is equal to the increase in investment times the multiplier, Rs. 20 crore × 4.

Figure 16.10 gives the diagrammatic picture of the IS curves where equation $Y = 520 - 8r$ is represented by IS_1 and equation $Y = 600 - 8r$ is represented by IS_2.

Solution 2

(1) Equation of the LM curve

In equilibrium, $m_d = m_s$

Thus,
$$0.20Y - 5r = 240$$
$$0.20Y = 240 + 5r$$
$$Y = 1200 + 25r$$

(2) Equation of the LM curve when the supply of money increases by Rs. 60 crore to Rs. 300 crore:

In equilibrium, $m_d = m_s$

Thus,
$$0.20Y - 5r = 300$$
$$0.20Y = 300 + 5r$$
$$Y = 1500 + 25r$$

(3) When the supply of money increases by Rs. 60 crore, the LM curve shifts horizontally by Rs. 300 crore, which is equal to $\frac{1}{k}\Delta m_s$, $\frac{60}{0.20}$ crore.

Figure 16.11 gives the diagrammatic picture of the LM curves where equation $Y = 1200 + 25r$ is represented by LM_1 and equation $Y = 1500 + 25r$ is represented by LM_2.

Solution 3

(1) Equilibrium income and the rate of interest:

Equation of the IS curve:
$$Y = C + I$$
$$Y = 0.75Y + 107.5 - 0.25r$$
$$Y - 0.75Y = 107.5 - 0.25r$$
$$0.25Y = 107.5 - 0.25r$$
$$Y = 430 - r$$

Equation of the LM curve:

In equilibrium, $m_d = m_s$

Thus,
$$0.25Y - 2.5r = 80$$
$$0.25Y = 80 + 2.5r$$
$$Y = 320 + 10r$$

Simultaneous equilibrium for the IS and LM curves:
$$IS = LM$$
$$430 - r = 320 + 10r$$

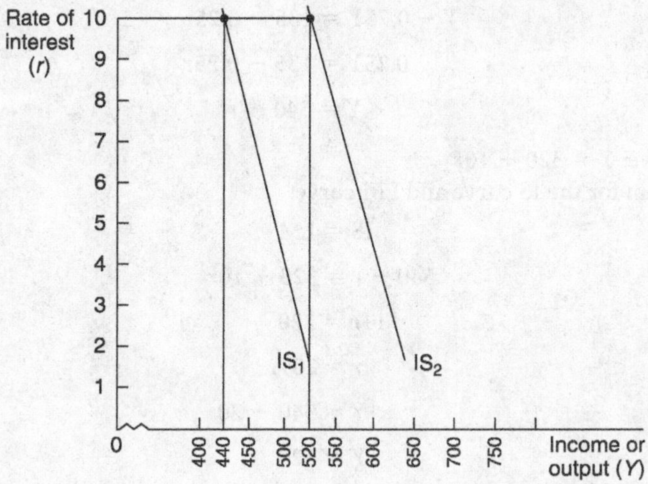

Figure 16.10 IS Curves of Equation $Y = 520–8r$ and $Y = 600–8r$

$$11r = 110$$

$$r = 10\%$$

$$Y = 430 - 10$$

$$Y = 420$$

Simultaneous equilibrium for the IS curve and LM curves exists when $Y = 420$ and $r = 10\%$.

(2) The equilibrium income and the rate of interest when autonomous investment increases to Rs. 135 crore:
Equation of the new IS curve:

$$Y = C + I$$

$$Y = 0.75Y + 135 - 0.25r$$

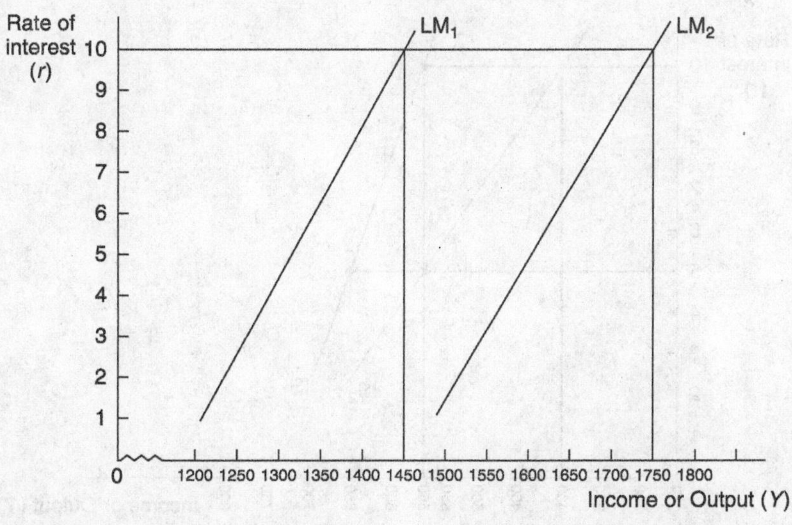

Figure 16.11 LM Curves of Equation $Y = 1200 + 25r$ and $Y = 1500 + 25r$

$$Y - 0.75Y = 135 - 0.25r$$
$$0.25Y = 135 - 0.25r$$
$$Y = 540 - r$$

Equation of the LM curve: $Y = 320 + 10r$
Simultaneous equilibrium for the IS curve and LM curve:

$$\text{IS} = \text{LM}$$
$$540 - r = 320 + 10r$$
$$11r = 220$$
$$r = 20\%$$
$$Y = 540 - 20$$
$$Y = 520$$

Simultaneous equilibrium for the IS curve and LM curves exists when $Y = 520$ and $r = 20\%$.

Solution 4

(1) Equation of the IS curve:
The consumption and investment functions are as follows:

$$C = 60 + 0.75Y$$
$$I = 120 - 4r$$

We have

$$Y = C + I$$
$$Y = 60 + 0.75Y + 120 - 4r$$
$$Y - 0.75Y = 180 - 4r$$
$$0.25Y = 180 - 4r$$
$$Y = 720 - 16r$$

This is represented by the IS_1 curve in the Figure 16.12.

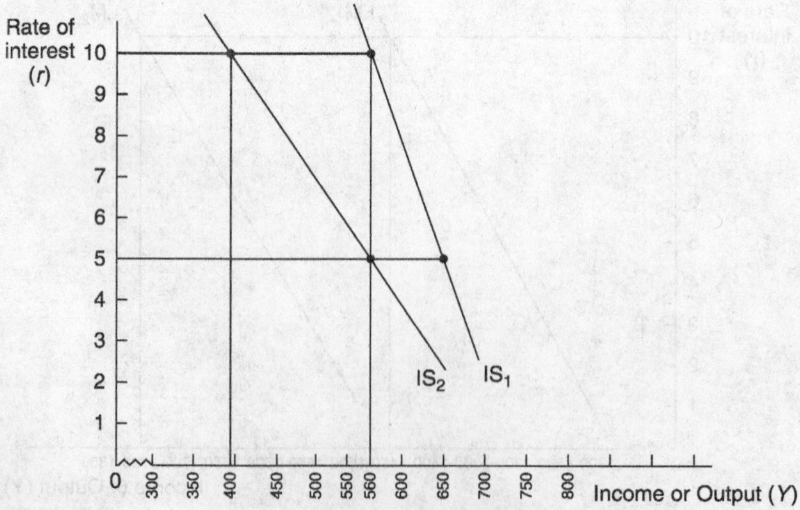

Figure 16.12 IS Curves of Equation $Y = 720-16r$ and $Y = 720-32r$

(2) Equation of the IS curve when h increases to 8.

The consumption and the new investment functions are as follows:

$$C = 60 + 0.75Y$$

$$I = 120 - 8r$$

We have

$$Y = C + I$$

$$Y = 60 + 0.75Y + 120 - 8r$$

$$Y - 0.75Y = 180 - 8r$$

$$0.25Y = 180 - 8r$$

$$Y = 720 - 32r$$

This is represented by IS_2 in Figure 16.12.

(3) The effect on the slope of the IS curve when the value of h increases: The slope of the IS_2 curve is less than that of IS_1.

Solution 5

(1) The direction and the amount of shift in the LM curve when the increase in the money supply is Rs. 10 crore:

Amount of shift in the LM curve: $\frac{1}{0.25} \times 20 = 80$

Since there is an increase in the money supply, the LM curve will shift to the right.

(2) The direction and the amount of shift in the LM curve when the decrease in the money supply is Rs. 25 crore:

Amount of shift in the LM curve: $\frac{1}{0.25} \times 25 = 100$

Since there is a decrease in the money supply, the LM curve will shift to the left.

Space	Goods Market	Money Market
Space 1	$S > I, Y > C + I$	$m_d < m_s$
Space 2	$S > I, Y > C + I$	$m_d > m_s$
Space 3	$S > I, Y < C + I$	$m_d > m_s$
Space 4	$S < I, Y < C + I$	$m_d < m_s$

UNSOLVED NUMERICAL PROBLEMS

1. Equation of the IS curve: $Y = 340 - 10r$

   Different values of r can be taken with the corresponding values of Y and then the IS curve can be plotted. When $r = 5$, $Y = 290$; $r = 7$, $Y = 270$; and $r = 10$, $Y = 240$.

2. (a) Equation of the IS curve: $Y = 280 - 10r$

   (b) Equation of the IS curve when investment changes:

   $Y = 280 - 20r$

3. (a) Equation of the IS curve by the aggregate demand–aggregate supply approach: $Y = 1680 - 10000r$

   (b) Equation of the IS curve by the saving–investment approach:

   $Y = 1680 - 10000r$

4. (a) Equation of the IS curve: $Y = 6400 - 40r$

   (b) Equation of the IS curve when the investment function changes to $I = 1500 - 5r$ while the consumption function remains the same: $Y = 6400 - 20r$

5. (a) IS equation: $Y = 8800 - 100r$

   (b) LM Equation: $Y = 6000 + 250r$

   (c) Simultaneous equilibrium for the IS and LM curves:

   $r = 8\%$, $Y = 8000$

The IS–LM Framework for a Three Sector Model

17

After studying this topic, you should be able to understand

- ✓ *In a three sector model, two new variables are included: government expenditure and taxation, G and T.*
- ✓ *There is only one combination of income and the interest rate at which there exists simultaneous equilibrium in the goods and money market.*
- ✓ *An increase in government expenditure by ΔG shifts the IS curve to the right by an amount equal to 1/1 − b × ΔG.*
- ✓ *The impact of taxes is felt through a change in the consumption level.*
- ✓ *A change in the money supply disturbs the money-market equilibrium causing a shift in the LM curve.*
- ✓ *By how much does the national income change in response to the monetary and fiscal policies depends on the elasticities of the IS and the LM curves.*
- ✓ *An expansionary fiscal policy shifts the IS curve to the right and leads to an increase in both the income level and the interest rate.*
- ✓ *An expansionary monetary policy shifts the LM curve to the right and leads to an increase in the income level but a decrease in the interest rate.*

INTRODUCTION

This chapter is an extension of Chapter 16 which extends the IS–LM two sector model to a three sector model where there exists the government sector in addition to the households and the firms. The shifts in the IS curve due to the changes in fiscal policy and the shifts in the LM curve due to changes in monetary policy are also analysed.

The chapter goes on to discuss the effectiveness of monetary and fiscal policies in the different ranges of the LM curve. (Refer to Appendix B for the IS–LM framework for a four sector model)

THE IS–LM MODEL FOR A THREE SECTOR ECONOMY

The construction of a three sector model involves the inclusion of two new variables which pertain to the government sector, government expenditure and taxation. The analysis is based on certain assumptions:

(1) The price level is constant.

(2) At that constant price level, the firms are willing to supply whatever output is demanded.

(3) The short-run aggregate supply curve is perfectly elastic till the full employment level of output.

(4) Government expenditure is autonomous; hence, $G = \overline{G}$.

(5) Taxes are a linear function of income. Thus, $T = \overline{T} + tY$ where $\overline{T}$ is the autonomous tax (which is independent of the income level) while t is the income tax rate.

BOX 17.1

The IS–LM model emerged as an aftermath of the Keynesian revolution. It showed how the economists from the period of the 1940s to the 1960s regarded the Keynesian economics and the classical economics. Later, many other macroeconomic models also came up like the Harrod–Domar growth model and the multiplier–accelerator business-cycle model. However, these failed to gain as much popularity as some of the other models like the IS–LM model.

THE GOODS MARKET EQUILIBRIUM IN A THREE SECTOR ECONOMY: THE IS CURVE

As already observed, there are two approaches to determine the equilibrium level of income. In a three sector economy, they can be expressed as

(1) Aggregate Demand–Aggregate Supply Approach

Aggregate demand = Total value of output (or income)

or
$$Y = C + I + G$$

(2) Injections equal Leakages Approach

$$I + G = S + T$$

We have consumption function as $C = C(Y)$; investment function as $I = I(r)$; government expenditure $G = \overline{G}$; saving function as $S = S(Y)$; tax as $T = \overline{T} + tY$ and equilibrium condition as $Y = C(Y) + I(r) + \overline{G}$.

The two equilibrium conditions can be used to develop a graphical approach to the derivation of the IS curve as in Figure 17.1.

In Figure 17.1 starting with a two sector model, Quadrant A shows the investment curve, *I*. Corresponding to the saving function S_1 in Quadrant C, the two sector goods market equilibrium is represented by the curve IS_1 in Quadrant D. The investment curve, *I* of Quadrant A and the savings curve, S_1 of Quadrant C yields the curve IS_1 in Quadrant D. Quadrant D shows the goods market equilibrium in a three sector economy where the IS curve depicts the different combinations of the interest rates and the output levels at which planned investment equals saving or planned spending is equal to the income.

Next assume the government sector is introduced in the model or, in other words, we have a three sector model. In Quadrant A, government expenditures have been added to the investment curve to get the $I + G$ curve. As government expenditures are independent of the interest rate, $I + G$ curve lies to the right of the investment curve as shown in the figure.

Quadrant B gives the injections leakages equality in the form of a 45 degree line drawn through the origin. At all points along this 45 degree line, injections equal leakages or $I + G = S + T$.

Quadrant C shows the saving function *S*. When a tax is imposed, the saving curve will shift to the right by the amount of the tax to get the adjusted saving curve S_2. When taxes are added to the adjusted saving function, we get the $S_2 + T$ curve in Quadrant C of Figure 17.1.

The investment curve *I* of Quadrant A and the saving curve *S* of Quadrant C yielded the curve IS_1 in Quadrant D. The investment plus government expenditure curve $(I + G)$of Quadrant A and the saving plus tax curve $(S_2 + T)$ of Quadrant C yields the curve IS_2 in Quadrant D.

THE MONEY–MARKET EQUILIBRIUM IN A THREE SECTOR ECONOMY: THE LM CURVE

In a three sector economy, the analysis of the money market will remain the same as in the two sector economy as government expenditure and taxes do not influence either the demand for money or the supply of money.

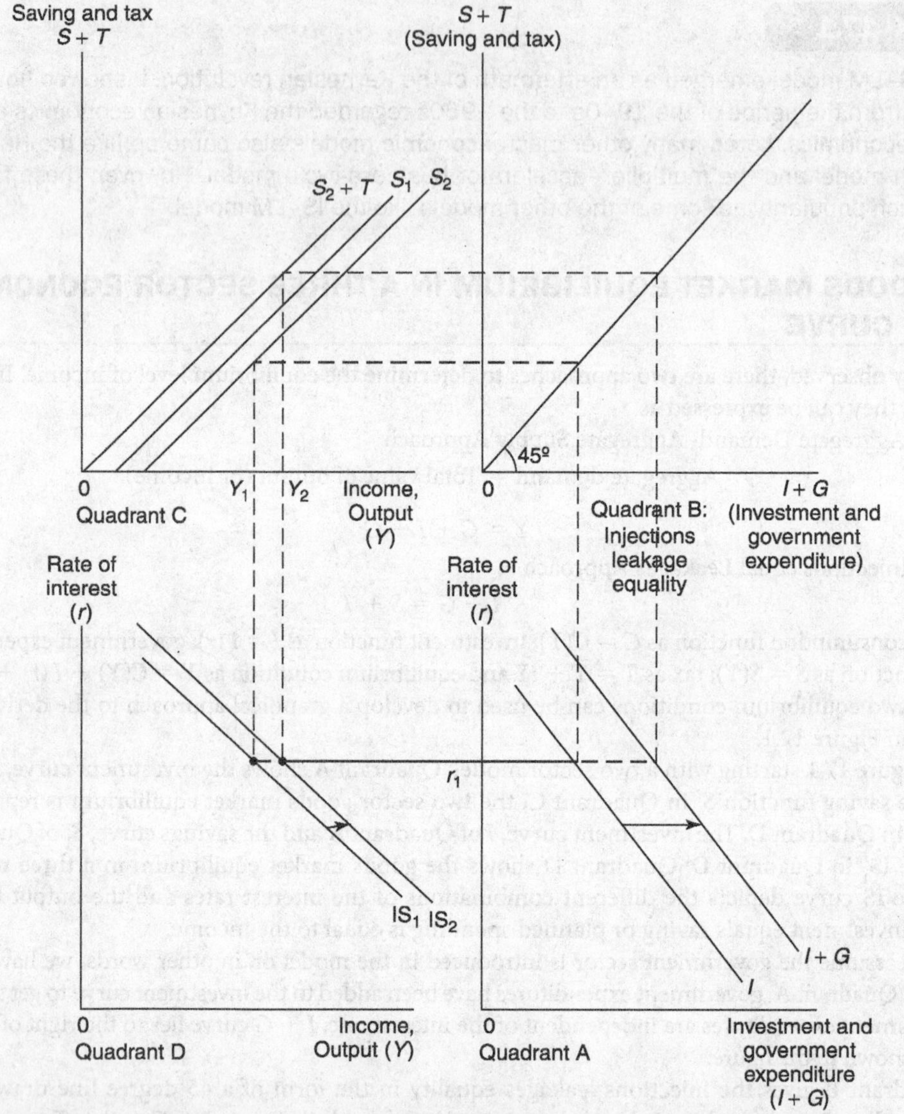

Figure 17.1 The Goods Market Equilibrium in a Three Sector Economy: The IS Curve

Equilibrium in the Two Markets: The Goods Market and Money Market

The IS Curve: An Algebraic Explanation

The goods market is in equilibrium when

$$\text{Aggregate demand} = \text{Total value of output (or income)}$$

or

$$Y = C + I + G$$

But,

$$C = C_a + b\,Y_d,$$

$$I = \bar{I} - hr,$$
$$G = \overline{G},$$
$$Y_d = Y - T,$$
$$T = \overline{T} + tY$$

Thus,
$$Y = C_a + bY_d + \bar{I} - hr + \overline{G}$$
$$Y = C_a + b(Y - T) + \bar{I} - hr + \overline{G}$$
$$Y = C_a + b[Y - (\overline{T} + tY)] + \bar{I} - hr + \overline{G}$$
$$Y = C_a + bY - b\overline{T} - btY + \bar{I} - hr + \overline{G}$$
$$Y - bY + btY = C_a - b\overline{T} + \bar{I} - hr + \overline{G}$$
$$Y(1 - b + bt) = C_a - b\overline{T} + \bar{I} - hr + \overline{G}$$
$$Y = \frac{1}{1-b(1-t)} C_a - b\overline{T} + \bar{I} - hr + \overline{G} \quad (1)$$

Equation (1) represents the IS curve in a three sector economy.

Numerical Illustration 1

Suppose the consumption and investment functions are as follows:

$$C = 10 + 0.5Y$$
$$I = 80 - 8r.$$

(a) Find the equation of the IS curve.

(b) Suppose the government sector is introduced in the model. Now $C = 10 + 0.5\,Y_d$ (where $Y_d = Y - T$), $I = 80 - 8r$, $G =$ Rs. 20 crores and $T =$ Rs. 30 crores. Find the equation of the IS curve.

Solution

(a) Equation of the IS curve

$$Y = C + I$$
$$Y = 10 + 0.5Y + 80 - 8r$$
$$0.5Y = 90 - 8r$$
$$Y = 180 - 16r$$

(b) Equation of the IS curve when the government sector is introduced in the model:

$$Y = C + I + G$$
$$Y = 10 + 0.5\,(Y - 30) + 80 - 8r + 20$$
$$0.5Y = 90 - 8r - 15 + 20$$
$$0.5Y = 95 - 8r$$
$$Y = 190 - 16r$$

The LM Curve: An Algebraic Explanation

The money–market equilibrium is similar to that of a two sector economy.

Thus,

$$m_d = m_s$$

But,

$$m_d = m_t + m_{sp}$$

where, m_d = total demand for money

$m_t = kY$ (transactions demand for money)

$m_{sp} = g(r)$ (speculative demand for money)

We assume that the speculative demand for money is a linear function (rather than a curve). Hence, we have $m_{sp} = \overline{m}_{sp} - g(r)$.

From the above, we have Supply of money $m_s = \overline{m}_a$

$$\text{Demand for money } m_d = kY + \overline{m}_{sp} - g(r)$$

The money–market equilibrium condition can be written as

$$\overline{m}_s = kY + \overline{m}_{sp} - g(r)$$

Thus,

$$Y = \frac{1}{k}\,[\overline{m}_s - \overline{m}_{sp} + g(r)] \tag{2}$$

Equation (2) represents the LM curve.

RECAP

- With the inclusion of the two new variables, *G* and *T*, the IS curve represents the goods market equilibrium whereas the LM curve represents the money–market equilibrium.

EQUILIBRIUM IN THE GOODS AND THE MONEY MARKET IN A THREE SECTOR ECONOMY

We have already observed in Chapter 16 that there is only one combination of income and the rate of interest at which both the goods and the money market are in equilibrium. This has been depicted in Figure 17.2. This combination exists at point E at which the IS and LM curves intersect to determine the equilibrium rate of interest at r^* and the equilibrium level of income at Y^*. It is important to note that at all other points, there exists disequilibrium in either the goods market or the money market.

All combinations of income and interest that lie above and towards the right of the IS curve, like point R, indicate a situation where $Y > C + I + G$ or saving plus taxes is greater than planned investment plus government expenditures. There exists an excess supply of goods. Hence, the level of income will fall.

BOX 17.2

The initial IS–LM model (as compared to the new IS–LM model) plays an important role in policy decisions. However, it is being subject to criticism in that it is an obsolete instrument of monetary policy. It is unable to explain the existence of a high inflation rate and high unemployment rate simultaneously in the economy. However, attempts are being made to revive the initial IS–LM model through the expectation concepts.

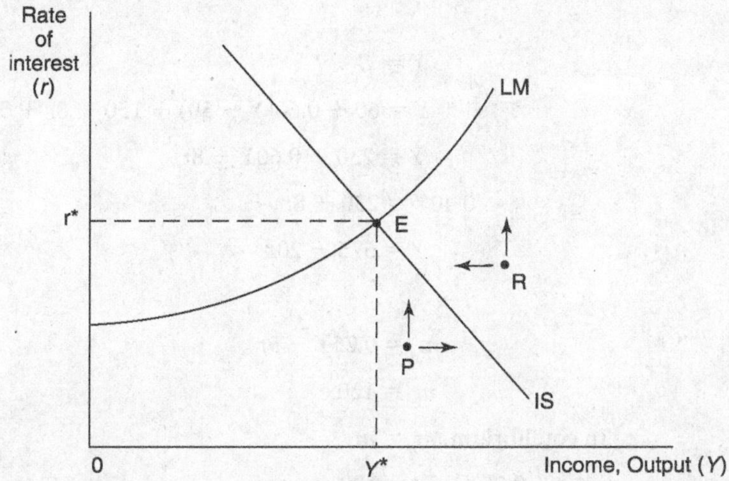

Figure 17.2 Equilibrium in the Goods and the Money Market in a Three Sector Economy

All combinations of income and interest that lie below and towards the left of the IS curve, like point P, indicate a situation where $Y < C + I + G$ or saving plus taxes is less than planned investment plus government expenditures. There exists an excess demand for goods. Thus, there will be an increase in the income level.

Similarly as far as the LM curve is concerned, at all combinations of income and interest that lie below and towards the right of the LM curve, like point R, the demand for money is greater than the supply of money or there is an excess demand for money. Hence, the rate of interest will rise.

At all combinations of income and interest that lie above and towards the left of the LM curve, the demand for money is less than the supply of money or there is an excess supply of money. Hence, the rate of interest will fall.

It is only at point E that there is equilibrium in both the goods and money markets which will remain unchanged until a shift in the IS or LM curve disturbs the equilibrium.

RECAP

- The point of equilibrium will remain unchanged until it is disturbed by a shift in the IS or LM curve.

Numerical Illustration 2

Suppose the consumption and investment functions are as follows:

$$C = 60 + 0.60Y_d \text{ (where } Y = Y_d - T)$$

$$I = 150 - 8r$$

Also, the government expenditure and taxes are

$$G = \text{Rs. 50 crores}$$

$$T = \text{Rs. 50 crores}$$

Assume that the supply of money is Rs. 120 crores. The demand for money function is $m_d = 0.25Y - 5r$. Find

(1) the equation of the IS curve.

(2) the equation of the LM curve.

(3) the simultaneous equilibrium for the IS curve and LM curves and plot it.

Solution

(1) IS equation:

$$Y = C + I$$

$$Y = 60 + 0.60(Y - 50) + 150 - 8r + 50$$

$$Y = 230 + 0.60Y - 8r$$

$$0.40Y = 230 - 8r$$

$$Y = 575 - 20r$$

(2) LM equation:

$$m_d = 0.25Y - 5r$$

$$m_s = 120$$

In equilibrium, $m_d = m_s$

Thus,

$$0.25Y - 5r = 120$$

$$0.25Y = 120 + 5r$$

$$Y = 480 + 20r$$

(3) Simultaneous equilibrium for the IS curve and LM curves

$$IS = LM$$

$$575 - 20r = 480 + 20r$$

$$40r = 95$$

$$r = 2.375\%$$

$$Y = 575 - 20 \times 2.375$$

$$Y = 527.5$$

Simultaneous equilibrium for the IS curve and LM curves exists when $Y = 527.5$ and $r = 2.375\%$.

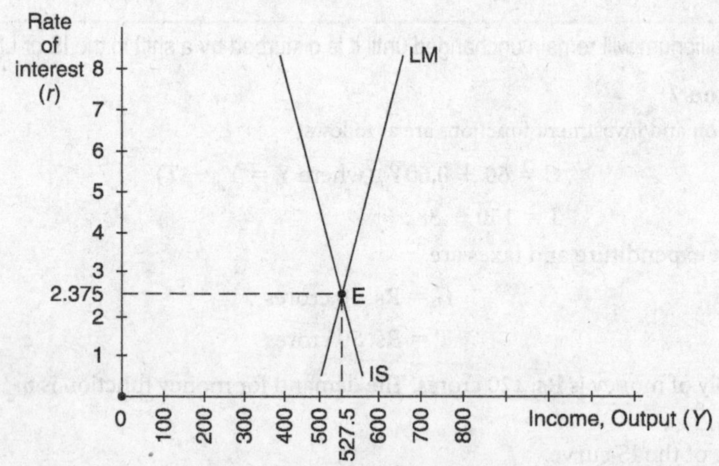

Figure 17.3 Simultaneous Equilibrium for IS and LM Curves Exist When $Y = 527.5$ and $r = 2.375\%$

SHIFTS IN THE IS CURVE DUE TO CHANGES IN FISCAL POLICY

In Chapter 16 we had observed that a shift in either the investment function or the consumption function leads to a shift in the IS curve. Similarly, the effects of a change in the fiscal policy can be analysed in terms of its influence on the IS curve and the resulting changes in income and the rate of interest. It is to be remembered that a fiscal policy relates to the government expenditures and its taxes.

A Change in Government Expenditure

In Figure 17.4, the initial equilibrium is at point E_1 determined by the intersection of the IS_1 and LM curves with the equilibrium income and the rate of interest at Y_1 and r_1 respectively.

An increase in government expenditure by ΔG shifts the IS curve to the right by an amount equal to the government expenditure multiplier times the change in government expenditure, $1/1 - b \times \Delta G$. (We had discussed in Chapter 7 that the government expenditure multiplier is $G_M = \Delta Y/\Delta G = 1/1 - b$). Thus, the new IS curve is IS_2 with the equilibrium at point E_2. The equilibrium income and the rate of interest are Y_2 and r_2, respectively.

The above analysis shows that an increase in government expenditure brings about an increase in income from Y_1 to Y_2 and an increase in the rate of interest from r_1 to r_2.

One would expect that the increase in the government expenditure would result in an increase in the income level by an amount equal to the multiplier times the increase in the government expenditure or, in other words, by an amount equal to $1/1 - b \times \Delta G$. In that case, equilibrium would be at point E′ on the IS_2 curve and the increase in income would be from Y_1 to Y'. Instead, the equilibrium is at E_2 while the increase in income is from Y_1 to Y_2 only. This is due to the crowding out effect.

Crowding Out

The level of government expenditure, *G*, is an important component of aggregate demand. As already discussed, Figure 17.4 analyses the effects of a shift in the IS curve due to an increase in aggregate demand. The initial equilibrium is at point E_1. Given the rate of interest at r_1, there is an increase in government expenditure and thus in the aggregate demand. To meet the increased demand, there will be an increase in the level of output. The IS curve will shift from IS_1 to

Crowding out is a situation which arises when an expansionary fiscal policy-for example, an increase in government expenditure-leads to an increase in the rate of interest, thus leading to a decrease in private investment.

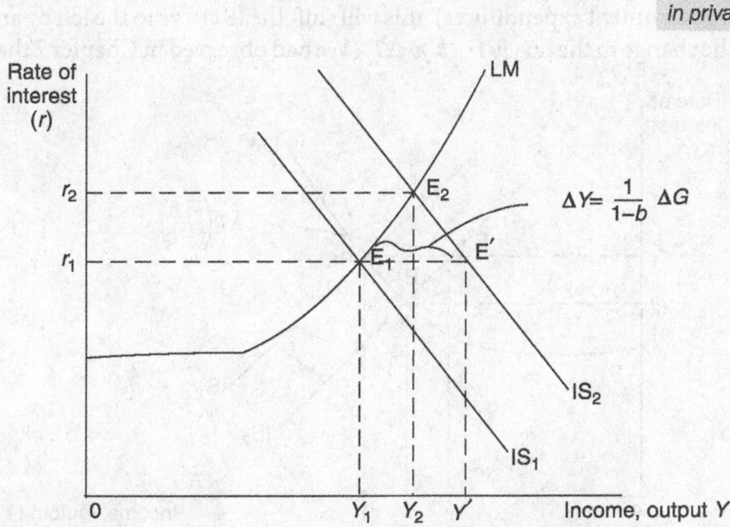

Figure 17.4 Shift in the IS Curve Due to Changes in Fiscal Policy

IS_2 and equilibrium will move from point E_1 to point E′ at the rate of interest, r_1. There will be an increase in the equilibrium income from Y_1 to Y'.

At E′ though there exists goods market equilibrium, there is disequilibrium in the money market. This is because the increase in the income has generated an excess demand for money. Therefore, there will occur an increase in the rate of interest leading to a decrease in investment and hence in the aggregate demand. After all the adjustments for the increase in the government expenditures and the dampening effects of the higher rate of interest on investment are taken into consideration, both the goods and the money market are simultaneously in equilibrium only at point E_2. It is only at this point that the planned spending equals income and the demand for money equals the supply of money. Thus, an increase in government expenditure (fiscal expansion) does lead to an increase in the income level, but it is to be noted that the increase in the rate of interest has a dampening effect on the expansion. In Figure 17.4, a comparison between the equilibrium at E_2 and E′ in the goods market shows that the increase in the government expenditure leads to an increase in the income level from Y_1 to Y_2 (and not Y').

Crowding out is a situation which arises when an expansionary fiscal policy–for example, an increase in government expenditure–leads to an increase in the rate of interest, thus leading to a decrease in private investment. Hence, the adjustments which occur in the rate of interest have a dampening effect on the increase in the output.

We consider two cases:

(1) In an economy with the level of output at the full employment level, an increase in government expenditures will cause an increase in aggregate demand and, hence, an increase in the rate of interest. This will continue till the initial increase in the aggregate demand is totally crowded out.

(2) In an economy with the level of output below the full employment level, whenever there is an increase in government expenditures firms will hire more workers to increase the level of output. Hence, there occurs an increase in both the interest rate and the income level. In such a situation, there will not be a full crowding out.

A Change in Taxes

The impact of taxes is felt through a change in the consumption level. In Figures. 17.5 and 17.6, which show the impact of a tax, the economy's initial equilibrium is at point E_1 determined by the intersection of the IS_1 and LM curves with the equilibrium income and the rate of interest at Y_1 and r_1, respectively.

Figure 17.5 depicts the impact of an increase in taxes. Suppose the government increases the tax by ΔT (there is no change in government expenditures), this will shift the IS curve to the left by an amount equal to the tax multiplier times the change in the tax, $b/1 - b \times \Delta T$. (We had observed in Chapter 7 that the tax multiplier is

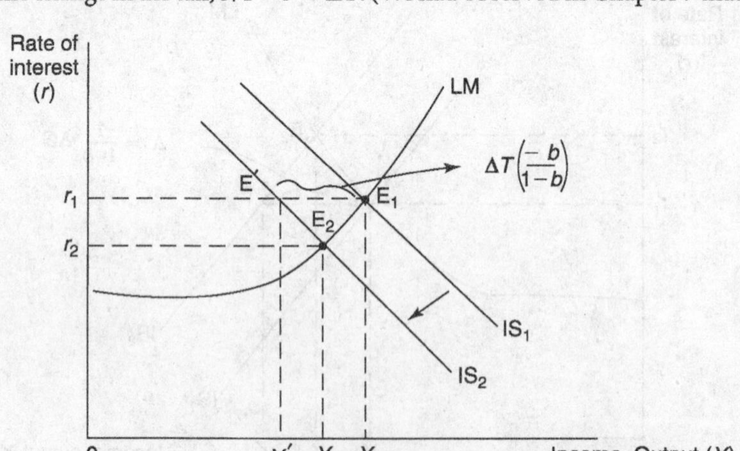

Figure 17.5 Shift in the IS Curve Due to an Increase in Tax

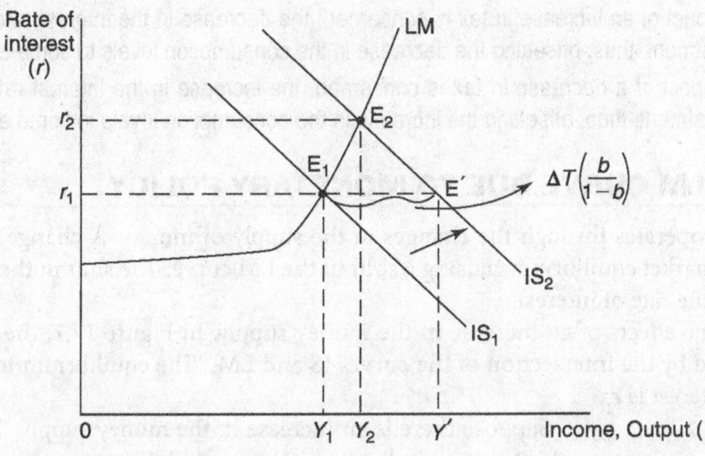

Figure 17.6 Shift in the IS Curve Due to a Decrease in Tax

$G_T = \Delta Y/\Delta T = b/1 - b$). Thus, the new IS curve is IS_2 with the equilibrium at point E_2. The equilibrium income and the rate of interest are Y_2 and r_2, respectively. Thus, an increase in tax brings about a decrease in income from Y_1 to Y_2 and a decrease in the rate of interest from r_1 to r_2.

One would expect that an increase in the tax would result in a decrease in the income level by an amount equal to the tax multiplier times the increase in the tax, or in words $b/1 - b \times \Delta T$. In that case, the new equilibrium would be at point E′ on the IS_2 curve and the decrease in income from Y_1 to Y'. Instead, the equilibrium is at E_2 while the decrease in income is from Y_1 to Y_2 only. The reason for this is that an increase in the tax results in a decrease in the consumption level which leads to a decrease in the production of the goods and services causing a decrease in the income levels. Hence, individuals demand less money leading to decrease in the interest rates. The decrease in the interest rates is responsible for an increase in investment, thus, offsetting the decrease in the consumption levels to some extent. The Keynesian model had ignored these effects and, thus, exaggerated the effects of an increase in the taxes.

Figure 17.6 depicts the impact of a decrease in taxes. Suppose that the government decreases the tax by ΔT (there is no change in government expenditures). This will lead to a shift in the IS curve to the right by an amount equal to the tax multiplier times the change in the tax, $b/1 - b \times \Delta T$. The new IS curve is IS_2 with the equilibrium at point E_2. The equilibrium income and the rate of interest are Y_2 and r_2, respectively. Thus, a decrease in tax brings about an increase in the income from Y_1 to Y_2 and an increase in the rate of interest from r_1 to r_2.

One would expect that a decrease in the taxes would result in an increase in the income level by an amount equal to the tax multiplier times the decrease in the taxes, or in words $b/1 - b \times \Delta T$. Then, the new equilibrium would be at point E′ on the IS_2 curve and the increase in income from Y_1 to Y'. Instead, the equilibrium point is E_2 while the increase in income from Y_1 to Y_2 only. The reason for this is that a decrease in the taxes results in an increase in the consumption level which leads to an increase in the production of the goods and services causing an increase in the income levels. Hence, individuals demand more money leading to an increase in the interest rates. The increase in the interest rates is responsible for the firms reducing their investments. The Keynesian model had ignored these effects and understated the effects of a decrease in the taxes.

RECAP

- The increase in the income due to the increase in the government expenditure should be equal to $1/1 - b \times \Delta G$.
- Due to the crowding out effect, the increase in income is much smaller than $1/1 - b \times \Delta G$.

- As far as the impact of an increase in tax is concerned, the decrease in the interest rates is responsible for an increase in investment, thus, offsetting the decrease in the consumption levels to some extent.
- As far as the impact of a decrease in tax is concerned, the increase in the interest rates is responsible for a decrease in investment, thus, offsetting the increase in the consumption levels to some extent.

SHIFTS IN THE LM CURVE DUE TO MONETARY POLICY

The monetary policy operates through the changes in the supply of money. A change in the money supply disturbs the money–market equilibrium causing a shift in the LM curve. The shift in the LM curve influences the income level and the rate of interest.

Let us examine the effects of an increase in the money supply. In Figure 17.7, the initial equilibrium is at point E_1 determined by the intersection of the curves IS and LM_1. The equilibrium income is Y_1 while the equilibrium rate of interest is r_1.

The mechanism by which the changes in the monetary policy affect the aggregate demand and, thus, the income level is called the monetary transmission process.

Suppose there is an increase in the money supply. Thus at the prevailing rate of interest r_1, individuals are now holding excess money in their portfolio which they will try to deposit in the banks, buy bonds, etc. Hence, there will be a decrease in the interest rates. The equilibrium moves to point E′ at which there is equilibrium in the money market and the individuals are willing to hold a larger quantity of money due to a decrease in the interest rate. However, at point E′ there is disequilibrium in the goods market. The decrease in the interest rate will encourage investment leading to an increase in the income level. As a result, there occurs a movement up the LM_2 until a new equilibrium is established at point E_2, determined by the intersection of the curves IS and LM_2. The equilibrium income increases to Y_2 while the equilibrium rate of interest falls to r_2.

The mechanism by which the changes in the monetary policy affect the aggregate demand and, thus, the income level is called the monetary transmission process.

RECAP

- A shift in the LM curve affects the income level and the rate of interest.

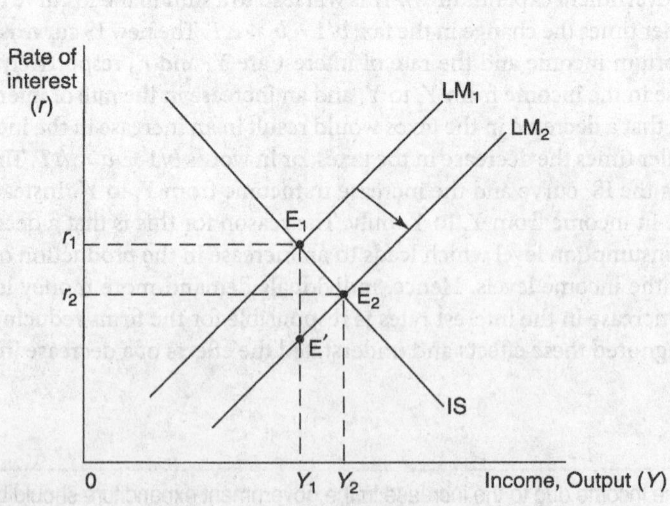

Figure 17.7 The Effects of an Increase in the Money Supply

THE ELASTICITIES OF IS AND LM CURVES AND THE EFFECTIVENESS OF MONETARY AND FISCAL POLICIES

We have observed the impact of the monetary and fiscal policies in bringing about changes in the national income. However, we have yet to determine by how much the national income will change in response to the policies. This responsiveness depends on the elasticities of the IS and the LM curves.

The Elasticities of IS and LM Curves

The Elasticity of LM Curve: Given the supply of money in an economy, the LM curve has a positive slope as in Figure 17.8. For most analytical purposes, it can be divided into three ranges:

(1) **Keynesian range:** At some very low rate of interest, say r_1 speculative demand for money becomes perfectly elastic or infinity. At this rate of interest, all expect the interest rate to increase in the future and, thus, become bears. Hence, all individuals prefer to hold only cash and no one prefers to hold bonds. In this range, no amount of monetary expansion can lower the interest rate. The extra liquidity, which has been created by the monetary authorities, is trapped in the asset portfolio of the public. This range is also called the liquidity trap. The rate of interest serves as the minimum and cannot fall any further. In this range, the LM curve is horizontal and the interest elasticity is infinity.

(2) **Classical range:** At some very high rate of interest, the speculative demand for money becomes perfectly inelastic. All expect the interest rate to fall in the future and become bulls. Thus, everyone prefers to hold only bonds and no one likes to hold cash. The speculative demand for money becomes zero. In this range, the LM curve is vertical. This is called the classical range as it is in accordance with the classical theory of money where money is demanded for conducting transactions. In this range, the LM curve is vertical and the interest elasticity is zero.

(3) **Intermediate range:** This is the range in between the Keynesian range and the classical range. Here, both the transactions and speculative demand for money exist. The interest elasticity in this range is greater than zero.

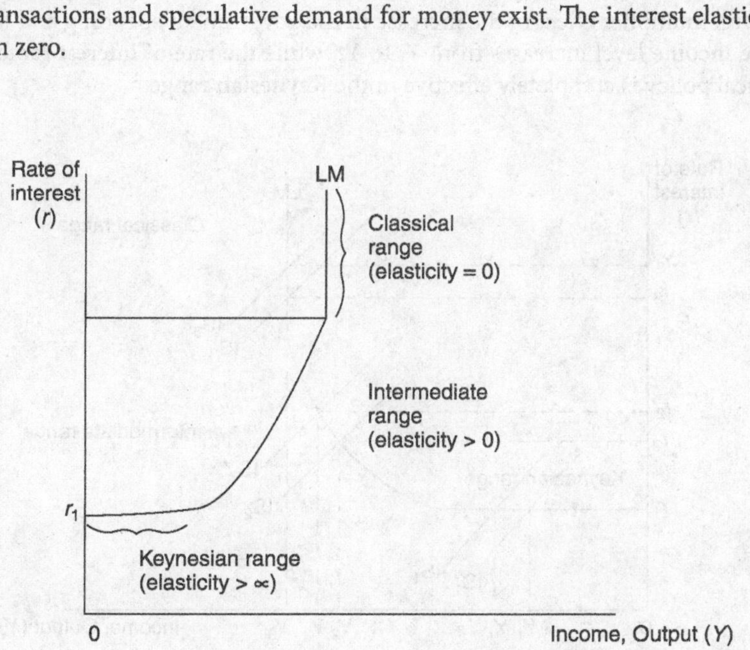

Figure 17.8 The LM Curve

The Elasticity of IS Curve: The IS curve has a positive slope. As far as the elasticity of the IS curve is concerned, it depends on the responsiveness of investment to changes in the interest rate and on the magnitude of the multiplier.

(1) If investment is insensitive (or independent) to the rate of interest, then the investment curve will be perfectly inelastic. The IS curve will be vertical or perfectly inelastic.

(2) If investment is sensitive to the interest rate, or in other words it is interest elastic, then the investment curve will be elastic. In that case the IS curve will be elastic; the elasticity being higher, the lower is the marginal propensity to save. (A lower marginal propensity to save implies a higher multiplier.)

Effectiveness of Monetary and Fiscal Policies

The effectiveness of a policy in achieving the economic objectives depends on the elasticity of the IS and LM curves. It is important to note that an expansionary fiscal policy, as it shifts the IS curve to the right, leads to an increase in both the income level and the interest rate. On the other hand, an expansionary monetary policy, as it shifts the LM curve to the right, leads to an increase the income level but a decrease in the interest rate.

Effectiveness of Fiscal Policy

Fiscal Policy relates to the utilization of government expenditure and taxation to achieve some well-defined objectives relating to growth, employment and many others. The fiscal policy has an immediate impact on the goods market and, thus, leads to shift in the IS curve.

In Figure 17.9, we examine the effectiveness of the fiscal policy in the three different ranges of the LM curve:

(1) **Keynesian range or the liquidity trap:** Here, fiscal policy is very effective. Initially, the equilibrium exists at the intersection of the IS_1 and LM curves to determine the equilibrium income at Y_1 and the rate of interest at r_1. A fiscal expansion, say an increase in the government expenditure, leads to a shift of the IS_1 curve to IS_1'. It is important to note that in the range of the liquidity trap, an increase in the government expenditure does not affect the rate of interest and, thus, the level of investment. Hence, there is a full multiplier effect of the increase in the government spending and no dampening effects occur. The income level increases from Y_1 to Y_1' while the rate of interest remains unchanged at r_1. Hence, fiscal policy is completely effective in the Keynesian range.

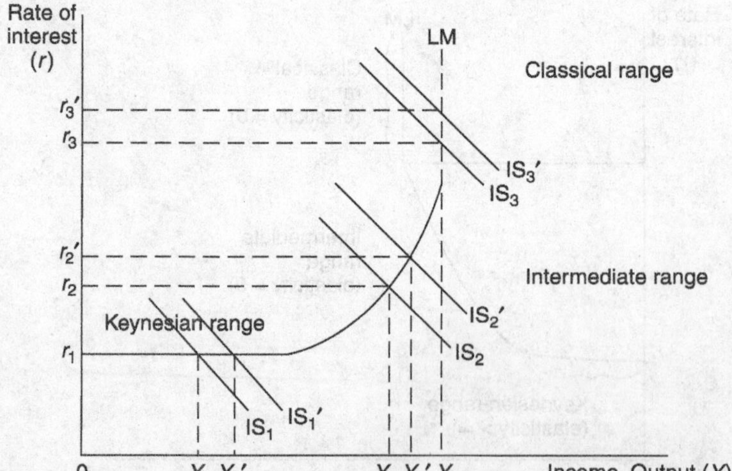

Figure 17.9 Effectiveness of Fiscal Policy

(2) **Classical range:** Here, fiscal policy is not effective. Initially, the equilibrium exists at the intersection of the IS_3 and LM curves to determine the equilibrium income at Y_3 and the rate of interest at r_3. A fiscal expansion, say an increase in the government expenditure, leads to a shift of the IS_3 curve to IS_3'. The income level remains unchanged at Y_3 while the rate of interest increases from r_3 to r_3'.
An increase in government expenditure and the interest rate and an unchanged income level imply that there occurs an offsetting decrease or crowding out of private investment which equals the increase in the government expenditure. Hence, there is full crowding out. Hence, fiscal policy is completely ineffective in the classical range.

(3) **Intermediate range:** Here, fiscal policy is effective but it is not as effective as in the Keynesian range. Initially, equilibrium exists at the intersection of the IS_2 and LM curves to determine the equilibrium income at Y_2 and the rate of interest at r_2. A fiscal expansion, say an increase in the government expenditure, leads to a shift of the IS_2 curve to IS_2'. Thus, the income level increases from Y_2 to Y_2' while the rate of interest increases from r_2 to r_2'.
In this range, the expansionary effect of the fiscal policy does succeed in raising the income level. However, the increase in the income is not as much as in the Keynesian range. This is due to the increase in the interest rate because of which investment decreases and, thus, the expansionary effect of the fiscal policy gets negated to some extent. Thus, fiscal policy is less effective in the intermediate range as compared to the Keynesian range.

Effectiveness of Monetary Policy

Monetary policy relates to changes in the supply of money by the central bank to achieve the objectives relating to growth, employment and others. Monetary policy has an immediate impact on the money market and leads to a shift in the LM curve.

In Figure 17.10, we examine the effectiveness of the monetary policy in the three different ranges of the LM curve with the help of two types of IS curves, one elastic and the other inelastic.

(1) **Keynesian range:** Here, monetary policy is completely ineffective.

(a) **Elastic IS curve, IS_1:** Initial equilibrium exists at the intersection of the IS_1 and LM_1 curves to determine the equilibrium income at Y_1 and the rate of interest at r_1. In this range a monetary expansion, a shift in the LM curve from LM_1 to LM_2, does not lead to an increase in the income

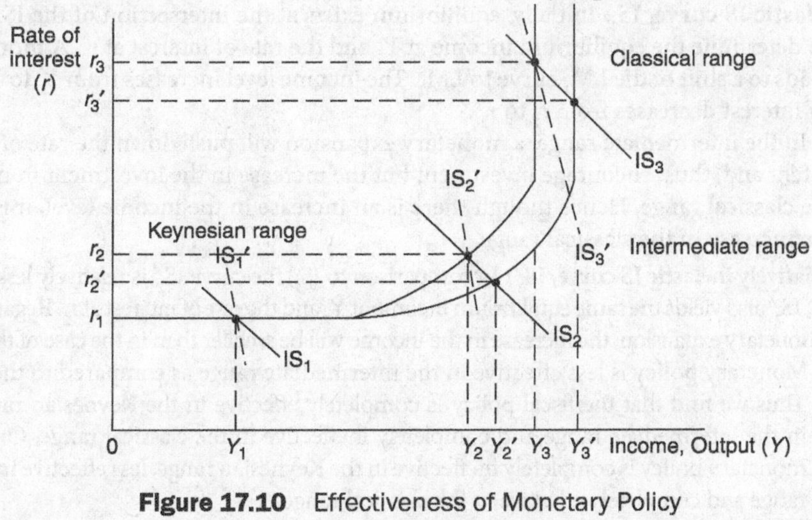

Figure 17.10 Effectiveness of Monetary Policy

level or any changes in the interest rate, which remain at Y_1 and r_1 respectively. All increases in the supply of money are held as speculative balances and no part of any increases in the money supply are diverted for transactions. Hence, there is no increase in the income level. Hence, monetary policy is completely ineffective in the Keynesian range.

(b) **Relatively inelastic IS curve, IS′:** As compared to IS_1, the curve IS_1' is relatively less elastic. However as with IS_1, IS_1' yields the same equilibrium income at Y_1 and the rate of interest at r_1. The effects of a monetary expansion are also similar.

Monetary policy is ineffective in the liquidity trap whatever the elasticity of the IS curve.

(2) **Classical range:** Here, monetary policy is completely effective.

(a) **Elastic IS curve, IS_3:** Initially, equilibrium exists at the intersection of the IS_3 and LM_1 curves to determine the equilibrium income at Y_3 and the rate of interest at r_3. A monetary expansion leads to a shift of the LM_1 curve to LM_2. The income level increases from Y_3 to Y_3' while the rate of interest decreases from r_3 to r_3'.

In the classical range, the speculative demand for money is zero due to the high interest rates. Money is demanded only for transaction purposes. In such a situation, a monetary expansion will push down the rate of interest and, thus, encourage investment leading to an increase in the income level. Monetary policy is totally effective in the classical range in bringing about an increase in the income level.

(b) **Relatively inelastic IS curve, IS_3':** As compared to IS_3, the curve IS_3' is relatively less elastic. Similar to IS_3, IS_3' also yields the same equilibrium income at Y_3 and the rate of interest at r_3. But as far as the effects of a monetary expansion are concerned, the increase in the income will be lower while the decrease in the interest rate will be much larger than for the elastic IS curve.

Monetary policy is completely effective in the classical range whatever the elasticity of the IS curve.

(3) **Intermediate range:** We had observed that in the Keynesian range, monetary policy is completely ineffective as the entire increase in the money supply is absorbed as speculative money balances. In contrast, in the classical range monetary policy is completely effective as the entire increase in the money supply is absorbed as transactions money balances.

As far as the intermediate range is concerned, monetary policy is effective but not as much as in the classical range because the increase in the money supply is absorbed partly as transactions money balances and partly as speculative money balances.

(a) **Elastic IS curve, IS_2:** Initially, equilibrium exists at the intersection of the IS_2 and LM_1 curves to determine the equilibrium income at Y_2 and the rate of interest at r_2. A monetary expansion leads to a shift of the LM_1 curve to LM_2. The income level increases from Y_2 to Y_2' while the rate of interest decreases from r_2 to r_2'.

In the intermediate range, a monetary expansion will push down the rate of interest to some extent and, thus, encourage investment but the increase in the investment in not as much as in the classical range. Hence though there is an increase in the income level, it is not as much as the increase in the classical range.

(b) **Relatively inelastic IS curve, IS_2':** In comparison to IS_2, the curve IS_2' is relatively less elastic. Similar to IS_2, IS_2' also yields the same equilibrium income at Y_2 and the rate of interest at r_2. Regarding the effects of a monetary expansion, the increase in the income will be smaller than in the case of the elastic IS curve.

Monetary policy is less effective in the intermediate range as compared to the classical range.

Thus we find that the fiscal policy is completely effective in the Keynesian range, less effective in the intermediate range and completely ineffective in the classical range. On the other hand, monetary policy is completely ineffective in the Keynesian range, less effective in the intermediate range and completely effective in the classical range.

RECAP

- Fiscal policy is most effective in the Keynesian range and ineffective in the classical range.
- Monetary policy is most effective in the classical range and ineffective in the Keynesian range.

SUMMARY

INTRODUCTION

1. The chapter extends the IS–LM two sector model to a three sector model.
2. The shifts in the IS curve and the shifts in the LM curve have also been analysed.

THE IS–LM MODEL FOR A THREE SECTOR ECONOMY

1. The construction of a three sector model involves the inclusion of government expenditure and taxation.
2. The analysis is based on certain assumptions: constant price level, perfectly elastic short-run aggregate supply curve till the full employment level of output, $G = \overline{G}$, and $T = \overline{T} + tY$.

THE GOODS MARKET EQUILIBRIUM IN A THREE SECTOR ECONOMY: THE IS CURVE

There are two approaches to determine the equilibrium level of income. In a three sector economy, they can be expressed as Aggregate demand–Aggregate supply approach and Injections equal Leakages approach.

THE MONEY–MARKET EQUILIBRIUM IN A THREE SECTOR ECONOMY: THE LM CURVE

In a three sector economy, the analysis of the money market will remain the same as in the two sector economy.

EQUILIBRIUM IN THE TWO MARKETS: THE GOODS MARKET AND MONEY MARKET

The equation of the IS curve in a three sector economy can be written as $Y = \frac{1}{1 - b(1 - t)} C_a - b\overline{T} + \overline{I} - hr + \overline{G}$

THE LM CURVE: AN ALGEBRAIC EXPLANATION

The equation of the LM curve in a three sector economy can be written as $Y = \frac{1}{k}[\overline{m}_s - \overline{m}_{sp} + g(r)]$

EQUILIBRIUM IN THE GOODS AND THE MONEY MARKET IN THREE SECTOR ECONOMY

1. There is only one combination of income and the rate of interest at which both the goods and the money market are in equilibrium.
2. This combination exists at the point at which the IS and LM curves intersect.
3. At all points towards the right of the IS curve, there exists an excess supply of goods and, thus, the level of income will fall.
4. At all points towards the left of the IS curve, there exists an excess demand for goods and, thus, there will be an increase in the income level.
5. At all points towards the right of the LM curve, there is an excess demand for money and, hence, the rate of interest will rise.
6. At all points towards the left of the LM curve, there is an excess supply of money and, hence, the rate of interest will fall.
7. The equilibrium in both the goods and money markets will remain unchanged until a shift in the IS or LM curve disturbs the equilibrium.

SHIFT IN THE IS CURVE DUE TO CHANGES IN FISCAL POLICY

1. An increase in government expenditure by ΔG shifts the IS curve to the right by an amount equal to $1/1 - b \times \Delta G$.
2. However, the resultant increase in the income level is much smaller than $1/1 - b \times \Delta G$. This is due to the crowding out effect.
3. The increase in the rate of interest has a dampening effect on the expansion in the income level.
4. Crowding out is a situation which arises when an expansionary fiscal policy, for example an increase in government expenditure, leads to an increase in the rate of interest, thus, leading to a decrease in private investment.
5. The impact of taxes is felt through a change in the consumption level.

6. One would expect that an increase in the tax would result in a decrease in the income level by $b/1 - b \times \Delta T$. However, the decrease is smaller. The decrease in the interest rates is responsible for an increase in investment, thus, offsetting the decrease in the consumption levels to some extent.
7. One would expect that a decrease in the tax would result in an increase in the income level by $b/1 - b \times \Delta T$. However, the increase is much smaller. The increase in the interest rates is responsible for a decrease in investment, thus, offsetting the increase in the consumption levels to some extent.

SHIFT IN THE LM CURVE DUE TO MONETARY POLICY

1. The monetary policy operates through the changes in the supply of money.
2. A change in the money supply disturbs the money–market equilibrium causing a shift in the LM curve.
3. The shift in the LM curve influences the income level and the rate of interest.
4. The mechanism by which the changes in the monetary policy affect the aggregate demand and, thus, the income level is called the monetary transmission process.

THE ELASTICITIES OF IS AND LM CURVES AND THE EFFECTIVENESS OF MONETARY AND FISCAL POLICIES

1. By how much does the national income change in response to the monetary and fiscal policies depends on the elasticities of the IS and the LM curves.
2. An expansionary fiscal policy shifts the IS curve to the right and leads to an increase in both the income level and the interest rate.
3. An expansionary monetary policy shifts the LM curve to the right and leads to an increase the income level but a decrease in the interest rate.

THE ELASTICITY OF LM CURVE

1. Given the supply of money in an economy, the LM curve has a positive slope. It can be divided into three ranges.
2. In the Keynesian range at some very low rate of interest, all expect the interest rate to increase in the future and thus become bears. In this range, the LM curve is horizontal and the interest elasticity is infinity.
3. In the classical range at some very high rate of interest, all expect the interest rate to fall in the future and become bulls. In this range, the LM curve is vertical and the interest elasticity is zero.
4. In the intermediate range, the interest elasticity is greater than zero.

THE ELASTICITY OF IS CURVE

The IS curve has a positive slope. The elasticity of the IS curve depends on the responsiveness of investment to changes in the interest rate and on the magnitude of the multiplier.

EFFECTIVENESS OF MONETARY AND FISCAL POLICIES

The effectiveness of a policy in achieving the economic objectives depends on the elasticity of the IS and LM curves.

EFFECTIVENESS OF FISCAL POLICY

1. Fiscal policy relates to the utilization of government expenditure and taxation to achieve some well-defined objectives relating to growth, employment and many others.
2. In the Keynesian range or the liquidity trap, fiscal policy is completely effective.
3. In the classical range, there is full crowding out and fiscal policy is completely ineffective.
4. In the intermediate range, fiscal policy is effective but it is not as effective as in the Keynesian range.

EFFECTIVENESS OF MONETARY POLICY

1. Monetary policy relates to changes in the supply of money by the central bank to achieve the objectives relating to growth, employment and others.
2. In the Keynesian range, monetary policy is ineffective whatever the elasticity of the IS curve.
3. In the classical range, monetary policy is completely effective whatever the elasticity of the IS curve.
4. In the intermediate range, monetary policy is effective but not as effective as in the classical range.

REVIEW QUESTIONS

TRUE OR FALSE QUESTIONS

1. All combinations of income and interest that lie above and towards the right of the IS curve indicate a situation where the demand for money is greater than the supply of money.
2. The increase in the income due to the increase in the government expenditure is equal to $1/1 - b \times \Delta G$.
3. The mechanism by which the changes in the monetary policy affect the aggregate demand and, thus, the income level is called the monetary transmission process.
4. Fiscal policy is most effective in the Keynesian range and ineffective in the classical range.
5. In the Keynesian range, the LM curve is vertical and the interest elasticity is zero.

VERY SHORT-ANSWER QUESTIONS

1. Why does there exist disequilibrium in the goods market at all combinations of income and interest that do not lie on the IS curve? Explain.
2. Why does there exist a disequilibrium in the money market at all combinations of income and interest that do not lie on the LM curve? Explain.
3. Derive the IS curve algebraically through the aggregate demand–aggregate supply approach in a three sector economy.
4. Derive the LM curve algebraically through the money–market equilibrium in a three sector economy.
5. 'In the classical range, all expect the rate of interest to fall in the future and become bulls'. Explain.

SHORT-ANSWER QUESTIONS

1. Write a short note on the simultaneous equilibrium in the goods and the money markets in a three sector economy.
2. What is crowding out? Discuss.
3. How does a change in the money supply disturb the money–market equilibrium? Explain.
4. Write a short note on the
   (a) elasticity of the IS curve.
   (b) elasticity of the LM curve.
5. Compare the effectiveness of monetary and fiscal policy in the Keynesian range or the liquidity trap.

LONG-ANSWER QUESTIONS

1. Examine the effects of a change in government expenditure on the equilibrium level of income and the rate of interest in a three sector economy. In this connection, throw some light on the crowding out effect.
2. Examine the impact of a tax on the equilibrium level of income and the rate of interest in a three sector economy.
3. 'Fiscal policy is most effective in the Keynesian range and ineffective in the classical range'. Explain.
4. 'Monetary policy is most effective in the classical range and ineffective in the Keynesian range'. Explain.
5. Discuss the simultaneous equilibrium in the goods and the money markets in a three sector economy by first discussing in brief the equilibrium in the goods market and the equilibrium in the money market.

SOLVED NUMERICAL PROBLEMS

Numerical Problem 1

Suppose the consumption and investment functions are as follows:

$$C = 50 + 0.80\,(Y - 0.25Y)$$

$$I = 200 - 5r$$

Also,

$$G = 100$$

Find

(1) the equation of the IS curve.

(2) the equation of the IS curve when government expenditure increases by Rs. 40.

Numerical Problem 2

Suppose the consumption and investment functions and the government expenditure are as follows:

$$C = 50 + 0.75(Y - 80)$$

$$I = 150 - 10r$$

$$G = \text{Rs. } 120 \text{ crores}$$

Also assume that the supply of money is Rs. 196 crores. The demand for money function is $m_d = 0.4Y - 6r$.

(1) Find the equation of the IS curve.

(2) Find the equation of the LM curve.

(3) Find the simultaneous equilibrium for the IS curve and LM curves.

(4) Find the simultaneous equilibrium for the IS curve and LM curves when government expenditure increases by Rs. 55 crores.

Numerical Problem 3

Assume that the consumption and investment functions are as follows:

$$C = 50 + 0.6Y_d$$

$$I = (I = 200 - 5r)$$

Also

$$G = 130$$

$$0 = 0$$

Find

(1) the equation of the IS curve.

(2) the equation of the IS curve when

(a) government expenditure increases by Rs. 50 crores.

(b) taxes increases by Rs. 50 crores.

(c) government expenditure increases by Rs. 50 crores and taxes increases by Rs. 50 crores.

(d) Plot all the curves.

Numerical Problem 4

In a three sector model, suppose the fundamental equations are:

$$C = \text{Rs. } 1000 + 0.80(Y - 0.25)$$

$$I = \text{Rs. } 1500 - 60r$$

$$G = \text{Rs. } 1000$$

$$L = 0.20Y - 20r$$

$$M = \text{Rs. } 1500$$

Find

(1) the equation of the IS curve.

(2) the equation of the LM curve.
(3) the simultaneous equilibrium for the IS and LM curves.

Numerical Problem 5
Find the simultaneous equilibrium for the IS curve and LM curves when

$$C = 200 + 0.80Y_d$$

$$I = 250 - 7.2r$$

$$G = 90$$

$$T = 0.20Y$$

$$m_s = 180$$

$$m_d = 0.2Y - 2r$$

UNSOLVED NUMERICAL PROBLEMS (WITH ANSWERS)

1. $$C = 500 + 0.80(Y_d)$$

$$I = 1500$$

$$G = 1000$$

$$T = 1000$$

$$L = 0.20Y - 100r$$

$$M = 2100$$

$$Y_d = Y - T$$

Find
(a) the IS equation.
(b) the LM equation.
(c) the equilibrium income and the interest rate.

2. In an economy, the consumption and investment functions and the government expenditure are as follows:

$$C = 180 + 0.80(Y - 100)$$

$$I = 280 - 5r$$

$$G = \text{Rs. } 100 \text{ crores}$$

Assume that the supply of money is Rs. 400 crores. The demand for money function is $m_d = 0.20Y$.
(a) Find the equation of the IS curve.
(b) Find the equation of the LM curve.
(c) Find the simultaneous equilibrium for the IS curve and LM curves.
(d) Find the level of investment.

3. In the Numerical 2 above, find the
   (a) IS curve when government expenditure increases by Rs. 20 crores.
   (b) LM curve.
   (c) equilibrium income level and the rate of interest.
   (d) level of investment.
4. Suppose,

$$C = 100 + 0.6Y_d$$

$$I = 220 - 10r$$

$$G = 100$$

$$T = 100$$

The supply of money is Rs. 110. The demand for money function is $m_d = 0.2Y - 5r$.
   (a) Find the equation of the IS curve.
   (b) Find the equilibrium of the economy.
   (c) Find the equilibrium of the economy if G increases from 100 to 200.
5. Find the simultaneous equilibrium for the IS curve and LM curves when

$$C = 100 + 0.70Y_d$$

$$I = 200 - 6.6r$$

$$G = 140$$

$$T = 0.20Y$$

$$m_s = 80$$

$$m_d = 0.2Y - 2r$$

ANSWERS

TRUE OR FALSE QUESTIONS

1. **False.** All combinations of income and interest that lie above and towards the right of the IS curve indicate a situation where $Y > C + I + G$ or saving plus taxes is greater than planned investment plus government expenditures.
2. **False.** The increase in the income due to the increase in the government expenditure should be equal to $1/1 + b \times \Delta G$. But due to the crowding out effect, the increase in income is much smaller than $1/1 - b \times \Delta G$.
3. **True.** Through this mechanism, monetary policy is able to influence aggregate demand and, thus, the income level.
4. **True.** While fiscal policy is most effective in the Keynesian range and ineffective in the classical range, monetary policy is most effective in the classical range and ineffective in the Keynesian range.
5. **False.** In the Keynesian range, the LM curve is horizontal and the interest elasticity is infinity.

SOLVED NUMERICAL PROBLEMS

Solution 1

(1) Equation of the IS curve

$$Y = C + I$$

$$Y = 50 + 0.80(Y - 0.25\,Y) + 200 - 5r + 100$$

$$Y = 0.80\,(0.75Y) + 350 - 5r$$

$$Y - 0.6Y = 350 - 5r$$

$$0.4Y = 350 - 5r$$

$$Y = 875 - 12.5r$$

(2) Equation of the IS curve when government expenditure increases by Rs. 40.

$$Y = C + I$$

$$Y = 50 + 0.80(Y - 0.25Y) + 200 - 5r + 140$$

$$Y = 0.80\,(0.75Y) + 390 - 5r$$

$$Y - 0.6Y = 390 - 5r$$

$$0.4Y = 390 - 5r$$

$$Y = 975 - 12.5r$$

Solution 2

(1) Equation of the IS curve $Y = C + I + G$

$$Y = 50 + 0.75(Y - 80) + 150 - 10r + 120$$

$$Y = 50 + 0.75Y - 60 + 150 - 10r + 120$$

$$Y - 0.75Y = 50 - 60 + 150 - 10r + 120$$

$$0.25Y = 260 - 10r$$

$$Y = 1040 - 40r$$

(2) Equation of the LM curve $m_d = 0.4\,Y - 6r$

$$m_s = 196$$

In equilibrium, $m_d = m_s$

Thus,

$$0.4Y - 6r = 196$$

$$0.4Y = 196 + 6r$$

$$Y = 490 + 15r$$

(3) Simultaneous equilibrium for the IS curve and LM curves

$$IS = LM$$

$$1040 - 40r = 490 + 15r$$

$$40r + 15r = 1040 - 490$$

$$55r = 550$$

$$r = 10\%$$

$$Y = 1040 - 40 \times 10$$

$$Y = 640$$

Simultaneous equilibrium for the IS curve and LM curves exists when $Y = 640$ and $r = 10\%$.

(4) Simultaneous equilibrium for the IS curve and LM curves when government expenditure increases by Rs. 55 crores

IS equation $$Y = C + I + G$$

$$Y = 50 + 0.75(Y - 80) + 150 - 10r + 175$$

$$Y = 50 + 0.75Y - 60 + 150 - 10r + 175$$

$$Y - 0.75Y = 50 - 60 + 150 - 10r + 175$$

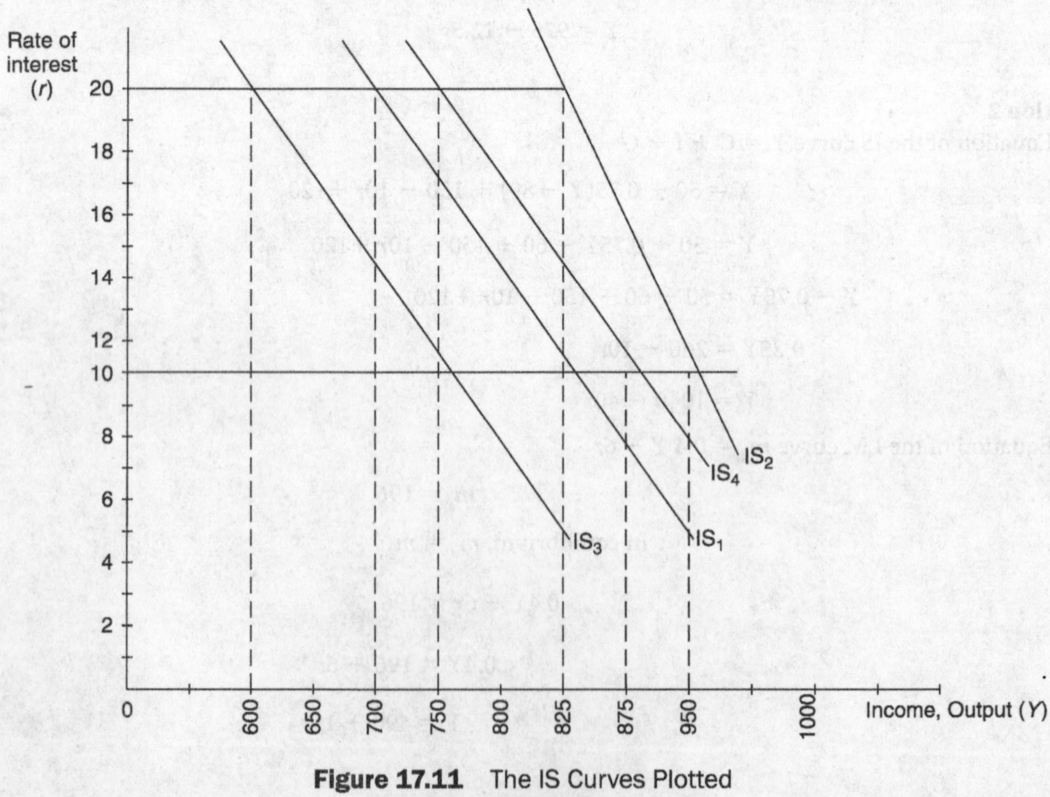

Figure 17.11 The IS Curves Plotted

$$0.25Y = 315 - 10r$$

$$Y = 1260 - 40r$$

LM equation will remain unchanged at

$$Y = 490 + 15r$$

Simultaneous equilibrium for the IS curve and LM curve

$$\text{IS} = \text{LM}$$

$$1260 - 40r = 490 + 15r$$

$$15r + 40r = 1260 - 490$$

$$55r = 770$$

$$r = 14\%$$

$$Y = 1260 - 40 \times 14$$

$$Y = 700$$

Simultaneous equilibrium for the IS curve and LM curves exists when $Y = 700$ and $r = 14\%$.

Solution 3

(1) Equation of the goods market equilibrium or the IS curve (i) $Y = C + I + G$

$$Y = 50 + 0.6Y_d + 200 - 5r + 130$$

$$Y = 50 + 0.6(Y - 0) + 200 - 5r + 130$$

$$Y = 50 + 0.6Y + 200 - 5r + 130$$

$$Y - 0.6Y = 380 - 5r$$

$$0.4Y = 380 - 5r$$

$$Y = 950 - 12.5r$$

(2) Equation of the of the IS curve

(a) Government expenditure increases by Rs. 50 crores

$$Y = C + I + G$$

$$Y = 50 + 0.6(Y - 0) + 200 - 5r + 180$$

$$Y = 50 + 0.6\,(Y - 0) + 200 - 5r + 180$$

$$Y = 50 + 0.6Y + 200 - 5r + 180$$

$$Y - 0.6Y = 430 - 5r$$

$$0.4Y = 430 - 5r$$

$$Y = 1075 - 12.5r$$

(b) Taxes increases by Rs. 50 crores

$$Y = C + I + G$$

$$Y = 50 + 0.6(Y - 50) + 200 - 5r + 130$$

$$Y = 50 + 0.6(Y - 50) + 200 - 5r + 130$$

$$Y = 50 + 0.6Y - 30 + 200 - 5r + 130$$

$$Y - 0.6Y = 350 - 5r$$

$$0.4Y = 350 - 5r$$

$$Y = 875 - 12.5r$$

(c) Government expenditure increases by Rs. 50 crores and taxes increases by Rs. 50 crores. This is the case of the balanced budget.

$$Y = C + I + G$$

$$Y = 50 + 0.6(Y - 50) + 200 - 5r + 180$$

$$Y = 50 + 0.6(Y - 50) + 200 - 5r + 180$$

$$Y = 50 + 0.6Y - 30 + 200 - 5r + 180$$

$$Y - 0.6Y = 400 - 5r$$

$$0.4Y = 400 - 5r$$

$$Y = 1000 - 12.5r$$

(d) In Figure 17.11,

(1) The initial IS curve, $Y = 950 = 12.5r$ is given by the curve IS_1.

(2) (a) The IS curve when government expenditure increases by Rs. 50 crores, $Y = 1075 - 12.5r$ is given by the curve IS_2. This indicates a horizontal shift of Rs. 125 crores.

(b) The IS curve when taxes increase by Rs. 50 crores, $Y = 875 - 12.5r$ is given by the curve IS_3. This indicates a horizontal shift towards the left of Rs. 75 crores from the IS_1 curve.

(c) The IS curve when government expenditure increases by Rs. 50 crores and taxes increase by Rs. 50 crores, $Y = 1000 - 12.5r$, given by the curve IS_4. This indicates a horizontal shift towards the right of Rs. 50 crores. This is because $\Delta G = \Delta T =$ 50 crores.

Solution 4

(1) Equation of the goods market or the IS curve

$$Y = C + I + G$$

$$Y = 1000 + 0.80(Y - 0.25Y) + 1500 - 60r + 1000$$

$$Y = 1000 + 0.80(0.75Y) + 1500 - 60r + \text{Rs. } 1000$$

$$Y = \text{Rs. } 3500 + 0.6Y - 60r$$

$$Y = \text{Rs. } 8750 - 150r$$

(2) Equation of the money market or the LM curve:

$$M = L$$

$$1500 = 0.20Y - 20r$$

$$Y = 7500 + 100r$$

(3) Simultaneous equilibrium for the IS and LM curves

$$\text{IS} = \text{LM}$$

$$Y = 8750 - 150r \quad (1)$$

$$Y = 7500 + 100r \quad (2)$$

Subtracting Eq. (2) from (1), we get

$$0 = 1250 - 250r$$

$$r = 5\%$$

$$Y = \text{Rs. } 8000$$

Solution 5

Equation of the IS curve

$$Y = C + I + G$$

$$Y = 200 + 0.80Y_d + 250 - 7.2r + 90$$

$$Y = 200 + 0.80(Y - T) + 250 - 7.2r + 90$$

$$Y = 200 + 0.80(Y - 0.20Y) + 250 - 7.2r + 90$$

$$Y = 200 + 0.80Y - 0.16Y + 340 - 7.2r$$

$$Y - 0.80Y + 0.16Y = 540 - 7.2r$$

$$0.36Y = 540 - 7.2r$$

$$Y = 1500 - 20r$$

Equation of the LM curve

$$m_s = 180$$

$$m_d = 0.2Y - 2r$$

In equilibrium, $m_d = m_s$.

Thus, $$0.2Y - 2r = 180$$

$$0.2Y = 180 + 2r$$

$$Y = 900 + 10r$$

Simultaneous equilibrium for the IS curve and LM curves

$$\text{IS} = \text{LM}$$

$$1500 - 20r = 900 + 10r$$

$$20r + 10r = 1500 - 900$$

$$30r = 600$$

$$r = 20\%$$

$$Y = 1500 - 20 \times 20$$

$$Y = 1100$$

Simultaneous equilibrium for the IS curve and LM curves exists when $Y = 1100$ and $r = 20\%$.

UNSOLVED NUMERICAL PROBLEMS

1. (a) Equation of the goods market equilibrium or the IS curve

   $Y = 11000$

   (b) Equation of the money-market equilibrium or the LM curve

   $Y = 10500 + 500r$

   (c) The equilibrium income and the interest rate:

   $Y = 11000$

   $r = 1\%$

   Simultaneous equilibrium for the IS curve and LM curves exists when $Y = 11000$ and $r = 1\%$.

2. (a) Equation of the IS curve

   $Y = 2400 - 25r$

   (b) Equation of the LM curve

   $Y = 2000$

   (c) Simultaneous equilibrium for the IS curve and LM curves

   $r = 16\ \%$

   $Y = 2000$

   (d) Simultaneous equilibrium for the IS curve and LM curves exists when $Y = 2000$ and $r = 16\%$.

   $I = 200$

3. (a) Equation of the IS curve when government expenditure increases by Rs. 20 crores

   $Y = 2500 - 25r$

   (b) Equation of the LM curve

   $Y = 2000$

   Hence, the equation of the LM curve remains unchanged as there is no change in the demand and supply of money.

   (c) The equilibrium income level and the rate of interest

   $r = 20\%$

   $Y = 2000$

   (d) Simultaneous equilibrium for the IS curve and LM curves exists when $Y = 2000$ and $r = 20\%$.

   $I = 180$

4. (a) Equation of the IS curve

   $Y = 900 - 25r$

   (b) Equation of the LM curve

   $Y = 550 + 25r$

   Simultaneous equilibrium for the IS curve and LM curves.

   $r = 7\ \%$

   $Y = 725$

   Simultaneous equilibrium for the IS curve and LM curves exists when $Y = 725$ and $r = 7\%$.

(c) Equilibrium of the economy if G increases from 100 to 200

Equation of the IS curve

$Y = 1150 - 25r$

Equation of the LM curve

$Y = 550 + 25r$

Simultaneous equilibrium for the IS curve and LM curves.

$r = 12\%$

$Y = 850$

Simultaneous equilibrium for the IS curve and LM curves exists when $Y = 850$ and $r = 12\%$.

5. Equation of the IS curve

$Y = 1000 - 15r$

Equation of the LM curve

$Y = 400 + 25r$

Simultaneous equilibrium for the IS curve and LM curves.

$r = 15\%$

$Y = 775$

Simultaneous equilibrium for the IS curve and LM curves exists when $Y = 775$ and $r = 15\%$.

Aggregate Demand and Aggregate Supply

18

After studying this topic, you should be able to understand

- ✓ *The aggregate demand curve charts out the IS–LM equilibrium while holding the nominal money supply and autonomous expenditures constant but allowing the prices to change.*
- ✓ *Shifts in the IS curve or the LM curve lead to shifts in the aggregate demand curve.*
- ✓ *Shifts in the IS and LM curves occur due to changes in the monetary or fiscal policy.*
- ✓ *According to the classical approach, the short-run aggregate supply curve is vertical.*
- ✓ *According to the Keynesian approach, the short-run aggregate supply curve is horizontal.*
- ✓ *It has also been put forward that the short-run aggregate supply curve is upward sloping.*
- ✓ *The intersection of the aggregate demand and aggregate supply curves determines the equilibrium price and output level.*
- ✓ *A monetary expansion leads to an outward (rightwards) shift of the aggregate demand curve.*
- ✓ *A decrease in the government expenditures leads to an inward (leftwards) shift of the aggregate demand curve.*
- ✓ *An adverse supply shock may lead an economy to a situation known as stagflation.*
- ✓ *Supply side economics has argued that decreasing the tax rates produces large increases in the aggregate supply.*

INTRODUCTION

This chapter introduces the model of aggregate demand and aggregate supply which can be used to study the joint determination of the output level and the price level. The aggregate demand curve has been derived from the IS–LM model. We attempt at examining why it slopes downwards and the reasons for the shifts in it. The aggregate supply curve has also been analysed in terms of the classical approach and the Keynesian approach. The intersection of the aggregate demand and aggregate supply curves determines the equilibrium level of output and the price level. The effects of a monetary expansion and supply shocks have also examined. (For further discussion on Aggregate Demand and Aggregate Supply refer to Appendix C)

THE AGGREGATE DEMAND CURVE

The aggregate demand curve shows the different combinations of output level and the price level at which the goods and money markets are simultaneously in equilibrium.

In the earlier chapters, we have examined the IS–LM model to explain the determination of the national income in the short run in two and three sector economies assuming a fixed price level. We now aim to study what will happen if the price level is allowed to vary in the IS–LM model. The aggregate demand curve shows the different combinations of output level and the price level at which the goods and money markets are simultaneously in equilibrium. We also attempt to derive the aggregate demand curve from the IS–LM model.

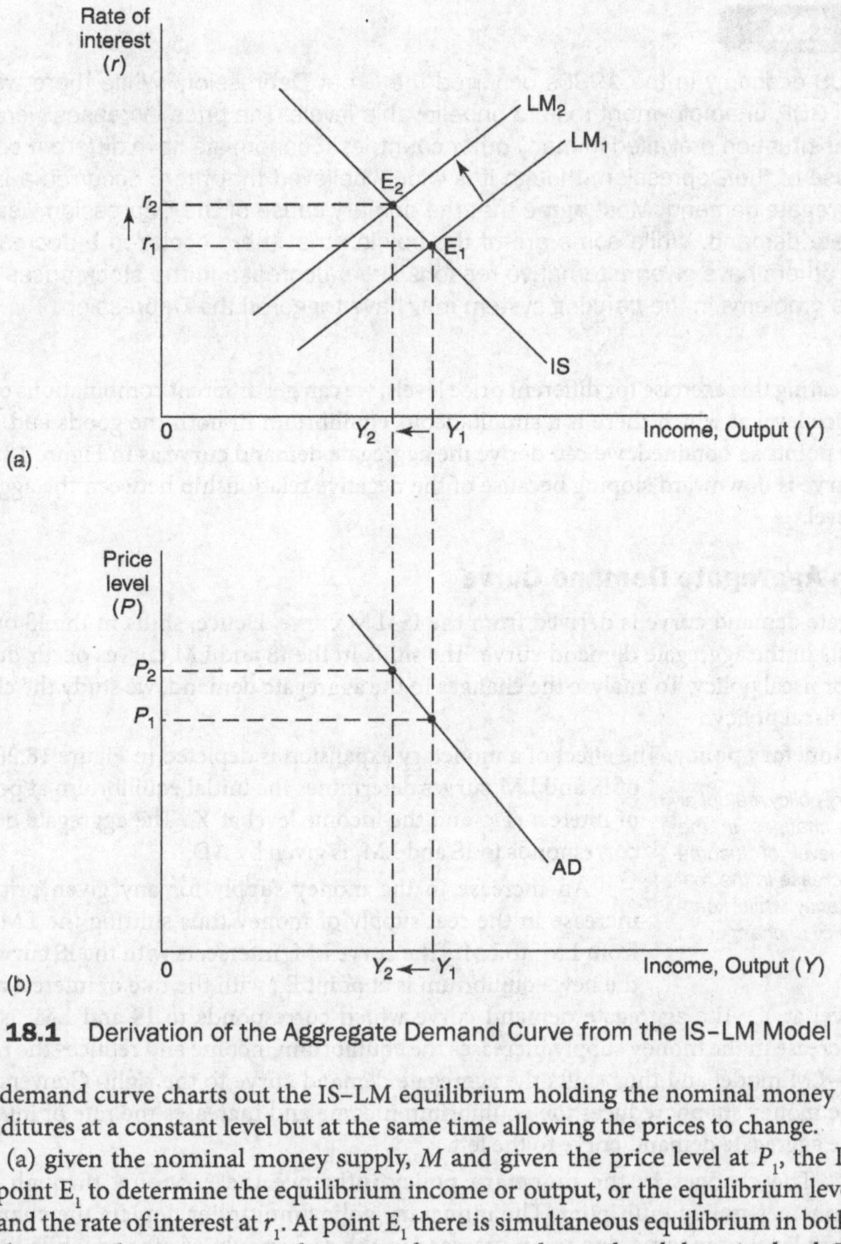

Figure 18.1 Derivation of the Aggregate Demand Curve from the IS–LM Model

The aggregate demand curve charts out the IS–LM equilibrium holding the nominal money supply and autonomous expenditures at a constant level but at the same time allowing the prices to change.

In Figure 18.1 (a) given the nominal money supply, M and given the price level at P_1, the IS and LM_1 curves intersect at point E_1 to determine the equilibrium income or output, or the equilibrium level of aggregate demand, at Y_1 and the rate of interest at r_1. At point E_1 there is simultaneous equilibrium in both the goods and the money markets. We, thus, get one combination of aggregate demand and the price level, Y_1 and P_1 as depicted in Figure 18.1 (b).

Suppose there is an increase in the price level to P_2 while there is no change in the nominal money supply. This increase in the prices will not have any impact on the goods market where all the variables are fixed in real terms and thus remain unaffected by any price changes. Hence, the IS curve will remain unaffected.

As far as the money market is concerned, given the nominal money supply, an increase in the prices will lead to a decrease in the real money supply. The LM curve will shift leftwards to LM_2. The curves IS and LM_2 intersect at point intersect at point E_2 to determine the equilibrium level of aggregate demand, at Y_2 and the rate of interest at r_2.We thus find another combination of aggregate demand and the price level, Y_2 and P_2 as in Figure 18.1 (b).

BOX 18.1

In the US economy in the 1930s occurred the Great Depression. While there was a decrease in the real GDP, unemployment rose to unbelievable levels. The price increases were also quite high. A similar situation prevailed in many other countries. Economists have different opinions regarding the cause of the Depression, though it is widely believed that there occurred a large decrease in the aggregate demand. Most agree that the primary cause of the Depression was a decline in the aggregate demand. While some are of the opinion that there occurred a decrease in the money supply, others have given alternative reasons like a decrease in the stock prices which combined with the problems in the banking system may have triggered the Depression.

By repeating this exercise for different price levels, we can get different combinations of aggregate demand and the price level at which there is a simultaneous equilibrium in both the goods and money markets. By joining the points so obtained, we can derive the aggregate demand curve as in Figure 18.1(b). The aggregate demand curve is downward sloping because of the negative relationship between the aggregate demand and the price level.

Shifts in Aggregate Demand Curve

The aggregate demand curve is derived from the IS–LM curve. Hence, shifts in the IS or the LM curve will lead to shifts in the aggregate demand curve. The shifts in the IS and LM curves occur due to changes in the monetary or fiscal policy. To analyse the changes in the aggregate demand, we study the changes in monetary policy and fiscal policy.

The monetary policy multiplier depicts the changes in the equilibrium level of income due to an increase in the real supply of money while keeping fiscal policy unchanged.

1. **Monetary policy:** The effect of a monetary expansion is depicted in Figure 18.2(a). The intersection of IS and LM_1 curves determines the initial equilibrium at point E_1, with the rate of interest at r_1 and the income level at Y_1. The aggregate demand curve which corresponds to IS and LM_1 is given by AD_1.

   An increase in the money supply for any given price level leads to an increase in the real supply of money thus shifting the LM curve downwards, from LM_1 to LM_2. The curve LM_2 intersects with the IS curve at point E_2. Hence the new equilibrium is at point E_2, with the rate of interest at r_2 and the income level at Y_2. The aggregate demand curve which corresponds to IS and LM_2 is given by AD_2. An increase in the money supply increases the equilibrium income and reduces the rate of interest in the IS–LM model and thus shifts the aggregate demand curve to the right. Conversely, any decrease in the money supply reduces the equilibrium income and increases the rate of interest and thus shifts the aggregate demand curve to the left.

   The changes in the monetary policy influence the economy through what is called the monetary policy multiplier. The monetary policy multiplier depicts the changes in the equilibrium level of income due to an increase in the real supply of money while keeping fiscal policy unchanged.

The fiscal policy multiplier depicts the changes in the equilibrium income level due to an increase in government expenditure, holding the real supply of money constant.

2. **Fiscal policy:** The effect of a fiscal expansion is depicted in Figure 18.2(b). The intersection of IS_1 and LM curves determines the initial equilibrium at point E_1, with the rate of interest at r_1 and the income level at Y_1. The aggregate demand curve which corresponds to IS_1 and LM is given by AD_1.

   An increase in the government expenditure or a decrease in taxes shifts the IS curve rightwards from IS_1 to IS_2. The curve IS_2 intersects with the LM curve at point E_2. The new equilibrium is at point E_2, with the rate of interest at r_2 and

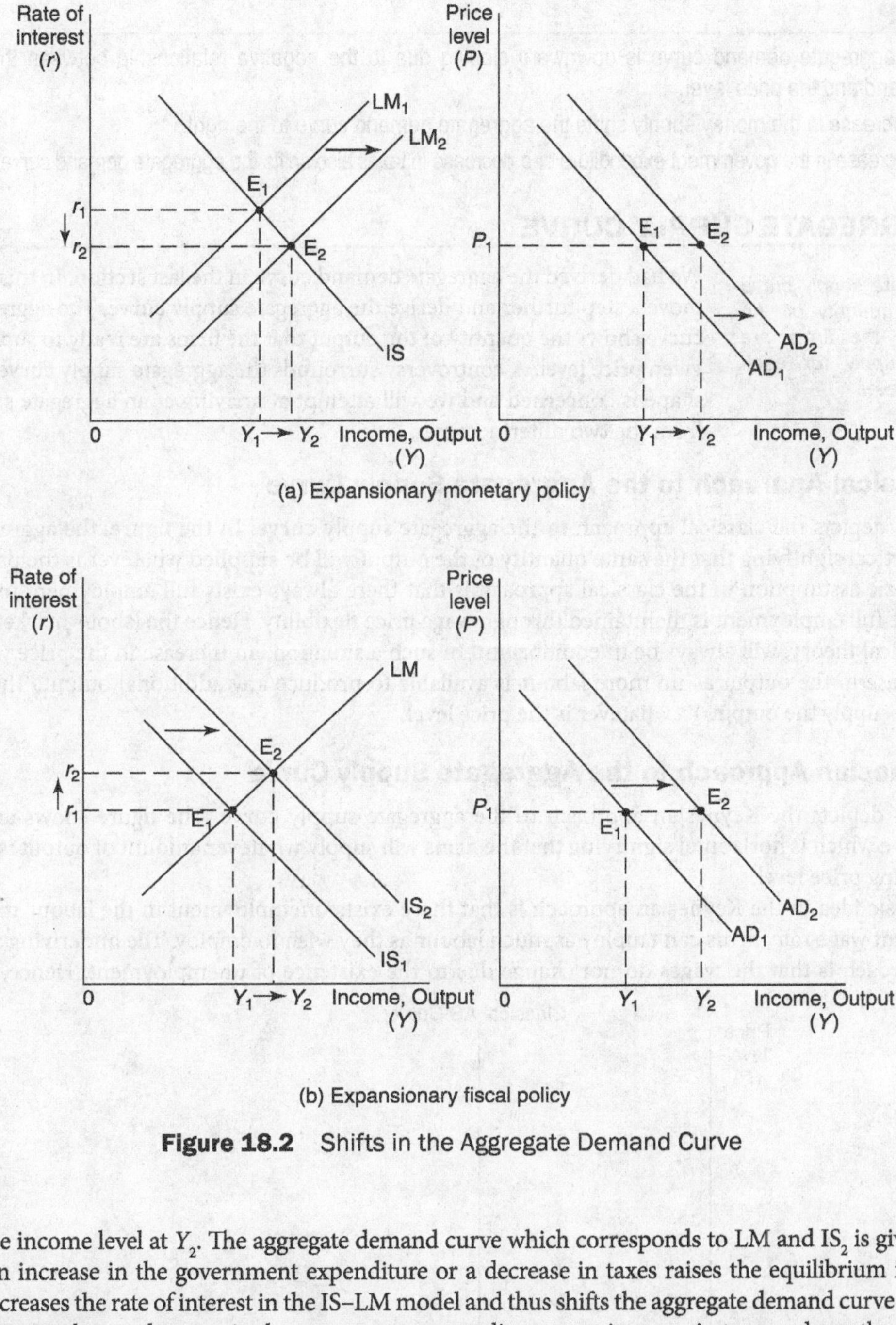

Figure 18.2 Shifts in the Aggregate Demand Curve

the income level at Y_2. The aggregate demand curve which corresponds to LM and IS_2 is given by AD_2. An increase in the government expenditure or a decrease in taxes raises the equilibrium income and increases the rate of interest in the IS–LM model and thus shifts the aggregate demand curve to the right. Conversely, any decrease in the government expenditure or an increase in taxes reduces the equilibrium income and decreases the rate of interest and thus shifts the aggregate demand curve to the left.

The changes in the fiscal policy influence the economy through what is called the fiscal policy multiplier. The fiscal policy multiplier depicts the changes in the equilibrium income level due to an increase in the government expenditure, holding the real supply of money constant.

RECAP

- The aggregate demand curve is downward sloping due to the negative relationship between the aggregate demand and the price level.
- An increase in the money supply shifts the aggregate demand curve to the right.
- An increase in the government expenditure or a decrease in taxes also shifts the aggregate demand curve to the right.

THE AGGREGATE SUPPLY CURVE

The aggregate supply curve shows the quantity of the output that the firms are ready to supply for each given price level.

We had derived the aggregate demand curve in the last section. In this section, we move a step further and derive the aggregate supply curve. The aggregate supply curve shows the quantity of the output that the firms are ready to supply for each given price level. A controversy surrounds the aggregate supply curve as far as its shape is concerned and we will attempt at arriving at an aggregate supply curve from the two differing views.

The Classical Approach to the Aggregate Supply Curve

Figure 18.3 depicts the classical approach to the aggregate supply curve. In the figure, the aggregate supply curve is vertical signifying that the same quantity of the output will be supplied whatever is the price level.

The basic assumption in the classical approach is that there always exists full employment in the labour market. The full employment is maintained through wage price flexibility. Hence the labour market, according to the classical theory, will always be in equilibrium. In such a situation, an increase in the price will not lead to an increase in the output as no more labour is available to produce any additional output. The firms will continue to supply the output Y^* whatever is the price level.

The Keynesian Approach to the Aggregate Supply Curve

Figure 18.4 depicts the Keynesian approach to the aggregate supply curve. The figure shows an aggregate supply curve which is horizontal signifying that the firms will supply whatever amount of output is demanded at the existing price level.

The basic idea in the Keynesian approach is that there exists unemployment in the labour market. Thus at the current wage rate, firms can employ as much labour as they wish to employ. The underlying assumption in this approach is that the wages do not change due to the existence of unemployment. Hence, there is no

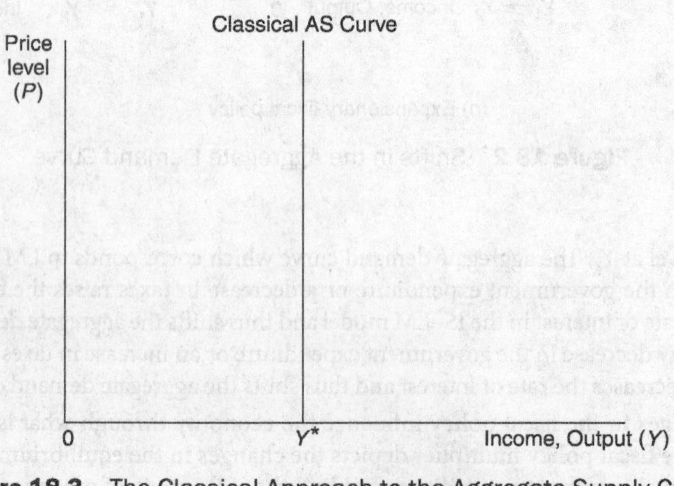

Figure 18.3 The Classical Approach to the Aggregate Supply Curve

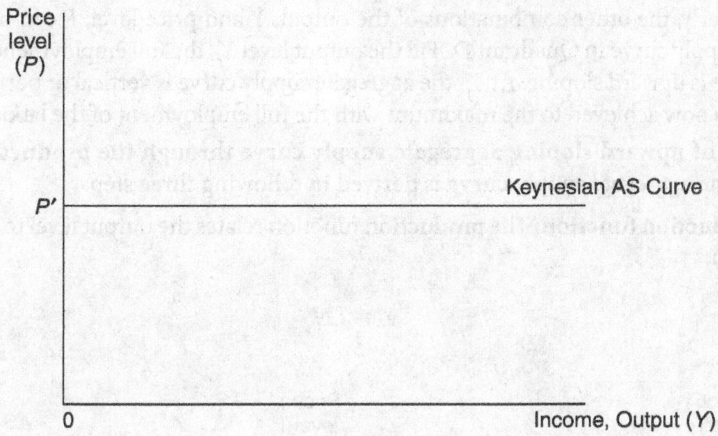

Figure 18.4 The Keynesian Approach to the Aggregate Supply Curve

change in the average costs of production in response to a change in the output level. At the existing price level, the firms are willing to supply whatever output is demanded. Hence according to the Keynesian approach, the aggregate supply curve is horizontal.

The Upward Sloping Aggregate Supply Curve

As is obvious from the above two approaches, the theory of aggregate supply is one of most controversial areas in macroeconomics. In a world which is ideal there is perfect wage price flexibility in the labour market and the economy would always be at full employment. This is the classical world. Reality is far different from this ideal world where the labour market adjusts at a very slow speed to changes in the aggregate demand.

A variety of models of aggregate supply have been put forward. All are of the same opinion that the short-run aggregate supply curve has a positive slope whereas the long-run aggregate supply curve is vertical. We derive the short-run aggregate supply curve with the help of following two approaches:

(1) **Derivation of the upward sloping aggregate supply curve through the change in real wage:** The approach assumes that the money wage rate is fixed and that the marginal productivity of labour is diminishing. Figure 18.5 depicts the derivation of the aggregate supply curve by this approach.

Quadrant A shows the aggregate production function for the economy as a whole with the axes having been reversed. It gives the aggregate output corresponding to a particular labour input.

Quadrant B depicts the demand curve for labour, D_N (which is actually the marginal physical product of labour curve as labour will be hired till the marginal physical product of labour is equal to the real wage). Quadrant B also shows the supply curve of labour as positively related to the real wage.

Quadrant C gives the various combinations of the price level and real wage. With the help of the curve W, one is able to identify the price level which will yield the indicated W/P on the basis of the money wage rate, W.

Quadrant D shows how the aggregate supply function has been derived from the other quadrants in the figure.

Starting with Quadrant A, when employment of labour is N_1 the output produced is Y_1. Quadrant B shows that N_1 units of labour will be demanded at a wage rate $(W/P)_1$. Quadrant C shows that producers must get a price level P_1 for an output of Y_1 to yield a wage rate of $(W/P)_1$, which is the wage at which the firms will hire labour of N_1 units to produce an output of Y_1 at a price level P_1. In Quadrant D, the Y_1 of Quadrant A and P_1 of Quadrant C combine to give the point H which is a point on the aggregate supply curve. Similarly, the other combinations of the output, Y and price level, P can be arrived at to get the aggregate supply curve in Quadrant D. Till the output level Y_f, the full employment output, the aggregate supply curve is upward sloping. At Y_f, the aggregate supply curve is vertical or perfectly inelastic because the output is now achieved to the maximum with the full employment of the labour force.

(2) **Derivation of upward sloping aggregate supply curve through the production function:** In this approach, the aggregate supply curve is derived in following three steps:

Step 1: Production function: The production function relates the output level to employment through the equation,

$$Y = l\,N$$

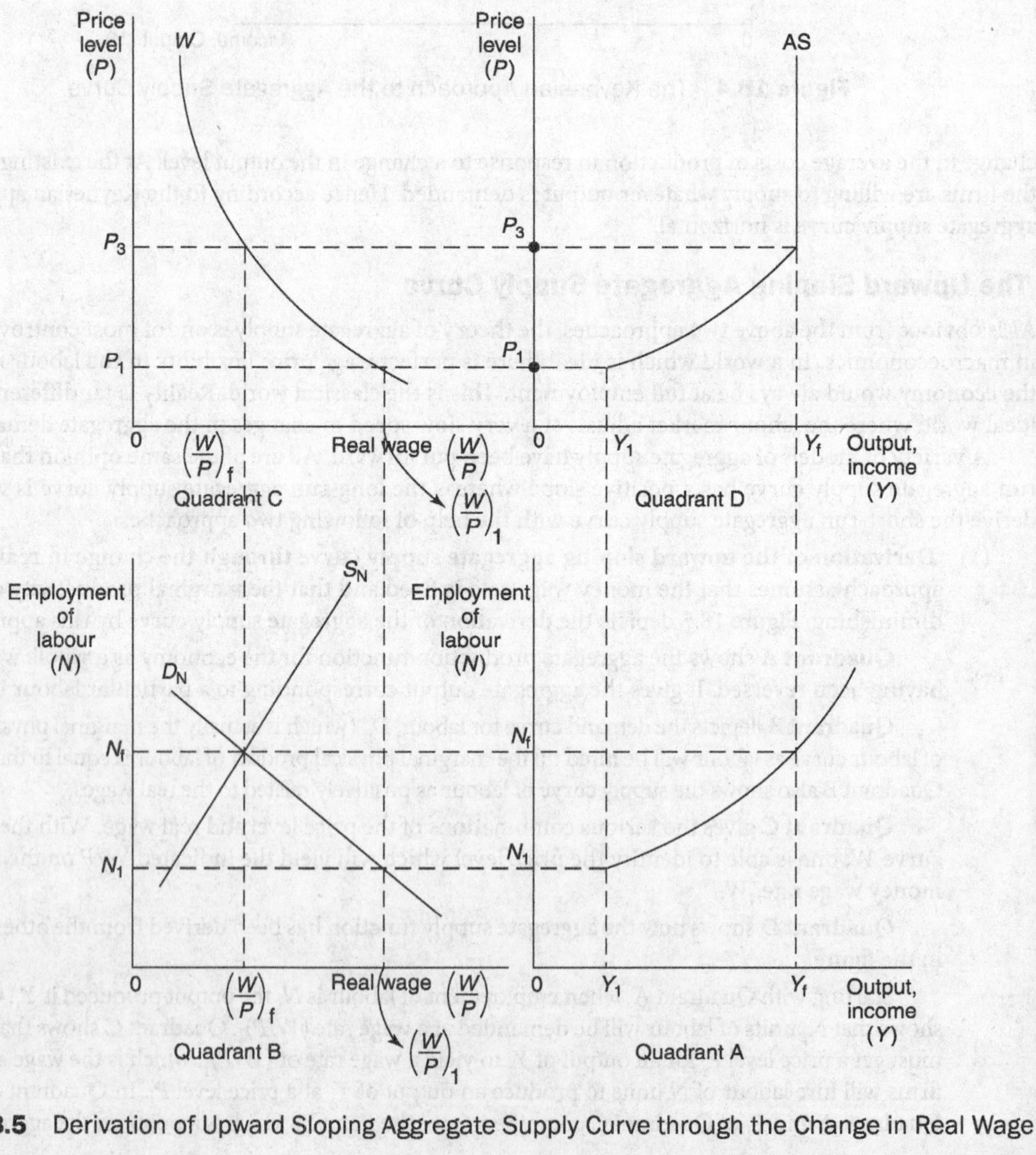

Figure 18.5 Derivation of Upward Sloping Aggregate Supply Curve through the Change in Real Wage

where, Y = output level

N = employment level

l = input coefficient or labour productivity (which is the output produced per unit of labour employed)

Step 2: Prices and cost: The main component of cost is the labour cost. A firm will supply an output such that the price it charges at least covers the cost. If W is the wages in the current period, then the cost per unit of labour is W/l. While determining the price the firms set a mark up, z over the price. The mark up z includes not only the costs of the other factors of production like raw materials but also includes the normal profits of the firm. Thus,

$$P = W/l + z\,W/l = (1+z)W/l$$

The above equation shows that the price level is proportional to the wage rate.

Step 3: Phillips' curve: The wages in the current period are linked to the wages in the previous period and to the employment level through the Phillips' curve. (The Phillips' curve has been analysed in Chapter 21).

Also from the production function, the level of output is proportional to the employment level. Using this analysis we can arrive at a relationship between price and output which yields the upward sloping supply curve as in Figure 18.6.

(For a more detailed explanation, see the Appendix to Chapter 18.)

RECAP

- The main assumption in the classical approach is that there always exists full employment in the labour market.
- The basic idea in the Keynesian approach is that there exists unemployment in the labour market.
- In most models of aggregate supply, the short-run aggregate supply curve has a positive slope while the long-run aggregate supply curve is vertical.

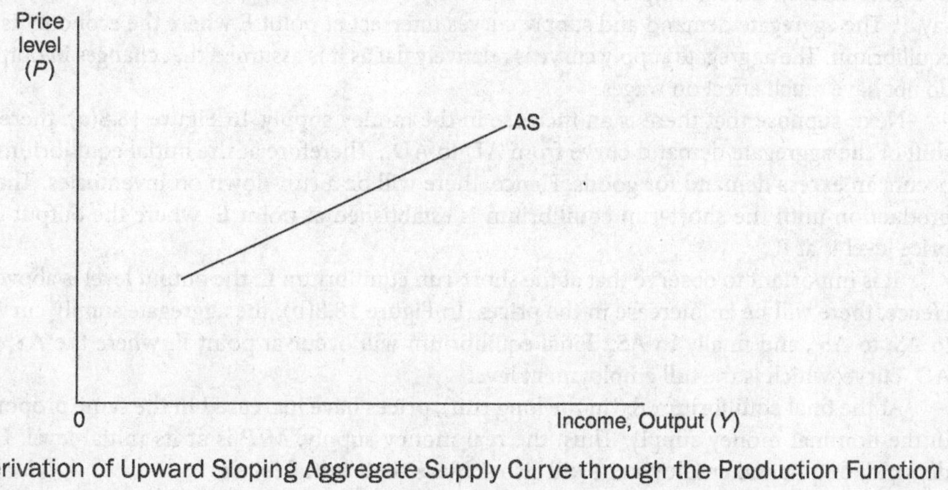

Figure 18.6 Derivation of Upward Sloping Aggregate Supply Curve through the Production Function

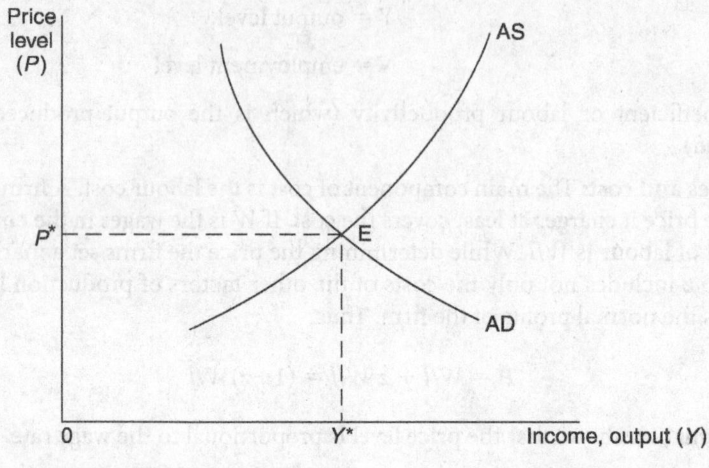

Figure 18.7 Determination of the Output Level and the Price Level

THE AGGREGATE DEMAND AND AGGREGATE SUPPLY MODEL

We now bring together the aggregate demand and aggregate supply curves, which we have derived earlier in Figure 18.7. The aggregate demand curve, AD and aggregate supply curve, AS intersect at point E to determine the equilibrium output level at Y^* and the equilibrium price level at P^*. By construction, at the equilibrium point E,

(1) The labour market is in equilibrium because point E lies on the aggregate supply curve.

(2) The goods and financial markets are in equilibrium because point E lies on the aggregate demand curve.

RECAP

- At the equilibrium point, the labour market is in equilibrium; the goods and financial markets are also in equilibrium.

THE EFFECTS OF A MONETARY EXPANSION

In Figure 18.8(a), the full employment level of output is Y^*. The aggregate supply curve is drawn with prices, at say, P. The aggregate demand and supply curves intersect at point E where the economy is in full employment equilibrium. The aggregate supply curve is relatively flat as it is assumed that changes in output and employment do not have much effect on wages.

Next, suppose that there is an increase in the money supply. In Figure 18.8(a), there will be an outward shift of the aggregate demand curve from AD to AD_1. Therefore at the initial equilibrium price level P, there occurs an excess demand for goods. Hence, there will be a run-down on inventories. The firms will increase production until the short-run equilibrium is established at point E_1 where the output level is Y_1 while the price level is at P_1.

It is important to observe that at the short-run equilibrium E_1 the output level is above the normal output. Hence, there will be an increase in the prices. In Figure 18.8(b), the aggregate supply curve will shift upwards to AS, to AS_1, and finally to AS_3. Final equilibrium will occur at point E_3 where the AS_3 curve intersects the AD_1 curve, which is the full employment level.

At the final equilibrium E_3 (in the long run), prices have increased in the same proportion as the increase in the nominal money supply. Thus, the real money supply, M/P is at its initial level. Hence the aggregate demand, output and employment will also achieve their initial levels.

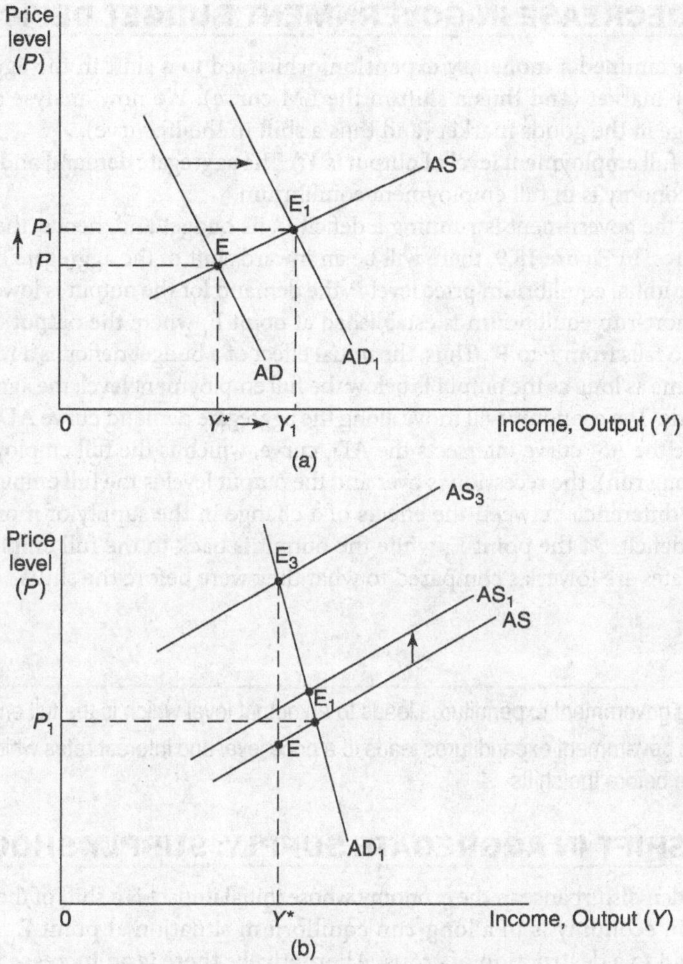

Figure 18.8 Effects of a Monetary Expansion

RECAP

- **A monetary expansion leads to an increase in price in the same proportion as the increase in the nominal money supply.**
- **The aggregate demand, output and employment achieve their initial levels.**

BOX 18.2

In the 1940s, there occurred a boom in the United States. The cause of the boom was the increased government expenditures required at times of war. This increase in aggregate demand led to an impressive increase in the domestic production and a radical fall in the unemployment levels. Prices rose minimally as the government had imposed price controls.

EFFECTS OF A DECREASE IN GOVERNMENT BUDGET DEFICIT

In the last section we examined a monetary expansion, which led to a shift in the aggregate demand due to a change in the money market (and thus a shift in the LM curve). We now analyse a shift in the aggregate demand due to a change in the goods market (and thus a shift in the IS curve).

In Figure 18.9, the full employment level of output is Y^*. The aggregate demand and supply curves intersect at point E where the economy is in full employment equilibrium.

Next suppose that the government is running a deficit in its budget and, hence, there is a reduction in the government expenditures. In Figure 18.9, there will be an inward shift of the aggregate demand curve from AD to AD_1. Therefore at the initial equilibrium price level P, the demand for the output is lower. The firms will reduce production until the short-run equilibrium is established at point E_1 where the output decreases from Y^* to Y_1 while the price level also falls from P to P_1. Thus, the initial effect of a budget deficit is a reduction in the output.

Over a period of time as long as the output is below the full employment level, the aggregate supply curve will keep shifting downwards. The economy will move along the aggregate demand curve AD_1. Final equilibrium will occur at point E_3 where the AS_3 curve intersects the AD_1 curve, which is the full employment level. At the final equilibrium E_3(in the long run), the recession is over and the output level is the full employment level Y^*.

There is a crucial difference between the effects of a change in the supply of money and the effects of a change in the budget deficit. At the point E_3 while the output is back to the full employment level, the price level and the interest rates are lower as compared to what they were before the shifts.

RECAP

- A decrease in the government expenditures leads to an output level which is the full employment level.
- A decrease in the government expenditures leads to a price level and interest rates which are lower as compared to what they were before the shifts

EFFECTS OF A SHIFT IN AGGREGATE SUPPLY: SUPPLY SHOCKS

A supply shock is a sudden disturbance in the economy whose initial impact is a shift of the aggregate supply curve.

In Figure 18.10, an economy is in a long-run equilibrium situation at point E_1. Suppose unfavourable weather conditions lead to a destruction of crops. Alternatively, there is an increase in the real prices of oil. Whatever the reason, the impact is an increase in the costs of production. This leads to an upward shift of the

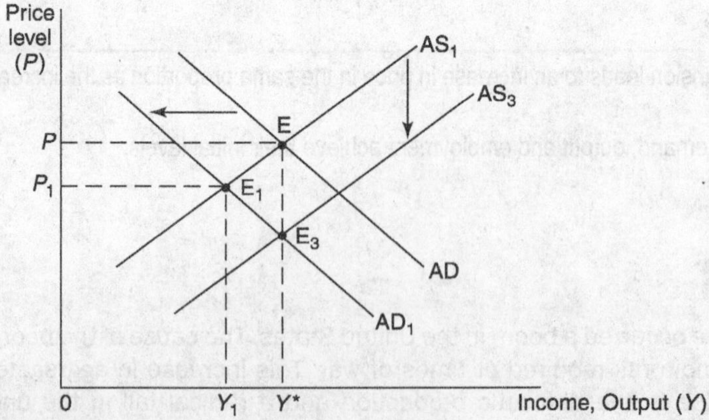

Figure 18.9 Effects of a Decrease in Government Budget Deficit

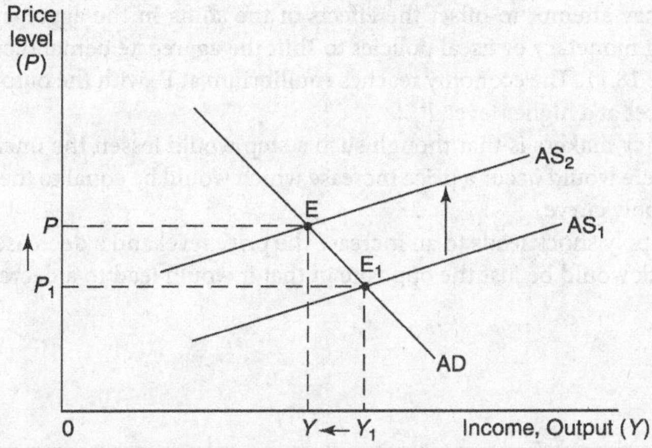

Figure 18.10 Effects of a Shift in Aggregate Supply: Supply Shocks

short-run aggregate supply curve from AS_1 to AS_2 as shown in Figure 18.10. The economy is now in unemployment equilibrium at E. The economy's output falls from Y_1 to Y while the price level rises from P_1 to P. Hence the economy is experiencing a falling output (stagnation) and increasing prices (inflation), a situation known as stagflation.

A supply shock is a sudden disturbance in the economy whose initial impact is a shift of the aggregate supply curve.

What should policy makers do in such a situation? There are two alternatives before the policy makers in such a situation:

(1) They can just let things take their normal course. Over time, the recession will cure itself. Wages and prices will adjust themselves slowly and the aggregate supply curve will shift back to AS_1. In the long run, the economy will move back along the aggregate demand curve to point E_1.

Stagflation is a situation when an economy experiences a falling output (stagnation) and increasing prices (inflation).

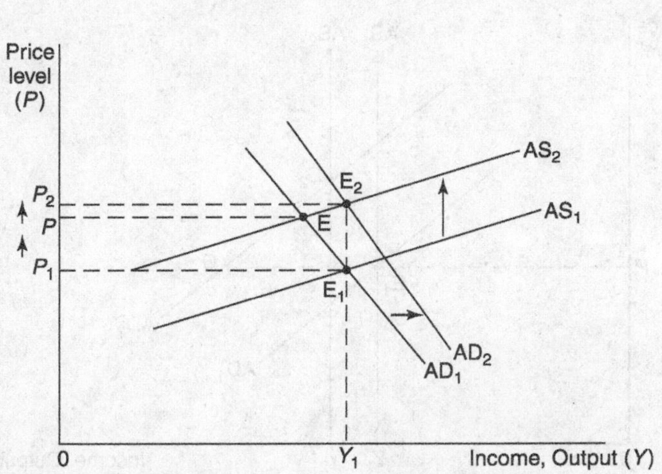

Figure 18.11 Adverse Supply Shock and Accommodating Monetary or Fiscal Policies

(2) Policymakers may attempt to offset the effects of the shifts in the aggregate supply curve by using accommodating monetary or fiscal policies to shift the aggregate demand curve from AD_1 to AD_2 as shown in Figure 18.11. The economy reaches equilibrium at E_2 with the output at the full employment level Y_1 and prices at a higher level, P_2.

The problem for the policy makers is that though such a step would lessen the unemployment effects of the adverse supply shock, there would occur a price increase which would be equal to the full extent of the upward shift in the aggregate supply curve.

While an adverse supply shock leads to an increase the price level and a decrease in the GNP, the effect of a favourable supply shock would be just the opposite in that it would lead to a decrease in the price level and an increase in the GNP.

RECAP

- Policymakers may attempt to offset the effects of the shifts in the aggregate supply curve by using accommodating monetary or fiscal policies to shift the aggregate demand curve.
- A favourable supply shock would lead to a decrease in the price level and an increase in the GNP.

THE SUPPLY SIDE ECONOMICS

We have already observed that the Keynesian short-run aggregate supply curve is horizontal indicating that the firms supply whatever goods are demanded at the existing level of prices. On the other hand, the classical short-run aggregate supply curve is vertical indicating complete wage price flexibility and an economy which would be always operating at the full employment level.

Supply side economics has proposed that decreasing the tax rates produces large increases in the aggregate supply. If one examines the truth one finds that tax cuts certainly lead to increases in the aggregate supply. However, the increases in the supply are much smaller than the increases in the aggregate demand.

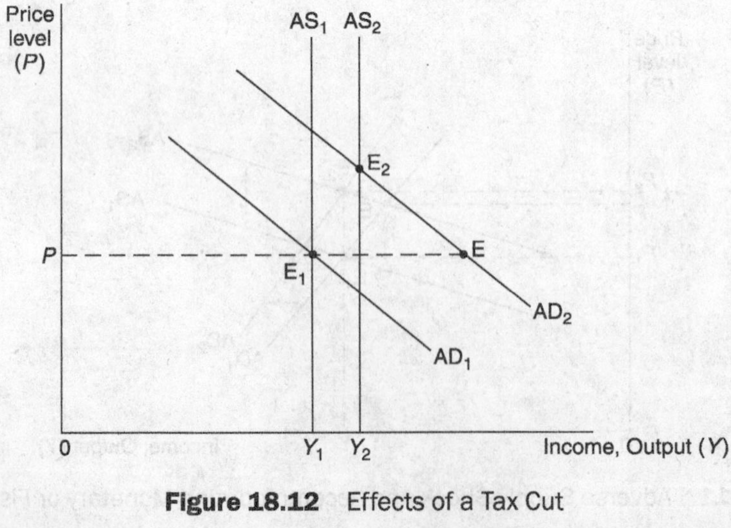

Figure 18.12 Effects of a Tax Cut

Figure 18.12 examines the effects of a tax cut on both the aggregate demand and the aggregate supply curves. As individuals have more money in their hands, the aggregate demand curve shifts outwards from AD_1 to AD_2. As the lower tax rates encourages individuals to work harder, though only to a small extent, the aggregate supply curve shifts outwards from AS_1 to AS_2. Hence while there occurs a large shift in the aggregate demand curve, there occurs only a small shift in the aggregate supply curve.

In the short run, the economy's equilibrium will move from E_1 to E with a considerable increase in the output level. However, this effect is completely due to a shift in aggregate demand curve alone. In the long run, the economy's equilibrium will move to point E_2. Here while there is a very small increase in the output level, there occurs a permanent increase in the price level. Therefore, the total tax collections decrease while there is an increase in the government's deficit. Some economists are in favour of reducing the government expenditures simultaneously with the tax cuts. Then the effect on the government deficit would be neutral.

RECAP

- Tax cuts certainly lead to increases in the aggregate supply.
- Due to tax cuts while there occurs a large shift in the aggregate demand curve, there occurs only a small shift in the aggregate supply curve.
- Some economists are in favour of reducing the government expenditures simultaneously with the tax cuts.

SUMMARY

INTRODUCTION

1. The chapter introduced the model of aggregate demand and aggregate supply.
2. While the aggregate demand curve has been derived from the IS–LM model, the aggregate supply curve has been analysed in terms of the classical approach and the Keynesian approach.
3. The effects of a monetary expansion and supply shocks have also been examined.

THE AGGREGATE DEMAND CURVE

1. We studied what will happen if the price level is allowed to vary in the IS–LM model.
2. The aggregate demand curve shows the different combinations of output level and the price level at which the goods and money markets are simultaneously in equilibrium.
3. The aggregate demand curve charts out the IS–LM equilibrium holding the nominal money supply and autonomous expenditures at a constant level but at the same time allowing the prices to change.
4. Suppose there is an increase in the price level while there is no change in the nominal money supply, the IS curve will remain unaffected while the LM curve will shift leftwards.
5. The aggregate demand curve is downward sloping because of the negative relationship between the aggregate demand and the price level.

SHIFTS IN AGGREGATE DEMAND CURVE

1. Shifts in the IS curve or the LM curve will lead to shifts in the aggregate demand curve.
2. The shifts in the IS and LM curves occur due to changes in the monetary or fiscal policy.
3. An increase in the money supply increases the equilibrium income and reduces the rate of interest in the IS–LM model and, thus, shifts the aggregate demand curve to the right.
4. The monetary policy multiplier depicts the changes in the equilibrium level of income due to an increase in the real supply of money while keeping fiscal policy unchanged.

5. An increase in government expenditure or a decrease in taxes raises the equilibrium income and increases the rate of interest in the IS–LM model and, thus, shifts the aggregate demand curve to the right.
6. The fiscal policy multiplier depicts the changes in the equilibrium income level due to an increase in government expenditure, holding the real supply of money constant.

THE AGGREGATE SUPPLY CURVE

1. The aggregate supply curve shows for each given price level, the quantity of output that the firms are ready to supply.
2. In the classical approach, the aggregate supply curve is vertical. The basic assumption in the classical approach is that there always exists full employment in the labour market.
3. In the Keynesian approach, the aggregate supply curve is horizontal. The basic idea in the Keynesian approach is that there exists unemployment in the labour market.
4. A variety of models of aggregate supply have been put forward. All are of the same opinion that the short-run aggregate supply curve has a positive slope whereas the long-run aggregate supply curve is vertical.
5. We can derive the short-run aggregate supply curve with the help of two approaches: through the change in real wages and through the production function.

THE AGGREGATE DEMAND AND AGGREGATE SUPPLY MODEL

1. The intersection of the aggregate demand and aggregate supply curves determines the equilibrium price and output level.
2. The labour market is in equilibrium at the equilibrium point.
3. The goods and financial markets are also in equilibrium.

EFFECTS OF A MONETARY EXPANSION

1. A monetary expansion leads to an outward shift of the aggregate demand curve.
2. At the final equilibrium in the long run, prices increase in the same proportion as the increase in the nominal money supply.
3. The aggregate demand, output and employment also achieve their initial levels.

EFFECTS OF A DECREASE IN GOVERNMENT BUDGET DEFICIT

1. A decrease in the government expenditures leads to a leftward shift of the aggregate demand curve.
2. A decrease in the government expenditures leads to a price level and interest rates which are lower as compared to what they were before the shifts.

EFFECTS OF A SHIFT IN AGGREGATE SUPPLY: SUPPLY SHOCKS

1. A supply shock is a sudden disturbance in the economy whose initial impact is a shift of the aggregate supply curve.
2. Due to an adverse supply shock, an economy may experience a situation known as stagflation.
3. Policymakers may attempt to offset the effects of the shifts in the aggregate supply curve by using accommodating monetary or fiscal policies to shift the aggregate demand curve.
4. While an adverse supply shock leads to an increase in the price level and a decrease in the GNP, the effect of a favourable supply shock would be just the opposite in that it would lead to a decrease in the price level and an increase in the GNP.

THE SUPPLY SIDE ECONOMICS

1. Supply side economics has proposed that decreasing the tax rates produces large increases in the aggregate supply.
2. However, the increases in the supply are much smaller than the increases in the aggregate demand.
3. While there is a very small increase in the output level, there occurs a permanent increase in the price level.
4. Therefore, the total tax collections decrease while there is an increase in the government's deficit.
5. Some economists are in favour of reducing the government expenditures simultaneously with the tax cuts. Then the effect on the government deficit would be neutral.

REVIEW QUESTIONS

TRUE OR FALSE QUESTIONS

1. The aggregate demand curve is upward sloping because of the negative relationship between the aggregate demand and the price level.
2. The fiscal policy multiplier depicts the changes in the equilibrium level of income due to an increase in the real supply of money while keeping fiscal policy unchanged.
3. An increase in the money supply increases the equilibrium income and shifts the aggregate demand curve to the right.
4. An increase in government expenditure or a decrease in taxes raises the equilibrium income and shifts the aggregate demand curve to the right.
5. A supply shock is a sudden disturbance in the economy whose initial impact is a shift of the aggregate supply curve.

VERY SHORT-ANSWER QUESTIONS

1. What is the aggregate demand curve? Why is it downward sloping?
2. What is the monetary policy multiplier?
3. What is the fiscal policy multiplier?
4. What is a supply shock?
5. What is stagflation?

SHORT-ANSWER QUESTIONS

1. What is the impact of an increase in the price level (while there is no change in the nominal money supply) on IS and LM curves?
2. Discuss the classical approach to the aggregate supply curve.
3. Discuss the Keynesian approach to the aggregate supply curve.
4. 'The intersection of the aggregate demand and aggregate supply curves determines the equilibrium price and output level.' Explain.
5. What are the effects of an adverse supply shock? Discuss.

LONG-ANSWER QUESTIONS

1. 'The aggregate demand curve charts out the IS–LM equilibrium while holding the nominal money supply and autonomous expenditures constant but allowing the prices to change.' Explain.
2. Examine the shifts in the IS and LM curves that occur due to changes in the
   (a) Monetary policy (b) Fiscal policy
3. Show the derivation of the upward sloping aggregate supply curve through the change in real wages.
4. How can an upward sloping aggregate supply curve be derived through the production function? Explain.
5. Discuss the effects of a monetary expansion on the aggregate demand and supply curves.

ANSWERS

TRUE OR FALSE QUESTIONS

1. **False.** The aggregate demand curve is downward sloping because of the negative relationship between the aggregate demand and the price level.
2. **False.** The monetary policy multiplier depicts the changes in the equilibrium level of income due to an increase in the real supply of money while keeping fiscal policy unchanged.
3. **True.** An increase in the money supply increases the equilibrium income and reduces the rate of interest in the IS–LM model and thus shifts the aggregate demand curve to the right.
4. **True.** An increase in government expenditure or a decrease in taxes raises the equilibrium income and increases the rate of interest in the IS–LM model and, thus, shifts the aggregate demand curve to the right.
5. **True.** Due to an adverse supply shock, an economy may experience a falling output (stagnation) and increasing prices (inflation), a situation known as stagflation.

UNIT VI INFLATION AND UNEMPLOYMENT

Inflation

19

After studying this topic, you should be able to understand

- ✓ *Inflation leads to a decrease in the purchasing power of money.*
- ✓ *The two ways in which inflation can be measured are through a change in the Price Index and the Gross National Product Deflator.*
- ✓ *In the real economy since all prices do not change proportionately, some members of the society gain from inflation while others may loose.*
- ✓ *A household's wealth depends on the difference between the value of its assets and debts.*
- ✓ *It has been observed in various countries that there exists a positive relationship between inflation and economic growth.*
- ✓ *Perfectly anticipated inflation exists when the rate of inflation is steady and perfectly predictable.*
- ✓ *Imperfectly anticipated inflation is that inflation, which people do not expect.*
- ✓ *India is the only major country that uses a wholesale index to measure inflation.*

INTRODUCTION

Inflation is a major economic problem, which plagues most of the countries in the world today. The present chapter and the next chapter analyse inflation and its related aspects.

The chapter starts with a simple definition of inflation, deflation and other related terms. It goes on to discuss the different measures of inflation, including the consumer price index and the wholesale price index. Inflation has widespread effects including economic and social effects, which have been discussed at length. The chapter also focuses on some features of inflation in India.

MEANING OF INFLATION

Inflation is a persistent and an appreciable increase in the general level of prices.

A sustained inflation takes place when the general price level continues to rise over a fairly long time period.

Disinflation is a situation where there occurs a decrease in the rate at which prices are rising.

Inflation is a persistent and an appreciable increase in the general level of prices. This leads to a decrease in the purchasing power of money. A sustained inflation takes place when the general price level continues to rise over a fairly long time period. Disinflation is a situation where there occurs a decrease in the rate at which prices are rising.

Deflation is the opposite of inflation. It is a situation where there exists a persistent decrease in the general level of prices. It leads to a decrease in the purchasing power of money.

RECAP

- Deflation is the opposite of inflation and leads to a decrease in the purchasing power of money.

MEASUREMENT OF INFLATION

Two measures of inflation are as follows:

(1) **Change in the Price Index:** The rate of inflation can be measured through change in the price index.

$$\text{Rate of Inflation} = \frac{\text{Price Index in period } (t) - \text{Price Index in period } (t-1)}{\text{Price Index in period } (t)}$$

Where, t = time period, which has been selected for measuring inflation

$t - 1$ = the preceding year

As far as the price index is concerned, following two indexes are often used:

(a) **Consumer Price Index (CPI):** Consumer price index (CPI) is a time-series index. It is a weighted average of prices of a specified basket of goods and services, which are purchased by the consumers. The CPI is a fixed quantity price index and often taken as a cost of living index. The CPI keeps a track of the changes in the price of a specified basket of consumer goods and services. By observing the changes in this index, inflation can be measured.

Consumer Price Index (CPI) is a weighted average of prices of a specified basket of goods and services, which are purchased by the consumers.

(b) **Wholesale Price Index (WPI):** The wholesale price index (WPI) or what is called the producer price index is used to measure the change in the average price of goods, which are traded in the wholesale market. In India, the WPI has been taken as an indicator of the inflation rate in the economy.

The Wholesale Price Index (WPI) or the Producer Price Index is used to measure the change in the average price of goods, which are traded in wholesale market.

(2) **Gross National Product Deflator (GNP Deflator):** The GNP deflator is not obtained directly like the CPI and WPI. It can be obtained as follows:

$$\text{GNP Deflator} = \frac{\text{Nominal GNP}}{\text{Real GNP}}$$

where, Nominal GNP = GNP at current prices

Real GNP = GNP at constant prices

The CPI is a weighted average of prices of a specified basket of goods and services, which are purchased by consumers whereas the WPI is used to measure the change in the average price of goods, which are traded in the wholesale market. In contrast, the GNP deflator is based on the prices of all the goods.

RECAP

- The CPI is a weighted average of prices of goods and services purchased by consumers and the WPI is average price of goods which are traded in wholesale market; the GNP deflator is based on the prices of all the goods.

BOX 19.1

Often in countries where the inflation rates are high and uncertain, the long-term nominal loans are risky. Thus, the lenders are not certain about the real worth of the repayments they will eventually receive. Hence in such situations, governments issue what is known as indexed debt. Indexed debt is a debt where the interest payments get adjusted upward each year to account for the inflation.

THE ECONOMIC AND SOCIAL EFFECTS OF INFLATION

In an economy where all prices change proportionately, no one is hurt and no one gains due to the changes in the price level. However, in the real economy all prices do not change proportionately. While some members of the society gain from inflation, others may loose. We can analyse the effects of inflation under two categories, economic effects and social effects.

Economic Effects of Inflation

We hereby examine the economic effects of inflation. They are as follows:

(1) **On the Distribution of Income:** The impact of an increase in the general price level is felt unevenly by the different groups of people, some of whom can be called the gainers whereas the others can be called the losers from inflation.

Gainers from inflation include the following:

(a) The producers as a group including the manufacturers, traders and the farmers whose income is derived from profits and thus they gain due to inflation.

As far as the manufacturers are concerned, they are able to sell their goods at high prices. No doubt there is an increase in the wages, interest rates, rent and the cost of the raw materials. However, it has been observed that the increase in the general level of prices is much more than the increase in the cost of production. Thus, the profit margin of the producer grows. Also there exists a time lag between the increase in prices and the wage increase, which again is in the interest of the producers.

The big farmers and traders again gain during times of inflation. It has been observed that the increase in the prices of the agricultural goods is much more than the increase in the prices of the industrial goods. Also, the demand for agricultural goods is less inelastic and the hoarding of these goods by the traders leads to further increase in their prices. In contrast to the big farmers the small farmers, who have just enough for subsistence, do not gain due to inflation.

(b) Those investing in equities benefit due to inflation. Due to the increase in the price, firms make large profits. The shareholders benefit in two ways: through the increased dividends that they earn and also due to the increase in the price of their shares, which enables them to make capital gains.

(c) The debtors gain during times of inflation. This is because the decrease in the value of money reduces the burden of the interest owed by them.

Losers from inflation include the following:

(1) The wage and salary earners (who are unorganized and without any wage contracts) lose due to inflation. The organized workers employed in large scale manufacturing units are able to pressurize and achieve wage increases through their unions whenever there is an increase in the price level. It is, however, the unorganized workers employed in small scale manufacturing units who are unable to achieve the wage increases. As a result, their real wages decrease during the times of inflation. Even the agricultural labourers, who are not only unorganized but also uneducated and ignorant, are badly affected due to inflation.

(2) Those investing in bonds lose due to inflation. Due to the increase in the general price level, investors holding fixed interest yielding bonds suffer. These bondholders lose in two ways: through the decrease in the real income from the bonds and also on account of capital losses if they decide to sell the bonds.

(3) The creditors lose during times of inflation. This is because the decrease in the value of money reduces the real worth of the interest that they get from their debtors.

(4) Recipients of incomes from rent are often hurt during inflation. However, this occurs only in cases when there are no escalator clauses, which enable the landlords to protect their interests.

In general, inflation leads to a redistribution of income from the creditors to the debtors and from the landlords to the tenants (provided there are no escalator clauses). It can thus be argued that inflation leads to a redistribution of income with the rich becoming richer and the poor becoming poorer.

(2) **On the Distribution of Wealth:** A household's wealth depends on the difference between the value of its assets and its debts.

The assets can be divided into two categories:

(a) Variable price assets include all types of physical assets like property, gold and silver jewellery, and financial assets like shares. To what extent does the household gain from these assets depends on the increase in the price of these assets vis-à-vis the inflation rate.

(b) Fixed claim assets include bonds, money, debentures and bank deposits. The money value of these assets is fixed in terms of money. Hence, their real worth declines during inflation. As far as debt is concerned, a household's debt includes housing loans and others, which are generally fixed in monetary terms.

To what extent an individual's wealth is influenced by inflation will depend on two factors: firstly on how the assets are divided between fixed claim assets and variable price assets, and secondly on the extent of its debts in comparison to its fixed claim assets.

(3) **On Output and Employment:** As far as the short run is concerned, economists are of the opinion that for an economy which is operating below full employment, inflation of the creeping or crawling type may prove to be favourable as long as it is unanticipated. The prices increase at a faster rate than the money wages resulting in higher profits and also providing an incentive to the firms to expand the output by hiring more workers. Thus at least in the short run inflation, if unanticipated, will lead to an increase in employment and thus in the output.

Inflation leads to an increase in the output not only through an increase in employment but also through a reallocation of the resources, including labour. Some economists, however, are of the opinion that inflation leads to a misallocation of the resources, in that the output of only those industries will rise whose prices rise the maximum. The other industries may, in fact, face a contraction in their output. But this is not necessarily true as most prices are flexible upwards and inflexible downwards. In such a situation, a better reallocation of resources is possible only through a price increase.

It can thus be argued that inflation leads to an improvement in the allocation of resources and thus to an increase in the employment and output.

However, this is subject to the following two qualifications:

(a) The benefits of inflation may be temporary. In the long run, once the money wages catch up with the rising prices or, in other words, labour finally anticipates the inflation and succeeds in increasing the real wages, the unemployment situation may be back again.

(b) The distortions in the resource allocation caused by inflation may in fact result in a slow down or may even lead to a minor recession.

(4) **On the Rate of Long Run Economic Growth:** It has been observed in various countries that there exists a positive relationship between inflation and economic growth.

During inflation, wages lagged behind prices. This resulted in

(a) Huge profit margins, which provided not only the incentive but also the resources to the firms to invest in the capital goods. The high profits were also responsible for the huge savings, given the fact that the high income group saves more than the low income group.

(b) A shift of resources away from the wage goods (whose demand were not increasing as rapidly) to the capital goods.

The result was an increase in the production of capital goods leading to an increase in the productive capacity and hence economic growth.

In the modern times, the situation seems to be different. Not only are the workers more organized which prevents the wages from lagging behind the prices, in addition savings may not rise because people may find their real net worth shrinking and thus may not increase the fraction of income that they save. Also in the modern world, besides inflation other factors like advances in knowledge are more important for growth.

Most economists agree that a moderate inflation is conducive to economic growth. Hyperinflation or inflation that occurs at a break neck speed may discourage saving and thus hinder economic growth.

In the opinion of James Tobin, a little amount of inflation is good for an economy. George L. Perry, George A. Akerlof and William T. Dickens have also argued that a little inflation of about say, 2 or 3 per cent per annum is good from the view point of an economy. It will, to some extent, help in achieving a lower rate of unemployment and thus economic efficiency. Thus, some economists believe that a little inflation 'greases the wheels' of the labour market and thus lubricates the economy.

Social Effects of Inflation

Besides the economic effects, inflation has some social effects also which result in problems for the society. To understand these problems, it is important to differentiate between the two types of inflation.

(1) Perfectly Anticipated Inflation: Perfectly anticipated inflation exists when the rate of inflation is steady, perfectly predictable and expected (for example, every month there is an increase in the price level, say by 2 per cent). Thus it is inflation, which people expect. Such inflation imposes certain costs on the society. These costs are:

Perfectly anticipated inflation exists when the rate of inflation is steady and perfectly predictable.

(a) Menu Cost: With a high rate of inflation, firms are expected to adjust their announced prices. This involves making changes in the catalogues and cash registers. The costs involved in these changes are called menu costs. The higher the inflation rate the more often the firms have to print the new menus. It has often been noticed that firms facing menu costs are not willing to change prices frequently. This may, in fact, lead to inefficiencies in the allocation of resources.

(b) Shoe leather Cost: The cost of holding money by an individual is the interest, which he foregoes by not holding an asset which could have earned him an interest. When there is a rise in the rate of inflation, there is an increase in the nominal interest rate and thus the interest lost by holding money rises. Hence, there is an increase in the cost of holding money. The demand for money balances falls. Individuals are now required to make more frequent trips to the bank to withdraw smaller amounts of money and leave the rest in interest earning assets. The frequent trips to the bank will involve more of walking to the bank which will make one's shoes to wear out more quickly. This is the shoe leather cost of inflation.

(c) Distortions in Taxation: Often the tax provisions do not take into consideration the effects of inflation. In India, indexation benefits are available while computing capital gains in respect of assets held over a longer term. However, income slabs and tax rates are generally not inflation linked and are only subject to periodic reviews as part of the government's annual budgetary exercise. As the tax codes measure the nominal income and not the real incomes, inflation can influence the individuals' real tax liability. Thus, inflation distorts taxes.

(d) Inconvenience in Using Money as a Yardstick: Money is the yardstick, which measures the economic transactions. However, this yardstick itself is affected by inflation. For example, when the value of the rupee itself keeps changing, then it is less useful in the measurement of economic transactions.

Imperfectly anticipated inflation is that inflation, which people do not expect.

(2) Imperfectly Anticipated Inflation: Imperfectly anticipated inflation is that inflation, which people do not expect. Such inflation imposes certain costs on the society. These costs are:

(a) An Arbitrary Redistribution of Wealth (Though already discussed under the economic effects, it is being discussed again with more emphasis on the social aspect). This redistribution occurs because an unexpected inflation:

(i) leads to a decrease in the real value of all assets fixed in nominal term like bonds, money, saving accounts and insurance contracts.

(ii) hurts individuals who have a fixed pension and can thus erode the purchasing power of an individual's lifetime savings.

(iii) often the agreements on loans are in terms of the nominal rate of interest, which is further based on the inflation rate existing at that time. If inflation is more than expected, then the debtors stand to gain whereas the creditors lose as the debtors certainly do pay back the loan but with less purchasing power. Thus, inflation leads to a redistribution of wealth between creditors and debtors.

(iv) with unexpected inflation, realized real interest rates are lower than nominal interest rates.

(b) An Unfavourable Effect on Decision Making. Due to inflation, while some gain others loose. Unanticipated inflation brings in an additional element of risk. Such an additional risk may affect adversely some of the attractive exchanges, which take place among the consumers and the businesses. This is an additional cost, which occurs due to an unexpected inflation.

RECAP

- The impact of an increase in the general price level is felt unevenly by the different groups of people, some of whom can be called the gainers whereas the others can be called the losers from inflation.
- It can be argued that inflation leads to an improvement in the allocation of resources and thus to an increase in the employment and output.
- Some economists believe that a little inflation 'greases the wheels' of the labour market and thus lubricates the economy.

INFLATION IN INDIA

Inflation continues to be a serious problem that plagues most economies of the world today. It is one of the most closely observed economic variables in India as it has a considerable influence on the life of an average consumer. A controversy that surrounds inflation in India is connected with the methodology used to calculate inflation.

Most of the developed countries use the CPI to calculate inflation, in India the WPI is used. According to the International Monetary Fund (IMF) statistics while 24 countries use the WPI, 157 countries use the CPI as the official measure to track down the inflation rate. India is the only major country that uses a wholesale price index to measure inflation. The CPI, in fact, is a measure of the increase in price that the consumer actually has to pay. In most countries, it is the official barometer of inflation. On the other hand, the WPI does not measure the increase in the price which the consumers actually experiences as it is based on the wholesale prices. Also, it is felt by some economists that a few of the commodities in the WPI are now less important from the consumer's point of view.

In India, the WPI method is still used because there are many problems associated with the CPI. Not only are there four different types of CPI indices in India (CPI Urban Non-manual Employees, CPI Industrial

Table 19.1 Annual WPI Inflation rate (%) (Base: 1993–94 = 100)

Year	March end annual inflation rate (per cent)					
	Primary articles	Fuel, power, light & lubri.	Manufactured products	All commodities	52-week Avg (All items)	Range of inflation during 52 weeks
Weights (per cent)	22.02	14.23	63.75	100.00	100.00	100.00
2000–01	1.5	15.1	4.0	5.5	7.2	4.9–8.8
2001–02	3.9	3.9	0.0	1.6	3.6	1.1–5.6
2002–03	6.1	10.8	5.1	6.5	3.4	1.4–6.5
2003–04	1.6	2.5	6.7	4.6	5.5	3.8–6.9
2004–05	1.3	10.5	4.6	5.1	6.5	4.3–8.7
2005–06	5.4	8.9	1.7	4.1	4.4	3.3–6.0
2006–07	10.7	1.0	6.1	5.9	5.4	3.7–6.7
2007–08	9.7	6.8	7.3	7.8	4.7	3.1–8.0
2008–09	5.2	−6.1	1.7	0.8	8.4	0.7–12.9

Source: Economic Survey 2008–09.

Workers, CPI Agricultural labourers and CPI Rural labour) but there also exists a lag in the reporting of the CPI numbers. Also, while the WPI is published on a weekly basis the CPI is published on a monthly basis. In India, the rate of inflation is calculated on a weekly basis. The WPI has an economy-wide coverage. Also, the weights used in the commodity basket in the case of the WPI are on the basis of the value of quantities which are traded in the domestic market. In the case of the CPIs, the commodity basket is based on consumer expenditure surveys.

Table 19.1 from the Economic Survey 2008–09 depicts the inflation trends by broad commodity groups from 2000–01 to 2008–09. The years 2000–01, 2004–05 and 2008–09 show the highest average rate of inflation with 2008–09 recording the highest average in the decade. As on 28 March 2009, the WPI overall inflation rate was just 0.8 per cent.

RECAP

- In India, the WPI method is still used to arrive at the inflation rate because there are many problems associated with the CPI.
- In India, the rate of inflation is calculated on a weekly basis.

SUMMARY

INTRODUCTION

Inflation is a major economic problem, which plagues most of the countries in the world today. The present chapter and the next chapter analyse inflation and its related aspects.

MEANING OF INFLATION

1. Inflation is a persistent and an appreciable increase in the general level of prices. This leads to a decrease in the purchasing power of money.

2. A sustained inflation takes place when the general price level continues to rise over a fairly long time period. Disinflation is a situation where there occurs a decrease in the rate at which prices are rising.

MEASUREMENT OF INFLATION

1. The two ways in which inflation can be measured are through a change in the price index and the gross national product deflator.
2. As far as the price index is concerned, two indexes are often used: Consumer Price Index (CPI) is a weighted average of prices of a specified basket of goods and services, which are purchased by the consumers; and Wholesale Price Index (WPI) is used to measure the change in the average price of goods, which are traded in the wholesale market.
3. The GNP deflator is not obtained directly like the CPI and WPI. It is based on the prices of all the goods.

THE ECONOMIC AND SOCIAL EFFECTS OF INFLATION

ECONOMIC EFFECTS OF INFLATION

1. As far as the distribution of income is concerned, some gain while others loose due to inflation.
2. The gainers from inflation are: producers including the manufacturers, traders and the farmers whose income is derived from profits; those investing in equities and the debtors who experience a decrease in the burden of the interest owed by them.
3. The losers from inflation are: unorganized workers and agricultural labourers; those investing in bonds; creditors and the recipients of incomes from rent.
4. It can thus be argued that inflation leads to a redistribution of income with the rich becoming richer and the poor becoming poorer.
5. As far as the distribution of wealth is concerned, a household's wealth depends on the difference between the value of its assets and its debts.
6. The assets can be divided into two categories: variable price assets and fixed claim assets. As far as debt is concerned, a household's debt includes housing loans and others which are generally fixed in monetary terms.
7. As far as output and employment are concerned in the short run, inflation if unanticipated will lead to an increase in employment and thus in the output.
8. It can be argued that inflation leads to an improvement in the allocation of resources and thus to an increase in the employment and output.
9. As far as the rate of long run economic growth is concerned, it has been observed in various countries that there exists a positive relationship between inflation and economic growth.
10. During inflation, wages lagged behind prices. This resulted in huge profit margins and a shift of resources away from the wage goods to the capital goods leading to an increase in the productive capacity and hence economic growth.
11. Most economists agree that a moderate inflation is conducive to economic growth. Hyperinflation or inflation which occurs at a break neck speed may discourage saving and thus hinder economic growth.

SOCIAL EFFECTS OF INFLATION

1. Perfectly anticipated inflation exists when the rate of inflation is steady, perfectly predictable and expected. Such inflation imposes certain costs on the society, which include menu cost, shoe leather cost, distortions in taxation and inconvenience in using money as a yardstick.
2. Imperfectly anticipated inflation is that inflation, which people do not expect. Such inflation imposes certain costs on the society. These costs are an arbitrary redistribution of wealth and an unfavourable effect on decision making.

INFLATION IN INDIA

1. Inflation is one of the most closely observed economic variables in India as it has a considerable influence on the life of an average consumer.
2. Most of the developed countries use the CPI to calculate inflation, in India the WPI is used.

3. In India, the WPI method is still used because there are many problems associated with the CPI.
4. Economic Survey 2008–09 depicts that the years 2000–01, 2004–05 and 2008–09 show the highest average rates of inflation with 2008–09 recording the highest average in the decade.

REVIEW QUESTIONS

TRUE OR FALSE QUESTIONS

1. Inflation is a persistent and an appreciable increase in the general level of prices.
2. Disinflation is a situation where there occurs an increase in the rate at which prices are rising.
3. Wholesale Price Index (WPI) is a weighted average of prices of a specified basket of goods and services, which are purchased by the consumers.
4. Perfectly anticipated inflation exists when the rate of inflation is steady, perfectly predictable and expected.
5. India is the only major country that uses a consumer price index to measure inflation.

VERY SHORT-ANSWER QUESTIONS

1. Write short notes on the following :
   (a) Inflation
   (b) Sustained Inflation
   (c) Disinflation
   (d) Deflation
2. Differentiate between the Consumer Price Index (CPI) and Wholesale Price Index (WPI).
3. What is Gross National Product Deflator (GNP Deflator)?
4. (a) What is perfectly anticipated inflation?
   (b) What is imperfectly anticipated inflation?
5. What is the shoe leather cost of inflation? Explain.

SHORT-ANSWER QUESTIONS

1. Discuss the following as measures of inflation:
   (a) Change in the Price Index
   (b) Gross National Product Deflator
2. 'Most of the developed countries use the CPI to calculate inflation, but in India the WPI is used.' Comment.
3. What is the impact of inflation on the distribution of income? Who are the gainers and the losers from inflation?
4. 'Inflation leads to an improvement in the allocation of resources and thus to an increase in the employment and output'. Comment.
5. What is the effect of inflation on economic growth? Does there exist a positive relationship between the two?

LONG-ANSWER QUESTIONS

1. Which are the two ways in which inflation can be measured? Discuss.
2. Analyse the economic effects of inflation
   (a) On the Distribution of Income
   (b) On the Distribution of Wealth.
3. How does inflation influence the
   (a) economy's output and employment?
   (b) rate of Long Run Economic Growth?
4. Examine the social effects of inflation.
5. Write a short note on inflation in India.

ANSWERS

TRUE OR FALSE QUESTIONS

1. **True.** Inflation is a persistent and an appreciable increase in the general level of prices whereas deflation is a persistent decrease in the general level of prices.
2. **False.** Disinflation is a situation where there occurs a decrease in the rate at which prices are rising.
3. **False.** Consumer Price Index (CPI) is a weighted average of prices of a specified basket of goods and services which are purchased by the consumers.
4. **True.** Perfectly anticipated inflation exists when the rate of inflation is steady, perfectly predictable and expected. Thus, it is the inflation which people expect.
5. **False.** Most of the developed countries use the CPI to calculate inflation, in India the WPI is used. India is the only major country that uses WPI to measure inflation.

20

Theories of Inflation

After studying this topic, you should be able to understand

- ✓ The proponents of the monetarist approach take the quantity theory of money as their basis and propose that the changes in the price level can be explained mainly in terms of the changes in the supply of money.
- ✓ According to Fisher's approach, change in the supply of money leads to proportional changes in the general price level.
- ✓ If Cambridge cash balance approach is emphasized as a theory of price, then P is determined from the quantity theory of money equation $P = \frac{M}{y}\frac{1}{K}$.
- ✓ The modern theory is an attempt by Friedman to present the quantity theory of money as a theory of demand for money.
- ✓ Keynes had argued that inflation occurs due to an increase in the aggregate demand.
- ✓ The inflationary gap is the amount by which the aggregate demand exceeds the aggregate output at the full employment level.
- ✓ According to the modern approach to inflation, when the increase in the price level is due to an increase in the aggregate demand it is called demand pull inflation and when it is due to an increase in the aggregate supply it is called cost push inflation.
- ✓ Demand pull inflation occurs due to a change in the real factors or the monetary factors.
- ✓ The theories of cost push inflation lay emphasis on an autonomous increase in some component of cost as the source of inflation and which leads to an upward shift in the supply curve.
- ✓ Three main kinds of cost push inflation include wage push inflation, profit push inflation and supply-shock inflation.
- ✓ Some economists are of the view that any inflationary process contains some aspects of both demand side and supply side inflation.
- ✓ As far as the demand side inflation is concerned, restrictive monetary and fiscal policies are commonly used to control the inflation.
- ✓ As far as the supply side inflation is concerned, restrictive monetary and fiscal policies are not appropriate for controlling inflation.
- ✓ Indexation reduces the reaction of people to inflation.

INTRODUCTION

One of the key economic questions that economists are concerned with are the causes of inflation. It is only after understanding the causes that attempts can be made to control it and keep it under acceptable limits. Hence, this chapter discusses the various theories of inflation. The theories explain the sources of inflation and thus, act, as a guiding factor in suggesting the different ways in which inflation can be controlled.

The theories can be broadly grouped under two approaches: the monetarist approach and the Keynesian approach.

The proponents of the monetarist approach take the Quantity Theory of Money (QTM) as their basis and propose that the changes in the price level can be explained mainly in terms of the changes in the money supply.

BOX 20.1

Historically, there existed a large amount of literature on the causes of inflation. In this connection, there were many schools of thought. They can all be placed under two broad areas: quality theories of inflation and quantity theories of inflation. According to the quality theory, a seller accepts currency so that he can later on exchange that currency for the goods that he desires to purchase as a buyer. The quantity theory of inflation is based on the quantity equation of money and the supply of money. David Hume and Adam Smith had presented a quality theory of inflation for production and quantity theory of inflation for money.

The Keynesian approach argues that an increase in the money supply will lead to only a modest increase in the price level if an economy is operating below full employment. In fact, it will lead to an increase in output and employment. However, when only once a situation of full employment is reached an increase in the money supply will lead to a considerable increase in the price level.

MONETARIST APPROACH TO INFLATION

Fisher's Approach to the Quantity Theory of Money

Though the QTM is associated with Fisher, economists like Jean Bodin and David Hume had formulated the theory much earlier. They all had emphasized that changes in the supply of money affects the general price level. Later, other quantity theorists like J. S. Mill had stressed that change in the supply of money leads to proportional changes in the general price level. This proportionality was later put forward by Fisher in his QTM.

In Chapter 13, Fisher's approach was discussed in the context of the demand for money. Some of the aspects of the theory are being repeated here to emphasize the relationship between money and prices. Fisher's famous equation of exchange is

$$MV_T = P_{TT} \tag{1}$$

where, M = total quantity of money in circulation

V_T = transactions velocity of money or the average number of times a unit of money changes hands to perform transactions during a given period of time

P_T = average price of all kinds of market transactions

T = aggregate of all transactions of goods and services during a given time period

The equation of exchange is a truism because each side of the equation depicts the value (in terms of money) of the total transactions during a given time period. Fisher's QTM is a tautology and does not make any assertions about the relationships between the variables in the real world. To develop the theory, certain assumptions are necessary; they are:

- Transactions, T: It is assumed that the total volume of transactions is a function of the basic physical and operational characteristics of the economy, namely capital, labour, the factors of production and technology, which are all independent of M, V_T and P_T.
- Money, M: It is assumed that the stock of money is determined by the monetary system.
- Velocity of circulation, V_T: V_T is assumed to be constant because payment practices (including the frequency with which people are paid and the irregularity in payments, etc.) change quite slowly.
- Prices, P_T: In the QTM, P_T is the only variable that is influenced by the changes in M. Hence, we get from Eq. (1),

$$P_T = \frac{MV_T}{T} \tag{2}$$

From the above analysis, with V_T and T as constants, and P_T as a passive variable, it is implied that P_T changes equiproportionately in response to changes in M.

It is important to note that this equiproportionate relationship between M and P_T will not hold true if there is a change in either V_T or T.

Cambridge Cash Balance Approach

The Cambridge economists Marshall and Pigou presented an alternative formulation of the QTM. In Chapter 13, the Cambridge approach was discussed in the context of demand for money as a function of money income. Here, we emphasize it as a theory of price.

In this neoclassical theory, the demand for money function is:

$$M_d = KY \tag{3}$$

where, M_d = money demanded

K = a constant

Y = the national income in money terms

We have $$y = \frac{Y}{P} \tag{4}$$

where, y = the real national income

P = general price level

Combining Eqs. (3) and (4), we get

$$M^d = KPy \tag{5}$$

The equilibrium condition in the money market is

$$M^d = M^s \text{ (or } M) \tag{6}$$

Thus, we get from Eqs. (5) and (6),

$$M = KPy$$

Hence, $$P = \frac{M}{y}\frac{1}{K}$$

In the above equation, P is determined from the QTM.

The Cambridge approach is considered to be advancement over Fisher's approach in many ways:

(1) In the Fisher's approach, money is treated as a flow variable whereas in the Cambridge approach money refers to the stock of cash balances at a particular point in time and is thus a stock variable.

(2) Fisher's approach emphasizes the strategic role of the supply of money in influencing the price level whereas the Cambridge approach lays emphasis on the demand for money or, in other words, the demand for cash balances.

(3) Fisher's approach lays emphasis on the medium of exchange function of money whereas the Cambridge approach lays stress on the store of value function of money. Hence, the Cambridge approach is consistent with the broader definition of money that includes not only currency and demand deposits but also time deposits in the definition of money.

The Cambridge approach is also superior in that it is in accordance with the demand supply analysis of the money market.

Modern Quantity Theory of Money

In 1956, Milton Friedman had presented his well-known article 'Quantity Theory of Money—A Restatement'. The modern QTM is a reformulation of the earlier QTM of Friedman. The modern theory is an attempt by Friedman to present the QTM as a theory of demand for money. The earlier versions of the QTM were suffering from the onslaught of the Keynesians who did not give much importance to money supply. Friedman's theory was an endeavour to save the QTM.

In Chapter 15, Friedman's theory was discussed in the context of the demand for money. It is sufficient to mention here, as emphasized by Friedman also, that this is clearly a theory of demand for money and not a theory of income or prices. Friedman rejects the view that the QTM is essentially a theory of prices. Friedman has expressed the demand for money in terms of the QTM.

Friedman's reformulation of the demand for money and, thus, of the QTM has been strongly influenced by Keynes and his liquidity preference theory. Hence, it lays more importance on money as an asset as compared to the earlier versions of the QTM that lay more emphasis on money as a medium of exchange.

Although it is possible to differentiate between the simple QTM and the Keynesian theory without much difficulty, the same cannot be said for the modern QTM. While Friedman sees the modern QTM as simply a statement of the old QTM, others agree that it is more close to the Keynesian theory.

RECAP

- Fisher's famous equation of exchange is $MV_T = P_T T$.
- In Fisher's approach, the equiproportionate relationship between M and P_T will not hold true if there is a change in either V_T or T.
- The Cambridge approach is considered to be advancement over Fisher's approach.
- Friedman's theory lays more importance on money as an asset as compared to the earlier versions of the QTM, which lay more emphasis on money as a medium of exchange.

KEYNESIAN APPROACH TO INFLATION

The classical economists had put forward the importance of the supply of money as the cause of inflation whereas Keynes had argued that inflation occurs due to an increase in the aggregate demand. An increase in the aggregate demand, given the full employment output, leads to an excess demand.

Keynes' analysis of excess demand was presented in terms of the 'inflationary gap' in his book, *How to Pay for the War* in 1940. It is, in fact, an application of his aggregate demand model to an inflationary situation.

Figure 20.1 depicts an inflationary gap with the help of a Keynesian cross. Initially, the aggregate demand represented by $C + I + G$ equals the aggregate supply at point B. The equilibrium output is Y_f, which is also the full employment output. Suppose there is an increase in the aggregate demand depicted by an upwards shift of the aggregate demand curve to $C + I + G + \Delta G$. This will create an excess demand equal to the amount AB. AB is the inflationary gap, which is actually the excess demand at the full employment output. The inflationary gap is the amount by which the aggregate demand exceeds the aggregate output at the full employment level.

The inflationary gap is the amount by which the aggregate demand exceeds the aggregate output at the full employment level.

If an economy is in the inflationary gap, then it is obvious that since the output level cannot be increased beyond the full employment level, the prices will increase leading to demand pull inflation.

Keynes had argued that for inflation to be controlled it is necessary that the aggregate demand curve must be shifted downwards such that it intersects

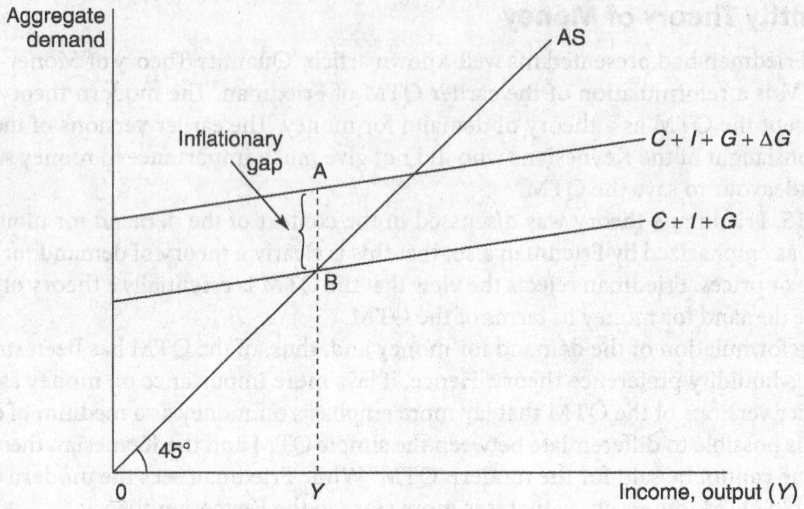

Figure 20.1 Inflationary Gap

the 45 degree line at point B. This can be achieved through appropriate policy measures like increasing taxes or reducing government expenditure.

It is important to note that Keynes' theory of inflation is a non-monetary theory as the increases in the money supply do not play any role in the theory.

RECAP

- An economy can come out of an inflationary gap through appropriate policy measures like increasing taxes or reducing government expenditure.
- Keynes' theory of inflation is a non-monetary theory as the increases in the money supply do not play any role in the theory.

MODERN APPROACH TO INFLATION

When the increase in the price level is due to an increase in the aggregate demand, it is called demand pull inflation.

As is obvious from the theories of inflation discussed so far, the prime concern of the economists is to identify the causes of inflation. The modern approach focuses on the fact that the price level is determined by the aggregate demand and the aggregate supply. Thus, changes in the price level can be related to changes in the aggregate demand and the aggregate supply.

BOX 20.2

Some post Keynesians have advocated the theory of endogenous money. They argue that the Central Bank has only a little control over the money supply. The money supply, according to these economists, adapts itself according to the demand for bank credit. However, not all economists accept this theory.

In Chapter 18, we had analysed the determination of the price level through the aggregate demand and aggregate supply analysis and it will form the analytical basis of our discussion in the present chapter. However, the theories of inflation will be explained in terms of the IS-LM framework.

When the increase in the price level is due to an increase in the aggregate supply, it is called cost push inflation.

According to the modern theory, as the price level is determined by aggregate demand and aggregate supply, any change in the price level is caused by a change in either aggregate demand or aggregate supply or both. When the increase in the price level is due to an increase in the aggregate demand, it is called demand pull inflation and when it is due to an increase in the aggregate supply it is called cost push inflation.

Inflation: Demand Side

One explanation of inflation is in terms of a generalized excess demand or, in other words, when too much of money is chasing too little of goods. Thus, at the existing price level the demand for goods and services exceeds the supply of goods (or the potential or full employment output) leading to an increase in the general price level.

We assume that

(1) The aggregate supply curve slopes upwards to the right and then becomes perfectly inelastic at the full employment output level.

(2) The economy is operating at full employment. Thus, a rightwards shift in the aggregate demand curve influences only the price level. In other words, it leads to a situation of pure inflation, without influencing the output level in any way.

In terms of the IS-LM analysis, excess demand that further leads to an increase in the price may occur due to

(1) a shift in the IS curve to the right due to a change in the real factors, including fiscal actions like a change in government expenditure and taxation;

(2) a shift in the LM curve to the right due to a change in the monetary factors like a change in the money supply.

An excess demand (which occurs due to the forces, which are operating only on the demand side of the commodity market) leads to demand pull inflation since the inflation occurs as the aggregate demand is pulled above what the economy's potential output is in the short run.

Demand Pull Inflation Arising From Real Factors

As already mentioned, demand pull inflation occurs due to a change in the real factors. A change in the real factors leads to a rightward shift of the IS curve. A change in the real factors includes:

(1) An increase in government expenditure with no change in tax revenue.

(2) A decrease in tax revenue with no change in government expenditure.

(3) An upward shift of the investment function.

(4) A downward shift of the saving function.

(5) An upward shift of the export function.

(6) A downward shift of the import function

Figure 20.2 illustrates the process by which demand pull inflation occurs due to a change in the real factors. The intersection of IS_1 and LM curves determines the initial equilibrium at point E_1, with the rate of interest at r_1 and the income level at Y_1, which represents the full employment real output. The aggregate demand curve, which corresponds to IS_1 and LM, is given by AD_1. The curves AD_1 and AS intersect to determine the equilibrium at E_1 with the income level at Y_1 and the price level at P_1.

An increase in investment expenditure shifts the IS curve rightwards from IS_1 to IS_2. The curve IS_2 intersects the LM curve at point E_2. The new equilibrium is at point E_2, with the rate of interest at r_2 and the income level at Y_2.

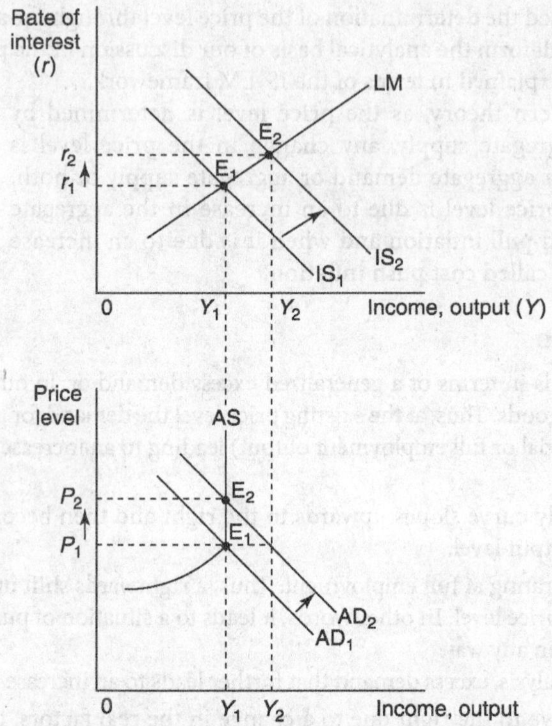

Figure 20.2 Demand Pull Inflation Arising from Real Factors

The aggregate demand curve, which corresponds to LM and IS_2, is AD_2. The intersection of curves AD_2 and AS determines the price level at P_2. The increase in the price level from P_1 to P_2 is required to eliminate the excess demand, equal to $Y_2 - Y_1$ that exists at the price level P_1. This excess demand is a result of a rightward shift in the IS curve. The increase in the price to P_2 eliminates the excess demand to re-establish equilibrium at the full employment income Y_1 and the price level P_2.

The analysis would be thc same with any of the other factors discussed above, which lead to a rightward shift of the IS curve.

Demand Pull Inflation Arising From Monetary Factors

Demand pull inflation also occurs due to a change in the monetary factors. A change in the monetary factors leads to a rightward shift of the LM curve. A change in the monetary factors includes

(1) an increase in the money supply, and
(2) a decrease in the demand for money.

In general, the increase in the money supply plays a more important role as far as the shift in the LM curve is concerned. Figure 20.3 illustrates the process by which demand pull inflation occurs due to a change in the monetary factors. The intersection of IS and LM_1 curves determines the initial equilibrium at point E_1 with the rate of interest at r_1 and the income level at Y_1. The income Y_1 represents the full employment real output. The aggregate demand curve, which corresponds to IS and LM_1 is given by AD_1. The intersection of the curves AD_1 and AS determines the equilibrium at E_1 with the income level at Y_1 and the price level at P_1.

An increase in the money supply shifts the LM curve rightwards from LM_1 to LM_2. The curve LM_2 intersects the IS curve at point E_2. The new equilibrium is at point E_2 with the rate of interest at a lower level of r_2 and the income level at Y_2.

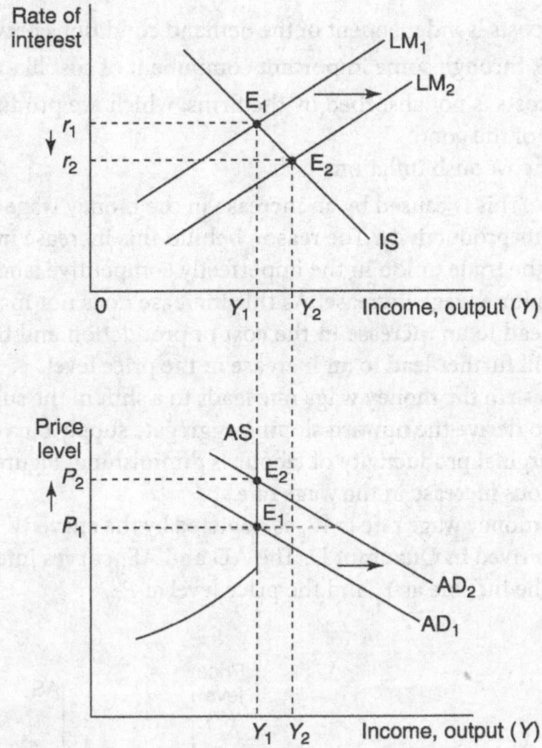

Figure 20.3 Demand Pull Inflation Arising from Monetary Factors

The aggregate demand curve, which corresponds to IS and LM$_2$ is given as AD$_2$; the curves AD$_2$ and AS intersect to determine the price level at P_2. Once again, the increase in the price level from P_1 to P_2 is required to eliminate the excess demand equal to $Y_2 - Y_1$ that exists at the price level P_1. This excess demand is a result of a rightward shift in the LM curve. The increase in the price to P_2 eliminates the excess demand to re-establish equilibrium at the full employment income Y_1 and the price level P_2.

For a persistent increase in the price level, there should be a persistent increase in the money supply. The analysis would be the same with any of the other factors discussed above, which lead to a rightward shift in the LM curve.

There is a disagreement among economists regarding the importance of the factors that cause inflation. Friedman is of the view that inflation is caused by monetary factors whereas Hicks is of the opinion that money plays only a supportive role as far as inflation is concerned. Thus, economists differ in their opinion as to the role performed by the real and monetary factors in the modern demand pull inflation.

Inflation: Supply Side

Another explanation of inflation is in terms of the supply side, called supply or cost push inflation.

Cost Push Inflation

The theories of cost push, also called mark up or seller's, inflation came in the 1950s. They appeared to refute the demand pull theories of inflation. These theories lay emphasis on an autonomous increase in some component of cost as the source of inflation and which leads to an upward shift in the supply curve. Three ingredients that are common to these theories are:

(1) The upward push in costs is independent of the demand conditions prevailing in the relevant market.
(2) The push forces work through some important component of cost like wage and profits.
(3) The increase in the costs is not absorbed by the firms, which are producing the good but are passed on to the consumers of the good.

There are three main kinds of cost push inflation:

(1) **Wage push inflation:** This is caused by an increase in the money wage rate, which is in excess of the increases in the labour productivity. The reason behind this increase in the money wage may be the monopoly power of the trade union in the imperfectly competitive labour markets, which may pressurize the employers for a wage increase. As this increase does not match an increase in the labour productivity, it will lead to an increase in the cost of production and thus to an upward shift in the supply curve. This will further lead to an increase in the price level.

To analyse as to how an increase in the money wage rate leads to a shift in the supply curve, the four quadrant diagram used in Chapter 18 to derive the upward sloping aggregate supply curve is being repeated here.

It is assumed that the marginal productivity of labour is diminishing. Figure 20.4 depicts cost push inflation arising from an autonomous increase in the wage rate.

Assume that the existing money wage rate is W_1 as depicted by the curve W_1 in Quadrant C. Corresponding to W_1, the AS_1 has been derived in Quadrant D. The AD and AS_1 curves intersect to determine the initial equilibrium at point E_1 with the income at Y_1 and the price level at P_1.

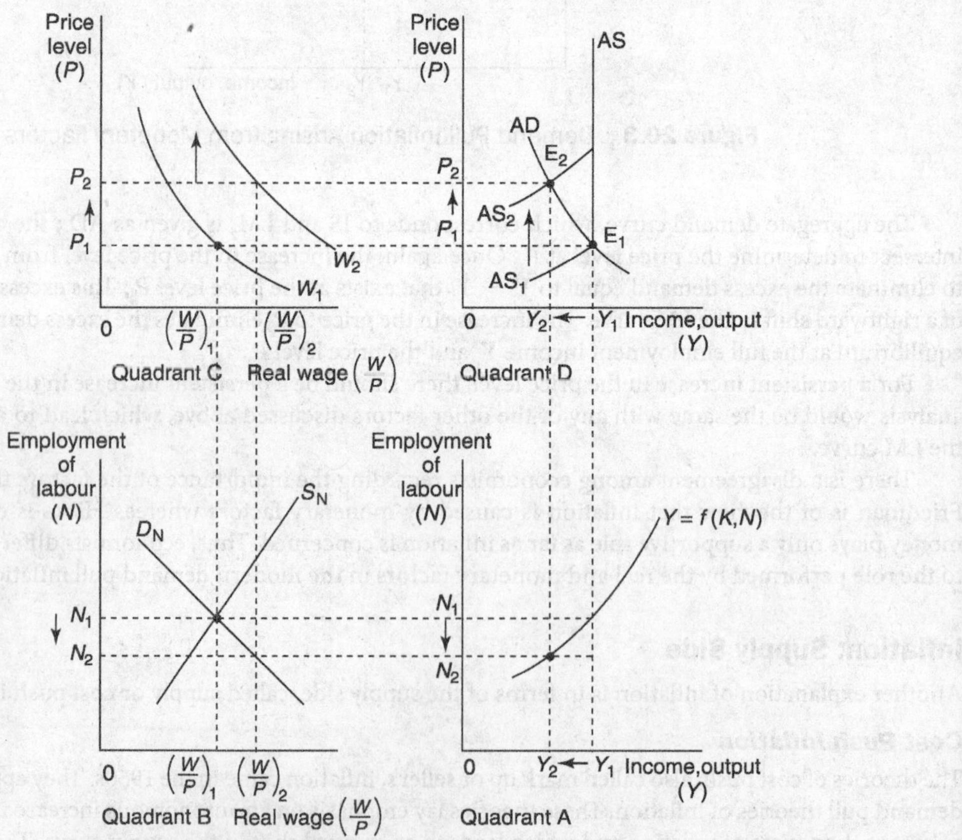

Figure 20.4 Cost Push Inflation Arising from an Autonomous Increase in the Wage Rate

Next suppose that there is an increase in the wage rate to W_2, which is entirely due to the monopoly power of the labour union and is in no way linked to increases in the labour productivity or any increase in the demand for labour. This leads to a shift in the money wage curve to W_2 in Quadrant C. With there being no shifts in the curves in Quadrant A and Quadrant B, the AS curve in Quadrant D will now shift to AS_2. At the price P_1 the aggregate demand exceeds the aggregate supply by $Y_2 Y_1$. Hence, there is an increase in the price level till a new equilibrium is established at point E_2. Thus, the AD and AS_2 curves intersect to determine the new equilibrium at point E_2 with the income at Y_2 and the price level at P_2.

It is to be noted from the above analysis that an increase in the money wage rate leads to

(a) a decrease in the income or output;

(b) an increase in the price level; and

(c) a decrease in the employment.

Wage inflation cannot occur in an economy where the labour markets are competitive. In such a market, the money wage rate will increase or decrease only in response to variation in the supply or demand for labour.

For a wage push inflation to occur, it is not necessary that the labour market is completely unionized. It is sufficient that a small segment of the labour market is unionized because then the effect of a wage push in the unionized industries may spread to the non-unionized industries. This is because the non-union wages are closely linked to the union wages.

It is not necessary that every increase in the money wage rate leads to a wage push inflation. An increase in the money wage rate does not lead to a wage push under certain conditions:

(a) When the increase in the money wage rate is matched by increases in the labour productivity.

(b) When an increase in the money wage rate results from an excess demand for labour, derived from the upward shift in the aggregate demand for goods (and not due to the monopoly power of the labour union).

(2) **Profit push inflation:** This is caused by the exercise of the monopoly power of the oligopolistic and monopolistic industries to enhance their profit margin. Thus, the monopolists and oligopolists may often go in for a price rise which is more than any increase in the costs.

We have observed that for a wage push inflation to occur, the existence of a unionized labour is necessary. Similarly for a profit push inflation to occur, the existence of imperfect competition in the sale of goods is a necessary condition. It is in such imperfect markets that the seller is successful in administering prices such that they increase at a rate much greater than the costs.

The process is the same as that described in Figure 20.4, which depicts wage push inflation. The aggregate supply curve shifts upwards from AS_1 to AS_2 in Quadrant D resulting in profit push inflation.

Some economists are of the opinion that a monopolist will not increase his price randomly. He has to take into consideration factors like demand for the good, sales and unit costs before he sets the price. It is often argued that the responsibility for supply side inflation rests more with the labour unions who are more concerned with increases in the wage rates than with other considerations.

(3) **Supply-Shock inflation:** This is caused by occurrences like the increase in the prices by the OPEC and even crop failures.

The process here again is the same as that described in Figure 20.4, which depicts wage push inflation and also profit push inflation. The aggregate supply curve shifts upwards from AS_1 to AS_2 in Quadrant D resulting in supply-shock inflation. The difference is in the driving force that leads to the inflation.

The monopolists and oligopolists on the one hand and the labour unions on the other hand exercise some kind of power that is different from the powers exercised by organizations like the OPEC. Unlike the monopolists and the labour unions, which are subject to the control of the authorities, the OPEC is a foreign organization which is outside the control of any authorities.

Similarly, crop failures and crop shortages are again subject to the vagaries of nature and thus beyond the control of any government. It is also important to note that supply shocks are unanticipated and unexpected.

Relationship Between Demand Side Inflation and Supply Side Inflation

Till now we have focused individually on the demand side and supply side inflation; however, some economists are of the view that any inflationary process contains some aspects of both demand side and supply side inflation.

It cannot be denied that there is an asymmetry between the two sides of inflation as depicted in Figure 20.5. Suppose, initially, the equilibrium is at point E with the output at Y_1, the full employment output and the price level at P_1. Two situations are possible:

(1) An inflationary process may begin with an excess demand and may continue as long as the excess demand persists. In the figure, this is depicted by the shifts in the aggregate demand curve from AD_1 to AD_2 and further to AD_3. The aggregate supply curve will remain unchanged at AS_1. Cost push factors are not playing any role whatsoever in the inflation process. As a result, the equilibrium shifts from point E to A to C. While the output will remain at Y_1, the prices will increase from P_1 to P_4 and so on. It is quite possible that in the extreme case there may occur a situation of hyperinflation.

It is quite possible that due to the rise in the aggregate demand, in a situation of full employment, the wage rates may increase. The increase in the money wage rate shifts the AS_1 curve to AS_2, which intersects AD_2 at point A. However, it is quite possible that the increase in the prices leads to a situation where the producers find their profits lower. Thus, they increase the administered prices. This creates a situation of a wage-price spiral where the general price level and the money wage rates follow each other in an upward spiral.

(2) An inflationary process may begin on the supply side but it will not continue unless there is an excess demand. In the figure, this is depicted by the shifts in the aggregate supply curve from AS_1 to AS_2 and further to AS_3. The aggregate demand curve will remain unchanged at AD_1. Demand pull factors are not playing any role whatsoever in this inflation process. As a result, the equilibrium shifts from point E to F to G. While the output (and thus the employment level) will decrease from Y_1 to Y_2 to Y_3, the prices will increase from P_1 to P_2 to P_3 and so on. The successive decreases in the output level and the growing unemployment levels will ultimately put an end to the inflation process.

The increase in the money wage rates leads to an increase in the prices. However, this increase in the prices will not be sustained unless it is followed by appropriate changes in the aggregate demand.

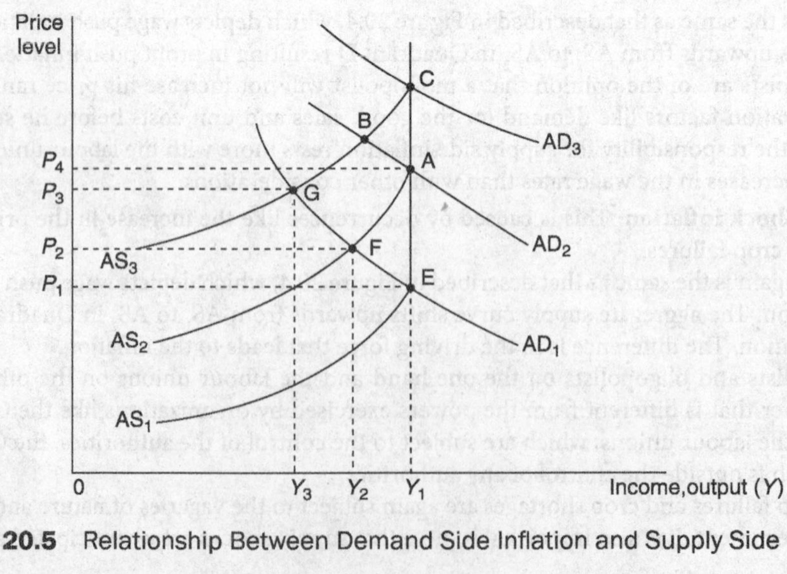

Figure 20.5 Relationship Between Demand Side Inflation and Supply Side Inflation

RECAP

- Friedman is of the view that inflation is caused by monetary factors whereas Hicks is of the opinion that money plays only a supportive role as far as inflation is concerned.
- For a wage push inflation to occur, it is not necessary that the labour market is completely unionized. It is sufficient that a small segment of the labour market is unionized.
- For a profit push inflation to occur, the existence of imperfect competition in the sale of goods is a necessary condition.
- It is often argued that the responsibility for supply side inflation rests more with the labour unions who are more concerned with increases in the wage rates than with other considerations.
- An inflationary process may begin with an excess demand and may continue as long as the excess demand persists.
- An inflationary process may begin on the supply side but it will not continue unless there is an excess demand.

CONTROL OF INFLATION

As far as the demand side inflation is concerned, restrictive monetary and fiscal policies are commonly used to control the inflation. Any increases in investment, government expenditure or foreign expenditures that lead to a rightward shift of the aggregate demand curve leading to an increase in the price level can be counteracted by restrictive monetary and fiscal policies. This is because such policies have an immediate impact on the level of the aggregate demand.

As far as the supply side inflation is concerned, restrictive monetary and fiscal policies are not appropriate for controlling inflation. This is because supply side inflation is accompanied by rising prices and an output below the full employment level.

In Figure 20.6, the intersection of the curves AS_1 and AD_2 at point E determines the full employment output at Y_1 and the price level at P_1. Assume an increase in the money wage rates, which leads to a shift of the AS_1 curve to AS_2. The intersection of the curves AS_2 and AD_2 at point F depicts a decrease in the output to Y_2 while the price level rises to the P_2.

An attempt at using restrictive monetary and fiscal policies to prevent the price rise will lead to a shift of the aggregate demand curve to AD_1. The intersection of the curves AS_2 and AD_1 at point G depicts a further

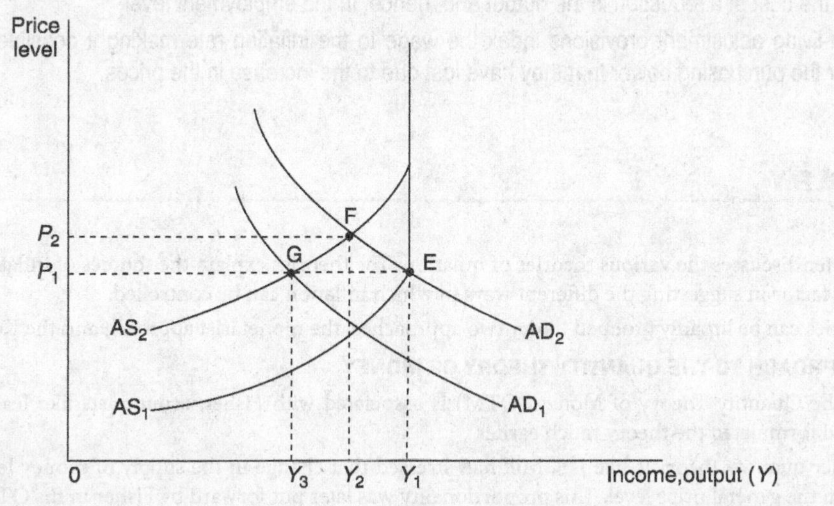

Figure 20.6 Supply Side Inflation and Restrictive Monetary and Fiscal Policies

decrease in the output to Y_3 while the price level remains unchanged at P_1. Hence, it is apparent that an attempt at controlling a supply side inflation through restrictive monetary and fiscal policies can be achieved only at the cost of a reduction in the output and hence in the employment level. Such an increase in the unemployment may not be socially acceptable and may, in fact, result in an economic slowdown. Thus in such cases, price stability can be achieved only at the cost of an increase in the unemployment rate.

Indexation

Indexation is a method by which there is an automatic adjustment of wages and prices according to the rate of inflation. Indexation reduces the reaction of people to inflation.

Indexed debt is a debt where the interest payments are adjusted upwards every year to account for inflation.

Indexation is a method by which there is an automatic adjustment of wages and prices according to the rate of inflation. Indexation reduces the reaction of people to inflation.

There are two kinds of contracts, which are especially affected by inflation. These are as follows.

(1) Long-term loan contracts, which are for a period of 25 to 30 years with a fixed nominal interest rate for the entire period like housing loan. For the long-term lenders and borrowers, the rate of inflation is of great importance for the next 25 or 30 years. Thus in countries where the inflation rates are not only high but also uncertain, the long-term nominal loans turn out to be very risky. The lenders are not certain about the real value of the repayments that they expect to receive. Hence to tackle such situations, the governments in such countries may issue what is called indexed debt. Indexed debt is a debt where the interest payments are adjusted upwards every year to account for inflation.

(2) Wage contract: Often, the labour contracts incorporate automatic cost-of-living adjustment (COLA) provisions. These provisions index the wage to the inflation rate. Hence, they make it possible for the workers to recover the purchasing power that they have lost due to the increase in the prices. Wage indexation is more widespread in the countries with high inflation rates.

RECAP

- An attempt at controlling a supply side inflation through restrictive monetary and fiscal policies can be achieved only at the cost of a reduction in the output and, hence, in the employment level.
- Cost-of-living adjustment provisions index the wage to the inflation rate making it possible for the workers to recover the purchasing power that they have lost due to the increase in the prices.

SUMMARY

INTRODUCTION

1. This chapter discusses the various theories of inflation. The theories explain the sources of inflation and, thus, act as a guiding factor in suggesting the different ways in which inflation can be controlled.
2. The theories can be broadly grouped under two approaches: the monetarist approach and the Keynesian approach.

FISHER'S APPROACH TO THE QUANTITY THEORY OF MONEY

1. Though the Quantity Theory of Money (QTM) is associated with Fisher, economists like Jean Bodin and David Hume had formulated the theory much earlier.
2. Later, other quantity theorists like J. S. Mill had stressed that change in the supply of money leads to proportional changes in the general price level. This proportionality was later put forward by Fisher in his QTM.
3. Fisher's famous equation of exchange is $MV_T = P_T T$.

4. Fisher's QTM is a tautology and does not make any assertions about the relationships between the variables in the real world. To develop the theory, certain assumptions are necessary.

CAMBRIDGE CASH BALANCE APPROACH

1. The Cambridge economists Marshall and Pigou presented an alternative formulation of the QTM.
2. In this neoclassical theory, the demand for money function is $M_d = KY$.
   Also, $M = KPy$ where, P is determined from the QTM as $P = \frac{M}{y}\frac{1}{K}$.
3. The Cambridge approach is considered to be an advance over Fisher's approach in many ways; for example, while Fisher's approach lays emphasis on the medium of exchange function of money the Cambridge approach lays stress on the store of value function of money. The Cambridge approach is also superior in that it is in accordance with the demand supply analysis of the money market.

MODERN QUANTITY THEORY OF MONEY

1. The modern theory is an attempt by Friedman to present the QTM as a theory of demand for money.
2. Friedman's reformulation of the demand for money lays more importance on money as an asset as compared to the earlier versions of the QTM, which lay more emphasis on money as a medium of exchange.

KEYNESIAN APPROACH TO INFLATION

1. Keynes had argued that inflation occurs due to an increase in the aggregate demand.
2. The inflationary gap is the amount by which the aggregate demand exceeds the aggregate output at the full employment level.
3. Keynes had argued that inflation can be controlled through appropriate policy measures, like increasing taxes or reducing government expenditure.
4. It is important to note that Keynes' theory of inflation is a non-monetary theory as the increases in the money supply do not play any role in the theory.

MODERN APPROACH TO INFLATION

1. The modern approach focuses on the fact that the price level is determined by the aggregate demand and the aggregate supply. Thus, changes in the price level can be related to changes in aggregate demand and the aggregate supply.
2. When the increase in the price level is due to an increase in the aggregate demand, it is called demand pull inflation and when it is due to an increase in the aggregate supply it is called cost push inflation.

INFLATION: DEMAND SIDE

1. One explanation of inflation is in terms of a generalized excess demand or, in other words, when too much of money is chasing too little of goods.
2. In terms of the IS-LM analysis, excess demand that leads to an excess demand inflation may occur due to a shift in the IS curve to the right due to a change in the real factors, or a shift in the LM curve to the right due to a change in the monetary factors.
3. Demand pull inflation occurs due to a change in the real factors. A change in the real factors leads to a rightward shift of the IS curve. For example, an increase in investment expenditure shifts the IS curve rightwards leading to a shift in aggregate demand. There occurs an excess demand, which leads to an increase in the price level. The increase in the price level eliminates the excess demand to re-establish equilibrium at the full employment income level but with a higher price level.
4. Demand pull inflation also occurs due to a change in the monetary factors. A change in the monetary factors leads to a rightward shift of the LM curve. In general, an increase in the supply of money shifts the LM curve rightwards leading to a shift in aggregate demand. There occurs an excess demand, which leads to an increase in the price level. The increase in the price level eliminates the excess demand to re-establish equilibrium at the full employment income level but with a higher price level.

INFLATION: SUPPLY SIDE

1. Another explanation of inflation is in terms of the supply side, called supply or cost push inflation.
2. The theories of cost push lay emphasis on an autonomous increase in some component of cost as the source of inflation and which leads to an upward shift in the supply curve.

3. There are three main kinds of cost push inflation.
4. Wage push inflation is caused by an increase in the money wage rate which is in excess of the increases in the labour productivity. For a wage push inflation to occur, it is not necessary that the labour market is completely unionized. It is sufficient that a small segment of the labour market is unionized.
5. Profit push inflation is caused by the exercise of the monopoly power of the oligopolistic and monopolistic industries to enhance their profit margin. For a profit push inflation to occur, the existence of imperfect competition in the sale of goods is a necessary condition.
6. Supply shock inflation is caused by occurrences like the increase in the prices by the OPEC and even crop failures. It is also important to note that supply shocks are unanticipated and unexpected.

RELATIONSHIP BETWEEN DEMAND SIDE INFLATION AND SUPPLY SIDE INFLATION

1. Some economists are of the view that any inflationary process contains some aspects of both demand side and supply side inflation.
2. An inflationary process may begin with an excess demand and may continue as long as the excess demand persists.
3. An inflationary process may begin on the supply side but it will not continue unless there is an excess demand.

CONTROL OF INFLATION

1. As far as the demand side inflation is concerned, restrictive monetary and fiscal policies are commonly used to control the inflation.
2. As far as the supply side inflation is concerned, restrictive monetary and fiscal policies are not appropriate for controlling the inflation.
3. Any attempt at controlling a supply side inflation through restrictive monetary and fiscal policies can be achieved only at the cost of a reduction in the output and hence in the employment level.

INDEXATION

1. Indexation is a method by which there is an automatic adjustment of wages and prices according to the rate of inflation. Indexation reduces the reaction of people to inflation.
2. There are two kinds of contracts, which are especially affected by inflation.
3. Long-term loan contracts are for a period of 25 to 30 years. In countries where the inflation rates are not only high but also uncertain, the long-term nominal loans turn out to be very risky. To tackle such situations, the governments in such countries may issue what is called indexed debt. Indexed debt is a debt where the interest payments are adjusted upwards every year to account for inflation. Wage contracts: Often, the labour contracts incorporate automatic cost-of-living adjustment (COLA) provisions. These provisions index the wage to the inflation rate.

REVIEW QUESTIONS

TRUE OR FALSE QUESTIONS

1. Fisher's QTM is a tautology and does not make any assertions about the relationships between the variables in the real world.
2. Fisher's approach lays emphasis on the store of value function of money whereas the Cambridge approach lays stress on the medium of exchange function of money.
3. Friedman's theory is a theory of demand for money.
4. The inflationary gap is the amount by which the aggregate output exceeds the aggregate demand at the full employment level.
5. When the increase in the price level is due to an increase in the aggregate demand, it is called cost push inflation.

VERY SHORT-ANSWER QUESTIONS

1. What is an inflationary gap? Discuss.
2. How can an economy move out of an inflationary gap?

3. (a) What is demand pull inflation?
   (b) What is cost push inflation?
4. How can demand pull inflation occur due to a change in the real factors? Explain.
5. How can demand pull inflation occur due to a change in the monetary factors? Explain.

SHORT-ANSWER QUESTIONS

1. 'The Cambridge approach is considered to be an advance over Fisher's approach in many ways.' Explain.
2. Write a short note on Friedman's modern quantity theory of money.
3. What is the Keynesian approach to inflation? Discuss.
4. How can inflation be controlled? Discuss.
5. What is indexation? Discuss.

LONG-ANSWER QUESTIONS

1. Compare Fisher's approach to the quantity theory of money with the Cambridge cash balance approach.
2. What is the monetarist approach to inflation? Explain.
3. What is demand pull inflation? Compare demand pull inflation arising from real factors with that arising from monetary factors.
4. What is cost push inflation? Which are the three main kinds of cost push inflation?
5. (a) Is there a difference between demand side and supply side inflation?
   (b) Analyse the relationship between demand side inflation and supply side inflation.

ANSWERS

TRUE OR FALSE QUESTIONS

1. **True.** As Fisher's QTM is a tautology and does not make any assertions about the relationships between the variables in the real world, to develop the theory certain assumptions are necessary.
2. **False.** Fisher's approach lays emphasis on the medium of exchange function of money whereas the Cambridge approach lays stress on the store of value function of money.
3. **True.** Friedman's theory is clearly a theory of demand for money and not a theory of income or prices.
4. **False.** The inflationary gap is the amount by which the aggregate demand exceeds the aggregate output at the full employment level.
5. **False.** When the increase in the price level is due to an increase in the aggregate demand, it is called demand pull inflation.

Unemployment

21

After studying this topic, you should be able to understand

- ✓ *The labour force consists of both the employed and the unemployed.*
- ✓ *The unemployment pool is formed by the unemployed persons at any point of time.*
- ✓ *The natural rate of unemployment is the average rate of unemployment around which any economy fluctuates in the long run.*
- ✓ *Frictional unemployment arises due to the time gap it takes for the workers to search for a job that best suits their individual skills and tastes, when the economy is at full employment.*
- ✓ *Wait unemployment is caused by wage rigidity above the equilibrium level of employment.*
- ✓ *Unemployment results in a loss in production and also leads to an undesirable effect on the distribution of income.*
- ✓ *The Phillips' curve shows that there exists an inverse relationship between the rate of unemployment and rate of increase in money wages.*
- ✓ *The modern Phillips' curve incorporates the concept of expected inflation to explain the relationship between unemployment and inflation.*
- ✓ *The sacrifice ratio is the percentage of output lost for a one point decrease in the inflation rate.*

INTRODUCTION

In the real world, full employment is just not possible. All economies experience some unemployment accompanied by low standards of living, hardships, psychological distress and mental agony. Side by side with unemployment, most countries are also plagued with inflation and its related consequences. This chapter deals with inflation and also the relationship between the rate of unemployment and the rate of inflation.

UNEMPLOYMENT AND RELATED TERMS

Unemployed

A person is unemployed if he is out of work and (1) has been actively looking for work during the previous four weeks, or (2) is waiting to be called back to a job after having been laid off.

A person is unemployed if he is out of work and (1) has been actively looking for work during the previous four weeks, or (2) is waiting to be called back to a job after having been laid off.

Employed

A person is employed if during the reference week (1) he did any work (at least one hour) as a paid employee, worked in his own business, profession, or on his own farm, or worked 15 hours or more as an unpaid worker in an enterprise operated by a member of a family, or (2) was not working but had a job or business from which he was temporarily absent, whether or not he was paid for the time off or was seeking another job.

Labour Force

Labour force consists of those people who are unemployed as well as those who are employed.

Unemployment can be defined more specifically as

Unemployment = Labour Force − Number of people employed

A person is employed if during the reference week: (1) he did any work (at least one hour) as a paid employee, worked in his own business, profession, or on his own farm, or worked 15 hours or more as an unpaid worker in an enterprise operated by a member of a family, or (2) was not working but had a job or business from which he was temporarily absent, whether or not he was paid for the time off or was seeking another job.

The Unemployment Rate

$$\text{Unemployment rate} = \frac{\text{Labour Force} - \text{Number of people employed}}{\text{Labour Force}} \times 100$$

We have, E = Total number of employed persons

U = Total number of unemployed persons

L = Total labour force

Labour force consists of those people who are unemployed as well as those who are employed.

Using the above notations, we get: $L = E + U$

Therefore, rate of unemployment $= \dfrac{U}{L}$

The Unemployment Pool

The unemployment pool consists of the number of unemployed persons at any point of time. As more and more people enter the pool, unemployment increases.

Unemployment pool consists of the number of unemployed persons at any point of time.

There are many reasons why a person may become unemployed. Some of them are as follows:

(1) He may be a new entrant or a re-entrant in the labour force.
(2) He may have quit the job in order to look for another job and may register as unemployed.
(3) He may be laid off.
(4) He may lose a job, either by being fired or due to the firm closing down.

Duration of Unemployment

The duration of unemployment is defined as the average length of time for which a person remains unemployed. It indicates whether unemployment is short-term or long-term.

BOX 21.1

Neither Employed Nor Unemployed: As per the International Labour Organization (ILO) definition, it is quite possible to be neither employed nor unemployed, i.e., to be outside of the "labour force." The people who belong to this category are those who do not have a job and are not looking for one. Many of these people may be going to college or may be retired. Some may be constrained due to family responsibilities where as others may have a physical or mental disability, which does not allow them to participate in the labour force activities.

Frequency of Unemployment

Frequency of unemployment is defined as the average number of times, per period, that the workers become unemployed.

The frequency of unemployment is defined as the average number of times, per period, that the workers become unemployed. It depends on two factors:

(1) The extent to which demand for labour varies across the different firms in the economy. More the variability, higher is the level of the unemployment rate and vice versa.

(2) The growth rate of the labour force. The higher the growth rate, the higher is the rate of unemployment and vice versa.

RECAP

- The duration of unemployment indicates whether unemployment is short-term or long-term.

TYPES OF UNEMPLOYMENT

Natural Rate of Unemployment

Natural rate of unemployment is the average rate of unemployment around which any economy fluctuates in the long run.

Natural rate of unemployment is the average rate of unemployment around which any economy fluctuates in the long run. Often it is known as NAIRU (Non-accelerating Inflation Rate of Unemployment). It is calculated as:

Natural rate of unemployment for any year = Average of unemployment rate for 10 years earlier to ten years later

Policies Aimed at Reducing the Natural Unemployment

The government must formulate policies to reduce the natural rate of unemployment. Some policies in this direction are as follows:

(1) Unemployment benefits should be reduced as they allow for a longer time period for searching for jobs. These benefits also reduce the urgency for an unemployed person to take up a job.

(2) Minimum wages should also be reduced.

(3) Incentives should be given to workers to take up technical training. This will make the workers more productive and side by side reduce the natural rate of unemployment.

(4) Unemployment hysteresis is a theory, which argues that recessions may permanently affect the natural rate of unemployment. Thus, efforts should be made to control recession.

BOX 21.2

Certainly a Unique Way of Solving Unemployment: Under the ancient system of slave labour, the slave-owners would see to it that their property (the slaves) was never unemployed for long. If anything occurred, they would sell the unemployed labourer rather than keep it unemployed. In the planned economies of the old Soviet Union typically, occupation was provided for everyone, even by overstaffing if it was so required.

Frictional Unemployment

Frictional unemployment is the unemployment, which arises due to the time gap it takes for the workers to search for a job that best suits their individual skills and tastes, when the economy is at full-employment. As neither are the workers identical nor are all the jobs identical, it becomes difficult to match the worker's skills, preferences and their abilities with the job profile. Hence, every economy will have to make do with some extent of frictional unemployment. If frictional unemployment is reduced, then natural rate of unemployment will also fall.

Frictional unemployment is the unemployment, which arises due to the time gap it takes for the workers to search for a job that best suits their individual skills and tastes, when the economy is at full employment.

Unemployment in excess of frictional unemployment is what is called cyclical unemployment.

Causes of Frictional Unemployment

(1) A sectoral shift is actually a change in the composition of demand among the different industries or regions. This occurs due to the advancement of technology and with new inventions. For example, suppose the demand for a good rises due to a fall in its price. This, in turn, leads to a rise in the demand for the labour in this particular industry. Thus, new workers will be attracted to this industry from another industry. This process will take some time. The gap between the time they leave one industry and join another results in frictional unemployment.

(2) Workers find themselves out of work unexpectedly due to many reasons; some of them are as follows:

(a) A particular skill in which a worker has expertise may no longer be needed.

(b) A firm may fail and lay off workers.

(c) A worker's performance may not be satisfactory and thus he is unexpectedly out of work.

Policies Aimed at Reducing Frictional Unemployment

(1) The employment agencies of the government can collect information on the workers' profile and also job profile. Then an effort can be made to match jobs and workers.

(2) To make the workers more efficient, retraining programmes can be designed.

(3) It is necessary that the terms of the employment insurance programme are not so soft and generous that they encourage the workers to turn down job offers, which they do not find very attractive. Such programmes reduce the uncertainty regarding the workers' income. However, they raise the level of frictional unemployment.

(4) Economists have proposed certain reforms to reduce the level of unemployment; some of them are as follows:

(a) A 100 per cent experience rated system where the firm, which lays off a worker has to bear the entire cost of that worker's unemployment benefits.

(b) A partially experience rated system where the firm that lays off a worker has to bear a part of the burden of the worker's unemployment benefits.

Wait Unemployment

Wait unemployment is the unemployment, which is caused by wage rigidity above the equilibrium level which in turn results in job rationing.

Wait unemployment is the unemployment, which is caused by wage rigidity above the equilibrium level which, in turn, results in job rationing.

Job rationing occurs when, at the going wage rate, the supply of labour is greater than the demand for labour. The workers are waiting for jobs to be made available to them. The extent of wait unemployment is shown in Figure 21.1.

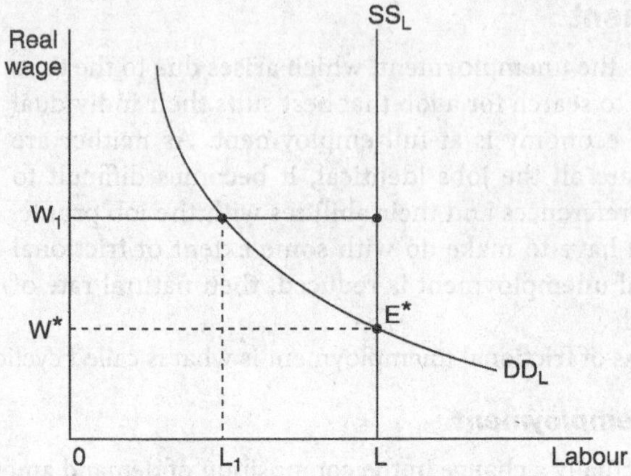

Figure 21.1 Wait Unemployment

where,

x-axis = Quantity of Labour

y-axis = Real Wage

OL = Number of labourers who are willing to take up work

SS_L = The supply curve of labour. It is perfectly inelastic at OL units of labour.

DD_L = The demand curve for labour. It is downward sloping.

E* = Equilibrium takes place at point E*, where $DD_L = SS_L$.

OW* = The equilibrium wage rate.

OW_1 = Let real wage level be rigid at OW_1. Here the demand for labour is OL_1 and supply of labour is OL. The supply of labour exceeds the demand for labour by L_1L. This excess supply of labour leads to wait unemployment. It is called so as L_1L units of labour are in the market searching and waiting for jobs.

Causes of Wait Unemployment

(1) Minimum wage laws aim at protecting and safeguarding the interest of workers against their exploitation by the employers. The minimum wage, or what is also called the floor wage, for certain industries and types of workers, especially the unskilled and inexperienced workers is fixed through legislation, at a level which is above the equilibrium wage rate. The Minimum Wage Law aims at promoting an equitable distribution of income.

The Minimum Wage Law, however, may add to the already existing level of unemployment. At the high wages, some workers are laid off due to lack of demand. Thus, there is an increase in the unemployment gap.

An alternative way to increase the income of the poor working class would be, as believed by many economists and policy makers, tax credit. In this scheme, the government makes payment or gives credit to low income families which is more than the tax that they owe to the government.

BOX 21.3

Minimum Wage Act was passed in India in 1948 and since then has been revised many times. The Act provides for fixation of minimum wages for notified scheduled employment. As per Government of India, for all the States, the minimum wages have been fixed at about Rs. 40 to 60 per day per person, average about Rs. 50 per day for 25 days per month. It has been successful in raising the level of wages for unskilled and some types of semi-skilled workers, thus improving their productive efficiency.

(2) The union is a worker's organization representing the collective preferences of the members. The union aims at improving the terms of employment, including wages and working conditions, for its members. The union has a strong influence on the social, political and economic life of any economy.

Often, the union aims at maximizing both employment and wage rate. However, given the downward sloping demand curve of labour, a higher wage rate is possible only with a lower level of employment. Hence, this results in a decrease in employment and an increase in wait unemployment.

(3) According to the Efficiency Wage Theory, high wages that are above the level that balances demand and supply often make the workers more efficient. Hence, firms may often give higher wages even at the expense of reducing employment. This again will lead to an increase in wait unemployment.

RECAP

- Natural unemployment can be reduced through policies aimed at reducing the unemployment benefits and minimum wages and by giving incentives to workers.
- Frictional unemployment can be reduced through collecting information on the workers' profile to match jobs and workers and through retraining programmes.

COSTS OF UNEMPLOYMENT

The costs of unemployment are as follows:

Loss in Production

It is very obvious that the unemployed do not produce. Thus, there is a lost output which involves a high cost. Arthur Okun has put forward an empirical relationship between unemployment and output. According to Okun's law, there is a negative relationship between unemployment and the real GDP.

According to this law, 1 extra point of unemployment costs 2 per cent of the GDP.

Okun's law is depicted in Figure 21.2 as a downward sloping curve showing an inverse relationship between unemployment and the real GDP.

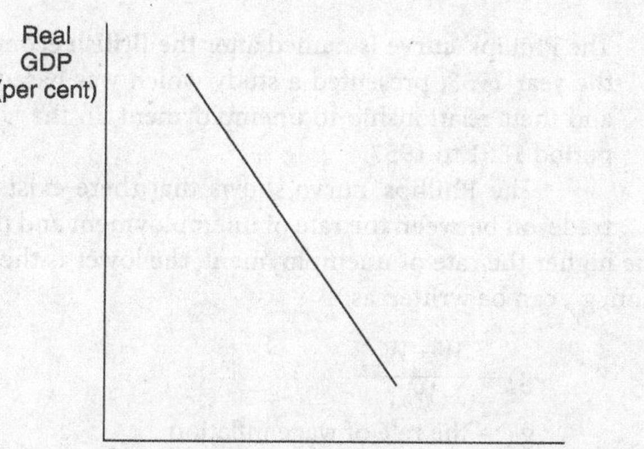

Figure 21.2 Okun's Law

BOX 21.4

The Miseries of the Unemployed: Those who are unemployed are unable to earn money to meet their financial obligations. Thus, they are not in a position to pay mortgage payments or to pay the rent. This may lead them to eviction and without a home. Unemployment also makes one susceptible to malnutrition, mental stress, illness, and loss of self esteem and may even lead to depression. Even the optimistic may find it difficult to remain so in the face of unemployment.

High unemployment can even create a fear of foreigners stealing jobs. Thus, efforts to preserve the existing jobs for the domestic and native workers may lead to barriers against "outsiders" who want jobs, and obstacles to immigration.

where, x-axis = Unemployment rate,
y-axis = Real GDP growth rate.

An Undesirable Effect on the Income Distribution and the Human Costs of Unemployment

The costs of recession are borne more by those individuals who have lost their jobs. In the less developed countries, the cost of unemployment is the human misery and poverty which the unemployed have to suffer. In the developed countries, people often have a high standard of living. Recession and the consequential unemployment resulting there from have led to high rates of suicides. Left with no work and thus no sources of income, people are increasingly turning towards crimes.

RECAP

- According to Okun's law, there exists a negative relationship between unemployment and the real GDP.
- In the less developed countries, the cost of unemployment is the human misery and poverty which the unemployed have to suffer.

RELATIONSHIP BETWEEN INFLATION AND UNEMPLOYMENT

Phillips' Curve

Phillips' curve shows that there exists an inverse relationship or trade-off between the rate of unemployment and the rate of increase in money wages or wage inflation.

The Phillips' curve is named after the British economist A. W. Phillips who, in the year 1958, presented a study which was based on the behaviour of wages and their relationship to unemployment, in the United Kingdom for the time period 1861 to 1957.

The Phillips' curve shows that there exists an inverse relationship or trade-off between the rate of unemployment and the rate of increase in money wages or wage inflation. The higher the rate of unemployment, the lower is the rate of wage inflation.

The rate of wage inflation, g_w, can be written as:

$$g_w = \frac{W - W_{-1}}{W_{-1}}$$

where, g_w = the rate of wage inflation
W = the wage in the current period
W_{-1} = the wage in the preceding period

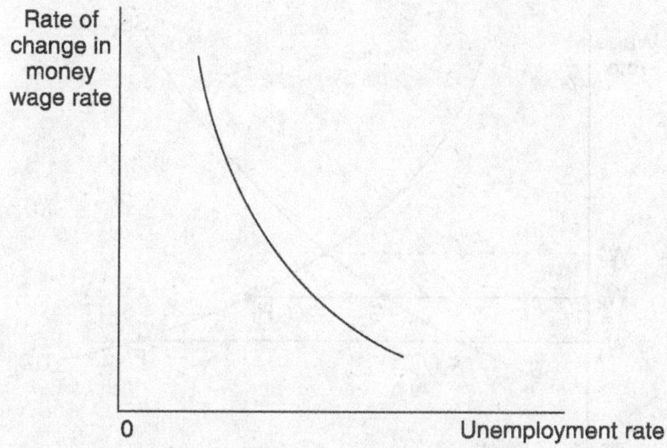

Figure 21.3 Phillips' Curve for the United Kingdom

The natural rate of unemployment is the amount of frictional unemployment that exists at the level of full employment. We denote it by U*. The Phillips curve can be presented as:

$$g_w = -e(U - U^*)$$

where,

e = It measures the responsiveness of wages to unemployment
U = the unemployment rate
U^* = the natural rate of unemployment
$U - U^*$ = the unemployment gap

From the above equation, the following results emerge:

1. If $U > U^*$, it implies that the unemployment rate is greater than the natural rate and, hence, the wages fall.
2. If $U < U^*$, it implies that the unemployment rate is lower than the natural rate and, hence, wages rise.

In Figure 21.3, the original Phillips' curve has been depicted (for the United Kingdom) as a downward sloping and flat curve showing an inverse relationship between the rate of unemployment and wage inflation.

where, *x*-axis = unemployment rate
y-axis = rate of change in money wage rate

The original Phillips' curve shows a negative relationship between the rate of increase in wages and the unemployment rate. Later it came to be described as negative relationship between the rate of increase in prices and the rate of unemployment.

The Phillips' Curve Relationship: an Explanation

Behaviour of the Organized Labour

An organized labour market can cause autonomous wage increases, which are in excess of the increases in the productivity of labour. This leads to an increase in the prices of goods, resulting in wage-push inflation.

The extent to which the labour market can push through these increases in wages will vary inversely with the unemployment rate in the labour markets:

(1) During situations of low unemployment rates and tight labour markets, there is a buoyant demand for goods and the firms are making profits. Under such conditions, an aggressive labour can demand higher wages and the employers often accede to these demands.

(2) Alternatively, during situations of high unemployment rates and low profits, the employers resist to even moderate increases in the wages.

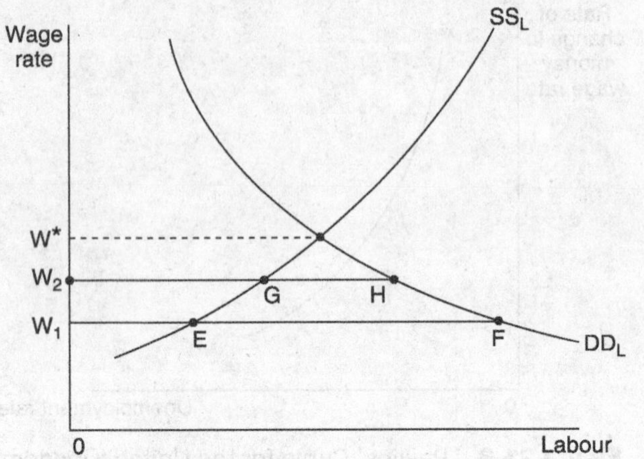

Figure 21.4 (a) Labour Market

An Excess Demand for Labour

Figure 21.4 (a) depicts the equilibrium in the labour market.

where, x-axis = quantity of labour
y-axis = wage rate
SS_L = the supply curve of labour
DD_L = the demand curve for labour
OW* = Equilibrium wage rate where the demand for labour is equal to the supply of labour.
OW_1 = Wage rate at which there is an excess demand for labour equal to EF.
OW_2 = Wage rate at which there is an excess demand for labour equal to GH.

It is quite obvious that when the wage rate is OW_1, and the excess demand for labour is EF, the increase in wages will be much greater than with the wage rate OW_2 and an excess demand for labour of GH. Thus, the rate of wage increase is inversely related to the amount of excess demand for labour.

This approach can also be expressed in terms of another argument put forward in terms of the Phillips' curve in Figure 21.4 (b). The amount of unemployment is inversely related to the amount of excess demand for labour.

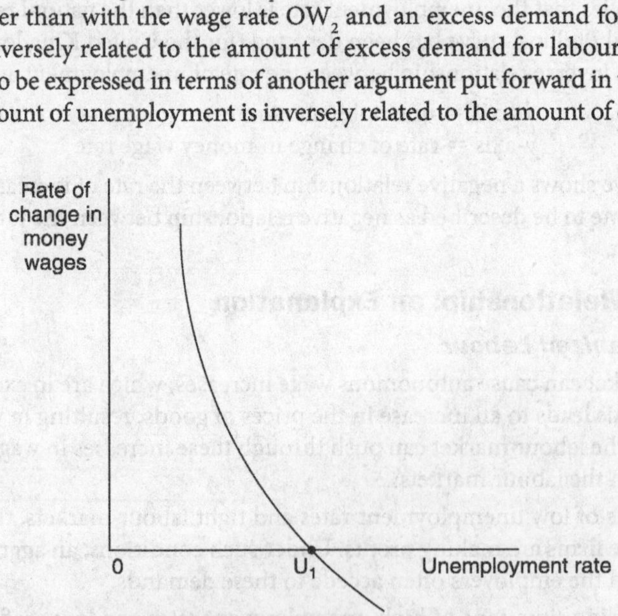

Figure 21.4 (b) The Phillips' Curve

Figure 21.4(b) shows
x-axis = unemployment rate
y-axis = rate of change in money wages
OU_1 = Unemployment rate at the equilibrium wage rate OW* where the demand for labour is equal to the supply of labour. At this level of unemployment, as there is neither excess demand nor excess supply of labour, the rate of wage increase will be zero. At a wage rate lower than OW*, there will be an excess demand for labour, or in other words, a lower rate of unemployment, and thus a greater increase in the wage rate. This will imply a movement up the Phillips' curve.

RECAP

- The explanation of the Phillips' curve can be expressed in terms of an excess demand for labour and the behaviour of the organized labour which can cause autonomous wage increases.

MODERN PHILLIPS' CURVE

The original Phillips' curve was unable to explain the behaviour of unemployment and inflation in the United Kingdom and in the United States after the 1960s. Something was missing from it—the concept of expected inflation. The modern Phillips' curve or the expectations-augmented Phillips' curve incorporates the concept of expected inflation.

Milton Friedman and Edmund Phelps have argued that the original Phillips' curve does not take into consideration the effect of expected inflation in the fixation of the wages. Workers are concerned with their real wages and want that their nominal wages should fully take into consideration the inflation they expect. Thus, workers want to be compensated for expected inflation. Firms, on the other hand, are willing to give higher wages because the goods will be sold in the market at higher prices. Thus, when they are fixing wages and prices, firms and workers take into consideration the expected increase in the price level.

Short-Run Modern Phillips' Curve

Figure 21.5 depicts the modern Phillips' curve.
where, x-axis = unemployment rate
y-axis = inflation rate
U* = natural rate of unemployment

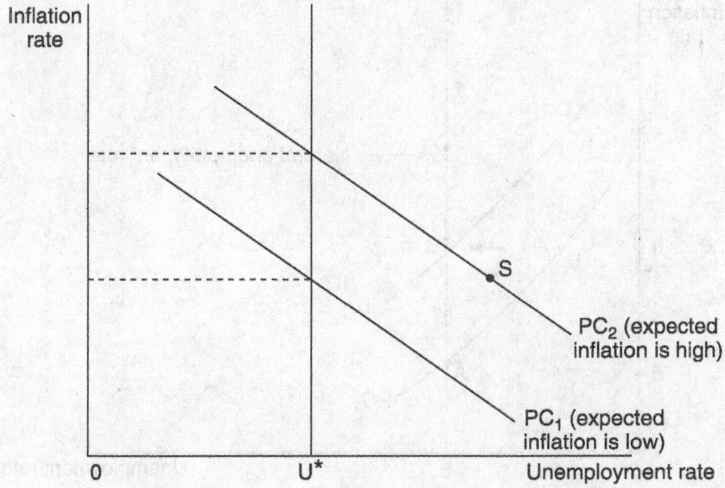

Figure 21.5 Modern Phillips' Curve: Short-run

PC_1 and PC_2 = These are the short-run modern Phillips' curves. They are downward sloping and, thus, show a negative relationship between inflation and unemployment in the short-run. The two curves have the same slope showing the same short-run trade-off. However, their height differs because it depends upon the level of expected inflation. The higher the curve higher is the expected inflation for any level of unemployment.

Stagflation is a situation where there is high unemployment and high expected inflation.

Pont S = It is a point of stagflation. Stagflation is a situation where there is high unemployment and high expected inflation.

Long-run Modern Phillips' Curve

Economists are of the view that the downward sloping Phillips' curve implying a trade-off between unemployment and inflation is only a short-run phenomenon. The relationship holds only as long as there is a discrepancy between anticipated and actual inflation rate. Once this discrepancy gets removed, the downward sloping Phillips' curve and the trade-off thereon no longer exist. Thus, in the long run the Phillips' curve is vertical, implying that the rate of unemployment is independent of the rate of inflation.

Figure 21.6 depicts the vertical or non trade-off Phillips' curve.

where,

x-axis = unemployment rate

y-axis = inflation rate

PC_1 = initial Phillips' curve

Point A = Initial point where the rate of unemployment rate is 6 per cent whereas the rate of inflation is 6 per cent.

The government pursues expansionary monetary and fiscal policies, which lead to an increase in aggregate demand. This creates an upward pressure on the rate of inflation, which increases to 8 per cent. The real wage rates experience a decline. This provides an incentive to producers to expand output. This, in turn, leads to an expansion in employment. Over a period of time, the unemployment rate falls and there is a movement upwards along PC_1 to point B.

Point B = The point at which there is an unemployment rate of 4 per cent and inflation rate of 8 per cent. It is reached due to the expansionary monetary and fiscal policies and thus leads to the conventional conclusion of a trade-off between the unemployment rate and inflation rate.

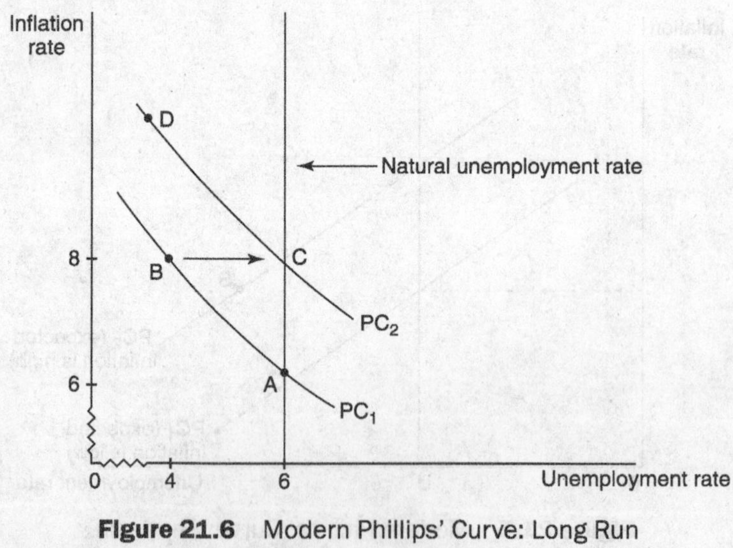

Figure 21.6 Modern Phillips' Curve: Long Run

However, this trade-off is just a temporary phenomenon. Workers do not take long to realize that inflation has caused a reduction in their real wages. Hence, they demand higher money wages. Once the employers accede to their demands, the real wage rate soon returns to its original level. Due to these adjustments, the Phillips' curve will shift upward and the unemployment rate will increase and come to its original level of 6 per cent.

PC_2 = The Phillips' curve after the impact of the monetary and fiscal policies.

Point C = The point at which there is an unemployment rate of 6 per cent and inflation rate of 8 per cent. It is thus showing that the unemployment rate has returned to its original position. Hence, there is now a situation of higher rate of inflation and higher rate of increase in the money wages and an unemployment rate which has not changed from its original 6 per cent rate.

Further expansionary monetary and fiscal policies will lead to movements from C to D, which is quite similar to the movement from A to B. But ultimately the unemployment rate will once again be at 6 per cent while the rate of inflation will rise further.

Thus, the conventional conclusion of a trade-off between the unemployment rate and inflation rate does not hold in the long run. The actual unemployment rate has a tendency to ultimately gravitate towards the equilibrium rate of unemployment, which Friedman calls the natural rate of unemployment, at which the demand for labour is equal to the supply of labour. The long-run Phillips' curve becomes vertical at 6 per cent, the natural unemployment rate.

Policy Implications of the Phillips' Curve

Of the many goals that every economic policy aims at achieving, two goals—low inflation and low unemployment—seem to be conflicting. Hence, there is a trade-off between the two goals of low inflation and low unemployment.

According to the Phillips' curve, policy makers could make a choice between different combinations of the rate of inflation and the rate of unemployment. They could have low inflation but at the cost of high unemployment, or they could maintain low unemployment but only at the cost of a high inflation.

But it has been found that empirical evidence for most of the countries goes against the findings shown by the Phillips' curve. It seems that even if there is a trade-off, it exists only in the short-run. There is no permanent inflation–unemployment tradeoff, and the policy makers can make a choice between different combinations of unemployment and inflation.

RECAP

- The short-run modern Phillips' curve is downward sloping showing a negative relationship between inflation and unemployment in the short-run.
- Stagflation is a situation where there exists high unemployment and high expected inflation.
- In the long-run the Phillips' curve is vertical, implying that the rate of unemployment is independent of the rate of inflation.
- Empirical evidence for most of the countries goes against the findings shown by the Phillips' curve. It seems that even if there is a trade-off, it exists only in the short run. There is no permanent inflation–unemployment trade-off, and the policy makers can make a choice between different combinations of unemployment and inflation.

SACRIFICE RATIO

Sacrifice ratio is the percentage of output, which is lost for a 1 point decrease in the inflation rate.

The sacrifice ratio is the percentage of output, which is lost for a one point decrease in the inflation rate. This ratio also depends on the time, place and methods which are used to reduce the inflation. Available estimates show a sacrifice ratio ranging from 1 to 10. Thus in the short-run, the government can

BOX 21.5

A Short-term Solution But Long-run Problem: A structural solution to unemployment could be in the form of a graduated retail tax, or "jobs levy", on the firms in which labour is more expensive than capital. This will shift the burden of the tax to capital intensive firms and away from the labour intensive firms. Theoretically, this will make the firms shift their operations to a more desired balance between capital intensive and labour intensive production. The tax revenue from the jobs levy could be used to finance the labour intensive public projects. However, the other side of the coin is that this would certainly discourage capital investment and thus economic growth. With less economic growth, long-run employment would be adversely affected. Hence, this would be just a very short-term solution to the problem.

reduce inflation but only at the cost of increasing the unemployment and reducing the level of output. Hence, the cost in terms of output of reducing inflation is very high.

As already mentioned, the Okun's law shows that there is a negative relationship between unemployment and the real GDP.

To be more specific, 1 extra point of unemployment costs 2 per cent of GDP.

RECAP

- Every extra point of unemployment costs 2 per cent of GDP.

SUMMARY

INTRODUCTION

In the real world, full employment is just not possible. Side by side with unemployment, most countries are also plagued with inflation.

UNEMPLOYMENT AND RELATED TERMS

Knowledge of the following terms is necessary:

1. Unemployed Person
2. Employed Person
3. Labour Force
4. Unemployment Rate
5. Unemployment Pool
6. Duration of Unemployment
7. Frequency of Unemployment

TYPES OF UNEMPLOYMENT

NATURAL RATE OF UNEMPLOYMENT

1. Natural rate of unemployment is the average rate of unemployment around which any economy fluctuates in the long run.
2. The government must formulate policies to reduce the natural rate of unemployment through:
   (a) a reduction in unemployment benefits;
   (b) a reduction in the minimum wages;
   (c) giving incentives to workers to take up technical training; and
   (d) efforts should be made to control recession.

FRICTIONAL UNEMPLOYMENT

1. Frictional unemployment is the unemployment, which arises due to the time gap it takes for the workers to search for a job that best suits their individual skills and tastes, when the economy is at full-employment.
2. The main causes of frictional unemployment are: a change in the composition of demand among the different industries or regions and workers being unexpectedly out of work.
3. Some of the policies for reducing frictional unemployment are:
   (a) Collection of information on the workers' profile and then an effort can be made to match jobs and workers.
   (b) Retraining programmes can be designed.

WAIT UNEMPLOYMENT

1. Wait unemployment is the unemployment, which is caused by wage rigidity above the equilibrium level which in turn results in job rationing.
2. The main causes of wait unemployment are:
   (a) Minimum wage laws,
   (b) The union monopoly power,
   (c) Efficiency wages.

COSTS OF UNEMPLOYMENT

The costs of unemployment are: a loss in production as depicted by Okun's law and an undesirable effect on the distribution of income.

PHILLIPS' CURVE

1. The Phillips' curve shows that there exists a trade-off between the rate of unemployment and the rate of increase in money wages or wage inflation.
2. The Phillips' curve has been depicted as a downward sloping and flat curve showing an inverse relationship between the rate of unemployment and wage inflation.
3. The two explanations for the Phillips' curve are in terms of
   (a) the behaviour of the organized labour, and
   (b) an excess demand for labour

MODERN PHILLIPS' CURVE

The modern Phillips' curve or the expectations augmented Phillips' curve incorporates the concept of expected inflation.

SHORT-RUN MODERN PHILLIPS' CURVE

1. It is downward sloping showing a negative relationship between inflation and unemployment in the short-run.
2. Stagflation is a situation where there is high unemployment and high expected inflation.

LONG-RUN MODERN PHILLIPS' CURVE

1. The downward sloping Phillips' curve implying a trade-off between unemployment and inflation is only a short-run phenomenon.
2. In the long-run, the Phillips' curve is vertical at the natural rate of unemployment, implying that the rate of unemployment is independent of the rate of inflation.
3. The conventional conclusion of a trade-off between the unemployment rate and inflation rate does not hold in the long run.

POLICY IMPLICATIONS OF THE PHILLIPS' CURVE

1. According to the Phillips' curve, the two goals of low inflation and low unemployment seem to be conflicting.
2. Empirical evidence shows that there is no permanent inflation-unemployment tradeoff, and the policy makers can make a choice between different combinations of unemployment and inflation.

SACRIFICE RATIO

The sacrifice ratio is the percentage of output, which is lost for a one point decrease in the inflation rate.

REVIEW QUESTIONS

TRUE OR FALSE QUESTIONS

1. Labour force consists of only those people who are employed.
2. Natural rate of unemployment is the average rate of unemployment around which any economy fluctuates in the long run.
3. Unemployment in excess of frictional unemployment is called the natural rate of unemployment.
4. Job rationing occurs when, at the going wage rate, the demand for labour is greater than the supply of labour.
5. The Phillips' curve shows that there exists a direct relationship between the rate of unemployment and the rate of increase in money wages.

VERY SHORT-ANSWER QUESTIONS

1. What is unemployment rate?
2. Write a short note on the unemployment pool.
3. What is the frequency of unemployment?
4. What is the Phillips' curve? What does it show?
5. What is the modern Phillips' curve? How is it different from the original Phillips' curve?

SHORT-ANSWER QUESTIONS

1. Write short notes on
   (a) Unemployed
   (b) Employed
   (c) Labour Force
2. Write short notes on
   (a) Wait unemployment
   (b) Frictional unemployment
3. The Phillips' curve shows that there exists a trade-off between the rate of unemployment and the rate of increase in money wages. Explain.
4. What is unemployment? What are the costs of unemployment?
5. Differentiate between frictional unemployment and wait unemployment.

LONG-ANSWER QUESTIONS

1. What is natural rate of unemployment? Suggest some policies to reduce natural rate of unemployment.
2. What is frictional unemployment? What are the causes of frictional unemployment?
3. What is wait unemployment? What are the causes of wait unemployment?
4. Discuss the relationship between Okun's law and the sacrifice ratio?
5. How do unemployment benefits increase the rate of unemployment? Discuss.

ANSWERS

TRUE OR FALSE QUESTIONS

1. **False.** Labour force consists of those people who are unemployed as well as those who are employed.
2. **True.** Often it is known as NAIRU, Non-accelerating Inflation Rate of Unemployment.
3. **False.** Unemployment in excess of frictional unemployment is called cyclical unemployment.
4. **False.** Job rationing occurs when, at the going wage rate, the supply of labour is greater than the demand for labour. The workers are waiting for jobs to be made available to them.
5. **False.** The Phillips' curve shows that there exists an inverse relationship or trade-off between the rate of unemployment and the rate of increase in money wages or wage inflation.

UNIT VII THE OPEN ECONOMY MACROECONOMICS AND THE FRAMEWORK OF MACROECONOMIC POLICIES

22 Foreign Exchange

After studying this topic, you should be able to understand

- ✓ *In a foreign exchange market foreign, currency (or foreign exchange) is purchased and sold by individuals, firms, commercial banks and the central banks of the different countries.*
- ✓ *Two types of foreign exchange transactions are spot transaction and forward transaction.*
- ✓ *The exchange rate reflects the purchasing power of one country's currency in terms of the purchasing power of another country's currency.*
- ✓ *Two nominal exchange rate systems are flexible or floating exchange rate system and fixed exchange rate system.*
- ✓ *As to how the exchange rate is determined, will depend on whether the exchange rates system is a flexible or a fixed exchange rate system.*
- ✓ *In a flexible exchange rate system the equilibrium rate of exchange is determined at the point at which the demand for foreign exchange equals the supply of foreign exchange.*
- ✓ *Under a fixed exchange rate, the exchange rate is set by the government in consultation with the other concerned countries.*
- ✓ *Both the major exchange rate systems, fixed and flexible exchange rates have inherent advantages and disadvantages.*

INTRODUCTION

In Chapter 8, we had focused on income determination in a four sector economy. At this stage of our analysis, we are in a position to go a step further and discuss the other important aspects which pertain to an open economy.

Today, all economies are open and dealing in transactions with the rest of the world. They all are involved in the export and import of goods and services. They are also engaged in borrowing and lending in the financial markets of the different countries.

All these different countries have their own currencies, which are generally (the exception being the Euro) legal tender only within the territories of the country. The rupee is acceptable within India where as the dollar is acceptable within the US economy. The problem occurs when one country trades with another. This problem can be solved be fixing the rate of exchange between the different currencies. Here, we discuss the determination of the foreign exchange rate and also the fixed and the flexible exchange rates.

FOREIGN EXCHANGE MARKET

The foreign exchange market is a market where foreign currencies (or foreign exchange) are purchased and sold by individuals, firms, commercial banks and the central banks of the different countries.

The foreign exchange market is a market where foreign currencies (or foreign exchange) are purchased and sold by individuals, firms, commercial banks and the central banks of the different countries.

Types of Foreign Exchange Transactions

Foreign exchange transactions are of two kinds:

A spot transaction is one where the seller of the foreign exchange has to deliver the exchange to the buyer on the spot, that is, within two days of the deal.

(1) **Spot transaction:** A spot transaction is one where the seller of the foreign exchange has to deliver the exchange to the buyer on the spot, that is, within two days of the deal.

(a) The spot market is one where there are spot sales and purchases of the foreign exchange.

(b) The spot exchange rate is the rate at which the foreign exchange is bought and sold in the spot market.

A forward transaction is one which involves an agreement between the buyer and the seller to purchase or sell a fixed amount of currency for a predetermined rate at a specified date in the future.

(2) **Forward transaction:** A forward transaction is one, which involves an agreement between the buyer and the seller to purchase or sell a fixed amount of currency for a predetermined rate at a specified date in the future. Usually, a forward contract is for a period of three months.

The forward exchange market is one where there is a forward sale and purchase of foreign exchange.

The forward exchange rate is the rate at which the foreign exchange is bought and sold in the forward exchange market.

Functions of the Foreign Exchange Market

The foreign exchange market performs many functions; some of the important ones are:

(1) **International transfer of purchasing power between the different countries:** In foreign trade, there are two types of transfers of purchasing power, which are as follows:

(a) From one country to another country.

(b) From one currency to another currency.

These transfers take place through a clearing mechanism. When a firm in a country exports some goods to a firm in another country, the exporting firm acquires a claim on the foreign firm where a the foreign firm is under a debt obligation to the exporting firm. Hence, there arise counter claims which are settled in the foreign exchange market through bills of exchange.

(2) **Provision of credit for foreign trade:** Similar to the domestic trade, credit is essential for the smooth functioning of the foreign trade. There is a considerable time gap involved in the movement of the goods between the exporter and the importer. Hence, there is need for some form of institutional credit to finance the transactions of the goods between the time periods.

(3) **Hedging risks of foreign exchange:** In a situation when the exchange rate fluctuates freely, any forward foreign exchange transaction will be subject to great risks. To avoid such risks, the buyers and sellers of foreign exchange resort to hedging facilities.

Hedging is an attempt at covering the risk involved in a foreign exchange transaction through a forward transaction.

Hedging is an attempt at covering the risk involved in a foreign exchange transaction through a forward transaction. The exporters and importers are subject to risks relating to the exchange rate in conducting their business. This risk can be avoided through a forward transaction where they can enter into an agreement regarding the buying and selling of goods at a future date at a contracted rate of exchange. However, where the rates of exchange are stable over long periods of time, hedging is not required.

Some Related Concepts

Arbitrage: It is the simultaneous buying and selling of different foreign currencies in the different foreign exchange markets to take advantage of the difference in the prices. An arbitrageur is the person who is engaged in such buying and selling of the foreign currencies.

Arbitrage is the simultaneous buying and selling of different foreign currencies in the different foreign exchange markets to take advantage of the difference in the prices.

Speculation: It is an activity related to the sale and purchase of foreign exchange in which risk is undertaken to take advantage of the fluctuations in the exchange rate. The speculative buying and selling of the foreign currency depends the speculator's expectations regarding the future exchange rates.

Speculation is an activity related to the sale and purchase of foreign exchange in which risk is undertaken to take advantage of the fluctuations in the exchange rate.

Speculative attacks: It is a situation, which causes a change in the investors' perception.

Currency board: It is an arrangement under which the central bank of a country holds enough amount of a foreign currency to back, in a fixed ratio, each and every unit of the domestic currency. Thus, under a currency board a country is in a position to commit itself to some strong currency like the dollar. Also whenever the need arises, it should be ready to convert its own currency to the foreign currency.

Currency board is an arrangement under which the central bank of a country holds enough amount of a foreign currency to back, in a fixed ratio, each and every unit of the domestic currency.

Dollarization: It is a step further than the currency board where a country abandons its domestic currency and adopts a strong foreign currency like the dollar. Thus, the domestic currency is converted into the US dollar.

Dollarization is a situation where a country abandons its domestic currency and adopts a strong foreign currency like the dollar.

RECAP

- The foreign exchange market performs many functions which include international transfer of purchasing power between different countries, provision of credit for foreign trade and hedging risks of foreign exchange.

EXCHANGE RATE SYSTEMS

The exchange rate is the rate at which one country's currency exchanges for another country's currency. Hence, it reflects the purchasing power of one country's currency in terms of the purchasing power of another country's currency. It is actually the price at which the residents of one country conduct trade with the residents of another country.

The exchange rate is the rate at which one country's currency exchanges for another country's currency.

One can distinguish between the nominal exchange rate and the real exchange rate. The nominal exchange rate is the rate at which the currency of one country is traded for the currency of another country. Thus, it signifies the relative price of one currency vis à vis the currency of another country. The real exchange rate is the rate at which the goods of one country are traded for the goods of another country. Hence, the real exchange rate takes into consideration the relative purchasing power of the currency as well. The real exchange rate is also called the terms of trade.

Two nominal exchange rate systems are:

(1) **Flexible or floating exchange rate:** Flexible or floating exchange rate is a system where the exchange rate fluctuates freely in response to the changes in the economic conditions and without any government intervention. Hence, the exchange rate is determined by the market forces.

(2) **Fixed exchange rate:** Fixed exchange rate is a system where the exchange rate does not fluctuate in response to the changes in the economic conditions. The exchange rate is maintained through government intervention in the foreign exchange market and also by the central bank through its buying and selling of currencies.

BOX 22.1

Till recently, the countries of East Asia experienced the most impressive growth rates ever possible. However, in the year 1997 there occurred the Asian Crisis when speculative attacks affected the currencies of these countries. Thailand was the first country which was forced to devalue its currency followed by South Korea, Indonesia and Malaysia. There was a financial and banking crisis. This attack on the currencies affected these economies adversely in many aspects. By 1999, the financial assistance from the IMF and the other world agencies embarked these countries on the path to recovery.

At this stage, a brief history of the exchange rate systems adopted by the different countries is required. When the Second World War ended, there was a need for a new international monetary and exchange rate system which would promote growth of world trade. Thus, at Bretton Woods New Hampshire, in the year 1944, delegates from 44 nations converged. They adopted the fixed exchange rate system in which each country pegged its currency to the dollar and as all currencies were pegged to the dollar, they were pegged to each other also. The International Monetary Fund (IMF) and the World Bank were two new organizations, which emerged from the Bretton Woods conference.

There occurred in succession many crises in the exchange rate. At a meeting held in 1971 at the Smithsonian Institution in Washington, D.C between the finance ministers of the leading countries of the world, the Bretton Woods system was officially dissolved. The dollar was devalued. The major industrial countries of the world adopted the flexible exchange rate in 1973. Thus as of today there are many exchange rate arrangements; while some countries operate under the flexible exchange rates, others operate under the floating exchange rates and there are some for whom the exchange rate systems lie somewhere in between.

RECAP

- The nominal exchange rate signifies the relative price of one currency vis à vis the currency of another country where as the real exchange rate takes into consideration the relative purchasing power of the currency as well.
- As of today there are many exchange rate arrangements; while some countries operate under the flexible exchange rates, others operate under the floating exchange rates and there are some for whom the exchange rate systems lie somewhere in between.

EXCHANGE RATE DETERMINATION

How the exchange rate is determined will depend on whether the exchange rate system is a flexible or a fixed exchange rate system.

Determination of Exchange Rate in a Flexible or Floating Exchange Rate System

As already mentioned, the exchange rate is the price of one currency in terms of another currency. In a flexible exchange rate system, the exchange rate is determined by the market forces of the demand and supply of foreign exchange. Here we will consider two countries, say India, as the home country and United States, as the foreign country and two currencies, rupee and the dollar.

Demand for Foreign Exchange

Foreign exchange is demanded by the citizens of a country to make payments outside the country. From the point of view of a country, say India, the demand for foreign exchange (say, dollar) arises to make payments for the following items:

(1) Imports of commodities.
(2) Imports of services, including banking, insurance shipping and tourism.
(3) Interest, royalties, payment for technical services and dividend payments on securities in India owned by the foreigners.
(4) Expenditures by the government abroad.
(5) Remittances by NRIs of capital out of India from realized capital gains.
(6) Exports of short-term capital.
(7) Exports of long-term capital.
(8) Unrequited payments including gifts to foreigners.
(9) Gold imports.
(10) Payment to foreign universities for education.

In all these items, perhaps the most important item is the imports of commodities since India, like any other developing country, imports commodities like petroleum and machinery which require huge amounts of foreign exchange. In the context of this analysis, as far as India is concerned the demand for foreign exchange is the demand for dollars.

Figure 22.1 depicts the derivation of the demand curve for foreign exchange. Suppose

(1) Initially the foreign exchange rate as determined at $1 = Rs. 50 (by autonomous factors). Suppose the price of a basket of goods imported from the United States is $5(or Rs. 250) per unit. Thus to import 100 units of the good, India's demand for dollars will be $500 or in other words Rs. 25,000.
(2) that the value of the rupee depreciates in terms of dollars to $1 = Rs. 60. Since the price of the basket of goods imported from the United States is in terms of dollars (which is not affected), it will remain at $5 (or Rs. 300) per unit. Thus to import 100 units of the good, India's demand for dollars will also remain unchanged at $500. But in terms of rupees, India will now have to spend Rs. 30,000 on its imports from the United States.

The net effect of the depreciation of the rupee will be an increase in the price of imports and, hence, a decrease in the demand for imports from the United States by India. Hence, there will be a decrease in demand for dollars by India.

In Figure 22.1, an increase in the price of the dollar (or depreciation of the rupee) from $1 = Rs 50 to $1 = Rs. 60 leads to a decrease in the demand for foreign exchange from OF to OF′. Hence, an increase in the exchange rate leads to a decrease in demand for the imports from the US leading to a decrease in demand for the foreign exchange (or dollars). It is obvious from this analysis that the demand curve for foreign exchange (or dollars) will be a downward sloping curve as in Figure 22.1.

The shape and slope of the demand curve for foreign exchange depends on certain factors, which are as follows:

(1) The extent of the decrease in the demand for foreign exchange, in response to an increase in the foreign exchange rate, will depend on elasticity of demand for the imported goods. This is because the demand for foreign currency is a derived demand in that it is derived from the demand for the foreign goods and services. For a given depreciation of the rupee,
    (a) if the elasticity of demand for the US goods is large then the decrease in demand for the US imports and thus for the dollar will be high. This is the case especially for luxuries and goods for which there exist substitutes.
    (b) if the elasticity of demand for the US goods is small then the decrease in demand for the US imports and thus for the dollar will be low. This is the case especially for necessities and raw materials.

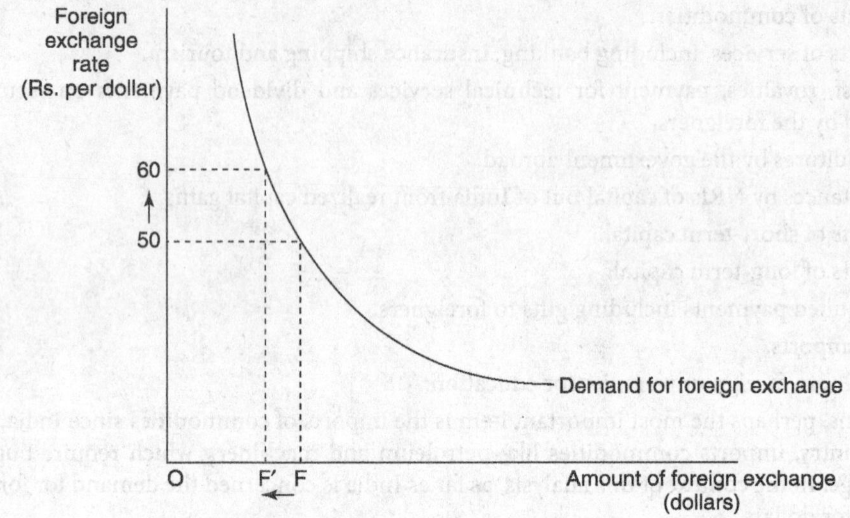

Figure 22.1 Demand for Foreign Exchange

(2) The existence of import competing industries in the country: If the import competing industries in the country are well developed, then the elasticity of demand for imports will be high. This is because any increase in the price of imports (due to the depreciation of the domestic currency) will be accompanied by an increase in the share of the import competing industries and decrease in the share of the imports.

(3) Time is also an important factor here because:

(a) In the short run, a reallocation of factors of production in response to a price change may be a difficult task. Hence, the elasticity of demand for imports may be low.

(b) In the long run, it is possible to reallocate factors of production in response to a price change, and thus change the production pattern accordingly. Hence, the elasticity of demand for imports may be high.

Supply of Foreign Exchange

The supply of foreign exchange to a country arises from the payments made by the foreigners to the residents of the country within a specified time period. From the view point of a country, say India, the supply of foreign exchange (the dollar) arises from payments made for the following items:

(1) Exports of commodities.
(2) Exports of services including banking, insurance, shipping and tourism.
(3) Interest and dividend payments on securities in the US owned by the Indians.
(4) Imports of short-term capital.
(5) Imports of long-term capital including foreign loans to India.
(6) Unrequited receipts including gifts from foreigners.
(7) Gold exports.

As far as India is concerned, the supply of foreign exchange is the supply of dollars.

Figure 22.2 depicts the derivation of the supply curve of foreign exchange. Suppose,

(1) Initially the foreign exchange rate as determined at $1 = Rs. 50 (by autonomous factors). Suppose the price of a composite of goods exported by India to the US is at Rs. 250 (or $5) per unit. Thus, if India exports 100 units of the composite good the supply of foreign exchange to India will be

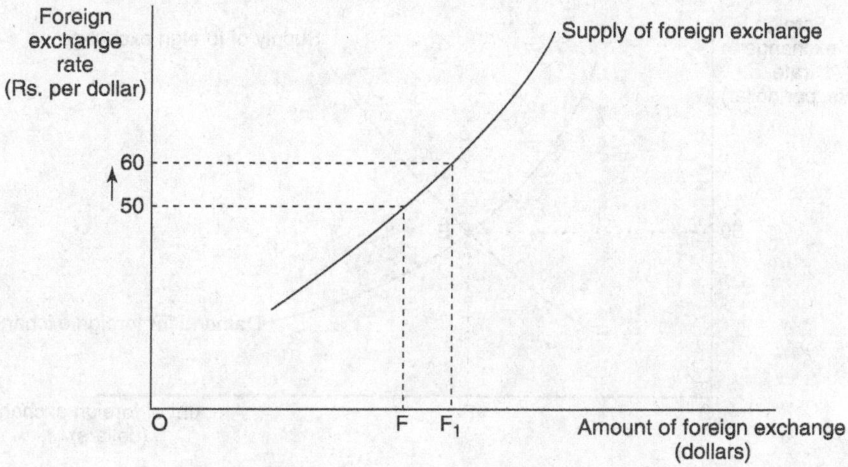

Figure 22.2 Supply of Foreign Exchange

$500 (25000/50). Since the price of the composite of goods imported from the US is in terms of dollars (which is not affected), it will remain at $5(or Rs. 300) per unit.

(2) that the value of the rupee depreciates in terms of dollars to $1 = Rs. 60. Since the price of the composite of goods exported by India to the US is in terms of rupees, it will remain at Rs. 250 (or $4.17) per unit. Thus, if India exports 100 units of the composite good the supply of foreign exchange to India will now be $416.7 (25000/60).

The net effect of the depreciation of the rupee will be a decrease in the price of the exports and hence an increase in the demand for exports to the US from India. Hence, there will be an increase in supply of dollars to India.

In Figure 22.2, an increase in the price of the dollar (or depreciation of the rupee) from $1 = Rs. 50 to 1$ = Rs 60 leads to an increase in the supply of foreign exchange from OF to OF_1. Hence, an increase in the exchange rate leads to an increase in demand for the exports from India to the US leading to an increase in supply of foreign exchange (or dollars). It is obvious from this analysis that the supply curve of foreign exchange (or dollars) will be an upward sloping curve as shown in Figure 22.2.

The shape and slope of the supply curve of foreign exchange will depend on the elasticity of demand for India's exports to the US. The supply of foreign currency is a derived demand in that it is derived from the demand for the exported goods and services. (India's exports to the US).

For a given depreciation of the rupee,

(1) If the elasticity of demand for India's exports to the US is greater than unity, then the supply of foreign exchange to India (or dollar) will increase. Hence, the supply curve for foreign exchange is upward sloping as shown in Figure 22.2.

(2) If the elasticity of demand for India's exports to the US is smaller than unity, then the supply of foreign exchange to India (or dollar) will decrease. Hence, the supply curve for foreign exchange will be downward sloping.

Exchange Rate: Equilibrium

The equilibrium rate of exchange is determined at the point at which the demand for foreign exchange equals the supply of foreign exchange. Thus, it is determined by the unregulated forces of the market demand and market supply. Graphically, it is determined at the point of intersection of the demand and the supply curves of foreign exchange.

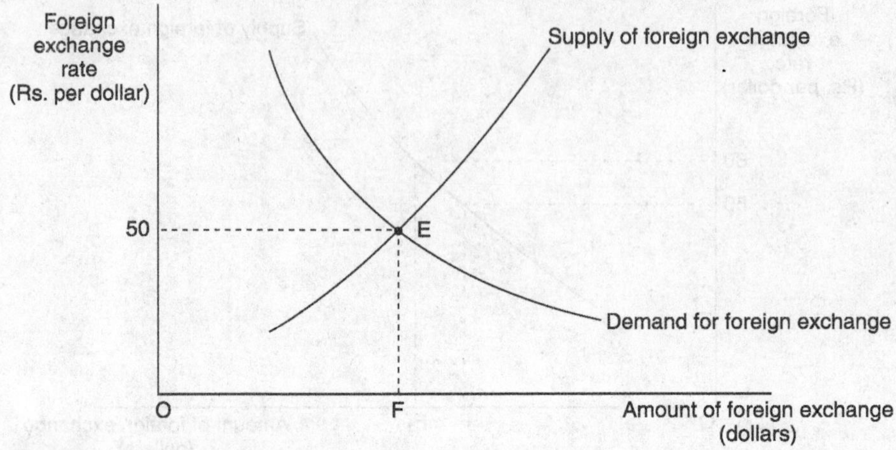

Figure 22.3 Determination of the Equilibrium Exchange Rate under a Flexible Exchange Rate System

In Figure 22.3, the demand curve for foreign exchange (demand for dollars) and the supply curve of foreign exchange (supply of dollars) intersect at point E. The equilibrium exchange rate is thus at $1 = Rs 50 with the equilibrium amount of foreign exchange at OF.

In such an exchange rate system, the government intervenes as and when required to make sure that the movements in the exchange rate are in order.

Exchange Rate: Disequilibrium

Figure 22.4 depicts the effect of a change in demand on the equilibrium rate of exchange. In the figure,

(1) Initially the demand curve for foreign exchange (demand for dollars) is given by the curve DD whereas the supply curve of foreign exchange (supply of dollars) is given by the curve SS.

The curves DD and SS intersect to determine equilibrium at point E. The equilibrium exchange rate is $1 = Rs 50 with the equilibrium amount of foreign exchange at OF.

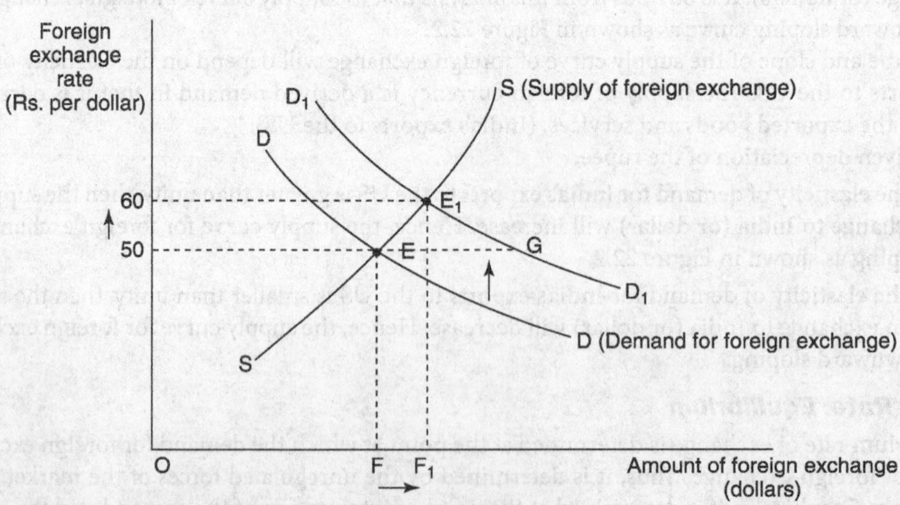

Figure 22.4 An Effect of a Change in Demand on the Equilibrium Exchange Rate

(2) Suppose the demand curve for foreign exchange shifts outwards to D_1D_1 due to perhaps a change in tastes in India in favour of US goods. The supply curve of foreign exchange (supply of dollars) remains at SS.

At the given exchange rate, there occurs an excess demand for foreign exchange (or dollars) equal to EG. The foreign exchange market will clear only if there is an increase in the exchange rate to $1 = Rs 60. Hence, the new equilibrium occurs at point E_1 where the curves D_1D_1 and SS intersect. The increase in the exchange rate (depreciation of the rupee), on the one hand, causes a decrease in the demand for India's imports and thus in the demand for dollars and on the other hand, an increase in the demand for India's exports and thus in the supply of dollars. At the new equilibrium exchange rate of $1 = Rs 60, the equilibrium amount of foreign exchange is at OF_1. Thus, an increase in the demand for imports leads to a depreciation of the domestic currency.

In a flexible exchange rate system, the exchange rate varies with changes in the demand and supply of foreign exchange. But there is always an equilibrium exchange rate at which the demand for foreign exchange equals the supply of foreign exchange creating an external equilibrium.

Fluctuations in the Exchange Rate

There are many factors that can lead to the change in the rate of exchange. One of the most important factors, which influence the exchange rate, is change in the demand and the supply of foreign exchange. However, the demand and the supply of foreign exchange are themselves dependent on the following factors:

(1) **Trade conditions prevailing in the country:** Whenever a country's exports are greater than its imports, the supply of foreign exchange is greater than the demand for foreign exchange leading to an increase in the value of the domestic currency in terms of the foreign currency. On the other hand, when a country's exports are smaller than its imports, the supply of foreign exchange is smaller than the demand for foreign exchange leading to a decrease in the value of the domestic currency in terms of the foreign currency.

(2) **Changes in the interest rate in the domestic country:** An increase in the interest rates attracts capital leading to an increase in the supply of foreign exchange. Given the demand for foreign exchange, this will lead to an increase in the value of the domestic currency in terms of the foreign currency. On the contrary, a decrease in the interest rates encourages the export of capital leading to a decrease in the supply of foreign exchange. Given the demand for foreign exchange, this will lead to a decrease in the value of the domestic currency in terms of the foreign currency.

(3) **Arbitrage operations:** As discussed earlier, an arbitrage involves the simultaneous buying and selling of different foreign currencies in the different foreign exchange markets. The purpose of this exercise is to take advantage of the difference in the prices in the two markets. These operations have a singular impact on the foreign exchange market and, in fact, help in ensuring that there exists no major variation in the exchange rates in different currency markets.

(4) **Stock exchange influences:** If the individuals of a country purchase stocks in another country, then there is an increase in demand for foreign currency. Given the supply of foreign currency, this will lead to a decrease in the value of the domestic currency in terms of the foreign currency. If on the other hand, foreigners purchase stocks in the country there is an increase in supply of foreign currency. Given the demand for foreign currency, this will lead to an increase in the value of the domestic currency in terms of the foreign currency. The fall in the value of rupee in the fiscal year 2008–09, thus, could partly be explained by the flight of foreign capital away from the Indian stock markets, which in turn also sent the market indices spiralling down.

Determination of Exchange Rate in a Fixed Exchange Rate System

Many countries have a fixed exchange rate system. In contrast to the flexible exchange rate system where the demand and supply of foreign exchange determine the exchange rate, under a fixed exchange rate system the exchange rate is set by the government in consultation with the other concerned countries.

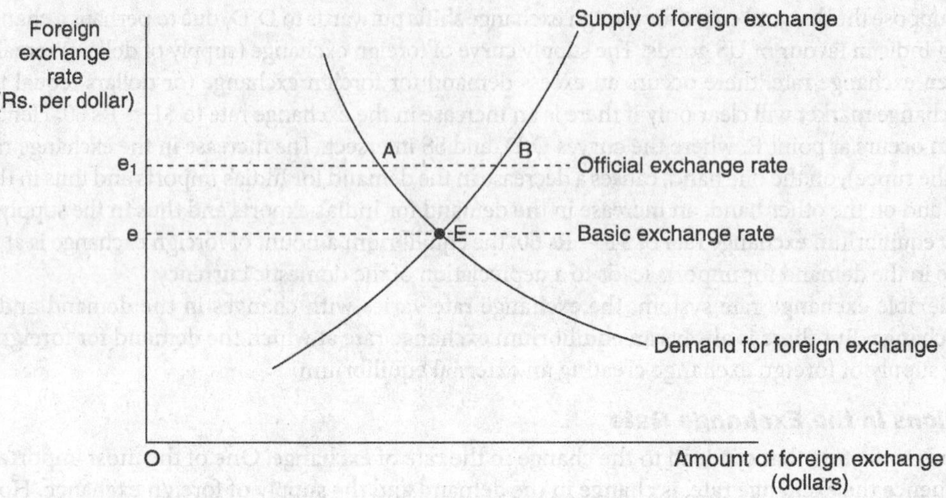

Figure 22.5 Determination of the Exchange Rate under a Fixed Exchange Rate System

It is not necessary that the exchange rate set by the government is one where the demand for foreign exchange is equal to the supply of foreign exchange. Figure 22.5 depicts the determination of the exchange rate under a fixed exchange rate system. The official exchange rate at e_1 is higher than the basic exchange rate determined by the demand and supply of foreign exchange at e_1. Thus, the exchange rate is overvalued.

The question arises as to what a country should do when its official exchange rate is higher than the basic exchange rate. It has several alternatives to choose from; they are as follows:

(1) Change the value of the official exchange rate so that it is equal to or nearer to the basic exchange rate. Thus, in Figure 22.5, the country can lower the exchange rate from e_1 to e.

(2) There can be a direct intervention on the part of the government to reduce imports through, say, taxation. Such a policy will decrease the demand for imports shifting the demand curve for foreign exchange raising the basic value of the exchange rate towards the fixed rate.

(3) The government of the country could supply or demand its currency in the foreign exchange market. For example, in Figure 22.5, at the official exchange rate the supply of foreign exchange is greater than the demand for foreign exchange by the amount AB. The government could in such a situation buy currency, using official reserve assets like gold.

It is important to note that when the exchange rate of a country is overvalued, then appropriate policy actions will have to be taken because an overvalued exchange rate cannot be sustained for long.

BOX 22.2

Often a group of countries come together to form a currency union, instead of fixing exchange rates. Under the currency union, the countries share a common currency and also agree to cooperate amongst themselves both economically and politically. They, thus, have a common currency which not only reduces the costs of trading but also prevents speculative attacks on the national currencies (which are eliminated in favour of a common currency). The major disadvantage of such a system is that the member countries have to share a common monetary policy and cannot use the monetary policy to pursue individual domestic goals. The euro was the common currency adopted by eleven countries in 1999.

RECAP

- Foreign exchange is demanded by the citizens of a country to make payments outside the country.
- The net effect of the depreciation of the rupee will be on the one hand an increase in the price of imports and hence a decrease in the demand for imports from the United States by India and, on the other hand, a decrease in the price of the exports and hence an increase in the demand for exports to the United States from India.
- The supply of foreign exchange to a country arises from the payments made for different items by the foreigners to the residents of the country within a specified time period.

FIXED VERSUS FLEXIBLE EXCHANGE RATE

Most major economies now follow the flexible exchange rate system. Even China, where the Yuan was historically pegged to the dollar, lifted the peg finally in the year 2005. The value of the Yuan is now a managed floating exchange rate based on market demand and supply with reference to a basket of international currencies.

It is now the appropriate time for us to evaluate the gains and losses connected with the two major exchange rate systems we have discussed.

Advantages and Disadvantages of the Fixed Exchange Rate System

Advantages of the Fixed Exchange Rate System

(1) It eliminates the uncertainties that are associated with international business transactions and, hence, creates a confidence in the foreign currency. A fixed exchange rate removes the uncertainties regarding the exchange rate.

(2) In comparison to the floating exchange rate system, the fixed exchange rate system is simpler to implement because the money supply adjusts itself automatically to the required level.

(3) It is often able to constrain the inflationary government policies and also acts as a safety device in controlling the import of inflation, which often accompanies a flexible exchange rate system. As a fixed exchange rate shields an economy from the occurrences in the other countries, it is able to prevent any import of inflation.

(4) It disciplines a country's monetary authority and, thus, improves the monetary policy preventing excessive growth in the money supply. Again, this may lead to a lower inflation rate in the long run.

(5) It facilitates the movements of capital between countries by providing a stability in the exchange rates and creating a confidence in the foreign currencies.

(6) It discourages speculative activity, which is an important feature associated with the flexible exchange rate.

It is important to observe that a fixed exchange rate can be maintained only between countries, which have similar basic economic conditions and similar types of macroeconomic policies.

Disadvantages of the Fixed Exchange Rate System

(1) It reduces a country's ability to apply its monetary policy to deal with recessions. This problem is more acute when the different countries under the fixed exchange rate system aim at different policy goals. In fact there may occur disagreements regarding the goals of monetary policy among the countries under the fixed exchange rate and may ultimately lead to a breakdown of the entire system.

(2) As is obvious from the experience of the gold standard and the Bretton Woods systems, a fixed exchange system is rigid and this has unfavourable effects on economies of the countries.

Advantages and Disadvantages of the Flexible Exchange Rate System

Advantages of the Flexible or Market Determined Exchange Rate System

(1) It enables countries to formulate their macroeconomic policies independent of the other countries. Hence, a country is not required to sacrifice full employment and other goals to achieve an external equilibrium.

(2) It allows monetary and the fiscal policies to attain goals such as employment, stabilizing prices, etc.

(3) It provides an automatic and smooth adjustment mechanism for correcting any disequilibrium in the balance of payments of a country concerned through the free market forces of demand and supply.

It seems that empirically the total amount of world trade has increased under the flexible exchange rate system.

Disadvantages of the Flexible Exchange Rate System

(1) It increases the uncertainty regarding the future exchange rates, thus, affecting adversely the volume of world trade.

(2) It may lead to speculation and may thus disturb the stability in the system.

(3) It not only imparts an inflationary bias to the system but is also not able to prevent any import of inflation, which often accompanies a flexible exchange rate system.

The exchange rate system that is ideal differs according to the circumstances. When a group of countries is able to avail huge benefits from an increased trade and is able to coordinate its monetary policies, a fixed exchange rate system is more suitable. However, countries which have their own policy goals relating to, for example, unemployment and inflation, should adopt a flexible exchange rate system.

RECAP

- A fixed exchange rate can be maintained only between countries, which have similar basic economic conditions and similar types of macroeconomic policies.
- It seems that empirically the total amount of world trade has increased under the flexible exchange rate system.
- Which exchange rate system is ideal differs according to the circumstances.

SUMMARY

INTRODUCTION

1. Today, all economies are open and dealing in transactions with the rest of the world.
2. Different countries have their own currencies that are generally (the exception being the Euro) legal tender only within the territories of the respective country. The rupee is acceptable within India where as the dollar is acceptable within the US economy.
3. The problem occurs when one country trades with another. This problem can be solved by fixing the rate of exchange between the different currencies. Here, we discuss the determination of the foreign exchange rate and also the fixed and the flexible exchange rates.

FOREIGN EXCHANGE MARKET

1. In a foreign exchange market, foreign currencies (or foreign exchange) are purchased and sold by individuals, firms, commercial banks and the central banks of the different countries.
2. Two types of foreign exchange transactions are spot transaction and forward transaction.

3. The foreign exchange market performs many functions which include international transfer of purchasing power between different countries, provision of credit for foreign trade and hedging risks of foreign exchange.
4. Hedging is an attempt at covering the risk involved in a foreign exchange transaction through a forward transaction.
5. Arbitrage is the simultaneous buying and selling of different foreign currencies in the different foreign exchange markets to take advantage of the difference in the prices.
6. Speculation is an activity relating to the sale and purchase of foreign exchange in which risk is undertaken to take advantage of the fluctuations in the exchange rate.

EXCHANGE RATE SYSTEMS

1. The exchange rate reflects the purchasing power of one country's currency in terms of the purchasing power of another country's currency.
2. The nominal exchange rate is the rate at which the currency of one country is traded for the currency of another country.
3. The real exchange rate is the rate at which the goods of one country are traded for the goods of another country.
4. Two nominal exchange rate systems are flexible or floating exchange rate and fixed exchange rate.
5. Flexible or floating exchange rate is a system where the exchange rate fluctuates freely in response to the changes in the economic conditions and without any government intervention. Hence, the exchange rate is determined by the market forces.
6. Fixed exchange rate is a system where the exchange rate does not fluctuate in response to the changes in the economic conditions.

EXCHANGE RATE DETERMINATION

1. How the exchange rate is determined will depend on whether the exchange rates system is a flexible or a fixed exchange rate system.
2. In a flexible exchange rate system, the equilibrium rate of exchange is determined at the point at which the demand for foreign exchange equals the supply of foreign exchange.
3. Foreign exchange is demanded by the citizens of a country to make payments outside the country.
4. The net effect of the depreciation of the rupee will be an increase in the price of imports and, hence, a decrease in the demand for imports from the United States by India.
5. The supply of foreign exchange is a derived demand in that it is derived from the demand for the exported goods and services.
6. The net effect of the depreciation of the rupee will be a decrease in the price of the exports and, hence, an increase in the demand for exports to the United States from India.
7. Under a fixed exchange rate, the exchange rate is set by the government in consultation with the other concerned countries.

FIXED VERSUS FLEXIBLE EXCHANGE RATE

1. There are gains and losses associated with both the major exchange rate systems, fixed and flexible exchange rate.
2. Advantages of the fixed exchange rate system are that it eliminates the uncertainties that are associated with international business transactions, is simpler to implement, and is often able to constrain the inflationary government policies.
3. Disadvantages of the fixed exchange rate system are that it reduces a country's ability to apply its monetary policy to deal with recessions and it is rigid.
4. Advantages of the flexible or market determined exchange rate system are: it enables countries to formulate their macroeconomic policies independently of the other countries, it allows monetary and the fiscal policies to attain goals such as employment and stabilizing prices and it provides an automatic and smooth adjustment mechanism for correcting any disequilibrium in the balance of payments.
5. Disadvantages of the flexible exchange rate system are: it increases the uncertainty regarding the future exchange rates. It may lead to speculation and also prevent any import of inflation.
6. When some countries are able to avail huge benefits from an increased trade and are able to coordinate their monetary policies, a fixed exchange rate system is more suitable. However, countries which have their own policy goals relating to, for example, unemployment and inflation, should adopt a flexible exchange rate system.

REVIEW QUESTIONS

TRUE OR FALSE QUESTIONS

1. A forward transaction is one where the seller of the foreign exchange has to deliver the exchange to the buyer on the spot, that is, within two days of the deal.
2. The foreign exchange market is a market where foreign currencies are purchased and sold.
3. Currency board is an arrangement where a country abandons its domestic currency and adopts a strong foreign currency like the dollar.
4. The exchange rate is the rate at which one country's currency exchanges for another country's currency.
5. The real exchange rate is the rate at which the currency of one country is traded for the currency of another country.

VERY SHORT-ANSWER QUESTIONS

1. What is a foreign exchange market?
2. What do you mean by an arbitrage? Explain.
3. How does speculation occur in the foreign exchange market? What is a speculative attack?
4. What type of an arrangement is the currency board?
5. 'The exchange rate reflects the purchasing power of one country's currency in terms of the purchasing power of another country's currency.' Explain.

SHORT-ANSWER QUESTIONS

1. What are the two types of foreign exchange transactions? Discuss.
2. What is hedging? Explain.
3. (a) What is the exchange rate? Differentiate between the nominal and real exchange rates.
   (b) Which are the two nominal exchange rate systems? Explain.
4. What are the factors that determine the shape and slope of the demand curve for foreign exchange in a flexible exchange rate system?
5. What are the factors that lead to fluctuations in the exchange rate under a flexible exchange rate system? Explain.

LONG-ANSWER QUESTIONS

1. What are the functions performed by the foreign exchange market? Discuss.
2. Which are the two nominal exchange rate systems? Analyse with the help of a brief history of the exchange rate systems adopted by the different countries.
3. Explain the determination of the demand for foreign exchange in a flexible or floating exchange rate system.
4. Analyse the determination of the supply of foreign exchange in a flexible or floating exchange rate system.
5. Discuss the relative advantages and disadvantages of the fixed and flexible exchange rate systems.

ANSWERS

TRUE OR FALSE QUESTIONS

1. **False.** A spot transaction is one where the seller of the foreign exchange has to deliver the exchange to the buyer on the spot, that is, within two days of the deal.
2. **True.** The foreign exchange market is a market where foreign currencies (or foreign exchange) are purchased and sold by individuals, firms, commercial banks and the central banks of the different countries.
3. **False.** Dollarization is a step further than the currency board where a country abandons its domestic currency and adopts a strong foreign currency like the dollar. Thus, the domestic currency is converted into the US dollar.
4. **True.** The exchange rate reflects the purchasing power of one country's currency in terms of the purchasing power of another country's currency.
5. **False.** The nominal exchange rate is the rate at which the currency of one country is traded for the currency of another country.

Balance of Payments

23

After studying this topic, you should be able to understand

- ✓ *The balance of payment is a statement which summarizes the exports and imports and the other international transactions between the countries.*
- ✓ *The transactions entering into the balance of payments can be grouped under three broad accounts: current account, capital account and official international reserve account.*
- ✓ *The current account of the balance of payments measures the flow of goods, services and income which occur across the national borders. The capital account of the balance of payments measures the outflow and inflow of capital into the economy.*
- ✓ *The balance of payments of a country will always balance because of the double entry system of book keeping.*
- ✓ *Autonomous transactions are transactions that take place for the satisfaction that they give or for the profit that they yield.*
- ✓ *Accommodating transactions take place for balancing a deficit or surplus in the foreign account.*
- ✓ *The macroeconomic policies are utilized for correcting disequilibrium in the balance of payments which include expenditure reducing policies and expenditure switching policies.*
- ✓ *Expenditure reducing policies can be divided under two broad groups: monetary and fiscal policy.*
- ✓ *Expenditure switching policies work mainly through changing the relative price of exports and imports.*
- ✓ *Once the global crisis deepened, it spread to most of the countries including India through the capital and current account of the balance of payments.*

INTRODUCTION

In Chapter 7, we had developed the model for a closed economy and in Chapter 8 to the model of an open economy. However, the discussion was limited to only the economy's exports and imports of goods and services and the affect of a change in the net exports on the aggregate demand and the equilibrium level of income and output. However, there is much more to the international economic relationships than just simple exports and imports of goods and services. Transfer payments between the individuals of the different countries and also the governments are of extreme importance. Capital flows between countries is again important.

The balance of payment is a statement which summarizes the exports and imports and the other international transactions between the countries. This chapter analyses the different aspects of the balance of payments.

MEANING AND STRUCTURE OF BALANCE OF PAYMENTS

The balance of payments is a summary statement of all the economic transactions between the residents of one country with the rest of the world during a particular period of time, which is usually a year.

The balance of payments is a summary statement of all the economic transactions between the residents of one country with the rest of the world during a particular period of time, which is usually a year.

In the balance of payments accounting, any transaction that involves a payment by the residents of a country will be shown as a debit item while any transaction that involves a receipt by the residents of a country will be shown as a credit item in the balance of payments of that country.

The transactions entering into the balance of payments can be grouped under three broad accounts:

(1) Current account

(2) Capital account

(3) Official international reserve account

Current Account

The current account of the balance of payments measures the flow of goods, services and income which occur across the national borders.

The current account of the balance of payments measures the flow of goods, services and income which occur across the national borders. The current account of the balance of payments includes the following items:

The balance of trade is the difference between the exports and imports of goods.

(1) **Balance of trade** which includes the export and import of goods (or merchandise). It is also called the balance of visible trade. The balance of trade is the difference between the exports and imports of goods. While exports of goods are entered as a positive entry or credit claims in the balance of payments, imports of goods are entered as a negative entry or debits in the balance of payments.

The balance of trade is one of the most important components of the balance of payments. It is not necessary for the balance of trade to be always in balance. If in a country:

(a) Exports are greater than the imports, there is a *trade surplus*. Hence, the country has a favourable balance of trade.

(b) Exports are smaller than the imports, there is a *trade deficit*. Hence, the country has an unfavourable balance of trade.

The balance of invisible trade is the difference between the exports and imports of services.

(2) **Balance of invisible** trade which includes the export and import of services. The balance of invisible trade is the difference between the exports and imports of services. The services include the following:

(a) Travel, for example, expenditure by foreign tourists in India on hotels will be a credit entry in India's balance of payments.

(b) Insurance, banking, shipping and freight services, and others, provided, for example, by Indian firms to foreigners will again be a credit entry in India's balance of payments.

(c) Expenditure abroad by the government agencies (in India) will be a debit entry in India's balance of payments.

(d) Interest and dividend on foreign investment earned by domestic entities will be a credit entry in India's balance of payments.

While the exports of services are entered as a positive entry or credit claims in the balance of payments, imports of services are entered as a negative entry or debits in the balance of payments.

Unilateral transfers (also called unrequited transfers) are one way transactions since there is no claim involved as far as repayment is concerned, either at present or in future.

(3) **Unilateral transfers** These are also called unrequited transfers since they are one way transactions as there is no claim involved as far as repayment is concerned, either at present or in the future. Unilateral transfers include gifts, personal remittances, indemnities and others. Unilateral transfers appearing on the:

(a) Credit side of the balance of payments include personal remittances of the emigrants to relatives in the country and gifts and grants which are received by the country from the individuals, institutions and governments of the foreign countries.

(b) Debit side of the balance of payments includes payments made by the country to the other countries in the form of personal remittances, gifts and grants.

The balance of current account or the current account balance includes the balance of trade, the balance of invisible trade and the balance of unrequited transfers or unilateral transfers. It represents the country's current receipts from abroad and unilateral receipts on the credit side and country's current international expenditures abroad and unilateral payments on the debit side. It has a flow dimension.

It is important to understand that

(1) If the sum of receipts (or credits) is greater than the sum of payments (or debits), then there will be a current account surplus. It implies that there is a net inflow of income into the country.

(2) If the sum of receipts (or credits) is smaller than the sum of payments (or debits), then there will be a current account deficit. It implies that there is a net outflow of income from the country. It not only leads to a loss of income from the country but also involves a problem in making payments.

The transactions in the current account have an effect on the national income and, thus, the income and output levels in the economy.

Capital Account

The capital account of the balance of payments measures the outflow and inflow of capital into the economy.

The capital account of the balance of payments measures the outflow and inflow of capital into the economy. The outflow of capital occurs due to the purchase of foreign assets by the households and firms in the domestic country. The inflow of capital occurs due to the purchase of assets in the domestic country by the households and firms of the foreign countries. The capital account has a stock dimension.

The capital account of the balance of payments includes the following capital transactions:

(1) **Long-term movements of capital:** This includes:

(a) Portfolio investment which refers to the purchase of long term securities by foreigners from the residents of the domestic country. The holding/maturity period is normally greater than a year. This involves the acquiring of an asset which does not give any control to the investor, for example purchase of the shares of a company in the country by a foreigner.

(b) Direct investment which refers to the private direct foreign investment in shares, bonds, plant and machinery in the country. In direct investment, the investor has a controlling power.

(2) **Short-term movements of capital:** This includes:

(a) Purchase of short-term government and corporate securities (with a maturity period of one year or less than one year); for example, commercial bills and treasury bills.

(b) Holdings of cash balances by foreigners due to, for example, political uncertainty.

(c) Purchase of foreign currency for speculation.

(3) **Loan repayments:** This includes:

(a) Loans by the international financial institutions to the government of a country.

(b) Loans received by the government of the country from the government of another country.

(c) Receipts of funds in the repayments of loans, for example, to loans extended to business firms and governments in the foreign countries.

All these involve an inflow of capital and are, thus, entered as a positive entry or credit claims in the balance of payments. Similarly, an outflow of capital is entered as a negative entry or debits in the balance of payments.

Table 23.1 Balance of Payments

Current Account	Capital Account	The Official International Reserve Accounts
1. Balance of Trade	**1. Long-term movements of capital**	(a) Foreign currencies
(a) Export and import of goods	(a) Portfolio investment	(b) Gold: Monetary and Non-monetary gold
(b) Non-monetary gold (according to which gold is a commodity and all exports and imports of gold are treated like any other commodity.)	(b) Direct investment	(c) Special Depository Receipts (SDRs)
2. Balance of Invisible Trade (includes exports and imports of services)	**2. Short-term movements of capital**	
(a) Travel	(a) Purchase of short-term government and corporate securities.	
(b) Insurance, banking, shipping and freight services, and others.	(b) Holdings of cash balances by foreigners.	
(c) Expenditure abroad by government agencies.	(c) Purchase of foreign currency for speculation.	
(d) Interest and dividend income.		
(e) Miscellaneous		
3. Unilateral Transfers	**3. Repayment of Loans**	
(a) Personal remittances	(a) Loans by the international financial institutions.	
(b) Transfers from the government	(b) Loans received by the government.	
	(c) Receipts of funds in the repayments of loans.	

Errors and Omissions: In the balance of payments accounts of any country, usually an item called errors and omissions is included to balance the balance of payments.

The transactions in the capital account influence the position of the economy as an international creditor or debtor.

The Official International Reserve Account

The official reserves of a country include:

(1) **Foreign currencies:** Most countries prefer to hold their foreign exchange reserves in dollars which is the most widely accepted and important currency in the world today.

(2) **Gold:** As far as gold is concerned, it can be divided into two categories:

   (a) Monetary gold, where the movements occur when gold is used as a means of payment. Hence, all monetary gold movements are included under the official reserves.

   (b) Non-monetary gold according to which gold is a commodity. Hence, all exports and imports of gold are treated like any other commodity in the balance of payments.

(3) **Special depository receipts:** (SDRs): When a country becomes a member of the IMF, it has to deposit a subscription of which 25 per cent is in the form of gold or even SDRs while the rest is in the form of the country's own currency. Depending on its subscription a country can draw other convertible currencies from the IMF, and this enters as a positive entry or credit claims in the balance of payments.

The foreign exchange reserves are maintained not only to make payments in case of deficits in the balance of payments but also to stabilize the foreign exchange rate.

The transactions in the international reserve account determine the foreign exchange reserves which are available for settling a deficit in the current or capital account of the country.

The different components of the balance of payments can be shown as in Table 23.1.

RECAP

- The current account of the balance of payments includes the following items: balance of trade, balance of invisible trade and unilateral transfers.
- The balance of trade is one of the most important components of the balance of payments.
- The transactions in the current account have an effect on the national income and, thus, the income and output levels in the economy.
- The transactions in the capital account influence the position of the economy as an international creditor or debtor.
- The transactions in the international reserve account determine the foreign exchange reserves which are available for settling a deficit in the current or capital account of the country.

DOUBLE ENTRY BOOKKEEPING

It is important to note that the balance of payments of a country will always balance and, thus, will always be in equilibrium. This is based on the double entry system of bookkeeping where each transaction is recorded twice, as a debit entry and as a credit entry.

Table 23.2 depicts a hypothetical example of the balance of payments of a country. The left side of the table shows the ways in which a country can acquire foreign currency while the right side of the table shows the ways in which the country spends the foreign currency.

Balance of trade: In Table 23.2, Row 1 indicates that the country earns Rs. 500 crores as foreign exchange by exporting goods. Similarly, Row 6 indicates that the country spends Rs. 600 crores of the foreign exchange by importing goods. These two rows depict the balance of trade equal to −100 crores as Row (a) in Table 23.3. This implies that there is an adverse balance of trade.

Balance of services: In Table 23.2, Row 2 indicates that the country earns Rs. 250 crores as foreign exchange by exporting services. Similarly, Row 7 indicates that the country spends Rs. 50 crores of the foreign

Table 23.2 Balance of Payments of a Country

Row No.	Receipts (credit)	Amount (Rs. crore)	Row No.	Payments (debit)	Amount (Rs. crore)
1.	Exports of goods	500	1.	Imports of goods	600
2.	Exports of services	250	2.	Imports of services	50
3.	Unilateral receipts	50	3.	Unilateral payments	80
4.	Capital receipts	100	4.	Capital payments	120
5.	Sale of gold	100	5.	Purchase of gold	150
	Total receipts	1,000		**Total payments**	1,000

exchange by importing services. These two rows depict the balance of invisible trade equal to 200 crores as Row (b) in Table 23.3. This implies that there is a favourable balance of services or invisible trade.

Balance of unilateral transfers: In Table 23.2, Row 3 indicates that the country earns Rs. 50 crores as foreign exchange from unilateral receipts. Similarly, Row8 indicates that the country spends Rs. 80 crores of the foreign exchange on unilateral payments. These two rows depict the balance of unilateral transfers or unrequited receipts equal to −30 crores as Row (c) in Table 23.3. This implies that there is an unfavorable balance of unilateral transfers.

Balance of current account: In Table 23.2, the balance of current account includes Rows 1, 2, 3 and 6, 7 and 8. In Table 23.3, the balance of current account includes Rows (a), (b) and (c) to depict a surplus on the current account equal to Rs. 70 crores as in Row (d).

Balance of capital account: In Table 23.2, Row4 indicates that the country earns Rs. 100 crores as foreign exchange from capital receipts. Similarly, Row 9 indicates that the country spends Rs. 120 crores of the foreign exchange on capital payments. These two rows depict a deficit in capital account. Table 23.3 shows a balance of capital account equal to Rs.−20 crores as Row (e).

Balance of official reserve account: In Table 23.2, Row5 indicates that the country earns Rs. 100 crores as foreign exchange from the sale of gold. Similarly, Row 10 indicates that the country spends Rs. 150 crores of the foreign exchange on purchase of gold. These two rows depict the balance of official reserve account equal to Rs.−50 crores as Row (f) in Table 23.3.

Balance of payments: In Table 23.3, the balance of payments includes Rows (d), (e) and (f) to depict a balance in the balance of payments in an accounting sense. The balance of current account equals Rs. 70 crores while the balance of capital account depicts a deficit equal to Rs. −20 crores. The official reserve account provides the balancing factor through a net purchase of gold equal to Rs. 50 crores.

RECAP

- The official reserve account provides the balancing factor in the balance of payments.

A DISEQUILIBRIUM IN THE BALANCE OF PAYMENTS

As we have already observed, the balance of payment always balances as it is prepared on the basis of the double entry system of bookkeeping. This leads us to the very important issue of how a surplus or a deficit occurs in the balance of payments, or in other words how disequilibrium occurs in the balance of payments. To understand this very crucial aspect of the balance of payments, we first examine autonomous and accommodating transactions.

Autonomous and Accommodating Transactions

One can distinguish between two types of transactions, autonomous and accommodating transactions.

Table 23.3 The External Balances in the Balance of Payments

1.	Balance of trade (Rows 1 and 6 of Table 23.2)	500 − 600 = − 100
2.	Balance of services (Rows 2 and 7 of Table 23.2)	250 − 50 = 200
3.	Balance of unilateral transfers (Rows 3 and 8 of Table 23.2)	50 − 80 = − 30
4.	Balance of current account (Rows (a), (b) and (c) of Table 23.3)	−100 + 200 − 30 = 70
5.	Balance of capital account (Rows 4 and 9 of Table 23.2)	100 − 120 = −20
6.	Balance of official reserve account (Rows 5 and 10 of Table 23.2)	100 − 150 = − 50
7.	Balance of payments (Rows (d), (e) and (f) of Table 23.3)	1000 − 1000 − 0

Autonomous transactions are those transactions that take place independently of other items in the balance of payments. Thus, these transactions take place for the satisfaction that they give or for the profit that they yield. They take place in both the current and the capital accounts.

Autonomous transactions are those transactions that take place independently of other items in the balance of payments.

(1) **Current account:** Here, autonomous transactions include the exports and imports of goods and services. Unilateral transfers are also included under autonomous transactions though they are not commercial transactions (since they do not, in any way, bring about a balance in the balance of payments).

(2) **Capital account:** Here, autonomous transactions include the long-term movements of capital because they are commercial transactions for the explicit purpose of making profits.

Accommodating transactions are those transactions that take place for the specific purpose of equalizing the balance of payments from an accountant's point of view. They take place for balancing a deficit or surplus in the foreign account. They are not motivated by profit. They include short-term movements of capital, monetary gold movements and variations in the foreign exchange reserves.

Accommodating transactions are those transactions that take place for the specific purpose of equalizing the balance of payments from an accountant's point of view.

To determine whether the balance of payments is in equilibrium or disequilibrium, only the autonomous transactions are considered.

(1) If the total receipts from autonomous transactions are equal to the total payments from autonomous transactions, then there is equilibriumin the balance of payments.

(2) If the total receipts from autonomous transactions are not equal to the total payments from autonomous transactions, then there is disequilibrium in the balance of payments. The disequilibrium is in the form of a

(a) Surplus if the total receipts from autonomous transactions are larger than the total payments from autonomous transactions.

(b) Deficit if the total receipts from autonomous transactions are smaller than the total payments from autonomous transactions.

Any disequilibrium in the balance of payments is offset by the accommodating transactions which make up for any deficit or surplus. Hence, the sum of accommodating transactions and autonomous transactions will always be zero. Thus, theoretically speaking, from an accountant's point of view the balance of payment always balances, yet there will exist disequilibrium in the balance of payments from an economist's point of view.

RECAP

- To determine whether the balance of payments is in equilibrium or disequilibrium, only the autonomous transactions are considered.

KINDS OF DISEQUILIBRIA IN THE BALANCE OF PAYMENTS

One can differentiate between different kinds of disequilibrium on the basis of the source of the disequilibrium.

(1) **Structural Disequilibrium:** This occurs due to structural imbalances caused by the shifts in the international demand and/or the supply of the factors of production, goods or services. They persist for a long time and are difficult to eliminate. Some causes of structural disequilibrium are:

(a) **Change in production pattern:** Some countries may experience a change in its factor endowments over long periods of time. This happened in the case of Britain which had to face competition in its exports, especially of manufactured goods, from countries of West Europe and US. Hence, there occurred a structural imbalance in its balance of payments which Britain could not tackle even by changing its production pattern and shifting to new industries.

(b) **Loss of capital:** A country may experience a loss of capital. For example, during times of war there is widespread destruction including that of industries. Hence, on the one hand, a country has to rely on imports not only for goods but also for capital at least over a short period of time. On the other hand, its exports will experience a slow down. All this will lead to a structural disequilibrium in the country's balance of payments.

(c) **Resource deficiencies:** Many countries have to go through a shortage of resources which prevents them from achieving the level of growth which they desire to achieve. Hence, they have to face an increased dependence on imports which creates a problem in their balance of payments. For example, India has to rely heavily on imports of petroleum for its development, thus, putting a strain on India's balance of payments.

(d) **A change in the supply of long-term flows of capital:** Often a country which depends heavily on foreign capital may find a change in that it may stop coming perhaps because the investor may find other avenues of investment more attractive. This may have a serious affect on the production structure and, thus, on the balance of payments of the country.

(e) **Change in the demand pattern:** Countries which experience growth and change in the income distribution experience a shift in the demand from agricultural goods to manufactured goods. Hence, countries whose exports are primarily based on agricultural goods suffer a setback as the demand for their exports fails to keep up with the growing world demand for exports. They face difficulties in their balance of payments. They can tackle this problem through a change in their production pattern and also through a diversification of their exports.

(f) **Changes in the political, economic and social environment:** This again plays a crucial role in influencing the relations between countries and, hence, their exports and imports.

(2) **Cyclical Disequilibrium:** Business cycles are another major cause of disequilibrium in the balance of payments. Business cycles, which are global, affect almost all the countries though to differing degrees. A recession and inflation is accompanied by a trade surplus in some countries and a deficit in the others depending on the nature of their exports and imports and also on the elasticity of demand for their exports and imports. Countries with a high marginal propensity to import experience huge trade deficits during inflation and smaller deficits during recession times.

(3) **Exchange Rate Disequilibrium:** There often occurs an overvaluation or an undervaluation of a currency on the foreign scenario.

Overvaluation of a currency is said to occur when the official value of a currency is fixed at a higher rate than what would have been determined by the free market forces of demand and supply.

Overvaluation of a currency is said to occur when the official value of a currency is fixed at a higher rate than what would have been determined by the free market forces of demand and supply. The effects of overvaluation are similar to that of inflation. It has an adverse affect on exports and a favourable effect on imports, thus, producing a deficit in the balance of payments.

Undervaluation of a currency is said to occur when the official value of a currency is fixed at a lower rate than what would have been determined by the free market forces of demand and supply.

Undervaluation of a currency is said to occur when the official value of a currency is fixed at a lower rate than what would have been determined by the free market forces of demand and supply. The effects of undervaluation are opposite to that of overvaluation. It has an adverse affect on imports and a favourable effect on exports, thus, producing a surplus in the balance of payments.

Capital flows are also influenced by disequilibrium in the exchange rate. An undervaluation of the currency attracts foreign capital, thus, adding to the surplus in the balance of payments.

(4) **Monetary Disequilibrium:** Inflation and deflation are the accompaniments of a monetary disequilibrium. Inflation has a two-fold effect on trade. On the one hand, inflation makes imports relatively cheaper leading to an increase in the demand for imports.

On the other hand, inflation makes exports relatively costlier leading to a decrease in the demand for exports. Thus inflation leads to a deficit in the balance of payments, which will persist if the inflation continues to persist.

THE PROCESS OF ADJUSTMENT IN THE BALANCE OF PAYMENTS

Disequilibrium in the balance of payments is a cause for concern for every economy, more so if the disequilibrium is in the form of a deficit. We here analyse the macroeconomic policies that are utilized for adjustment in the balance of payments. Since deficit is more of a basis for concern, our analysis will focus on a deficit. They can be grouped under two heads:

(1) Expenditure reducing or Expenditure changing policies:
  (a) Monetary policy
  (b) Fiscal policy
(2) Expenditure switching policies:
  (a) Devaluation: The elasticity approach
  (b) Devaluation: The absorption approach

Expenditure Reducing or Expenditure Changing Policies

Expenditure reducing policies are aimed at bringing about a change in the aggregate expenditure in the country. To simplify our analysis, we exclude autonomous capital movements. Thus, the balance of payments can be written as

Expenditure reducing policies are aimed at bringing about a change in the aggregate expenditure in the country.

$$B = Y - E$$

where, B = balance of payments (net)

Y = domestic output

E = domestic expenditure

If in a country:

(1) $Y > E$: The domestic output is greater than the domestic expenditure and there will be a surplus in the country's balance of payments.
(2) $Y = E$: The domestic output is equal to the domestic expenditure and there will be balance of payments equilibrium.
(3) $Y < E$: The domestic output is smaller than the domestic expenditure and there will be a deficit in the country's balance of payments.

It is a deficit in the balance of payments that is of concern for the policy makers. The deficit can be eliminated in two ways: either by increasing the domestic output, Y or by reducing the domestic expenditure, E. However in the short run, it may be difficult to increase the output if there are structural constraints. Hence,most economies prefer to resort to expenditure reducing policies to reduce a balance of payments deficit.

Expenditure reducing policies can be divided under two broad groups: monetary and fiscal policy.

Monetary Policy

During the gold standard monetary policies were quite popular in correcting disequilibrium in the balance of payments. However, in the 1930s they were not successful in bringing about stabilization during the Depression and they lost popularity. It was only in the 1950s that interest and belief in the effectiveness of monetary policy was once again revived.

The instruments of monetary policy are discussed in depth in Chapter 25. Here, we will throw light only on some of these instruments.

To tackle a deficit in the balance of payments, a contractionary or tight monetary policy is followed. The instruments of monetary policy which are most effective and used often include:

(1) **Changes in interest rates**: The effect of an increase in the interest rates on the level of investment will depend on the general economic situation. Suppose there is a boom in the economy and,

  (a) If the producers expect prices and thus the interest rate to fall in the future, they will postpone all investments. Through the multiplier effect, this will lead to a decrease in the national income and thus a reduction in the imports which will, to some extent, reduce the deficit in the balance of payments.

  (b) If the producers expect prices and thus the interest rate to rise in the future, they will go ahead with all investments. Through the multiplier effect, this will lead to an increase in the national income and thus an increase in the imports which will increase, rather than decrease, the deficit in the balance of payments.

(2) **Open market operations:** Suppose the central bank sells bonds and securities in the open market. Commercial banks, insurance companies and others purchase it with liquid money. This will not only reduce the liquidity in the banking system but will also decrease the availability of credit. The interest rates will also increase. This will have an adverse effect on investment and the national income, leading to a fall in the imports.

Other instruments of monetary policy like changes in reserve requirements are also often applied to correct a deficit in the balance of payments.

Fiscal Policy

Fiscal policies can also be used to reduce expenditure. They can be divided into two groups:

(1) **Those that work on the income side of the government budget:** Here, the most important instrument is taxation. As far as taxes are concerned

  (a) an increase in direct taxes—for example, income tax—reduces the incomes of households leading to a decrease in consumption (and also in savings) and thus a decrease in imports.

  (b) an increase in indirect taxes—for example, sales tax—leads to a decrease in consumption and thus a decrease in imports.

(2) **Those that work on the expenditure side of the government budget:** As far as government expenditure is concerned,

  (a) a reduction in transfer payments will immediately decrease consumption since it is the low income group, with a high marginal propensity to consume, which is the main beneficiary of transfer payments.

  (b) a decrease in public consumption expenditure will lead to a fall in income and thus in imports.

  (c) a decrease in public investment expenditure will—similar to private investment—lead to a decrease in national income and imports.

Monetary and fiscal policies are the two most important ways of implementing an expenditure reducing policy. To eliminate a deficit in the balance of payments, a country can pursue a contractionary monetary policy or a restrictive fiscal policy. Both policies lead to the following:

(a) On the one hand, a deflationary impact on the national income leading to a decrease in imports.

(b) On the other hand, a positive effect on exports and the import competing industries.

Thus, an expenditure reducing policy affects exports favourably and imports adversely leading to a positive effect on the balance of payments.

BOX 23.1

In the 1980s the US dollar appreciated quite strongly, reached a peak in 1985 and then decreased for the next three years and then became stable at nearly the same rate as in the 1980s. The Keynesians explain these fluctuations in terms of the macroeconomic policies, which were a blend of expansionary fiscal policy and a tight monetary policy. The classical economists argue that the US dollar appreciated because of the increase in the desirability of the US assets as compared to the other foreign assets. However later when the foreign savers were satiated with the US assets, there occurred a decrease in the value of the dollar.

Expenditure Switching Policies: Devaluation–the Elasticity Approach

The expenditure switching policies work mainly through changing the relative price of exports and imports.

The expenditure switching policies work mainly through changing the relative price of exports and imports. This is achieved through a change in the exchange rates that is a revaluation or devaluation of the domestic currency. One can include direct controls, which includes commercial controls (like limiting the volume of imports), financial controls and exchange restrictions, also as a switching device.

In a flexible exchange rate system a country with a deficit in the balance of payments experiences depreciation, or in other words a lowering in the value of its currency with respect to other currencies. Similarly, a country with a surplus in the balance of payments experiences appreciation, or in other words a rise in the value of its currency with respect to other currencies.

Devaluation refers to a conscious action by the monetary authorities to lower the value of a currency with respect to the price of gold.

Under a stable exchange rate system in case of a deficit or a surplus in the balance of payments, the authorities have to take a conscious decision to bring about changes in the value of the currency with respect to the price of gold or to some primary asset. Devaluation refers to a conscious action by the monetary authorities to lower the value of a currency with respect to the price of gold.

Devaluation leads to a change in the relative prices. A devaluation of 10 per cent leads to

(1) an increase in the price of imports by 10 per cent in the home currency which will, on the one hand, discourage imports and, on the other hand, encourage the import competing industries which will be in a better position to compete.

(2) a decrease in the price of exports by 10 per cent in the foreign currency which will encourage exports.

Devaluation of a currency improves the balance of payments by encouraging exports and discouraging imports. The extent to which devaluation encourages exports and discourages imports depends on the elasticity of demand for its exports and imports.

The traditional approach to the effects of devaluation has been analysed in the Marshall Lerner condition in terms of elasticity. According to the Marshall Lerner condition, for a devaluation to have a positive effect on a country's balance of payments the sum of the absolute values of the elasticity of demand for its exports and imports should be greater than one. If the sum of the absolute values of the elasticity of demand for its exports and imports is less than one, then a country can improve its balance of payments through a revaluation.

The Marshall Lerner condition can be expressed as follows:

$$\Delta B = k\,X_f(e_{1m} + e_{2m} - 1) \quad (1)$$

where, ΔB = change in the trade balance

k = devaluation in percentage terms

X_f = value of exports in terms of foreign currency

e_{1m} = the elasticity of demand for imports of the devaluing country

e_{2m} = the elasticity of demand for exports (imports of the foreign country) of the devaluing country

A devaluation leads to a

(1) an increase in the price of imports: The larger is the elasticity of demand for imports, the greater will be the decrease in the volume of imports. The value of the elasticity of demand for imports will depend on the type of good that the country imports. In case a country imports goods like necessities and raw materials, the elasticity of demand for imports will be low and devaluation may not be effective in correcting a balance of payment deficit.

(2) a decrease in the price of exports: The larger is the elasticity of demand for exports of a country, the greater will be the increase in the volume of exports. The value of the elasticity of demand for exports will depend on the type of good that the country exports and also the conditions in the market. In case a country exports goods like necessities and raw materials, the elasticity of demand for exports will be low and devaluation may not be effective in correcting a balance of payment deficit. On the other hand, if a country exports industrial goods the elasticity of demand for exports will be high and devaluation will be very effective in correcting a balance of payment deficit.

The Marshall Lerner condition is based on some conditions which should be satisfied:

(1) The supply elasticities should be large: This may be true in times of a recession when there are unemployed resources. However, when there exists full employment an increase in the price of exports will fail to increase the supply of exports.

(2) When devaluation takes place the trade balance is in equilibrium, which again is not always possible.

Devaluation has some adverse effects on the economy. It has an inflationary impact which is, to some extent, limited if devaluation is pursued with a contractionary monetary and fiscal policy. It is also felt that devaluation leads to a redistribution of income from the labour class to the others.

In spite of all the restrictions and adverse effects, the Marshall Lerner condition holds in that the larger are the elasticities of demand for a country's exports and imports, the greater is the favourable effect of devaluation on the balance of payments.

Expenditure Switching Policies: Devaluation–the Absorption Approach

Sidney Alexander in 1952 presented an alternative approach, the absorption approach, to the effects of devaluation. The approach is in macro terms.

$$B = Y - A \tag{2}$$

where, B = balance of trade

Y = national income

A = total absorption or total expenditure or total demand.

Since total demand includes consumption and investment, for a two sector economy $A = C + I$.

Devaluation affects the balance of trade, B either by influencing the national income, Y or by influencing the total absorption, A. We have

$$\Delta B = \Delta Y - \Delta A \tag{3}$$

The effect of devaluation on absorption can be split into two parts:

(1) Direct effect on absorption which depends mainly on the real income at which the devaluation occurs, ΔD.

(2) Indirect effect on absorption which depends on the propensity to absorb, c out of real income, $c\Delta Y$.

$$\Delta A = \Delta D + c\Delta Y \tag{4}$$

where, ΔA = change in absorption

ΔD = direct effect on absorption

$c\Delta Y$ = indirect effect on absorption

Combining Eqs. (3) and (4), we get

$$\Delta B = \Delta Y - (\Delta D + c\Delta Y)$$

$$\Delta B = \Delta Y(1 - c) - \Delta D \tag{5}$$

It is obvious from the above equation that the effects of devaluation on the balance of trade depend on three factors. These three factors depend on how devaluation effects the

(1) national income, Y

(2) propensity to absorb, c

(3) direct absorption, D

The effects of devaluation will be different according to whether there is full employment in the economy or whether there exist unemployed resources.

When there is full employment in the economy, devaluation will not have any influence on the national income. However, it will affect the economy to some extent through its affect on absorption.

When there are unemployed resources in the economy, devaluation leads to an expansionary effect on exports and hence on income and absorption. If the increase in income is greater than the increase in absorption, then there will be an improvement in the trade balance.

Policy Mix and a Simultaneous External and Internal Balance

Trevor Swan had developed a diagrammatic analysis to explain the impact of expenditure changing and expenditure policies on the external and internal balance of a country, in what is called the **Swan diagram.**

Figure 23.1 depicts the impact of expenditure changing and expenditure policies on the external and internal balance of a country.

where x-axis = domestic absorption

y-axis = real exchange rate (amount of the domestic currency that is required to purchase one unit of the foreign currency)

Curve IB = combinations of the real exchange rate and domestic absorption at which there exists an internal balance.

Curve EB = combinations of the real exchange rate and domestic absorption at which there exists an external balance.

An increase in R, the real exchange rate (amount of the domestic currency that is required to purchase one unit of the foreign currency) implies a devaluation of the domestic currency. A decrease in R, the real exchange rate implies a revaluation of the domestic currency.

Curve IB is downward sloping with negative slope because a lower rate of exchange worsens the balance of trade and, thus, a higher domestic absorption is required for the economy to maintain an internal balance. Curve EB is upward sloping with a positive slope because a higher rate of exchange improves the balance of trade and, thus, a higher domestic absorption is required for the economy to maintain an external balance.

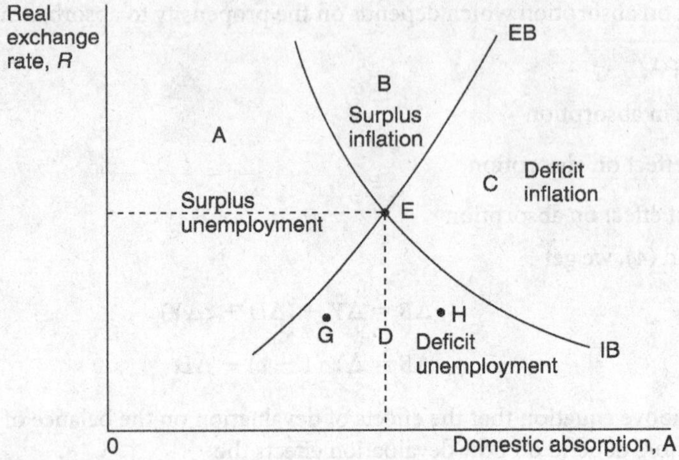

Figure 23.1 Policy Mix and a Simultaneous External and Internal Balance

In Figure 23.1,

(1) At all points to the right (and above) of the IB curve, there exists an inflationary situation while at all points to the left (and below) of the IB curve, there exists unemployment.

(2) At all points to the left (and above) of the EB curve, there exists a surplus in the balance of payments while at all points to the right (and below) of the EB curve there exists a deficit in the balance of payments.

In Figure 23.1, there are four quadrants:

Quadrant A: Unemployment and balance of payments surplus
Quadrant B: Inflation and balance of payments surplus
Quadrant C: Inflation and balance of payments deficit
Quadrant D: Unemployment and balance of payments deficit

At a point like G in Quadrant D where there exists unemployment and a deficit in the balance of payments, a movement to point E (where there exists a simultaneous external and internal balance) would require a devaluation of the currency on the one hand and an increase in domestic absorption (expansionary fiscal policy) on the other hand. Thus, a combination of two policies is usually required to achieve two goals.

At a point like H in Quadrant D where there again exists unemployment and a deficit in the balance of payments, a movement to point E would require a devaluation of the currency on the one hand and a decrease in domestic absorption (contractionary fiscal policy) on the other hand.

Thus, we have observed that in most cases a combination of both expenditure reducing and expenditure switching policies is required to achieve both external and internal balance in a country.

BOX 23.2

In the year 1991, there occurred the worst possible balance of payments crisis in India. The excess of domestic expenditure over income was responsible for a rapid increase in foreign borrowing. The double digit inflation and the increase in oil prices made the situation even worse. India's credit rating came down. The situation, however, improved later on when economic reforms were undertaken and the exchange rate was devalued.

RECAP

- Often economies prefer to resort to expenditure reducing policies to reduce a balance of payments deficit.
- The expenditure switching policies work through a change in the exchange rates, that is, a revaluation or devaluation of the domestic currency.
- The extent to which devaluation encourages exports and discourages imports depends on the elasticity of demand for its exports and imports.
- A combination of both expenditure reducing and expenditure switching policies is required to achieve both external and internal balance in a country.

Table 23.4 Balance of Payments

(US$ million)

Sl. No.	Items	2004–05	2005–06	2006–07	2007–08	2008–09	Apr–Sept. 2008	Apr–Sept. 2009
						PR	PR	P
1	Exports	85206	105152	128888	166162	189001	111085	81139
2	Imports	118908	157056	190670	257629	307651	175483	139356
3	Trade Balance	−33702	−51904	−61782	−91467	−118650	−64398	−58217
4	Invisibles (net)	31232	42002	52217	75731	89923	48549	39599
	Non-factor Services	15426	23170	29469	38853	49631	25110	15371
	Income	−4979	−5855	−7331	−5068	−4507	−1646	−2353
	Private Transfers	20525	24493	29825	41706	44567	25091	26695
5	Goods and Services Balance	−18276	−28734	−32313	−52614	−69019	−39288	−42846
6	Current Account Balance	−2470	−9902	−9565	−15737	−28728	−15849	−18618
7	External Assistance (net)	1923	1702	1775	2114	2637	869	571
8	External Commercial Borrowings (net)	5194	2508	16103	22609	7941	3166	745
9	Non-resident Deposits (net)	−964	2789	4321	179	4290	1072	2864
10	Foreign Investment (net) of which	13000	15528	14753	43326	3467	8349	32088
	(i) FDI (net)	3713	3034	7693	15893	17498	13867	14142
	(ii) Portfolio (net)	9287	12494	7060	27433	−14030	−5518	17946
11	Other Flows (net)	9476	2427	9219	39673	−9687	−106	−8117
12	Total Capital Account (net) (including errors and omission)	28629	24954	46171	107901	8648	13350	28151
13	Reserves [increase (−) /decrease (+)]	(−)26159	(−)15052	(−)36606		(+)20080	(+)2499	(−)9533

PR: Partially Revised **P: Preliminary**

Source: Indian Economic Survey, 2009−10.

ANALYSIS OF PERFORMANCE OF INDIAN ECONOMY IN THE EXTERNAL SECTOR

The Indian economy suffered adverse developments in the external sector in the year 2008–09. This economic slowdown was a reflection of the global financial crisis. Most emerging economies of the world were affected by the unfavourable conditions in the global market. The impact of the global financial crisis, perhaps the worst since the Great Depression, spread from the developed to the emerging economies through the financial and trade channels.

In the beginning, the impact was not very significant in India. In fact, it was more or less positive in the beginning. However once the global crisis deepened, it spread to most of the countries including India through the capital and current account of the balance of payments. Despite these adverse developments in the balance of payments of India, including a sharp deceleration in the net capital flows and a slowdown in the demand for exports, the foreign sector of the Indian economy showed resilience. India continued to remain an attractive destination for foreign direct investment while its foreign exchange reserves continued to be in comfortable position.

Table 23.4 gives India's balance of payments as in the Indian Economic Survey, 2008–09.

RECAP

- Despite the adverse developments in the global scenario, the foreign sector of the Indian economy showed resilience and India continued to remain an attractive destination for foreign direct investment.

SUMMARY

INTRODUCTION

The balance of payment is a statement which summarizes the exports and imports and the other international transactions between the countries. The present chapter analysed the different aspects of the balance of payments.

MEANING AND STRUCTURE OF BALANCE OF PAYMENTS

1. The balance of payment is a statement which summarizes the exports and imports and the other international transactions between the countries.
2. The transactions entering into the balance of payments can be grouped under three broad accounts: current account, capital account and official international reserve account.
3. The current account of the balance of payments measures the flow of goods, services and income which occur across the national borders.
4. The capital account of the balance of payments measures the outflow and inflow of capital into the economy.

CURRENT ACCOUNT

1. The current account of the balance of payments includes the following items: balance of trade which includes the export and import of goods (or merchandise); balance of invisible trade which includes the export and import of services; unilateral transfers which are one way transactions as there is no claim involved as far as repayment is concerned, either at present or in the future.
2. The transactions in the current account have an effect on the national income and, thus, the income and output levels in the economy.

CAPITAL ACCOUNT

1. The capital account of the balance of payments measures the outflow and inflow of capital into the economy.
2. The capital account of the balance of payments includes the following capital transactions: long-term movements of capital which further includes portfolio investment and direct investment; short-term movements of capital which includes items like purchase of short-term government and corporate securities and loan repayments which include loans by the international financial institutions.
3. The transactions in the capital account influence the position of the economy as an international creditor or debtor.

THE OFFICIAL INTERNATIONAL RESERVE ACCOUNT

1. The official reserves of a country include foreign currencies, monetary gold and SDRs.
2. The transactions in the international reserve account determine the foreign exchange reserves which are available for settling a deficit in the current or capital account of the country.

DOUBLE ENTRY BOOKKEEPING

1. The balance of payments of a country will always balance because of the double entry system of bookkeeping and thus will always be in equilibrium.
2. The official reserve account provides the balancing factor in the balance of payments.

A DISEQUILIBRIUM IN THE BALANCE OF PAYMENTS

1. Autonomous transactions are those transactions that take place independently of other items in the balance of payments. Thus, these are transactions that take place for the satisfaction that they give or for the profit that they yield.
2. Autonomous transactions include exports and imports of goods and services, unilateral transfers and long-term movements of capital.
3. Accommodating transactions are those transactions that take place for the specific purpose of equalizing the balance of payments from an accountant's point of view. They take place for balancing a deficit or surplus in the foreign account.
4. Accommodating transactions include short-term movements of capital, monetary gold movements and variations in the foreign exchange reserves.
5. To determine whether the balance of payments is in equilibrium or disequilibrium, only the autonomous transactions are considered.
6. Any disequilibrium in the balance of payments is offset by the accommodating transactions which make up for any deficit or surplus. Hence, the sum of accommodating transactions and autonomous transactions will always be zero.

KINDS OF DISEQUILIBRIA IN THE BALANCE OF PAYMENTS

1. Structural disequilibrium occurs due to structural imbalances caused by the shifts in the international demand and/or the supply of the factors of production, goods or services.
2. Cyclical disequilibrium is caused by business cycles.
3. Exchange rate disequilibrium: Overvaluation of a currency has an adverse affect on exports and a favourable effect on imports, thus, producing a deficit in the balance of payments. Undervaluation of a currency has an adverse affect on imports and a favourable effect on exports, thus, producing a surplus in the balance of payments.
4. Monetary disequilibrium: Inflation makes exports relatively costlier leading to a decrease in the demand for exports. Thus, inflation leads to a deficit in the balance of payments.

THE PROCESS OF ADJUSTMENT IN THE BALANCE OF PAYMENTS

The macroeconomic policies that are utilized for correcting disequilibrium in the balance of payments include expenditure reducing policies and expenditure switching policies.

EXPENDITURE REDUCING OR EXPENDITURE CHANGING POLICIES

1. Expenditure reducing policies are aimed at bringing about a change in the aggregate expenditure in the country.
2. Expenditure reducing policies can be divided under two broad groups: monetary and fiscal policy.
3. To tackle a deficit in the balance of payments, a contractionary or tight monetary policy is followed.
4. Fiscal policies can be divided into two groups: those that work on the income side of the government budget and those that work on the expenditure side of the government budget.

EXPENDITURE SWITCHING POLICIES: DEVALUATION - THE ELASTICITY APPROACH

1. The expenditure switching policies work mainly through changing the relative price of exports and imports.
2. Under a stable exchange rate system in case of a deficit or a surplus in the balance of payments, the authorities have to take a conscious decision to bring about changes in the value of the currency with respect to the price of gold or to some primary asset.
3. Devaluation refers to a conscious action by the monetary authorities to lower the value of a currency with respect to the price of gold.
4. Devaluation of a currency improves the balance of payments by encouraging exports and discouraging imports.

5. The extent to which devaluation encourages exports and discourages imports depends on the elasticity of demand for its exports and imports.
6. According to the Marshall Lerner condition, for a devaluation to have a positive effect on a country's balance of payments the sum of the absolute values of the elasticity of demand for its exports and imports should be greater than one.

EXPENDITURE SWITCHING POLICIES: DEVALUATION–THE ABSORPTION APPROACH

1. Sidney Alexander in 1952 presented an alternative approach, the absorption approach, to the effects of devaluation.
2. Devaluation affects the balance of trade, *B* either by influencing the national income, *Y* or by influencing the total absorption, *A*.
3. The effects of devaluation will be different according to whether there is full employment in the economy or whether there exist unemployed resources.

POLICY MIX AND A SIMULTANEOUS EXTERNAL AND INTERNAL BALANCE

1. Trevor Swan had developed a diagrammatic analysis to explain the impact of expenditure changing and expenditure policies on the external and internal balance of a country, in what is called the Swan diagram.
2. In most cases, a combination of both expenditure reducing and expenditure switching policies are required to achieve both external and internal balance in a country.

ANALYSIS OF PERFORMANCE OF INDIAN ECONOMY IN THE EXTERNAL SECTOR

1. Once the global crisis deepened, it spread to most of the countries including India through the capital and current account of the balance of payments.
2. Despite these adverse developments in the balance of payments of India, including a sharp deceleration in the net capital flows and a slowdown in the demand for exports, the foreign sector of the Indian economy showed resilience.
3. India continued to remain an attractive destination for foreign direct investment while its foreign exchange reserves continued to be in comfortable position.

REVIEW QUESTIONS

TRUE OR FALSE QUESTIONS

1. The capital account of the balance of payments measures the flow of goods, services and income which occurs across the national borders.
2. Autonomous transactions are those transactions that take place independently of other items in the balance of payments.
3. To determine whether the balance of payments is in equilibrium or disequilibrium, only the accommodating transactions are considered.
4. Structural disequilibrium occurs due to business cycles.
5. According to the Marshall Lerner condition, for a devaluation to have a positive effect on a country's balance of payments the sum of the absolute values of the elasticity of demand for its exports and imports should be greater than one.

VERY SHORT-ANSWER QUESTIONS

1. Define the balance of payments.
2. What are unilateral transfers?
3. What do you understand by autonomous transactions?
4. What are accommodating transactions?
5. Which two macroeconomic policies are utilized for correcting disequilibrium in the balance of payments?

SHORT-ANSWER QUESTIONS

1. Write short notes on the
   (a) Balance of Trade
   (b) Balance of Invisible Trade
2. Write a short note on the official international reserve account.

3. Differentiate between autonomous and accommodating transactions.
4. Briefly discuss the different kinds of disequilibria in the balance of payments.
5. Discuss the effectiveness of monetary and fiscal policies as expenditure reducing policies in tackling a balance of payments deficit.

LONG-ANSWER QUESTIONS

1. What does the current account of the balance of payments measure? Discuss the constituents of the current account of the balance of payments.
2. What does the capital account of the balance of payments measure? Discuss the constituents of the capital account of the balance of payments.
3. The balance of payments of a country will always balance because of the double entry system of bookkeeping'. Explain.
4. 'To determine whether the balance of payments is in equilibrium or disequilibrium, only the autonomous transactions are considered.' Explain.
5. What is devaluation? Discuss the conditions under which it is expected to improve a deficit in the balance of payments of a country?

ANSWERS

TRUE OR FALSE QUESTIONS

1. **False.** The current account of the balance of payments measures the flow of goods, services and income which occurs across the national borders. The capital account of the balance of payments measures the outflow and inflow of capital into the economy.
2. **True.** Autonomous transactions are those transactions that take place independently of other items in the balance of payments. Thus, these are transactions that take place for the satisfaction that they give or for the profit that they yield.
3. **False.** To determine whether the balance of payments is in equilibrium or disequilibrium, only the autonomous transactions are considered.
4. **False.** Structural disequilibrium occurs due to structural imbalances caused by the shifts in the international demand and/or the supply of the factors of production, goods or services.
5. **True.** If the sum of the absolute values of the elasticity of demand for its exports and imports is less than one, then a country can improve its balance of payments through a revaluation.

24

Macroeconomic Policies

After studying this topic, you should be able to understand

- ✓ *Macroeconomic policy is the action taken by the government to achieve the macroeconomic objectives of the economy.*
- ✓ *Monetary policy is an operation by the monetary authority where as fiscal policy is an operation by the government.*
- ✓ *The objectives of macroeconomic policy differ from country to country.*
- ✓ *The objectives of macroeconomic policy are determined by the government keeping in mind the economic and social needs of the country.*
- ✓ *The targets are the variables, which should be controlled to achieve the macroeconomic objectives.*

INTRODUCTION

Monetary policy is an operation by the monetary authorities of the country and it operates through changes in the quantity of money. Thus, its immediate impact is felt in the money market.

Fiscal policy is an operation by the government and it operates through changes in the government expenditure and tax collections. Thus, its immediate impact is felt in the goods market.

At many points, in the course of this book, we have observed that the right combination of fiscal and monetary policies can help an economy come out of a recession, an inflationary situation and tackle problems relating to growth and even those on the trade front. Besides these policies, there exist other policies like income policy, growth policy employment policy and others which all fall under the heading of macroeconomic policy. However, our focus will be on the two most important policies, fiscal and monetary polices which we will examine at length in the following chapter.

In spite of the success of the different policies, there appears to be frequent demands indicating that policy makers are highly conservative and restrained in their approach to the implementation of the different policies. Are they really restrained or are they being extra cautious? In the present chapter, we attempt at answering this question and many other questions as well.

MEANING AND THE ADVENT OF MACROECONOMIC POLICY

Macroeconomic policy refers to the action taken by the government through the different policies to achieve the macroeconomic objectives of the economy.

Macroeconomic policy refers to the action taken by the government through the different policies to achieve the macroeconomic objectives of the economy. These macro goals include economic growth, economic development, full employment, equality in the distribution of income, controlling the inflation in the economy through maintaining price stability and others. The most popular macroeconomic policies are the fiscal policy and the monetary policy.

Monetary policy is an operation by the monetary authorities of the country and it operates through changes in the quantity of money. Thus, its immediate impact is felt in the money market. Fiscal policy is an operation by the government and it operates through changes in the government expenditure and tax collections. Thus, its immediate impact is felt in the goods market.

Before the Second World War, there was a strong conviction that a laissez faire economy was the best. The government's role should be at a minimum and the economy should function on the basis of the principle of the invisible hand as mentioned by Adam Smith in his famous 1776 book, *An Inquiry into the Nature and Causes of the Wealth of Nations* where each individual aimed at the maximization of his own welfare and in the process the society's welfare was maximized. Smith was deeply religious, and saw the invisible hand as the device by which a generous and kind God administered a universe where happiness was at a maximum.

With the advent of Keynes, the role of the government in achieving the macroeconomic objectives was realized. The authorities in the United States and the other countries realized as to how important a role the government played in achieving the objectives of growth, employment and price stability besides the other goals. Thus, laws were passed in many countries underlying the importance of the government in the different aspects of economic activity. Though there were still doubts and differences relating to the extent of responsibility that the government should be assigned in achieving the different goals, but it certainly was the beginning of an era where the role of the government in economic activity gained importance. Slowly, as time passed, the role of the government encompassed the different aspects of life.

To what extent the government has been successful in achieving the macroeconomic objectives over the period is a subject open to debate and differing from one country to another. Nevertheless, the importance of the government cannot be undermined even in today's world. Hence, we examine it in some depth in the following chapter, which examines the monetary and fiscal policy.

RECAP

- The role of the government in achieving the macroeconomic objectives was realized only with the advent of Keynes.

OBJECTIVES OF MACROECONOMIC POLICY

The objectives of macroeconomic policy differ from country to country. While an underdeveloped country may aim at growth and development, an industrialized country may aim at providing employment or at achieving a situation near full employment, and also price stability by keeping inflation under control. Hence, the policy makers in the different countries have to consider all these aspects while framing their policies. Hence, policies have to be framed accordingly.

In general, we can categorize the different objectives of macroeconomic policy as below:

(1) **A High and sustainable economic growth:** In the simplest terms, the economic growth can be defined as the increase in an economy's output over a period of time. One of the best ways of measuring the economy's output is the real GNP, the word 'real' implying that the effects of inflation have been adjusted for. Sometimes, the GDP is used which is quite similar to the GNP.

Economic growth can be defined as the increase in an economy's output over a period of time.

If the real GNP is corrected for the increases in the population another useful concept in economic growth, the real GNP per capita can be obtained. From the real GNP per capita various other related concepts of economic growth can be arrived at, each of which emphasizes some aspect of economic growth. For example, the real consumption per capita indicates the growth in the economic welfare of the consumer.

One of the main objectives of macroeconomic policy is to achieve a high rate of economic growth, especially in the developing countries. However, achieving a high rate of economic growth is not sufficient. It is important that this rate is sustained for a sufficiently long period of time.

BOX 24.1

The attainment of full employment was considered to be very important for the policy makers after the Second World War. For the socialist government of the 40s, the attempt at achieving full employment was one of the primary objectives and continued to remain so for the next three decades. The problem of unemployment became more acute in the 80s. However, it was seen to be an unavoidable consequence of the structural changes which accompanied industrial development but which were necessary to make the industries more efficient. The lower levels of unemployment, which persist in the west today, are a consequence of the industrial development achieved at that time.

(2) **Low unemployment or a high rate of employment:** Most economies are in a situation where they face some level of unemployment, which may be at a higher level in the less developed countries and at a lower level in the more developed countries. Unemployment is generally accompanied by low living standards, hardships and mental agony.

As already discussed in Chapter 21, a person is unemployed if he is out of work and (a) has been actively looking for work during the previous four weeks, or (b) is waiting to be called back to a job after having been laid off.

One of the main objectives of macroeconomic policy has been not only to achieve full employment but also to maintain it at that level. This was especially important after the Second World War. Keynes was one of the first economists who pointed out the need to achieve full employment. However, today the objective of full employment is given much less importance as compared to the other objectives in many countries. Most countries have achieved a situation of near full employment. Not everyone has been able to get a job but the situation is improving every day and the unemployment levels are falling to levels that some consider to be close to the situation of full employment.

(3) **Price stability:** Inflation is defined as a sustained and appreciable increase in the general level of prices. For price stability, it is necessary for the inflation rate to be zero or near zero. Most economies aim at keeping the inflation rates at low levels. Macroeconomic policy has the control of inflation as one of its primary objectives. In fact if one had to single out the most important objective of macroeconomic policy today, then it would certainly be inflation. A large part of the government's efforts in every economy are devoted to controlling inflation.

If one were to analyse the evils of inflation, the foremost among them would be the arbitrary way in which the income and wealth distribution is affected by inflation. It can, in fact, wipe out the purchasing power of individual's total savings earned in his whole life.

Economists have put forward the view that a little amount of inflation is good for an economy because a little inflation of about 2–3 per cent will lead to a rise in real wages and thus act as trigger, which will pep up the entire economy.

Nevertheless, it is a generally accepted fact that high levels of inflation are bad for an economy and thus need to be controlled. A rapid rate of inflation that is unanticipated and thus to which adjustment is not feasible is without doubt harmful for any economy. Inflation at a mild rate may be good for an economy but it is subject to uncertainty. In the light of these arguments, it seems that it is a better option to aim at controlling inflation and maintaining stable prices or a zero inflation rate.

Balance of payments of a country is a record of all flows of money into and out of the country.

(4) **Equilibrium in the balance of payments:** As already discussed in depth in Chapter 23, balance of payments of a country is a record of all flows of money into and out of the country. It includes the following two categories of transactions:

BOX 24.2

During the 1960s, the balance of payments was regarded as the litmus test. In Britain, a deficit was unpalatable and considered not befitting a world power. Under the 'Bretton Woods' fixed exchange rate system when international free movement of capital was not there, a sustained deficit was sure shot indicative of potential erosion in the pound sterling. As years passed with emergence of large global capital flows and with a floating pound, the surpluses or deficits in balance of payments ceased to matter as much. The sustained deficits in balance of payments during the 90s did not result in any discomfort among the economists in Britain.

(1) Current transactions that include exports and imports of goods and services or, in other words, the visible and invisible trade.

(2) Capital transactions that include the inflows and outflows of capital; for example foreign investments and foreign exchange reserves.

Perhaps, the more important of the two is the current account as it records how well a country is performing in terms of its exports of goods and services as compared to its imports-A country has to keep earning sufficient currency through its exports, if it has to not only provide for its imports but all the more important if it has to rise as a nation and take its place in the world.

One of the primary objectives of macroeconomic policy is, thus, to maintain a stable balance of payments position.

Which is the Most Important Objective?

After the Second World War till the 80s, full employment was considered the number one objective of the socialist governments in Britain. This belief, however, crumbled under Thatcher in the 80s when unemployment was accepted as an unavoidable outcome pursuant to the steps undertaken to make industry more efficient. Also, the relative de-industrialization that has since been occurring throughout the developed world has made higher unemployment inevitable. Consequently, this objective has now become less important than it used to be.

Two other objectives, which have always been important in most economies, are a low level of inflation and growth. Peoples' standard of living will increase only if there is growth. However, a high inflation will wipe out any increase in the standard of living as there will be a decrease in the value of money.

The most important objective today is inflation, and macroeconomic policy in most countries is oriented towards achieving this objective.

The objectives discussed are the primary objectives and the secondary ones, though equally important from the view point of the society, have been emphasized in the conflicts between the different objectives.

The Conflicts Between the Objectives

Unfortunately, it is very difficult for any government to achieve all the objectives simultaneously. This is because, often, there are conflicts between the different objectives such as:

(1) **A healthy growth and a low rate of inflation:** If an economy grows too quickly and that too due to an excessive increase in the consumer demands, then there will be an increase in the prices. Thus, there will be growth but accompanied by inflation.

On the other hand if steps are taken to control inflation, for example, high rates of interest, then investment spending will be discouraged thereby hampering growth.

Hence, it is difficult to achieve both the objectives of low inflation and healthy growth simultaneously.

(2) **A healthy growth and equilibrium in the balance of payments:** In a growing economy consumer spending is high, especially on foreign goods in comparison to domestic goods. This leads to a worsening of the trade deficit and disequilibrium in the balance of payments. Earlier governments would use import controls to tackle the problem. However, due to the World Trade Organization (WTO) and the move for globalization such controls are no longer feasible.

It is difficult to achieve both the objectives of healthy growth and equilibrium in the balance of payments simultaneously.

(3) **A low rate of inflation and low unemployment:** The conflict between inflation and unemployment has been a reason of worry for the economists. As already mentioned in Chapter 21, the short-run modern Phillips' curves are downward sloping showing a negative relationship between inflation and unemployment in the short run. Thus if the government attempts at controlling a high inflation through high rates of interest and a reduction in government expenditures, then there will occur a decrease in consumption expenditures and also investment spending will be discouraged. This will result in decrease in the demand for labour and, thus, in unemployment.

A reduction in inflation is possible but only at the cost of a high rate of unemployment. A situation where there is high unemployment and high expected inflation is known as stagflation.

However, it is important to note that the downward sloping Phillips' curve implying a trade-off between unemployment and inflation is only a situation which exists in the short run. In the long run the Phillips curve is vertical, implying that the rate of unemployment is independent of the rate of inflation.

(4) **A healthy growth and an equal distribution of income and wealth:** Often, it has been observed that a country may grow but the effects of the growth may not trickle down to the common man. The rich may just become richer. The socialist countries attempted to improve the lot of the common man. But this meant a slower rate of growth.

Hence, it is difficult to achieve equality in the distribution of income and wealth side by side with growth because forcing equality can have an adverse effect on the incentives for work and thus lead to inefficiencies.

(5) **A healthy growth and a healthy environment:** Environment is an objective, which most economies are now realizing as important for macroeconomic policy. However, it is still not being given the importance that it deserves.

The faster is the growth the higher is the pollution because of the smoke emanating from the factories and cars, disappearance of forests to make way for the new factories and houses, etc. Hence, although growth is taking place but it is at the cost of increasing the levels of pollution.

RECAP

- The most important objective today is inflation, and macroeconomic policy in most countries is oriented towards achieving this objective.
- It is very difficult for any government to achieve all the objectives simultaneously because, often, there are conflicts between the different objectives.

Objectives of Macroeconomic Policy in India

'From a macroeconomic perspective, low levels of budget deficits and public debt are generally considered as key ingredients for economic growth, reducing poverty and improving social outcomes. This owes to the stabilization models attributing resource–expenditure imbalances as the trigger for economic problems of many emerging/developing economies. The fiscal reforms initiated in 1990s as a part of economic liberalization reflected this point of view. Fiscal consolidation began in the early 1990s with fiscal deficit declining from 6.6 per cent of GDP in 1990–91 to 4.1 per cent of GDP in 1996–97; however, it faltered and started deteriorating in 1997–98 and reached a level of 6.2 per cent of GDP in 2001–02. It was against this background, that operationalization of the Fiscal Responsibility and Budget Management Act of 2003 (FRBMA) assumed urgency leading to the notification of the rules under the Act in July, 2004. In the post-FRBMA period, progress in fiscal consolidation was more or less close to the targets envisaged thereunder'. — India Economic Survey 2008–09.

THE FORMULATION OF THE MACROECONOMIC POLICY

The responsibility of formulating the macroeconomic policy in any economy falls on the shoulders of the government. It is the government who has to not only determine the objectives of the macroeconomic policy but has to keep in mind the conflicts between the different objectives also while making the decisions on the instruments and the target variables to be used in the implementation of the policy objectives.

As far as the objectives of macroeconomic policy are concerned, they are determined by the government keeping in mind the economic and social needs of the country. As already mentioned, in an underdeveloped country the policy objectives are oriented towards growth and development where as in an industrialized country it is oriented towards achieving a situation of full employment, and price stability. Thus, the policy makers have to consider all these aspects while framing the policies, deciding on the policy instruments and the target variables.

Targets, Instruments and Indicators of Macroeconomic Policy

We have already discussed at length the objectives of monetary policy. Once the objectives have been decided, the immediate problem before the policy makers is how to achieve the objectives.

The targets are the variables, which are to be controlled to achieve the macroeconomic objectives. In other words, these are the means to achieve the end result. They are the recognized goals of the policies. The targets of monetary policy, for example, include money supply, interest rates and bank credit. The targets of fiscal policy, for example, include consumption expenditure, investment expenditure and savings.

Targets can be further divided into the ultimate targets and the intermediate targets. An ultimate target for an economy could be to attain a zero level of inflation.

To be able to serve as a target, a variable should have four qualifications:

(1) The variable should have a relationship with the objectives and this should be clearly understood.
(2) The variable should be directly affected by the policy instruments.
(3) The influence of any non-policy factors should be minimal compared to the policy instruments.
(4) The variable should be measurable and there should be no time lag involved.

The government uses a variety of instruments to achieve the macroeconomic objectives. The instruments are the tools with the policy makers to achieve the target. For example to achieve an exchange rate target, the instrument available with the central bank is the sale or the purchase of foreign exchange.

The instruments of monetary policy include open market operations, cash reserve ratio and statutory liquidity ratio. These instruments of monetary policy influence the target variables of monetary policy to achieve the macroeconomic policy objectives. The instruments of fiscal policy include government expenditure, taxation and deficit financing. Similar to the instruments of monetary policy, the instruments of fiscal policy influence the target variables of fiscal policy to achieve the macroeconomic policy objectives.

Indicators are those economic variables that are signals, which indicate whether we are moving closer to achieving the targets.

Indicators are those economic variables that are signals, which indicate whether we are moving closer to achieving the targets. Thus they are a feedback that provides the necessary information to the policy makers as to whether they are approaching the targets, or adjustments are required to achieve the target.

The government faces many problems in trying to attain the objectives it has decided upon; some of them are as follows:

(1) The effects of the policies on the objectives are delayed and distributed over time in the uncertain dynamic world.

(2) There may exist a delay in obtaining the full and complete information about the actual state of the objectives; for example, about the real income and the employment.

(3) The processing and analysis of the information may involve a lot of time.

(4) The objectives may be affected not only by the policy instruments but also by developments, which are not related to the policies.

These innumerable problems act as a hurdle in the task of making the different policies. Hence, often, the policy makers have to rely on what we can think of as proxies for the objectives/goals.

RECAP

- The instruments of monetary policy influence the target variables of the monetary policy to achieve the macroeconomic policy objectives.
- The instruments of fiscal policy influence the target variables of the fiscal policy to achieve the macroeconomic policy objectives.

SUMMARY

INTRODUCTION

1. The right combination of fiscal and monetary policies can help an economy to come out of a recession and an inflationary situation.
2. In spite of the success of the different policies, there appears to be frequent demands indicating that policy makers are highly conservative and restrained in their approach to the implementation of the different policies.

MEANING OF AND THE ADVENT OF MACROECONOMIC POLICY

1. Macroeconomic policy is the action taken by the government to achieve the macroeconomic objectives of the economy.
2. Monetary policy is an operation by the monetary authorities where as fiscal policy is an operation by the government.
3. With the advent of Keynes, the role of the government in achieving the macroeconomic objectives was realized.

OBJECTIVES OF MACROECONOMIC POLICY

1. The objectives of macroeconomic policy differ from country to country.
2. An underdeveloped country may aim at growth and development where as an industrialized country may aim at providing employment or at achieving a situation near full employment, and also price stability by keeping inflation under control.
3. One of the main objectives of macroeconomic policy is to achieve a high rate of economic growth, especially in the developing countries.
4. Another main objective of macroeconomic policy has been to not only achieve full employment but to maintain it at that level. Keynes was one of the first economists who pointed out the need to achieve full employment. However, today the objective of full employment is given much less importance.
5. Inflation is defined as a sustained and appreciable increase in the general level of prices. In fact, if one had to single out the most important objective of macroeconomic policy today, then it would certainly be inflation.
6. Balance of payments of a country is a record of all flows of money into and out of the country. It includes two categories of transactions: current transactions and capital transactions. One of the primary objectives of macroeconomic policy is, thus, to maintain a stable balance of payments position.

WHICH IS THE MOST IMPORTANT OBJECTIVE?

1. After the Second World War till the 80s, full employment was considered the number one objective of the socialist governments in Britain.
2. The most important objective today is inflation, and macroeconomic policy in most countries is oriented towards achieving this objective.

THE CONFLICTS BETWEEN THE OBJECTIVES

1. A healthy growth and a low rate of inflation: If an economy grows too quickly and that too due to an excessive increase in the consumer demands, then there will be an increase in the prices. Thus, there will be growth but accompanied by inflation.
2. A healthy growth and equilibrium in the balance of payments: In a growing economy consumer spending is high, especially on foreign goods in comparison to domestic goods. This leads to a worsening of the trade deficit and disequilibrium in the balance of payments.
3. A low rate of inflation and low unemployment: The short-run modern Phillips' curves are downward sloping showing a negative relationship between inflation and unemployment in the short run. In the long run the Phillips curve is vertical, implying that the rate of unemployment is independent of the rate of inflation.
4. A healthy growth and an equal distribution of income and wealth: It is difficult to achieve equality in the distribution of income and wealth side by side with growth because forcing equality can have an adverse effect on the incentives for work and, thus, lead to inefficiencies.
5. A healthy growth and a healthy environment: The faster is the growth the higher is the pollution because of the smoke emanating from the factories and cars, disappearance of forests to make way for the new factories and houses, etc.

THE FORMULATION OF THE MACROECONOMIC POLICY

The objectives of macroeconomic policy are determined by the government keeping in mind the economic and social needs of the country.

TARGETS AND INSTRUMENTS OF MACROECONOMIC POLICY

1. The targets are the variables, which are to be controlled to achieve the macro economic objectives. The targets of monetary policy, for example, include money supply, interest rates and bank credit. The targets of fiscal policy, for example, include consumption expenditure, investment expenditure and savings.
2. The government uses a variety of instruments to achieve the macroeconomic objectives. The instruments of monetary policy, for example, include open market operations, cash reserve ratio and statutory liquidity ratio. The instruments of fiscal policy, for example, include government expenditure, taxation and deficit financing.
3. The government faces many problems in trying to attain the objectives it has decided upon.

REVIEW QUESTIONS

TRUE OR FALSE QUESTIONS

1. Macroeconomic policy refers to the action taken by the government through the different policies to achieve some macroeconomic objectives of the economy.
2. Monetary policy is an operation by the government and it operates through changes in the government expenditure and tax collections.
3. If the real GNP is corrected for the increases in the population, the real consumption per capita can be obtained.
4. Balance of payments of a country is a record of all flows of money into and out of the country.
5. In the short-run the Phillips curve is vertical, implying that the rate of unemployment is independent of the rate of inflation.

VERY SHORT-ANSWER QUESTIONS

1. Define macroeconomic policy.
2. What are fiscal policy and monetary policy?

3. What does the objective of a high and sustainable economic growth imply? Explain.
4. 'One of the main objectives of macroeconomic policy has been to not only achieve full employment but to maintain it at that level.' Explain.
5. 'If one had to single out the most important objective of macroeconomic policy today, then it would certainly be inflation.' Comment.

SHORT-ANSWER QUESTIONS

1. What do you mean by macroeconomic policy? Which are the two most popular macroeconomic policies?
2. Discuss any two objectives of macroeconomic policy.
3. Which is the most important objective of macroeconomic policy?
4. Does the objective of a healthy growth conflict with any of the other objectives?
5. 'The objectives of macroeconomic policy are determined by the government keeping in mind the economic and social needs of the country.' Comment.

LONG-ANSWER QUESTIONS

1. Write a short note on the meaning of and the advent of macroeconomic policy.
2. What are the objectives of macroeconomic policy? Discuss.
3. Are there any conflicts between the different objectives? Discuss.
4. Write a short note on the targets and instruments of macroeconomic policy.
5. What are the objectives of macroeconomic policy in India? Discuss.

ANSWERS

TRUE OR FALSE QUESTIONS

1. **True.** Macroeconomic policy refers to the action taken by the authorities to achieve some macroeconomic objectives of the economy. The most popular macroeconomic policies are the fiscal policy and the monetary policy.
2. **False.** Fiscal policy is an operation by the government and it operates through changes in the government expenditure and tax collections. Thus, its immediate impact is in the goods market.
3. **False.** If the real GNP is corrected for the increases in the population, the real GNP per capita can be obtained.)
4. **True.** Balance of payments of a country is a record of all monetary flows into and out of the country. It includes two categories of transactions: current transactions and capital transactions.
5. **False.** In the long-run the Phillips curve is vertical, implying that the rate of unemployment is independent of the rate of inflation.

Monetary Policy and Fiscal Policy

25

After studying this topic, you should be able to understand

- ✓ *Monetary policy aims at achieving certain well-defined macroeconomic objectives.*
- ✓ *To achieve the objectives of monetary policy, the central bank has at its disposal the quantitative and the qualitative measures of monetary policy.*
- ✓ *The effective working of monetary policy is hindered due to the existence of different obstacles.*
- ✓ *Fiscal policy refers to the government's policy regarding government expenditure, taxation and public borrowing with the view to achieving certain well-defined macroeconomic objectives.*
- ✓ *To implement fiscal policy, the government has at its behest several instruments which include taxation, government expenditure and public borrowing. Fiscal policy actions which can tackle the problem of instability include: automatic stabilizers and discretionary fiscal policy.*
- ✓ *The full employment budget and actual budget differs due to the cyclical factor in the budget.*
- ✓ *The full employment budget surplus differs from the actual budget surplus only in respect of tax collections.*
- ✓ *The increase in government spending crowds out private investment spending.*

INTRODUCTION

This chapter examines the monetary policy and the fiscal policy and their functioning. An attempt has also been made at understanding the goals which these policies aim at achieving. Are they successful in achieving these goals or do they face some limitations which prevent them from achieving them? All these issues will be examined at length in the chapter.

MEANING OF MONETARY POLICY

Monetary policy is an operation by the monetary authorities of the country to achieve certain well-defined macroeconomic objectives/goals. It is generally the central bank of the country which undertakes the implementation of the monetary policy. It operates through changes in the quantity of money. Hence, monetary policy has its immediate impact in the money market.

Monetary policy is an operation by the monetary authorities of the country to achieve certain well defined macroeconomic objectives.

Excess reserves are reserves in excess of the required reserves.

Monetary policy, it is to be noted, has much wider connotations than the credit policy. While both are administered by the central bank of the country, the credit policy is concerned with changes in the supply of credit and the monetary policy with changes in the supply of money. To avoid confusion, often the two are clubbed together under the head of monetary policy.

RECAP

- The central bank of the country undertakes the implementation of the monetary policy through changes in the quantity of money.

INSTRUMENTS OF MONETARY POLICY

The main objectives which the monetary policy aims at achieving include economic growth, a higher rate of employment, stable prices, equality in the distribution of income and wealth, a stable balance of payments and many others depending on the need of the time.

To achieve these objectives, monetary policy has at its disposal instruments which give the central bank the power to control the money supply and hence achieve these objectives.

These instruments can be divided into two categories:

(1) Quantitative or general measures
(2) Qualitative or selective measures

Quantitative or General Measures of Monetary Policy

Open Market Operations

Open market operations are the sale and purchase of government securities and treasury bills by the central bank.

It is the sale and purchase of government securities and treasury bills by the central bank. It is an instrument of monetary control which is most powerful and which is most widely used by the central bank. The central bank carries out the open market operations through the commercial banks. Hence, these operations affect the bank deposits and reserves and thus influence their capacity to create money.

Suppose the central bank follows:

(1) **A contractionary monetary policy:** It aims at reducing the supply of money in the hands of the public and also at decreasing the creation of credit. To achieve this, it offers government securities and treasury bills for sale through the commercial banks. When the public and other institutions purchase these securities through cheques drawn on the commercial banks, there is a withdrawal of money from their accounts with the banks. Hence, there occurs a decrease in the cash reserves of banks thereby reducing their capacity to create credit. There is, thus, a decrease in the money supply.

(2) **An expansionary monetary policy**: It aims at raising the supply of money in the hands of the public and also at increasing the creation of credit. To achieve this, it purchases government securities and treasury bills through the commercial banks. When the public and other institutions sell these securities, there is an increase in the flow of money to their accounts with the banks. Hence, there occurs an increase in the bank's deposits and also in their cash reserves. This improves their capacity to create credit. There is, thus, an increase in the money supply.

Effectiveness of open market operations: Open market operations are one of the most popular instruments of monetary policy. In the UK, USA and other countries, they are regarded as one of the most efficient instruments of monetary control.

Advantages of open market operations

(1) They are highly flexible and can be used in widely varying amounts.
(2) They are easily reversible in time.
(3) They can be often used in widely differing amounts.

(4) Unlike the other instruments of monetary policy, they do not involve any public announcements. Hence, they do not have any announcement effects. i.e. there are no reactions in the market consequent to open market operations.

For open market operations to be successful at least three conditions need to be satisfied:

(1) It is necessary that the market for government securities, the gilt edged market is well-developed and well-organized.
(2) It is necessary that the central bank has enough capacity to buy and sell government securities.
(3) It is necessary that in the pursuit of these operations, the chief consideration for the central bank is only of monetary control.

In India, it seems that out of all these conditions only condition (b) seems to be satisfied. The central bank of the country, the Reserve Bank of India has sufficient capacity to buy and sell securities. As for condition (a), the market for government securities is not well organized. Regarding condition (c), the RBI has often been weighed down by considerations other than monetary control and more towards, say, public debt management.

Variations in Reserve Requirements

Commercial banks maintain a certain proportion of their time and demand liabilities in the form of cash reserves. These can be divided under two heads:

(1) **Required reserves:** These are cash balances which banks hold to meet their statutory reserve requirements. This is a legal requirement imposed on the banks by the central bank. The purpose of these reserves is to safeguard the interest of the depositors and to prevent the banking system from a total collapse. It also enables the central bank to control the liquidity. As per these requirements, the banks have to maintain a certain minimum reserve deposit ratio. Hence, a fraction of each bank's total deposits have to be maintained as cash balances with the central bank.

Required reserves are cash balances which banks hold to meet their statutory reserve requirements.

When the central bank pursues

(a) a contractionary monetary policy, it raises the cash reserve ratio (CRR). With an upward revision in the CRR, banks are required to hold larger proportion of their cash balances with the central bank for the same amount of their liabilities. This reduces the bank's ability to extend loans leading to a decrease in the money supply. In essence, the CRR impounds funds available with the banks.
(b) an expansionary monetary policy, it will reduce the CRR. With a reduction in the reserve requirement ratio, banks are required to hold a smaller proportion of their cash balances with the central bank for the same amount of their liabilities. This improves the bank's ability to extend loans leading to an increase in the money supply.

BOX 25.1

As per the existing law, the central bank of India, RBI has the power to impose statutorily a cash reserve ratio (CRR) on banks which can be anywhere between 3 and 15 per cent of their net demand and time deposits. The RBI has been using this instrument often for monetary control. When the RBI hiked the CRR by 25 basis points to 8.25 per cent effective 2008 May 24, the small -almost token-CRR hike led to a withdrawal of around US$ 2.22 billion from the banking system. During the fiscal year 2008–09, frequent changes in the CRR were resorted to in tandem with current and evolving macroeconomic situation and liquidity conditions in the global and domestic financial markets. In 2008 November CRR was down to 5.5 per cent. 2009 January saw another reduction of 50 basis points in CRR in order to gear up the economy to cope up with the global recession. CRR stood at 5 per cent at fiscal close.

(2) **Excess reserves:** These are reserves in excess of the required reserves. A part of these may be held as cash on hand or in the form of vault cash with the banks themselves. The rest may be kept as excess balances with the central bank. They are held by the banks for meeting basically two purposes:
   (a) Currency drains which is the net withdrawal of currency by the depositors.
   (b) Clearing drains which is the net loss of cash due to the interbank clearing of checks.

Effectiveness of Variations in Reserve Requirements: As compared to open market operations, it is often alleged that variations in reserve requirements are an inferior tool of monetary policy because:

(1) They lead to lumpy and discontinuous changes in the deposits and the reserves.
(2) Changes in reserve requirements are newsworthy, they produce announcement effects.

However, the counter argument given in support of variations in reserve requirements is that:

(1) Banks can be given sufficient notice of the changes so that they can be introduced gradually with banks having sufficient time to adjust their portfolios in accordance.
(2) During times of inflation, the reserves of banks would be increasing rapidly. Hence, banks would not find it difficult to meet a higher CRR and thus they would not face any problems in giving their complete cooperation to the monetary authorities in controlling the money supply.
(3) Often, the central bank is unable to use open market operations for the purposes of monetary control. Hence, it has to resort to variations in reserve requirements if it wishes to ensure monetary stability in the economy.

It is increasingly felt that the variable reserve ratio, on its own, is not a sufficient instrument of controlling the money supply. Thus, to make it an effective instrument it needs to be supplemented by the other instruments of monetary policy.

The statutory liquidity requirement is a statutory requirement where the banks are required to maintain a certain fixed proportion of their demand and time liabilities in the form of designated liquid assets.

The Statutory Liquidity Requirement

Besides the CRR, banks are subject to control through yet another requirement, the statutory liquidity ratio, the SLR as it is often known.

Under the SLR, banks are statutorily required to maintain a certain fixed proportion of their demand and time liabilities in the form of designated liquid assets. This ratio of liquid assets to demand and time liabilities is known as statutory liquidity ratio. The SLR can be defined as:

$$\text{SLR} = \frac{\text{ER} + I^* + \text{CB}}{L}$$

where,
ER = excess reserves which are total reserves minus the required reserves with the central bank
I^* = investment in encumbered securities which are securities against which no loans have been taken by the bank from the central bank
CB = current account balances with other banks
L = total demand and time liabilities of the bank

BOX 25.2

In India, the SLR was first imposed on the banks in the year 1949. It was fixed at 20 per cent. It remained at this level for about a period of 15 years until it was increased to 25 per cent in the year 1964. After that, it was often changed and stood at 24 per cent at end of fiscal year 2008–09. RBI is empowered to increase this ratio up to 40 per cent.

The purpose behind the SLR was to prevent the commercial banks from negating the impact of an increase in CRR by converting their liquid assets into cash so that their loanable funds remain intact. An increase in SLR thus impedes the bank's leveraged capacity to pump more money into the economy.

By increasing the SLR, the central bank attempts to allocate an increasingly larger share of bank resources to the government and the specified public sector agencies. However, the central bank has not been very successful in its effort because in meeting the SLR, the banks have preferred to acquire other approved securities, rather than the government securities since these other securities give higher yields.

Effectiveness of SLR: In India, like the CRR, the SLR has not been very successful as an instrument of monetary policy. Also, it has not been a very flexible instrument of monetary policy and has often been revised in the upward direction for considerations other than monetary control.

Bank Rate Policy

Bank rate or the discount rate is the rate of interest at which the central bank rediscounts eligible bills of exchange or other commercial papers.

The bank rate or the discount rate is the rate of interest at which the central bank rediscounts eligible bills of exchange or other commercial papers. When the banks are short of reserves, they borrow from the central bank by getting their bills of exchange rediscounted. In simpler terms, the bank rate is the rate of interest charged by the central bank on the loans and advances made by it to the commercial banks. The central bank is a 'lender of the last resort' for the commercial banks.

It is at the discretion of the central bank to change the bank rate.

(1) When the central bank pursues an expansionary monetary policy, it lowers the bank rate. Hence, it becomes cheaper for the commercial banks to borrow from the central bank's discount window. Thus, a decrease in the bank rate increases the money supply. A decrease in the bank rate is followed by a fall in the market rates of interest all along the line since the banks revise their lending rates downwards. This is followed by an expansion in bank credit and is a sign for the onset of a cheap money policy in the economy.

(2) When the central bank pursues a contractionary monetary policy, it raises the bank rate. Hence, it becomes costlier for the commercial banks to borrow from the central bank's discount window, discouraging them to borrow from the central bank. Thus, an increase in the bank rate decreases the money supply. An increase in the bank rate is followed by a rise in the market rates of interest all along the line since the banks revise their lending rates upwards to absorb the higher cost of borrowed reserves. This is followed by a tighter bank credit and is a sign for the onset of a tighter money policy in the economy.

Effectiveness of Bank Rate Policy: In reality, it is difficult to predict the effect of the changes in the bank rate on the amount of the banks borrowings. This effect will depend on a number of factors:

(1) The extent to which the bank is dependent on borrowed reserves.
(2) The extent to which the differential between the banks lending rates and borrowed rates is sensitive to the bank's demand for borrowed reserves.
(3) The extent to which the other rates of interest change in response to the changes in the borrowed reserves.
(4) The demand for loans and the extent to which loans are available from other sources.

Limitations of the Bank Rate Policy

(1) The bank rate is often more sticky in comparison to the other rates. Also, the changes in it are discontinuous.

BOX 25.3

Changes in the bank rate in India in the initial years were not very frequent. Since 1962, it has been varied more often. From 10 per cent in 1990–91 it came down to 6 per cent in 2006–07 and remained at that level till 2009 March. The repo rate (in 2009 April) stood at 4.75 per cent while the reverse repo rate at 3.25 per cent. Between 2008 October and 2009 March, the central bank cut the repo rate at which it lends to banks by 425 basis points in desperate attempts to help boost economic activity.

(2) Changes in the bank rate have announcement effects, i.e. there are reactions in the market due to a mere announcement of a change being brought about in the bank rate. Hence, the central bank may avoid bringing about changes in the bank rate.

(3) Over the years, the flexibility in the money market has gone down. Hence, the response of the money and credit markets to changes in the bank rate is not very adequate for monetary policy to be effective.

(4) Most commercial banks nowadays are often financially self reliant and thus not fully dependent on the central bank for finance.

(5) In certain countries, there has developed a private market for loans and those banks which are in need of loans borrow from those who have excess reserves.

Repo (Repurchase) Rate and Reverse Repo (Repurchase) Rate

Repo rate is the rate at which the central bank infuses short-term liquidity into the system.

Reverse repo rate is the rate at which banks park their short-term excess liquidity with the central bank in exchange for government securities.

The repo rate is the rate at which the central bank infuses short-term liquidity into the system. In simpler terms, it is the rate at which the central bank lends to the banks.

The reverse repo rate is the rate at which banks park their short-term excess liquidity with the central bank in exchange for government securities. It is the rate at which the central bank borrows from the banks. Hence, the reverse repo rate is the return earned by the banks on their excess funds with the central bank. An increase in this rate tempts banks to park their short-term excess liquidity with the central bank thus squeezing out loose cash from the system which in turn helps in reducing inflationary pressures. When yields on government securities go up, the financial markets feel liquidity crunch and lending rates to retail and corporate sector harden.

BOX 25.4

Difference between Bank Rate and Repo Rate: Bank rate is the rate at which RBI provides finance to commercial banks in India. Banks can avail different types of refinance from RBI at rates that are linked to bank rate. Thus, banks can borrow at this rate depending on their eligibility for refinance.

Repo, on the other hand, is a money market instrument, which enables collateralized short-term borrowing and lending through sale/purchase operations in debt instruments. Under a repo transaction, a holder of securities (a bank) sells them to an investor (RBI, in this case) with an understanding to repurchase the same at a predetermined date and rate. Thus, in repo, the forward clean price of the bonds is determined in advance at a level which varies from the spot clean price by accounting for the disparity between repo interest and coupon earned on the security. Thus, a bank can borrow under repo provided it has the extra securities which it can lend temporarily to RBI for borrowing short-term funds.

The reverse repo rate is linked to the repo rate. The spread between the reverse repo rate and the repo rate is maintained generally at 100 basis points with the repo rate being the higher of the two.

Qualitative or Selective Measures of Monetary Policy

The quantitative measures control the total volume of credit and the cost of credit in the economy and, hence, the expansion or contraction in the total amount of credit and thus the supply of money.

On the other hand, the qualitative measures control the direction and distribution of credit in the economy. This can have two aspects:

(1) Positive aspect in that these measures can be used to encourage the flow of credit in particular directions.

(2) Negative aspect in that these measures can be used to restrict the flow of credit to particular sectors.

Some qualitative credit control measures are:

Rationing of Credit

This has been often used in many countries. Credit rationing is resorted to when there occurs a shortage of institutional credit. The more powerful and the financially strong sectors, which in fact may not really need the credit, may be able to capture the major share of the credit. The sectors which may in fact be in dire need of funds may not be able to procure them. To prevent such a situation from occurring, the central bank may resort to credit rationing. They may do so by

(a) Charging higher rates of interest on the bank loans which go beyond certain limits.

(b) Setting limits on the quantum of loans to larger firms and industries.

Change in Margin Requirements

This is a tool of monetary policy that works indirectly to influence lending and, thus, regulate the capital markets. The margin requirement specifies the minimum maintainable ratio of the value of the securities charged to the amount borrowed.

Changes in margin requirements are used to control speculative activities. If the wholesalers start hoarding some particular essential goods so that they can create a shortage and push up the price of these goods, then in that case the central bank can raise the margin requirement for these goods.

Moral Suasion

This is a combination of persuasion and pressures which a central bank asserts to bring the erring banks in line so that they function in accordance with the central bank's directives. The central bank can exercise these through letters, meetings and discussions with the banks on the various matters. In fact, moral suasion is the only instrument which can be used both for quantitative and qualitative credit control.

Moral suasion is a combination of persuasion and pressures which a central bank asserts to bring the erring banks in line so that they function in accordance with the central bank's directives.

Direct Action

This refers to the coercive actions resorted to by the central bank against those banks who do not function according to its directives. These may be by way of denial of discretionary rediscounting facilities, charging of penal interest rates, etc.

Direct action refers to the coercive actions resorted to by the central bank against those banks who do not function according to its directives.

Effectiveness of Qualitative Credit Control Measures, this will depend on a number of factors:

(1) The extent of restrictions on the credit: These may not be sufficient. The selective credit controls are generally security oriented and not purpose oriented. Hence, the influential borrowers may succeed in using the borrowed funds for purposes like speculation in the stock markets rather than for the priority sectors.

(2) The availability of finance from other sources: Besides the availability of finance from banks, another major source of funds for the traders is the unregulated credit market. Further, the existence of black money constraints the ability of the central bank to curtail speculative hoarding and other such activities.

(3) The extent to which supply is not able to fulfill the demand: The greater is the shortage of funds, the more will be the speculation in the market. Hence, it is necessary that the credit controls are imposed well in advance so that timely action can be taken.

It is increasingly felt that the selective credit controls cannot be successful on their own. They need to be supplemented with the general credit controls. Also, they are more in the form of short-term rather than long-term solutions.

Deficit Financing: Government's Instrument of Monetary Control

It refers to ways in which the deficit in the government's budget is financed. In the less developed countries, it is financed by credit from the central bank. The central bank merely prints more currency and then puts them into circulation on behalf of the government.

Deficit financing leads to an increase in the money supply leading to an increase in the expenditure in the economy. Thus, whenever there exists a slack in demand, deficit financing is resorted to increase the aggregate demand in the economy. Hence, deficit financing fills up the gap in the government expenditure and the revenue that it gets from taxation, public borrowing and external finance.

However, one major problem that is associated with deficit financing is that it always results in inflation. The increase in the money supply leads to an increase in the money in the hands of the public. This creates a demand for goods and services. However, the supply of goods is not able to keep up with the demand. Hence, there occurs an inflationary pressure in the economy.

RECAP

- Quantitative measures of monetary policy include open market operations, variations in reserve requirements, bank rate policy and repo rate.
- Qualitative measures of monetary policy include rationing of credit, change in margin requirements, moral suasion and direct action.

MONETARY POLICY DEVELOPMENTS IN INDIA

In the first six months of 2008–09, the monetary policy of the RBI was oriented towards controlling the monetary expansion. The government also implemented various fiscal measures to control inflation in the economy. The major policy rates were also changed accordingly by the RBI to pursue a contractionary monetary policy. The repo rate (RR) was increased from 7.75 per cent in the beginning of 2008 April to 9.0 per cent with effect from 2008 August. However, the reverse repo rate was left the same at 6.0 per cent. The cash reserve ratio was increased from 7.50 per cent at the beginning of 2008 April to 9.0 per cent with effect from 2008 August.

However, the situation underwent an abrupt change in the latter half of the year. Due to the international financial crisis, there occurred an outflow of foreign exchange. There was a reversal of policy by the RBI in the form of decreases in the repo and reverse repo rate, the cash reserve ratio and also the statutory liquidity ratio. The repo rate was decreased from 9.0 per cent in 2008 August to 5.0 per cent in 2009 March. The reverse repo rate was also reduced from 6.0 per cent to 3.5 from 2009 March. SLR was decreased from 25 per cent of the net demand and time liabilities to 24 per cent from 2008 November. The CRR was also reduced from 9.0 to 5.0 per cent from 2009 January.

LIMITATIONS OF MONETARY POLICY

(1) **The Existence of a time lag:** This is perhaps one of the major problems in the path of the working of monetary policy. There exists a substantial time lag between the time that there is a realization for the need for a monetary policy and the time by which the response of the policy in bringing about changes in aggregate demand is felt.

The time lags can be divided under two heads:

(a) **Inside lags:** These include the recognition lag and the action lag. The recognition lag relates to the considerable time taken by the central bank in realizing that there are problems and, hence, a need to tackle them through the monetary policy. The action lag may occur due to the considerable time gap involved during the recognition phase and the actual implementation of the policy.

(b) **Outside lags:** Once the policy has been implemented, the problem occurs in that it may take a considerable time for the households and firms to respond to those policies. Hence, there may occur a considerable time lapse for the impact of these changes to be felt on aggregate demand and the output.

The issue of time lags is very important for the success of the monetary policy in achieving its various goals. If the time lag is short, then the chances of monetary policy being successful are strong. However, with long time gaps it is quite possible that the situation may have undergone a complete change and implementation of the policy may worsen rather than improve the situation.

(2) **The presence of non-bank financial intermediaries:** Besides commercial banks, the other entities which play a major role in the money and capital markets are the financial intermediaries, other than the banks. These include the development banks, mutual saving funds, insurance companies, etc. Like banks, these intermediaries cannot directly create money. However, they can influence money indirectly through their actions. Suppose the central bank is pursuing a tight monetary policy, these non-bank financial intermediaries can, to some extent negate the impact of such a policy through an increase in the velocity of money, and also by attracting idle funds and converting them into active balances.

(3) **The underdeveloped nature of the money and capital markets:** One of the major problems in the implementation of monetary policy in the less developed countries is that their money and the capital markets are highly fragmented, disconnected and disorganized. In such economies, sectors like the agriculture sector is unorganized and its main source of funds are the moneylenders who do not fall under the supervision of the central bank and, hence, are outside its control.

The presence of these factors not only increases the time lag involved but also to some extent limits the effectiveness of monetary policy in achieving its goals.

RECAP

- The existence of a time lag, presence of non-bank financial intermediaries and the underdeveloped nature of the money and capital markets limit the effectiveness of monetary policy in achieving its goals.

MEANING OF FISCAL POLICY

The government of a country can influence the economy not only through the monetary policy but also through the fiscal policy. Fiscal policy refers to the government's policy regarding government expenditure, taxation and public borrowing with the view to achieving certain well-defined macroeconomic objectives.

Fiscal policy refers to the government's policy regarding government expenditure, taxation and public borrowing with the view to achieving certain well-defined macroeconomic objectives.

It was only with the coming of Keynes that fiscal policy gained importance. Prior to Keynes, monetary policy was more popular. Also, economists like Adam Smith strongly propagated the belief that in an economy the role of the government should be kept at a minimum. An economy which functioned on its own without any interference of any kind would be an ideal economy. It was believed that an economy would always function at the full employment level and hence the government's role should be limited to maintaining law and order and in providing the essential services.

The coming of the Great Depression and the failure of monetary policy to tackle the severe unemployment problems arising from it made one realize the need for fiscal policy. Further, the 'new economics' by Keynes with the emphasis on aggregate demand strengthened the belief that the time was right to renew the dwindling faith of the public in the effectiveness of fiscal policy. Also, government expenditure and taxation were gaining importance. It was obvious that the government could increase or decrease aggregate demand through its expenditures, taxation and transfers. However, the monetarists attacked this argument because they believed that with the exception of some circumstances, in general, increases in government expenditures do not add to aggregate demand but in fact are responsible for crowding out private investment of an equal amount.

Most economists do not agree with the crowding out arguments and promote the view that fiscal policy is certainly an effective instrument in achieving the macroeconomic policy objectives. In the developed nations of the world, fiscal policy is effective in maintaining economic stability while in the developing countries its role is all the more important in achieving economic growth, development and also in tackling employment and the problems emanating from it.

RECAP

- In the developed nations, fiscal policy is effective in maintaining economic stability while in the developing countries it is important in achieving economic growth, development and also in tackling employment.

INSTRUMENTS OF FISCAL POLICY

To implement fiscal policy, the government has at its behest several instruments:

Taxation

One of the most important sources of revenue for the government in most countries is taxation. In the developing countries, the government is making an attempt at increasing the proportion of the national income which is collected as taxes. Taxes can be analysed under two headings:

Direct Taxes

(1) **Corporate income taxes** which are collected from firm's economic profits. These form a very small proportion of the total revenue of the government for many reasons:

(a) Since the corporate sector forms a very small part of the economy, its contribution to the total revenue will also be small.

(b) Often to encourage industrial development, the government offers incentives in the form of tax rebates and investment subsidies.

However, it is important to note that in spite of all problems corporate income taxes are easier to collect as compared to the personal income tax.

(2) **Personal income tax** again account for a very small proportion of the total revenue of the government for many reasons:
   (a) A large proportion of the people have low incomes and are thus not in a position to pay tax.
   (b) There are administrative weaknesses which are responsible for tax evasions.

(3) **Taxes on wealth and property** can account for a large proportion of the total revenue of the government for many reasons:
   (a) Since they are collected from the rich class which has property, they are not likely to have an adverse influence on the incentive to work.
   (b) Such taxes can reduce the income and wealth inequalities to some extent.

Indirect Taxes

(1) **Sales tax and excise duty** which are paid by all, the rich and the poor. However, luxury goods are taxed at a higher rate than the necessities.

(2) **Customs duty** includes exports duty and imports duty. They are easy to implement as the number of commodities involved in trade are limited and easy to monitor.

   In the developed countries, the direct taxes are a more important source of revenue for the government as compared to the developing countries where indirect taxes are more important.

Government Expenditure

Since the Great Depression, the government's role in economic activity is continuously on the increase for several reasons:

(1) It was realized that the private sector was not in a position to pull the economy out of the Depression on its own.

(2) The private sector did not posses either the ability or the willingness to embark on the ambitious projects which were necessary to put the economy on the path of growth and development.

   Hence, it was realized that government expenditure is imperative for an economy in the form of investments in capital goods industries, building the infrastructure and payments of wages and salaries. Besides, the government has to fulfill various social obligations which include expenditure on education, public health services, unemployment compensations, pensions and other welfare considerations.

Public Borrowing

Though public borrowing is the second most important source of revenue (taxation is the most important source of revenue) it is unlike taxes. All the borrowings from the public must be repaid in the future.

Public borrowing can take two forms:

(1) Compulsory loans where bonds are issued by the government for a period varying from five to ten years. Employees' contribution to provident fund falls under this category.

(2) Voluntary loans where bills and securities are issued by the government.

   Since taxation is insufficient to finance the growing public expenditures, the government in most countries has to resort to borrowing from the public. The developmental expenditures are increasing at such a great speed that in most countries the government has to finance these expenditures by raising loans from the public.

(Deficit financing has also often been included as an instrument of fiscal policy. Since it has already been discussed earlier in this chapter it is not repeated again.)

RECAP

- One of the most important sources of revenue for the government in most countries is taxation
- Public borrowing is the second most important source of revenue.

FISCAL POLICY AND STABILIZATION IN THE ECONOMY

In any economy, due to the business cycles there are many ups and downs causing instability in the economy.

An Automatic Stabilizer

An automatic stabilizer is a built-in mechanism in any economy which automatically reduces the change in the output in response to a change in the level of the autonomous demand.

An automatic stabilizer is a built-in mechanism in any economy which automatically reduces the change in the output in response to a change in the level of the autonomous demand. The changes in the taxes and in the government expenditures vary automatically and in the desired direction to bring about stability in the economy.

The business cycles are often caused due to the changes in the level of the autonomous demand, particularly investment. Sometimes, the investors are optimistic and go in for high levels of investment while at other times the investors are pessimistic and go in for low levels of investment. The automatic stabilizer diminishes the effects on the output level due to the swings in the investment. There is no deliberate action or interference by the government to bring about stability.

Two automatic stabilizers are:

(1) **A proportional income tax:** When the gross national product of an economy increases, the tax revenue increases automatically because some tax payers progress into the higher income and tax brackets. When the gross national product of an economy decreases, the tax revenue decreases automatically because some tax payers retreat into the lower brackets. Hence, the tax revenues automatically move in the requisite direction thus bringing about stabilization in the economy.

(2) **Unemployment benefits:** In many economies, unemployment benefits are paid to the workers who are without a job. These make it possible for the unemployed to consume even during a recession. Hence, there is no decrease in the level of consumption and in aggregate demand. As a result, output remains stable even during recessions due to the unemployment benefits.

On the other hand, during a boom the number of unemployed falls and hence there is a decrease in the unemployment benefits. Hence, the increases in the level of consumption and in aggregate demand are controlled to some extent. Thus, output remains stable even during periods of boom.

Existence of automatic stabilizers reduces the fluctuations which occur in the output due to the business cycles. However, a major limitation of automatic stabilizers is that though they can prevent a downturn in the output level from becoming worse but they cannot prevent a downturn from taking place. This is because they come into effect only when a downturn has occurred. Hence, they cannot on their own prevent a downturn and initiate an upturn.

Discretionary Fiscal Policy

Discretionary fiscal policy refers to the deliberate changes in the government expenditure and the tax rates by the government in an economy in order to bring about stability in the economy.

It is important to note that the above explanation of discretionary fiscal policy is more applicable for a developed country where the main concern is with stabilization. However, as far as a developing country is concerned, the discretionary fiscal policy would be designed more towards achieving economic development.

A major limitation in the implementation of fiscal policy is the time lag involved in its implementation. Not only is there a delay in making decisions relating to the fiscal policy actions to achieve a particular goal, even once the decision has been made there are innumerable delays in the implementation and the execution of the policies. The time lag involved at the different stages of the fiscal policy actions leads to a decrease in the effectiveness of the policy.

RECAP

- A major limitation of automatic stabilizers is that though they can prevent a downturn in the output level from becoming worse but they cannot prevent a downturn from taking place.
- A major limitation in the implementation of fiscal policy is the time lag involved in its implementation.

FULL EMPLOYMENT BUDGET SURPLUS

In an economy, the effect of any fiscal plan on the economic activity is associated with the size of the fiscal budget:

(1) When the government expenditure is greater than government revenues, there exists a deficit in the budget and the government policy is stimulative or expansionary.

(2) When government expenditure is smaller than government revenues, there exists a surplus in the budget and the government policy is restrictive or contractionary.

However, it is incorrect to measure the direction of the fiscal policy as expansionary or contractionary by analysing a budget deficit or a budget surplus. A budget may be in deficit during a recession when there is a decrease in the tax revenue. On the other hand, a budget may be in surplus during a boom when there is an increase in the tax revenue.

To measure the effect of fiscal policy on the level of output, a policy measure is necessary which is independent and not related to the business cycles. The full employment budget surplus is often quoted to be such a policy measure.

A related concept is the budget surplus, BS. The budget surplus is the excess of government revenue over its total expenditures.While the government revenue is in the form of taxes, its total expenditures are in the form of purchases of goods and services and transfer payments.

The budget surplus is the excess of government revenue over its total expenditures.

Thus, $$BS = TA - G - TR$$

where,

BS = budget surplus

TA = tY = proportional tax

G = government expenditure on goods and services

TR = transfer payments

Thus, $$BS = tY - G - TR$$

A negative budget surplus is an excess of government expenditure over government revenue. In simpler terms, it is a budget deficit.

The full employment budget surplus measures the budget surplus at the full employment level of income. It is also known as the high employment surplus, the standardized budget surplus or the cyclically adjusted surplus (or deficit). If Y* is the full employment income level, then $BS^* = tY^* - G - TR$.

The full employment budget surplus measures the budget surplus at the full employment level of income.

Thus, $$BS^* - BS = t(Y^* - Y).$$

It is important to note that

(1) If the actual output level is higher than the full employment level, then the full employment budget surplus is smaller less than the actual surplus.

(2) If the actual output level is smaller than the full employment level, then the full employment budget surplus is larger than the actual budget surplus.

While the full employment budget and actual budget differ due to the cyclical factor in the budget, the full employment budget surplus differs from the actual budget surplus only in respect of tax collections.

The full employment budget surplus is a convenient way of analysing the impact of the budget and the effect of any fiscal plan on the economic activity.

The full employment budget surplus has been depicted in Fig. 25.1 where BS is the line depicting the budget surplus. It has been plotted as a function of income, given the fiscal policy choices in terms of t, G and TR. When the income level is high, the budget is in surplus or the budget surplus is high as the government revenue from tax is large. When the income level is low, the budget is in deficit or there is a budget deficit as the government revenue from tax is small.

In the figure suppose that the full employment level of output or income is at Y^*. The full employment budget surplus is BS*.

(1) At an income level of Y', the government will have a balanced budget where the government expenditure matches the government revenue.

(2) At lower levels of income, for example, if the income level is below the full employment level at Y_1, the budget will be in a deficit or there is a negative budget surplus. This occurs in spite of there being a surplus at the full employment level. This may happen, for example during recessions, when G + TR are larger than the collections from taxes.

(3) At higher levels of income, G + TR is smaller than the collections from taxes.

The changes in the budget often occur due to changes in fiscal policy:

(1) **An increase in the government expenditure:** An increase in government expenditures will decrease the budget surplus.

Change in income due to the increase in government expenditures can be expressed as $\Delta Y = G_M \Delta\overline{G}$.

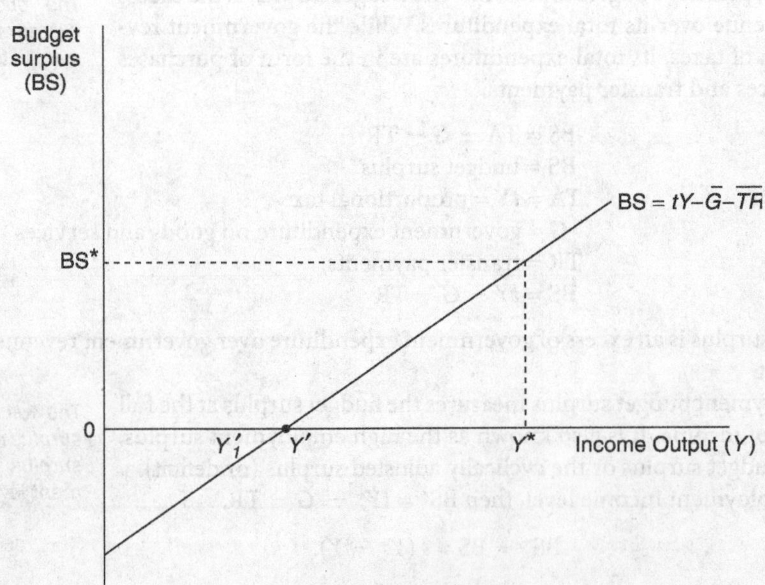

Figure 25.1 Budget Surplus

But a fraction of this increased income is collected as taxes. Thus, there is an increase in tax revenue equal to $\Delta T = tG_M \Delta M \overline{G}$

Change in budget surplus: $\Delta BS = \Delta T - \Delta\overline{G}$

$$= tG_M \Delta\overline{G} - \Delta\overline{G}$$

$$= \Delta\overline{G}\,(tG_M - 1)$$

$$= \Delta\overline{G}\,[\frac{t}{1 - b\,(1 - t)} - 1]$$

$$= \frac{-(1 - b)\,(1 - t)}{1 - b\,(1 - t)}\,\Delta\overline{G}$$

The change in the budget surplus is clearly negative. Thus, an increase in the government expenditure will decrease the budget surplus.

(2) **A rise in the tax rate:** An increase in the tax rate reduces the disposable income but increases the budget surplus.

We have observed that while an increase in the government expenditure decreases the budget surplus, an increase in the tax rate increases the budget surplus. It may appear that the budget surplus is a suitable measure of analysing the directions and effects of fiscal policy.

Besides the fiscal policy choices relating to *t*, *G* and TR, the budget deficit or surplus also depends on factors that affect the level of income. Thus, the budget surplus suffers from a serious defect in case it is used to measure the effects of fiscal policy. The problem is that there can occur a change in the budget surplus even due to a change in autonomous private investment expenditure. An increase in investment expenditures increases the income level. This leads to an increase in tax revenues and hence there is an increase in budget surplus or a decrease in the budget deficit. In this, it is quite obvious that the government has played no part in bringing about a change in the deficit.

RECAP

- An increase in the government expenditure or a decrease in the tax rate will decrease the budget surplus.
- Besides the fiscal policy choices relating to *t*, *G* and TR, the budget deficit or surplus, also depends on factors that affect the level of income.

LIMITATIONS OF FISCAL POLICY

(1) **The existence of a time lag** Similar to monetary policy, this is perhaps one of the major problems in the path of the working of fiscal policy. There exists a considerable time lag between the time there is a realization for the need for a fiscal policy and the time by which the response of the policy in bringing about changes in aggregate demand is felt.

The time lags can be divided under two heads:

(a) **Inside lags** These include the considerable time taken by the parliament or the state legislatures in giving their consent to the changes in the fiscal policy. There are long bureaucratic procedures which govern the changes required in taxation and government expenditures.

(b) **Outside lags** Once the approvals have been given, the changes in the fiscal policy act directly on aggregate demand and the output.

It is imperative to observe that in case of fiscal policy, inside lags are longer than the outside lags. However, the existence of the lags is certainly responsible for reducing the effectiveness of the fiscal policy. The policy makers, keeping in mind the existence of the lags, may often try to take the future into consideration in their attempts to bring about stability in the economy. But since the future is uncertain and difficult to predict, they may actually land up doing just the opposite, that is destabilize the economy. Hence, the policymakers should refrain from intervening in the functioning of the economy unless it is absolutely necessary to do so since they may do more harm than good.

(2) **The underdeveloped nature of the less developed countries limits the effectiveness of the fiscal policy** The major problems in the implementation of fiscal policy in the less developed countries are:

(a) In such economies, sectors like the agriculture sector are often non-monetized. It is difficult for the administrators to asses the taxes to be paid by this sector which is formed mainly by the farmers and the self employed. Often, the agricultural sector is either exempt from taxation or subject to a minimal tax. Hence, the entire burden of the tax has to be borne by the monetized sector which is unjust and inequitable because the rich and the powerful landowners are able to get away without paying little or no tax.

(b) In most such countries, the tax laws are highly complicated with various types of exemptions and deductions. As a result, many interpretations and loopholes coexist which in turn make the tax laws a fertile ground for long drawn litigation. The tax rates which ideally should be progressive end up being regressive favouring the smart, who incidentally are also rich, and who are able to take advantage of the loopholes while the general public and fixed income group bears the brunt of the tax. There are problems even at the level of the tax enforcement. The tax machinery is generally highly inefficient and prone to corruption which results in revenue leakages from the government coffers.

(c) **The excessive burden of public debt:** Often, the resources which are generated through tax and other sources may prove to be insufficient for the ever increasing expenditures necessary for development of the economy. Hence, the authorities have to raise public debt, or in other words borrowings, both internal and external.

The problems associated with public debt are innumerable. Not only have the loans to be paid back, the interest payments have also to be made at regular intervals. The problem is more acute in the case of external borrowings where all repayments are in terms of foreign currency. This will necessitate that the country earns sufficient foreign exchange to be in a position to pay back the debt. Often, a country may be caught in an external debt trap where it is forced to take on a fresh loan to pay back just the interest on the earlier loan. Even with internal borrowings, the government may have to take recourse to deficit financing which leads to inflation and related problems.

RECAP

- The existence of a time lag, underdeveloped nature of the less developed countries and the excessive burden of public debt limit the effectiveness of the fiscal policy.

CROWDING OUT AND ITS IMPORTANCE

Crowding out is a situation which takes place when an expansionary fiscal policy causes an increase in the rate of interest leading to a decrease in private spending, especially the investment level.

Crowding out is a situation which takes place when an expansionary fiscal policy causes an increase in the rate of interest leading to a decrease in private spending, especially the investment level.

In Figure 25.2, the effects of an expansionary fiscal policy have been analysed in terms of the IS–LM framework. The initial equilibrium is determined by the intersection of the curves IS_1 and LM at point E_1. Due to an expansionary fiscal policy, the equilibrium shifts to E_2 and not E'. The income level increases to Y_2 and not Y'. The reason for this can be explained in terms of the rise in the

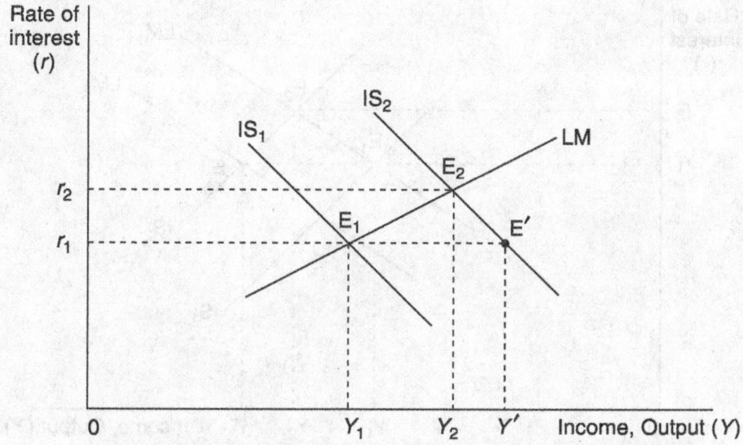

Figure 25.2 Effects of Expansionary Fiscal Policy

rate of interest from r_1 to r_2. This has a contractionary effect on investment. Thus, the increase in government spending crowds out private investment spending. The adjustments which occur in the interest rate have a dampening effect on the increase in output which is caused by the increase in government spending. It is to be noted that the higher the increase in the rate of interest rate due to increase in government spending, the greater will be the crowding out effect.

The crowding out depends on certain factors:

(1) The flatter is the LM curve, the lower is the increase in interest rates and thus the higher is the increase in income.

(2) The flatter is the IS curve, the lower is the increase in the interest rate and thus the lower is the increase in income.

(3) The larger the value of the multiplier, the higher the increase in the interest rate and the income.

The importance of crowding out can be analysed by considering following three cases:

(1) In an economy where there exist unemployed resources, a fiscal expansion may increase the level of output but it may not increase the interest rate, as shown in Fig. 25.3. The reason may be the increase in the supply of money by the monetary authorities in order to accommodate the fiscal expansion. This would prevent the rise in the interest rate.

Monetary accommodation is also described as monetizing the budget deficit. It involves the printing of more money by the monetary authorities. Such a situation has been depicted in Figure 25.3 where both the IS and LM curves shift to the right and equilibrium shifts from E_1 to E′. The income level increases from Y_1 to Y' while the rate of interest remains unchanged at r_1. There need not occur a decrease in investment and hence there may not be any crowding out.

(2) In an economy where the level of output is below the full employment level, a fiscal expansion increases the level of aggregate demand but now the firms can hire additional workers to increase the output level. There will be an increase in both the rate of interest and income level. However, there occurs an increase in savings in the economy which will make possible the financing of a larger budget deficit without there being a total displacement of private investment. Hence, there will not be a full crowding out.

(3) In an economy where the level of output is at the full employment level, a fiscal expansion increases the level of aggregate demand which will lead to an increase in the price level. This will decrease the real money balances causing the LM curve to shift to the left, raising interest rates until the initial increase in the aggregate demand is totally crowded out.

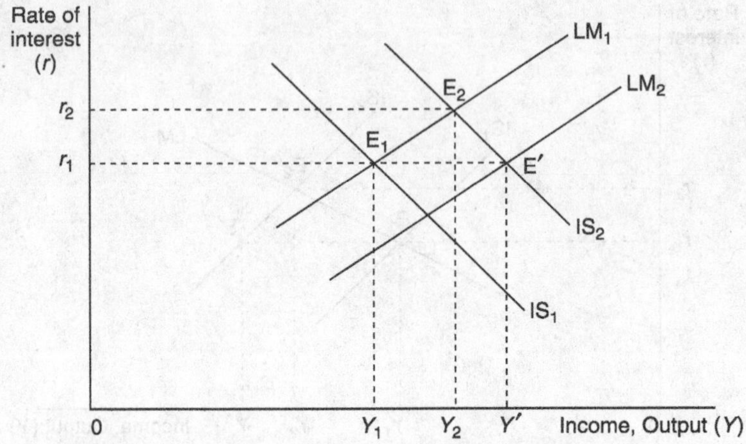

Figure 25. 3 A Fiscal Expansion and Monetary Accommodation

RECAP

- **In an economy where there exist unemployed resources, there may not be any crowding out.**
- **In an economy where the level of output is below the full employment level, there will not be a full crowding out.**
- **In an economy where the level of output is at the full employment level, there will be complete crowding out.**

SUMMARY

INTRODUCTION

1. **This chapter examined monetary policy and fiscal policy and their functioning.**
2. **An attempt has also been made at understanding the goals which these policies aim at achieving.**

MEANING OF MONETARY POLICY

1. **Monetary policy is an operation by the monetary authorities of the country to achieve certain well-defined macroeconomic objectives/goals.**
2. **It is generally the central bank of the country which undertakes the implementation of the monetary policy. It operates through changes in the quantity of money.**

INSTRUMENTS OF MONETARY POLICY

1. **The main objectives which the monetary policy aims at achieving include economic growth, a higher rate of employment and price stability.**
2. **To achieve the objectives of monetary policy, there exist various instruments which can be divided into two categories: quantitative or general measures and qualitative or selective measures.**
3. **Quantitative or general measures of monetary policy control the total volume of credit and the cost of credit in the economy and thus the supply of money. They include open market operations, variations in reserve requirements, statutory liquidity requirement,bank rate policy, repo rate and reverse repo rate.**
4. **Open market operations refer tothe sale and purchase of government securities and treasury bills by the central bank. It is an instrument of monetary control which is most powerful and which is most widely used by the central bank.**
5. **The advantages of open market operations are: they are highly flexible, easily reversible in time and do not have any announcement effects.**

6. Variations in reserve requirements can be divided under two heads, required reserves and excess reserves.
7. Required reserves are cash balances which banks hold to meet their statutory reserve requirements. The purpose of these reserves is to safeguard the interest of the depositors. It also enables the central bank to be able to control liquidity.
8. Excess reserves are reserves in excess of the required reserves. They are held by the banks for meeting currency drains and clearing drains.
9. It is often alleged that variations in reserve requirements are an inferior tool of monetary policy because they lead to lumpy and discontinuous changes in the deposits and also in that they produce announcement effects.
10. Under the statutory liquidity requirement,banks are statutorily required to maintain a certain fixed proportion of their demand and time liabilities in the form of designated liquid assets.
11. In India, like the CRR, the SLR has not been very successful as an instrument of monetary policy.
12. Bank rate policy or the discount rate is the rate of interest at which the central bank rediscounts eligible bills of exchange or other commercial papers.
13. The limitation of the bank rate policy is that it is more sticky in comparison to the other rates and the changes in it are discontinuous and have announcement effects.
14. The repo rate is the rate at which the central bank infuses short-term liquidity into the system. In simpler terms, it is the rate at which the central bank lends to the banks. The reverse repo rate is the rate at which banks park their short-term excess liquidity with the central bank in exchange for government securities. It is the rate at which the central bank borrows from the banks.
15. Qualitative or selective measures of monetary policy control the direction and distribution of credit in the economy. They include rationing of credit, change in margin requirements, moral suasion and direct action.
16. Credit rationing is resorted to when there occurs a shortage of institutional credit.
17. Change in margin requirements works indirectly to influence lending and thus regulate the capital markets.
18. Moral suasion is a combination of persuasion and pressures which a central bank asserts to bring the erring banks in line so that they function in accordance with the central bank's directives.
19. Direct action refers to the coercive actions resorted to by the central bank against banks who do not function according to its directives.
20. Deficit financing refers to ways in which the deficit in the government's budget is financed. The central bank merely prints more currency and then puts them into circulation on behalf of the government.
21. One major problem that is associated with deficit financing is that it always results in inflation.

LIMITATIONS OF MONETARY POLICY

The limitations of monetary policy are the existence of a time lag, presence of non-bank financial intermediaries reducing the impact of the monetary policy through an increase in the velocity of money and the underdeveloped nature of the money and capital markets.

MEANING OF FISCAL POLICY

1. Fiscal policy refers to the government's policy regarding government expenditure, taxation and public borrowing with the view to achieving certain well-defined macroeconomic objectives.
2. It was only with the coming of Keynes that fiscal policy gained importance.
3. The monetarists believed that with the exception of some circumstances, in general, increases in government expenditures do not add to aggregate demand but in fact are responsible for crowding out private investment of an equal amount.

INSTRUMENTS OF FISCAL POLICY

1. To implement fiscal policy, the government has at its behest several instruments which include taxation, government expenditure and public borrowing.
2. Taxation is one of the most important sources of revenue for the government in most countries. Taxes can be analysed under two headings: direct taxes which include corporate income taxes, personal income tax and taxes on wealth and property and indirect taxes which include sales tax, excise duty and customs duty.

3. In the developed countries, the direct taxes are a more important source of revenue for the government as compared to the developing countries where indirect taxes are more important.
4. Since the Great Depression, the government's role in economic activity is continuously on the increase. It was realized that government expenditure is imperative for an economy in the form of investments in capital goods industries, building the infrastructure and payments of wages and salaries.
5. Though public borrowing is the second most important source of revenue, it is unlike taxes. All the borrowings from the public must be paid back in the future. Public borrowing can take two forms: compulsory loans and voluntary loans where bills and securities are issued by the government.

FISCAL POLICY AND STABILIZATION IN THE ECONOMY

1. In any economy, due to the business cycles there are many ups and downs causing instability in the economy. Fiscal policy actions can tackle the problem of instability.
2. Two automatic stabilizers are: a proportional income tax and unemployment benefits. A major limitation of automatic stabilizers is that though they can prevent a downturn in the output level from becoming worse but they cannot prevent a downturn from taking place.
3. Discretionary fiscal policy refers to the deliberate changes in the government expenditure and the tax rates by the government in an economy in order to bring about stability in the economy. A major limitation in the implementation of fiscal policy is the time lag involved in its implementation.

LIMITATIONS OF FISCAL POLICY

1. The effective working of fiscal policy is hindered due to the existence of different obstacles.
2. The existence of a time lag which includes inside lags and outside lags. In case of fiscal policy, inside lags are longer than the outside lags.
3. The underdeveloped nature of the less developed countries limits the effectiveness of the fiscal policy. It is difficult for the administrators to asses the taxes to be paid by agriculture sector. In most countries, the tax laws are highly complicated.
4. Often, the resources which are generated through tax and other sources may prove to be insufficient and the authorities may have to resort to public debt.

CROWDING OUT AND ITS IMPORTANCE

1. Crowding out is a situation which takes place when an expansionary fiscal policy causes an increase in the rate of interest leading to a decrease in private spending, especially the investment level.
2. An increase in government spending crowds out private investment spending. It is to be noted that the higher the increase in the rate of interest rate due to increase in government spending, the greater will be the crowding out effect.
3. The importance of crowding out can be analysed by considering three cases.
4. In an economy where there exist unemployed resources, a fiscal expansion may not lead to any crowding out.
5. In an economy where the level of output is below the full employment level, there will not be a full crowding out.
6. In an economy where the level of output is at the full employment level, there will be a full crowding out.

REVIEW QUESTIONS

TRUE OR FALSE QUESTIONS

1. Monetary policy is an operation by the monetary authorities of the country.
2. The two categories of instruments of monetary policy at the disposal of the central bank are the quantitative or general measures and the qualitative or selective measures.
3. Required reserves are cash balances which the central bank holds to meet its statutory reserve requirements.
4. According to the statutory liquidity requirement, banks are required to maintain a certain fixed proportion of their liabilities in the form of designated liquid assets.
5. Reverse repo rate is the rate at which the central bank infuses short-term liquidity into the system.

VERY SHORT-ANSWER QUESTIONS

1. What is the difference between monetary policy and credit policy?
2. Mention the main objectives which the monetary policy aims at achieving.
3. Name the two categories of instruments of monetary policy at the disposal of the central bank.
4. What are excess reserves? Why are they held by the banks?
5. What is the difference between the repo rate and the reverse repo rate?

SHORT-ANSWER QUESTIONS

1. What is the meaning of monetary policy?
2. What is an open market operation?
3. What is fiscal policy? Discuss.
4. Why are variations in reserve requirements said to be an inferior tool of monetary policy as compared to open market operations?
5. Write a short note on the bank rate policy.

LONG-ANSWER QUESTIONS

1. What are the instruments of monetary policy? How are the two categories different from each other?
2. 'Open market operation is an instrument of monetary control which is most powerful and which is most widely used by the central bank.' Discuss.
3. How can fiscal policy actions tackle the problem of stabilization in the economy?
4. 'To implement fiscal policy, the government has at its behest several instruments which include taxation, government expenditure and public borrowing.' Comment.
5. What is crowding out? Why is it important?

ANSWERS

TRUE OR FALSE QUESTIONS

1. **True.** Monetary policy is an operation by the monetary authorities of the country to achieve certain well-defined macroeconomic objectives.
2. **True.** These instruments give the central bank the power to control the money supply and, hence, achieve the macroeconomic objectives.
3. **False.** Required reserves are cash balances which commercial banks hold to meet their statutory reserve requirements.
4. **True.** This is a statutory requirement where the banks are required to maintain a certain fixed proportion of their demand and time liabilities in the form of designated liquid assets.
5. **False.** Reverse repo rate is the rate at which banks park their short-term excess liquidity with the central bank in exchange for government securities.

Appendix A

An Alternative Formulation of the IS–LM Model: The Recent Approach to the IS–LM Model

THE GOODS MARKET EQUILIBRIUM: THE *IS* CURVE

The equilibrium in the goods market is represented by the IS curve. The IS curve is a graphic representation of the goods market equilibrium showing the different combinations of the output levels and the interest rates at which planned spending is equal to income.

The derivation of the IS curve can be done in two stages:

Stage 1: The Investment Demand Curve

Investment is expenditure on the additions to the firm's capital in the form of building, machinery, etc.

In the earlier chapters, investment has been assumed to be exogenous. However as the interest rate is being introduced in our analysis, investment is now taken as endogenous.

Investment is expenditure on the additions to the firm's capital in the form of building, machinery, etc. Firms borrow for purposes of making investments. The higher is the rate of interest on the borrowings, the lower are the profits of the firm. Hence at high rates of interest, the firm will borrow and invest less as compared to low rates of interest. Thus, the investment function can be expressed as

$$I = \bar{I} - br \qquad (1)$$

where,

$\bar{I}$ = autonomous investment spending (or investment spending that is independent of both the income level and the interest rate)

b = responsiveness of investment spending to the rate of interest

r = the rate of interest

Equation (1) states that

(1) The lower the interest rate the higher is the planned investment.

(2) A large b implies that a relatively small increase in the rate of interest will lead to a large decrease in the level of investment.

Figure A.1 shows the firm's investment demand curve showing the firm's investment at different rates of interest. The position of the curve depends on the following:

(1) $\bar{I}$ or the level of autonomous investment spending. A change in $\bar{I}$ will lead to a shift in the curve. A rise in $\bar{I}$ implies a higher investment at each level of the rate of interest. A fall in $\bar{I}$ implies a lower investment at each level of the rate of interest.

(2) b or the responsiveness of investment spending to the rate of interest.

(a) A large b implies that the responsiveness of investment to the rate of interest is high. Thus, a small decrease in the rate of interest will lead to a large increase in the level of investment. Hence, the investment demand curve is nearly flat.

(b) A small b implies that the responsiveness of investment to the rate of interest is low. Thus, a small decrease in the rate of interest will lead to a small increase in the level of investment. Hence, the investment demand curve is nearly vertical.

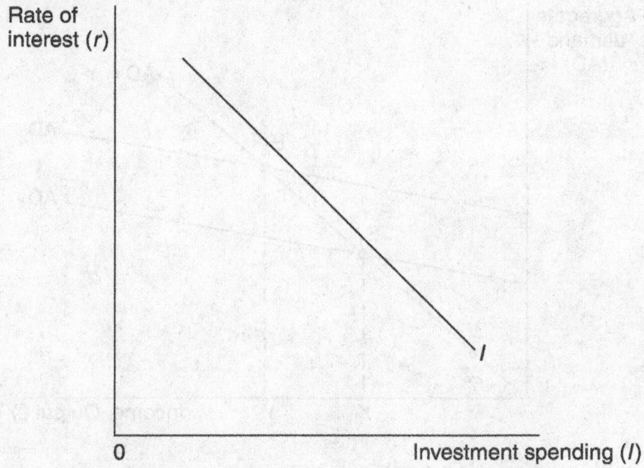

Figure A.1 Investment Demand Curve

Stage 2: The Investment Demand Curve and the Aggregate Demand Curve

In the earlier chapters in a two sector economy, investment was defined to include consumption and investment but with investment as exogenous. We now include investment as a function of the interest rate in the aggregate demand function. Thus,

$$\text{AD} = C + I$$

where,

$$C = \overline{C}_a + bY \text{ (consumption function)}$$

$$I = \bar{I} - br \text{ (investment function)}$$

Substituting in the aggregate demand function for the consumption function and the investment function, we get

$$\text{AD} = \overline{C}_a + bY + \bar{I} - br \tag{2}$$

A Derivation of the IS Curve

Figure A.2 shows the derivation of the IS curve.

Suppose the rate of interest is r_1. The aggregate demand curve will be

$$\text{AD}_1 = \overline{C}_a + bY + \bar{I} - br_1 \tag{3}$$

In equation (3), the term $\overline{C}_a + \bar{I} - br_1$ is a constant. Hence, the intercept of the aggregate demand curve, AD_1 is equal to $\overline{C}_a + I - br$. AD_1 intersects the guideline at point E_1 to determine the equilibrium level of income at Y_1. (Y_1, r_1) form one combination of income and the rate of interest at which planned spending is equal to income or at which the goods market is in equilibrium. This can be plotted as in Figure A.2(b) to obtain point E_1.

A decrease in interest rate to r_2 leads to a shift in the aggregate demand curve from AD_1 to AD_2. The intercept of the aggregate demand curve, AD_2 is equal to $\overline{C}_a + I - br_2$. AD_2 intersects the guideline at point E_2 to determine the equilibrium level of income at Y_2. Thus, (Y_2, r_2) form another combination of income and the rate of interest at which the goods market is in equilibrium. This again can be plotted in Figure A.2(b) to obtain point E_2.

Similarly, the other combinations can be derived. Joining these points at which the goods market is in equilibrium we can arrive at the IS curve as in Figure A.2(b). At each and every point on the IS curve, the goods market is in equilibrium. The IS curve is downward sloping indicating the negative relationship between income and the rate of interest.

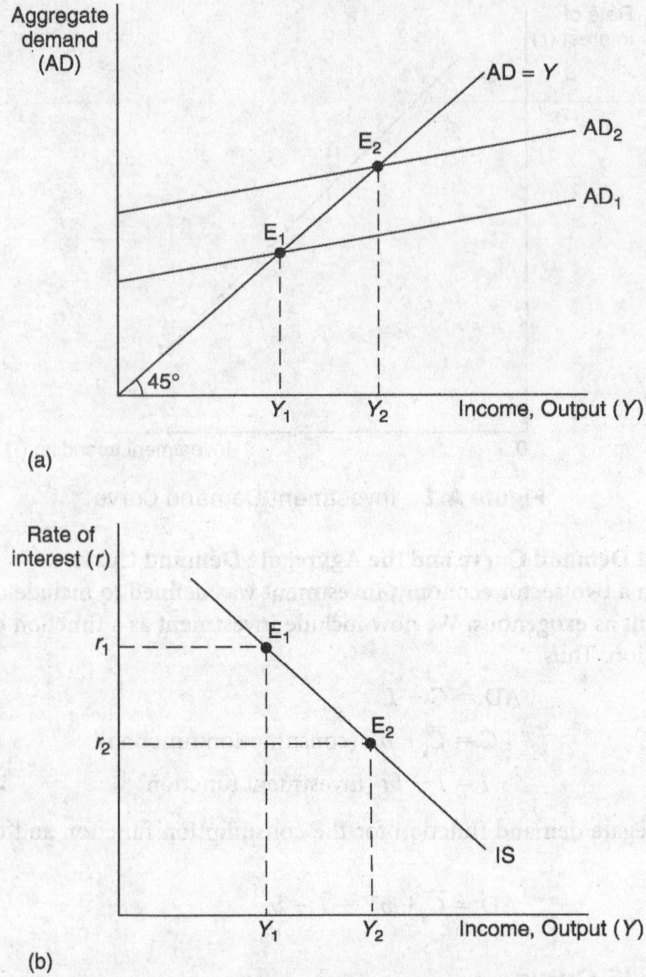

Figure A.2 A Derivation of the IS Curve

THE MONEY—MARKET EQUILIBRIUM: THE LM CURVE

The equilibrium in the money market is represented by the LM curve. The LM curve is a graphic representation of the money—market equilibrium showing the different combinations of the output levels and the interest rates at which the demand for money is equal to the supply of money.

A Derivation of the LM Curve

The derivation of the LM curve can be shown in two stages:

Stage 1: The Demand for Money

The demand for money is actually a demand for real (and not nominal) money. The demand for real money depends on two factors:

(1) Real income, as individuals hold money to finance their expenditures which depend on their real income.

(2) Rate of interest which is the opportunity cost of holding money. Thus, at a high interest rate the demand for money is low.

Thus, the demand for real balances can be expressed as

$$L = kY - hr \tag{4}$$

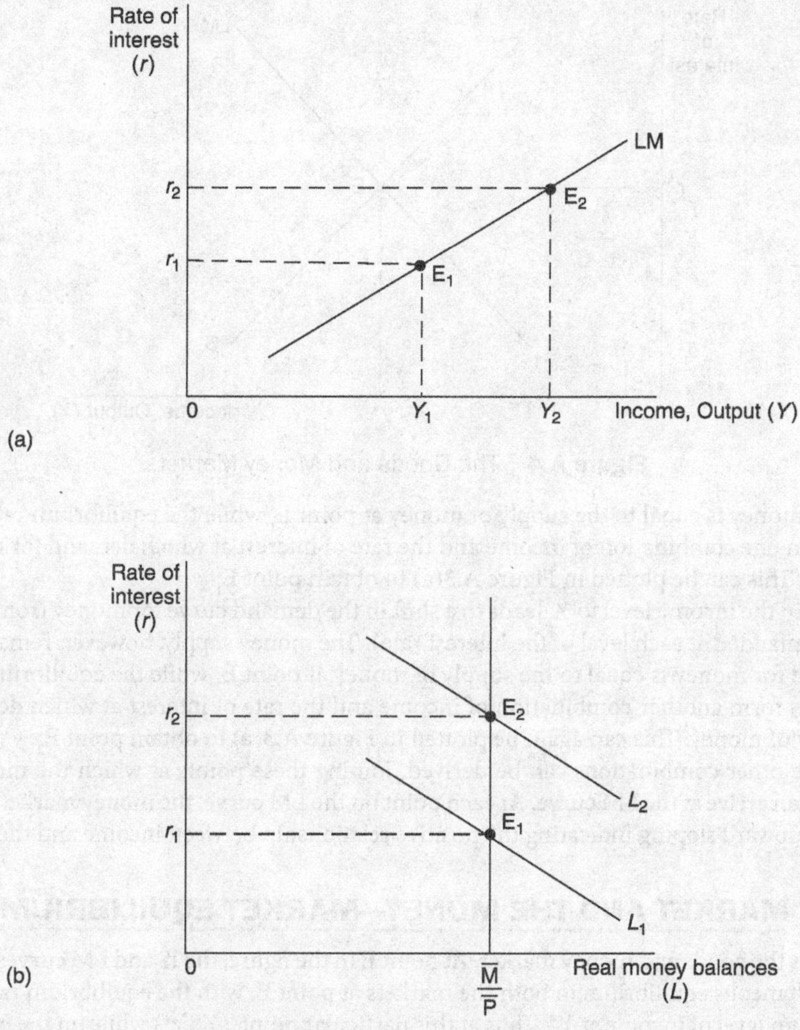

Figure A.3 A Derivation of the LM Curve

where, L = demand for real money balances

k = responsiveness of demand for real money balances to the income level

Y = income level

h = responsiveness of demand for real money balances to the interest rate

r = rate of interest

Stage 2: The Equilibrium in the Money Market-Demand for Money Equals the Supply of Money

As far as the supply of money is concerned, the nominal quantity of money, M in an economy is determined by the central bank. Given the price level, the real supply of money is at the level $\overline{M}/\overline{P}$. Hence, the supply of money curve is a vertical line, independent of the rate of interest in Figure A.3(b).

As far as the demand for money is concerned, initially suppose the income level is Y_1. The corresponding demand curve for money is

$$L_1 = kY_1 - hr.$$

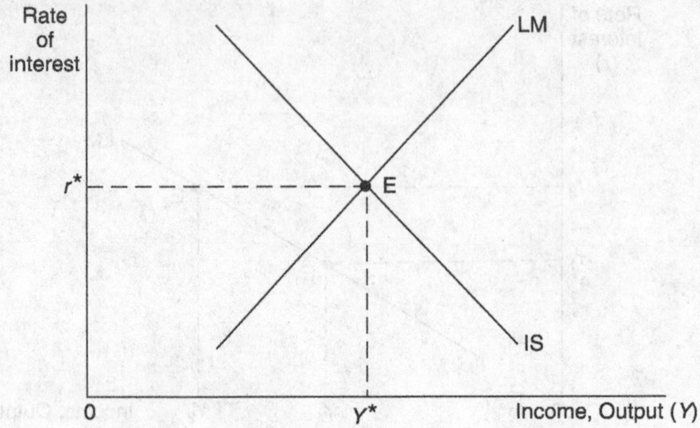

Figure A.4 The Goods and Money Markets

The demand for money is equal to the supply of money at point E_1 while the equilibrium rate of interest is r_1. Thus, (Y_1, r_1) form one combination of income and the rate of interest at which demand for money equals the supply of money. This can be plotted in Figure A.3(a) to obtain point E_1.

An increase in the income level to Y_2 leads to a shift in the demand curve for money from L_1 to L_2 (as more money is now demanded at each level of the interest rate). The money supply, however, remains unchanged at $\overline{M}/\overline{P}$. The demand for money is equal to the supply of money at point E_2 while the equilibrium rate of interest is r_2. Thus, (Y_2, r_2) form another combination of income and the rate of interest at which demand for money equals the supply of money. This can again be plotted in Figure A.3(a) to obtain point E_2.

Similarly, the other combinations can be derived. Joining these points at which the money market is in equilibrium, we can arrive at the LM curve. At each point on the LM curve, the money market is in equilibrium. The LM curve is upward sloping indicating the positive relationship between income and the rate of interest.

THE GOODS MARKET AND THE MONEY—MARKET EQUILIBRIUM

Figure A.4 depicts the goods and money market. At point E in the figure, the IS and LM curves intersect. Hence, there exists simultaneous equilibrium in both the markets at point E, with the equilibrium rate of interest at r^* and the equilibrium level of income at Y^*. Thus at this particular point, (Y^*, r^*) while on the one hand, planned spending is equal to income, on the other hand the demand for money is equal to the supply of money.

APPENDIX B

The IS–LM Framework for a Four Sector Model

INTRODUCTION

In Chapters 16 and 17, we have focused on a closed economy. We are now in a position to relax this assumption and focus on an open economy in which there are four sectors: households, firms, government and the foreign sector.

THE IS–LM MODEL FOR A FOUR SECTOR ECONOMY

In the construction of a four sector model, two new variables which pertain to the foreign sector are included, exports and imports. The analysis is based on certain assumptions, some of which are the same as in the earlier models:

(1) The price level is constant.

(2) At that constant price level, the firms are willing to supply whatever output is demanded.

(3) The short-run aggregate supply curve is perfectly elastic till the full employment level of output.

(4) Government expenditure is autonomous. Hence, $G = \overline{G}$.

(5) Taxes are a linear function of income. Thus, $T = \overline{T} + tY$, where T is the autonomous tax (which is independent of the income level) while t is the income tax rate.

(6) Exports involve an outflow of domestic goods and services and, hence, an inflow of income. It is assumed that exports are constant, or $X = \overline{X}$.

(7) Imports involve an inflow of foreign goods and services and, hence, an outflow of income. It is assumed that imports are a function of income, or $M = \overline{M}_a + mY$.

THE GOODS MARKET EQUILIBRIUM IN A FOUR SECTOR ECONOMY: THE IS CURVE

As already discussed, there are two approaches to determine the equilibrium level of income. In a four sector economy, they are:

(1) **Aggregate Demand—Aggregate Supply Approach**

$$\text{Aggregate demand} = \text{Total value of output (or income)}$$

or
$$Y = C + I + G + X - M$$

(2) **Injections equal Leakages Approach**

$$I + G + X = S + T + M$$

We have consumption function as $C = C(Y)$

Investment function as $I = I(r)$

Government expenditure $G = \overline{G}$

Saving function as $S = S(Y)$

Tax as $T = \overline{T} + tY$

Exports as $X = \overline{X}$ (where exports are constant)

Imports function as $M = \overline{M}_a + mY$ (where M_a represents autonomous imports and m is the marginal propensity to import)

The equilibrium condition can be written as

$$Y = C(Y) + I(r) + \overline{G} + \overline{X} + M(Y)$$

The two equilibrium conditions can be used to develop a graphical approach to the derivation of the IS curve.

In Figure B.1, in Quadrant A exports have been added to the $I + G$ curve to get the $I + G + X$. As exports are independent of the interest rate, $I + G + X$ curve lies to the right of $I + G$ curve of the three sector economy.

Quadrant B gives the injections—leakages equality in the form of a 45 degree line drawn through the origin. At all points along this 45 degree line, injections equal leakages or $I + G + X = S + T + M$.

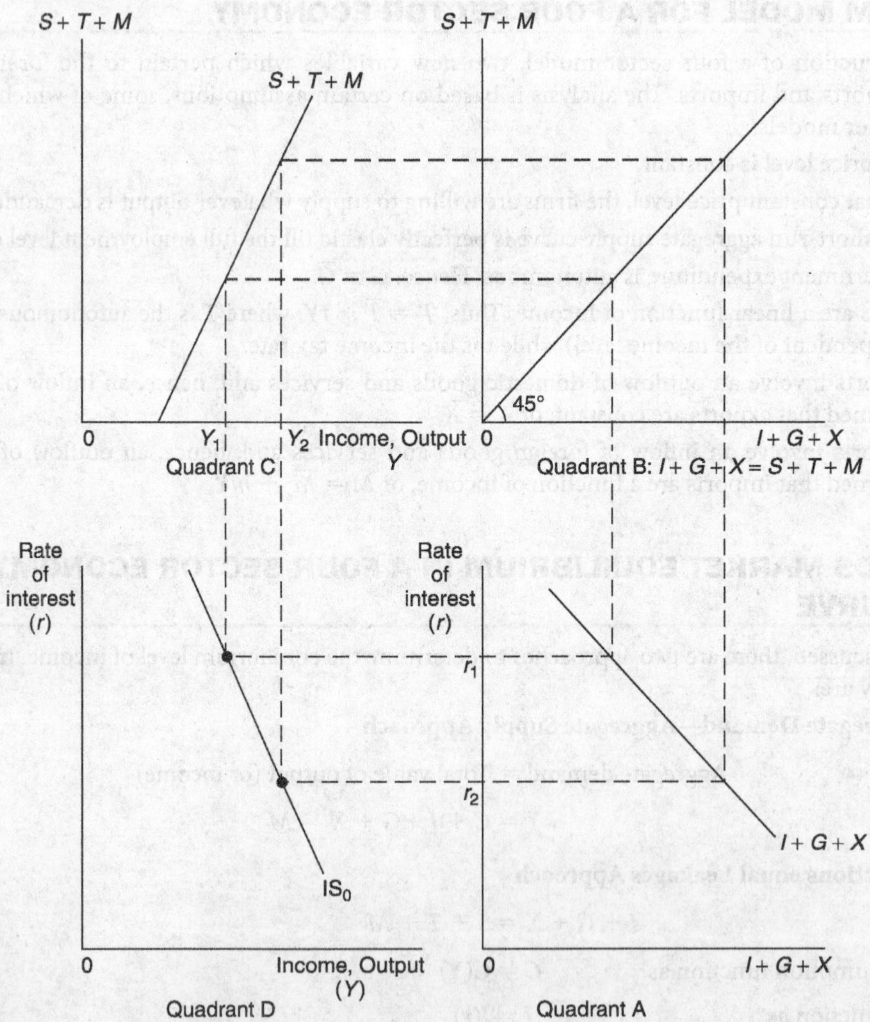

Figure B.1 The Goods Market Equilibrium in a Four Sector Economy: The IS Curve

Quadrant C shows the saving plus tax plus imports function. To introduce imports in the model, imports are added vertically to the $S + T$ curve to get the $S + T + M$ curve.

The investment plus government expenditure plus exports $(I + G + X)$ curve of Quadrant A and the saving plus tax curve plus imports, $(S + T + M)$ curve of Quadrant C yields the curve IS_0 for the open economy in Quadrant D.

As compared to the IS curve of the closed economy, the slope of the IS_0 curve is greater than the IS curve of the closed economy.

THE MONEY–MARKET EQUILIBRIUM IN A THREE SECTOR ECONOMY: THE LM CURVE

In a four sector economy, the analysis of the money market will remain the same as in the two and three sectors economy since the introduction of the foreign sector does not influence either the demand for money or the supply of money.

EQUILIBRIUM IN THE TWO MARKETS: THE GOODS MARKET AND MONEY MARKET

The IS Curve: An Algebraic Explanation

The goods market is in equilibrium when
Aggregate demand = Total value of output (or income)

or $$Y = C + I + G + X - M$$

But

$$C = C_a + bY_d,$$
$$I = \bar{I} - hr,$$
$$G = \overline{G},$$
$$Y_d = Y - T,$$
$$T = \overline{T} + tY$$
$$X = \overline{X}$$
$$M = \overline{M}_a + mY$$

Thus,

$$Y = C_a + bY_d + \bar{I} - hr + \overline{G} + \overline{X} - (\overline{M}_a + mY)$$
$$Y = C_a + b(Y - T) + \bar{I} - hr + \overline{G} + \overline{X} - (\overline{M}_a + mY)$$
$$Y = C_a + b[Y - (\overline{T} + tY)] + \bar{I} - hr + \overline{G} + \overline{X} - (\overline{M}_a + mY)$$
$$Y = C_a + bY - b\overline{T} - btY + \bar{I} - hr + \overline{G} + \overline{X} - \overline{M}_a - mY$$
$$Y - bY + btY + mY = C_a - b\overline{T} + \bar{I} - hr + \overline{G} + \overline{X} - M_a$$
$$Y(1 - b + bt + m) = C_a - b\overline{T} + \bar{I} - hr + \overline{G} + \overline{X} - \overline{M}_a$$
$$Y = \frac{1}{1 - b(1 - t) + m} C_a - b\overline{T} + \bar{I} - \text{hr} + \overline{G} + \overline{X} - \overline{M}_a \quad (1)$$

Equation (1) represents the IS curve in a four sector economy.

The LM Curve: An Algebraic Explanation

The money market equilibrium is similar to that of a two and three sector economy. Thus,

$$m_d = m_s$$

But

$$m_d = m_t + m_{sp}$$

where,

$$m_t = kY$$

$$m_{sp} = g(r)$$

We assume that the speculative demand for money is a linear function, $\overline{m}_{sp} = m_{sp} - g(r)$

We have

Supply of money as

$$m_s = \overline{m}_a$$

Demand for money as

$$m_d = kY + \overline{m}_{sp} - g(r)$$

The money—market equilibrium condition can be written as

$$\overline{m}_s = kY + \overline{m}_{sp} - g(r)$$

Thus,

$$\frac{Y}{k} = 1\,[\overline{m}_s - \overline{m}_{sp} + g(r)] \qquad (2)$$

Equation (2) represents the LM curve.

Equilibrium in the Goods and the Money Market in Three Sector Economy

We have already observed in Chapter 17 that there is only one combination of income and the rate of interest at which there exists a simultaneous equilibrium in the goods and the money markets in a four sector economy. This has been depicted in Figure B.2. This combination exists at point E_0 at which the IS_0 and LM curves intersect to determine the equilibrium rate of interest at r_0 and the equilibrium level of income at Y_0. At all other points, there exists disequilibrium in either the goods market or the money market or both the markets.This disequilibrium will remain unchanged until a shift in the IS or LM curve disturbs the equilibrium.

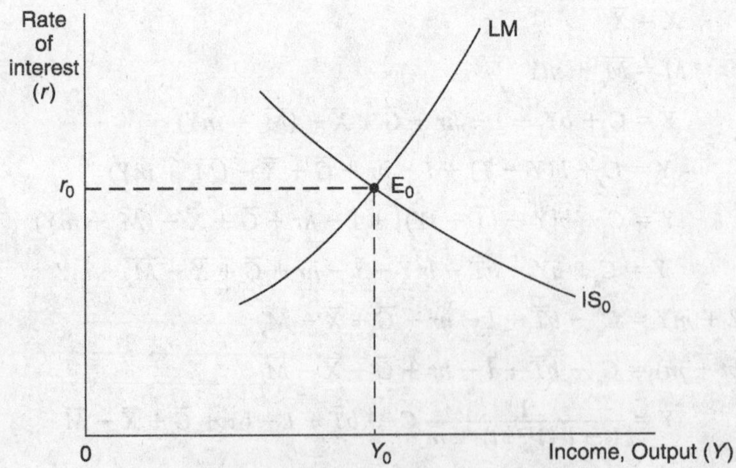

Figure B.2 Equilibrium in the Goods and the Money Market in a Four Sector Economy

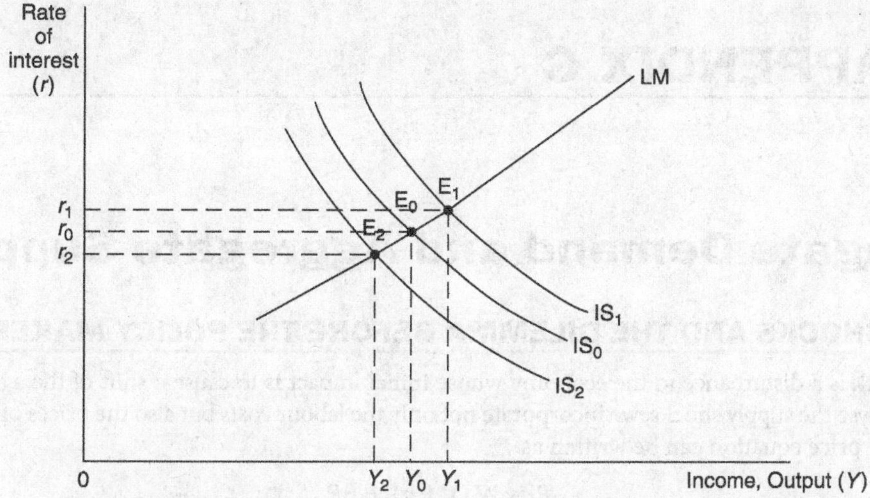

Figure B.3 Shifts in the IS Curve in a Four Sector Economy

SHIFTS IN THE IS CURVE IN A FOUR SECTOR ECONOMY

A shift in the IS curve can occur due to a change in both internal and external factors. Here, we are focusing on only the external factors or the foreign sector, as we have already analysed the internal factors in much detail.

In Figure B.3, the initial equilibrium exists at point E_0 at which the IS_0 and LM curves intersect to determine the equilibrium rate of interest at r_0 and the equilibrium level of income at Y_0.

Assume now that there occurs a rightward shift in the IS curve from IS_0 to IS_1. This could occur due to:

(1) An increase in exports which could arise due to
   (a) a change in the tastes in the other countries in favour of exports.
   (b) an increase in the incomes in the other countries.
   (c) a decrease in the duties on imports in the other countries.

(2) A decrease in imports which could arise due to
   (a) a change in the tastes in the domestic economy in favour of the domestic goods.
   (b) an increase in the duties on imports from the other countries.

Given that there is no change in the relative price levels or any other changes, the new equilibrium will occur at point E_1 at which the IS_1 and LM curves intersect. The equilibrium rate of interest will be r_1 and the equilibrium level of income will be Y_1. Hence, there will occur an increase in both the equilibrium income and the rate of interest. Similarly, it can be shown that a leftward shift in the IS curve will lead to a decrease in both the equilibrium income and the rate of interest.

APPENDIX C

Aggregate Demand and Aggregate Supply

SUPPLY SHOCKS AND THE DILEMMA BEFORE THE POLICY MAKERS

A supply shock is a disturbance in the economy whose initial impact is to cause a shift of the aggregate supply curve. To analyse the supply shocks, we incorporate not only the labour costs but also the prices of raw materials.

Thus, the price equation can be written as

$$P = W(1 + z) + \theta P_m$$

where,

P = Price

W = Wage in the current period

z = Mark up over labour costs

θ = Material requirement per unit of output

P_m = Prices of the materials

θP_m = Input cost of the materials.

Analysing the above equation, we observe that

(1) The wage rate, W, and thus the price increases with the output level. Therefore, the aggregate supply curve is upward sloping.

(2) Given the wage rate, an increase in the price of the materials, P_m, leads to an increase in the price level. This again will lead to an upward shift of the aggregate supply curve.

An Adverse Supply Shock

An adverse supply shock leads to an upward shift of the aggregate supply curve. For example, an increase in the real prices of oil will lead to an upward shift of the aggregate supply curve from AS to AS′ in Figure C.1. The economy's equilibrium shifts from E to the unemployment equilibrium at E′, increasing the prices and reducing the output level. Also, now at each level of output the production costs are higher.

Over a period of time, due to the existence of unemployment there occurs a decrease in the wages and hence in prices. Slowly, the economy returns to the initial equilibrium at point E, which is the full employment level.

At point E, though the price level is the same as before the shock, the nominal wage and, thus, the real wages are lower as compared to before the shock. Thus, an adverse supply shock reduces the real wage rate.

An adverse supply shock can be dealt with by macroeconomic policy. Accommodating fiscal or monetary policies could shift the aggregate demand curve from AD to AD′. This would shift the economy to E*, which is the full employment level.

Such a policy would certainly decrease the unemployment effects of the supply shocks. But there would be an increase in prices by the full extent of the upward shift in the aggregate supply curve. This happens due to the trade-off between the inflationary impact and the recessionary effects of a supply shock.

Although an adverse supply shock leads to an increase in the price level, a decrease in the GNP and in the real wages, a favourable supply shock would have just the opposite effect—a decrease in the price level, increase in GNP and in the real wages.

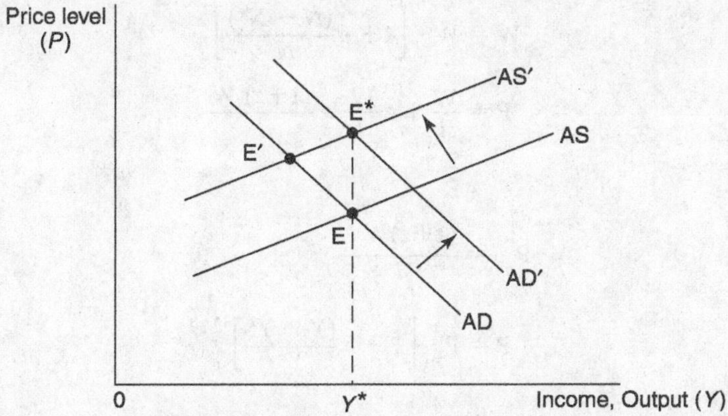

Figure C.1 An Adverse Supply Shock

DERIVATION OF THE UPWARD SLOPING AGGREGATE SUPPLY CURVE THROUGH THE PRODUCTION FUNCTION

Step 1: Production Function

The production function relates the output level to employment through the equation

$$Y = lN \tag{1}$$

Step 2: Prices and Cost

$$P = \frac{W}{l} + z\frac{W}{l} = \frac{(1+z)\,W}{l} \tag{2}$$

Step 3: Phillips' Curve

According to the Phillips' curve,

$$g_w = \frac{W - W_{-1}}{W_{-1}} \tag{3}$$

where,

g_w = Rate of wage inflation

W = Wages in the current period

W_{-1} = Wages in the previous period

The simple Phillips' curve can be written as

$$g_w = -\,e\,(u - u^*) \tag{4}$$

where,

u = Unemployment rate

u^* = Natural rate of unemployment

e = Responsiveness of the wages to unemployment

From the above equations, we get

$$W = W_{-1}\,[1 - e\,(u - u^*)]$$

But

$$u = \frac{N^* - N}{N}$$

where, N^* = Full employment

N = Actual employment

Thus

$$g_w = \frac{W - W_{-1}}{W_{-1}} = e\frac{(N^* - N)}{N}$$

or
$$W = W_{-1}\left[1 + e\frac{(N - N^*)}{N^*}\right]$$

Now
$$P = \frac{W}{l} + z\frac{W}{l} = \frac{(1+z)\,W}{l}$$

also
$$P_{-1} = \frac{(1+z)W_{-1}}{l}$$

Hence,
$$P = P_{-1}\left[1 + e\frac{(Y - Y^*)}{Y^*}\right]$$

This can be written as
$$P = P_{-1}\left[\frac{1 + e\,(Y - Y^*)}{Y^*}\right]$$

This is the equation of the aggregate supply curve.

Glossary

Absolute income hypothesis: The basic principle of absolute income hypothesis is that the individual consumer will determine the fraction of his current income that he will allocate to consumption on the basis of his absolute income level.

Accelerator principle: The basic relationship that exists between the investment and the change in the output level is known as the accelerator principle.

Accelerator: The capital output ratio, k, is known as the accelerator.

Accommodating transactions: Accommodating transactions are those transactions that take place for the specific purpose of equalizing the balance of payments from an accountant's point of view.

Aggregate demand curve: The aggregate demand curve shows the different combinations of output level and the price level at which the goods and money markets are simultaneously in equilibrium.

Aggregate demand: Aggregate demand is the total amount of goods demanded in an economy.

Aggregate supply curve: The aggregate supply curve shows the quantity of the output that the firms are ready to supply for each given price level.

Arbitrage: Arbitrage is the simultaneous buying and selling of different foreign currencies in the different foreign exchange markets to take advantage of the difference in the prices.

Autonomous investment: Investment that does not change due to a change in income and the interest rate is called autonomous investment.

Autonomous transactions: Autonomous transactions are those transactions that take place independently of other items in the balance of payments.They take place for the satisfaction that they give or for the profit that they yield.

Average Propensity to Consume (APC): The APC is defined as the ratio of consumption to income for different levels of income.

Balance of invisible trade: The balance of invisible trade is the difference between the exports and imports of services.

Balance of payments: The balance of payments is a summary statement of all the economic transactions between the residents of one country with the rest of the world during a particular period of time, which is usually a year.

Balance of trade: The balance of trade is the difference between the exports and imports of goods.

Balanced budget multiplier: The balanced budget multiplier is the increase in the output as a consequence of equal increases in the government expenditure and taxes. It is equal to one.

Balanced budget: The budget is in balance when the government expenditures plus transfer payments equal the gross tax receipts or, in other words, $G = T$.

Bank rate: Bank rate or the discount rate is the rate of interest at which the central bank rediscounts eligible bills of exchange or other commercial papers.

Bears: Bears are those who expect that the price of bonds will fall in the future.

Bond: A bond is an asset that carries a promise to pay to its owner a fixed amount of income per annum. This income entitles the owner of the bond to a future income stream.

Budget surplus: Budget surplus is the excess of government revenue over its total expenditures.

Bulls: Bulls are those who expect that the price of bonds will rise in the future.

Capital: Capital is the accumulated stock of plant and equipment, which is held by the business firms.

Capital account of the balance of payments: The capital account of the balance of payments measures the outflow and inflow of capital into the economy.

Consumer Price Index (CPI): Consumer Price Index (CPI) is a weighted average of prices of a specified basket of goods and services, which are purchased by the consumers.

Consumption function: The consumption function is a relationship between income and consumption expenditure.

Cost push inflation: When the increase in the price level is due to an increase in the aggregate supply, it is called cost push inflation.

Credit multiplier: Credit multiplier is the ratio of the change in the amount of credit to the change in reserves.

Crowding out: Crowding out is a situation which takes place when an expansionary fiscal policy causes an increase in the rate of interest leading to a decrease in private spending, especially the investment level.

Currency: Currency includes both coins and paper notes, though paper notes are the more predominant of the two.

Currency board: Currency board is an arrangement under which the central bank of a country holds enough amount of a foreign currency to back, in a fixed ratio, each and every unit of the domestic currency.

Currency deposit ratio: Currency deposit ratio is the currency held by the public as a fraction of their demand deposits.

Current account of the balance of payments: The current account of the balance of payments measures the flow of goods, services and income which occurs across the national borders.

Demand deposits: Demand deposits of banks are current account deposits, which are payable on demand either by cheque (with no restrictions) or otherwise.

Demand pull inflation: When the increase in the price level is due to an increase in the aggregate demand, it is called demand pull inflation.

Deposit money: Deposit money or chequeable deposits are entries in the ledgers of the bank to the credit of the holder.

Deposit multiplier: Deposit multiplier is the ratio of the change in deposits to the change in reserves.

Devaluation: Devaluation refers to a conscious action by the monetary authorities to lower the value of a currency with respect to the price of gold.

Direct action: Direct action refers to the coercive actions resorted to by the central bank against those banks who do not function according to its directives.

Direct taxes: Direct taxes are levied directly and include personal income and corporate income taxes.

Disinflation: Disinflation is a situation where there occurs a decrease in the rate at which prices are rising.

Disposable Personal Income: Disposable personal income is the amount, which is actually available to the households and to the non-corporate businesses after they have fulfilled their tax obligations to the government.

Dollarization: Dollarization is a situation where a country abandons its domestic currency and adopts a strong foreign currency like the dollar.

Dynamic Models: Dynamic models are those models that trace the changes that occur in the values of the different variables over time.

Economic growth: Economic growth can be defined as the increase in an economy's output over a period of time.

Employed: A person is employed if during the reference week: (a) he did any work (at least one hour) as a paid employee, worked in his own business, profession, or on his own farm, or worked 15 hours or more as an unpaid worker in an enterprise operated by a member of a family, or (b) was not working but had a job or business from which he was temporarily absent, whether or not he was paid for the time off or was seeking another job.

Equilibrium: Equilibrium is a state of balance or a state where there is no change.

Excess reserves: Excess reserves are reserves in excess of the required reserves.

Exchange rate: The exchange rate is the rate at which one country's currency exchanges for another country's currency.

Expenditure reducing policies: Expenditure reducing policies are aimed at bringing about a change in the aggregate expenditure in the country.

Expenditure switching policies: The expenditure switching policies work mainly through changing the relative price of exports and imports.

Fiscal policy multiplier: The fiscal policy multiplier depicts the changes in the equilibrium income level due to an increase in government expenditure, holding the real supply of money constant.

Fiscal policy: Fiscal policy refers to the government's policy regarding government expenditure, taxation and public borrowing with the view to achieving certain well-defined macroeconomic objectives.

Flow: Flow is a quantity measured over a period of time.

Foreign exchange market: The foreign exchange market is a market where foreign currencies (or foreign exchange) are purchased and sold by individuals, firms, commercial banks and the central banks of the different countries.

Forward transaction: A forward transaction is one which involves an agreement between the buyer and the seller to purchase or sell a fixed amount of currency for a predetermined rate at a specified date in the future.

Frequency of unemployment: The frequency of unemployment is defined as the average number of times, per period, that the workers become unemployed.

Full employment budget surplus: The full employment budget surplus measures the budget surplus at the full employment level of income.

General Equilibrium Approach: General equilibrium approach involves a state where all the markets and the decision-making units in the economy are in a simultaneous equilibrium.

Gross Domestic Product: Gross Domestic Product is the total value of all the final goods and services produced by all the enterprises within the domestic territory of a country in a particular year.

Gross National Product: Gross National Product is a measure of the value of goods and services that the nationals or residents of the country produce regardless of where they are located.

Hedging: Hedging is an attempt at covering the risk involved in a foreign exchange transaction through a forward transaction.

High-powered money: High-powered money is the money, which is produced by the government and the central bank and held in the hands of the public and the banks.

Imperfectly Anticipated Inflation: Imperfectly anticipated inflation is that inflation, which people do not expect.

Indexation: Indexation is a method by which there is an automatic adjustment of wages and prices according to the rate of inflation. Indexation reduces the reaction of people to inflation.

Indexed debt: Indexed debt is a debt where the interest payments are adjusted upwards every year to account for inflation.

Indicators: Indicators are those economic variables that are signals, which indicate to us whether we are moving closer to achieving the targets.

Indirect taxes: Indirect taxes are levied indirectly and include sales tax and excise tax. They are paid as a part of the price of the goods.

Induced investment: Investment that changes due to a change in income and the interest rate is called induced investment.

Inflation: Inflation is a persistent and an appreciable increase in the general level of prices.

Inflationary gap: The inflationary gap is the amount by which the aggregate demand exceeds the aggregate output at the full employment level.

Injection: Injection is an amount of money, which is spent by the different sectors in the economy and which is in addition to their incomes generated in the circular flow of income.

Interest: Interest is the price, which is paid by the borrower to the lender of borrowed funds.

Investment: Investment can be defined as the value of that portion of an economy's output for any period of time that takes the form of new producer's durable equipment, new structures and the change in inventories.

IS curve: The IS curve is a graphic representation of the goods market equilibrium showing the different combinations of the output levels and the interest rates at which saving equals investment (or planned spending is equal to income).

Labour force: Labour force consists of those people who are unemployed as well as those who are employed.

Life cycle hypothesis: The life cycle hypothesis puts forward the view that consumption is related to the present value of the individual's income or wealth.

Liquidity: Liquidity can be defined as the ease with which an asset can be converted into cash at short notice and without any/least loss. Money is the only asset, which is perfectly liquid.

Liquidity trap: The liquidity trap is a situation when at some very low rate of interest all asset holders become bears.

LM curve: The LM curve is a graphic representation of the money market equilibrium showing the different combinations of the output levels and the interest rates at which the demand for money is equal to the supply of money.

Macroeconomics: Macroeconomics is the study of how the national economy as a whole grows and the changes that occur over time.

Macroeconomic policy: Macroeconomic policy refers to the action taken by the government through the different policies to achieve some macroeconomic objectives of the economy.

Marginal efficiency of investment schedule: The marginal efficiency of investment schedule depicts the relationship between the economy's investment and rate of interest when the change in the price of capital goods is taken into consideration.

Marginal Propensity to Consume (MPC): The MPC is defined as the increase in the consumption per unit of increase in the income.

Marginal propensity to import: The marginal propensity to import is the fraction of any change in income that will be devoted to imports.

Microeconomics: Microeconomics is that branch of economics, which analyses the market behaviour and decision-making process of the individual consumers and firms.

Monetary policy multiplier: Monetary policy multiplier depicts the changes in the equilibrium level of income due to an increase in the real supply of money while keeping fiscal policy unchanged.

Monetary policy: Monetary policy is an operation by the monetary authorities of the country to achieve certain well-defined macroeconomic objectives.

Monetary transmission process: The mechanism by which the changes in the monetary policy affect the aggregate demand and, thus, the income level is called the monetary transmission process.

Money flows: Money flows include the monetary flows between the different sectors.

Money: Money is anything that is generally accepted as a means of payment in the settlement of transactions.

Moral suasion: Moral suasion is a combination of persuasion and pressures which a central bank asserts to bring the erring banks in line so that they function in accordance with the central bank's directives.

Multiplier: The multiplier can be defined as the amount by which there occurs a change in the equilibrium level of income due to a change in autonomous aggregate expenditure by one unit.

National saving certificates: National saving certificates is a tax saving instrument for purposes of investing long-term savings available at all post offices in India being a combination of both high safety and adequate returns.

Natural rate of unemployment: Natural rate of unemployment is the average rate of unemployment around which any economy fluctuates in the long run. It is often known as NAIRU (Non-accelerating Inflation Rate of Unemployment).

Net Investment: Net investment is an accretion to the stock of capital.

Nominal GDP: Nominal GDP is the total of the value of the goods and services calculated at current prices.

Open economy: Open economy is an economy, which is engaged in trade with the rest of the world.

Open market operations: Open market operations are the sale and purchase of government securities and treasury bills by the central bank.

Overvaluation: Overvaluation of a currency is said to occur when the official value of a currency is fixed at a higher rate than what would have been determined by the free market forces of demand and supply.

Partial Equilibrium Approach: Partial equilibrium approach involves the determination of the equilibrium price and output in each market, *ceteris paribus.*

Perfectly Anticipated Inflation: Perfectly anticipated inflation exists when the rate of inflation is steady and perfectly predictable.

Permanent income hypothesis: According to the permanent income hypothesis, consumption is related to the permanent income.

Personal Income: Personal income is the income received by the households and the non-corporate businesses.

Phillips' curve: Phillips' curve shows that there exists an inverse relationship or trade-off between the rate of unemployment and the rate of increase in money wages or wage inflation.

Precautionary demand: The precautionary demand for money is the demand for cash by the public for contingencies, which may involve unexpected expenditures and opportunities.

Present value of a capital asset: The present value of a capital asset is the sum obtained after discounting the expected future yields over its entire life at the market rate of interest.

Private investment: Private investment refers to the investment in the private sector.

Production function: The production function describes input-output relationship.

Public investment: Public investment refers to the investment in the public sector.

Real flows: Real flows include the flows of the factors of production and the goods and services between the different sectors.

Real GDP: Real GDP is the total of the value of goods and services calculated at constant prices.

Relative income hypothesis: According to the relative income hypothesis, the fraction of a family's income that will be allocated to consumption will depend on its income level relative to the income level of the other families with which it classifies itself.

Repo rate: Repo rate is the rate at which the central bank infuses short-term liquidity into the system.

Required reserves: Required reserves are cash balances which banks hold to meet their statutory reserve requirements.

Reserve deposit ratio: Reserve deposit ratio is the reserves held by the banks as a fraction of their deposits.

Reverse repo rate: Reverse repo rate is the rate at which banks park their short-term excess liquidity with the central bank in exchange for government securities.

Sacrifice ratio: Sacrifice ratio is the percentage of output, which is lost for a one point decrease in the inflation rate.

Saving account deposits: Savings account deposits are payable on demand and withdrawable by cheques, though the chequing facilities are limited and in addition they earn an interest.

Say's law: The most famous tenet of Say's law is 'supply creates its own demand'.

Speculation: Speculation is an activity relating to the sale and purchase of foreign exchange in which risk is undertaken to take advantage of the fluctuations in the exchange rate.

Speculative demand for money: The speculative demand for money arises due to the existence of an uncertainty about the future.

Spot transaction: A spot transaction is one where the seller of the foreign exchange has to deliver the exchange to the buyer on the spot, that is, within two days of the deal.

Stagflation: Stagflation is a situation when an economy experiences a falling output (stagnation) and increasing prices (inflation).

Static Models: Static models are those models where the relationship between the different variables relates to the same period in time.

Statutory liquidity requirement: The statutory liquidity requirement is a statutory requirement where the banks are required to maintain a certain fixed proportion of their demand and time liabilities in the form of designated liquid assets.

Stock: Stock is a quantity, which is measured at a point in time.

Supply price of a capital asset: The supply price of a capital asset is the cost of replacing the capital asset, which is under consideration, with a new one.

Supply Shock: A supply shock is a sudden disturbance in the economy whose initial impact is a shift of the aggregate supply curve.

Sustained inflation: A sustained inflation takes place when the general price level continues to rise over a fairly long time period.

Time deposit ratio: Time deposit ratio is the ratio of time deposits to demand deposit.

Time deposits: Time deposits of banks are fixed-term deposits where the term of the deposit may vary and in addition they are not payable on demand.

Transactions demand for money: The transactions demand for money is the demand for cash by the public for carrying on its various current transactions.

Transfer payments: Transfer payments are those government payments, which do not involve any direct services by the recipient; for example, welfare payments, unemployment insurance and others.

Undervaluation: Undervaluation of a currency is said to occur when the official value of a currency is fixed at a lower rate than what would have been determined by the free market forces of demand and supply.

Unemployed: A person is unemployed if he is out of work and (a) has been actively looking for work during the previous four weeks, or (b) is waiting to be called back to a job after having been laid off.

Unemployment pool: The unemployment pool consists of the number of unemployed persons at any point of time.

Unilateral transfers: Unilateral transfers (also called unrequited transfers) are one way transactions as there is no claim involved as far as repayment is concerned, either at present or in the future.

Wholesale Price Index (WPI): Wholesale Price Index (WPI) or what is called the producer price index is used to measure the change in the average price of goods, which are traded in the wholesale market.

Withdrawal: Withdrawal is the income, which is generated in the production of the national output and which does not become a part of the circular flow of income.

Index